[OCT 9-63-]

Graeme Park

Hatboro

Horsham

Willow Grove

Norristown

Conshohocken

Chestnut Hill

Cliveden

Germantown

Stenton

Andalusia
The Castle

Villanova

Rosemont

Bryn Mawr

Haverford

Ardmore

Narberth

Pencoyd

Merion

Strawberry Mansion

Wynnewood

Overbrook

Mount Pleasant

Girard College

Pont
Reading

Pa. R.R. 30th St. Sta.

MARKET ST

Upper Darby

Woodlands

CAMDEN

Lansdowne

Powelton

Bartram's Garden

PHILADELPHIA

Corinthian Yacht Club

DELAWARE RIVER

SCHUYLKILL RIVER

FAIRMOUNT PARK

WISSAHICKON CREEK

GERMANTOWN PIKE

Pennsylvania R.R.

Pennsylvania R.R.

Pennsylvania R.R.

PA. 30

PA. 309

P.&R. R.R.

P.&R. R.R.

P.&R. R.R.

U.S. 611

U.S. 1

COBB'S CREEK

NEW JERSEY

D1158251

Philadelphia and Vicinity

0   5   10

by Nathaniel Burt

THE PERENNIAL PHILADELPHIANS

Novels

SCOTLAND'S BURNING

MAKE MY BED

Poetry

ROOMS IN A HOUSE

QUESTION ON A KITE

THE PERENNIAL PHILADELPHIANS
The Anatomy of an American Aristocracy

THE PERENNIAL

PHILADELPHIANS

The Anatomy of an American Aristocracy

BY NATHANIEL BURT

 *with photographs*

LITTLE, BROWN AND COMPANY · BOSTON · TORONTO

COPYRIGHT © 1963 BY NATHANIEL BURT

ALL RIGHTS RESERVED. NO PART OF THIS BOOK MAY BE REPRO-
DUCED IN ANY FORM WITHOUT PERMISSION IN WRITING FROM THE
PUBLISHER, EXCEPT BY A REVIEWER WHO MAY QUOTE BRIEF PAS-
SAGES IN A REVIEW TO BE PRINTED IN A MAGAZINE OR NEWSPAPER.

LIBRARY OF CONGRESS CATALOG CARD NO. 63-14956

FIRST EDITION

Certain selections from this book have
appeared in somewhat different form in
Horizon.

*Published simultaneously in Canada
by Little, Brown & Company (Canada) Limited*

PRINTED IN THE UNITED STATES OF AMERICA

To

ANNA INGERSOLL

JAMES AND RUTH MAGILL

GEORGE AND ANNIE NORRIS

HAMILTON AND PHOEBE GILKYSON

Philadelphienses Optimi

Foreword

THIS BOOK DOES NOT pretend to be a full-length study or portrait of the whole big city of Philadelphia. That is a vaster and more complex subject, a full-length affair indeed. This particular portrait is of the head only — of Philadelphia's upper class; a head of such importance in the city that the portrait turns out to be a rather elaborate one. It can be justified on the assumption that Philadelphia, even more than most places, is characterized and dominated by its head — that is, its upper class, the "Old Philadelphians"; what they are, how they got that way. But it is not a thesis; it is not meant to prove or demonstrate, merely to present, to introduce.

In this very presentation there may, however, be a certain element of thesis. It is not, for instance, universally acknowledged that upper classes and class distinctions do actually exist in America. It is not uncommon to find statements in print — newspapers, magazines — more or less to that effect. How such doubts ever came to exist, above all *why* they exist would indeed make a pretty thesis. But there can or should be no doubt that Philadelphia is one of the many American communities where an hereditary upper class has existed continuously from the beginning — as soon as it got a chance to get started — and where it proposes to keep right on going whether anyone believes in or approves of its existence or not.

Like many portraitists, I had trouble with changes in my subject as I went along. Above all I had trouble with the passage of time. For Philadelphia is, for all its slowness, a slowly *fluid* city. I began to look at it closely in 1956, and since then much has happened there. Things are still happening, but as of let us say January 1962, the books have been closed. A few flagrant obituaries and developments have to be accounted for; but on the whole this

[ix]

sketch of the head-of-a-city remains more or less untouched since.*

Meanwhile, every day, Philadelphia does continue to change. Perhaps, as many people think, notably many Old Philadelphians, the change is always and inexorably in the direction away from Old Philadelphia control and influence. This may well be so. It is of course the nature of things to change, and Old Philadelphians are notoriously inhospitable to changes; at least they think they are. But it must be remembered that many things that are hallowed Old Philadelphia traditions now were considered horrid innovations not so long ago, and the process of time and change works both ways: old things are created out of new things. Families parvenu in 1860 are inbred in 1960; houses considered blatant eyesores then become historical landmarks now. I'm rather inclined to believe that the status of Old Philadelphia and the amount of "Old Philadelphianism" current in any one time remains pretty constant. It does not seem improbable that at least some members of a younger generation of Old Philadelphians, leaping on the bandwagon of whatever is current, will be able to have a good deal to say about directing and driving that bandwagon. They've done it before, they can do it again.

However, part of the very charm of Philadelphia is a perpetual feeling of nostalgia, loss, regret for the old days. So it can be hoped things won't improve to such an extent that this most typical complex of Philadelphia and Old Philadelphia emotions will disappear in the excitement of the Philadelphia Renaissance. E. B. White has indicated that only places that are a bit decadent are pleasant to live in. Charm, especially Philadelphia charm, wouldn't be the same without this tinge of decadence.

* See Appendix.

Contents

Contents

Illustrations

(Between pages 306 and 307)

[xiii]

Illustrations

A modern Nicholas Biddle, Jr., on the steps of the Bank. (*Photograph by Tom Hollyman, reproduced by permission of* Holiday *Magazine, copyright Curtis Publishing Company, 1957.*)

John Hare Powel's Powelton. (*Courtesy of the Historical Society of Pennsylvania.*)

Girard College.

"The Fairman Rogers Four-in-hand," by Thomas Eakins. (*The Philadelphia Museum of Art. Photograph by A. J. Wyatt, Staff Photographer.*)

Henry S. Drinker on the steps of the Art Museum. (*Photograph by Tom Hollyman, reproduced by permission of* Holiday *Magazine, copyright Curtis Publishing Company, 1957.*)

"Max Schmitt in a Single Scull," by Thomas Eakins. (*The Metropolitan Museum of Art, Alfred N. Punnett Fund and gift of George D. Pratt, 1934.*)

View of Fairmount Dam and Josiah White's lock.

C. W. Peale's self-portrait with his Museum. (*Pennsylvania Academy of the Fine Arts.*)

"Christ Healing the Sick in the Temple," by Benjamin West. (*Courtesy of the Pennsylvania Hospital.*)

The façade of Frank Furness's Pennsylvania Academy of the Fine Arts. (*Courtesy of the Pennsylvania Academy of the Fine Arts.*)

Bust of Dr. Benjamin West, by William Rush. (*Courtesy of the Pennsylvania Hospital.*)

Eakins's picture of William Rush carving his allegorical figure of the Schuylkill. (*The Philadelphia Museum of Art. Photograph by A. J. Wyatt, Staff Photographer.*)

"Gross Clinic," by Thomas Eakins. (*Courtesy of the Jefferson Medical College, Phila., Pa. Photographed by Philadelphia Museum of Art.*)

Mrs. Bingham, unfinished portrait by Gilbert Stuart. (*Courtesy American Heritage — Dr. Francis Fisher Hart, Ambler, Pa.*)

Fanny Kemble, by Thomas Sully. (*Pennsylvania Academy of the Fine Arts.*)

Mrs. Harry Ingersoll, by Sully. (*Courtesy of the Historical Society of Pennsylvania.*)

BOOK

I

BOOK

I

1

i. "Thar' She Blows"

THERE USED TO BE a time when people didn't really believe in Philadelphia, especially in the 'twenties and 'thirties and in New York. Of course they knew there was such a city. They sometimes passed through it on the train. Otherwise it was just a statistic; and so safely ignored. When people heard stories of the kind of thing that still existed there, they didn't like it and refused to accept it. Typical was the reaction of one of the more brittle female members of New York's Algonquin group. Caught by mischance at a Philadelphia dinner party during the 'thirties, she went around muttering, "Moss, moss on everything!"

Certainly Philadelphia between the two World Wars did lie across the path of the roaring 'twenties and the sophisticated 'thirties like a big black fossil. It was neither exciting like Manhattan, quaint like Boston, nor picturesque and glamorous like the South and West. It was not even conspicuously awful like the Midwest. It was, in fact, like some forbidden Oriental city. John Gunther in his *Inside U.S.A.* quotes J. David Stern, publisher in the 'forties of the now defunct Philadelphia *Record,* as saying that Philadelphia was "the most Chinese city in the United States," surrounded by its own impenetrable wall. This feeling of being isolated behind such a wall was, even still is, a characteristic bit of Philadelphia psychology.

But things have changed. In 1939 Philip Barry's play *The Philadelphia Story* hit Broadway, and Christopher Morley's novel *Kitty Foyle* the best-seller list and, later, the movies. As with the opening up of Oklahoma, or Perry's mission to Japan, the walls of this Forbidden City were breached and the rush was on. Foreign Devils have been making a killing out of it ever since.

Other books began to appear, most notably the two by Struthers Burt in the 'forties. In the 'fifties Grace Kelly, obviously a princess brought up in a magic tower of some kind, took over Hollywood; and for a climax in 1956-57 there was first The Wedding, then the simultaneous success of *Happy Hunting* and *The Happiest Millionaire,* both intended to be Philadelphian, and along with these another best-selling novel called point-blank *The Philadelphian.* The end is not in sight.*

One gets the feeling of a sudden curiosity, as of children gathered about on the beach to stare at a stranded sea monster. Nobody seems quite sure of what it is; but it's there all right — a big vague crusty old Something which upon even superficial examination turns out to be not quite like everything or anything else.

And of course Philadelphia really and truly is there and has been all along. Thar' she blows, a fresh-water whale wedged up on the silt between two dirty rivers; America's most inland (and second largest) seaport, at first glance a forbidding, perhaps, but scarcely anything as romantic as a Forbidden City — still America's fourth largest,† a huge, sprawling, dirty Industrial Fact that would seem to have nothing to do with shining princesses and magic towers.

Certainly the first impact is not of anything slim, tall or shining; rather the exact opposite, a wide, flat dinginess, for Philadelphia is above all big and flat and drab. The traveler approaching from north or south, especially by train, sees mile after mile of run-down industrial muck and run-down working-class slum; long, identical flat rows of brick houses, redolent of the worst aspects of the nineteenth century. To the traveler from abroad the first thought must be "Birmingham." So from the beginning an

---

* When I have mentioned to a Philadelphian that I'm "writing a book on Philadelphia" the stock retort is, "What, another?"

† But third before the 1960 census, when Los Angeles finally caught up.

English character, that of the England of the Midlands, is declared. Birmingham has been called the Tory City and the nickname would be appropriate to Philadelphia too, but the difference between the two cities appears as one approaches the center. Philadelphia, unlike Birmingham, has a skyline. That skyline represents the difference; for Philadelphia is not just an industrial well from which money and prestige are siphoned off to the capital; Philadelphia is a financial, cultural, social capital in its own right, and the skyline, though a Tory skyline perhaps, testifies to this.

Every American city except Los Angeles and Washington has its skyline, and of each skyline there is one characteristic photographic "shot" — New York or San Francisco from the harbor, Boston across the Common or the Charles, Kansas City over grain fields, Chicago from Lake Shore Drive. The characteristic shot of Philadelphia is from Fairmount Park, the great reach of trees and lawns, once country estates, that borders Philadelphia's smaller river the Schuylkill and goes almost to the center of the city. If you pick the right spot, the foreground is all country still, a rolling richness of greenery, smooth open spaces, barriers of old woods. Then, surprising over this rural prospect, a blue range of buildings, tall but square, as unlike the pointed soaring sawtooth of New York as possible; a skyline that squats. The highest thing in it remains the tower of City Hall, completed in 1894.

The traveler arriving by train (and the proper, the traditional way to approach Philadelphia is always by train) debouches into the somewhat dingy spaciousness of 30th Street Station, an impressive neoclassic building that is not as impressive as it is meant to be; a Grand Gesture somehow incomplete, curiously empty, echoing, too big for its uses.

What a contrast to New York or Washington. What lack of excitement, how desultory the crowds. The main concourse, for all its grandeur, has a casual, almost rooming-house air. Pretty, faded touches of color, "Philadelphia taste," relieve the blankness. A nice war memorial by a local sculptor whom "Everybody

[5]

knows" used to be lit by a spotlight. The spotlight has long gone out. Respectable matrons in overalls drift about tidying the place up, half parlormaid, half brakeman. Ambling to a portico where taxis are congregated, and there are nearly always taxis there, one finds that patience and order prevail. A parrot voice on a record urges one to "Take a check please," elderly gentlemen starters call out the numbers in turn. It's eminently sensible. You get your cab no sooner and no later than your proper turn, with none of the mad piratical scramble that attends the similar function in New York. The taxi driver then takes you to your destination in what seems merely minutes. He does not lean out the window to curse a truck driver or an old lady pedestrian. He does not tell you his political views and his private grievances, though he may show you a photograph of his children. When you arrive he climbs out and opens the door. He often says "Thank you" with what seems like deep sincerity when you give him a tip.*

The visitor, especially the New York visitor, stunned as it were by silence, finds nothing to destroy the mood — a sinking of the spirit perhaps, certainly a lack of exhilaration — as he emerges into the rather thick air of the city itself. The impression from inside is still that of dingy size and of the nineteenth century. Philadelphians themselves are so used to the look of their city that they sometimes fail to appreciate the initial effect of it on sensitive observers from more self-conscious places.

It is not gay. In the very center of the business and shopping district, among those flat-topped skyscrapers and blocking the two broadest and busiest streets, Broad Street that runs due north and south, Market Street that runs due east and west, sits extraordinary City Hall, an enormous tower with a statue of William Penn on top of it blooming in the center, and below a building in the most extravagant of late Victorian styles. It is massive, craggy, gray. On the hour a solemn bell tolls, with vast, wonderful, funereal bongs and long pauses between strokes. One would not be surprised if everyone stopped and took off his hat during the

---

* Of all the Philadelphia taxi drivers I've been back of these last years, not one has been surly or rude. How is it possible?

performance. Nobody does, but one senses over everything a certain solemn heaviness. A serious city, and important.

Then, all around the center of skyscrapers and importance, stretch blocks of miscellaneous drabness and dreary nondescript streets of nondescript shops, broken here and there by the raw emptiness of asphalt parking lots. The aspect is pretty dreadful, described once as being like an old whore with her teeth kicked out. Not gay. Not even important, in these back parts of the commercial district. Where is the chic of New York, the marbled sweep of Washington, the brisk, pink-cheeked conservatism of Boston? The streets are filthy with old newspapers. Venture too far down or up Broad Street and one enters what are obviously Negro slums of the grimiest sort. A sally east or west on Market Street brings one to a honky-tonk movie or a cut-rate department store.

For a total, hotel-dwelling, unacquainted stranger, in Philadelphia say on a bleak drizzling midwinter evening, this initial effect can be overwhelmingly depressing.

Gradually, however, even for the total stranger, if he stays long enough and is curious, compensations do emerge. Beginning with the comparative calm of 30th Street Station and the politeness of taxi drivers, one goes on to notice the pervasiveness of that comparative calm. The main shopping streets, Walnut, Market, Chestnut, are as crowded and pushing as any others, but elsewhere one can stroll. Other people stroll. If one bothers to look into those nondescript shops they can be fascinating: old coins and stamps, saddles and leather goods, everything in the way of odd educational toys, custom tailors, a shop devoted exclusively to health foods and candies made of figs and nuts and honey, theatrical costumers. Greek shops, Jewish shops, Italian shops, and along every one of these raddled byways an old house, an old church, a Friends meeting house, an odd club or society. The more one explores and the more one gets to know, the more one sees. Sooner or later one is bound to find the Hidden City, those numberless little back streets of old houses, or old houses newly restored — Clinton and Camac, Delancey and Panama, Addison,

Sartain, Waverly, Iseminger, Fawn Court, Elfreth's Alley — that slip through the city from one river to the other, mostly to the south between Locust and Lombard Streets.

It is on this part of town that the sun seems to smile, making the tiny secluded gardens green, the occasional big old trees sleepy. Sometimes a rickety wagon goes by, drawn by a clopping horse driven by an old Negro. Rows and rows of Old Curiosity Shops on Pine Street cause one inevitably to loiter. Suddenly one realizes: this is the South. And in fact Philadelphia is, for all its northern industrial Victorianism, the high tide of the South. Hence the relaxed charm, the slovenliness, the brick, old-fashioned, easy humanity.

The weight of the past is heavy, and most of Philadelphia is decidedly not up-to-date. But there are startling exceptions. From City Hall westward to 30th Street something is happening. There are a lot of gleaming new business buildings on a sort of concrete plaza with little trees in tubs. This obviously is something Civic; another, and still unfinished, Grand Gesture. Alongside is a new hotel, garish as Miami, with decor of fearsome moderneness, and stuffed with the kind of exotically inappropriate eating places — a Cheshire Cheese, for instance — that one might find on an ocean liner. It's a puzzlement. It all seems so jostlingly, deliberately different. And then catty-corner northwestward stretches a vast avenue, the Benjamin Franklin Parkway, different too from anything else, a Champs Élysées of trees and an occasional fountain. At the end, far, far away, remote as a dream up on an acropolis, sits a great tawny Greek building, the Art Museum, all columns, steps and pediments. This Washingtonian effect also doesn't seem to fit the Birmingham of America, the important gloom of City Hall. Obviously another Grand Gesture.

ii. Myths

THE IMPRESSIONS of Philadelphia — industrial if old-fashioned might and muck, financial and commercial might and gloom, the equally but more charmingly old-fashioned tucked-away Southern-

ness, and the sudden contrasting evidences of civic Grand Gestures — are striking enough, even contradictory enough, to keep
the total stranger occupied with conjecture. Few strangers, however, come to the facts absolutely cold. Almost invariably they
bring with them, along with their briefcases, some preconceptions;
two in particular, two highly developed Philadelphia myths; for
as the city lies caught between its two rivers, so the fact lies
caught between its two fictions.

These two myths might be labeled the "Dead Burg" myth and
the "Fox-hunting Aristocracy" myth; the one the idea that Philadelphia is utterly lacking in gaiety, a town of Quaker slowness
and sobriety; the other that it is the citadel of an extremely
frosty upper class almost wholly devoted to snobbishness and
horses. Like many myths, both of these are based on solid fact.

There is no doubt, for instance, that Philadelphia has the least
rewarding night life of almost any city in the world. It is an
axiom that Philadelphia has "no good restaurants," and that its
boîtes are lively as wet flannel, its theater spotty and secondhand.
It is not Fun; it is the Salesman's Graveyard.

There are, as the myth has it, "no good night clubs"; but there
are actually lots of night clubs. In some of them National Figures
perform. There are strip-tease joints aplenty, and places where
girls who look good in the gloom will be glad to make your
acquaintance. But this is all for sailors and outsiders, for traveling
salesmen, for the expense account. Philadelphians themselves
never go there except when rowdy, young and male. Most Philadelphians don't even know they exist.

Until 1961 you could not get a drink on the Sabbath. "I went
to Philadelphia on Sunday, but it was closed." And it was. The
blue laws, puritan heritage of the Quakers and others, saw to it
that Philadelphia was kept closed. One effect of these laws has
been to create so-called "bottle clubs" where one can drink on
Sunday. They have picturesque names like the Vesper Club and
the Mercantile Literary Association, and serve the best food in the
city; but you have to belong.

Otherwise, there are "no good restaurants." Anybody will tell you this. There are actually quite a few nice places to eat in public. The Barclay and Warwick Hotels have a most elegant hotel menu; the Bellevue is nice if not chic; a restaurant called the Three Threes on one of the tucked-away streets is informally delightful. Dante's, way down in South Philadelphia, must be one of the finest, really indigenously Italian restaurants in America, as old Bookbinders over near the Delaware is indigenously seafood. The golf champion Helen Sigel Wilson runs a restaurant where Everybody Goes. But if you want to take a visitor out to a show place for a big evening — somehow none of these quite fits the occasion. At least Everybody says that there are no good restaurants in Philadelphia.

The second myth is true also. There is very definitely a fox-hunting gentry in Philadelphia, and Philadelphia really is a center of fox hunting. More, older and better hunts are still scattered about Philadelphia than any city in the country; perhaps one should say in the world, for in England and Virginia, those other world centers of the pink coat, hunting is an exclusively rural pastime, whereas in Philadelphia it is suburban; the fox hunters being, on the whole, people who may live in or go out to the country, but who are essentially identified with the city itself.

However, there is not much evidence of this on Broad Street. No pink coats are worn there, and in fact there is not much visible evidence of the existence of any kind of gentry, fox-hunting or otherwise. One sees well-set-up, well-dressed, out-doorsy gentlemen coming out of offices at noon and at five, but no more of them than one sees on Wall Street or State Street or Michigan Avenue. There is a definite lack of the chic matronage one sees on Park Avenue or Lake Shore Drive. There is no really "smart" shopping section. "Smartness" is just what Philadelphia deliberately avoids, and except for a few small dress shops, downtown Philadelphia totally lacks a modish appearance.

This does not mean, however, that the gentry doesn't exist, or even that a good many of them aren't smart, after their fashion. Their comparative invisibility in town can be accounted for in at least two ways.

For one thing, there are so few of them. The *Social Register,* that handy but not always reliable index of upper-classness, lists, out of a metropolitan area population of some four million, no more than thirty thousand individuals (but more than any other city except New York). This is less than one per cent of the total population; of these only a fraction, ten per cent of this one per cent, would be acknowledged by Philadelphians themselves as really upper-class. In any case a good many of the genuine gentry, particularly the older and odder ones, might be more or less unrecognizable as such on the street or anywhere else, since Philadelphia doesn't hold with "distinction" any more than it does with "smartness."

But even more important than sheer lack of numbers is the fact that nearly all the gentry, in a proportion of ten to one, live out of the city and prefer to stay there. "I'm just a country girl from Villanova. I never get into town," a young matron might say; and when approached by a stranger in the perennial American game of "Where do you live," she is liable (like the Philadelphia girl being presented at Court who was asked by the Queen where she lived,) to reply simply, "The Main Line." It is often a great surprise to Philadelphians to realize that there are people who don't know that "the Main Line" is the main line westward of the Pennsylvania Railroad, "on" or along the tracks of which a great many of the Philadelphia fox-hunting gentry actually do live.

Nonetheless, despite the small numbers, deliberate unostentatiousness and distant residence of this gentry, a curious and contradictory observable fact is that there are no streets in America where the gentry, when they are visible, stand out with such striking and sore-thumb obviousness. In Boston, everybody takes on a Proper Bostonian look, in New York the real gentry is lost in the crowd of people trying to look like Somebody, and succeeding. In Philadelphia people tend to look exactly what they are. It is the only city in America, for instance, where the lower middle class looks exactly the way a lower middle class is expected to look; again, as in England, the streets are full of slightly anemic, slightly crushed, rather neatly and badly dressed but, at the same time, overwhelmingly self-satisfied people who, one feels, are thoroughly smug about the meekly stolid condition to which God has called them. They are *respectable;* nowhere is the subway more respectable than in Philadelphia. Among them one sees occasionally people of an obviously different, and again obviously native race, taller, often handsomer, usually healthy, with bright cheeks and sound teeth, well-dressed in a somewhat careless and tweedy way; but at one with the lower orders in that same supreme satisfaction with things as they are. A quite fascinating spectacle is the calm, natural aplomb of an upper-class Philadelphian strolling along the street in an off hour quite sure that Nobody Else is there.

Both this comparative absence and curious conspicuousness of the gentry on the streets of Philadelphia are significant; probably, in fact, the crucial symptoms of Philadelphia's whole present existence. For this is a city that has been owned by and managed *for* (not *by*) one of the few, if not the only, still-established hereditary oligarchies in America, perhaps in the Western world; certainly one of the few whose tenure extends without any real break from the early eighteenth century to the present; a tenure, however, that has tended to become more and more, until very recently, an absentee landlordship.

The stamp of both the presence and absence of this owning oligarchy is everywhere visible. In almost every case the overt characteristics of the city can be traced back to the influence — or obvious lack of influence — of this class. Take, for instance, Philadelphia's reputation as a "Dead Burg." One reason Philadelphia's public evening life doesn't glitter is that those who have the money and taste to make it glitter have no interest in public appearances. Before- and after-theater parties, such as they are, have dinner at clubs in the bosom of their friends and hidden from public view. Afterwards they go to somebody's house. Except for the Barclay Hotel, where "people" do go all dressed up, and aside from dances, galas and theaters, most of the social life of Philadelphia takes place "in the country," again in people's houses.

Or take, for another example, the disreputable snaggle-toothed obsolescence of so much of Philadelphia's real estate. This is traceable directly to the fact that the owners and administrators of it live elsewhere, shielded from the sight of what their absence has done to the basis of their fortunes. A half-century of neglect is bound to show sooner or later.

On the other hand, the back-street charms, the trees, the few nice streets of old houses, the unexpected little gardens, public and private, anything in fact that makes for that tucked-away, elusive "Philadelphia Taste" is entirely the residual traces of its gentility. The minute you get beyond the central citadel, north of Market, south of Pine, all this disappears. The graces are gone, the charms are of a different and grimmer kind.

Or take Philadelphia's assets, the Grand Gestures, the public monuments. Each one bears, like a thumbprint, the impress, usually, of some one prominent Old Philadelphian family: the Free Library, spiced with statues and portraits of Peppers; the Franklin Institute, Philadelphia's museum of science, of which one of the proudest exhibits has been the Bible of the Duane family, descended so casually from Benjamin Franklin; or the Academy of Natural Sciences, where has stood preeminent a large habitat group with a moose shot by a Biddle and stuffed by a Cadwalader. Even such a plebeian and aggressively proletarian institution as Temple University cannot resist having a corner devoted to those Philadelphia companions — the portrait and the grandfather's clock, as inevitable as fountains in Rome. (Usually, to complete this shrine to the Founding Fathers, there is an eighteenth-century chair. If you wanted to make for some Academy of Human Sciences a habitat group of a stuffed Biddle or Cadwalader, this would be certainly the setting — portrait, clock and the appropriate specimen sitting in the chair.)

Even the new civic Penn Center and its concrete manifestoes, for all its aggressive defiance of traditional Philadelphiansm, is the product of this dominant class. These changes are the result, to a large extent, of a rebellion against old corruption and a change of heart within the ranks of the gentry itself — a realization that absentee landlordship and delegated politics were leading to ruin; and of a valiant effort, led by a member of said gentry, Mayor (now Senator) Joseph Clark, to lift Philadelphia out of a depression caused largely by the lack of aggressive and up-to-date Old Philadelphia leadership.

The Old Philadelphia gentry is then, at most, still the real owner and ruler of the city; at least, the drop of Tabasco that gives character and flavor to the whole. It is certainly, by either presence or absence, a very important factor, perhaps the most important single factor, in the life of the city.

iii. Position

NO ONE, OF COURSE, is more serenely aware of this than the Old Philadelphian himself. This awareness may be hidden under layers of careful indoctrination, a rigorous training in modesty, cordiality and relaxed, cheerfully casual good manners. But buried under it all, like the Church's one Foundation, the hidden majority of the iceberg, lies a subconscious veneration for his own Position. It is the fact of this venerable Position, into which he is born and to which he must react in one way or another, that largely determines the upper-class Philadelphian's attitudes and career. He can take advantage of it or escape it, love it or loathe it, maintain it or rebel against it, but it is *there*, like Philadelphia itself, and as long as he stays in Philadelphia he's in for it. Whether he likes it or not, he will be enmeshed in a sense of belonging at once cosy and asphyxiating. "People know who he is," as Philadelphians would put it; even if they don't actually do very much about it.

This sense of Position, of being an important member of an important community of other such people of importance, is the firm core about which the Old Philadelphian's psychology is built. It is sense of Position that gives to so many Philadelphians that air of condescension which can be infuriating, or amusing, but which continually tends to peep out from under the good humor and the good manners. It is sense of Position, in fact, that defines them as "Old Philadelphians," though this designation in actual practice is always reserved for somebody else, and always used in a deprecating way about oneself. "Of course I'm not an Old Philadelphian," Senator Clark will say; meaning that, though the Clarks have belonged to everything worth belonging to in Philadelphia for several generations, they are a nineteenth-century, not an eighteenth-century family. In a similar manner other people who have Position too, but who perhaps don't actually belong to the inner circle of the Philadelphia Club (the city's oldest and best) and the Assembly (the antique annual dance), will use the phrase to mean just that, always preceded by the "of course." Or as Miss Gertrude Ely, one of Philadelphia's charming and indomitable octogenarians, puts it, "Of course I have the advantage of not being an Old Philadelphian." This doesn't mean she isn't important, or distinctly Philadelphian.

Actually all but the most liberated of these people consider themselves, and refer to each other, not as "Old Philadelphians" of course, but as just plain Philadelphians. *The* Philadelphians. When they refer to someone as a Philadelphian they don't mean for a minute just any one of the city's four million residents. They mean one of their thousand friends, connections or relations. As far as they are concerned, there are no other *real* Philadelphians and there is no other real Philadelphia except those particular areas where these particular Philadelphians live or have lived. The rest of the city is *terra incognita*, a something that surrounds the real city like a natural phenomenon, a forest or a swamp.

Since they all (theoretically) know just who is a Philadelphian and since anyone they don't know really isn't, any such qualifying adjective as "old," or much less "proper," is mere impertinence; "proper," that term so felicitously used by Cleveland Amory for

Boston, being precisely the wrong word for Philadelphia anyway. It conveys, first of all, a sort of prim and meticulous uprightness which is the very antithesis of Philadelphia's relaxed, fuzzy, social *Gemütlichkeit*, and it also proposes a moral sternness which is quite out of key. Philadelphia has always been very, very careful about appearances, but quite tolerant about acts and consciences. It believes in conventions, not convictions, and in form, not character. Charlotte Wilcocks, a well-brought-up young Victorian, had no compunction about recording in her diary for 1842, "Ellen confided me that Mr. Butler kept a mistress. I suspected as much. I might have informed her that her uncle kept *two*. Decent conversation for two young women!" Such gossip has always been the staple of Philadelphia dinner conversation; and in such goings-on, from the marital difficulties of Pierce Butler and the dashing Fanny Kemble down to the latest divorces of Unionville and Penllyn, the Philadelphians ("old" perhaps but certainly not "proper") have always evinced a thoroughly malicious and whole-hearted delight.*

This attitude toward the designation "Philadelphian" has not been wholly popular with the rest of Philadelphia's millions, needless to say. Philadelphia is a big and various city, and includes a great deal that is not "Old Philadelphian." To the Old Philadelphian however, the Philadelphian who lives secluded behind the walls, largely social now, of his Inner City, Philadelphia is a small and exceedingly homogeneous place. Although actually nowadays families may be spread over a fifty-mile radius, one child near West Chester down towards Wilmington, and the other a two-hour motor ride away up in Bucks County near Trenton, to Philadelphians Philadelphia is still pretty small and still pretty close-knit; at least they talk and act as if it were, whatever they may think or say on the subject.

---

* Dr. Kinsey, examining Philadelphia, said it was the last American stronghold of the established mistress, professional or amateur. Elsewhere either puritanism still held, divorce had caught up, or vice was casual. The apropos story is that of two old codgers in the window of the Union League, good friends but only as clubmates. Said one, "I'm so relieved to see my wife hasn't found me out yet; there she goes down Broad Street with my mistress." "Isn't that a coincidence," said the friend. "I was just going to say exactly the same thing!"

iv. *"Not"*

ALTHOUGH THESE Old, these Inner Philadelphians certainly are a distinct tribe, it is not so easy to pin down the characteristic markings of the species; and in fact that very lack of the charac-- teristic is part of the characteristic. They have little of the crotch- ety indigenous distinctiveness of Bostonians of this sort, nor the brittle or richly dowdy learned-in-finishing-school elegance of Little Old New Yorkers; not for them the flowery graces of the South.

In fact, negativeness itself is typical. What Owen Wister called the "instinct of disparagement" that makes Philadelphians habitually run everything down, especially things Philadelphian, is a form of this negative. This has the advantage of modesty; it also is a blight on creative effort, on reform, on any new enthu- siasm. And it is perhaps in negatives, in the places and peoples Philadelphia is *not* like, that Philadelphia can most easily be bracketed.

It is, for example, *not* like New York. Certainly no two large cities so close together, in one country and speaking the same language, could be more different. If Philadelphians can be said to be self-conscious about anything, and their principal aim in life is to be unself-conscious, it is in their desire not to be like New Yorkers, or what they think of as New Yorkers. This is more than mere antipathy; New York is too close, and represents too strong an economic threat to be ignored as Philadelphians would prefer to ignore it. It represents too easy an escape for the rebel- lious, talented, ambitious youth who finds opportunities there he can't find at home. From the point of view of the Stock Exchange or the theater, Philadelphia is just a suburb of New York. Phila- delphia women go there when they want to buy clothes, and their men when they want to buy women. The remark Gunther quotes in *Inside U.S.A.* of the Philadelphian who described New York as "simply an island full of clip joints" is typical enough; but there is an element of uneasiness in having the world's largest city on one's doorstep.

New York represents serious competition, but Philadelphia is damned if it's going to compete. Even without the threat, the antipathy would be great enough. The whole aspiring, pushing, ostentatious, inhuman showcase quality of the city, the raucous glitter, the avidity for the novel, the insistence on the high pitch, everything about it in fact rubs Philadelphians the wrong way. Put a "not" in front of any of these New York characteristics, and you get a Philadelphia one. Philadelphians make a conventional reservation in favor of what they call Old New Yorkers, but the actual remnant of "Old New York Society" with its tinge of the Gilded Age still seems as aspiring as the Stock Exchange itself to Philadelphians, who may be uneasy about New York economically, but are perfectly secure in their disdain for it socially.

In all this, naturally, Philadelphia is one with New York's more distant northern neighbor, Boston, and it would seem that these two would have much in common. Both Philadelphia and Boston are comparatively old-fashioned cities, both dominated by local aristocracies, both given to good works and antiquarianisms. They are both of the same coin, all right, but opposite faces; almost everything that is true in detail of Boston is untrue of Philadelphia. A comparison of the two cities' respective Athenaeums illustrates the conflict between them on such subjects as books and food. Both are private subscription libraries to which one has to belong, usually by descent, as a "shareholder." Both occupy their original buildings, though the one in Boston has been altered and enlarged. Both contain books; here the resemblance ends. The Athenaeum in Boston is a thriving affair, busy with researchers from Harvard and its nooks and crannies thick with learning, if not necessarily shareholders. At one time refreshments were served: tea or bouillon, with three plain crackers, could be had for three cents; cheese cost two cents more. Each additional sweet cracker was an extra penny. Even this has been considered too orgiastic, and nowadays, there are no refreshments at all.

The Philadelphia Athenaeum,* on the other hand, which occupies a stately high-ceilinged brownstone building on Philadelphia's Washington Square, is usually empty. Hardly anyone used
it for years, until quite recently. Under the influence of an ambitious new young director, and as part of the stir of the Philadelphia Renaissance, the Athenaeum cleaned out its attic for the
first time in the twentieth century, and discovered there a priceless collection of early American novels, preserved only because
nobody had bothered to throw them away. All the shareholders
turn out once a year, however, for the Athenaeum lunch. After
passing through a receiving line of patronesses, they are served
a feast of turtle soup, pressed duck, spoon bread, tomato aspic and
meringue cake † — after which all leave quickly so as not to be
caught by their more unfortunate relatives. The cause of Literature has thus been served, and nobody need crack a book for the
rest of the year.

Boston and Philadelphia, for all their radical differences, are
quite willing to join forces, but never quite make it. They keep
"discovering" one another with surprise, pleasure, but a slight
uneasiness. A Boston court tennis team was recently amazed at
the cordial entente that emerged after the matches in Philadelphia; the New Yorkers all hurried home, presumably to "clip
joints," while the Bostonians stayed and enjoyed themselves. But
there was a lingering doubt as to whether Philadelphia still kept
up a proper respect for wines.

As for the West, to Philadelphians, of course, it remains a
stranger that has not been properly introduced and therefore
does not exist. The Far West, the Wyoming of Wister and *The*

---

* The Philadelphia *Athenæum*, as it is actually written, is careful to spell itself
with the a and e joined, in proper classical fashion. This causes a bit of turmoil
among shareholders when annual checks are drawn; surely among the few in
America containing that classic "æ." Checks in Philadelphia, incidentally, are
usually "cheques."

† In recent years, as part of the Renaissance, the shareholders and book readers
have increased, but the menu has been reduced. There is considerable discussion
as to whether this is a good thing.

Virginian, is loved and admired as a sort of Shangri-La, and a surprising number of Philadelphians have gone there and even settled. But the Midwest is just a blank. People go to weddings in Lake Forest and find it vulgar. The fact that Philadelphia has a kinship with cities like Cincinnati, Indianapolis and above all St. Louis, which stretch in a sort of belt of sympathetic vibration across the middle of the country, has seldom been acknowledged by either Philadelphia or its kindred cities. St. Louis especially, with its Southern tinge, German influence, cultural pretensions, cosy prosperity combined with dinginess, love of good living and disdain for parvenu Chicago and Kansas City (substitute New York and Pittsburgh), is simply a somewhat later edition of Philadelphia, even down to having streets named after trees, Walnut, Chestnut, Locust, Spruce and Pine. But the relationship goes more or less unacknowledged these days, though Governor Pennypacker of Pennsylvania did make a speech at the St. Louis World's Fair of 1904 in which he actually called St. Louis "the Philadelphia of the West."

Hating New York, unacquainted with and basically unsympathetic in some ways to Boston, ignoring the Midwest, Philadelphia, the Philadelphia of the Old Philadelphians, does look with kindness upon two sections of the globe, the South and England. Links with the South have always been very strong, and Philadelphia regards Southern ways, that is Old Southern ways, with somewhat the same mixture of envy and disapproval as that with which no doubt the Prodigal Son was regarded by the boy who stayed home. The South is the black-sheep cousin, reckless, ruined, but oh how romantic! A Southerner with good connections is almost sure to be welcomed with open arms, and the best marriages have been made from the earliest times across the Mason-Dixon line, with Virginia Lees and Charleston Middletons. Philadelphia admired and still admires nothing more than the South's landowning patriarchal quality, the horse raisin' and fox huntin', the lavish hospitality, the fragrance of belles and juleps, the high-minded disdain for mere mercantilism. Nothing pleases the secret soul of the Philadelphian more than to be known as John Smith of Smithside, his country place, like the Marylander Charles Carroll of Carrollton or the Carters of Carter's Grove.

But alas, Philadelphia cannot approve. Disdain of mercantilism is one thing; recklessness and shiftlessness are another. Having a good time is delightful, but being a wastrel is something else again. And there is always the dark shadow of slavery, stubbornly opposed from the very beginning by the Quaker conscience. When the Civil War came, Philadelphia, at first reluctantly, went for the Union,* and has since been the bedrock of unreconstructed Republicanism. (Once more one has to add "until recently.") Glamour is all very well, but common sense, caution and even that Quaker conscience have to count in the end. The moral is plain: the plantation South is ruined, whereas Philadelphia is still doing quite nicely, thank you, though you will hardly get an Old Philadelphian to admit it.

As for England, that other land of the Old Philadelphian's heart's desire, it has the inestimable advantage of not being American, and hence pleasantly removed from the actual concerns of this world. The England that Philadelphia loves is, of course, never, never the England of Birmingham, which Philadelphia most nearly resembles, but a sort of Gilbert and Sullivan England, or the country, more or less gone in fact, that is imperishably preserved in Trollope, or Agatha Christie. Many Philadelphians, like many Englishmen no doubt, wish they lived in Barsetshire, and in old-fashioned circles there still remains the conviction that any joke in *Punch* is ipso facto funnier than any joke in *The New Yorker*. The English-Speaking Union flourishes as it does in Boston and Virginia, and a company of amateur Savoyards receives the yearly devotion of the best people.

In many ways Philadelphia remains exactly what it used to be: the second largest city of the British Empire. In its flatness, its

---

* Though Copperheadism was rife, and the Philadelphia Club had to maintain two separate bars, one for Southern sympathizers, one for Northern. Even afterwards a few of the best families remained, at least till F.D.R., sort of protesting Democrats, whose children were not permitted to walk on the sidewalk in front of the clubhouse of the arch-Republican Union League on Broad Street.

monotony of row-houses, its grim industrialism, it is as English as can be. In the love of country and country values cherished by the upper classes and in the equal cherishing of the upper classes by themselves, it is also English. In all sorts of traits of English descent, from a style of blond good looks, negligent arrogance and casual high living derived from eighteenth-century English inheritance, to a rather fundamental trust in a sort of Establishment of Church, Government and Culture to be presided over by the aristocracy, Philadelphia is very like an antique Toryish England; the England perhaps of Galsworthy, but nothing whatsoever to do with the England of Aldous Huxley, Bernard Shaw, Harold Laski or Evelyn Waugh.

On the other hand, like Philadelphia's Copperheadism, Philadelphia's colonialism is ambivalent. As Philadelphia turns out to be the first home of the Union League and the center of Eastern Republicanism, so it was also the "cradle of Independence," and the first capital of the new Republic.

Philadelphians are quite happy to admire England from afar, and rather loathsomely cuddle illusions of English superiority in taste and manners; but when it comes down to brass tacks, as it did in 1776, they are not going to give up any local perquisites, or take any guff from the Lords Proprietor. For the English visitor of rank or charm nothing is too good; but woe to the visiting Anglican Bishop who began his lecture "I take it I am addressing members of the middle class." Philadelphia would be quite happy to return to the Empire except for Imperials. And then it might be bad for business. As in its relations with the South, Philadelphia finds lands and titles splendid, but the city's prosperity is not based on them. And yet, though Philadelphia's aristocracy is a mercantile and professional one, the Philadelphian's fateful image of himself as a country gentleman, a hard-riding hereditary country squire; a tinge of the South and of England, a sort of subdued but real romanticism prevents him from being wholehearted about his role of Merchant Prince. The tug of war between Country Seat and Counting House, acute even before the Revolution, endures to this day.

v. *Recherché and Solid*

SAYS SIDNEY FISHER: "The proper pursuit for a man of my position is the life of a gentleman farmer"; and Sidney himself represents this conflict and many other Philadelphia attitudes in their
fine flower. It is not untypical that though he has been dead for
some ninety years his attitudes are still much alive. He was a
gentleman of romantic good looks, the best family connections
(his grandmother was a Logan) and not enough money, who led
a rather querulous and useless life in Philadelphia during the
nineteenth century. A representative "disappointed man," he
dabbled at law and poetry, tried to live beyond his income,
married an Ingersoll — and kept a diary. The diary, discovered
among the effects of his son, has almost daily entries from 1834
to 1871, and has been transcribed, all seventy-nine volumes of it,
into typescript. Like the George Templeton Strong diary for
New York and the William Appleton diary for Boston, it covers
the details of nineteenth-century life with thoroughness and local
emphasis. There is an enormous amount about houses and furniture and parties and people, nothing about God and Mr. Fisher's
conscience.

Like Strong and Appleton, Sidney Fisher worried constantly
about money, but very unlike them could never lower himself to
making any. When he wasn't worrying about himself, he cast a
cold, dispassionate and surprisingly judicial eye upon the world
and events about him. His opinions are of course a good deal
more ferocious and exaggerated than even the thoughts of the
most die-hard Old Philadelphian nowadays; but they are the
same opinions, basically, and in almost every superior Old Philadelphian there is a taint of Sidney somewhere or other.

His feeling about position and family of course was quite
unequivocal: "Luckily my fortune small as it is and my social
position command respect from the mass," and "I am somewhat
proud of my family, as on both sides my ancestors for five or six
generations have held the stations of gentlemen and men of
property and education — which is something in this country of

parvenus." This country as opposed, of course, to England, which he never saw and knew only by hearsay, but which he regarded in true Tory-colonial fashion as his spiritual home; the England of the landed gentry, not of Reform Bills and Gladstone and such, whose ". . . grandeur, wealth and splendour, pervading comfort" (now that the shoe is on the other foot this is usually referred to as "American materialism") "make one repine that one's lot is cast anywhere else. We are poor and coarse and unrefined and there are so many things to disgust and feel ashamed of, that I really think the true way is to insist on our claim of relationship to England and feel proud of her glory and greatness, and keep our complacency in that way for the next hundred years." Many Philadelphians seem to have followed his advice.

Part of this somewhat nauseating snobbism was political; that is, derived from his Federalist hatred of democracy in theory and of Jackson in practice.

My hatred of democracy is stronger than my love of country. Truly, as the newspapers say, we live in a favored country. The cold of Russia, the heat of Africa; drought, disease, and democracy make up a combination of blessings. Nothing is done with reference to the wishes or opinions of the educated classes; hence the war against the Bank [of the United States] and the cry against the rich and the "aristocrats." I always vote *against* the popular side on principle.

These are sentiments which could have been uttered almost word for word by any good New Deal-hating Old Philadelphian a century later in the 1930's, before the Second World War, like the Civil War, stirred up a latent patriotism.

To one with such an attitude, naturally, politicians are a low sort of vermin, and engagement in public life is no fit occupation for a gent. Mr. Ramsey, an acquaintance from Dickinson College days,

is now on his way to Washington, a member of Congress. This sounds great but nowadays political success implies little merit of any kind. On the contrary the most educated and virtuous men avoid public life and from the interior of our Boeotian State [that is, western Pennsylvania] the favorites of the democracy are seldom distinguished for anything but vulgarity, want of principle, etc. I did not know Ramsey well . . . but he seems more of a gentleman than could be expected.

Having met the Governor of Pennsylvania, Fisher feels kindly disposed, since he is after all not a Democrat and hence at least on the right side. "Ritner is a bluff good-humored, honest-looking fat Dutchman, without the slightest approach to the appearance or manner of a gentleman. This however is not to be expected in a Governor of Pennsylvania."

The city of Philadelphia itself is not exempt from this rampant, all-consuming Instinct of Disparagement. In fact, Old Philadelphians love nothing better than to run down Philadelphia, as compared, at least, to London and Paris:

Philadelphia is a great village, with all the narrowness of mind, the dullness, the vulgarity, the little passions and meddling gossip of a village. There are none of the refined pleasures of a metropolis, no brilliant and elegant society, no luxury and splendour, no public amusements, no fine arts, no great interests and exciting movements which dazzle and impress and give such spirit to London and Paris. Our cities are the provincial towns of Europe, Liverpool or Marseilles.

This attitude of a superior soul caught in a closet, a big, spiritual frog in a muddy puddle, is a perennial pattern among slightly intellectual Old Philadelphians, and gives to the mouth of many a bluestocking matron and white-mustached bon viveur the upthrust lower lip expressive of cynical superiority. After a party at Nicholas Biddle's in 1836 when Sidney was still a gay bachelor, he writes,

So much for the first dance of the season. Rather stupid. How could it be otherwise with our society. We have some married women certainly who are interesting, but of young ladies very few whose character and qualities are sufficiently elevated to induce a young man to exert himself to please, and who indeed can properly appreciate such exertion.

And in summer, during the depressed year of 1842, "Nothing but a village in the West can be more stupid, triste and village-like than Philadelphia now."

That is to say, Philadelphia is dreadful, but as compared with a village in the West, or in fact anywhere *else* in America, Philadelphia is at least redeemed by having in it other Old Philadelphians. One still hears people say things like "Of course, there's nothing west of the Schuylkill."

Sidney's diatribe against New York could again be quoted word for word by a modern Philadelphian and nobody would really know the difference. After a description of the "vulgarity, meanness and ostentatious parade of parvenuism" of the metropolis *ca.* 1837 (bear the date in mind) :

. . . this shows the difference between the best Philadelphia and New York society. The first unpretending, elegant, cordial and friendly, containing many persons not rich, but few whose families have not held some station for several generations, which circumstance has produced an air of refinement, dignity and simplicity of manner wanting in New York and also a great degree of intimacy among the different families who compose our society as their fathers and grandfathers knew each other. Wealth is not the only passport; this probably will not last long.

For Philadelphia, like New York, is plagued with

vulgar, nouveau riche people who are now crowding into society and are seen at all the parties. The good, respectable old-family society for which Philadelphia was once so celebrated is fast disappearing and persons of low origin and vulgar habits are introduced because they are rich who a few years ago were never heard of. If they were agreeable, cultivated, intelligent or beautiful there would be some compensations, but they are all commonplace and uninteresting, many of them vulgar, stupid and ugly. . . .

And their descendants, having become agreeable and cultivated, are now saying precisely the same thing about modern Philadelphia society and other, later, horrid nouveaux riches. The patterns of change in Philadelphia, as in so many things, seem to be quite changeless.

All this, of course, does not for one minute prevent Sidney, or any other Philadelphian then or now, from going to the houses of the horrid nouveaux riches, admiring the décor, eating the sumptuous repasts and coming away to disparage:

On Friday evening [February 14, 1841] went to a small party at Mrs. Hutchinson's. They live in a fine new house in Spruce above 10th and their rooms are the most beautiful I ever saw. *All* the furniture from Paris of the most costly description and in admirable taste and keeping. The front room is in rosewood and some rich fawn colored stuff for drapery and sofas, with immense mirrors and splendid chandeliers, candelabra, lamps, bronze ornaments, etc. The back room, which is the dress-room, is in blue and white damask and gold. The woodwork of the chairs, etc. is massy gilt, the chandelier and candelabra, etc. ormolu of exquisite taste and execution. The designs for the various articles required the genius of an artist.

One thing struck me as very pretty, a fire screen composed of a large plate of glass, very thick and set in a rich and massy gilt frame, so that you see the fire and are protected from the heat. This frame corresponds with that of the mantel mirror, so that the whole, the blazing fire thus framed in, the gold ornaments on the mantel and the large mirror above, glittering with lights from candelabra and chandeliers produces a very beautiful effect.

Another novelty was very pretty. The top of the mantelpiece was covered with a cushion of crimson velvet with a rich fringe of gold hanging from its edge and heavy gold tassels from the corners. On this were placed ornaments of ormolu of the most beautiful description.

The refreshments and service correspond to all this. I noticed two or three pieces of plate remarkable for their elegance of shape and beautiful carving. They belonged to some monastery in Spain and Hutchinson was lucky enough to get them whilst there. The furniture in short, as Willing said, is just such as you see in the palaces in Europe, but the *company* is very different. Instead of the courtly and highbred crowd, who have been accustomed to this splendour all their lives, you see here merchants and lawyers who work all day in counting houses and offices and when they go into such a house, stare about them and seem out of their element. Here it is a show, there the habitual scene of daily life.

Hutchinson tho a very worthy man, has no education or mind and his family is obscure. He made his fortune in Lisbon and resided there many years. His marriage with Miss Hare introduced him into society. She is a very agreeable and pretty woman, he is fond of her and proud of her and she is attached to him tho he is more than twenty years her senior. It was a good match for her as she was poor. Spent the evening pleasantly talking with Mrs. Harry Ingersoll.

This illustrates the process of infusion which keeps the Philadelphia, or any other, oligarchy going. By now the Hutchinsons are very Old Philadelphian indeed.

But even as late as the 1840's Sidney could find reservoirs unpolluted and yet equally luxurious:

A small but very beautiful recherché party at Mrs. Geo. Cadwalader's. It was made for Mrs. Harrison. The rooms very rich and splendid and also in excellent taste; frescoes by Monachesi, curtains, chairs, divans of the richest white damask silk *embroidered* [italics are Sidney's], vases, candelabra, chandeliers, enormous mirrors in great profusion, in two large rooms brilliantly lighted and filled with about fifty well-dressed and well-bred men and women, sitting in quiet talk, made a pretty scene. The supper was in the same style of sumptuous elegance, without profusion. They have been accustomed to this sort of thing all their lives, and so do it with ease, propriety and grace. Very different from the gaudy show, crowded glitter and loaded tables of certain vulgar people here who by mere force of money have got into a society to which they are not entitled by birth, education or manners.

In other words, the only proper society is an hereditary one. He speaks of a family Christmas dinner at Wakefield, the old Fisher place, with his country relatives.

Their manners though plain and Quakerlike are . . . by no means vulgar. Far superior in this to those of much of the flashy society in town [nowadays substitute "Main Line"] and for this reason, that the family is in position, fortune and education what they have been all their lives and what their fathers were before them. They live on the estate which they inherited and the furniture of the house, plain compared with modern luxury, belonged to those who lived there before them. They are not *parvenus* and this one thing gives a man qualities which *nothing* else can. I always feel socially superior to a man who is not a gentleman by birth and I never yet saw one who had risen to a higher position whose mind and character as well as his manners did not show the taint of his origin. Early impressions are too powerful to be removed by the influence of after life.

This presents the Philadelphia ideal of a society of birth in about as forthright a way as the human sensibilities can stand. Nobody can honestly deny that there is something in it. However, a certain chicken-and-egg confusion, or law of diminishing returns does set in. When does the process of automatic hereditary social virtue begin? Are the children of parvenus also parvenus? Somebody has to start the family ball rolling somewhere. When Adam delved and Eve span, who was then the gentleman?

Actually, for Philadelphia, the second generation will do quite well if it conforms gracefully to the mores of the already established, and above all if, like Mr. Hutchinson, it marries "into society."

This is all somewhat unfair to both Philadelphia and Sidney, as it presents them at their most exasperated. Sidney at his best (and Old Philadelphia too) was and is really sincerely devoted to country life and appreciative of rural beauties; Sidney was also devoted to his family and friends even when they were a bit crude. He almost forgave his father-in-law C. Jared Ingersoll for being a Democrat, and his brother Henry for going into trade and making a million, and he was not actually quite as impeccably awful as he would like to have been. He also had a good enough mind, read contemporary poets and novelists and philosophers with understanding and sense, had a shrewd eye for the actualities of character, even public character, and a devotion to poetry which did not, however, help him to write it very well. In the end, he even accepted and admired Lincoln, that apostle and representative of dreadful Democracy, and so presumably changed some of his opinions a little bit.

On the whole, however, Sidney, and most Old Philadelphians, are more inclined to subscribe to his pithy statement, "If we must submit to democracy in the government, let us at least keep it away from our social circles."

As an antidote to Sidney Fisher, and as representative of another, and opposite side of Old Philadelphianism, we can cite old John F. Watson of the *Annals*. He was a very different kettle of Philadelphian. There is nothing fancy about John.

John Fanning Watson during the 1830's was a citizen of Germantown (he worked in a bank there) who made it his duty to ask questions of everyone over eighty in the city, and thus acquired a mass of fact and fable, which he collected in three fat volumes. *Watson's Annals*, as these volumes are called, remain a sort of basic text of Philadelphiana. Though full of Honest John's own conceits and whimsies, latter-day researchers usually find that about details of fact — which old house stood where and who lived in it — Watson is almost unfailingly right. He covers not only "Rare Old Houses," but "Education in Early Times." (Sample: a news item of 1733. "Last Tuesday night Mr. Thomas Makin, a very ancient man, who for many years was a schoolmaster in this city, stooping over a wharf to get a pail of water, unhappily fell in and was drowned.") He writes of "Superstition and Popular Credulity," "Auction Sales," "Stoves, Public Stages, Tomatoes etc," and gives an enormous mass of detail presented in no order or sequence, about taverns, ponds, mansions, churches, streets and people.

In the course of his antiquarian rambles he delivers impromptu discourses, some of which parallel Sidney Fisher's. Watson's attitudes are equally Philadelphian; in fact the two take the same view of most things, in their conservatism, but for quite different reasons. Sidney despairs of the present because it is vulgar, and loves the past for its gentility. John equally deplores present luxuries, but because they are inconsistent with "Republican simplicity," and loves the past for what he imagines to be its sturdy sobriety. At any moment he is apt to say, "In primitive days, when culprits were few and society simple and sincere . . ." or of an ancestral education, "What they aimed to impart was solid and substantial. But since then solid reading is less sought after. The ephemera of England flutter across the water . . ."; or of female singing on the part of ancestresses, "They not only sang far more *natural* and in the character of their sex, but . . .

with far more good sense and *solid entertainment*. None then had heard or dreamed of a singing which was to be *screamed*, *secundum artem*, in alto voices, or shivered into trills of thirty-two demisemiquavers in a breath." "Solid" is John's favorite word.

How changed to John, for instance, appeared the status of apprentices from those honest old days. The gaudy modern apprentice (*ca.* 1835 or so)

must have his suit of fine broadcloth . . . ; his hat of the finest fur . . . ; his overcoat . . . with capes enough for another, or at least to clothe a whole family of children . . . ; his stock of the most approved patent stiffened stuff, with the exact tie in front, and his unmentionables brought up tight about him with the patent double roller gum elastic suspenders. Now what a contrast does this afford to the dress of the apprentice of seventy years since. Only figure to yourselves, readers, a young man of eighteen years of age, of good proportions, handsome face and blooming with beauty, dressed in a pair of deerskin breeches coming hardly down to his knees. . . . Imagine, that the leather breeches, after several years' wear, got greasy as they grew old, and were only flexible so long as they were on and kept warm by the superflux of youthful heat.

Imagine, that in the morning of a cold day in January, when the snow which had blown into the bed chamber through the broken pane . . . had filled up the breeches with snow, and stiffened them up almost into horn, . . . the poor hapless wight . . . had to warm them into flexibility by some of that superabundant heat which had been acquired by lying warm in a straw bed . . . before he could move his legs down stairs to kindle a fire for his master.

On the increasing luxury of "modern times" and the parvenu ostentation of which Sidney speaks, John is no less severe. As of 1836 he gives up. "I can no longer employ my pen to illustrate the changing manners and times in our city. The traces of the past are . . . wholly effaced. The former was an age . . . of homely and domestic comfort . . . and this is now an entire age of luxury and cumbrous pomp. Now our 'merchants are princes' and our tradesmen are 'men of fortune': *all dwell in palaces.*" Is this progress? queries John. He doubts it. "The lesson of universal history has been that luxury always produces its own downfall and ruin. Shall *we* ever see this? Self-love and self-confidence answer *No!* Nous verrons," answers John for himself.

"I admire splendour . . . but above all things I *do love comfort*." Solid comfort. It is this which divides John and Sidney and their kindred Old Philadelphians to this day; for though Sidney likes comfort well enough, it must be elegant. Both tend to despise the present and adore the past, to dislike ostentation and admire simplicity; but the bias differs.

This split and ambivalence of Plain and Fancy is seen throughout the make-up of Old Philadelphia. Watson and Fisher are fairly good contemporary representations of the two. Sidney wants "good family" and a "recherché" ease of taste and manner. John prefers "good stock," and — "solid comfort." The split between Plain and Fancy shows up in most phases of Old Philadelphia life — Quaker (plain) versus Episcopalianism (fancy), Germantown versus Main Line, even to some extent between Philadelphia's two "first families," Morris versus Biddle. Depending often as much on personal characteristics as on background or family or place of residence, Old Philadelphians tend to divide themselves into these two sects, though of course seldom as extreme in either direction as Sidney Fisher or John Watson. The two influences balance each other, and many Old Philadelphians, pulled in both directions, as a result occupy a middle ground between them.

vi. *The Middle of the Middle of the Middle*

PERHAPS ESPECIALLY in relation to the surrounding extremes, the key to the constitution of the Philadelphian is that word "middle." It is in the middle of that most unregional of American regions, the "Middle Atlantic." Its climate is at least comparatively (only comparatively) "moderate"; and the same comparative middleness exists in its personalities.

Moderation in fact, according to Owen Wister, has been the one extreme, the vice of the city. In a fragment of an unfinished novel, in which he called Philadelphia "Monopolis," Wister dilates on the theme of Philadelphia's excess of moderation.

In the midst of moderation, amplitude and fecundity did the settlers found their city; . . . ease, won with ease, was the lot of Monopolis. The ironic gods now looked down on the City of Moderation and forthwith planned their jest — how to bring about excess? Here then was the jest: out of moderation's very heart excess had been created — too much moderation.

Moderation, middleness of social warmth, is the principal quality and indeed the principal charm of its manners. At its best, and within its limits, the social temperature of Philadelphia is almost perfect; none of the orneriness of Boston, the hard, glittering animation of New York which can get so tiresome, nor on the other hand the gush and punctilio and recklessness and constant play-acting (at least for Northerners) of the South. This is all part of "Philadelphia Taste," which is as much a social as a decorative thing. Consciousness of this "Taste" is one of the things that makes Philadelphians condescend. Sally McKean, writing to a New York friend in the eighteenth century, says of a Philadelphia party: "You never could have had such a drawing-room. It was brilliant beyond anything you can imagine. And though there was a great deal of extravagance, there was so much of Philadelphia taste in everything, that it must have been confessed the most delightful occasion of the kind ever known in this country." The New York reaction to this is unfortunately not extant.

There is in actual fact a natural, relaxed, live-and-let-live about Philadelphia taste and manners at their best which demands nothing of you but an equal simplicity and casualness. It is almost impossible not to have a convivial good time among Philadelphians, so long as you don't expect too much in the way of stimulation.

And so long, of course, as you are really in *with* them, not just alongside. For this enveloping warmth is reserved for people they know, the society of relations, friends or strangers properly introduced. As for the non-introduced, they simply do not exist. The non-existence of the unknown in Philadelphia is quite a frightening affair, for Philadelphians have been trained to see only what they recognize. You could be put naked on a pedestal in the middle of the room revolving slowly under searchlights, and the surrounding Philadelphians, if they didn't recognize you, still wouldn't see you. Outsiders can be made to feel quite transparent, as though people were going to walk right through them.

An illuminating advertising campaign conducted by N. W. Ayer, Philadelphia's leading advertising agency, for the *Evening Bulletin*, Philadelphia's leading newspaper, manages, surely not completely unintentionally, to take off a good many of Philadelphia's most stubborn qualities. The cartoon advertisement always involves the same situation: a strange long-nosed individualist is jumping up and down in excitement, shouting and pointing at some odd event. All around him are seated complacent and happy Philadelphians with faces buried in the *Bulletin* and paying no attention to him whatever. The fact that the "odd event" often involves considerable threat to their own immediate safety does not influence them in the least. In this one concise cartoon the artist, Richard Decker, has been summing up Philadelphia for years. First and foremost of course is the Philadelphia lack of curiosity, the inability and unwillingness to observe the unknown, no matter how spectacular. Then there is Philadelphia's enormous self-satisfaction, the delight in the status quo; above all, the intense groupiness, the cheerful conformity and oneness of the readers of the *Bulletin*, and their complete exclusion of the oddball, the intense, the enthusiastic and the alarmed — no matter how proper his concern. This all comes under the head of that modestly modulated *Bulletin* slogan, "Nearly everybody reads the *Bulletin*." Nearly everybody, that is, except the peculiar.

Certainly one of the most acute aspects of Philadelphia middleness is the strong desire to be in the middle of a group. As a Boston woman who moved to Philadelphia remarked, "At home all my friends say 'I' this and 'I' that. Here in Philadelphia they always say 'we.'" For a school or herd, acceptance or non-acceptance by those of the same species is a matter of life and death; it is abnormally important in Philadelphia too. This accounts for the completely contradictory accounts of Philadelphia by different reporters. John Gunther, as a Midwestern New Deal liberal, found Philadelphia full of obsolete privilege and chilly snobbery. Sean O'Faolain, a cultivated and clubbable Irishman, found it a haven of old-fashioned geniality and culture. By contrast, an anonymous Nebraskan was moved to Philadelphia as president of a Philadelphia branch of a great national company. A party was given for him and his wife. The party was a great success, but nobody spoke to the guests of honor, who went home, packed up and took the plane back to Omaha. On the other hand, Bostonians and Southerners with the right kind of social and college backgrounds, and attached to the right banks or companies in Philadelphia, are assimilated so quickly that they are inclined to believe that the fabled crustiness of Philadelphia, or even the existence of Old Philadelphia itself, is a myth. It depends entirely on one's protective coloring.

Another critical aspect of Philadelphia's middleness, middle-of-the-groupness and middle-of-the-roadness is what Philadelphians are fond of calling their "conservatism." If a rather sentimental nostalgia for the past, a cynicism about the present and an abject gloom about the future can be called conservative, Philadelphians, almost to a man and woman, are conservative; this, of course, without reference to period, and just as true of Sidney Fisher in 1840 as of a typical Old Philadelphian in the 1960's. When it comes to really conserving anything, however, Philadelphians have always been flagrantly lax. Old houses, old neighborhoods, old customs, old restaurants, old reputations are abandoned just as soon as they are out-of-date, out-of-date in Philadelphia being usually just the moment when they become picturesque and fashionable everywhere else. The last gas lamps, for instance, were just removed from Philadelphia streets a year or so ago. There was a good deal of nostalgic newspaper work about it, but the lamps went. Meanwhile, almost everywhere else,

Greenwich Village, the suburbs of New York, people are wildly buying up and installing identically "quaint" gas lamps. As opposed to real conservatives, Southern Bourbons or Morganatic New Yorkers or Die-hard Bostonians, who will stick by styles and places and opinions just *because* they are completely untenable, Philadelphians are downright Boosters. Their motto is never "The old at any cost," or "King Charles to the death"; instead the Philadelphia motto is, "Don't be the first to cross a new bridge, or the last to leave an old one." Philadelphia boys do not stand on burning decks, whence all but they have fled. They flee when and not before or after Nearly Everyone Else, Nearly Everyone Else in Philadelphia that is, does. That this happens to be about twenty years after the rest of the country does not mean they are conservative, just slow. "Conservatism" and "inertia" or even "nostalgia" are not all quite the same thing.

This essential lack of conservatism is most conspicuous in the way Philadelphians have abandoned the residential quarters of their city, allowing them to go to the dogs and the wreckers, in striking contrast to Boston or Charleston. The fact that many Philadelphians sold their town houses at the very bottom of the depression is quite typical too. This, in fact, is part of another Philadelphia virtue, which like moderation has become a vice by being carried to excess: common sense. In *The Peterkin Papers,* it is the Lady from Philadelphia who rescues the over-transcendentalized New England family from their peculiar quandaries by the application of a little simple practicality. At home, however, the practicality of Philadelphians can be carried to absurdity.

Mrs. Keith is an example. Mrs. Keith was a famous Philadelphia dowager who lived in what was known as the old Physick house. Dr. Physick was, believe it or not, a famous eighteenth-century doctor, and though Mrs. Keith was not necessarily a descendant, she did, not so long ago, live in his house. Like many Philadelphia dowagers, she had a hat, but one day decided to buy a new one. When she got the new hat home she found she couldn't tell where the front of it was. She wore it out to parties, turned a different way each time in hopes that one of her friends would tell her she had it on wrong. But none of her friends could tell which was the front either, so she went back to her old hat.

The Physick house was famous for having beautifully and elaborately paneled eighteenth-century doors. One day Mrs. Keith had a carpenter come and shave off all the paneling. When asked in horror why she had done it, she said, "I can't get a maid nowadays to dust them properly, and I'm certainly not going to dust them myself; so I just shaved them clean." She also owned a beautiful set of Queen Anne dining-room chairs; one day she had them all burned up in the furnace. Her relations, who had been eyeing them expectantly, were outraged of course. She told them, "You were all quarreling so about who'd get them when I died that I just got rid of them to keep peace in the family."

The Keiths had a country cousin, whom they both disliked, who kept threatening to visit. Finally she was really coming. "She can't use my bathroom," said Mr. Keith. "Nor mine," said Mrs. Keith; so they built an extra bathroom especially for the cousin's visit. Mrs. Keith also not only always referred to, but addressed her husband as "Mr. Keith." When at last a member of the family dared ask her why, she said, "Well, I really don't know him well enough to call him anything else."

A by-product of this exaggerated common sense is Philadelphia aplomb, which consists in simply not recognizing untoward incidents, in the same fashion that one does not recognize unfamiliar people. There is a whole string of pants stories, of varying authenticity, which underline this quality; someone who was following a Miss Cadwalader in the receiving line of a wedding noticed that her underpants had fallen down. She stepped out of them, he picked them up and put them in his pocket and they went through the line without missing a step. (The man who told me this said I really couldn't use it, "The Cadwaladers wouldn't like it.") Henry Savage, one of Philadelphia's favorite eccentrics, was something of a miser. He economized by never wearing suspenders, his trousers being held up by bits of string. Introduced to a lady, he rose from his chair, the strings broke, his pants fell in horrid disclosure, he pulled them up, bowed gracefully and sat down, quite undisturbed. Mrs. George Woodward of Krisheim, one of the great ladies of Chestnut Hill, used to give musicales. At one of these her underpants fell down as she was receiving guests. She merely handed them to a footman without comment and went on receiving.

One of the best authenticated, most flagrant and recent examples of Philadelphia aplomb was the case of Mrs. Isaac Clothier and the burglar. For several years the Main Line has been enlivened by the raids of a man known as the "Bandana Bandit." * Presumably once a butler, he robbed only the best people, seeming to know not only who they were, but where they cached the stuff. It was, in fact, a sort of painful honor to be robbed by him. The Clothiers' turn came when Mrs. Clothier was alone in the house and in bed. The bandit walked into her bedroom. She turned on the light, sat up and said, "Now, my dear man, you know I never keep any money in the house. There's nothing but those little things on the bureau my children gave me, they really wouldn't be worth your while. Why don't you just go downstairs and have a glass of milk?" He did, and left.

Perhaps the most peculiar aspect of Philadelphia middleness is the concentration of Philadelphians generally upon the middle parts of the body, particularly the seat and the stomach. The stories of Philadelphia aplomb in situations involving the loss of pants are only one tiny facet of a really odd complex, a complex which should eventually interest a good psychiatrist. The two principal aspects of this fixation are the Philadelphia concern for food and drink, and their interest in the sedentary, in all its forms. The motif of the Chair turns up everywhere; at the dinner party, old Philadelphia's principal ritual, which combines admirably both stomach and seat; in sports, where Philadelphia's two most cherished sports, riding and rowing, both involve sitting; and in

---

* He was finally caught.

professional life, where being Chairman of the Board is the ultimate in respectability.

Middle age too is another Philadelphia middle. For if Boston is an old city, firm, formed, "finished" in the sense of "completed" as Arnold Bennett called it, crotchety, permanently set in its convictions, and New York, if not a young, is at least a perennially would-be youthful city, Philadelphia is essentially middle-aged; still full of activity but slowing down, still fluid but fond of its comfortable routines, no longer adventurous but quite happy to do the same cosy things over and over again, reveling in the security of a pattern. The young, if they have any imagination or ambition, are usually rebellious in Philadelphia. It is only later on that they begin to appreciate the values of the relaxed, the intimate, the non-competitive, the familiar. The slowness that drives youth crazy suits the middle-aged perfectly. It's such a relief.

Even the Philadelphia accent, such as it is, remains a sort of middle. Halfway between North and South, too closely related for comfort to the barbarities of the Midwestern accent in its tendencies to nasality and hard *r*'s, it still does have peculiarities all its own. One is a drawl; another a cockneyish tendency to turn all vowels to diphthongs. Both these effects are of course common in the South too, but the Philadelphia versions are quite different. The word "no" is almost universally, among high and low, pronounced "nao." The key phrase is "the lonely road to the dark park," which in Philadelphia tends pretty generally to come out something like "the laonely raoad to the daork paork." It is not on the whole a pretty accent, but at its nicest is relaxed, unaffected and curiously soothing, without the harshness of more northern and western brogues. On the other hand it's not a *special* accent in the way that the New England, the Southern, the Colony Club or the Toity-Toid New York, the cowboy Western accents are all special. Philadelphians, of course, assume that everybody *else* has the accent. They actually in a way do come closer to being right than most Americans.

About the only middle in fact which is not appreciated by Old

Philadelphians is the middle class, and Philadelphia is certainly one of the remaining places in America where the term "middle class" is still distinctly derogatory. Obviously the Philadelphia upper class is sociologically and essentially an upper middle class. That is, it is a mercantile and professional *haute bourgeoisie,* not a feudal, landowning, arms-bearing nobility. However, when the old Philadelphians say "middle class" they don't mean themselves. Not for a moment. They mean the middle middle, nongent bourgeoisie, that is, any prosperous person who lives in Philadelphia but isn't related or connected to anybody, and of whom they have "never heard." (There would be a further distinction between "perfectly nice people" whom one doesn't know and hasn't heard of, but who, for some strange reason, seem to have all the earmarks of the upper class, and those who are obviously non-upper.) A Philadelphia matron who had out-of-town relations visiting her insisted that they dress for dinner. "I have a new couple," she explained, "and I don't want them to think we're middle class."

Exactly as in England, this Forsyte upper middle class of Old Philadelphians has become the real ruling class, the determiner of upper-class standards, the possessor of upper-class privileges. The difference in Philadelphia is not one of title or money, but between those with an hereditary acquaintance with the usages of "ladies and gentlemen," and those to whom this world of "breeding" seems alien and affected. Superficial manners, educational background, acquaintanceship with the right people and belonging to the right things all have some bearing on whether one is "upper" or "middle" class in Philadelphia; but fundamentally what really counts is Family. Birth is still the criterion and Family, in the somewhat broad Philadelphia sense, is still the center of the Philadelphia cosmology.

vii. Family

BASICALLY, the ideal Philadelphia in-group, the group Philadelphians above all prefer to be in the middle of, the ultimate club, is the Family; not the immediate family circle but the total family of in-laws and connections —"kin." The Philadelphia tone of good-humored, relaxed chumminess is exactly that of a merry family Christmas party, in which everyone knows everything about everyone, and there is nothing in the atmosphere that can't be taken entirely for granted.

Almost all the functions of upper-class Philadelphia life reflect this standard. Business is to be conducted as though a family council were managing the estate, with the help of family lawyers. Pleasure consists in clan gatherings. Whether at small dinner parties or at massive teas or at informal gettings-together in local country clubs, the ideal of a family group coming together to celebrate their mutual affection and self-esteem is basic, no matter how diluted by actual suburban dispersion and the intrusion of newcomers.

As in any family-centered Establishment, most personal judgments tend to be made from the point of view of "The Family." Being an ornament or support of said family is a good deal more important than just being Important in any public sense; which is certainly one reason for the chronic dissatisfaction of creative or ambitious native Philadelphians.

Even deeper than this feeling of the family group and its atmosphere as being the measure of social life and the ideal of social tone, is the sense that family status is the basis of one's own standing in the world. For that venerable Position of which the Philadelphian is so confident is based first of all on Family.

The derivation of family status anywhere is fairly uniform: tenure of power and wealth, a record of distinction somewhere along the line, and connections with other such families of status. In this Philadelphia is certainly not different from Rome or Kalamazoo. The way to found a family is traditional and summed up by that formula attributed to Quakers, "In the first generation thee * must do well, in the second marry well, in the third breed well; then the fourth will take care of itself." If Philadelphia does differ from other centers it is in its emphasis on that

* Every Quaker story must work a "thee" in somehow.

marrying second generation. It is not, as a rule, family founders who are remembered and worshipped, but members of a later generation. What this means is that in Philadelphia inherited position is better than self-made position. Inherited money is better than made money. Where the money came from is something, no matter how honorable or even exciting, that one usually prefers to forget. A real Family just *has* money; and almost the same thing might be said of distinction.

The mere acquisition of wealth, particularly in Trade, may create individual Position, but does not make a Family. The idea is "wait and see." If a son turns out well, that is, takes the opportunity to become a full-fledged gentleman and marries into an already good family, the chances are that it's a safe bet. His children merely have to consolidate, marry within this same circle and have lots of properly educated children. Then the Family Position is fairly secure; somebody along the line is bound to turn up rich and distinguished again to keep things going.

There are some pretty acute words on all this in Richard Powell's novel, *The Philadelphian.*

Philadelphia society had long ago worked out a procedure for taking in new members. Money and power were important, but Philadelphia wanted to see if you could produce children and grandchildren who could handle money and power. Marrying well was part of it, but Philadelphia wanted to find out if the blood lines would run true from generation to generation. Proving that you had poise and culture was part of it, but would your children have the same qualities, or would they be freaks and eccentrics. Philadelphia society didn't care for freaks and eccentrics. It had produced very few of them in its two hundred and fifty years of existence. Those few had been removed quietly and quickly, the way a gentleman farmer who was proud of his stock might dispose of a two-headed calf.

As important as being an actual member of a Family, perhaps more important, is being caught in the Web. You may yourself be totally undistinguished, have a totally undistinguished name; but being related in good standing to Everybody through your grandmother is quite enough. The important thing is to be related, *and* in good standing, which means that Grandmother's marriage was acceptable and Grandfather joined the Family, rather than Grandmother leaving it. Since Everybody is related or at least connected (it is a safe bet that there is nobody in this circle who is not related or connected by at least two or three removes to everyone else) and since Everybody remembers just exactly how Everybody is related and connected to each other, one's in-ness or out-ness is a pretty well-established fact. One's place at the center or the periphery of the Web has nothing to do with name, personal charm or prowess, or real ancestral worth. What counts is the number and closeness of connecting strands. Older people in Philadelphia develop a phenomenal memory for this sort of thing, and *no* protracted Philadelphia conversation ever takes place anywhere among Philadelphians remotely caught in the Web, except perhaps the very young, in which somewhere along the line the question of who she was before she was married or the reference to a cousin or an in-law or a progenitor does not emerge. Often whole evenings can be given over to this sort of thing; and one must not assume that this is necessarily dull, since Philadelphians can lavish an enormous amount of anecdotal fancy on decking the family tree with displays of scandalous humor.

Even the most diaphanous web however has to have moorings, and there do emerge certain specific families whose positions make a sort of focus for the whole shebang. No two Philadelphians will ever give you, if pressed, the same answer to a question about which are Philadelphia's first families. It is, of course, an unseemly question; the particular Philadelphian's own family is naturally one of them, but modesty compels him to omit his or any other family too obviously related or connected. Outside of this the choice is among hundreds, and variable; but certain names are bound to come up — if only to be dismissed.

viii. *"Where Scrapples Eat Biddle"*

WHEN EDWARD VII was Prince of Wales, and had visited Philadelphia, he is said to have remarked, "I met a very large and interesting family named Scrapple, and I discovered a rather delicious native food they call biddle." This is the hoariest of all Philadelphia jokes, one with "Here's to dear old Boston" with its reference to Cabots and Lowells. However the fact that it *is* one of the oldest of Philadelphia chestnuts has significance. Jokes about Philadelphia being a city founded at the confluence of the Biddle and Drexel families, and about the qu'est-ce que c'est Cassatts, are outmoded. Drexels and Cassatts, both fairly recent families anyway, have now more or less receded into the background.

Biddle and Cadwalader seem, in fact, to be about the only names nowadays that non-Philadelphians recognize as being typically Philadelphian. There are jokes about this too: "When a Biddle gets drunk he thinks he's a Cadwalader" is an old one to Philadelphians, but just recently printed by Bennett Cerf as a new one. Rittenhouse and Pennypacker, names once good for jokes, have also become unfamiliar. None of them would probably be given nowadays in a Philadelphian's list of absolutely first families. Cadwalader definitely would. And Biddle would invariably be mentioned — to be almost invariably dismissed.

The Biddles serve the function, peculiar to the Philadelphia psychology, of being a lightning rod. As Benjamin Franklin (the inventor of the lightning rod) is Philadelphia's Great Man for public consumption, so nobody else has to try, the Biddles act as Philadelphia's First Family for public consumption. Everybody knows, everybody in Philadelphia, that such names as Hopkinson and Roberts are really older and better; or that, as the ancient rhyme, rather out-of-date now, called the Philadelphia Rosary goes:

> Morris, Norris, Rush and Chew,
> Drinker, Dallas, Coxe and Pugh,
> Wharton, Pepper, Pennypacker,
> Willing, Shippen and Markoe

— or names such as Hare, Hart, Fox, Montgomery, Harrison, etc., are all of them more historically Philadelphian names than Biddle.

The barbarians (and the Biddles) can go on thinking the Biddles are First Family if they want to. It saves Philadelphia a lot of trouble.

The Biddles may not be the center of the Web, the point being that this web has no real center; but they are certainly one of its recognized attachments. They are after all related to most of the better families like the Cadwaladers, and if any family can be cited as an example of the Quaker formula worked out in fact, it is the Biddles.

They are "of course" not Oldest Philadelphians, though they don't as a rule admit this in the usual disarming Philadelphia way. They come, in horrid fact, from New Jersey, whence so many other Philadelphia families like the Coxes and the Stokeses and the Wetherills also came.

The original Biddle was a Quaker shoemaker who suffered for conscience's sake in English jails. Painful research has dug up the supposition that he was a younger son of a gentleman soldier of titled connections, but it seems unlikely that even the youngest son of a gentleman, even a Quaker, would descend to shoemaking at that time. However, Quakers always made much of the dignity of labor, and had no contempt for being "in trade." This Biddle emigrated to New Jersey in 1681, took up large lands, and both he and his son were important early colonial figures there.

However, two restless grandchildren, William and John, moved across the river to the big city. John prospered in a modest way as an importer. William, as a disastrous failure and an irascible plunger, went bankrupt. However, he had the good sense to marry a Mary Scull (the Sculls are still about, one of them now married to a Biddle, another to a Cadwalader). He died and left his widow with nine children. She brought them up to be founders of the Biddle family fortunes.

It was the Revolutionary generation of Biddles that "did well," not singly, but in quintuplicate. John the importer had two sons who became famous Revolutionary officers: Owen, a Quaker watchmaker and amateur astronomer, whose conscience forced him to fight for liberty, but who later apologized to his Meeting for it; and Clement, who was Washington's aide-de-camp and close personal friend. Both Owen and Clement had innumerable children; Clement's in particular both married well and did well. His sons, Thomas and Clement Jr., were eminent bankers, Mary began all the Cadwalader business (the story, incidentally, that Biddles were at any time gardeners of the Cadwaladers seems purely apocryphal) by marrying a General Thomas and John played safe by marrying his second cousin Mary Biddle, thereby inaugurating another Biddle custom. (There have been at least two modern Biddle–Biddle marriages.) Most of Clement's nine married children, following the Quaker prescription for the third generation, bred like rabbits, and this Clement branch became known as the Solid Biddles, involved in law and finance and marrying everybody in sight worth marrying.

The children of William the Bankrupt were the Romantic Biddles. Three of them made their mark. Edward, the first Biddle to shine, became a politician of note in Reading, and something of a pre-Revolutionary firebrand, who died from the effects of a rumpus with a tavernkeeper over politics. His younger brother Nicholas joined the infant American Navy, and when, during an engagement with the British, he was blown up on his ship the *Randolph,* he provided America with its first authentic naval hero. Ballads were written about him. Another brother, Charles, did survive, though he was shipwrecked many times under the most harrowing circumstances, was a prisoner of the British during the Revolution, and altogether led a life of watery daring and hardship. Mutinies, hurricanes, duels, murders, drownings, plagues, he took in his energetic stride. His description, in his autobiography, of the incident that broke him of "a vile habit I had of striking with anything I laid my hands on . . . at any of the crew that did not move briskly as I thought they should" gives the general impression.

When we first discovered the ship had sprung a leak I ordered Mr. Corry the Chief Mate to turn out all hands. They were all soon upon deck except John Walsh, a very stout, lazy fellow. I called him myself, but he not answering, I jumped into the steerage with a belaying pin in my hand, and going up to his berth I struck him on the head. He soon after began to groan. Feeling him about the head I found I had struck him in the mouth, and that it was bleeding. I felt the pains of the damned for I concluded he was mortally wounded. It determined me to break myself of the abominable practice of striking with what might indanger [sic] the life of a man, and from that time I never gave a sailor a blow with anything but a piece of rope.

After the war, with pioneer adaptability this salty character adjusted himself to life ashore, made a fortune as banker and merchant, entered politics, was a friend of both Washington and Burr, practiced as a lawyer, and in 1785 was Vice President of the State of Pennsylvania under the old constitution, while Dr. Franklin himself, another friend, was President. Charles Biddle died in the odor of Philadelphia sanctity and respectability at seventy-six, leaving a number of children who also distinguished themselves and gave the Biddle name its final coat of Philadelphia fixative.

All these three sons of William and Mary had a touch of picturesque violence about them, not characteristically Philadelphian, and this drop of spice seems to have been inherited in more or less each generation afterward.

The paragon of all Biddles, certainly the man who gave the name its cachet, and certainly one of Philadelphia's essential and symbolic figures, was Charles's son Nicholas. Nicholas the Great was in every way the *beau ideal* of the Philadelphia second generation. Charles, his father, may have been a diamond somewhat in the rough, but Nicholas was as polished as a diamond could be. Nicholas began life with everything. His father was by now rich and respectable, and he himself was, if the miniatures of him do not lie, a model of Byronic beauty. He was so brilliant that he finished his course at the University of Pennsylvania by the time he was thirteen, and was sent to Princeton, where he did advanced work in the classics and graduated as valedictorian with the class of 1801.

The general family expectation, unusual in Philadelphia, seems to have been that he would be a writer. But, like any good literary Philadelphian, he first studied law under his older brother William; and though he did join the circle about Joseph Dennie, founder and editor in Philadelphia of America's first successful egghead journal, the *Port Folio,* and wrote articles for the magazine, his life along these lines was continually interrupted by other opportunities. He went abroad, first as secretary to the Minister to France, and then as secretary to the Minister to England, James Monroe. He made the grand tour, and strengthened his passion for the antique by travels in Greece. On his way home he stopped in England long enough to amaze the dons of Cambridge with his comparisons between ancient and modern Greek. This was considered a great coup for America.

Back in Philadelphia his association with the *Port Folio* was interrupted again, this time by politics and his election to the state legislature. While there his friend Monroe, now President, persuaded him to become a director of the newly rechartered Bank of the United States. Nicholas, though he had had no previous practical business experience, felt he was obligated. He boned up on banking, and it was not long before he was, like other Biddles in other banks, the president of this one.

The Bank of the United States was a rather special bank, however. Although run like a private institution for the profit of private stockholders, it was at the same time the real Treasury of the United States, in default of any other. All the government funds were entrusted to it, and though some of the directors were appointed to act in the government interest, the bank was really run by Biddle, and very well too, largely in the interests of the majority stockholders.

The Bank became a bulwark of security and conservatism in the feverishly speculative and expansive commercial world of the young republic. As such, it quickly acquired enemies, both in the West, where concentration of capital on the seaboard was ipso facto a sinister thing, and where the cautious control of the Bank hampered the more exuberant dreams of western speculators, and in New York. Thanks to the Erie Canal, New York had succeeded

Philadelphia as America's commercial center, and New York bankers resented the fact that Philadelphia, in the person of Biddle, still held the purse strings. When Jackson, a Westerner, and Van Buren, a New Yorker, came to power, the attack on the Bank grew bitter. The assault was made in the name of Democracy. There is certainly something rather odd about a semi-private institution under the virtual dictatorship of one private citizen, Biddle, controlling all the funds of a democratic government. Nonetheless, the system worked, and might have been in fact, with more public support, a model for an orderly government-supervised development of the American economy.

Biddle, like so many of the Philadelphia oligarchy, though a Jeffersonian liberal, was not exactly a Jacksonian Democrat. He certainly underestimated the power and skill of the Wild Man from the West. He forced the issue with Jackson by asking for the recharter of the Bank before the recharter was due. Jackson saw to it that the Bank was not rechartered, and the government funds were withdrawn. They were turned over to a group of "pet banks" in the various states, and the result was inflation, chaos and the panic of 1841 which in the end brought down the Bank of the United States too.

Though Biddle had retired before the crash, an investigation of the Bank's doings resulted in a court action. Biddle was accused of various things, the most spectacular being the snatching of some $400,000 of the Bank's funds. He was never brought to trial, but he was blamed for all the disasters leading up to the Bank's collapse, and retired, a thoroughly hated and discredited figure, to his country place, Andalusia. He had acquired Andalusia in proper second-generation fashion by marrying the heiress Jane Craig, and in the 1830's he had remodeled it into what is still one of the most beautiful of America's Greek temple mansions, prototype of so many southern plantation houses. His last years were spent there in lettered seclusion, entertaining distinguished visitors, writing an occasional paper. When he died in 1844 he was still in disgrace, already half forgotten.

The obituary on Biddle that Sidney Fisher wrote into his diary

(February 18, 1844) gives a contemporary and contemplative, if
a bit flowery, picture of the man and his fate:

Yesterday morning Nicholas Biddle died. The event created some
sensation; very slight however compared to that which it would have
produced a few years ago. There have been few instances of a more
complete reverse of fortune. . . . His manners, talents, varied accomplishments and the triumphant success which appeared for a long
time to attend all his measures, gave him a degree of influence and
popularity among the monied and educated classes equalled only by
that of Genl. Jackson with the populace. . . . How he was followed,
praised, worshipped, can scarcely be conceived by those who did not
witness the scenes in which he was an actor.

I saw but little except that which was exhibited in Society. Wherever he appeared there was a sensation and a crowd immediately
formed around him. His manner was gracious, smiling, easy, gentle-
manlike, a little condescending and exhibited supreme self-satisfaction
and elation.* His conversation was ready, fluent, elegant and witty.
His language was always choice and happy, without approaching the
vile habit of haranguing, flowed in free, sparkling and harmonious
periods. His figure was short, round and fat, yet his carriage was erect
and not ungraceful and his head and face were stamped with the marks
of character and intellect. His features were regular and chiselled, his
mouth remarkable for beauty and expression, his eyes grey, full and
beaming. He wore his hair very long, hanging around his face in
silken curls and he was very neat and recherché in his dress.

Whilst he was in the Bank he kept two establishments, always open,
with a full equipment of furniture, servants, horses etc, one in town
in Spruce St. above 7th and one at Andalusia, his seat on the Delaware near Bristol. His income then was very large and his expenditure lavish.

In the midst of this career of prosperity came the financial embar-
rassments of the Bank and of the country, speedily followed by the
wreck of the institution and, as a consequence, by a general destruction of private fortunes and universal prostration of business. . . .
The great object of democratic hatred had fallen, the "monster" had
verified the predictions of its enemies, it had ended in bankruptcy
and ruin, its corruption and abuses were now exposed in open day.

---

* As Bray Hammond puts it, "He liked to be irresistible." — Au.

The arch enemy of "the party," of "the people" had met with a deserved fate. His true character was now brought to light with all his tricks and intrigues, together with the frauds, speculations, extravagance and luxury of the money mongers and gamblers, the mushroom "aristocracy" with whom he was connected. . . .

The story of Biddle's disgrace to this day is not really clear, and he remains one of the most controversial, picturesque, important and incomprehensibly neglected figures in American history. Until recently he has been nothing but a contemptible footnote in the career of Andrew Jackson, and is represented in modern liberal discussions of Jackson as a sort of defeated Black Prince of Reaction, leader of the nasty moneybags and oligarchs worsted by the Champion of the People.

There is no doubt that he became the leader of the conservative rich and of various anti-Jackson forces, that power went to his head, and that the downfall of the Bank was in some measure due to his lack of political caution, skill and common sense. The picture of him as a scaly dragon in chains beneath the feet of Our Andrew, All-American Heavyweight, is a mite distorted however. In the first place he was himself personally a liberal, pro-Jefferson, pro-French, who took up banking in a purely democratic political dollar-a-year fashion. His earliest and latest and only really successful enemies were not the Peepul, who got nothing out of his defeat but ruin and suffering, but laissez-faire capitalists and Wall Street. For them the defeat of the Bank meant freedom of enterprise, freedom from government control and from government in business. It was not really until the days of that other Champion of the People, F.D.R., that Biddle was vindicated, in fact if not in name, that finance was again brought back into the federal fold, and that Biddle's enemies, the freelance exploiters of the American economy, were brought to heel again after a century of rapine.

This revaluation of Biddle's role * is a new thing. But what-

---

* Bray Hammond's *Banking and Politics in America* (Princeton University Press, 1957) gives the pro-Biddle side of the case. Thomas Govan's *Nicholas Biddle* (University of Chicago Press, 1959) is a most persuasive total defense of Biddle and his

ever the rights and wrongs, the man as a character and as a potent Philadelphia symbol emerges with a classic, or at least appropriately neo-classic clarity. He makes a fine figure, the darling of the gods who at the very height of his glory, at the top of his pride, his hubris, is struck down by the lightning of Nemesis. Against the almost ludicrously apt marble columns of his bank and his mansion he plays out this Greek drama with just the right lordly and humane brilliance and dignity. What could be better staged than this vignette, for instance, again from Sidney Fisher:

> The superiority of Biddle's character was made evident during these trying scenes. He had always been noted for courage and firmness, for calmness and self possession. When the Bank stopped payment, and crowds were collected around it, and the public were expecting the mob to attack it every moment, he walked quietly thro the throng with the unconcerned air of a stranger, tho he risked his life by doing so.

When Biddle retired for good to Andalusia the political and financial hopes of Philadelphia retired with him. Once capital of the United States and of Pennsylvania, largest, richest, most luxurious of American cities, center of fashion and intellect, Philadelphia had lost everything but Biddle and the Bank. When the Bank broke, when Biddle closed the classic doors of Andalusia against the world, Philadelphia closed its doors against the nation as a whole. The nation had rejected the leadership of Old Philadelphia; very well, Old Philadelphia rejected the nation. Like Biddle, Old Philadelphia retired into itself. Henceforth let vulgar Washington take over politics and vulgar New York take over finance. Philadelphia gentlemen would at least remain Philadelphian and gentlemen. Let even schoolmarmish Boston be first in books. Philadelphia would no longer be first at anything. But

---

Bank. Although for the lay reader (which certainly includes me), it is rather technical-economic-banking, it seems a most important book, not only for the understanding of Biddle but also for the understanding of Jackson, laissez faire, the modern New Deal, American liberalism and any number of other things.

by turning its back on the rest of the country, it would at least remain Philadelphian.

ix. *Later Biddles*

LATER BIDDLES have not been remiss in carrying on the family name, the family fortune and the family glamour. Nicholas the Great's own son, Charles John, managed the right blend of military dash and political intransigence. He carried on, for instance, the family's military tradition as exemplified in naval Nicholas. He served with gallantry as a captain in the Mexican War. At the siege and capture of Chapultepec he was, never a very robust person, flat on his back with a tropical fever. He was unable to rise, and his regiment had to leave him behind. However, he managed to crawl out, find and mount an old horse that had been left behind too, and dressed as he was, clutching a ramrod for his only weapon, joined his regiment, and led them in the attack. He was the second American to set foot on the ramparts. After the Civil War he capped his career of courage by being the foremost Democratic newspaper editor in a rabidly Republican city.

His sister Meta did the right thing by marrying her first cousin James Biddle, also a distinguished naval officer, but not to be confused with their mutual uncle, a Commodore James. Charles John's grandson, Charles John, a lawyer, still lives in Nicholas's pillared Andalusia on the banks of the otherwise industrialized Delaware.

In a still later generation of this Romantic branch of the Biddles, Anthony Drexel Biddle, great-grandson of Nicholas, maintained the Biddle glamour with a touch of plain eccentricity. His father had married into the comparatively parvenu but exceedingly famous and rich Drexel family. Inheritor of a large fortune in trust, Anthony devoted himself with equal energy to publishing and boxing, the collection of alligators as pets, and to parlor theatricals; his homemade version of Dr. Jekyll and Mr. Hyde, where he ended writhing on the floor and purple in the face, was evidently an experience.

He wrote books, which he published himself, of a bewildering variety. His book on the Madeira Islands, *The Land of Wine* (1901), is quoted by the *Encyclopaedia Britannica* as an authority. His *Life of Corbett* the boxer was his greatest literary success. His *Froggy Fairy Books* and *Shantytown Sketches,* the kind of dreadful dialect stories for which Philadelphians always seem to have a weakness, are better forgotten.

As a boxer and athlete he was not only known as a participant and patron, but also as the organizer of sort of YMCA-like Bible Classes, which combined mayhem and Christianity for the young in a highly appetizing manner. The climax of his career came when, in his sixties, he made a name for himself teaching Marines hand-to-hand combat during the Second World War. He was said to know more ways of killing a man than anybody else in history.

This strain of flamboyance, always latent in this branch of the Romantic Biddles, flowered mightily in Anthony's children. His daughter Cordelia's marriage to Angier Duke, the North Carolina tobacco heir, in 1915 was a scene of quite un-Philadelphian hoopla. Over a thousand people crowded into Holy Trinity on Rittenhouse Square, twenty-two hundred guests attended the reception, the display of wedding presents was capped by a half-inch sapphire given by the Stotesburys, and the railyards were choked with the private cars of the Dukes. With such a start the marriage was almost doomed to collapse, and the Duke–Biddle children, pried loose from Philadelphia moorings, exposed to the overstimulation of New York, and from the Philadelphia point of view decidedly adrift on a wash of somewhat unfortunate publicity, have carried on this tradition of marital failure. The last great house built in Tuxedo Park was contrived for the newlyweds Angier Biddle Duke and Priscilla St. George. They were divorced almost immediately and both remarried in no time to people who also had been divorced. The chain reaction of former wives and husbands, their new wives and husbands and these new spouses' former spouses, as listed in the paper to describe who had been who, along the way, included at least twenty names.

Despite the searchlights and scandals (including the public undressing of the family achieved by Cordelia in her book, *My Philadelphia Father,* from which the hit play *The Happiest Millionaire* was made) this branch of Biddles has nonetheless to be credited with solid achievement too. Anthony's son Anthony was Ambassador to Poland when the Second War broke out, and continued thereafter in the ticklish post of Ambassador to the Governments in Exile in London. He was for years Deputy General of Pennsylvania, and under the Kennedy Administration was brought out of this semi-retirement, just before his death, to be appointed Ambassador to Spain. Angier Biddle Duke has also done well as a diplomat, and as envoy to San Salvador was the youngest ambassador in American history. He is now Chief of Protocol for the State Department.

Anthony the boxer's brother, Livingston, stayed within the Philadelphia fold. As a gentlemanly, handsome and self-effacing sportsman and patron of literature and music, his one indiscretion, the publication of a book of poems, was easily forgiven. His son Livingston Jr. is, however, more suspect as being the Biddle's one really serious professional writer. His novel *Main Line* created something of a sensation in 1950 and is a worthy adjunct to the list of the "Philadelphia Novel." His brother Ernest is a renegade too as a well-thought-of professional portrait painter.

The most distinguished, and by far the most rebellious of all creative Biddles has been a sport from the other, or Solid branch, never heretofore marked by the sinister taint of aesthetic talent. George Biddle, in a long and crotchety career as painter, promoter of the WPA for artists during the depression, war correspondent and writer, has never failed to indicate his rejection of Philadelphia and Philadelphia values. He has not been too popular at home, and has lived for many years in self-imposed exile up the Hudson. His brother, Francis, has made himself equally distinguished and equally unpopular in the comparatively more respectable field of the law, as Franklin Roosevelt's Attorney General. They have both carried on the Biddle traditions of intransigence, Democratic politics and literary skill. George's autobiography and his *Artist at War* are vivid pieces of recollection and reportage respectively, and Francis Biddle's novel *The Llanfear Pattern* is one of the earliest and best of the Philadelphia Novels.*

Their paternal grandfather George Washington Biddle, a grandson of the Revolutionary Clement, was one of the leaders of the Philadelphia bar in the last half of the nineteenth century. He was what was always referred to as a "ripe" classical scholar, and translated Demosthenes for his amusement. This bookish Biddleism was inherited by two other brothers of Francis and George, Sydney, one of Philadelphia's earliest and most reputable psychoanalysts, and Moncure. Both Sydney and Moncure stayed in Philadelphia. Moncure in fact was an investment banker, but was also famous as a bibliophile, connoisseur of editions of the classics and an eccentric in his own right, who managed to collect about him a good many anecdotes, some probably aprocryphal. A particularly Biddle one concerns his meeting with a gentleman called Bible at a Dickens rally. Mr. Bible, a learned but thoroughly unworldly gentleman, when introduced remarked that he had heard the name Biddle somewhere before. In fact had met a Charles Biddle (the present incumbent of Andalusia). Was Moncure any relation? "Well, Mr. Bible, it's like this. At the Club they say to me 'Charles is *a* Biddle; but you, Moncure, are *the* Biddle.' " "Ah," said Mr. Bible. "Of course with a name like mine I don't run into these little contretemps." Those who knew Moncure Biddle best, however, insist that this is most uncharacteristic; for all his Biddle-mindedness, he was personally modest about his own personal Biddleness.

Though never approaching the political stature of the Adamses, Roosevelts, Tafts, or Byrds, the military glory of the Lees or the literary éclat of the Lowells, nor even the sheer continuing aristo-

---

* And in 1961, Francis published *his* autobiography, *A Casual Past,* with its sequel *In Brief Authority* (1962).

A BIDDLE GENEALOGY
(enormously simplified)

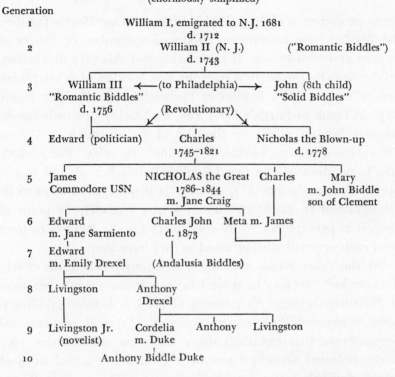

Generation

1   William I, emigrated to N.J. 1681
d. 1712

2   William II (N. J.)   ("Romantic Biddles")
d. 1743

3   William III ←—(to Philadelphia)—→ John (8th child)
"Romantic Biddles"   "Solid Biddles"
d. 1756   (Revolutionary)

4   Edward (politician)   Charles   Nicholas the Blown-up
1745–1821   d. 1778

5   James   NICHOLAS the Great   Charles   Mary
Commodore USN   1786–1844   m. John Biddle
m. Jane Craig   son of Clement

6   Edward   Charles John   Meta m. James
m. Jane Sarmiento   d. 1873

7   Edward
m. Emily Drexel   (Andalusia Biddles)

8   Livingston   Anthony
Drexel

9   Livingston Jr.   Cordelia   Anthony   Livingston
(novelist)   m. Duke

10   Anthony Biddle Duke

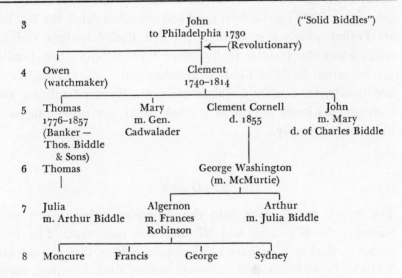

3   John   ("Solid Biddles")
to Philadelphia 1730
←—(Revolutionary)

4   Owen   Clement
(watchmaker)   1740–1814

5   Thomas   Mary   Clement Cornell   John
1776–1857   m. Gen.   d. 1855   m. Mary
(Banker —   Cadwalader   d. of Charles Biddle
Thos. Biddle
& Sons)

6   Thomas   George Washington
(m. McMurtie)

7   Julia   Algernon   Arthur
m. Arthur Biddle   m. Frances   m. Julia Biddle
Robinson

8   Moncure   Francis   George   Sydney

cratic prominence of New York's Livingston or Morris families, the Biddles have nonetheless produced a number of figures of interest and of standing. It is probably just this very distinction, mild as it is by comparison with the first families of other places, that tells against the Biddles in Philadelphia itself. The Pirate Captain Hook in Barrie's *Peter Pan,* meditating upon his career, consoles himself with the thought of his distinction: "Fame, Fame, that glittering bauble, it is mine!" he cries. But he had, alas, been educated at a Good English Public School, and within him there stirs the horrid question, "Is it quite good form to be distinguished at anything?" From a true Philadelphia point of view, it is perhaps not really good form for the Biddles to have been even as gently distinguished as they have been.

On the other hand, something facetiously called the Koch-Votichenko* Law may be at work here, as it often is in other areas of Philadelphianism. An example of the law is this: (a) Everybody thinks cannibals eat missionaries. (b) All sophisticated people know that cannibals don't really eat missionaries. (c) Anthropologists actually know of a good many actual cases of actual cannibals eating actual missionaries. The same really applies here: (a) The common herd and outsiders think the Biddles are Philadelphia's first family. (b) All Philadelphians and insiders know the Biddles really aren't Philadelphia's first family. (c) In actual fact the Biddles probably really are Philadelphia's first family, have more social connections, financial solidity and local and national esteem as a whole than any other one such Philadelphia family.

x. Others

THE NAME BIDDLE sank into the American subconscious with Nicholas the Blown-up and Nicholas the Bankrupt. The Cadwaladers, God save us, have never done anything that spectacular. Their claim to reputation, however, among Philadelphians them-

---

* The names of two playful Princeton professors.

selves, is impeccable. They, first of all, belong to that Welsh
Quaker settlement, known as the Welsh Tract or Barony, that
actually still provides the central enduring core of Philadelphia
aristocracy. This "Barony," comprising some 50,000 acres in
what is now the Main Line, was granted by Penn in one piece to
a group of Quakers from Wales who wanted to settle together.
Their isolation in this voluntary Welsh ghetto did not last long,
and marriages were made first with other Welsh Quaker families
and then with almost everybody. Some well-known Philadelphia
place names, Radnor, Haverford, Merion, Bryn Mawr, are vestiges
of this settlement, and are now Philadelphia's most famous suburbs; many of Philadelphia's oldest and best family names, Roberts, Pugh, Price, Evans, Lewis, Lloyd and others come from the
settlers in this same area.

Of these Cadwalader is and was one of the best. The name itself
is something of a lucky accident. Many Welsh emigrants of the
period had no last names, being Owen ap (son of) Robert, John
ap Owen, and suchlike. In some generation the patronymic
froze as a last name and Owen ap Robert would become Owen
Roberts, or Rhys ap John became plain Rhys Jones. This happened to John ap Cadwalader who followed the family of his
uncle John ap Thomas to the Barony in 1697, and there became
John Cadwalader, his descendants thus missing by a generation
the fate that overtook the children of his uncle, who became ordinary Jones. As one can see, this adds just one more insane complication to the already complicated genealogy of these Welshmen.
The Cadwaladers themselves — or the Thomases or the Joneses or
whatever you want to call them — trace their family tree right
back through ninety-five generations to Adda ap Duw; that is,
Adam son of God. From there the Cadwaladers go on down
Biblical history via Noah and his descendants, then make a surprising shift into classical mythology. Coelus, Saturn and Jupiter
bring them shortly into the royal house of Troy and thence to
Aeneas and Brutus. Brutus having settled in England as everyone knows, the rest of the ancestors are people like King Arthur
and King Lear. (It is interesting to note that the Cadwaladers, of

Lear's three daughters, spring from nasty Regan, not nice Cordelia.)

Of all early Cadwaladers the most respectable was Dr. Thomas (ap John) whose career spanned the eighteenth century, from 1708 to 1779. Apprenticed first to his uncle who bore the not un-Welsh name of Dr. Evan Jones, one of the first medical men of the city, he then studied abroad. He returned to a large practice and a long, useful, public career. As a doctor he was known as America's first anatomist, performer of America's earliest autopsies and perhaps the earliest experimenter in the therapeutic uses of electricity. He was a friend of Franklin and associated with him in his various projects, particularly the Library Company of 1731. He married (good second generation that he was) an heiress, Hannah Lambert, and came into possession of great lands in New Jersey near Trenton.

Two of the Doctor's sons, John and Lambert, fought with distinction in the Revolution; equipping and leading companies of their own, and even providing them with Madeira during drills. In the next generation, John's son Thomas, usually referred to, like his father, as General, was the agent for the Penn family's vast American estates, and married Mary Biddle, daughter of Clement.

His sons, in turn, the brothers John and George, were the principal nineteenth-century Cadwaladers. John, a lawyer, studied with Horace Binney, Philadelphia's grand old man of the bar, was counsel for his cousin, Nicholas Biddle, and his Bank of the United States and raised and commanded a company of city militia during the riots of 1844, a gesture not without some risk. Through it all he remained, along with his Biddle and Ingersoll contemporaries, a firm Democrat (which was not entirely without risk either). George, his brother, was a more dashing fellow. He made and spent fortunes, his house was the grandest in town, his carriages the most elegant, his trotter Ned Forrest the fastest in the world. Whenever there was trouble he fought in it, was shot at as an officer of the City Troop in the riots, and was a General in the Mexican War. He was also the first head, in 1834, of the newly organized Philadelphia Club. Sidney Fisher, who knew both the brothers well, describes George as a "handsome animal," and gives a good deal of detail about both of them, ranging from John's politics to George's mistresses, of neither of which he approves. The two were dominant social figures in their time, and are neatly representative of two stock Old Philadelphia masculine roles — the radical but imbedded legal-literary intellectual and the don't-give-a-damn sportsman and bon viveur, both of whom, because of their social security, get away with breaches of conformity which would not be permitted to the merely respectable or the merely middle class.

In this century, a Richard Cadwalader, though otherwise a shy soul, owned the largest yacht in the world. But the most prominent and beloved of Cadwaladers has been Dr. Williams Cadwalader of the Zoo. Actually Williams Biddle Cadwalader was a distinguished neurologist, professor of the subject at the University of Pennsylvania and president of the American Neurological Society. Around Philadelphia, however, he was more famous for his love of animals. Besides endless and very successful efforts to stimulate interest in the Zoo and raise money for it, he spent hours there getting to know not only the employees but the inmates. Few nature lovers have gone so far in this direction. A woman friend of his touring the Zoo one day came upon him inside one of the cages holding a conversation with Frankie the hippopotamus. After a few fond embraces he left. Later she saw him again, talking to the shoebill stork. This time he picked the stork up and gave it a good-by kiss on the bill. However the animals may have responded, among the employees of the Zoo and in Philadelphia generally the hippopotamus-hugging Dr. Williams was, till he died in 1957, one of the city's very favorite sons. His brother Lambert was chief patron of the Academy of Natural Sciences for years, and he and Williams frequently indulged in heated lunchtime arguments over the respective merits of live versus stuffed animals. At the Philadelphia Club, where these tussles took place, the two were known as the Quick and the Dead.

These careers can easily be matched by any number of members of any number of other Philadelphia families. What has distinguished the Cadwaladers has been first of all the long span, going back to the very beginnings of Philadelphia settlement, then the more or less invariable quality of local professional and social eminence, and last and probably most important their peculiarly central position in the Philadelphia Web. The roots of almost all family trees cross at the Cadwaladers, and families that have no especially close ties with each other, the Biddles and Morrises for instance, are all connected to the Cadwaladers. As genealogical glue the Cadwaladers can't be beat.

The Morrises' claim to Philadelphia station is rather similar to the Cadwaladers', with whom they are connected and related by various cross-fertilizations. Though never quite as exalted, they too came from that same original stock of Welsh Quakerism, although the Morrises did not settle in the Barony or come direct from Wales.

The original Morris, Anthony, emigrated from London and settled in Philadelphia itself. There he soon became one of the richest men in the city, largely as a brewer, and prominent as weighty Friend, Justice of the Court of Common Pleas, Mayor of Philadelphia in 1703. He also found time for four wives and fifteen children, most of whom also married and had children. The Morrises have done well (though the only one really famous Philadelphia Morris, Robert, who helped finance the Revolution, was no relation) and married well, but above all they have bred well, and perhaps their central position, even beyond that of the Biddles, is based on sheer numbers. If one asks what the Morrises are really famous for, the answer is "being there." Of the original Anthony there are probably 30,000 descendants, most of them not active of course in Philadelphia social circles. Of his descendant Captain Samuel's procreation there have been at least 5,000. The *Social Register* now contains over sixty Morris listings, of whom all but a couple are of the same family.

The particular Morris from whom most of Philadelphia's present-day socially eligible Morrises descend, and who "represents" the Morrises, somewhat as Nicholas the Great "represents" the

Biddles, was Samuel, variously known as Captain Morris, Samuel junior, to distinguish him from an uncle, Samuel senior, or as "Christian Sam." Descendant of four Anthony Morrises in a row, he remains the Chief Morris, one of the guardian spirits of the Philadelphia mythology, Philadelphia's great Club Man. Yet he was not even distinguished enough in his time to make the *Dictionary of American Biography,* as four other Morrises have, which for any man active in the Revolution is pretty damn undistinguished; but at least in Philadelphia his fame is secure. He was, and is still, famous first of all as a fox hunter, Master of the Gloucester Hunt from its inception in 1766 to his demise in 1812, which was about the time of the demise of the club too. Since this was America's first organized hunt, one can see how important Sam's place is in history; Philadelphia history, that is. He was second Captain of the City Troop, America's oldest and most socially eligible volunteer cavalry corps; and there Samuel earned his sobriquet "Christian Sam" for his benign but sporting qualities as a leader. Beyond all this he was Governor of the State in Schuylkill, America's oldest club, for forty-six years from 1765 on, and it is still the custom at all meetings of the club for members to drink standing to the memory of "our late Governor Morris." Samuel was otherwise active in civic affairs, and in his business as a sugar refiner. He had ten children, most of whom did well, married well and bred well. But it is as a sort of kindly Santa Claus of sport, an upper-class Old John Peel of the chase and the toast, that he is enshrined in the hearts and memories of Old Philadelphia; everybody's pink-coated ancestor.

This close association with Philadelphia's favorite institutions, the benign aura of Christian Sam as soldier, fox hunter and gourmet, the universal family connections with every possible Old Philadelphia family of any accepted vintage (except the Biddles and Ingersolls) , and above all the blend of national obscurity and local prestige make the Morrises a far more representative, one could even here say typical, Old Philadelphia family than the Biddles.

Although the best of relations have always persisted between these two most prominent and most prolific first families, no one named Biddle has ever married anyone named Morris. This is somewhat incredible considering the numbers and the propinquity, but it is a fact. Perhaps the species have become too distinct, like robins and wrens, to mate.

There are more exotic Philadelphia strains too. Morrises may represent the cloth, but there is much colorful embroidery. There are naturally many Germans, with that pleasing but sometimes sinister blend of fey religion, solid learning and rock-bottom worldly practicality which fits so well into the Quaker pattern (Pepper, Wistar–Wister, Lewis, Rittenhouse, Pennypacker — all anglicized — and the Drexels who were Austrian). There is also a considerable infusion of French, especially French West Indian, blood (Borie, Geyelin, Vauclain, Nalle). The ultimate in this line are the Markoes, or rather were, since there are no longer any male Markoes in Philadelphia. The Markoes were originally Marcous, French Huguenots who came to the Virgin Island of St. Croix, in the West Indies, in the seventeenth century. When the island itself was turned over to Denmark, the Marcous assimilated and became Markoes. The first Markoe to come to the United States was Abraham, who, as a sympathizer with the Revolution, joined up with the City Troop in Philadelphia and was its first Captain. However, as he was still a Danish citizen, he was forced to resign; Denmark was neutral and made it clear that anyone caught fighting would have his property confiscated. Abraham still owned plantations in St. Croix, so he quit fighting in 1776 and turned his command over to Christian Sam Morris.

For many years Markoes were among the first families of the city. The great J. P. Morgan, among his other Philadelphia connections, had as intimate friends no less than three dowager Mrs. Markoes. They each shared a different interest with him, and were known respectively as his Art Markoe, his Church Markoe and his Bed Markoe. The last lived in New York, of course. One of the final elegant private houses built in town in Philadelphia was the pleasantly neo-colonial Markoe house of 1901 on the corner of 17th and Locust Streets, now the Wellington Fund headquarters. And though the Markoes are gone, their memory lingers on through their innumerable connections and cousins.

The family is more or less gone from St. Croix too; or at least somewhat changed. All the Markoes there now are colored. Mrs. Gordon Fetterman, a Philadelphia descendant of the Markoes, went to St. Croix unprepared for this. She looked up one of the last of the Markoes in Frederiksted, a doctor who lived in an elegant small house. When he greeted her it was something of a shock. She explained her visit, stating that Abraham Markoe was her several times great-grandfather. "How delightful! Mine too, dear lady," the doctor said and gave her a cousinly embrace.

The Danes insisted that all children adopt the name of their father, regardless of the mother's race, color, creed or previous condition of matrimony. It was not the usual thing, however, to marry one's colored mistress. One Markoe defied custom and did. Everyone was shocked, and above all pitied his four beautiful daughters. He showed the islanders, however. He had all his girls educated in Switzerland, brought them out in the Danish court (where even white West Indians were bound to be comparatively darker than Danes anyway) and married them all off to Danish nobility; so that many unsuspecting Philadelphians have not only Negro but Danish-noble-Negro not-too-distant relations.

Even more odd and exotic are the Jewish names, both Portuguese and German, that have become inextricably woven into the Philadelphia Web (Rosengarten, Etting, Horwitz and others). This is such a well-known aspect of Philadelphia life that many quite un-Jewish family names like Markoe and Newbold are persistently confused in this group. In any case Nearly Everybody is by now related or connected to them. They are members in good standing of everything Philadelphians should be members of, and are mostly pillars of the right Episcopalian churches. As among the English aristocracy (see du Maurier's *Trilby*), a little touch of Jewishness is almost requisite. This, of course, does not mean that the usual upper-class anti-Semitism is not rampant, and that "real Jews," emigrant, unassimilated, synagogue-going, Polish-Russian Jews are not rigorously excluded wherever possible.

There are other mildly odd notes. There is the usual bit of Dutch (Van Pelt, etc.). There is a residue of Swedish (Sinnickson, Ryerson), some of it derived from the region's first settlement by Swedes and Finns in the early seventeenth century, before Penn. The Swedish-American Society is very choice, though few of the members have any connection with Sweden, except by good will. There is a touch of Swiss (Wurts), of Spanish in the Biddle family (Sarmiento) and elsewhere (Muñoz), and, of course, many of Philadelphia's most embedded families were originally Southern (Drayton, Bullitt) or even from New England (Shippen, Ingersoll). Many more have roots in New Jersey and Delaware.

The truth of the matter is that the Old Philadelphia aristocracy has one of the least homogeneous backgrounds, with the most varied strains in it of any American groups of this sort (compared particularly with Boston). It is a typical paradox that it is now one of the most homogeneous, the most local, the most completely blended and the most resistant to foreign infiltration.

Like scrapple itself, which is made of all sorts of unmentionable things from pigs, the end product of Philadelphia's national and racial blend has turned out to be something smooth, rich and of a nice even consistency. In the big happy Philadelphia family it is the Web, the total kinship that really counts, rather than any few outstanding, separate, famous family names.

2

i. Born Retired

A RATHER SILLY STORY, told not for its worth but for its appropriateness, concerns a Princeton graduate surrounded after dinner by a group of Yale men. The Elis discoursed at length about the vast sums of money donated to the Old Blue by their highly successful classmates. In the lull the Princetonian was finally moved to observe, "We certainly have to envy you Yale men, always so ambitious, doing big things. Of course you have this incentive of making your Y in life — gives you that urge to *go* places. The trouble with us Princetonians is that we've already made our P's." Substitute New York for the Y and Philadelphia for the P and you have a fairly accurate and not just coincidental picture of some differences.

The Philadelphian, the Old Philadelphian, a central member in good standing of the Web, is equipped from the beginning with a sort of blank check on life. All he has to do is cash in (this, naturally, much more so in the past than the present). He is born retired. His education and training are not designed to make him Get Ahead. He's already Ahead. Nor to make him Somebody, since he's already as Somebody as anyone ought to be, or even to make him develop and discover himself, which might be in very poor taste. He is meant to turn out a credit to the Family, a pillar of the Establishment, and if he can't be an outstanding member, he can always be a member in good standing.

One should not imagine, however, that being "born retired" means that one just sits around enjoying oneself. By no manner of means. Being a "credit to the family," even a "member in good standing," not to mention an outstanding member, is a rather arduous undertaking really. It involves a code of life, formulas which are fairly complicated and which cover every aspect of liv- / ing, the economic, the spiritual, the aesthetic and the alcoholic.

The end toward which this code, these formulas, are directed is not Achievement, but Maintenance. Even from its beginnings Philadelphia took easily to Maintenance and looked a bit askance on Achievement. By now it is safe to say that traditional Old Philadelphia psychology is entirely dominated in every way, for good and for evil, by these attitudes of the maintainer, as that of New York is still dominated by those of the attainer. The results are obvious: New York has won the race, but from a Philadelphia point of view has lost its soul, *i.e.* its gentility.

Maintaining position takes just as much work and effort, of a totally different kind, as attaining Position. The Family Founder must be clever, aggressive, imaginative in a practical way at least, a risk-taker, an adventurer. His eye is on the future and the main chance. The Family Maintainer must be a cautious conservative with his eye on the past, who does his best to discourage too much cleverness, aggressiveness, imagination and risk-taking, either among his own or among newcomers. The formulas for getting ahead are fluid, but involve getting there fustest with the mostest. The formulas for staying ahead are rather elaborately fixed but involve principally staying there lastest with the bestest.

These formulas apply all around in every possible direction, but one can divide the area of life into provinces, where the code of Maintenance applies in different ways.

First of all there is education. One does not become a good Maintainer simply by the accident of birth. One has to be groomed and trained like a horse for it. After education comes Life, and life too can be blocked off into various almost equally important areas — Work, Good Works, Play and just plain Living. Formulas apply.

Nowhere does the Code of Maintenance function more oddly in Philadelphia, but more logically, than in the area of "work." What "work" means to an Old Philadelphian is a rather special sort of thing, but it does still involve the ordinary professions and vocations and labors of mankind. These various activities from time immemorial and in all societies have been graded and pigeonholed in a hierarchy of status and prestige. Philadelphia is no exception.

However, in Philadelphia the customary professional hierarchy of the English upper classes — a pyramid topped by a career in Politics, the Army or Navy, and the Church — has been inverted. Not for Philadelphia the devotion of New England to the pulpit and its offshoots, professorship and the more moral literature; nor the Southern respect for soldiers and statesmen. As far as Philadelphia is concerned, the Church, the Armed Forces and Politics are not for the Philadelphia well-born. For one thing, as a clergyman, soldier, politician or teacher, one stands a good chance of being moved *away* from Philadelphia! A career *away* from Philadelphia is out of bounds, doesn't count. This is one of the basic reasons for these prejudices.

Instead, the Old Philadelphian is supposed to confine himself to certain specific callings. First come Medicine and Law. Nothing in Philadelphia is more sacred than these two sacred professions. Next comes Insurance and Banking, with brokerage as a dubious modern adjunct. After this, running the Family Firm, no matter what its nature, is correct, especially if it falls in the area of the Iron Triangle — iron or steel making, railroads and coal. Even just a job in any of these directions is all right. But nearly anything else, no matter how respectable or lucrative, is taboo. Within this very limited area of choice the Old Philadelphian can, or could, expect to grow in favor with God and the Family. Outside of it he was always taking a big chance, and had to prove himself doubly successful.

Old Philadelphia families, then, have from the beginning been medical families, legal families, then banking families, iron, railroad and coal families, and proud of it. There are no strictly church families, like the Potters of New York, no political families like the Adamses of Quincy, few military families like the Lees of Virginia. Bishop White, first Episcopalian Bishop of

Pennsylvania, was a most prominent Old Philadelphian of his time, and his relations and descendants are deeply enmeshed; but not as clergymen. General McClellan during the Civil War was of Family; but of medical, not martial, family. Only the Meades might count as a truly military line. The Biddles and Cadwaladers produced their quota of generals and commodores; but one can scarcely call either clan a "military family." One of the Dallases, George, was Vice President under Polk, and Boies Penrose, of the Penrose family, was perennial Senator from Pennsylvania, but both these men, particularly Penrose, were exceptional. A Wharton was for years and years Mayor of Philadelphia; but only in the good old days. No Wharton has been Mayor of Philadelphia in a century. So it goes.

This of course does not mean that one is not interested in religion, politics, arms or learning. On the contrary, as an Old Philadelphian one is absolutely required to have definite prejudices and associations. One must belong to the City Troop, one must serve on the vestry, one must collect books; but always as a layman and an amateur.

The prejudices in fact, particularly religious and political ones, are basic. In politics, until the recent local revolution known as the Philadelphia Renaissance, one had to be a McKinley Republican, worshipful of the high tariff. In religion one had to be either a Quaker, or, if more fashionable, an Episcopalian.

ii. Plain and Fancy

EVERYBODY KNOWS two things about Philadelphia: it was founded by Quakers, and Benjamin Franklin lived there. Benjamin Franklin being a Deist and a firm anti-sectarian had no influence on religious attitudes except a negative one. He was, of course, never, never a Quaker and most Quakers despised him. The Quakers themselves ceased to be a numerical majority early in Philadelphia's history, and by 1750 had pretty much lost majority control of the legislature; but their influence has been and even continues to be enormous, and most basic Philadelphia attitudes are thoroughly conditioned by Quakerism.

There was for instance Penn's Plan. Like Boston, Providence and Baltimore, though unlike New York and Washington, Philadelphia was founded in the name of God as a refuge for an oppressed religious minority and has become a stronghold of conservative finance. Mammon has very comfortably taken over. Philadelphia differs from all the other older American cities, however, in that it was not only intended, but planned; planned in great detail.

It was for instance America's first large-scale gridiron. Whereas other cities "just growed," Philadelphia from the beginning was laid out in regular squares, right across the narrow waist between the Delaware and Schuylkill Rivers. In the very center was Penn Square, for generations a wilderness, where City Hall now stands. Four other squares, now called Washington, Franklin, Rittenhouse and Logan, were placed at equal distances from this center in four different directions. What's more, this simple but practical plan was followed, right from the seventeenth century until, about 1900, all the original blocks were finally built up. It has been adopted, without, alas, the saving grace of the little parks, by most later American villages, towns and cities. This is one of the legacies of Penn and the Quakers to Philadelphia and the country.

Penn's plan however embraced much more: he actually planned the whole life of the city. His design envisaged not only the central gridiron, but around it, to the north and south, two suburban districts called the "Liberties," and beyond them an area of larger farms and landed estates. He granted lots in town or in the Liberties to each person who took up a grant of the larger country acreages out beyond, hoping in this way to create a community of interest between town and country. What Penn encouraged has remained to this day the basic psychology of the Old Philadelphian, who remains a city-dweller, but whose heart is in the country, a country landholder with roots in the city.

Penn did not think of his precious plantation as a settlement of free pioneers, organizing their own civilization. Not at all. Pennsylvania was a private property on which all comers were *allowed* to settle. A very different concept from that which governed, say, the sterner independence of the settlers in New England. New England was intolerant, but independent. As for Pennsylvania, tolerant, yes, independent no. And this concept of a benign patriarchy still influences the minds of Old Philadelphians.

Penn of course was very soon disillusioned by the ingratitude of his wards. The Proprietors lost most of their powers; but this still did not mean democracy. It meant aristocracy, "rule of the best," or at least oligarchy, "rule of the few." The "best" in this case meant the richest, the men of probity and property. Till the American Revolution the franchise was limited by property qualifications and only one Philadelphian out of fifty could vote. Since the majority of these property owners were Quakers, "rule of the best" meant rule by the Meeting.

Pretty soon, however, all sorts of people, Anglicans, Presbyterians, even Catholics and Jews and Germans began to settle, and make money too. Quakers ceased to be a majority of even the oligarchy. They then devised a more indirect method of retaining power: control by board. Quakers of course were used to boards since they ran their meetings and indeed their lives by them. As a meeting could be controlled by a few, with, of course, the consent of the many, so could public and cultural affairs. All one needed was a three-fifths majority of any given board, to be handed down in a self-perpetuating family fashion. In this way, long after the Quakers were outnumbered and outvoted in the Assembly, they continued to dominate the cultural, financial, judicial, charitable and intellectual world of Philadelphia.

Though most of the Old Philadelphia Quaker families have by now converted to Episcopalianism, the façade that Philadelphia still presents to the world is a Quaker façade — subdued, careful, moderate, puritanical but never ascetic, honest but shrewd, modest but firm. Philadelphia kindness, Philadelphia conscience, Philadelphia temperance, that famous Philadelphia aplomb and equally famous Philadelphia moderation are all certainly as Quaker as Quaker can be. Unfortunately, along with these virtues inevitably have gone certain characteristic vices, the defects of the virtues. The most flagrant of these are conformism, anti-intellectualism, materialism and lack of enthusiasm.

There is, for instance, that "we-ness." In most groups decisions are taken by rule of the majority or rule of the strongest. In Quaker assemblies, decisions, like those of a jury, must be unanimous; what is called in that wonderful phrase "the sense of the meeting." This is admirable, but one can easily see how strong individuality must be curbed, and how agreeable the atmosphere is to the group-conscious, the "other-directed," the conformist mentality.

The same "sense of the meeting" that breeds conformism also breeds anti-intellectualism. Theological disputation, legalism, abstruse commentary have no place among those who consider themselves the flock of God, led by the inspiration of a still small Voice. One doesn't argue, one listens. It was theology that led in every case *except* that of the University of Pennsylvania to the founding of the early colleges of America. The Quakers founded schools, but they very deliberately did not found a colonial college.

Worldly culture, the arts, superfluous knowledge were discouraged, but unlike the Puritans, self-mortification was never part of the Quaker psychology. Instead, busyness was next to godliness, and the fruits of busyness were godly. This meant that both the materialisms of making money and of having money were encouraged. The successful laborer was obviously God's favorite. Of course pride, ostentation or luxurious idleness and frivolity were unthinkable, but enjoying one's sanctified rewards was almost a virtue. "Work for the night is coming" and "Plain but rich" are two essentially Quaker mottoes. Prosperity and Watson's "solid comfort" were canonized as signs of a spiritual grace. But they are, after all, thoroughly material blessings.

Another quality, and one that would seem the very antithesis of the nickname "Quaker," is a fondness for lack of enthusiasm. For a religion that depends absolutely upon divine guidance and divine inspiration, this would seem to be an abrupt contradiction. Nevertheless, it is a fact. "Enthusiasm," particularly of the Methodist or sectarian character, is and seems always to have been frowned on. Perhaps the dangers of this sort of enthusiasm in upsetting applecarts and above all in causing controversy have been experienced. In any case, Quakers are dead set against it. And so are Philadelphians. "Caution" and "calm" are the Quakers', and the Philadelphians', middle names.

All these qualities combine in "Quaker plainness," and Quaker plainness is to be credited for the Philadelphia modesty, lack of show, refusal to be panicked by the "latest thing," much of the quiet refinement of Philadelphia taste. It is also to be blamed for Philadelphia drabness, the frequent utter disregard of aesthetic values, the prevailing atmosphere of dreariness that hangs over much of the city. Some Quaker meetings are very beautiful in their total simplicity. Others are very depressing in their total bareness.

Completely opposed to "Quaker plainness" is Old Philadelphia's other, and now greatly preferred religion, Episcopalianism, and certainly that Philadelphia split between Plain and Fancy owes its origin to the opposition between Friend and Churchman. Though the Philadelphia upper classes have long ceased to be predominantly Quakers, there are still prominent Quaker families. Some are "in the world" like the Strawbridges and Clothiers of the store. Others, not in the world, exist as a sort of hidden clique of old solid Quaker families, Scattergoods, Emlens and others, who live an almost minority group existence, eschewing the shows of Philadelphia society and sticking close to one another.

The typical Philadelphia family pattern, however, is that of Quakers turned Episcopalian, and nobody could deny that by now the overwhelmingly preferred profession of the Philadelphia upper classes is Episcopalianism. Presbyterianism is respectable, solid and worthy, though a little bourgeois. The Philadelphia application of an old story is "Presbyterianism is not a sin; it's just a social error." Lutheranism has a nice old Germantown cachet. The other Protestant sects are not to be considered, and Roman Catholicism is still the wolf with privy paw. Though Catholicism in Philadelphia has not lacked for very distinguished representatives and very distinguished converts, it has not got the basic foundation of old families, French or English, which gives the sect tone in New York or Baltimore. In Philadelphia it is Irish or worse, and socially outcast.

How unlike Episcopalianism. There have been, of course, families, like the Simses, Willings, and McCalls, that have been Anglican from their beginnings, but by far the largest number of Philadelphia's old families — Cadwaladers, Biddles, Morrises, Whartons, Robertses, etc. — were once Quakers and are now Episcopalians. One cannot credit this mass conversion to any very spiritual causes. No revival such as the great awakening led by Presbyterian George Whitefield in the mid-eighteenth century emptied the meeting houses and filled the churches. It was a gradual but relentless process of ejection and seduction. Quakers were ejected from meeting for warlike activities in the Revolution and even the Civil War. They married Episcopalians and were kicked out for that. They got tired of the constant concern of Quakers over worldly pleasures and show, broke loose and joined the enemy. They bought pianos for their daughters — and out they went. Episcopalianism is almost designed to be a religion for the Best People, for English-speaking ladies and gentlemen, and though most sincere Episcopalians are revolted by the stigma, it remains. The Anglican society was from the beginning always the best, the most luxurious, the fashionable society of Philadelphia. (So much so, for example, that Sidney Fisher can speak of the total cessation of all social life during Lent, as of the 1840's.) When Quakers got rich, they got into it. Social snobbery or worldly sophistication, one fears, made as many conversions as conviction.

Nothing, of course, could represent a greater contrast to Quakerism than Episcopalianism: dogmatic, hierarchical, ceremonial, ornamental, generally unpuritan in outlook, though sometimes ascetic. Nonetheless the traditions of the British world which surround and pervade its established church do tend to breed, from utterly different causes, the same virtues and vices; that is: good manners, restraint, good taste, assurance, liberalism, moderation; and also — conformism, anti-intellectualism, materialism, lack of enthusiasm.

The term which covers and explains most of these Anglican attitudes is Good Form — what "is done" and what "isn't done." The conformism of the gentleman who wouldn't be seen dead without a fine linen handkerchief thrust negligently (but not too negligently) into the breast pocket of his coat is different from that bred by a Sense of the Meeting, but it is still conformism. The anti-intellectualism of the man who thinks any show of knowledge, acrimony of debate or intellectual passion is ill-bred isn't precisely the same as the scorn of the quietist for superfluous religious quibbling, but it has about the same result in discouraging intellectual agility. Concern for appearances is certainly not rich plainness, but it does make a virtue of furniture polish, and the good form of "nil admirari," of not getting too excited, comes to about the same thing as Quaker caution.

There's more to it, however, than just "good form." Certain actual denominational characteristics are involved. The services of the Anglican communion are far more "conformist," in allowing no individual prayers, for instance, than the services of say Congregationalism. Emphasis on rich vestments and stained glass may not be exactly materialism, but it's certainly not an ascetic rejection of material beauty. Above all there is that "lack of enthusiasm" for which Anglicanism has always been so famous, and which the tombstone of an English prelate of the eighteenth century celebrates: "Sacred to the memory of the Very Reverend Dean of this Cathedral, who in this Place, pursued the Cure of Souls, for Forty Years, without the least suspicion of Enthusiasm."

The great Episcopalian preacher Phillips Brooks, looking back from Boston on his happy years as Rector of Holy Trinity on

Rittenhouse Square, liked to compare religious life in Philadelphia to the "temperate zone," and a "broad Pennsylvania valley" as opposed to the "rough New England hillside" of religious Boston. In that fertile and peaceful religious valley have comfortably settled nearly all the members of Philadelphia's upper class, and though Episcopalianism has a small membership in Philadelphia compared to Catholicism, Baptism or even Judaism, all the positions of power on boards that were formerly occupied by Quakers are now occupied by their Episcopalian descendants.

iii. Home and Away

ONE OF THE WAYS in which both Quakers and Episcopalians maintain their influence over the Philadelphia upper classes is by their control over schools, foreign and domestic. All the "best schools" to which Old Philadelphians go are sectarian. The preferred New England boarding schools are Episcopalian church schools, the preferred local day schools are Episcopalian or Quaker. It is in such schools, boarding or day, that the young Old Philadelphian, at least the male Old Philadelphian, has been traditionally trained for Maintenance. Of late years, of course, the traditional patterns have been more and more difficult to maintain, but the general training of the young idea still remains fairly formalized.

The day of the nanny, or of the governess such as the formidable Annie Deane, described by George Biddle as having dominated his youth, is more or less past. Having no knowledge of French or music, she could not quite qualify as a full-fledged governess, a Fraülein or a Mademoiselle. On the other hand, she was firm in her insistence that she was not a nurse. She compromised on "nursery-governess," and if she did not eat with the family, she would not eat with the servants either, and had her meals alone in her bedroom. However lax or liberal parents and family might be socially, it was the privilege and duty of governesses to wallow in snobbery, and Miss Deane was evidently no mean wallower. For Annie Deane religion was essentially a "splendid ritual of social stability"; of the guests that entered the Biddle household, "there were but two that Annie Deane conceded to be young ladies." Miss Anna Ingersoll was one. Biddle forgot the other.

This kind of social starch is seldom available nowadays, and the function of the "nursery-governess" is taken over, in Philadelphia as it is everywhere else, by the nursery school. There are an endless variety of these; some of the best of them are run by Old Philadelphians, such as that of Mary Morris Rawle (Mrs. James) on the Main Line. Others are attached, somewhat grudgingly, to the local day schools, so that nowadays these day schools begin almost at birth.

The English pattern, however, of packing children off to boarding school at eight has never prevailed in Philadelphia or America, and is considered pretty barbarous. In Philadelphia, in fact, it used to be, and still is to the very slightest degree, a bit swank to go off to boarding school, and being swank in Philadelphia is one of those things that one has to be cautious about. It depends on who you are. To be traditionally swank, like the Cadwaladers, is wonderful, but parvenu swank makes people snicker, and to be snickered at in Philadelphia can be a dreadful fate. The old-fashioned, crusty, true-blue Old Philadelphian went, and still traditionally goes to certain local day schools. Usually he then graduates in late years to a boarding school; sometimes not.

In ancient days, schools were either conducted as charities for the poor, usually under sectarian and especially Quaker auspices, or were more fashionable private ventures by gentlemen, often scholars as well, who proposed to make a living off teaching the rich. These private ventures, and the somewhat dubious floggeries of an earlier time — like the school run by the fierce and misnamed Dr. Dove — merged in the nineteenth century with the charitable schools, grown more respectable and less charitable, to form various well-established, small, in-town academies. They became fewer, larger and better as the nineteenth century wore on. Of these, one of the best known bore the unfortunate name of Blight's; it merged into another, the Delancey Street School, and this in turn merged into the oldest and best established of all, Episcopal Academy.

There were, of course, others, but most of these city academies perished in the exodus of their patrons to the suburbs; those that survived, like Episcopal, moved too. Thus present generations have been spared the earlier city education in self-reliance, democracy and class distinctions supplied the boys who attended the older academies as they walked back from school. They were invariably waylaid in the alleys by non-academy-attending toughs, and the toughs and the little gentlemen happily engaged in rumbles with bricks in summer and snowballs in winter that remained a cherished memory in after years. Now the little gentlemen, and the ladies too, are taken vast distances by buses and car pools, or even the Paoli Local, and the toughs have only themselves to maim.

Old Philadelphia education at present divides itself firmly into the two suburban categories, Chestnut Hill and Main Line. Whereas in the old days the body of Old Philadelphia youth grew up together, they nowadays grow up separately, in two groups, and hardly ever do the twain get to meet. There is a Main Line set of good boys' day schools, of which Episcopal is the most highly considered, (also Haverford, Friends Central and others), and a Chestnut Hill set, of which Penn Charter is the most famous, (also Chestnut Hill Academy, Germantown Academy, Germantown Friends and others). As for girls' schools, the Main Line has Shipley, Agnes Irwin and Baldwin; Chestnut Hill, less well supplied for young ladies, supports Springside and Stevens. A good many of the best Friends schools are coeducational.

No day schools in the United States have more social and scholastic prestige than these, especially Episcopal and its rival across the river, Penn Charter. Both originally sectarian (Penn Charter is still run by an anciently established Quaker Board of Overseers), they now provide a direct channel to the best colleges or to the best boarding schools, the latter for Old Philadelphians, meaning preferably St. Paul's or St. George's. Both are "church schools," that is, Episcopalian, both are in New England, St. Paul's in New Hampshire, St. George's in Rhode Island. Of the two, St. Paul's is older and more "traditional," St. George's younger and more "smart." For girls, the boarding school is unexpected; those Philadelphia parents who do send their girls away seem to have no particular preferences.

The split between those boys who took their last years at St. Paul's or St. George's and those who stayed on at Episcopal and Penn Charter used to be fairly meaningful, and divided sheep from goats, fancy from plain, and rich from poor. Nowadays it is a less definite split. A similar division took place at the college level between those who went to the University (plain) and those who went to Princeton or, less often, Harvard and Yale (fancy). Nowadays this division too is all messed up by forces over which Old Philadelphia has little control; but the bias remains.

iv.   1740 and All That

PHILADELPHIA'S upper-class secondary schools may still be in the hands of Quakers and Episcopalians, but Philadelphia's two preferred colleges, the University of Pennsylvania and Princeton, are not. One was founded as non-sectarian, the other as New Light Presbyterian. Perhaps this lack of direct connection with either of the oligarchy's pet religions is part of the cause of Philadelphia's college dilemma.

The dilemma might be expressed in two questions: "Boston has its Harvard, New York has its Columbia, what is the matter with Philadelphia?" or "Why is the University of Pennsylvania neither the Harvard nor the Columbia of Philadelphia?" Any Philadelphian, even the most rabid devotee of the University, will agree that the University of Pennsylvania is *not* either Harvard or Columbia, but nobody knows just why.

The University (Philadelphians, like Virginians, always refer to their peculiar institution as just "the University") is rich, old and distinguished. Of the country's nearly two thousand institutions of higher learning, there would certainly not be much doubt of the University's place in the top fifty on the basis of its historical and social background, its famous schools of law, medicine and business. It might be acknowledged as one of the top dozen; but beyond this it would not really be safe to go.

It is rich, old and distinguished. It was "founded by Benjamin Franklin," like so many other things in Philadelphia; but unlike many other things in Philadelphia it is not *the* oldest, richest and most respected of American universities. It is only the sixth oldest, for instance, and in a city that prides itself on its firsts, this has been a bitter pill. Its medical school is the country's oldest (1765), but as an undergraduate college it is outranked chronologically by Harvard (1636), William and Mary (1693), Yale (1701), Princeton (1746) and even Columbia (1754). Nothing much can be done about this. After all, Philadelphia itself didn't exist when Harvard was founded. What could be done however has been done, and by one of the most ingenious, if silly, examples of Philadelphia's famed legalism, the actual date of the university's founding (1755) has been put back to 1740, thus circumventing Columbia, and Princeton too, always the object of Pennsylvania's most active jealousy.*

The claim is, of course, almost completely spurious. The foundation of the University in 1755 under the impetus of Franklin and the Presidency (or Provostship) of the Reverend William Smith, is surrounded by a glow of historical publicity; there is nothing mysterious about the whole thing. The College of Philadelphia as it was called, received its charter and enrolled its first students in 1755; graduated its first class in 1757, and everybody knows it. However (and here the law begins) this college was added to a secondary school, The Academy of Philadelphia, with which it shared a board of trustees. The Academy was proposed

* This sort of genealogical faking has always been a Philadelphia weakness, as demonstrated by the illegitimate claims of the *Saturday Evening Post* on Benjamin Franklin; there are plenty of other examples.

by Franklin in 1749, chartered in 1750 and actually opened in 1751. This is better than 1755 but not much. It gets around Columbia's 1754, but still doesn't get around Princeton's 1746.

In the 1890's when the University and the Philadelphia Oligarchy were experiencing a boom and also when interest in Philadelphia's historical primacy was peculiarly intense, a council was formed, under the leadership of the sometime Governor of Pennsylvania Samuel W. Pennypacker, an active alumnus, to look into the matter. Though nobody could possibly push back the date of the school, Franklin's Philadelphia Academy, before 1749, the *building* into which the school moved in 1751 was found to have been built in 1741, and the *trustees* of the organization which built the building, originally intended for a charitable school, date themselves from 1740. Eureka! Alleluia! The day was saved: *whereas* the University of Pennsylvania was an outgrowth of Franklin's Academy and *whereas* a charitable school was eventually added to the said Academy and *whereas* said charity school occupied a building originally intended for that purpose and built in 1741 and *whereas* said building was planned in 1740 *therefore* the University of Pennsylvania was founded in 1740. So the law triumphed over common sense. Governor Pennypacker's arguments were received with fervid applause, and in 1899 the pleased council voted to make 1740 the new, older date of the University's founding. A few crusty curmudgeons complained, but public opinion was against them. The seal says 1740, a bicentennial was officially celebrated in 1940. In academic processions, where protocol goes by seniority, University of Pennsylvania dignitaries are always pushed ahead of Princeton dignitaries, to the probable annoyance of both parties, and no doubt the smug amusement of dignitaries from Harvard, Yale and William and Mary.

This little incident is an unfortunate index to something which is, and always has been, wrong with the University of Pennsylvania. The character of very real worth, real literature, real intellectual distinction, real social prestige, combined with envy of other institutions, restless and unfulfilled ambitions, controversy, pettiness and reaction, is foreshadowed and embodied in the University's first Provost, the Reverend William Smith. This remarkable man might be summed up as a radical intellectual Scotch educator whose life's ambition was to become the first Anglican Bishop of America.

Smith began as Franklin's protégé, and ended up as his bitterest enemy. He left his native Scotland in his twenties after his Episcopal ordination and emigrated to the New World, where he hoped his talents would have fuller scope. They did. He wrote a blueprint for a Utopian but practical experiment in higher education called "The General Idea for a College of Mirania" which earned the approval of Franklin. The latter brought Smith to Philadelphia, and saw to it that he became the head of his new College. This was not enough for Smith, however. He entered into all phases of Philadelphia's teeming eighteenth-century intellectual life, and his influence was everywhere important and stimulating. In his curiosity, talent, breadth of interest, he was the equal of Franklin himself, or of other such Philadelphia "universal men" of the period as Charles Willson Peale and Francis Hopkinson. He married well, the daughter of William Moore, a great landowner, bastion of the Proprietary, or pro-Penn party in politics; as son-in-law of a rich man and head of Philadelphia's first institution of higher learning, he had Position all right. But he ruined it all by his ambition.

In his zeal to become Bishop and please the Anglican Philadelphian aristocracy and his trustees, he made over Franklin's secular, practical school, which was intended to guide the intelligent sons of merchants and mechanics toward wisdom and science, into a gentleman-factory on the English model, teaching largely the "useless ornaments of the dead languages." This, of course, quite contradicted Smith's own "College of Mirania" and the switch disgusted Franklin, as well it might. Meanwhile Smith had more or less disgraced himself by being thrown into jail for political libel, and by his intemperance, verbal and alcoholic.

When the Revolution came along his enemies turned on him; he was accused, quite falsely, of being a Tory traitor. His final effort to become the first Episcopal Bishop of Maryland (rather than Pennsylvania) after the Revolution was defeated when at a church council in New York he drank too much.

His university has never really quite recovered from Smith's debacle. Its charter was taken away during the Revolution, and the city fathers set up a rival University of the State of Pennsylvania to supplant it. Eventually, in 1791, the two rivals joined, and the present University of Pennsylvania was founded; but too much had been lost. Despite a great boom at the end of the nineteenth century, when the whole works moved to West Philadelphia and into some fantastic new buildings, the undergraduate college has never quite been able to match either the scholastic prestige of the University's own graduate schools of medicine and law or the national social prestige of its rivals, Harvard, Yale and Princeton.

v. Ivy

As THE BRILLIANT SMITH was a disappointed man, the University may be in some ways a "disappointed college." Nonetheless, it has an enviable reputation, particularly in science and economics. The famous Philadelphia doctors like Rush, and many others, held the chairs of chemistry, natural philosophy and such from the earliest times. The Wharton School of Finance was the first of its kind, and remains one of the best. In mathematics there were the redoubtable Pattersons, who for generations held the chair at the University and the presidency of the American Philosophical Society simultaneously. The tradition of Franklin in these directions may be said to have been admirably cherished right up to the present.

Nonetheless, though the slim majority of Old Philadelphians has gone to the University, the majority speak of it now with a sort of tolerant contempt. Unlike Boston or even New York, where a prominent professor is *somebody*, the faculty of Penn seems to have lived in seclusion, and its intellectual concerns never seem to have touched Philadelphia's dinner tables. Though the University is definitely a member in good standing of the "Ivy League," its student body is as a whole socially déclassé. Too many city boys and city girls (for it is coeducational in a way) attend, and Old Philadelphian undergraduates huddle within a few fraternities for protection. For the Old Philadelphian, the fraternity used to be actually more important than the college. Of these, Delta Psi (St. Anthony), Delta Phi (the St. Elmo) and Zeta Psi, the Peppers' fraternity, remain the conservative best. Zeta Psi, in fact, is so conservative that in the fall of 1958 it took in no new pledges at all. There are a few others of repute, and it is no longer a matter of life and death to belong to a good one; but it's pretty damn important.

The whole picture of the upper-class Philadelphian attitude to the University, and college education in general, was most forthrightly presented by an exceptionally acute, not to say somewhat cynical Old Philadelphian with a son to educate. This son was dear to his father's heart as a splendid athlete, but unfortunately for modern conditions he wasn't terribly bright. He was in a famous but not very exclusive large boarding school, and there his father went to see him play some crucial game of something. While on the grounds a gentleman who was known as the Dean of Admissions, *i.e.*, admissions *from* the school *to* colleges, took him aside and said, "We're worried about your son. He refuses to put down any college except Princeton in his list of college preferences, and he won't be able to make Princeton on account of his English. Have you any other suggestions for him?" The father didn't seem to have any other suggestions. "Do you mind if I make some then? How about the University of Rochester?" "That," said the father, "is where they make film, isn't it?" and so disposed of the University of Rochester. "Well, then," said the Dean, "where do you have influence?" "Oh, I know Whit and everybody up at Yale." "If he can't make Princeton, he can't make Yale," countered the Dean. "How about some good second-rate university? How about the University of Pennsylvania?" "Well, naturally I know all the Board of Trustees there. . . ." And there the boy eventually went, graduating successfully from the Wharton School and joining the family business.

After the interview had been thus satisfactorily concluded, the Dean said, "I know you're a Harvard graduate, yet you never mentioned Harvard when we were talking." "I wouldn't want any son of mine to go to Harvard. It's too snobbish. When I was up there I just joined the Club and I never met anybody else the whole time I was in college. But how did you know I went to Harvard?" "Don't you remember me?" said the Dean. "I was in your class." A fairly frank coverage of the Philadelphia attitude, especially when told by the father himself.

This instance of Philadelphia fatherly concern makes quite clear that the ambivalence of the old Philadelphia attitude toward the University is due as much to the rivalry of other institutions as to any internal problems. It is, above all, the national social prestige of the Big Three which is in competition with the purely local social prestige of the University. Upper-class boys from all over the country, including Philadelphia, go to Harvard, Yale and Princeton. Only from Philadelphia do upper-class boys go in any significant numbers to Penn.

This is of course a universal national phenomenon. The pattern of upper-class male college preference, as deduced from a counting * of noses in the various *Social Registers*, can be summed up as "The Big Three and a Local Favorite." That is, every city sends or has sent its Socially Registered sons to Harvard, Yale and Princeton, in some particular preferred order, and to one local institution. This order varies. New York sets the pattern with Yale first, Harvard second, Princeton third, then Columbia. Saint Louis and Baltimore are Princeton towns. Most other cities (Chicago, Cleveland, Cincinnati, etc.) are Yale towns. Only

* My counting. If you don't believe my results, check them yourself.

Boston, and occasionally Washington, are Harvard cities. Of course many other places don't have *Social Registers* — newfangled Los Angeles and Detroit for instance. Southern Richmond and New Orleans scorn such social carpetbagging. Still, it is not unlikely that the pattern prevails there too.

Of all the cities that are Socially Registered, only two are exceptional in giving first place in their affections to Local Favorites. These two cities are San Francisco, whose sons are loyal to the University of California and Stanford (not one, but two) — and Philadelphia. The condescension, then, of Old Philadelphians toward Penn is a mixed emotion. The chances are that from 1880 to 1900 at least, the majority of old Philadelphians actually went there. Around 1900 Harvard attracted the Fancy (as opposed to the Plain). From 1910 on the drift was overwhelmingly toward Princeton; even sons of University trustees went there. Nowadays, with the increased pressure of applications, it has become so hard to get into the Big Three that many Old Philadelphia youths are drifting back to Penn again.

But there is one aspect of the University that has never lost any of its prestige down through the centuries. This is the Board of Trustees. The faculty may be kept in purdah, the undergraduate body may be looked down upon as incurably mixed, but the éclat of the Board itself remains undiminished. This is, in fact, one of Philadelphia's superlative boards. Sometimes one gets the impression, among Old Philadelphians, that the only legitimate purpose of the University is to provide an excuse for the existence of such a Board.

A courteous old gentleman, himself a graduate of the University, was giving me the names of Philadelphians of importance to be looked up. I mentioned that I had met President Harnwell, and that he seemed a man of much insight, particularly into Philadelphia. "Oh you don't want to bother with people like that," said my gentleman. "I can introduce you to the Board of Trustees." As in any other Philadelphia institution or bank or company, it's the directors, not the hired men — presidents and "people like that" — who count. The anecdote could be applied anywhere in Philadelphia, but nowhere is the power of trusteeship more evident than in the history of the University.

vi. Country Club

IT MAY BE THEN the Board of Trustees that has prevented the University of Pennsylvania from being Philadelphia's Columbia; that is, a great metropolitan and cosmopolitan center of advanced learning, full of John Deweys, Irwin Edmans and Jacques Barzuns. It is certainly the nearness and competition of Princeton that has prevented the University of Pennsylvania from being Philadelphia's Harvard; that is, an undergraduate college of national social and intellectual prestige dominated by a local aristocracy.

A young Texas doctor married to a very Proper Bostonian was trying to get her to move with him way out west to Cambridge (Massachusetts). She demurred. "Priscilla says it's ra-ight fa-ar to Cambridge," he quoted her. "I never said anything of the sort," said Priscilla. "I just said that Cambridge was a very different sort of place." Similarly, Princeton is "right far" from Philadelphia; nonetheless relations are and have been terribly close, and the parallels very striking. Princeton was founded under Philadelphia auspices, as a result of the preaching of the eighteenth-century revivalist George Whitefield, whose followers, especially the Philadelphian preacher Gilbert Tennant, called themselves New Light, and broke from the conservative Old Light Presbyterians in Philadelphia. Their followers in turn went on to found the College of New Jersey, in protest, as more or less a seminary for New Light ministers. Philadelphians, notably the distinguished Shippens, were early and continuing patrons and trustees, and there has always been a constant group of upper-class Philadelphia boys, Shippens, Rushes, Biddles, Ingersolls, Pauls, Morrises, Roberts, etc., in residence. However, it *was* the College of New Jersey, not of Pennsylvania, and there was just as much or more New Jersey and New York influence

there as Philadelphian. Princeton has immemorially been described as a college paid for by New Yorkers, populated by
Jerseymen and patronized by Philadelphians and Baltimoreans.

Besides this definite connection, the fortunes of the college
have also exactly followed those of Philadelphia. Princeton was
the parvenu of early American colleges as Philadelphia was of
colonial cities. It too quickly rose and surpassed its rivals and was,
as Philadelphia was before the Revolution, if not the largest, certainly the most heterogeneous, cosmopolitan, liberal of American
institutions. Like Philadelphia, it too was occupied by the enemy
during the Revolution, was restored, was even for a brief while,
like Philadelphia, the capital of the country. Then, exactly like
Philadelphia, from the beginning of the nineteenth century till
the 1830's it declined, lost its primacy as a liberal, cosmopolitan
and national center and became parochial, reactionary and decadent.

Then followed a long, slow revival, a painful separation from
the South and Southern ties during the Civil War, and a boom of
rather timid intellectual distinction combined with a vast material
expansion from the 'seventies up to the First World War. The
climax of the Philadelphia oligarchy around 1900 was also the
climax of Princeton's standing as a "gentleman's college," and
it was during that period that the college took on the atmosphere
of so-called "country-club" leisure which has haunted it ever
since.

It was precisely this "country-clubbism" which was Princeton's
closest bond with Philadelphia. The air of "casualness" of suburban amenities and easy high living, the carefully tended lawns,
expert landscaping, flannels, boat races, drinking, houseparties,
and the more gentlemanly sports, was a perfect collegiate parallel
to the life of the Philadelphia suburbs and its cricket clubs. The
same sort of amateur booklover, amateur intellectual attitude
towards thought and literature prevailed, an adulation of England
(Tennyson) and a condescension to more native flavors. Like
Philadelphia, Princeton also has never produced an established
Great Writer (except perhaps Scott Fitzgerald) but has peren-

nially been represented by contemporary famous and successful ones. The same vice of lack of enthusiasm and its twin virtue, amiable relaxation, have both been the despair and delight of generations of observers, both also products of that same "psychology of being third" — of having made one's P's and being perfectly content with the station into which one has lapsed; not arrogant first, nor envious and ambitious second, but still condescendingly above anyone *else*.

Even more characteristically Old Philadelphian has been the Princeton undergraduate's notorious clubbiness, conformism, convention-mindedness, insistence upon appearances, that same Philadelphia "we-ness," the dreadful importance of belonging and being accepted, which unlike more cosmopolitan but less intimate places, takes in everyone, affects the whole tone and temper of life.

And the look of Princeton, its commanding Nassau Hall, a Grand Gesture of the eighteenth century, its complex of neo-Gothic dormitories, is a thoroughly Philadelphian look. Nassau Hall was originally designed by a Philadelphian, one Robert Smith, and was remodeled into its present form by another, John Notman. The Gothicry was initiated by the very Old Philadelphian firm of Cope and Stewardson, who tried their hand at this sort of thing first at Bryn Mawr, and then, in brick, at the University; so that these three institutions have a strong family resemblance, especially Bryn Mawr and Princeton. Certainly the lawns and big trees and flowering bushes which surround the buildings at Princeton are thoroughly Philadelphian in feeling.

Philadelphians, even Old Philadelphians, do of course go to Harvard and Yale. In fact it is almost a tradition that, like Francis Biddle and William Bullitt, Joseph Clark and Richardson Dilworth, those Philadelphians, native or adopted, active in politics and civic causes should be graduates of Harvard and Yale, not Princeton and Penn. This, however, is merely another index of comparative "foreignness"; the conventional Philadelphian doesn't go into politics. Harvard and Yale to Philadelphians are acceptable but exotic. Harvard is a bit precious, quaint and tarred with radicalism. Its very intellectual aliveness is a detriment as far as Philadelphians are concerned. One of Penn's most famous Old Philadelphian teachers of law was finally seduced away from the University up to Cambridge. Everything was done to make him happy, but after a couple of years in exile, he announced that he was quitting. The Harvard officials were upset. They asked him what had gone wrong. Had anybody offended him? "Oh no," he said, "everybody's been fine. It's just all this goddam intellectual conversation."

As for Yale, it's considered a bit nouveau riche, get ahead, New Yorky or even Chicagoan; too smart and loud by half.

At Princeton Philadelphians feel at home, and though no official bonds are recognized except for a permanent Philadelphia representation on the Board of Trustees (two trustees as a rule, one to represent Old Philadelphia, one non–Old Philadelphia), Princeton remains Old Philadelphia's natural social collegiate expression. Fiction writers, more sensitive to this sort of thing than most people, have celebrated this subterranean bond in terms of their heroes, or hero-villains — Morley in *Kitty Foyle*, Michener in *South Pacific*, Powell in *The Philadelphian* — the type of the "Main Line–Princetonian." Actually the number of Old Philadelphians studying there at any one time is not and never has been large; but it has always been consistent and in the past a tight little group that roomed together, together joined Ivy or Colonial Clubs and upon graduation immediately married one another's sisters.

Nowadays all this is supposed to be changed. Colleges are hard to get into — particularly Princeton, and even those who think they have an hereditary right there sometimes can't make it. Also, inside the college itself there has been a ferment of "democratizing" so that the instinctive group movement of an Old Philadelphian clique into Ivy and Colonial is no longer as well thought of or as automatic.

Nonetheless, Princeton is still psychologically a Philadelphia college, and Philadelphia is still socially a Princeton town (for example, Princetonians tend to dominate the best local Philadelphia clubs numerically), and though Philadelphians cherish and bewail their own local University, in the same way that Episcopalianism has been seducing the Quakers, so Princeton has been skimming the cream of young Old Philadelphians from the past two or three generations, and Penn has been suffering from it.

vii. Rights of Passage

FOR WOMEN IN PHILADELPHIA, things are somewhat different. It has always been obligatory for the Old Philadelphia boy to go to college, usually with the professions in mind. College education for women was unheard of, and, until after World War II, was still considered a radical or frumpy sort of thing to do. This makes all the more ironic the position of Bryn Mawr. Of all Philadelphia's many educational institutions, this is the only one that has a prestige comparable to, say, the Big Three among men's colleges. There is no Big Three among women's colleges, but in a list of the best, Vassar, Radcliffe, Smith, Wellesley and so forth, Bryn Mawr would always be included. Not for Philadelphia girls however. In the old days, only if she were distinctly plain, intellectual, rebellious or otherwise exceptional would the daughter of an Old Philadelphia family go to Bryn Mawr, or indeed to any other college. Even now, when every girl *has* to go to college (what else is there to do all winter?), Philadelphia girls seem to prefer to go farther away. They leave Bryn Mawr to girls from the first families of other places. As for girls from Philadelphia first families going to the female part of Pennsylvania, they would sooner *die* — or at least until very recently. Now the prohibition is somewhat relaxed, and there is even one "good sorority."

All this business about schools, colleges and clubs may be important for boys, but for girls it is all secondary. For girls a far more bloodcurdling and elaborate tribal rite of passage has been devised — the debut and all the preliminary hurdles of the Dancing Classes. A boy's social life might conceivably be made or marred by his school-college-fraternity affiliations, but a girl *has* to go to the Dancing Classes. There can be no such thing as the "right" dancing classes. In Philadelphia there are only *The* Dancing Classes.

The social position of a debutante has already been crystallized, long before her actual debut, by her attendance or non-attendance at these obligatory series of classes, again divided in two by the Schuylkill River into Main Line and Chestnut Hill. On the Main Line, for instance, come first the Tuesday Afternoon Dancing Classes, which snatch the buds as early as the second grade, and keep hold of them through the age of twelve. After these come Friday Evenings (ages thirteen to fifteen) for two years, still split in two suburban divisions; then finally two successive dances, the Friday and Saturday Evenings, which are held in town and unite the Main Line and Chestnut Hill. After that, the debut.

The transfer from one dancing class to the next represents each time a social hurdle, since each has a different committee, and attendance at one does not guarantee an invitation to the next, though it helps. A certain amount of pruning goes on during the process, and those girls who make the finish, or the Saturday Evening, about ninety of them at any one time, are pretty well qualified as socially eligible. (About 250 boys also get asked to each of the later Evenings.) Invitations are issued entirely at the discretion of the various committees — Tuesday, Friday, Saturday. One doesn't ask or write letters. One just waits. There are about a dozen members on each committee, and by the time they get through seeing that their own daughters and cousins and best friends' daughters make the course, there isn't much room for anyone else. Mere abstract social position or Old Philadelphianism is obviously less important here than knowing, or preferably being, a member of a committee. Of all Philadelphia's boards, these Dancing School Boards are unquestionably the most socially powerful.

The Dancing Classes have always been going on in Philadelphia, and the origins of the "Evenings" seem to be quite literally lost. Mrs. Boker, daughter-in-law of the playwright George Boker, was famous as committee member and arbiter of such a class at the end of the nineteenth century. Elizabeth Pennell, in her *Our*

Philadelphia, describes "the Dancing Class at the Natatorium" where Willie White, the aging beau of those occasions, once danced with her. This seemed to qualify, in those days, as a debut. At any rate, even in the 1880's, the Dancing Class, then on a Monday, "always had been."

Modern Philadelphia's dancing classes owe everything to a winsome but dynamic little Baltimorean, Mrs. Duer. She did not originate her classes, but took over the original one for its committee and expanded it. She did this professionally, and, in fact, had a whole chain of dancing classes from Virginia up to New Jersey along the Eastern seaboard. Her tiny, springing, bright-eyed presence was familiar to almost every suffering, well-brought-up child in the lower Middle Atlantic states, and it is the system of dancing classes once run by her that still holds Philadelphia in its somewhat icy grip. The invitations to the Tuesday Afternoons today read "in memory of Josephine Poe Duer." George Wharton Pepper's poem, "Rings on her fingers and springs on her toes, Josephine dances wherever she goes," written to her on her eightieth birthday, is one testimony to the place she held in Philadelphia hearts.

There have been attempts to break up this monopoly of the Dancing Classes. The William de Rham classes of New York have opened a Philadelphia branch, which seems to do well. In older echelons this blossoms into some things called the Dancing Assemblies at the Merion Tribute House. Those who go to these instead of the Saturday Evenings consider them "more fun"; those that go to the Saturday Evenings know that "fun" has nothing whatever to do with it.

After the Dancing Classes comes the debut. As of 1960–61, one hundred and seventy Philadelphia girls had formal debuts, registered in February on an official list kept by Caldwell, the jewelers. Most of these were private, tea dances and dinners mostly, as opposed to the mass debuts now popular in New York at big Charity Balls; although there is a June Ball which lets forth a dozen girls or so in one fell swoop, and some others like it. Of these debutantes only ninety of course have been finally graduated from the Saturday Evening Dancing Classes. Twenty or twenty-five * of these are then selected for invitation to the Assembly. There is no connection at all between the Assembly and the Dancing Classes. In the Assembly it's birth, not knowing people, that is decisive. A girl could perfectly well go to the Assembly without having been to any of the Dancing Classes; but it's not very likely. (It is actually a good deal more important for a boy to be asked to the Assembly than for a girl. A girl can always marry in; a man, theoretically, can't.) Still, by the time a debutante gets through the Assembly she has earned her right to be considered Old Philadelphian; by then, if everybody doesn't know where she and everybody else stands, they are either so low down in the social scale that they don't count, or they are singularly unaware.

Contrary to some outside impressions, the Assembly is in no sense a debutante ball; it is quite different from, say, New York's Junior Assembly, which is. The Philadelphia Assembly is a big two-hundred-year-old dance for grownups. It is probably still the most august of America's social occasions, and is only incidentally a part of training for the young; but attendance at the Assembly serves also as the final hurdle for the Old Philadelphia debutante.

A girl or a boy who has gone successfully through the whole business — for the boy, right school, right college, right club or fraternity in college, then right club in Philadelphia, for the girl the gamut of the Dancing Classes — the Assembly is the final accolade. He or she is then *in,* and few societies anywhere offer such a final and conspicuous kiss of approval. After that one can just relax permanently, as far as social position is concerned, for the rest of one's life. The mature Old Philadelphian's aplomb is based largely on having passed these youthful examinations with high marks. Now groomed for Maintenance, his or her "status-seeking" days are done.

* But this number has been increasing over the years.

BOOK

II

II

i. Sacred Professions

WHEN THE PROCESSING is finished, and the male animal has been broken and groomed, there then comes: Work. Work obviously means something quite different from merely "a job." Horatio Alger, or from newsboy to tycoon, will hardly do. On the other hand, the life of a Gentleman of Leisure, as the wails of Sidney Fisher indicate, was and is frowned on by this Quakerized society.

Work, then, becomes a compromise between realities and ideals. That is, there's no real question of making money, or of getting ahead; on the other hand, a man must Do Something. A man who doesn't "work" is considered a trifler and contemptible. But at the same time most of one's real money is probably inherited and most of one's real standing and prestige, that fine flower of distinction, is based on extracurricular, even leisure-time, activities. Just being a successful industrious man of business and nothing else may be respectable, but is definitely not awe-inspiring. As in the double standard of upper-class Philadelphian Victorian sexual life, which pretended to absolute heartfelt monogamy, but practiced a taken-for-granted illegal polygamy, so there exists a similar sort of rather hypocritical double standard in the world of careers. Philadelphia is full of people of considerable standing who are hereditary presidents and directors of savings fund societies, family companies and members of law firms, who though nominally "working" at these positions, and making quite a fuss about it too, are really busy with all sorts of other things, from deep-sea fishing to reforming Philadelphia politics.

The life of Dr. William Camac is a Victorian and somewhat

exaggerated summing up of the attitudes, the processes — and the dangers — of this double standard. Born of distinguished and very rich parents, he fell in love with a girl of strict and substantial Quaker background. She encouraged him; but at the last moment came the dreadful question: what was young Camac going to *do*? He had, it seems, no idea. He wasn't going to do anything. "I could never marry a do-nothing," said his fiancée, and turned him down. Camac, being of a scientific bent, thereupon went to the Jefferson Medical College, got his degree as a Doctor of Medicine, and presented the diploma to his beloved on bended knee. She took him. The formalities over with, he never thereafter did one stroke of medical work, though always known by his title as Dr. Camac. He devoted himself to botanizing and natural history. He had a magnificent country house with a conservatory famous for its palms and exotic plants; he was one of the earliest backers and first president of the hundred-year-old Philadelphia Zoological Society (needless to say, the first of its kind in the country) and is usually credited as its founder. Finally in a sunset burst of opulence he took his entire household, wife, children and servants, to Egypt, hired a large houseboat and sailed up the Nile. He entrusted his affairs at home to a dear friend, and as is so often the case in Philadelphia (this is a perennial story) the dear friend absconded. When Camac got home he was ruined, and that was the end of conservatories and houseboats on the Nile. More or less the end of the Camacs too; at least they emigrated to New York.

The Paul family has been especially rich in these nineteenth-century non-practicing doctors. John Marshall Paul, for instance, began fairly busily in Philadelphia, but in his forties moved to a country place up the Delaware. "He gradually retired from the practice of his profession," wrote his son and biographer.

His office became filled with fishing tackle rather than patients, as he settled down to the life of a country gentleman. His place sloped down to the river on the edge of which was a little boathouse. On a summer afternoon he would seek out some of the children, procure bait and rod, and row up the river to the cliff of Manunkachunk in the hope of catching a black bass, which so far as my experience went was never taken.

This idyllic afternoon landscape contrasts strongly with the career of his friend and first cousin, John Rodman Paul, who was a non-practicing doctor of another Philadelphia kind, that of the busy Boardsman. He too retired at forty, but not to fish. He was President of the Board of Managers of the Wills Eye Hospital, Treasurer of the College of Physicians, a Director of the Philadelphia Contributionship for Insurance of Houses from Loss by Fire, a Trustee of the University of Pennsylvania, a Director of the Bank of Commerce, President of the Gloucester Land Company, Treasurer of the Washington Manufacturing Company (a cotton mill), Inspector of the County Prison, and What Have You.

Even more conspicuously non-practicing was a somewhat later James Paul, usually known by his nickname of James the Marquis. Rusticated from Princeton for idleness, too much smoking and the reading of French novels, he was reinstated only on condition that he give up these pleasures. He did, graduated and went on through medical school. As a reward for all this virtue, his stern parent gave him a trip abroad for a present. He returned from his grand tour, bringing with him the largest consignment of French novels ever to enter the country, and devoted all the rest of his long life to smoking cigars, reading French novels and having lunch at the Philadelphia Club.

The cases of Dr. Camac and the Pauls were unusual in that they were flagrantly non-practicing doctors. Much more common is the non-practicing lawyer, and it is almost routine for a gifted young man, especially one with literary tastes, to study law, practice a year or two, then go into whatever he pleases, his duty done. But at least a gesture towards work, and preferably towards the two Sacred Professions, is mandatory. As examples, one can cite among others Nicholas Biddle, George Boker, and Owen Wister.

Actually the hardest-working and most distinguished Philadelphians are the really successful practitioners of these two Sacred Professions, Law and Medicine. Their prestige is far, far above that of the mere artist, politician, professor, clergyman, business executive or plain millionaire. Though the few Philadelphians who have become really world famous have usually not been lawyers or doctors, in Philadelphia itself to be its leading lawyer or leading doctor is almost automatically to be its leading citizen. The position held, for example, by the two Peppers, Senator George Wharton Pepper and Dr. Oliver Hazard Perry Pepper, as deans of law and medicine respectively, has been about as high as a human can get in Philadelphia estimation. The fact that they were both Peppers clinches it: but even Jacob Da Costa, a West Indian Jew, or John J. Johnson, a blacksmith's son from South Philadelphia, were in their day recognized as leaders of the Philadelphia world on the strength of their professional eminence, as leading doctor and leading lawyer respectively.

Between the two, the law is more Solid, medicine more Noble, and since Philadelphia on the whole prefers the solid to the noble, law does perhaps have the edge.

ii. *Medicine*

JUST THE SAME, medicine was Philadelphia's first love among the professions. From 1682 till about 1900 it is safe to say that *every* prominent Philadelphia doctor either was or became an established Old Philadelphian, or at least his descendants did. The exceptions could probably be counted on one's fingers. Nowadays medicine may not have quite the same power and éclat as the law, nor is it as much dominated by Old Philadelphia; but the prominent Old Philadelphia doctor is still a pretty hallowed personage.

For especially Quaker reasons, the title "Doctor" in itself has always been an honor. It was the only title of any kind that Quakers would recognize. It also represented as nothing else could the practical-humanitarian-scientific bent of Quakerism, though to this originally idealistic aroma was later added a more worldly edge. The first emigrant doctors had been educated in England or Scotland. The second generation, finding no medical schools or facilities in America, had to go back to England, or particularly Scotland, to acquire thorough training. This took money, money and leisure; so this second generation of doctors came, on the whole, from the already well-established upper classes who could afford to send their more intelligent offspring across the ocean for a tour of several years. Thomas Cadwalader and the Shippens represented the fine flower of this match between humanitarianism and social prestige. Medicine, in the eighteenth century and in Philadelphia, was off to a good start.

A group of Welsh Quaker practitioners, leaders in the Welsh Barony, can be considered the founders of Philadelphia medicine, both scientifically and socially. Of these, Thomas Lloyd was the first, chronologically and in importance. A Welshman, of course, and a graduate of Oxford in 1662, he was, with Penn himself, one of the few really upper-class converts to Quakerism, for this was a religion that appealed primarily to artisans rather than to the gentry. Lloyd brought with him a coat of arms of many quarterings, if not a genealogy straight from God like the Cadwaladers. After he arrived in America, he was too busy with politics and with the administration of the affairs of his friend Penn to do much actual practicing; but he still was a doctor, and as he was also probably the leading citizen of Pennsylvania, the combination was thought seemly.

Dr. Thomas Wynne was another, though less weighty, Quaker medical leading citizen. His claims to both medicine and gentility, unlike Dr. Lloyd's, were a bit suspect. His title of Doctor was assumed. He had not studied at the University like Lloyd, but was merely a self-taught "barber-surgeon," though evidently a capable one. His coat of arms he had casually borrowed from the deceased first husband of his third wife; surely a remote family connection. However, in the New World people weren't too particular, and he grew into his pretensions easily. His children, like those of Lloyd, married properly, and what is more, married medically. Dr. Edward Jones, an equally Welsh doctor of the early settlement, married a daughter of Dr. Wynne, and from them might be said to have descended Philadelphia medicine. It was Edward's son Evan who taught nephew Thomas Cadwalader his first rudiments; a Dr. John Jones, great-grandson of Dr. Wynne, became a famous surgeon, wrote the first American treatise on the subject, taught and practiced in New York at the infant King's College, and finally returned home to Philadelphia where he ended as the friend, physician and confidant of both Franklin and Washington. The descendants of this Jones family complex, among them Dr. Owen Jones Wister, father of the writer Owen Wister, have proliferated to this day; some of them are still doctors, Dr. Owen Jones Toland, for example.

In the early eighteenth century an immigration of English doctors, better trained, better educated, and more polished men of the world, challenged the earlier and seventeenth-century Welsh medical supremacy. Chief among them was Dr. John Kearsley, who arrived in 1711. He was not only the best practitioner of his day; he was also one of those universal men so common in Philadelphia's great days. An amateur architect, he designed Christ Church, Philadelphia's oldest and most beautiful Anglican place of worship. He was an amateur scientist, too, a politician, and above all a teacher: among his pupils were Thomas and Phineas Bond, William Shippen the elder, John Redman and (again) Thomas Cadwalader. The Bonds in particular became rich, influential and socially important, but they were Marylanders; it was only in the next generation that most of Philadelphia's prominent doctors were native-born.

Four names in this golden age of the revolutionary generation stand out, not only medically but socially: Shippen, Morgan, Kuhn and Rush. There may have been other distinguished contemporary physicians in Philadelphia, the appropriately named Dr. Physick, father of American surgery, for one, but none are better remembered now as persons or ancestors than the Great Four. They sum up in their backgrounds the principal ethnic strains that form the basis of Old Philadelphia — English, Welsh and German — and also illustrate various levels of "family." Shippen was already a fourth generation member of the upper classes, and a son of a doctor. Morgan was of dubious ancestry, but the most perfect gentleman of the world in Philadelphia of his time; real fancy. Kuhn was the son of a doctor too, solid Germantown. Rush was the son of a farmer. Every single one of them married well, William Shippen a Lee of Virginia, John Morgan the sister of his college classmate Francis Hopkinson, Adam Kuhn the widowed Elizabeth Hartman Markoe of St. Croix, Benjamin Rush a Stockton of Princeton. They all studied abroad and took the grand tour, meeting famous people, acquiring manners, and when they came home, they all fought the British as Patriots, fought each other as competitors, and founded institutional medicine in America. Descendants of Shippen, Kuhn and Rush still litter the Philadelphia landscape, though only the Rushes have survived as a family.

Of these four founders, Benjamin Rush was certainly the greatest, in fact he is undoubtedly Philadelphia's most famous man of medicine, though not solely as a doctor. He was born of poor parents in Byberry, then a fairly remote country district, now notorious, ironically enough considering Rush's reputation as a pioneer in psychiatry (he was one of the first to acknowledge the influence of the mind on the body), as the site of one of our more scandalous public insane asylums. His father did not amount to much, but, as in the case of so many great men, his mother Susanna did. She saw to it that he received the best education then possible in the region; in fact it followed that of rich William Shippen. First Nottingham School, a private boarding school in Maryland, then the College of New Jersey (Princeton), and after an apprenticeship with Dr. John Redman (pupil of Kearsley) on to the University of Edinburgh. After he got his medical degree he paid a brief but exciting visit to London. There Benjamin West, the Philadelphia-born painter, introduced him to Joshua Reynolds, who in turn introduced him to Dr. Johnson. He dined with the great man, and had opportunity to observe his rudeness to Goldsmith. He also ate a meal with the political agitator Wilkes in his rather comfortable jail. In Paris, as in London, he visited all the hospitals and doctors he could, and was introduced by Franklin to the elder Mirabeau and the philosopher Diderot.

Thus educated, broadened and stimulated, he returned in 1769 to Philadelphia and there he spent the rest of his long, various and generally inquisitive and acrimonious career. He became a member of the Continental Congress, and, having married Julia Stockton of the first family of Princeton, when he came to sign the Declaration of Independence for Pennsylvania, it was almost a family affair, with his father-in-law, Richard Stockton from New Jersey, signing right alongside. During the Revolution he served his country as a surgeon general of the army, building up a fine feud with William Shippen in the process. Shippen and Morgan were, of course, fighting each other too by this time over their medical school and other matters. After the war, Rush returned to practicing, teaching and quarreling. By 1789 he was Professor of the Theory and Practice of Medicine at what was soon to become the University of Pennsylvania, succeeding the deceased John Morgan.

Rush's second great hour occurred in 1793 when yellow fever, already a familiar visitor, struck Philadelphia in devastating force. Thousands died, many more were seriously ill, and by October when the plague was at its height nearly half the population of 45,000 had fled the city. Foremost among the handful of doctors who stayed was Benjamin Rush, who, supported by a fanatical though quite erroneous belief in the perfection of his method of treatment, fearlessly visited, encouraged and purged every person he could reach. Ill himself, with his young assistants dying about him, nothing shook his faith in himself as God's medical agent, and the courage and cheer that this faith gave him. He broke with everyone who disagreed with his cure, and permanently soured his reputation with the greater part of Philadelphia's doctors, but to the people in general he was an angel unafraid, the almost supernatural embodiment of medical invincibility. Many of his patients did die, some no doubt merely of his violent methods, which included copious bloodletting; but enough lived to buttress his own confidence. Certainly his example, if not his methods, did more to keep up morale in Philadelphia than any other one thing. As a medical hero, if not a medical scientist, he takes a high place in the profession.

He lived till 1813, a revered and controversial figure, Treasurer of the United States Mint, vice president of the American Philosophical Society, bitter controversialist (his successful lawsuit with the English newspaperman William Cobbett finally drove Cobbett from the country) and mystical non-sectarian. Though intensely and personally religious, sure of the private guidance of God, he could never be satisfied with any of the known sects, and shifted restlessly about from Presbyterianism to Episcopalianism without settling. His *Autobiography,* at first rather inadequately edited by his great-grandson Louis Biddle, and since reprinted in a more scholarly edition by the Princeton University Press, gives an extraordinary glimpse of this odd and powerful personage, bigoted and tolerant, benign and fierce, mystical and doubting. He belongs, like Dr. Kearsley, in that Philadelphia succession of "universal men" which the city has somehow managed to produce or shelter, with occasional lapses, right down to the present.

Rush's children achieved fame too: Richard as Minister to England and France, Attorney General and Secretary of the Treasury, a suavely gracious public figure; James as an eccentric antiquarian and husband of Phoebe Ridgeway, wealthy and flamboyant hostess of Philadelphia's mid-nineteenth century. William was a respectable doctor, Samuel a not-so-respectable lawyer. A descendant and namesake, Benjamin Rush, became in the twentieth century as president of the Insurance Company of North America, a formidable financial power. There is still a Dr. Alexander Rush, and a couple of non-doctor Benjamins.

iii. *Chaste Fellowship*

AMONG ALL the accomplishments of the Great Four, Shippen, Morgan, Kuhn and Rush, none has had a more powerful influence on medicine in Philadelphia than their efforts as founders of the College of Physicians. Under their leadership twenty-four of the most prominent doctors of the city first met in 1787, determined to produce an American version of the already venerable Royal College of Physicians in London. They elected Dr. John Redman, pupil of Kearsley, teacher of Rush, their first President. Dr. John Jones, of the Welsh medical line, was vice president and a Dr. Hutchinson, later one of the heroic victims of the great plague, was secretary. Censors were: Shippen, Morgan, Kuhn and Rush. One job of these Censors was to keep up the standards of the college by excluding the unfit. As Rush himself expressed it, "if we are as chaste as we should be in the admission of members, a fellowship in our college will become in time not only a sign of ability, but an introduction to business and reputation in Physic." He was correct, and the "chastity" of the College of Physicians distinguished it throughout the nineteenth century. Rush himself resigned, however, during the tense and acrimonious days of the Great Plague, when he maintained that the infection was of local origin and the majority of the College, led by Kuhn, insisted it was imported. The dispute raged on and on without benefit of facts.

Despite the loss of its most famous member, the College of Physicians continued to grow in size and prestige. Even today, when the number of Fellows and Associates has increased from a chaste twenty-four to a somewhat more licentious 1,200, Fellowship is a badge of honor. This 1,200 is a lot of doctors, but out of the approximately 3,600 medicos of Philadelphia, it still represents a selection of some chastity. Moving from building to building, in 1909 the College finally settled in a grand neo-Georgian edifice on South 22nd Street. In somewhat bedimmed marmoreal splendor it houses a fine medical library, a museum of gruesome specimens and over a hundred portraits of medical celebrities by artistic ones. Next to it is a charming herb garden, a living dictionary of healing plants, given in memory of Dr. Wharton Sinkler by Eckley Coxe. The great rooms themselves are all dedicated to Philadelphia doctors, nearly all of them Old Philadelphians. The auditorium is the S. Weir Mitchell room, and there are

Cadwalader, Wood, Packard and Norris rooms. The Family touch is as apparent here as elsewhere. Weir Mitchell, for instance, was the third in a line of doctors; his father, John Kearsley Mitchell, was, like his son both poet and litterateur, and as his name indicates, a collateral descendant of old John Kearsley.

Not only have there been doctors of distinction in nearly every Old Philadelphia family — Cadwalader and Morris in particular; Dr. Nathaniel Chapman, kin of the Biddles, was first president of the American Medical Association — but there are a good dozen famous Philadelphia medical families. The Woods have been doctors and Fellows of the College of Physicians for four generations in direct line. The Wood family tree, which embraces the equally distinguished Packards and Bacons, has included altogether fourteen respected men of medicine since the eighteenth century. The handing on of the name Horatio Curtis Wood has reached a sort of impasse in various branches; there being now a Dr. Horatio C. Wood, Jr. (Pennsylvania '97), a Dr. Horatio C. Wood IV (Haverford '50), a Dr. Horatio Curtis Wood, Jr. (Pennsylvania '26), and a plain Mr. H. Curtis Wood III (Yale '54). Whither?

As prolific and confused as the Woods, though less consistently medical, is the Wistar–Wister complex. Two brothers, Caspar and Johannes Wüster, emigrated separately from Germany in the early eighteenth century, allowing their names, more or less by accident, to be Anglicized in two different forms: Caspar Wist*ar* and John Wist*er*. This in time has led to a certain inevitable rivalry between branches. Caspar Wistar became first a glass manufacturer and then a Quaker, and his grandson and namesake, Caspar Wistar, became one of Philadelphia's great doctors, a contemporary of Rush, a Censor of the College of Physicians, President of the American Philosophical Society, and something of an amateur of natural history. Wist*aria* (*not* Wist*eria*) was named in his honor and it is ironic that this purple flowering oriental vine, now so domesticated in Philadelphia, should commonly be misspelled after the *wrong* branch of the family and pronounced Wist*eria* (as in hysteria). It should, of course, be

Wist*a*ria (as in malaria). It behooves all Philadelphians, except maybe the Wist*e*rs, to *get it right.**

Both Wisters, Wistars and their Morris and other cousins are thick in the history of Philadelphia medicine. On the staff of the Pennsylvania Hospital, for instance, have been not only Dr. Caspar himself, but later on a Dr. Caspar Morris, a Dr. Mifflin Wistar, a Dr. Morris Lewis, and another Dr. Caspar Morris (grandson), all kin. A great-nephew of Caspar Wistar, Isaac Jones Wistar, founded and endowed a Wistar Institute of Anatomy in Caspar's honor, which is still flourishing. (It devotes itself to biological research; in the process it bred a famous brand of disease-free white rat, for experiments. Possums too.)

In more direct succession have been the Meigses, from Charles, born in 1792, through Arthur, President of the College of Physicians, who died in 1912; and the Norrises, with George Washington Norris, born in 1808, his son William Fisher Norris (no kin of Sidney) and his grandson George William Norris, still very much alive in 1960, covering a span of 150 years in three generations of medical distinction.

The Norrises, like the Cadwaladers, are not just a "medical family" — they are Norrises who are doctors, a subtle difference. Since the original progenitor, Isaac Norris, came to Philadelphia from Jamaica in 1692, they have occupied Position, first as grandest of Quaker grandees, then as gentlemen of late-eighteenth-century fortune, finally as nineteenth-century doctors. The Norris country house Fair Hill rivaled Logan's Stenton, and their town residence, the Slate Roof House, originally used by William Penn, rivaled the mansion of the first Edward Shippen. Shippen was called "the biggest man with the biggest coach and the biggest house in town." (It was, incidentally, during the term of Isaac Norris II as Speaker of the Pennsylvania Assembly in 1751 that

---

* Unfortunately there is good scientific basis for this mistake. A British botanist, Thomas Nuttall, living in Germantown, first published the name in 1818 as "Wisteria," crediting it however to Dr. Caspar Wist*ar*. Nobody knows just why he made that mistake. Ignorance of the difference? Friendship for the Wist*e*rs of Germantown? Though the error was later corrected by Gray, it still persists. But it *is* an error.

the Liberty Bell was ordered for the new State House, and at his suggestion, inscribed with those prophetic words, "Proclaim Liberty in all the Land"; what Isaac had in mind, of course, was religious, definitely not political, liberty.)

The list of Presidents of the College of Physicians is, with a few exceptions, a list of Old Philadelphians, or of those whose families quickly became Old Philadelphian. In fact, a little genealogical digression, a sample of the density of the Philadelphia Web, might be exhibited here just to show how very dense and how very medical it all is:

First, the genealogical nightmare of the Welsh Barony, in which John Cadwalader, progenitor of that family, married Martha Jones, daughter of Dr. Edward Jones and his wife Mary, daughter of Dr. Thomas Wynne. Then another Mary, daughter of Dr. Thomas Lloyd, married out of the Barony to Isaac Norris I. Issac II married Sarah Logan, daughter of James. Their daughter, Mary Norris, married John Dickinson, famous Revolutionary figure, after whom Dickinson College was named. Dickinson's mother was still another Mary: Mary Cadwalader, daughter of John the founder. Dickinson's brother, Philemon, in his turn married not one but two Cadwaladers in succession: Mary, daughter of Dr. Thomas (ap John), and then her sister Rebecca. (Genealogy, the sport of Kings.) Meanwhile John and Philemon's great-uncle John Dickinson had married Rebecca Wynne, daughter of Dr. Thomas Wynne, sister of Mary who married Dr. Edward Jones. The confusion here of Thomases, Johns, Marys and Rebeccas is extensive. Thank the Lord for Philemon.

General John Cadwalader, second son of Dr. Thomas (Thomas *Cadwalader*, you fool, not Thomas Lloyd or Thomas Wynne), as his second wife married Williamina Bond, daughter of Dr. Phineas Bond. Anthony Morris the first and Edward Shippen the first had married sisters, Mary and Rebecca, from New York. Both widows themselves, they were widower Morris's third and widower Shippen's second wife respectively, and both Morris and Shippen went on to one more wife apiece. Divorce was really unnecessary in those days when the turnover was so great. Edward Shippen, "biggest man" in town, was, of course, the great-grandfather of Dr. William Jr., Rush's contemporary and enemy.

Luke Morris, great-grandson of Anthony the Founder, married Anne Willing, daughter of Charles Willing, Jr., who was the son of Charles Willing and his wife Anna Shippen, granddaughter of Edward the Founder. Luke's stepbrother, Christian Sam, married Rebecca Wistar, daughter of the original Caspar Wistar. Sam's daughter Sarah married Richard Wistar, grandson of Caspar. All or nearly all of Captain Sam's ten children carried the middle name Wistar; the youngest, Israel Wistar Morris was living until 1870, and there are two Israel Wistar Morrises alive today; relations. Daniel Wist*er*, son of the original John Wist*er*, brother of Caspar Wist*ar*, married Lowery Jones, daughter of Owen Jones, grandson of Dr. Edward Jones, whose daughter Martha married John Cadwalader, etc., etc.

This gives just a small glimpse of what has been going on and why so many Philadelphians feel kin. If you aren't related, who are you? It also gives some idea of the inbred quality of Philadelphia medicine.

Despite the degree to which the early doctors were Webbed, the man of genius from the sticks or foreign parts has always been received and honored in Philadelphia solely on the basis of his talents. Jacob Da Costa, to take one example, was born a member of a Virgin Islands family of Spanish Jews, and after a wandering but complete education, most of it abroad, settled in Philadelphia to become the city's best-known diagnostician. He was a pillar of both the Jefferson Medical School and the Pennsylvania Hospital, where his picture by Thomas Eakins, who liked to do doctors, now hangs. Since Jacob himself had married a Brinton, sister of a colleague, who was also a member of a famous medical family, he was doubly in, and Da Costas are still about and Socially Registered.

Dr. Samuel Gross, the most famous doctor of his time, a surgeon, and subject of Eakins's most famous picture, "The Gross Clinic," came from Easton, up the Delaware, which is right far from Philadelphia socially. He ended up not only painted by

Eakins, but especially enshrined in the College of Physicians, where his library is preserved intact. Dr. Gross's son, another Samuel, became a doctor in his own right, and not one, but two Gross girls married Horwitzes, still another medical family, represented today in Philadelphia by Orville Horwitz, a most respected and socially prominent doctor. Then a Horwitz married a Bullitt, a Bullitt descendant married an Ingersoll, and so it goes.

But of all these medical dynasties, surely the most thoroughly identified with and beloved by Old Philadelphia is that of the Peppers. Like the Wüster–Wister–Wistar family, the Pfeffer–Peppers were German, though of a later, just pre-Revolutionary vintage. Like the Morrises, but with a German accent, the Peppers made theirs in beer, invested it in real estate, and distributed it to worthy causes, notably the University of Pennsylvania. It was in the third generation that the Peppers, having done well, and married well (for example, a Henry Pepper of the nineteenth century married a Norris girl, and a Pepper girl married a Norris boy), turned to medicine. There they have stayed ever since.

Peppers over a span of more than a century have generally dictated the destinies, medical and otherwise, of the University. William Pepper the first, born in 1810, succeeded Dr. George Wood in 1860 as Professor of Medicine. His son William graduated there in 1862 and joined the faculty in 1868, eventually succeeding his father as Professor of Medicine. After years of practice and teaching he became provost of the University in 1880, an office then corresponding to president, and is generally credited with the tremendous growth in size and prestige the University experienced at the end of the century.

The dynasty has been continued to this very day, thus rounding out a full century of eminence since 1860, by the original William's two grandsons, William and Oliver Hazard Perry Pepper. William, followed right in his father's and grandfather's footsteps: University of Pennsylvania '94, M.D. '97, faculty '99, and finally Dean of the Medical School in 1912. His younger brother Oliver, after a career along the same lines, was president of the College of Physicians of Philadelphia, member of the Philosophical Society, and until his death in 1962, remained one of Philadelphia's most characteristic and genial Grand Old Doctors.

Despite all this intense family background, it cannot be said that medicine in Philadelphia at present is in any real way dominated or even significantly represented now by Old Philadelphia. Through the College of Physicians, the Medical School of the University of Pennsylvania, and the Pennsylvania Hospital, the influence and traditions at least of Old Philadelphia medicine are conserved and spread abroad. Such present-day figures as Dr. Oliver Pepper and Dr. George Norris have demonstrated the position of Old Philadelphia in the profession. In the younger generations, however, there seems to be less and less connection. There are still medical Woods, still a younger Dr. Rush and a younger Dr. Pepper; Dr. Owen Jones Toland, obstetrician and fox hunter, continues into the present the Welsh medical strain that has persisted unbroken in family descent from seventeenth-century Drs. Lloyd, Wynne and Jones — surely an American medical record of some sort. A Dr. Brooke Roberts (see Iron & Railroads), married to an Ingersoll (see Law) is considered one of the most brilliant young doctors in the city. But there are no younger Wister–Wistars or Meigses as doctors in Philadephia; a few older but no younger Morrises. In general, the tender bonds between the oligarchy and the art of healing seem to be dissolving; but the memory lingers on.

iv. Law

THIS GRADUAL SEPARATION in modern times between the Oligarchy and the Sacred Professions is also somewhat evident in the case of the Law; but though young Old Philadelphians may no longer fill up the legal ranks, their parents and grandparents still definitely occupy the command positions, and on the whole Law is still pretty much an Old Philadelphia preserve.

It is odd, considering the enormous importance of the law in Philadelphia, past and present, that it was not until the middle of the eighteenth century that lawyers began to emerge at all into respectability. This was due to the Quakers, of course. Controversy and acute intellectual agility did not fit in with the Quaker view of things. Differences between Friends were to be settled by forgiveness, compromise and a committee of arbitration; lawyers were agents of the World, and it was unseemly for Quakers to have anything to do with them, much less practice law themselves.

The rise of the law coincides with the retirement of Quakers from active control of the city and the province. Philadelphia's first real lawyer, Andrew Hamilton, was not a Quaker, and his career indicates the increasing control of the city by other strains, notably the Anglican, but also the Scotch and German, to whom controversial bitterness was the breath of life. How the Colonials, like the Founding Fathers, loved a good fight, complete with pamphlets, dogmatic differences, political chicanery and personal invective!

The unfavorable modern connotations of the phrase "Philadelphia lawyer," have caused in Philadelphia itself a good deal of bewilderment and heartburn. According to local mythology, the phrase is honorable and ancient, and was first applied to Andrew Hamilton himself, when, as a man in his eighties, he defended the printer Peter Zenger in the courts of New York and won the case. Zenger, a New York newspaper publisher, was being tried in 1735 for seditious libel as representative of the popular party, critical of the Royal Governor. The Governor managed to have all the defending New York lawyers disbarred. Hamilton, secretly smuggled in from Philadelphia to take on the case, got Zenger acquitted, amid great furore, and thus has become an historic defender of the freedom of the press. It became a catch phrase that to win a case, one had to "bring in a Philadelphia lawyer," much as the distraught Peterkins of the *Peterkin Papers* had to bring in the Lady from Philadelphia. It is only in later years that the phrase came to be used — by outsiders — in the derogatory sense, like "sea-lawyer," either to indicate sharp

and devious practice, or to suggest a sort of over-legal, complicated, law-proud stuffiness — the fine print that taketh away what
the large print giveth.

In Philadelphia itself the "Philadelphia lawyer" is a figure of
the greatest importance, and famous Philadelphia lawyers are still
revered as divines were in Puritan Massachusetts, or Herr Professors in prewar Germany. This is indicated by the Philadelphian usage of "Esq." after the name of an accredited member
of the bar. Of course the title is still used, largely by the older
generation, in a purely social way as a form of address, but it is
also used specifically nowadays to indicate a lawyer. In a general
list of patrons, for instance, one notices sometimes that while
everyone else is Mr., the lawyers stand out down the line by the
"Esq." after their names.

Law, like medicine, established itself right at the start, and
Philadelphia's first legal family lost no time in becoming part
of the Web. Andrew Hamilton is generally revered as the founder
of the Philadelphia bar. When, in 1952, the Philadelphia Bar
Association celebrated its 150th Anniversary references to him
were thick. To quote one orator of several, "It is Andrew Hamilton to whom we look as our great exemplar." Born so obscurely
that his parents are quite unknown, he ended up with a fine
country place, Bush Hill, north of town, and was one of the pillars of the non-Quaker community. His children's rather violent
Toryism kept them away in England during Revolutionary years,
but like so many good Philadelphians they came back and took
up their social position again. They lost Bush Hill, which was
commandeered in their absence as a hospital during the plague
of 1793, thus starting a juicy lawsuit, but another grand country
place, Woodlands, stayed in the family and still survives today
as the nucleus of a cemetery of that name. A descendant in the
female line married Hartman Kuhn, son of Dr. Adam, and their
daughter married a Morris, and so we are tied up again.

Andrew's successor as Attorney General and leading lawyer was
Tench Francis, who was also related to everybody, and Francis
was succeeded by Benjamin Chew. Horace Binney summed up

the history of the law in the earlier eighteenth century in these three names: Hamilton, Francis and Chew. "Although there are a few other names at the same epoch to be added to these three, yet the narrowness of the tradition . . . had caused that Bar to disappear from nearly all memories at the beginning of the present century." This could scarcely have been said by a nineteenth-century leader of medicine, with the memory of Cadwalader, Kearsley, the Bonds, the Shippens and many others still green, about Philadelphia's earlier eighteenth-century medical tradition.

In Andrew Hamilton, Tench Francis, and Benjamin Chew, however, not only did the law have its beginnings, but also numberless Families; and though the actual names of Hamilton and Francis are gone, they live on in their innumerable descendants.

The Chews, on the other hand, are far from extinct, and survive today as among the very oldest of Old Philadelphians. With the Rawles, they form the principal tie between the feeble pre- and the powerful post-Revolutionary bar. In the case of the Chews the tie was heavily genealogical; in the case of the Rawles, extremely legal. Both families were established in the Hamiltonian period. The Chews landed in Virginia in the 1600's, worked up through Maryland, and in 1754 Benjamin (1727–1810) came to Philadelphia. He studied with Hamilton, and before the Revolution he had succeeded Tench Francis as State Attorney General and leading legal figure. He bought Thomas Willing's great mansion in town and built a splendid country place called Cliveden (pronounced Clivden) for himself near Germantown. He was a very big wig; but unfortunately also a semi-Tory. He was exiled during part of the Revolution to New Jersey. Cliveden was occupied by the British and served them as a fort during the battle of Germantown. The Americans attacked it but were repulsed, and the walls still bear the marks of gunfire. When the fighting was over, Benjamin cautiously returned to the city, and finding the climate of opinion favorable — Philadelphia was extraordinarily tolerant about this sort of thing — went back to law and ended his career as a respected judge again.

His son, Benjamin, Jr., proved a very model of Philadelphia second-generationism, and though not much of a lawyer, planted the Chews' social position securely. He married an heiress, inherited four or five different fortunes himself, and when he died left an estate of above half a million. He devoted his life to doing nothing much, but doing it well. The Chews seem to have been able to keep right on, in battle-scarred Cliveden, not doing very much about law, but doing it well, and belonging to all the right things ever since.

The Rawles, though perhaps not quite as socially expansive as the Chews, were certainly far more significant legally. For over two hundred years, from the time the first Rawle joined the bar in 1725 till the last legal Rawle died in 1930, there has been a Rawle active in the Philadelphia courts. The first Rawle, Francis, a lawyer who *was* a Quaker, came out from England in 1686. His career really was not in law but in business, local politics and economics. His treatise with the downright title "Ways and Means for the Inhabitants of Delaware to Become Rich" was not so much a manual of self-help as an essay on economics. It was, as such, the first in North America, and advocating as he did a protective tariff to encourage native industry, Rawle was the progenitor of a long line of Philadelphia economists, whose theories based on tariffs finally bore fruit in the politics of the Republican party after the Civil War. Philadelphians, however, have always been a bit hurt that Rawle seemed to direct his good advice to Delaware. He no doubt meant what is nowadays called the Greater Delaware Valley.

Rawle's admission to the bar in 1725 was something of an afterthought; he died in 1726. His son William, however, was admitted in 1728 and continued to practice. But like the Chews, the Rawles were tainted with Toryism. Like the Chews, they too were on "vacation" during the fighting, most notably William, grandson of William and great-grandson of Francis, who spent the war years studying in London (Middle Temple). Just like Chew, he also hesitantly returned to Philadelphia in 1783 and also found the atmosphere favorable. He resettled and became, before his death in 1836, one of Philadelphia's greatest men. He married a kin of the Coateses, had twelve children, and remained an active and earnest Friend. The firm of Rawle and Henderson still exists. No Rawles are now in it, though a Henderson is.

William Rawle had the final distinction of being the first Chancellor of what is now the Philadelphia Bar Association. This was organized in 1802 as the Law Library Company, and occupies exactly the same position in the legal profession of Philadelphia as the College of Physicians does in that of Philadelphia medicine. Being in Philadelphia it claims, of course, to be the first such legal organization in America, if not in the world. But the company was, in fact, just a library in 1802 and not until 1827 did it become the Law Association of Philadelphia with a Chancellor, Rawle, a Vice Chancellor, and above all a Committee of Censors, thus fulfilling the requirements of a real bar association. Brushing such quibbles aside, however, the Philadelphia Bar Association celebrated its hundredth anniversary in 1902 and will no doubt be at it again in 2002, God willing.

There had been earlier attempts to form a bar association. A Society for the Promotion of Legal Knowledge and Forensic Eloquence was founded in 1821, but unfortunately when the day appointed for the first meeting arrived, the lawyers gathered for the occasion found the janitor had forgotten to unlock the door of the meeting room, and the body adjourned *sine die*. Forensic eloquence seemed to survive this blow.

From 1827 on, however, the Law Association of Philadelphia (which at last changed its name to Bar Association in 1931) not only controlled the profession in the city but very adequately maintained the prestige and power of Old Philadelphia over the law. The list of Chancellors, Vice Chancellors, Treasurers, Secretaries, Censors, even Librarians, is a roll of Philadelphia distinction socially as well as legally. Family would seem to have been just as important as forensic eloquence.

No single name is more conspicuous on these rolls, or better typifies both family and forensic eloquence in the post-Revolutionary law, than that of Ingersoll. Second to that of the Rawles only because it begins later, the legal reign of the Ingersolls has continued through six consecutive generations down to the present, and they have remained the most purely legal family in Philadelphia's existence. Even the Rawles began with an economist, but the first Ingersoll to settle in town was a lawyer, and all the prominent Ingersolls since have been lawyers, though some were non-practicing.

The Ingersolls differ from other Philadelphia families in being really indigenous New Englanders. The Shippens came to Philadelphia from Boston, but Edward had only been there for a while, and the Shippens were never a "Boston family." The Ingersolls, however, were first a "Salem family" (so much so that later generations lived in the House of the Seven Gables and were related to Hawthorne), and later a Connecticut family. Also, once they moved to Philadelphia, they tended to marry northward into Boston or upstate New York, rather than southward as some other Philadelphia families have done, and have consequently earned a reputation for being a bit aloof, special and even peculiar.

The life histories of some of the more prominent men of the clan have tended to underscore this separateness. The fact that Jared Ingersoll the first was a conspicuous Loyalist could hardly be held against the family in view of the Chews and Rawles. However, being a New Englander, Jared was perhaps a bit more decisive and uncompromising about it. Sent over to England from Connecticut, where he then lived, to protest the Stamp Act, he became converted to its virtues and returned home a so-called "Stamp Master" for his state. As such, to his surprise he found himself wildly unpopular. Riding to the capital to get approval from the Connecticut Assembly, he was waylaid by a mob of former friends, who forced him to resign. He left for Philadelphia where he had a judicial appointment, spent a few cautious years, and finally was sent back to Connecticut on parole as a Tory, where he died.

Unlike the Rawles, who just sort of slid back into Philadelphia after the war, the Ingersolls were saved by the split between generations. Jared, Jr., who had been sent to London and the

Middle Temple by his father for a "Revolutionary vacation" and safekeeping, there turned against his father's political views and came back to America a confirmed Patriot. In 1781 he settled in Philadelphia for good, and soon became a leader of the bar. He was Attorney General of Pennsylvania (1811–17) in a day when this was considered pretty distinguished, and later a judge. His opinions grew more conservative as he grew older, and he was an ardent Federalist, nominated at one time for Vice President of the United States.

The Ingersolls in any given generation seem to have had a talent for eventually picking the losing side without somehow damaging their reputations. Jared's son Charles Jared was less a practicing lawyer than a man of affairs, of letters and an all-around Philadelphia gentleman. He supported Jackson during the Bank business when every right-thinking Old Philadelphian was supporting Biddle. He was elected to Congress as a Democrat, and during the War of the Rebellion was a states' rights sympathizer with the South. In fact he was Philadelphia's leading Copperhead; but not because he sympathized with slavery. He was one of the few men in public life who saw that war was insanity, and who hoped the Middle States could keep the country together as a mediator between the abolitionist North and the slaveholding South. Nobody paid much attention to him. If they had, it might have saved a lot of trouble. The result of his good sense was to make him a thoroughly controversial figure in Philadelphia. Being an Ingersoll, however, he could get away with it.

Charles Jared's conservative brother, Joseph, was agin him on every issue. Joseph stuck closer to the profession, and until his death in 1868 stood for everything that was elegant, chiseled and courtly in the Philadelphia law; he was an active boardsman, and also served briefly as Minister to England in Fillmore's administration.

A son of Charles Jared, Edward, carried on the family tradition of intransigence, devoting his life, much like his father, to unpopular causes, the most unpopular being the cause of states' rights Democracy in the North during the Civil War. Like his great-grandfather, Jared the Loyalist, he was mobbed. After a Jefferson dinner in 1865 where he made derogatory remarks about the administration, he was attacked by the exasperated citizens, arrested and thrown into jail for disturbing the peace. Though educated as a lawyer, he never really practiced, and after the War devoted himself not too propitiously to belles-lettres.

R. Sturgis Ingersoll, present-day partner in the law firm of Ballard, Spahr, Andrews and Ingersoll, and President of the Philadelphia Art Museum, has expressed the family intransigence in this generation by introducing Picasso to Philadelphians, more or less over their dead bodies. His brother, Charles Jared Ingersoll, is not a lawyer, but is represented on so many business, charitable and institutional boards that a full page could be pretty well filled up just listing them (P.R.R., U.S. Steel, etc.). Unfortunately for continuity, none of the next younger generation are now practicing lawyers; but since they in turn are producing Ingersolls in adequate supply, there's still hope the line won't be broken.

There are, of course, plenty of other legal families of Revolutionary vintage and later, some of them still extant. The Tilghmans, for example, originally from Maryland, are still going strong in both places. An innocent stranger once asked a Maryland Tilghman if he were related to the Philadelphia family. "No," he answered, "they are related to me." Then there are the Reads and the Reeds. George Read signed the Declaration of Independence for Delaware, but studied and even practiced in Philadelphia. Joseph Reed came from Trenton to become a Philadelphia lawyer and anti slavery leader. Both founded legal successions which flourished for at least three generations; Reads and Reeds were related to everyone and persist to this day as families, if not legal ones.

The Hopkinsons too have persisted. Francis, brother-in-law of Dr. John Morgan and graduate too in that famous first class of 1757 at the College of Philadelphia, among his many other accomplishments was a lawyer and judge. His son Joseph, though less universally talented, was a judge too, one of the best friends of Joseph Bonaparte, brother of Napoleon, during Bonaparte's exile in America. Hopkinson died of a stroke while reading in the Athenaeum. Today Edward Hopkinson, who began as a lawyer but has shifted to banking, occupies as senior partner of Drexel and Company the position of Grand Old Man of Philadelphia succeeding the late Senator George Wharton Pepper.

v. Chancellors

THE BIDDLES and the Cadwaladers, along with their other interests, were also important nineteenth-century legal families. The chief legal Cadwalader was John, grandson of Dr. Thomas, who spanned the nineteenth century for law and Cadwalader as Thomas did the eighteenth for Cadwalader and medicine. Cadwalader never made Chancellor of the Bar Association, Philadelphia's highest legal accolade, however, as chief legal Biddle, George Washington did. The succession of Chancellors pretty well covers not only the Law, but also Family in its full Philadelphia–Victorian effulgence. From William Rawle, who occupied the post first, to George Tucker Bispham, who held it till 1899, the Chancellors have been acknowledged not only as professional leaders, but also as leaders socially. Most of them were, of course, connected or related to each other in some way. Only the second Chancellor, Peter Du Ponceau, escaped from the Web, and although he was specifically *not* an Old Philadelphian, he is an ingratiating character, who sheds a piquant light on an otherwise fairly stuffy prospect. He can't be neglected, even if he is a digression.

His history was odd. Born the son of a French army officer, he was sent to a Benedictine seminary and actually became an abbé at some incredibly early age. However, having taught himself English and met various English families, he became infected with Protestantism, and left the Church and France, coming to America with the German Baron Steuben. He got a commission and served with Steuben at Valley Forge and elsewhere, but had to resign after four years of service when his health broke down. He had then reached the ripe age of twenty-one. He was afterward an assistant to Robert Livingston, United States Secretary for Foreign Affairs. Since he spoke English, Latin and French perfectly, understood German, Italian, Spanish and could translate Danish and low Dutch, he made himself useful. He was admitted to the bar in 1785 and practiced for thirty years, dying at the age of eighty-four in 1844.

His vignette of a group of Philadelphia lawyers en route to Washington is refreshing. He wrote:

In the beginning of the present century, during the reign of the embargo, non-intercourse and other restrictive measures, a great number of cases were carried up from this city to the Supreme Court of the United States. The counsel engaged in those causes were in the habit of going together to Washington to argue . . . before that tribunal. These were Mr. [Jared] Ingersoll, Mr. [Alexander] Dallas, Mr. [William] Lewis, Mr. Edward Tilghman, Mr. [William] Rawle and myself, who am, alas, the only survivor of that joyous band. We hired a stage to ourselves, in which we proceeded by easy journeys. The court sat then . . . in the month of February; so that we had to travel in the depth of winter, through bad roads . . . in no very comfortable way. Nevertheless, as soon as we were out of the city, and felt the flush of air, we were like schoolboys in the playground on a holiday; and we began to kill time by all the means that our imaginations could suggest. Flashes of wit shot their coruscations on all sides; puns of the genuine Philadelphia stamp were handed about; old college stories were revived; macaroni Latin was spoken with great purity; songs were sung — even classical songs — among which I recollect the famous Bacchanalian of the Archdeacon of Oxford, "Mihi est propositum in taberna mori": in short, we might have been taken for anything but the grave counselors of the celebrated bar of Philadelphia.

Sometimes they went too far, as Du Ponceau's account of a return trip testifies.

To such a degree was our mirth carried, that our Irish driver, listening to us, did not perceive a stump that was before him; the carriage made a terrible jolt, our Phaeton was thrown from his seat, the horses took fright and ran away with us at a dreadful rate. A river or creek was before us, and the bridge was not very safe. It was determined to jump out of the carriage. I was pressed to show the example, but I did not choose to do it, intending to take my own course. I have heard it related, that at that moment, I took a pinch of snuff very leisurely; but that I do not remember, and I very much doubt the truth of the fact. Be that as it may, all except myself jumped out of the carriage. Being then left alone, I collected all my presence of mind, looked about me, chose my position, and jumped out so fortunately, that I fell upon my feet without the least injury. Turning back to look behind me, the first thing I saw was my friend Lewis, sprawling upon the ground, and not able to rise alone. I raised him on his feet, and presently came our companions, who all complained of being more or less bruised.

He concludes, "I am now left alone on the stage of life, which they were doomed also to leave before me." The thought of the bearers of such arch-Philadelphia names as Ingersoll, Dallas, Tilghman and Rawle, every one a revered lawyer, all tumbling promiscuously in the mud does give one pause, and a certain amount of pleasure.

The third Chancellor, John Sergeant, was generally conceded to be the greatest lawyer of them all in that first half of the nineteenth century. He spent a great deal of his time in politics, however, this being before the days when politics was completely taboo for a gent. He served a half-dozen terms in the United States Congress and in 1832 he even, like Ingersoll, ran for Vice President with Henry Clay against Jackson. He went back to Congress after his defeat, declined a seat in Harrison's cabinet and the position of Minister to England, and returned to Philadelphia, the law and the Chancellorship of the Law Association.

His successor as Chancellor was Horace Binney, perhaps the Representative Philadelphian of the nineteenth century, who came to the bar in 1800, at the age of twenty, and for seventy-five more years dominated the city, though he actually withdrew from active practice when he was only fifty. Binney declined, as any good Philadelphian should, an appointment to the United States Supreme Court and then, in 1869 after the death of Taney, the Chief Justiceship of same. His tenure of the Chancellorship was brief, only two years, from 1852 to 1854. Yet despite, or perhaps even because of this seeming avoidance of responsibilities, he remained till he died in 1875 unquestionably Philadelphia's leading citizen, giving advice, active on boards, writing the eulogies of his less durable friends, honored and beloved by all. "It would be difficult to mention a death that caused a sensation more widespread than his," said his eulogist, the Honorable William Strong of the United States Supreme Court.

It might be somewhat difficult to understand why the death of a lawyer of ninety-five, retired for almost half a century, should cause a "sensation" of any kind. It is the Philadelphia tradition of the Father Image that is involved here. There is always in Philadelphia at least one, often more than one, Grand Old Man who sums up for Philadelphia, and especially Old Philadelphia, everything that it wants to have summed up: professional prominence, devotion to city, extensive extracurricular participation, impeccable reputation, personal charm and physical handsomeness, the best social and, of course, family connections, an extreme but active senescence — and preferably lots of money. Nobody ever embodied all this better than Horace Binney.

Joseph Ingersoll succeeded Binney, but was busy with other things and only held the post for a few years. William Morris Meredith, the next in line, was unlike Sergeant and Binney in that he accepted things: he was Secretary of the Treasury under Taylor, and during the Civil War Attorney General of Pennsylvania, a position of crucial importance, but by that time already considered "politics" of a fairly low sort, though Meredith is described as having first "satisfied himself of the purity of the administration" before accepting the post. He was redeemed from these adventures by his election as first President of the Union League, though even this at that time was a controversial post. A big, clumsy man quite devoid of Ingersoll—Binney courtliness, who chawed tobacco in court and spat from the rostrum, he was nonetheless kin to the Biddles.

Peter McCall, who succeeded Meredith as Chancellor, was

thoroughly courtly and thoroughly typical. Of a family highly involved with Cadwaladers and Ingersolls, his one indiscretion was a term as Mayor of Philadelphia in 1844. After that he settled down to practice, delivered papers before the Historical Society, taught in the law school of the University of Pennsylvania, and was famous for his aplomb and manners. We are given a seashore sample of these:

Standing one summer day in front of the bath houses of the Stockton Hotel at Cape May [recounts a Law Association memorialist], I heard a gentleman say to two elegantly dressed ladies, "Here comes Mr. McCall now"; and as Mr. McCall, just out of the water, came up, the gentleman, with great lack of tact, stopped him and presented him to the ladies. [You had to be so careful in Victorian days.] A bathing suit is not a thing of beauty now, and was still less so then. But no prince in his robes of state could have been more courtly than Mr. McCall in his wet and unkempt hair and dripping flannels. With no excuse or apology for his appearance, no sign of irritation or even disturbance at the maladroit introduction, he stopped a moment, exchanged a few sentences with the party, and then bowed and passed on to his bath house as serenely as if he had been at a state ball.

A thoroughly Philadelphian model of calmness.

Charlotte Wilcocks, a young diarist and future sister-in-law of McCall's, whom we have already quoted apropos mistresses, gives an earlier and somewhat less dignified picture of him.

Went out to "Forest Hill" with oh! thrillin' Peter! We talked about — his *girls* and the way they should be educated. Aunt W. is evidently anxious for Peter and May to make a match; but Peter is quite too squinney, Mary and I both think, to fall in love with and so I dare say thinks Miss Swann, and then Peter's legs are so short, and his tooth blue, to say nothing of having lost his bloom and being too ladylike, and he is so horribly afraid of Harry and I coming together, he constantly advises me not to marry a lawyer. I set his mind at ease by telling him I was dying to be a widow.

Oh, the cold, cruel gaze of a young Victorian maiden! Evidently Peter in a bathing suit was more courtly than thrillin'; but alas for Charlotte, she failed to take Peter's advice, married his brother

Harry, and had a pretty slim time of it. Peter evidently derived some of his manners from his mother. According to Charlotte, "Mrs. McCall is such a funny old lady, so bland and suabacious." An hereditary suabaciousness, obviously.

George Washington Biddle, translator of Demosthenes, grandfather of Francis and George, succeeded thrillin' Peter. Biddle's brother-in-law Richard McMurtrie succeeded him. He is, like Meredith, famous for being a somewhat brusque character, and is also oddly distinguished for his sisters, who kept Philadelphia's most famous genteel boardinghouse, which combined the elegant conversation of a salon with good cheap board and bed, and at one time or another put up nearly everyone of consequence.

The two other Chancellors who filled up the century, Joseph Townsend and George Tucker Bispham, were lawyers and family men both. But after them this intimate blend of family and fame was interrupted, and Chancellors in this century have been men such as Joseph Gaffney, himself a sufficiently prodigious man of family, as well as a great lawyer, but within a strictly Irish Catholic circle, or the Jewish Bernard Segal, Chancellor when the 150th anniversary of the Association rolled around in 1952.

There have, of course, been lawyers, Philadelphians, members in the best standing of the Web, who refused to follow the Philadelphia fashion of declining and eagerly accepted all the offices that came their way. Thus Thomas McKean signed the Declaration and then was re-elected Governor of Pennsylvania again and again, seeing to it that his lawyer son Joseph Borden McKean was Attorney General of the state for eight years. Thomas Mifflin was Governor for three terms before McKean, and married a Morris. The Dallases rose even higher, or fell further, from a Philadelphia point of view. Alexander, one of those lawyers who rode with Du Ponceau in the merry stage to Washington, had a son, George Mifflin Dallas, who actually permitted himself to become Vice President of the United States under Polk, the only Philadelphian in history who risked getting even that close to the White House. He paid for it. Dallas, Texas is named for him, and cowgirls come to lay flowers on his grave. George

Dallas was, of course, a Democrat, which explains things. Later he was Minister to England. His father had started off badly by being a most successful Secretary of the Treasury under Madison. Secretary of the Treasury, along with Attorney General, seem to have been the only Cabinet positions Philadelphians would permit themselves, and Vice President (Ingersoll, Sergeant) the highest office for which they would consent to run.

vi. Outsiders

A GENEALOGICAL TANGLE even more fearsome than that of medicine, though not as antique, could be presented involving lawyers, and proving how Tench Francis was related to the Tilghmans, Tilghmans to Chews, Chews to Rawles, Rawles to Binneys and Cadwaladers, Cadwaladers, prime genealogical glue that they are, firmly stuck to Reads and McCalls, in turn stuck to Ingersolls. McMurtries were kin to Francises, Tilghmans, McCalls, Biddles and everyone else. Townsends married Bisphams, Bisphams married McKeans, and so on and on and on.

This gives, or certainly ought to give, a pretty fair picture of the identification of Family and Law. Of the seventy-odd lawyers who signed as original incorporators of the Law Library in 1802, a good many more than half bear Old Philadelphia names of one kind or another, some Jewish. This list included all the respectable lawyers of the city at that time. Pretty much the same is true of the one hundred and some men who served as officers, Censors, or even Librarians of the Law Association from 1827 to 1902.

There are exceptions, such as Peter Du Ponceau, as there were in medicine, and a certain few stand out like isolated promontories from the total mass of First Family professionalism. James Wilson, for instance, appointed by Washington to the first Supreme Court of the United States, Signer of the Declaration, a chief architect of the American Constitution and the Constitution of Pennsylvania, looms as one of the great figures of the nation and the state during those great days. Born in

Scotland, educated in the law in the office of John Dickinson, he had a varied, not to say checkered, career. He practiced in Philadelphia, then Reading and finally Carlisle, Pennsylvania, with immense success, and married Rachel Bird, sister of Mark Bird of Birdsboro, then one of the state's greatest ironmasters. He and his brother-in-law both had a mania for land speculation, and they were both ruined. Mark disappeared southwards, having sold his ironworks. James, at the end of his life, though still a Supreme Court Justice, had to escape from Philadelphia, then the capital, to New Jersey to avoid debtor's prison. He, too, finally fled to North Carolina and there died. An influential radical before the Revolution, he became so conservative that during the war itself, in 1779, he was branded as a Tory and his house, thereafter nicknamed Fort Wilson, was attacked by a mob. He and some friends barricaded it, and several people were killed and wounded in the tumult. He was only saved by the timely arrival of his friend Joseph Reed, then President (*i.e.* Governor) of the State, and the City Troop.

Wilson was a conspicuous non-decliner, and in fact suggested himself to Washington as first Chief Justice of the Supreme Court. He was obviously miffed when Washington failed to take him up on it. He was ambitious, cantankerous and greedy; but he was the first to formulate as a matter of actual American law the concept that sovereignty resides not in the rulers but the ruled, not in the state but in the people.

He also gave the first law lectures at the University of Pennsylvania in 1789, and so is usually cited as the founder of the Law School there. The lectures opened with great éclat, with Washington in the audience. They flourished for a while; but as Wilson got more involved in politics and debt, the lectures languished and the project died out, not to be revived until Sharswood reorganized things in the middle of the nineteenth century; but 1789 will do very nicely as date of origin, and Wilson as Founder.

Next to Wilson, the most famous and non–Old Philadelphian of all Philadelphia lawyers has been the great John G. Johnson.

What his friend J. P. Morgan was to finance, J. G. Johnson was to corporation law. The Trusts and Moguls of the Gilded Age 1900 wouldn't move without his advice, and Standard Oil and American Tobacco were merely two among his many similar clients. Once more the statement that one had to "bring in a Philadelphia lawyer" was applicable. His opinions were considered equivalent among financiers to judicial decisions. Despite his non–Old Philadelphianism, Johnson was the greatest decliner of them all, equal at least to Binney. He declined the United States Attorney Generalship offered by McKinley, and two separate places on the Supreme Court tendered by Garfield and by Cleveland. He spent his spare time and money acquiring art masterpieces at bargain prices, and his extraordinary collection now forms the core of that of the Philadelphia Museum of Art.

Last but by no means least of Philadelphia's non–Old Philadelphia giants was the late Owen J. Roberts (no kin to the Old Philadelphian Robertses of Pencoyd). A graduate of the University of Pennsylvania, who achieved fame as a prosecutor in the Teapot Dome oil scandals, and no decliner, he accepted a seat on the United States Supreme Court in 1930, the first important Philadelphian to do so since James Wilson himself. He was considered one of Philadelphia's most honored native sons, though living mostly in Washington. He was a trustee of the University and later Dean of its Law School, President of the Philosophical Society, and collector of about a dozen honorary degrees. His death in 1955 left a large gap in Philadelphia's unofficial council of Senior Citizens.

vii. Forensic Eloquence

THE EMINENT GENTLEMEN of the Law Association, as well as being interested in Family and making good marriages, were also interested in actual law cases, and the tradition is full of famous ones, such as the squabbles over Stephen Girard's will (which involved Meredith, Binney and Sergeant), murders, arguments before the Supreme Court and other disturbances. Most of these cases, however, are of strictly professional interest — the Bush Hill case, for example, a suit on the part of Andrew Hamilton's heirs to get back what was left of Bush Hill after it had been taken over as an emergency plague hospital in 1793. Sergeant and Edward Tilghman cashed in on this one, "which grew out of a common recovery." Meredith achieved great renown by ejecting from Franklin Square the bones of German Lutherans who had been buried there since 1763. Far more entertaining, however, are some equally famous but rather absurd *causes célèbres* that engaged these great minds, among them the case of the bells of St. Mark's.

St. Mark's on Locust Street near Rittenhouse Square was for years, and perhaps still can be considered, Philadelphia's most fashionable church; Episcopalian of course. Designed by the architect John Notman and finished in 1851, it was complete except for its handsome belfry, which may have contained bats, but had no bells. The rector, Dr. Eugene Hoffman, remedied that defect in the 1870's. The English-made bells were installed and began to ring, beginning at 6:45 A.M. on Sunday and three times thereafter for a half hour at a time. Opposite the church and nearby lived all the best of Old Philadelphia, and they were furious. According to Richard McCall Cadwalader, one of these nearby victims, "the bells are loud and harsh, and are rung by a person or persons unskilled in such matters." According to Charles Hutchinson, who lived at 1703 Locust (the rich Hutchinson domicile in 10th Street so lovingly described by Sidney Fisher having long been outmoded and left behind), the bells of St. Mark's were "a positive nuisance." "My baby," complained a mother, "starts up out of his sleep at the sound of the bells, and it is impossible to put him to sleep again."

Dr. Gross, standing on the street one day talking to friends, was appalled. "Who would live in such a neighborhood?" he exclaimed. "The church seemed almost to shake with the disgusting sound." Since Everybody lived in just this neighborhood, something had to be done. The Rector was adamant; the residents sued.

They hired William Henry Rawle. The church hired George Washington Biddle. Forensic eloquence never had a better day. Rawle compared the bells, as a nuisance, to abattoirs and pigsties, citing ancient precedent. He impugned the character and motives of Mr. Biddle, all in fun of course, since they were bosom friends. He quoted Shakespeare, "Methought I heard a voice cry 'sleep no more, Macbeth doth murder sleep,' " and intimated that the Reverend Dr. Hoffman, "a high-handed priest," was the Macbeth of Locust Street. As for the witnesses, Rawle refused to contrast "the affidavits of Harrison and Cadwalader and Norris" with those of "Michael Fitzgerald, Catherine Harkins, Adeline Blizzard and Patrick Malony, many of whom cannot even read and write," and whose signatures had been collected by the church as of those who positively liked bells.

Biddle on the other hand quoted Cowper, "How soft the music of those village bells." His brother-in-law Richard McMurtrie, who was Rawle's associate, promptly countered that those were *distant* village bells. Biddle, however, made the most of Rawle's class-conscious remarks about the witnesses. "Blizzard perhaps is not a highly aristocratic name," he admitted, but such people, who, after all, have to stay in town all year, "have their rights and should not have their little pleasures disturbed." Let the rich plaintiffs move on. Let them cross the Schuylkill and go West, let them follow Horace Greeley's advice, he said, and cease their petty wranglings, which would do more harm to their delicate systems than any amount of bell-ringing.

Despite this appeal to Democracy and the Little People, the court judged that the bells *were* a nuisance, quite apart from the social station of the people involved. The rich people happened to live right opposite the church, the poor people in sheltered back alleys. The court granted an injunction restraining the defendants from ringing their bells. The neighborhood is no longer the habitat of Cadwaladers, who have, in fact, followed

Greeley's advice to move West, but the injunction against the bells of St. Mark's still stands.

viii. Grand Old Men

THE DAYS when all the Chancellors, Attorneys General or Chief Justices of the city and state were inevitably at least cousins-in-law have long passed. Of the more than four thousand lawyers now practicing in Philadelphia, only a minute fraction are conceivably Old Philadelphian; but, whereas in medicine the few seldom occupy the high places, in law Old Philadelphians are still in the first rank, not so much as officials, Judges or Attorneys General or even Chancellors, but rather as senior partners of the best, largest, oldest and richest city law firms.

Until the twentieth century, the law firm was not characteristic of Philadelphia. Lawyers practiced by themselves, in offices that were often their houses. Fourth Street, down near where Locust comes to its end, saw John Cadwalader's house and office facing those of Sergeant, Binney and Ingersoll. Today, of course, the enormous complexity of law prevents any one man from being a master of it all; the modern law firm is thus a partnership of specialists. A big law firm can, as such, meet any legal emergency, but only by deploying a different set of its lawyers. So that now it is firms, rather than individuals, who corner the big business, and the biggest lawyers, on the whole, are those who have the senior positions in the biggest and best law firms.

There are about a dozen of such firms all told, and between them they pretty well get the lion's share of any really important legal business that passes through the city. A mere list of the present names of some of these firms discloses the grip that Old Philadelphia still maintains on the law, either as represented by actual partners, or by the names of former partners now deceased, but alive in name at least. Examples:

Ballard, Spahr, Andrews and Ingersoll (R. Sturgis Ingersoll is, as before mentioned, in the sixth generation of Ingersoll lawyers; the Ballards too are a formidable Old Philadelphia legal clan).

Drinker, Biddle and Reath (Henry Drinker, nephew of the painter Cecilia Beaux, brother of the writer Catherine Drinker Bowen, is of a family descended from one of the claimants of the title "first white child born in Philadelphia";* Charles Biddle is the present occupant of Nicholas the Great's Andalusia).

Duane, Morris and Heckscher (Morris Duane is a descendant of Benjamin Franklin and, as his name also indicates, a Morris; the Morris in the firm's name, however, goes back to the late Roland Morris, the Morris family's greatest lawyer of the twentieth century).

Montgomery, McCracken, Walker and Rhoads (both Montgomery and Rhoads are among the very oldest of Philadelphia names); Townsend, Elliott and Munson (a Townsend was Chancellor of the Association at the end of the nineteenth century; Munson married a Townsend). . . . and others. There are large and famous firms whose partners include no specifically Old Philadelphian names; many of the names and partners of the firms already mentioned are not Old Philadelphian. Other firms, such as that of Thomas Raeburn White, are Old Philadelphian but in a really Quaker, non-social sort of way. At least one of the oldest Old Philadelphia firms, that of Wolf, Block, Schorr and De Solis-Cohen is Old Philadelphia Jewish. But even when the senior partners are not strictly Old Philadelphian, the lower echelons are bound to contain some really antique monikers, and the descendants of the present non–Old Philadelphian senior partners have a pretty good chance of getting into and marrying into the Web.

As Old Philadelphian as any firm in the city, as large and as powerful, is that of Pepper, Hamilton and Scheetz. The senior partner was for years, until he retired shortly before his death in 1961, Old Philadelphia's chief citizen, the town's Father Image, Senator George Wharton Pepper. Perhaps no man in modern times was so well thought of, and so well represented the virtues,

---

* An Edward Drinker was born in a cave along the Delaware before Philadelphia was even built. (There is, needless to say, another claimant for this title of "First Born.")

and also some of the failings, of the Old Philadelphia state of mind as did this charming and venerable gentleman.

Born in 1867 of the same family as his first cousin, Dr. Oliver Pepper, George's father was a doctor too. His mother was a Wharton, daughter of a lawyer; her mother had been a Markoe. As the Peppers had already been famous in medicine during the nineteenth century, so the Whartons had been a weighty clan of Friends, producing in the eighteenth century Friends and merchants, and in the nineteenth, mayors, lawyers and millionaires. Of the Markoes we have heard. The Peppers at the time of the Civil War may not have been really quite Old Philadelphian, but the Whartons certainly were.

George had a somewhat sickly childhood. For years his mother was his only teacher. He learned much about literature, but little about mathematics and what he describes as the "habit of abstract thought." He pored over volumes of *Punch,* and was properly exposed to cricket and Gilbert and Sullivan. His aunt Mrs. Thomas McKean, in fact, arranged a production of *H.M.S. Pinafore,* performed by the children of the family. But he grew in strength and grace, and by the time he went to the University he was able to shine at cricket himself, as well as football, track and crew. That he should go to the University was predetermined. As he says in his memoirs, "those were the days when the son went to his father's college pretty much as a matter of course. In our case the ties . . . were unusually strong. My grandfather Wharton had been a trustee, my grandfather Pepper a professor in the Medical School. My father and my uncle Dr. William Pepper had . . . graduated from the college and its professional schools." As he said, the Peppers at the University were "not a mere succession but a dynasty."

Making the choice of a professional career also somewhat predetermined between law and medicine, he chose law. He studied at the law school, of course, and in the office of George W. Biddle. As his ancestors had been gradually weaned from a firm Quakerism to Episcopalianism, in a like fashion George Pepper was converted to Republicanism, though surrounded on all sides by old-line, states' rights residual Democrats of that stamp rather peculiar to the most upper-class of Old Philadelphians, like the Biddles, Ingersolls and Whartons. In those two faiths, Episcopalianism and Republicanism, he remained constant, active and undeviating from his youth on.

His rise in the law was slow and steady; not meteoric but solid. By 1900 he was safely niched in *Who's Who,* where he remained for the next sixty years; one of the longest tenures of that minor honor. He approached politics cautiously, but with eventual success, and despite his open scorn of Bossism, as represented by Senator Penrose and the Vare brothers, he was appointed by the Governor to be Senator from Pennsylvania, filling the vacancy caused by the death of Penrose himself in 1921, and then was elected for a term of his own. In those corrupt and politically stagnant years of the Harding and Coolidge administrations, he avoided the scandals, approved and fought for the economies, and somehow managed to preserve his faith not only in Republicanism, but in Harding and Coolidge themselves. Harding, he thought, had something of the "wisdom and tact of McKinley. I liked Harding because he showed a lively and unselfish interest in the political welfare of his friends" (and how!). Nothing is more revealing, in many ways, than his comment on Silent Cal. "He will," he says in his autobiography, "of course be denied by posterity the rank of Pitt, but he may in time be recognized as the Palmerston of our political history . . ." if there remain any other American, even Philadelphian, posterity to whom the comparison would occur, or even have any meaning.

He was defeated by his own party. The Vares not only squelched his nomination when he tried to run for a second term, but Vare got himself elected in Pepper's place. The Senate refused Vare his seat because of his over-lavish campaign expenses (that was the official reason) and he died unseated, a bitterly disappointed man. Pepper, who felt it his first duty to take his "licking like a gentleman," never again ran for active office.

He remained, like Nicholas Biddle, a perfect warning to Philadelphians of what happens when an honest gentleman gets into
politics.

This political failure merely enhanced his reputation at home.
From this point on he could always be referred to as "Senator"
but have no more political contretemps. He moved steadily higher
in Philadelphia esteem and legal prominence, became more and
more in demand as presider and speechmaker, and amassed a total
of fifteen honorary academic degrees. In 1938 he was president
of the American Law Institute, and around Philadelphia was on
the board of almost everything worth boarding. After the death
of Thomas Gates in 1948, Old Philadelphia banker and president
of the University of Pennsylvania through the 1930's, Pepper was
by common consent unquestionably Old Philadelphia's Grandest
Old Man.

In his hatred of Roosevelt and the New Deal he came near to
losing his urbanity, as he never did over the Teapot Dome Scandals or about Penrose and Vare. The packing of the Supreme
Court was "a measure conceived in hate, drafted with cunning
and projected with reckless disregard of consequences." Sensitive
to all the legal implications of the New Deal, he seems to have been
utterly insulated from the actual "great emergency" of the depression and from the disasters which caused Roosevelt's triumph.
He found it difficult, for instance, to "appreciate the anxieties of
the so-called 'underprivileged,'" and "simply could not imagine
what it is like to be an elevator boy or a share cropper." During
the war he was torn between his love for England and his anti-
Roosevelt isolationism (Japan had been "forced into war" by
That Man, etc.) .

Despite this core of bitterness, life remained serene. In his
seventies he still rose at 6:45 A.M., did his setting-up exercises,
took the 7:57 train in from his country place in Devon on the
Main Line, and worked at his office. Despite his years, the
crowded conditions of wartime travel still occasionally forced him
to give his seat to a standing woman. "When she protests I am
tempted to tell her the simple truth — which is that something

inside makes me positively uncomfortable if I continue to sit while a woman stands." His summers on Mount Desert Island in Maine were equally active, with hikes in the hills; "A mountain a day keeps the tummy away" was his motto. A ritual raising and lowering of the flag bracketed each day at his simple camp there.

Several years ago a friend of mine had occasion to lunch with the old gentleman at the Midday Club, a large modern businessman's lunch club on top of a skyscraper on Broad Street; anything but a cosy, intimate sort of place. When Senator Pepper walked in, and was observed, the entire body of lunchers stood up in respect. As in the case of Horace Binney, it is somewhat difficult to determine exactly what the basis of all this reverence really was. Certainly Senator Pepper's brief political career was admirable enough but not outstanding. As compared with those of John G. Johnson, whom he knew when he was younger, or Owen J. Roberts, friend of later years, or even his political enemy and younger fellow townsman Francis Biddle, his legal career attained comparatively little national fame or notoriety. Other people also serve on boards and collect academic degrees.

There was of course the charm, when not over-disturbed by animosities, the gentle, a bit cynical, modestly mock-modest, just a bit sarcastic humor, the evidently total social warmth and ease, the handsomeness and vigor of person, the fondness for poetry and the old-fashioned best of English literature, the gift for making witty impromptu verses, the sporting and the sportsmanship, and above all the manners — these add up. The very beginning of his autobiography sets a tone which only breaks down when he is discussing Roosevelt. The autobiography was "ostensibly written for the pleasure of friends. Actually, of course, the dominant motive has been self-gratification." Or his comments on Walnut Street after the Civil War.

To mention Walnut Street to an Old Philadelphian is to awaken memories of a departed glory. On bright Sundays, after church there was always an informal parade of fashion on the South side of this thoroughfare . . . of the blended congregations of half a dozen mid-city churches. They made upon the onlooker an impression of urbanity, of social experience and of entire self-satisfaction. If during church-time they had confessed themselves miserable sinners, by the time they appeared on parade their restoration to divine favor was seemingly complete.

There are few more succinct snapshots of the Old Philadelphia façade.

His politics may have been totally ineffective, but they represented — blind, bitter hatred of Roosevelt included — just what Old Philadelphia could admire. His religion, sympathetic to "all those who instinctively recoil from extremes and find wisdom in the old Greek proverb 'nothing too much,' " a quotation quite definitely not from the Old or New Testaments, may give offense to the mystical or the devout; but it certainly exemplifies the Philadelphia attitude toward God, shared by both Episcopalians and Friends. The activities on behalf of good causes, the boardsmanship, the Anglomania, the intimate associations personal and hereditary with the University, success at the law, which involved economic success too, personal charm, extreme old age — and the fact that, a Pepper himself, his mother was a Wharton and his grandmother a Markoe — "Nothing too much"; but a total summation of Old Philadelphia's idea of what a Grand Old Man should be. It was this balance of powers that made him so representative. The very multiplicity and harmoniousness of the parts, the right parts, the complete adaptation to an environment, no doubt inhibits real greatness in any one line; but "is it good form to be too distinguished?" That would imply a certain "too much" of trying, perhaps. The Code of Maintenance has seldom had a more perfect advocate. Like so many other Philadelphians, Senator Pepper probably ended up being a better Philadelphian than he was any other one thing.

2

i. Insurance: The Memory of Washington

NOBODY COULD question the primacy of Medicine and Law in the hearts and minds of Old Philadelphians. But very close to the Sacred Professions in Philadelphia esteem are the somewhat less intellectual pastimes of Banking and, oddly enough, Insurance. These activities also have the advantage of not requiring any college training: well-groomed and active but unscholarly Old Philadelphians can get in on the ground floor at an age when their professional brothers are still struggling with textbooks. Both banking and insurance have, too, the advantage of being pretty obviously profitable. Though fortunes certainly can and have been made in law and even medicine, banking and insurance are more direct routes for Rawle's "inhabitants of Delaware" to become rich. They are also more obviously "maintenance," guardianships of Philadelphia fortunes.

The relationship of Insurance to Banking is just faintly like that of Medicine to Law, though of course on a much more crass and worldly level. Insurance is older in Philadelphia, has a longer and more elegant tradition, is surrounded by more of an aura, and even has a halo of beneficence and altruism about it. Banking is more solid, was more inextricably bound up with Old Philadelphia in the nineteenth century, and now, along with the law, is probably the chief bastion of those Old Philadelphian guardianships. Insurance has faint medical connections, and doctors have often decorated the boards of prominent insurance companies. The connection of the law and banking is and has been umbilical, and many of the most prominent bankers, ancient and modern, began as successful lawyers.

Philadelphia can hardly claim to be the original homestead of law and medicine, even in this country, but it was very definitely First and Oldest in both insurance and banking.

Insurance, which antedated banking by a good half century, began in Philadelphia and America where so many other things began: with Benjamin Franklin. It was, like most of the great Benjamin's ideas, a combination of altruism and practicality, a combination one likes to think of as peculiarly American, or at least Anglo-American, and peculiarly effective. It is also especially, if not peculiarly, Philadelphian.

Franklin was interested in the problem of fires. Philadelphia was not troubled by floods or earthquakes; the yellow fever plague was later, but fire in the day of the open hearth and universal brick-and-wood construction was a real menace. Philadelphia by 1750 was becoming the largest metropolitan area in North America, second largest in the English-speaking world, so the threat of fires also increased. As early as 1736 Franklin had instigated the Fire Companies. The only fire-fighting organizations then known, and the only ones to exist in Philadelphia for a good hundred years longer, these companies were volunteer groups, like those of a modern small town. But whereas most modern fire companies are coordinated under City Hall, these were entirely separate and private; in fact, private clubs, each owning its own pretty but primitive hand-drawn, hand-pumped, hand-filled fire engine, and having its own name, insignia, uniforms, social complexion and status.

The Union Fire Company, the one started by Franklin, was first, but others soon followed: the Fellowship, the Hand-in-Hand, the Heart-in-Hand, the Friendship, the Hibernia and many more. Philadelphia's inveterate penchant for clubbiness, as well as ethnic solidarity, as represented by the Hibernia, is clear from the names. Of them all, the Hand-in-Hand became the most prominent socially, and after the Revolution had on its board four Signers of the Declaration, the Chief Justice of Pennsylvania, the Episcopalian

Bishop of Pennsylvania and the Provost of the University. One doubts if they all ran to fires.

It was obviously only a logical step from these fire companies to fire insurance, and Franklin was just the man to take it. In 1752 he formed his company, called, and still called, the Philadelphia Contributionship for the Insurance of Houses from Loss by Fire. This resoundingly full title is usually shortened to the Contributionship, or the company is referred to by its nickname, the Hand-in-Hand. This nickname is not derived from the fire company of the same name. Actually the personnel of Franklin's own Union Fire Company supplied half of the membership of the Contributionship's first board; but in order to indicate which houses were insured by the company, it placed on each front wall, according to established English custom, a small lead plaque. On this plaque was a device of four cross-clasped hands, hence Hand-in-Hand. These plaques or markers show today on countless Philadelphia houses; some indicate that the house is still insured by the company, others are merely decorative. Later insurance companies followed suit, so that a house may be spotted by a whole variety of these insurance markers.

The Contributionship gave and gives (more or less) insurance only on brick and stone buildings in Philadelphia and adjacent counties. The insurance is perpetual. One pays down a lump sum covering risks on a certified building, and after a while dividends are paid back. It is one of the few modern ways of making Philadelphia real estate pay. These limitations have of course prevented the Hand-in-Hand from being comparatively large, and a general company policy of great caution and selectiveness has kept it solvent but small. It remains, however, by far the oldest successful insurance company on the continent and is considered a "peculiarly Philadelphia institution."

It is not, one has to confess, the very first, and as usual there is some quibble about its being the very oldest. One hardly dares mention it, but Charleston, South Carolina, always a dangerous rival in such matters, had a Friendly Society for Mutual Insurance in 1735. Fortunately it had failed by 1750. Also there was and is a "Corporation for Relief of Poor and Distressed Presbyterian Ministers and of the Poor and Distressed Widows and Children of Presbyterian Ministers," of 1717, but this was at first more a church charity than the commercial insurance company it is now.

On the first board of directors of the Contributionship, with Franklin, were William Coleman, Samuel Rhoads, Hugh Roberts, Joseph Morris, Joseph Fox, William Griffits — all important gentlemen at the time, all of them Quakers, all representing families that are to this day leaders in affairs and society, though few of them are now Quakers. At present the chairman of the board is a Roberts, Isaac W.; William Logan Fox is on the board and also Morris Duane.

Franklin, as was his way, got the thing going, stayed on the board for a few years, then left his brainchild to shift for itself. He had other fish to fry. The Contributionship experienced rough going for the first ten years; there was a big turnover of boardsmen, business was slim. After 1760, however, things settled down to a quiet and even conservatism which persists to the present. Theaters were not insured on moral grounds; business buildings were looked on somewhat askance, and the Contributionship urged that wooden buildings be prohibited by law as risks, which helps account for Philadelphia's universally red-brick appearance. The treasurer in those early years, a rather eccentric old-timer called Caleb Carmalt, was himself so conservative he continued to keep the company accounts in English currency, shillings and pence, until 1815.

The Quaker influence remained predominant, and during Treasurer Carmalt's long years of service, of forty-five directors, only six were definitely not Quaker by conviction or birthright. In 1831, however, our non-Quaker legal friend, Horace Binney, joined the board, which had functioned all this time without benefit of chairman. This defect was remedied in 1844 when Binney was elected first chairman, a post he held for nearly thirty years till 1870.

Under his direction the company came its closest to expansiveness and boosterism. A building of its own was erected in 1836, on 4th Street near where Locust ends, more or less opposite Binney's own house and office. Thomas Walter, architect of the national Capitol, designed the building, a large red-brick neo-classic structure that looks like a modestly pretentious private house, with a small, columned porch and curving steps. Surrounding it and reaching out back is a bosky old garden. The treasurer, from 1842 on, usually a James Somers Smith in some generation, lived in the house, where he gardened and kept bees.

The custom of giving dinners to the directors after board meetings had been established in 1761, and these directors' dinners are still held in the house, complete with champagnes and other wines, hams supplied as always by Todd in Richmond, terrapin from Cape May, segars from the old family firm of Wagner. At a table furnished with monogrammed linen, engraved silver and special china, the directors feast about once a month in winter, accompanied by one or two exceptionally fortunate guests. The menu for December 18, 1867, lists oysters, two soups, fish, chops, turkey, bouillé, ham, chicken and oyster pie, sweetbreads, croquettes, duck, grouse, partridge, terrapin, and omelette. Where did they put it all? Nowadays the menu is as elegant but certainly more chaste.

Binney's reign represented something of a revolution. He wasn't a Quaker, and in disgust with him and his newfangled building at least three die-hard directors resigned. Binney also had a somewhat regrettable penchant for stirring up business, so that at one time in mid-century, the assets of the Contributionship were not far behind the million-dollar figure of the now gigantic Insurance Company of North America. In 1849, for the first time, the board departed from its custom of investing in government and municipal bonds and dared to subscribe to the shares of the Pennsylvania Railroad.

Gradually the Quaker, though certainly not the Old Philadelphian, control weakened, and Wisters, Yarnalls, Biddles and other such converts to Episcopalianism began to predominate. The famous scientist Joseph Leidy decorated the board, though admitting he knew nothing about insurance and cared less. "I am too busy to make money," he said.

This faintly progressive Binney tendency simmered down as the century wore on, and by the 1880's the company actively discouraged business. At that time they paid no dividends to the subscribers, and were only interested in avoiding risks, maintaining assets and giving dinners. Theaters continued to be taboo, high buildings were considered unsafe and Philadelphia's first skyscraper, the Bullitt building of 1887, was turned down — the height of conservatism. In general the Hand-in-Hand was said to be interested only in fire insurance on "pig iron below high water mark."

In 1894 this somnolent state of affairs was rudely shattered by an attempt on the part of a minority of lesser Old Philadelphian policyholders to upset the directorship, and make the company "progressive." The attitude of the board, they declared, was "that of a mouse snugly ensconced in a rich old cheese." The attempt was quashed. Old Philadelphia stockholders left their deathbeds to vote their confidence in the old order and its taste in Madeiras. Henry Paul, president of the Pennsylvania Company for the Insurance on Lives and Granting Annuities, and himself a thorough Old Philadelphia Madeira man, tried to vote 106 times as a trustee for the policies held by his company. When the smoke of battle cleared, the Old Guard was in more firmly than ever; but one great concession had been won: dividends were to be paid the policyholders, as envisaged in the charter of Franklin's original proposal.

From that day to this, nothing has really changed. An "annual collation" given to the policyholders was dropped during the Second World War. Brokers had first been permitted, with considerable reluctance, to handle business for the company in 1888. Later on a collation was given them too, but again in 1940 these had to be discontinued. Too many brokers. The directors' dinners, of course, continued as ever; there being only twelve directors, there has been no problem of overcrowding.

In 1905 the Madeira cellar, which contained wines dating back to the 1830's, was pronounced decadent, and the contents were bottled and sold. Prohibition wrought havoc. The spirits still on hand were distributed among the twelve directors and near beer was served at the Annual Collation and the Brokers' Luncheon in place of champagne and punch. What was served at the directors' dinners was not discussed. (Flasks were sometimes brought.)

Even the depression and the liquidation of real estate values in Center City failed to disturb the equanimity of the company. The usual ten per cent continued to be paid to the policyholders through the 1930's, and the million dollars' worth of mortgages were cleaned up by 1948. Assets increased during the first half of the twentieth century from 4 to 14 million, and insurance from 14 to 76 million. Smoke and accident damages have been included; the Philadelphia Contributionship for the Insurance of Houses from Loss by Fire continues to concentrate (more or less) on perpetual fire insurance on brick and stone buildings, preferably dwellings, in Philadelphia and adjacent counties.

One would think in the America of the 1960's, supposedly dominated by gigantic jet-age chromium-plated corporations, that even in Philadelphia one such insurance company as the Contributionship would be enough. But no; there are two. Another one, equally barnacled and Old Philadelphian, is the Mutual Assurance Company for Insuring Houses from Loss by Fire, which is the second oldest insurance company in the country. It was started in 1784 as a protest against the Contributionship.

At the time, the Contributionship rejected any building that had a tree next to it. Too risky. Penn's "Greene Country Towne" had been more or less founded on the principle of the tree-shaded street. The very names, Spruce, Pine, Locust, Walnut, celebrated this pleasant conception. Then as now, trees had their allies. Among them was Dr. Benjamin Rush. He and his tree-loving friends were furious about the Hand-in-Hand's arbitrary rule. Trees were not that much of a risk. Fires usually started inside houses, not outside, especially if the houses were protected by Dr. Franklin's lightning rod. The tree-lovers formed their own insurance (or assurance) company. It had its marker, just like the Contributionship's, which appropriately enough bore the device of a bushy tree. This insignia decorated the fronts of respectable houses, as did the clasped hands of its rival, and similarly the board of trustees of the Mutual (the Contributionship has directors; the Mutual, trustees) is completely Old Philadelphian, gives itself dinners, and tends to discourage business except on brick and stone dwellings in Philadelphia and adjacent counties. Charitable institutions are much favored as risks, but they have recently given up all their business buildings.

The nickname of the Mutual is, naturally enough, the "Green Tree," and the Green Tree and the Hand-in-Hand have long buried the hatchet, especially after the latter gave up its prejudice against trees; but they have never merged. In the early twentieth century the Mutual bought Judge John Cadwalader's old house on 4th Street, also near the end of Locust, and next to it the even older Dr. Caspar Wistar house. There they now do such business as has to be done, maintain a pretty garden, house their secretary and give dinners.

If anything, the dinners of the Mutual are even more special than those of the Contributionship. There are certainly few things in America, at least, that exceed them in sheer perfection of traditional taste. The Cadwalader house itself is a flawless specimen of early nineteenth-century neoclassic elegance, modest but still noble. The dining room upstairs, in what was originally the front parlor, is simply but perfectly furnished. The walls there and elsewhere in the house carry one of the choicest small collections of Philadelphia portraiture in the city. Eakins's fierce picture of George Cadwalader (the picture is probably fiercer than the man), a good Washington by Rembrandt Peale and a famous French Duplessis portrait of Franklin are the chief items. The whole line of Philadelphia portraiture is represented with the curious omission of Sully. (One of the best pictures is John Sargent's portrait of S. Weir Mitchell, even if it does make him look rather like a goat. The story is that as Sargent painted it he kept muttering to himself, "Mustn't make him look like a goat! Mustn't make him look like a goat!")

The trustees dress for dinner and after cocktails and caviar sit down to a meal, choicer perhaps though not as gargantuan as the Hand-in-Hand banquet of 1867. After sherry with soup, wine with the fish or meat, champagne with dessert, the table is cleared; this, incidentally, being no mean feat. Two serving men have to roll up the heavy linen and table padding from under the wine glasses, candelabra, silver tankards and other paraphernalia which still decorate the table, revealing the glowing mahogany underneath. Each guest then gets a big finger bowl (really a glass washer or Monteith) with two sherry glasses in it, turned upside down. Around the table, always clockwise, are passed port and Madeira. The chairman raps on the table and calls out, "Gentlemen, are you charged?" The glasses being filled, and the gentlemen therefore "charged," the first toast, "To The Mutual Assurance Company," is drunk. After a suitable pause comes the second toast, "To the memory of Washington"; then the cigars and brandy.

The toast to Washington has been traditional since 1799 when a messenger interrupted a Mutual dinner with the news of the General's death.

Nothing is more beautifully characteristic of Old Philadelphia at its best than these insurance dinners, with their masculine simplicity, good taste in food, liquor and setting, combination of old forms and perfect informality, convention and casualness, total lack of pretentiousness and strong feeling for ritual. Certainly if one wanted to pick one single ceremony as the perfect flowering of Old Philadelphia, a good insurance dinner would be it; beginning with the fact that it *is* a dinner and given by an insurance company. Perhaps as characteristic as anything is the fact that they are so secluded, private, comparatively unheard of, at least outside the inner circles of Old Philadelphia and Philadelphia finance. Of all Philadelphia's hidden treasures, they are most to be treasured and most hidden.

Each chair in the Mutual dining room has on its back a copper plate on which is inscribed the succession of trustees for each post. The laying on of hands (or sitting on of seats) in each case represents, as in the directorships of the Hand-in-Hand, an unbroken succession of Old Philadelphianism. Biddles have abounded on both boards. Morrises too; one such succession in the Contributionship has consisted of a dozen Morrises, with a few Norrises, Whartons and Biddles snuck in between. Then there are the Ingersolls; they balance neatly at present, C. Jared being a trustee of the Mutual and his brother R. Sturgis a director of the Contributionship. If there is any difference between the Contributionship and Mutual, aside from a feeling of seniority on the part of the former, it is in the Mutual's high-minded indifference to the business background of its chairmen; among these have not only been S. Weir Mitchell, doctor and novelist, but also Owen Wister, just plain novelist, who was succeeded by Dr. George W. Norris, just doctor, none of these people being specialists in insurance.

Though these are the boards of business corporations, not clubs or charities, their chief real function is, like that of the Chancellorship and directors of the Bar Association, or the presidency of the College of Physicians, the granting of honor and the setting of standards. Nowadays to be a director or trustee, much less a chairman of one of these boards, is one of the highest compliments that can be paid a Philadelphian of affairs. A man may get to be president of another big insurance company or a bank, may make the Philadelphia Club, may be in *Who's Who* and the *Social Register* and loaded with honorary degrees, but the final Philadelphia accolade and stamp of approval remains his election to the board of one of these commercially fairly negligible insurance companies.

There are of course other insurance companies, most of them far larger and more active. Philadelphia is probably the third largest insurance center in the country, after New York and Hartford. Some of these companies even involve themselves in the sordid businesses of life and accident insurance, which in the old hierarchies of insurance were beyond the pale. Casualty, as one embattled old-timer forcefully if ungrammatically put it, was "a low down business of ambulance chasing that no decent fire-insurance man could be expected to soil his fingers with." Nowadays it's become respectable, along with insurance brokerage.

Largest and oldest and most Philadelphian of these other companies are the Insurance Company of North America, founded in 1792, and the Penn Mutual. Both of these have beautiful boards and boardrooms, but they follow the pattern of big Philadelphia companies: Old Philadelphia directors, with a minority of carefully screened "new blood," and hired-man, self-made presidents.

An exception, and a rather significant one, to this pattern was the incumbency as president of the Ins. Co. of N. Amer. of a Benjamin Rush. He was a great-grandson of the Doctor, and something of a renegade, as the first member of his family to descend to trade; but he was merely one of a whole group of Old Philadelphians who, at that particular time after the Civil War, suddenly and with brilliant success left the family professions and took over the Philadelphia economy. Rush had the foresight as early as 1905, while still vice president, to sell insurance on that rich man's toy, the automobile. The then president, Charles Platt, objected violently to having anything to do with those "noisy stinking things," but finally gave in. By the time Rush became president in 1916 his foresight had already been amply justified. It was Rush who conceived the idea of the new building out on the Parkway. Rush instructed his architect, George Page, to build him a place where "George Washington would find himself at home." Page did the best he could, but one doubts if Washington would have felt quite at home in any skyscraper, no matter how colonial the boardroom or how full of collections of old fire engines.

ii. Banking: "Saviors of Their Country"

THE CROSSING of Broad and Chestnut Streets is the very center of Philadelphia's modern business district. The four corners are occupied by four banks: the Girard Trust Corn Exchange Bank, the Provident Tradesmen's Bank and Trust Company, the Western Saving Fund Society, and the Philadelphia National Bank. This is a very adequate symbol of the dignity and central position of the bank in Philadelphia. Like the learned professions and insurance, banking in Philadelphia is ancient and honorable. Philadelphia was America's first real financial center, and remained so up to the splendid debacle of Nicholas Biddle. Though nowadays it scarcely compares to New York, it is still one of the country's soundest financial bastions, and its great banks are still comparatively important in the state and even in the nation. Philadelphia still ranks fourth, after New York, San Francisco and Chicago in the number of its large banks.

Though the history of insurance in Philadelphia is essentially a history of institutions, the history of banking is a history of men. The line of the city's great bankers, Willing, Morris, Girard, Biddle, Drexel, Cooke, is as vital, picturesque and significant a succession as that of any dynasty of European monarchs. The impact of these men on the history of the United States was enormous, yet they are all of them neglected or even forgotten outside of Philadelphia; nothing, in fact, more perfectly exemplifies the peculiar fate of Philadelphia than the faint national reputations of these men. As the essence of Philadelphia charm is tucked away in back alleys and in the dining rooms of its old insurance companies, so the grandeur of Philadelphia is concealed in the dust of ledgers. The essentially puritan contempt and envy which shows itself in American attitudes towards bankers, and the fact that it is hard to make financial history, as compared with political and military history, seem very vital and poetic, especially if the bankers are honest, has accounted for some of this dimness. Paul Revere is famous entirely because Longfellow wrote a poem about him. Nobody has performed, or is likely to perform, a similar service for Morris or Biddle.*

Except for Willing and Drexel, the careers of these men were

---

* Though Biddle himself wrote at least one pretty cute poem about himself as poet turned banker.

on the whole tragic. Morris, Biddle and Cooke went bankrupt.
Girard ended as a lonely misanthropic philanthropist; the unsuccessful hero is not easily taken to the bosom of the people unless he's awfully glamorous. But heroes, in their money-oriented
way, these bankers were; heroes both patriotically and roman-
tically.

Some of these great figures were or became Old Philadelphians.
Some didn't. Morris and Girard failed to establish families.
Drexel and Cooke very definitely did. Biddle and Willing were
of families already established; but their careers made the establishment permanent, and descendants of both men survive today
in Philadelphia in about as exalted a Position as sheer heredity
can maintain in a democracy.

Thomas Willing in particular, First Bank President of these
United States, and certainly a parfit gentil model of same, had just
about everything, and kept it through the turmoil of the Revolution by a combination of caution and tact. In the first place he
looked like his good friend George Washington, and was often
mistaken for him. He cultivated the resemblance by an equally
dignified deportment. In the second place he was well and richly
born. His father, Charles Willing, an Englishman, had done well
in America, married well, and bred well, all in the first generation.
He made a fortune in importing, married a Shippen, and sired
eleven little Willings. (Willing and able.) Nearly all these children married well too.

Thomas carried right on where his father Charles left off. He
inherited the business, took in an orphaned waif called Robert
Morris and made him a partner. By the time of the Revolution,
the partnership of Willing and Morris was the greatest financial
power in America. Thomas married a McCall, and outdid even
his father when it came to breeding. He had thirteen. During
the time when Philadelphia was the capital, the Willings and
their kin, Powels, Hares, Shippens, McCalls, Francises and others,
represented "good society" both in Philadelphia and in the
country at large, and formed the local nucleus of Washington's
Republican Court.

Queen of this court was Thomas's beautiful daughter Anne, married to William Bingham, richest man in the country. Their magnificent house, with its marble staircases and footmen, Anne's fascinating social gift, demure and dignified with Washington, daring and delightfully risqué with visiting Frenchmen, earned and kept her at the head of female affairs.

King was not Mr. Bingham, estimable fellow though he was, but his father-in-law Thomas. Thomas had gotten through the Revolution without offending anybody, largely by a process of not signing things. He balked at signing the Declaration, he refused to subscribe to the Oath of Allegiance to the King during the British Occupation. He just entertained everyone at dinner, impartially and elegantly. The result was that when the shooting was over, he and his partner remained the greatest financial powers in America.

When it came time to start banks, Willing, so obviously safe and sound, was obviously the man for president. He was President of all three of America's first banks, a flimsy war emergency affair called the Pennsylvania Bank, a more durable institution called the Bank of North America, which lasted as the oldest bank in the country into modern times, and finally the First Bank of the United States. This was the original edition of that "hydra-headed monster" that Jackson destroyed. Willing retired from its presidency in 1797 after a few upsetting years; but lived on and on, growing richer and richer and more and more dignified, and by the time he died in 1821 he was one of Philadelphia's Grand Old Men — first American banker. The reward of virtue was an estate of well over a million.

If Willing exhibited to the Young Republic an example of the secure and conventional Capitalist, his friend and partner Robert Morris could be cited, perhaps in warning, as the Entrepreneur. Morris's career was scarcely exemplary, but it was certainly not dull.

By the time of the Revolution Morris was already a financial and social success. His origins were so obscure that his mother's name is still unknown, but his ebullient personality had won him friends everywhere. Unlike his partner Willing, he was a forth-right patriot. He came out forcefully against the Stamp Act, was a member of the Council of Safety set up in Philadelphia when war seemed imminent, and from the beginning controlled arms and supplies for the new Revolutionary Army. Though he actually voted, like Willing, against the Declaration of Independence in July, 1776, thinking it premature, he changed his mind and signed in August, thus achieving an immortality his partner Willing missed. Throughout the war he provided the Continental Army with a moral support and material assistance without which it would certainly have disintegrated. He made large profits doing so, but the risks were enormous. He was bitterly criticized for these profits, but no one was more grateful or valued him more highly as financier and friend than Washington himself, who offered him the position as first Secretary of the Treasury. In good Philadelphia fashion he declined, and the post went to the New Yorker Alexander Hamilton as second choice.

After the Revolution he devoted himself to working for a federal constitution and a central bank. He saw both these efforts successful, and was himself one of the two first Senators from Pennsylvania in 1789 when the Constitution was adopted. This was the top of the wave for him, at the beginning of the 1790's when the capital moved to Philadelphia. With his wife, the charming Mary White, sister of the future Bishop White, he entertained extravagantly at his country place, now Lemon Hill, on the Schuylkill and at his town mansion on High (now Market) Street.

In a final splurge of pride and ostentation, he started to build a new town house, a great marble palace which was to occupy the whole square between Chestnut and Walnut, 7th and 8th Streets. It was designed in grandiose neoclassic fashion by L'Enfant, who planned the grandiose neoclassic city of Washington, and was on a scale undreamed of then in Philadelphia for a private house, even by the Powels and Binghams. Two wings were completed before the crash came. He had, like his fellow Signer of the Declaration, Supreme Court Justice James Wilson, whom

Morris resembled in so many ways, speculated enormously in lands — in Washington, D.C., Pennsylvania, New York. With the outbreak of the Napoleonic Wars he was caught short; he couldn't pay his land taxes or sell his lands. His palace, on which he had already spent a fortune, remained unfinished, and in 1798 he was arrested and thrown into jail for debt. Like those of Biddle and Cooke later on, this purely private disaster was the signal for a public one, and Morris's bankruptcy marked the beginning of America's first real depression.

America has often been accused of ingratitude to its first financial savior. It was certainly a reflection on the times that this man was permitted to rot in a cheap jail for three long years and to die in comparative poverty and neglect. Still, like Nicholas Biddle after him, Morris did certainly invite his neoclassic fate and the lightning of the gods. His own extravagance and lack of caution, freed from the influence of Willing, were almost sure to lead him to disaster.

Willing and Morris between them set a pattern for Philadelphia and the nation of the Banker and the Entrepreneur, the opposite poles of Safety and Risk, which have defined the world of American finance ever since. It is not surprising that with these two examples before it, Philadelphia has grown on the whole to prefer safety.

Morris did not found a family dynasty. After the collapse, his sons went elsewhere and married girls from upstate New York and other barbarous places, so that in Philadelphia nowadays "Morris" means Anthony, not Robert.

The Willings of course were a different matter. Established as they were by the position of Thomas as the Father of Banking, and by their marital connections, they have ever since been considered as Philadelphia's almost-first family. A sister of Thomas Willing married Robert Hare, who did well in beer, and another married Samuel Powel, arbiter of elegance during Philadelphia's Golden Age. When Powel died in 1793, having no sons, he left all his immense estate to a nephew, John Powel Hare. Hare

changed his name about to John Hare Powel, and did his best
to follow his uncle's footsteps. Samuel Powel had taken the grand
tour to Europe in the 1760's, becoming a connoisseur of art in
Italy, nurse of the gentler arts; he also became an Anglican convert from Quakerism, in England. Nephew John, attached to
the American Legation in London, was known there as the
"handsomest man ever seen," and was painted as such by Sir
Thomas Lawrence. Samuel had built the most beautiful town
house in Philadelphia, on 3rd Street, still extant; John built the
most magnificent country house of its time in West Philadelphia, called Powelton, which still gives its name to a whole district there. Samuel, in his spare time, was a politician, and became known as the "patriot mayor" because he served as the
last mayor under the King and the first mayor under the Republic. John condescended to be a State Senator for a while,
full of Internal Improvements. Samuel patronized the Society
Meeting Weekly in the City of Philadelphia for their Mutual
Improvement in Useful Knowledge. John was the firebrand of
the Philadelphia Society for the Promotion of Agriculture, and
wrote pamphlets on sheep. They both, in other words, like the
later Chews, did nothing, and did it well. They were, in fact,
the perfect specimens, in two generations, of everything a Philadelphia gentleman aspires to be. Even their deaths had a bit
of a cachet. Samuel was one of the most prominent victims of
the Great Yellow Fever Plague. John fell on the ice, was all
broken up and died in his elegant summer villa at Newport, he
being one of the first of the Sidney Fishery visitors there.

The close connection of the Willings to these two dashing
gents did no social harm to any of them. The marriages of not
one but two of Thomas Willing's granddaughters, the Bingham
girls, into the Baring family did no harm either. The Barings
were (and are) England's greatest banking family, and though
one of the Bingham–Baring marriages ended in a divorce,
descendants of these unions still grace all of England's "red
books" — *Burke's Peerage* and the like — with their titles of

Baron Ashburton, Earl of Cromer and half a dozen others. Something still called the Bingham Estate left in trust by William for his descendants, remains a juicy plum, not only for said descendants who are scattered all over the world as nationals of various countries, but to the lawyers and Philadelphia trustees who still administer it.

There are Willings left. The elder Edward Shippen Willing (married to a Rawle) was President of the Philadelphia Club and for years a recognized embodiment of the Philadelphia gentleman of the Old School in dress, looks and deportment. His son Edward, Jr., caused a certain lifting of the eyebrows by becoming, of all things, a schoolteacher, for a good many years one of the most popular at Episcopal Academy, and has now gone as far afield as Seattle, Washington.

The French sea captain Stephen Girard, successor to Willing and Morris as financial leader of Philadelphia, was, of course, never an Old Philadelphian, nor did he have surviving children. He married a poor but pretty slum girl who went mad, and Stephen remained faithful to her in spirit if not in flesh. He was a remarkable character, learned, secretive, immensely generous to those he liked, implacable in hunting down and punishing those he felt had wronged him. Already rich as an importer and shipowner, he took over Thomas Willing's First Bank of the United States when it failed to be rechartered in 1811. Its beautiful little neoclassic building (architected incidentally by Samuel Blodgett, the first president of the ICNA) became thereafter known as Girard's bank. During the interval between the First (Willing) and Second (Biddle) Banks of the United States, Girard himself financed the country. Like Morris before him, Girard floated a war, that of 1812. When he died in 1831, run over by a dray while crossing the street, he was the first of America's multimillionaires, as Willing and Bingham had been its first millionaires.

His will, in which he left most of his money to the city of Philadelphia, caused much comment and a famous lawsuit. His character, an odd one, remained a mystery to his fellow townsmen, and for all his generosity, his reputation was always that of a cold, hard, one-eyed misogynist.

After Girard came Nicholas Biddle, who "liked being irresistible" and who ran the Second Bank of the United States and the finances of the whole country like "a rich young person good naturedly ordering the servants about," as Bray Hammond puts it. Biddle, as great financier, was the inheritor of Morris and Girard, until his fall; and when he fell, Chestnut Street was succeeded by Wall Street, and New York became at last the financial, as it had already become the commercial, capital of the United States.

This did not mean the end of finance in Philadelphia. Even contemporary with Morris, Girard and Nicholas the Great there were other, lesser but more durable banking houses, often private family enterprises. There were other banking Biddles; Thomas Biddle's sons. And an Enoch Clark founded a particularly solvent house; his family continued it. The Clarks later branched out into law, coal, cricket, tennis and eventually politics, as represented now by United States Senator Joseph Sill Clark, formerly Mayor of Philadelphia and most effective champion of reform in Philadelphia history. Another Clark political connection is Governor Nelson Rockefeller, whose ex-wife is Senator Clark's first cousin. (The Rockefellers were from Cleveland, and in oil.)

By far the most glamorous and important of these family banking houses was the house of Drexel, which also still exists. If Girard may be said to have come into banking sideways as a sea captain, Francis Drexel, debonair Austrian portrait painter, could be described as strolling into banking backwards. Though born in the Tyrol and educated in painting and the ways of the world in Italy and elsewhere on the Continent, there is still something awfully Philadelphian in the transformation from portrait painter to international money man. Like the change from Wüster to Wistar, Drexel was no doubt originally something like Drecksel, which means, in German slang, a little, no-account piece of dirt.* That Franz, or Francis, emphatically was not. He arrived in

---

* In fact the spelling "Drexel" goes back to the sixteenth century at least.

Philadelphia in his twenties, already experienced professionally and socially, and quickly became professionally and socially popular. He married a Philadelphia girl ("nobody in particular"). One of his patrons, an elder member of the Paul family, pointed out to him the example of Rembrandt Peale, who had made a good thing out of painting innumerable portraits of Washington. There was no end to the demand. Paul indicated to Drexel that in South America there was another man, Simon Bolívar, whose portrait might also be in demand, for the same reasons. Drexel went to South America. In his four years there, whether or not he painted Bolívar, he did discover a new art, the manipulation of currency exchange. By his painting and by what would now probably be called black market money operations, he got together some capital, and when he returned to America, decided that money, rather than miniatures, was his real talent.

He began his ventures in Louisville, but soon returned to Philadelphia and settled there. His career somewhat paralleled that of Girard; as Girard filled the vacuum left by the closing of the First Bank of the United States, so Drexel filled that caused by the closing of the Second. His business gradually shifted from currency brokerage to investment banking; with the assistance of his sons, Anthony and Joseph, the firm sent out tentacles to New York, London and Paris, and became in time the single most important American international banking house.

Francis Drexel the founder died at seventy-two, when he too, like Girard, was run over; being up-to-date, he was run over by a railroad train. He had educated his sons at home and in the office. They spoke many languages as fluently as their father, and like him knew something about painting and music. Joseph, the elder, married a Wharton and went to New York. He was a partner of Drexel, Harjes, the firm's subsidiary in Paris; then picked up young J. P. Morgan and was senior partner of Drexel, Morgan of New York till his retirement in 1876. He was a particular patron of art and music, left an extensive collection of musical manuscripts and was President of the Philharmonic Orchestra.

His younger brother, Anthony, who stayed in Philadelphia, was equally rich and philanthropic. He founded the Drexel Institute of Technology, Philadelphia's largest technical college, and owned part of Philadelphia's greatest paper, the *Public Ledger*. He was a staunch Union man, and was one of the "kingmakers" of the Grant regime, though of course he never ran for office or accepted an appointment. It was not till he died in 1893 that J. P. Morgan became actual senior partner of the New York branch of the firm, and could change the name of it from Drexel and Morgan to just plain Morgan; this subservience of New York to Philadelphia having been, it would seem, easily forgotten by all New Yorkers and biographers of the Great J. P.

Drexel and Company is still extant and important financially in Philadelphia, but the Drexel family itself has dwindled to the point where the joke about their "confluence" with the Biddles doesn't mean much any more. The New York branch is much more lively and Drexels give and patronize balls and, with their Biddle and Duke cousins, still show up in gossip columns and on society pages. One of the most lavish debuts of modern times was that of Pamela Drexel in Newport in the summer of 1959. The newspaper accounts stressed an artificial pond alive with ducklings and paragraph after paragraph of genealogical background, most of it Philadelphian; but this is all in New York and not, definitely not, Philadelphia.

Francis and Anthony Drexel were terribly important Philadelphians, but the real successor to Philadelphia's great financial dynasty of Morris–Girard–Nicholas Biddle was Jay Cooke. Cooke labored under the disadvantage, from a Philadelphia point of view, of being not only a non-Philadelphian, not even a romantic foreigner like Girard and Drexel, but of all things a Midwesterner. He came from Ohio. His father was named Eleutheros Cooke, a name which was not handed down in the family. In fact his father suffered so on account of it that he saw to it his son had a name which could not be trifled with: Jay. Jay started out in the Clark banking house, but branched out for himself just as the Civil War began; he had a brother who was a great friend of Governor Chase of Ohio. When Chase became Lincoln's Secretary of the Treasury, this was good for Cooke, and also good for the country. The Government's war bond issue was dying on the vine when Chase was persuaded to turn over the sale of it to Cooke. Cooke sold five hundred million dollars' worth of one issue and six hundred million of another, and thus, like Morris and Girard before him, saved the country financially. His career even modeled itself on that of Morris to the point of bankruptcy. He too, after the war, speculated, in railroads, not lands, and lost his shirt. When Jay Cooke folded in 1873, this also brought on a national panic. Unlike Morris, however, he was not thrown into jail. He somehow managed to repay all his creditors, and though never a financial power again, he got back some of his money, and left, unlike Morris and Girard, a family in Philadelphia. His descendants, now safely integrated, still flourish in Penllyn, alongside the Ingersolls, Foxes and Coxes.*

Last of Philadelphia's flamboyant financiers, it would seem was Edward Stotesbury, senior partner of Drexel in Philadelphia, and next to the Great J. P. himself as senior partner of Morgan in New York. Stotesbury was unique in one way: he was definitely a Philadelphian, but also fairly definitely not an Old Philadelphian, despite a good old-fashioned semi-Quaker family background; and so his social row was harder to hoe than that of any of his predecessors. Jokes are still told about the Stotesburys' bulldozing tactics as social climbers; when he finally achieved the Assembly, it is said, Stotesbury had the invitation framed under glass and enshrined, floodlit, in the front hall of his immense marble château, Whitemarsh Hall. He never made the Philadelphia Club. When he got drunk his favorite pastime, as a little man, was to bang on a drum as loud as he could, presum-

---

* In 1960 a modern Jay Cooke succeeded the late John Kelly as President of the Fairmount Park Commission; interesting Philadelphia juxtaposition somehow.

ably in memory of his days as a drummer boy in the Civil War. His second wife in particular, a widowed Mrs. Cromwell, taught him, as they say, to "play," and play he did in Palm Beach, where for lack of competition the Stotesburys were the Social Leaders, and at Bar Harbor, where their attempt to take over as Social Leaders drove the Old Philadelphians to Northeast Harbor, where they have been ever since.

Stotesbury and Morgan, representing Drexel in Philadelphia and Morgan in New York, filled somewhat the role of Morris, Girard and Jay Cooke in floating the First World War. Stotesbury died in his nintieth year, after a routine day at his offices in Drexel and Company, and the Reading Railroad, of which he was the longtime chairman. He left many of his works of art to the Museum; his vast palace is now a research center for Pennsalt, the Lewis chemical firm, and the surrounding acres have been somewhat unfortunately "developed"; but his memory lingers on as Philadelphia parvenu par excellence.

Drexel and Company and Morgan and Company split up in 1940, shortly after Stotesbury's death. Drexel continues in Philadelphia; Morgan, joined with the Guaranty Trust, in New York. Since Stotesbury's time no one in Philadelphia has ever achieved quite the same national or international position, or, locally the dubious social brilliance.

The senior partner of Drexel and Company is now Edward Hopkinson, Jr. (still usually referred to as "Junior" to distinguish him from an important but long-dead father). As a Hopkinson, descendant of Francis the Signer, as director and member of just about everything, as a cautious but persistent city reformer, he is the successor to Senator Pepper in the role of First Citizen, Father Image, Grand Old Man. Like many other Philadelphians, he began as a lawyer and switched to banking in midstream. Graduate of the College and Law School, and now trustee of the University of Pennsylvania, he is one of its most influential representatives. He is a member of all the right clubs and boards, and there has never been any question, as there might have been about Morris, Girard, Drexel and Cooke, and

as there certainly was about Stotesbury, of his essential Old Philadelphianism.

iii. In Girard We Trust

THE FOUR BIG BANKS nowadays, as represented by the four corners
of Chestnut and Broad, are big but no longer very weighty nationally. Even such a figure as Hopkinson is more a local than
a national power. The big old banks are dear to everybody's
hearts, but even dearer are the somewhat more specialized trust
companies and savings funds. That's where the Philadelphia Nest
Egg is incubated.

It is, of course, a bit hard to delimit and describe the dimen-
sions of the Philadelphia Nest Egg. It is the great complex of
inherited trust funds and personal savings upon the income of
which Old Philadelphia lives. As can be seen, many Old Philadelphians are still making money; but fundamentally the efforts
of Old Philadelphia lawyers, bankers and insurance men are devoted to the care and feeding of this Nest Egg; and the Nest
Egg, several billion dollars worth of it, is devoted to the care
and feeding of the Old Philadelphian heir. What with taxes
and the times, inflation, death duties and all the perils that assail
inherited wealth, this Rock of Gibraltar has been eroded till it
produces a lot less lavish care and feeding for the heirs than it
used to. But it is still there, in trust, in savings, in shares of
railroads and family businesses, groomed and guarded by the institutions with self-made presidents and hereditary directors that
are delegated to this care and feeding. Most of the Old Philadelphians who do work, work somewhere in this enormous old
Nest Egg guardianship; most of them have some hereditary financial interest in it too. A young Old Philadelphian who starts off
his career in a bank or bond house, in law or insurance, knows
that he is, however obscurely, working to defend His Own.

Two (there must be always two) trust companies especially
and two savings funds are particularly Old Philadelphian. These
are the Girard Trust, now after various mergings the Girard Trust

Corn Exchange Bank, and the Provident Trust, also hyphenated into the Provident Tradesmen's Bank and Trust; the Philadelphia Saving Fund Society, and the Western Saving Fund Society are the two savings banks. The two trust companies are referred to as the Girard and the Provident; the savings funds abbreviated into their initials, the PSFS and WSFS. Their boards of directors are little lower than the angels, that is, only a bit less flawlessly Old Philadelphian than those of the Hand-in-Hand and Green Tree, but unlike those venerable parties, they are big and rich and powerful and fairly up-to-date. They actually go out for business. They even advertise, discreetly of course.

They are housed in skyscrapers; in fact that skyline of Philadelphia, such as it is, flat-topped, square-shouldered, utterly unspired, uninspired and unaspiring, clustered closely about City Hall in the shadow of William Penn, stands as the castellated modern bastion of the Nest Egg. From a distance this skyline looks like a group of heavy, important old men clustered at a conference, their heads together and their backs turned resolutely against the low-lying outside world; a defensive huddle of conservatism. This is not a particularly deceptive appearance.

The Girard Trust is not the oldest bank or trust company or anything else in Philadelphia or even in the country, and thus, for such a very Old Philadelphian institution, is something of a black sheep. It was founded as late as 1836, when Philadelphia had already ceased to be City Number One. It was not founded by Stephen Girard either, who was dead by then, but by one Benjamin Richards, at various times Mayor of Philadelphia, who was a member of the Board of Commissioners administering Girard's estate. In the 1830's Richards started his own company to handle insurance, savings and eventually trusts. He called it the Girard Beneficial Association, largely because the name Girard had a pleasing sound to Philadelphians and indicated prestige, integrity and money money money. It did not become the Girard Trust till 1899.

Of all Philadelphia's banking institutions, the Girard Trust is nowadays the one most identified with Old Philadelphia and the

Nest Egg. It has been said that Philadelphians would prefer their coinage altered to "In Girard We Trust." Nearly Everybody, all those readers of the *Bulletin,* has a bit of money tied up in it. Hardly a block of central city real estate is free from the sometimes excessively cautious supervision of the Girard's trust officers, and one of the reasons for Philadelphia's obsolescence is the enormous amount of it held by heirs in estates administered by trust companies, a form of fractional and absentee ownership that does not make for tidy and progressive property dealings.

There is an agency in England called Universal Aunts, which helps people with baby sitting, housecleaning and moving. The Girard is by way of being one of Philadelphia's Universal Uncles, a protector always there with careful advice, safeguarding by sound investment the funds of a reckless younger generation. The reckless younger and even older generation is sometimes not too pleased, and one of Philadelphia's perennial indoor sports is suing the Girard; all of which the Girard and its brother trusts take with philosophic and somewhat condescending patience.

Besides Richards, the founder and first President (who married a Lippincott), the great figure in the history of the Girard was a modern president, Effingham Buckley Morris (1887–1928). Effingham Morris, like the later Benjamin Rush of the Insurance Company of North America, was another example of that curious flowering of Old Philadelphia in business around the turn of the century. He was a genuine Morris, and though Morrises were thick as thieves (to put it perhaps unfortunately) on all the boards of all the institutions, Effingham was the first to become actual president of an important one, and as such something of a renegade and self-made man. Like Rush, he was worshipped when alive, and still remains in memory as the Girard's Great President. Like Rush, too, he patronized architecture and under his personal direction the new building on Broad Street was built, after the model of the Pantheon in Rome. Mr. Morris on one of his jaunts abroad saw the original, and thought it would make a nice bank. McKim, Mead and White, New York architects, thought so too. There it sits, today dwarfed by surrounding skyscrapers, just like the Pantheon except that the Pantheon is round and the Girard is square, the Pantheon has no windows and the Girard has lots, etc.; a permanent, or semi-permanent memorial to a Morris. Just lately cleaned up, it really does look very pretty.

The PSFS is even more so. For one thing, we are back home again: the PSFS is the First and Oldest savings bank in the United States. Started in 1816 by Condy Raguet, one of those émigré Frenchmen like Du Ponceau and Girard who did so much for post-Revolutionary Philadelphia, but who didn't seem to found families, the PSFS immediately assumed a place as "the most eminently respectable institution in our city," as Rawle, the most eminently respectable lawyer in it, said in its praise.

What made it so respectable was its curiously philanthropic atmosphere. The Saving Fund was the "child of benevolence and political economy," a most respectable union. It began, of course, in Scotland in the late eighteenth century, though the first corporation was not chartered there till 1810. Saving funds were either cooperative ventures of poor but thrifty mechanics, or were created and administered by a board of the kindly well-to-do *for* poor but thrifty mechanics. This, equally of course, was the somewhat condescending version preferred by Philadelphians. "The design," said the founders, "is to afford a profitable mode of investment to mechanics, tradesmen, laborers, servants and others who have no friends competent or sufficiently interested in their welfare to advise and assist them." If masters would communicate to their servants the good news would be sent abroad. Meanwhile, "no views of individual interest prevailed among the persons who originated and who now conduct" the Philadelphia Saving Fund Society. In other words, it was actually a Good Work. At once to do good and to condescend — what sweeter avocation for an Old Philadelphian?

Thus, unlike an ordinary money-making bank, it soon became not only a badge of merit to be on the board, but even stylish to be president. Today, meeting on top of the most elegant and still tallest of Philadelphia's skyscrapers on 12th and Market Streets, now become something of an architectural classic, the PSFS board remains one of Philadelphia's very best. Isaac Roberts, Henry Drinker, Edward Hopkinson, R. Sturgis Ingersoll, Orville Bullitt, Morris Duane and others who combine Family and Achievement in equal proportions are joined (unlike the boards of the old insurance companies) by a few carefully selected non–Old Philadelphian self-made presidents — Roy G. Rincliffe, chairman of the board of the Philadelphia Electric Company; Courtney Smith, president of Swarthmore College; Richard C. Bond, president of John Wanamaker. This democratic and inclusive policy permits an osmosis of new blood, though old blood always predominates. As inclusion on the board of the Hand-in-Hand is the end of the line for an Old Philadelphian of affairs, so the board of the PSFS is for a non–Old Philadelphian newcomer.

The presidency in the past has usually been the reward of a long life of Philadelphia virtue, and even was accused of being something of a sinecure. When, for instance, Stacy Lloyd was president, it was said the initials PSFS stood for "Pretty Soft For Stacy." The present incumbent, Stewart Rauch, is certainly a contradiction of all these traditions. Still in his forties, he is generally looked on as Philadelphia's most active and ambitious young Old Philadelphian — a sort of Old Philadelphia White Hope. He has used the PSFS as a mere incentive to higher efforts in the field of Good Works, including his presidency of the United Fund campaign. No one has suggested that things are "Pretty Soft For Stewart."

The other Old Philadelphia trust companies, like the Provident, and savings funds, like the Western, follow the same pattern. As they shade off in size, respectability and antiquity, they tend to be less and less Old Philadelphian; but it is safe to say that all the surviving important ones are pretty well dominated by boards of the Best People. It must not be thought, incidentally, that the "Western" in WSFS stands for California, or even Pittsburgh. It means that the institution, started only a bit later than the PSFS, had an office a short walk west of the PSFS office. This was considered pretty daring. Until the Girard moved to Broad Street, any location west of 3rd Street for a respectable business was as awkward as a residence north of Market was for a respectable family.

iv. *Family Firms*

THOUGH BANKERS and lawyers and insurance men may manage and control money, they don't create it. Trade may be vulgar, still somebody has to pump the water. To be able to do so without too obviously soiling the hands requires another sort of Victorian compromise. That is, trade is vulgar, but a Family Concern is always respectable. Obviously somebody, the poor founder, has to start things off, but again it's the second generation that makes it all right. Trade becomes then hereditary, and even the manufacture of cookies or toilet paper (Scott Paper Company) is not debasing so long as it's all in the family. If the family itself is, or becomes, a member of the Philadelphia Web and is properly connected, then acceptability is secure.

As a rule, the best Old Philadelphia families begin in such family firms, then gradually move over into the higher realms of the professions or the "guardianships." The Morrises, the Hares, the Peppers, for instance, all began as brewers, but none of them are brewers now. The company begun by Anthony Morris I still exists, however, in the Perot Malting Company, founded in 1687, the oldest business in the United States, it claims. The Perots got in by marriage, of course.

Philadelphians are awfully proud of these Old Family Firms; but on the whole the mortality has been high. Like the conversion from Quaker to Episcopalian, as a family settles down and moves up, it tends to shed even hereditary trade. Despite protestations to the contrary, the proper root for a family is felt to be really in trusts and estates, not in the risks of commerce. If a really well-established family does continue with the Firm, it is then almost in a spirit of sentimental patronage, of loyalty to tradition, of duty rather than with base motives of making lots of money.

The nature of these family firms is and always has been most diverse. No single aspect of economic life dominates Philadelphia as, say, shipping and seafaring dominate the background of New England, or as gold does that of San Francisco, . . . or meatpacking of Chicago. As Morrises and others go back to drink, so do other family fortunes go back to food. Quaker flour was famous in early days; Philadelphia is even yet probably America's chief ice cream center. The Supplee dairies are more than just locally prosperous and are by now a "family concern." For years the Wagners from their picturesque cave on Dock Street supplied all good Philadelphians with cigars and condiments, and supplied the Wagners with wherewithal, now translated into horses and membership in clubs. Seed firms, like Landreth, Dreer and Burpee, listed in order of seniority, have made money over the generations, and made families too, especially Landreths (thirteen listings in the *S.R.*).

Drugs have made and still are making fortunes and families in Philadelphia. John Harrison began in the eighteenth century; but no family has been better established by drugs than that of the Rosengartens. George Rosengarten, son of a Westphalian banker ruined by Napoleon, emigrated in 1819. He took over the management of a distraught local drug firm, and by 1900 the Rosengartens were among the richest and best-established of Old Philadelphians. When the family firm finally merged with Merck and Company, Rosengartens continued prominently on the board of directors. Nobody really thinks of them as druggists nowadays, however, but rather as huntsmen, patrons of art and the University, devout Episcopalian laymen and relations of Everybody.

Pennsalt, the chemical firm, was a province of the Mordecai Lewis family. Now headed by Leonard Beale, it is still one of the larger corporations in the country.

Another very important and thoroughly family-and-Old-Philadelphia firm is that of Smith, Kline and French, recently the object of some unwelcome publicity when the Senate investigated drug prices. Whatever the pros and cons of the investigation, it was obvious that Smith, Kline and French were doing all right; and the board, officers, and even employees are so Old Philadelphian that the firm has been referred to as being itself an annex of the Philadelphia Club.

Lea and Febiger (medical books) and J. B. Lippincott Company are publishing firms of various vintages, all pretty much still family-owned and family-controlled affairs.

Bromleys no longer make carpets (though they do still make lace) nor Disstons saws, but as families the Bromleys and Disstons are securely established and no longer really need the backing of manufactures. The Stetsons of Stetson hats, on the other hand, still keep their hands, to the extent of a directorship at least, on a business that has done so much to make the Western cowboy glamorous. A Stetson big hat, made in Philadelphia, is still, along with the fancy belt buckle, handmade boot and stamped saddle, one of the extravagant necessities on which the cowhand spends his hard-earned cash. Like the writer Owen Wister, or the painter Thomas Eakins, the Stetson hat remains one of those curious connections which link the Old West with Old Philadelphia.

Perhaps as representative as any of these examples of family firmness have been those companies involved in clothes. Of these the two department stores, Strawbridge and Clothier, and Wanamaker's, have created institutions and families of rather startlingly high prestige. It was common in Philadelphia Republican circles to refer to Truman as a "little haberdasher"; nobody in Philadelphia refers to Wanamakers, Strawbridges or Clothiers as "big haberdashers," which is what they are.

Of the two, Wanamaker's is unquestionably the great and beloved store of Philadelphia, even yet the shopping Mecca of Philadelphians of all kinds and classes. The Wanamaker family itself, resplendent and respected though it may be, is still however, a bit parvenu. The Strawbridges and the Clothiers, on the other hand, though their store is far more subdued, and its patronage more solid middle-class than Old Philadelphian, are both as fam-

ilies by now quite crustily and prolifically established: Socially
a kind of hare and tortoise situation, in that the far more modest
S & C's seem now to be more quietly accepted than the high-
flying W's. The fact that Strawbridge and Clothier is very Quaker
certainly has much to do with this. It seems to be a Philadelphian
rule that families with strongly Quaker roots do better on the
whole and survive longer than many more lordly non-Quaker
families. The firm of Strawbridge and Clothier, as Philadelphia
things go, is pretty recent, dating only from 1868, less than a hundred years ago. This has not prevented both families from getting
into several generations of establishment. There is an Isaac
Clothier IV and a Francis Strawbridge III, both in fourth generations down from a Founder. There is no sign of either family's
dying out, and as the saying goes, four generations is enough and
five is aplenty.

The main store of Strawbridge and Clothier itself is housed
in a big solid dull handsome respectable pre–War II building at
8th and Market, the location of the original 1868 store. The firm
is proud of still being there, though admittedly it is way downtown these days for the average suburban shopper. Nonetheless
it remains prosperous and still completely under family control
(Strawbridges, that is, though no longer Clothiers).

As for the families themselves, they too remain prosperous;
still Quaker, but getting distinctly less plain and more fancy as
the generations go by. The two families are, in fact, probably
Philadelphia's most conspicuous examples of "wet" or worldly
Quakerism today. Older generations went to Swarthmore and
Haverford, younger generations to Princeton or Harvard. The
reputation of the late William Clothier as United States Amateur
Tennis Champion and Master of the Pickering Hunt and bon-
vivant sporting gent seems a bit un-Quakerlike. Still, on the
whole, these two families have approached fanciness with caution, and have been rewarded with Philadelphia security.

The Wanamakers, by contrast, leaped into pleasure with aban-
don, and came pretty close to running their Philadelphia course
— once more, the tortoises versus the hares. They did well and

married well, but have not conspicuously bred well; just squeaked through.

The Wanamakers are exact economic contemporaries of the Strawbridges and Clothiers. John Wanamaker the Great, Founder of The Store, civic reformer, patron of the arts and religion, started his first store, named Oak Hall, in 1861 and was rich by the end of the Civil War. When he died in 1922 he was a multi-millionaire. Whereas the Strawbridges and Clothiers began with the discreet social advantages of Quakerism, Wanamaker, son of a bricklayer, labored under the disadvantages of militant Baptism, and though he went Presbyterian, he was still pretty sectarian and YMCA for Old Philadelphia taste. He was in any case a grimly ostentatious person. "Pious John," as he was called, crusaded for political reform, unsuccessfully but still nobly, against the bossism of Quay and Penrose, and as a reward was appointed Postmaster General of the United States by President Benjamin Harrison. He and his son Rodman decorated the store with hand-painted oils; as a result the Store owns, or owned, probably the largest collection of French turn-of-the-century Salon art in the world, though very little of it is still visible.

The aura of success and sanctity was pretty thick. Whereas Strawbridge and Clothier contents itself with a chaste self-congratulatory plaque or two, the Big Store celebrates itself and its founder with a huge portrait in the main lobby, a Statement of Ideals and other such sundry self-given honors. "Let those who follow me continue to build with the plumb of honor, the level of truth and the square of integrity, education, courtesy and mutuality," declares the Founder in letters of gold, drawing his similes from his father's profession.

There is no doubt that as a religious man he was sincere, though given to publicity, and as a store builder a genius, though not a modest one. In an age of conscienceless robber barons he had a conscience, and aired it on all possible occasions in the interests of advertising. As a youth, when he was the first paid secretary of the YMCA, he had thought of going into the clergy, but God told him, when asked, to become a merchant, and backed him to the hilt. The Founder had no doubts on that score. The merchant's profession had something sacred about it, and was certainly as worthy as law or medicine. As for idlers living on their incomes who sneer at trade! He lost no opportunity of putting *them* in their place. (John Wanamaker and Sidney Fisher would *not* have seen eye to eye.) Of course it depended a bit on the size of the trade. "Anyone can be a shopkeeper," he declaimed, "but a merchant is as much different as . . . an eagle from a mouse." The bronze statue of an eagle in the center of the great court of the Philadelphia store symbolizes this difference. Strawbridge and Clothier, in retaliation, should put up a statue of a large, fat, gray Quaker mouse.

Wanamaker made no pretension to Old Philadelphianism; neither he nor his wife had social ambitions, but his sons, the somewhat obscure financial genius Thomas and the large-scale art patron Rodman, both married into the Web. Thomas married a Welsh, usually referred to by her nickname of "Pretty Minnie," Rodman a Henry. The daughters married equally well, notably Mary, who as Mrs. Warburton was a recognized hostess of no mean distinction. Rodman, who spent ten years in Paris and many years more in New York, embraced Art with somewhat the same bear hug of idealism and merchandising with which his father embraced Religion. A dapper, moustached, sporting and distinctly urbane gentleman, Rodman, when in Paris, distinguished himself by driving his coach-and-four from Paris to London (with the help of shipping across the Channel, of course), a feat unduplicated in the annals of that particular sport. He bulldozed culture into the stores. In addition to buying some six hundred pictures from the French Salons of the early 1900's, he installed the World's Largest Organ in the Great Court of the Store (somehow everything has to be capitalized when talking about the early Wanamakers) and gave concerts there and in New York of organ and orchestra music conducted by everybody from Richard Strauss to Leopold Stokowski, a man after his own heart. He collected dozens of antique violins, Stradivarii and others, and financed a "capella" of artists to play on

them, and filled his stores in Philadelphia and New York with
European and Oriental knickknacks, all of which was as good
advertising for merchandise in the early twentieth century as his
father's Sunday School had been in the late nineteenth.

Unfortunately in the third generation Flair and Finance, so
admirably wed in both the Founder and his sons, parted company.
The Principles of Maintenance took something of a beating, particularly compared to those paragons, the S's & C's. Rodman II,
son of Thomas, had flair all right, and as a very handsome and
proficient man of pleasure married and divorced Old Philadelphia maidens, shipped polo ponies back and forth to Europe, and
in general, disobeying all his grandfather's principles, supported
the Life Glamorous. He had nothing to do with the store, and
not much to do with Philadelphia, his centers being preferably
New York or the Riviera. His first cousin, John, son of Rodman I, had finance without flair, and although on the board of
the store, was not, it seems, particularly effective. His son John
has given hope that the fourth generation in this case *will* take
care of itself. He has shown no particular evidence of flair, but
as chairman of the Wanamaker board has been active, respected
and popular. He remains the last Wanamaker in control.

The only Wanamaker with much flair in Philadelphia at present is John's sister Fernanda Wanamaker, formerly Mrs. Wetherill, now Mrs. Donald Leas. She is famous for her looks and
dresses and parties and jewels and entertainments in Chestnut
Hill and above all in Southampton, Long Island, not otherwise
at all a Philadelphia resort. There, at costume balls attended
by the late Gary Cooper, Henry Ford II and Angier Biddle Duke,
she has battled her way to Number One Hostess, assisted by a
house full of chimpanzees. In her spare time, not being able
to repress an hereditary talent for merchandise, she runs a chain
of resort clothes stores. Blood will tell.

The store itself goes on, playing it safe, generally a solid, conservative, not very imaginative concern to which Old, and other,
Philadelphians remain loyal. The New York store went out of
business; in the Old Store in Philadelphia the pictures from the

French Salons have, with about a dozen exceptions, been relegated to the cellars, the organ contents itself with playing Viennese waltzes at the lunch hour and Christmas carols when appropriate, the restaurant serves as bad food as one can buy in Philadelphia, which is saying something, but John Wanamaker, Philadelphia, remains one of the biggest and best department stores in the country, a Family Firm that has almost outlived and outshone its family.

v. Rusty Cranes

PHILADELPHIA never seems like a seaport; but it is. As center of the great Delaware River basin, it is the second largest seaport in America. Though very few Old Philadelphia families now make their living from the sea, many owe their present position to shipping and shipbuilding. The Penroses launched their first ship in 1707, with the Penns as partners, and kept it up until the mid-nineteenth century. The Winsors operated a Winsor Line to Boston, the Dalletts a Red D Line to Venezuela, but while there are now lines of Winsors and Dalletts, there is now no Winsor Line and no Red D. The China trade was as brisk from Philadelphia as from New England, and Willings, Walns, Fishers and Coxes all cashed in on it. The West Indies were considered almost a Philadelphia monopoly. For all this, very little salt air seems to get up that long sluggish estuary, and Philadelphia's face is turned resolutely inland. Nonetheless, there were the Cramps.

They began in 1830 and flourished up through the First War. During Philadelphia's great Iron Age from 1840 to 1920, the Cramp shipyards were a bulwark of economic strength, and an especial point of economic pride. "Cramp builds the ships of the world as Baldwin builds the locomotives," Philadelphia orators were fond of boasting, and they were right. Cramp was the greatest American builder of steel ships, constructed numbers of battleships for the United States as well as for Russia, Venezuela, Japan and Turkey. When, around the turn of the century, the second Cramp in the succession took his six sons as partners into a business employing 8,000 men and dealing with many of the major world powers, one would certainly have thought the Cramps a secure dynasty. But by the outbreak of the Second World War the shipyard was deserted, the great cranes had rusted, and the Cramps themselves had died out, victims of the general collapse of American merchant shipping after World War I.

Cramp built the ships of the world; Baldwin the locomotives. From 1831, when Mathias Baldwin, a former jeweler's apprentice and designer of stationary steam engines, first exhibited a small model engine running on a circular track in Peale's Museum, Baldwin, his partners and their descendants were America's foremost manufacturers of the iron horse. They supplied locomotives to the English and even to the Czar of all the Russias. When the Civil War broke out, the desperate need for rail transportation by the North was supplied largely by Baldwin, and it was the ability of firms such as Baldwin to rise to such occasions that in the end won the war for the industrialized North.

Baldwin himself, abolitionist, teetotaler, like the Cramps a North Philadelphian, never got into Society, or tried to. His later partners, and their later partners and successors, Bairds, Vauclains and Converses, all did, and are still there. After a final boom during and after the First World War, the fortunes of the firm itself declined. The Age of the Iron Horse was pretty well over. By now, the control of the company has ceased to be Philadelphian, and its principal manufacture has ceased to be locomotives. But the various families concerned continue to exist. The original Baird began as an emigrant Irish bricklayer; in later years the Bairds have been identified as a clan of loyal Princetonians. A Vauclain, André Constant, is one of Philadelphia's most distinguished native-born composers and teachers of music. Converses were known, in a somewhat older generation, for polo. Nobody makes locomotives any more.

There are and have been hundreds of other family firms; and there have been and still are plenty of Old Philadelphians who just plain go into business — any old business. However, even when this is done, there is liable to be some sort of special twist to it. Firms with Old Philadelphia connections are still preferred, and when families like the Disstons sell out, some young Old Philadelphians prefer to quit good jobs rather than continue under a new alien management.

Of all family firms, however, those bounded by a holy trinity of Coal, Iron and the Railroads have been most indigenous, most Family, most effective in setting up families. This was the core of Philadelphia's nineteenth-century industrial prosperity, and the basis of most of Philadelphia's nineteenth-century wealth. The roots of this prosperity go far back into the eighteenth century, and today a good proportion of the Nest Egg is derived from money made under the sanction of this "Iron Triangle."

3

i. The Iron Potts

PENNSYLVANIA has always been America's Iron State. Though there is and has been competition elsewhere, the mining and forging of iron and steel was and is Pennsylvania's primary occupation. Pennsylvania is to the rest of America what the Midlands are to England or the Ruhr to the European continent. The center of this industry is now west in Pittsburgh, but it was first established in the east up the valley of the Schuylkill, and nothing is more honorable and respectable in Philadelphia than to have among one's ancestors one of the ancient baronial ironmasters.

The ironmasters best represent for Philadelphia that touch of the feudal which seems to be, probably unfortunately, an almost necessary ingredient in the background of an aristocracy. "Hence the superiority of the South; it has a gentry founded on land, not on money or professional success. Land is the only foundation for a gentry," says Guess Who (Sidney Fisher), and it better be inherited land too. "The only way to have property is to inherit it, and the universal feeling of the world that makes this the basis of the position of a gentleman is founded in truth and nature." The truth, of course, being that most landed aristocracies are founded either on force or slavery or both, and tend by nature to produce a race of reactionary boors, unless mitigated by commerce and urbanity. Nonetheless, this English sentimentality of the soil has to a rather fatal extent permeated the American upper-class psychology, and nowhere more than in Philadelphia, where the aristocracy is so patently founded on money and professional success.

One can trace this theme of the "landholder as aristocrat" in the formation of American regional psychology. The ideals of the Planter, in the South, and the Cattleman, in the West, have dominated the emotions of these particular regions to a formidable extent. In both cases, in both regions, this "ideal stereotype" may have set up all sorts of false standards and created fatal illusions, but still it provides a local pattern and a local pride, an "aristocratic role" which seems to be vital for the production of a healthy collective ego in any given social order. At least one sometimes senses the absence of such an ideal in the inferiority complexes of a region like the Middle West. In the East, though, it is impossible to ignore the merchant prince or the learned professional (in New England the clergyman, in Philadelphia the lawyer or doctor) as the fundamental source of family fortune, distinction and pride, in New England he should have a touch of salt, in Philadelphia it helps to have a touch of soot. In New England the shipowner and the ship captain do what the cattleman and cowboy have done for the West: they give money an aura of heroism and glamour, that is to say, Romance. (Notice, for instance, how the Texas oil billionaire invariably seems to adopt the quite inappropriate trappings of the ranchman.) The same can't quite be said of the Pennsylvania ironmaster, but along with the New York patroon and the New England shipowner, he does provide something of a landowning equivalent to offset the more purely trading wealth of the region's old families.

Coventry, Colebrookedale, Pool Forge, Pine Forge, Warwick, Reading, Mount Pleasant, Mount Hope, Mount Joy, Cornwall, Hopewell, Elizabeth, Maria, Rebecca, Mary Anne, Joanna — in a crude, frontier and rough-and-ready fashion these and so many other early forges and furnaces were almost Utopian models of the self-contained, feudal-commercial, capitalist-agrarian, autocratic-cooperative life. Set in tracts of woodland, ranging from three hundred to ten thousand acres, they were almost entirely self-supporting communities. The ironmaster himself lived in a handsome but not oppressive stone mansion, always referred to as the "manor," with formal gardens outside and imported furniture inside. Close by were barns, root cellars and springhouses, and beyond stood the furnace, a great pyramidal stone chimney whose smokeless glare at night illuminated the wilderness for miles about. Here the iron mined on the property was melted into pig iron, so called from the sand molds into which the metal flowed at the base of the furnace. They looked like so many suckling pigs nursing at the belly of a sow. This crude iron was then hammered and refined at the nearby forge. The charcoal for the fires was made from the surrounding woodlands; water power ran the bellows of the furnace and the hammer of the forge. The workmen, in various degrees of skill and prosperity from the lordly and expert forgemen to the lowly and ignorant woodcutters, lived in quarters beyond the furnace area, each with his own patch of garden. Wheat, corn and barley were grown in the surrounding fields, and a company store supplied what could not be made on the place, from buttons to rum. Schooling was supplied for the ironmaster's children by a tutor, who sometimes gave instruction to the more promising boys of the working population. Religion was handled largely by itinerant hell-fire Methodist evangelists. Occasionally the ironmaster had his own chapel and chaplain, as did the Grubbs at Mount Hope. As a rule, though, the ironworker preferred to get along without salvation or learning, and stuck to hard liquor and hunting.

It was a life of almost complete isolation, cut off from the world by distances of wilderness and bad roads. As the ironmasters progressed in prosperity, they tended to acquire town houses for the winter in Lancaster, Reading or Philadelphia itself. In summer they managed as many visitors and visits as they could. It was a life of hard work for everyone. The furnace presents a vigorous contrast to the plantation, with its glamorous but sultry and rather debased atmosphere, all profligate luxury on top and sordid misery below, or to the eternal conflict between tenant and patroon along the Hudson. The number of people involved was small (Hopewell Furnace seems usually to have been run with a working force of about sixty-five), each man had his own specialty and rank, and the ironmasters themselves were like as not boys from the furnaces who had worked up. Skill and brains and industry were obviously rewarded; there was no permanent gap between owner and worker of race or hereditary privilege. Even compared to a more model and modern setup like the Fairless Mills and adjacent Levittown, below Trenton on the Delaware, the old furnaces had a rugged human dignity and unity which few industrial or even agricultural complexes have ever achieved anywhere at any time. Pride of craft and family, aristocracy and democracy, industrialism and agrarianism were successfully combined. Of the many hundreds of these iron plantations that dotted Pennsylvania, few are still working iron centers.

Charcoal failed as a fuel when the forests were exhausted; one had to be near coal and railroads. Some works, like those at Birdsboro, converted to coke, expanded and survived. Others, like Hopewell, shriveled away and were abandoned. Most of the actual furnaces and forges have disappeared. The manor houses are left, and have been bought and remodeled and restored by suburbanites or historical societies. They are as handsome and livable now as then. Hopewell Furnace in the hills west of Birdsboro, on the Schuylkill, is now a National Park, and is being completely resurrected as a model of what one of these plantations was like. It is well worth a visit.

Besides the manor houses, the families also survive, and most Philadelphia families somewhere along the line relate themselves to the iron business or to the iron families, Potts, Rutter, Ross, Grubb, Brooke, Whitaker, Reeves, Roberts, Wood, Lukens, Huston and others.

Of these iron names, two best represent Iron to Old Philadelphia — Potts and Brooke. The Pottses are the oldest ironmaking family still involved in iron. The Brookes, though not nearly as old, still operate iron plants at Birdsboro. The Pottses represent perhaps "solid"; the Brookes, at least in later generations, "fancy." The Pottses consolidated their position in iron by marrying Rutters. The Brookes consolidated their social position by marrying everybody except the Pottses.

The earliest owner of ironworks in the Schuylkill valley was "Thos. Rutter, blacksmith," as he preferred to sign his name, even when a rich man. A Quaker immigrant to Philadelphia, he got into trouble there during the Keithian Schism, first split in the American Quaker ranks, went upstream and spawned, in 1716, Pennsylvania's first ironworks. He and his partners were joined up there by one Thomas Potts, who had managed ironworks for the capitalist Anthony Morris, and who then branched out on his own. Both Pottstown downstream and Pottsville upstream (hometown of John O'Hara and original of his fictional Gibbsville) were both founded and laid out by Pottses. In time the Rutter–Potts combine owned Colebrookedale, Mount Pleasant, Warwick, Coventry, Rutter's Forge, Spring Forge, Pool Forge, Pine Forge, Little Pine Forge, McCall's Forge, Valley Forge and many others, as well as thousands and thousands of surrounding acres of farm and woodland.

The principal center for all their doings was the chief Potts seat, Pottsgrove in Pottstown. (One can imagine the jokes once current about all this.) Here Martha Washington stayed while her husband was suffering at that other Potts seat, Valley Forge, and here the General himself often visited.

There are still plenty of Pottses, some active in iron, and plenty of Rutters. The plant of the Horace C. Potts firm is visible from the tracks of the Pennsylvania Railroad in North Philadelphia. A Peter Rutter, as a member of the American Legation in London, has a son who was a boxing partner of Prince Charles. (The Windsors, a German family, were in Empire).

The Brookes may not be as old in Iron as the Potts, but they concentrated their energies mostly in one place. Birdsboro nowadays is a rather prettily decadent old mill town on the river bank. Down by the water are the big black mills. Up on the hill are the vestiges of the various Brooke manors, now either ruins or rest homes. No Brookes now live there.

The original works there were started not by the Brookes, but by William Bird, a self-made ironmaster who began as a humble woodchopper for the Rutters; as low as one could get in the business. After working up to partner, he established his own furnaces in the 1740's, and soon became Rutters' chief competitor. His son Mark took over, and in fine second-generation fashion, married well (Mary Ross of Lancaster, whose ironmaster brother George Ross signed the Declaration) and proceeded to turn his father's modest house into a mansion complete with a surrounding pleasance of box and peacocks. Mark played a fairly prominent and patriotic role in the Revolution, but like his brother-in-law, James Wilson, he overspeculated in lands and lost everything.

When Bird failed, the works were batted about from distinguished hand to distinguished hand — Morrises of both families, (Anthony and Robert,) and others. The man who actually ran them was an unlikely Captain John Barde, scion of a Swiss family, who had served in the British army. While on duty in Florida he had eloped with the fourteen-year-old daughter of the late Governor, Major Robert Farmer, and soon found himself exiled. The Spaniards, in one of the world's most obscure campaigns, drove the English out of Florida, and the Bardes went up North to the United States. Somehow, in 1788, he got a job as tenant and manager of the Birdsboro works. He finally bought them himself in 1796 and promptly died. His still young widow, Anne, carried on alone. She married her daughters, in typical ironmistress style, into iron, and one of her sons-in-law, another self-made younger iron man called Matthew Brooke, bought the business from her.

All during the nineteenth century Brookes made iron, mostly at Birdsboro. The works got larger and larger, the family more and more high-toned. In various branches it connected itself with most of the other great iron families: the Heber Smiths of Joanna, the Grubbes of Cornwall. Brookes in Philadelphia have improved the strain not only by marriage into iron but by marriages into Morris. The one thing the Brookes have never done is marry Pottses. It's one of those curious rifts like the gap between Morris and Biddle. Difference of specie.*

In 1940 Birdsboro was able to celebrate its bicentennial with bands, parades, pretty girls in costumes, and Brookes. By 1960 no Brookes owned anything there. A George Clymer Brooke of Reading is President of a Birdsboro Steel Foundry and Machine Company, but the E. & O. Brooke Iron Company is owned by the Colorado Fuel and Iron Corporation, with headquarters right far from the Schuylkill. This side of the Iron Triangle has pretty well rusted away. Two other, but later, family iron and steel works, however, still flourish around Philadelphia. These are the Lukens works in Coatesville and the Alan Wood Steel Company in Conshohocken. The chief figure in the Lukens works was a strong-jawed woman of the early nineteenth century, Rebecca Pennock Lukens. She inherited the works from her father, ran them herself with a minimum of opposition from her doctor husband, who died early, and handed them on to her son-in-law Doctor Huston. The Hustons still own and run the company, still named Lukens in honor of Rebecca, and it is still one of the country's large organizations.

The Lukens works go back to the later eighteenth century. The Wood company dates only from the earlier nineteenth, but unlike the Brookes and other local ironworks that sold out to big business in the twentieth century, the Woods still run their own company. The present President, Harleston Wood, in his forties, is the sixth generation. Woodmont, the grandly gargoyled château built across the river from Conshohocken at the turn of the century by Alan, the third Wood, is, however, no longer inhabited by Woods. It is owned and occupied now by Father Divine and his Angels.

Both the Lukens–Hustons and the Woods follow pretty much in the feudal-family tradition of the Pottses and Brookes. Philadelphia's greatest man of iron, Joseph Wharton, belongs more in the modern tradition of large-scale operators, or of such early capitalists as Anthony Morris. His center of operations was not a

* But there existed a John Rutter Brooke who became a general.

"manor" on a hill, but Philadelphia itself, and his career belongs in the realm of Big, not Family, Business. Owners of Walnut Grove, famous during the Revolution for that party given by the British officers in occupation, the Meschianza, the Whartons produced a steady stream of reputable professional men and merchants, and married into all the other similar families. Though none of the Whartons is really very distinguished or glamorous, the *Dictionary of American Biography,* that Bible of who was who, contains seven Whartons, more than any other single Philadelphia family; for whatever that is worth. This, of course, is a comparatively meager showing next to the fifteen Virginia Lees, and nearly a dozen Boston Lowells and New York Livingstons, but then — is it really good form to be so distinguished? Along with the Morrises and the Norrises, Cadwaladers and Roberts, the Whartons are among the genuinely, unapologetically, old, Old Philadelphians, as opposed to such upstarts and newcomers as the Biddles and Ingersolls.

Joseph was one of ten children, born in a house on Spruce Street in Society Hill that belonged to his mother's family, she being a Fisher. Unlike his litterateur relation Sidney, though Joseph himself was also a facile poet, he had no disdain at all for sordid mercantile pursuits. He loved them. He was, after all, a Quaker. He first went into lead and paint, like those other Quakers, the Wetherills, and then into iron, and his company, the Bethlehem Iron Company, was the original of the now colossal Bethlehem Steel Company. He also had a personal monopoly on the American production of nickel, which came in handy. He is memorialized today as a philanthropist: creator of the Wharton School of Finance at the University of Pennsylvania, first of its kind, and one of the founders, benefactors and trustees of the Quaker co-educational college of Swarthmore.

He is an odd and unlikely Nickel King. That is, many Steel Barons were noted, like Joseph, for their piety; but few were so definitely, if quietly, well-born, and I suspect none was able so gracefully to turn a serious sonnet, an address to a college, or a tender poem to a dead mother. Besides the Business School and

Swarthmore, Joseph is remembered in connection with something called the Wharton Tract. This is a huge acreage in the pine barrens of New Jersey, bought by Wharton with the idea that the city of Philadelphia might someday use it in connection with water supplies. For years the tract remained in family hands; only recently it has become a New Jersey State Park, full of odd wildlife, swamps and the remains of Revolutionary bog-ironworks.

Wharton is still another of that group, perhaps the most outstanding of them all, that though Old Philadelphian by birth, nonetheless were self-made men too. Effingham Morris, Benjamin Rush, George Roberts, Joseph Wharton, all of families well-known in Philadelphia's Golden Age of 1770–1800, all became rich and powerful in that other age of Old Philadelphia's glory, the Iron Age of 1880–1910. This was also the period of Philadelphia's greatest artists, Thomas Eakins and Mary Cassatt, and of its preeminence in its two most characteristic sports, cricket and fox hunting; an oddly smothered sort of Philadelphia Renaissance.

ii. *The Iron Triangle II: Railroads*

RAILROADS IN PENNSYLVANIA were never exactly family firms. They were Big Business from the very beginning, and state-owned or state-sponsored big business at that. At least, that was the background of the state's biggest line, the Pennsylvania Railroad. That did not prevent it from devolving into the hands of Philadelphia's best families.

The Pennsylvania Railroad is still the "greatest railroad in the world." This is one of those broad statements that needs endless qualifications, *i.e.* the Trans-Siberian Railroad undoubtedly has more trackage, as does even the Santa Fe; but generally speaking, it seems to be true in all other respects that the Pennsylvania Railroad is the greatest railroad in the world — still. The crucial word is "still." The Pennsylvania Railroad in over a century has never failed to pay its dividend. This is another statement, true all right, but needing also a bit of qualification. In these last years it has come as near as a corporation can come to not paying its dividend, squeaking through at the last minute with twenty-five cents on the share. The record has been maintained, but as brokers say, this is no longer a stake for widows and orphans — a far cry from the days when good Philadelphia children were taught to pray for the Republican Party, the Girard Trust and the Pennsylvania Railroad. Then the Railroad was the Gibraltar of Philadelphia's economy, and indeed more than any other single factor, it rescued Philadelphia from the disasters of 1840, and set the city once more on the road to prosperity.

In 1840, as in 1950, Philadelphia was in a bad way. Through the eighteenth century the most prosperous port, the richest trading center of the continent, it had been steadily declining. With the opening of the Erie Canal in 1825 the produce of the booming West began to go to New York, or by river down to New Orleans, or by the newly constructed and macadamized National Road over the mountains to Baltimore. In the depression that followed the debacle of Biddle, in the 1840's, Philadelphia lost its financial leadership as well. The only salvation obviously lay in somehow getting the riches of the West over the mountains and into the port of Philadelphia.

Canals were tried, but one couldn't get canals over those damn mountains. A system of elevators called "inclined planes" was conceived, by which cargoes and cars transferred from canal barges were hitched to cables and dragged up the slopes on rails. The system was ingenious, but time-consuming. On the "Main Line of Public Works" between Harrisburg and Pittsburgh there were some ten stages or sections of these inclined planes, with level track between, and the delays in hitching and unhitching the cars can be imagined.

It took Philadelphians a long, long time to see the obvious: that the only way across those mountains was by steam locomotive. Short rail lines had been built here and there, so that one *could* get to Pittsburgh by steam, canal, inclined planes and canal again, but this hardly offered the smooth continuous passage of barges on the Erie to New York. At last in 1845, fighting the canal lobby tooth and nail all the way, with the threat of the new Baltimore and Ohio Railroad creeping up towards Pittsburgh from the South, the Pennsylvania Railroad got going.

First there was a mass meeting in the Chinese Museum, a cabinet of curiosities used as a lecture hall. Worthies sat on platforms. Thomas Cope, famous Quaker shipowner, presided. The address was made by tobacco-chewing lawyer William Meredith. A charter was suggested. In 1846 a Charter for a "Pennsylvania Central Railroad" was squeezed through the legislature, and the Baltimore and Ohio specifically enjoined from laying any tracks through Pennsylvania. Thirteen directors were anointed — a Lea, a Patterson, a Cope, a Wright, a Toland — and a dynamic Yankee and Unitarian, Samuel Vaughn Merrick, who manufactured hand engines for volunteer fire companies, among other things, was made President.

Now all they needed was a railroad.

None of these estimable gentlemen of course knew anything about railroads. A young surveyor called John Edgar Thomson set to work. The line he laid out, including the famous Horseshoe Curve, has never had to be re-surveyed. By 1855 a railroad existed between Harrisburg and Pittsburg, though not until 1861 did the Pennsylvania Railroad actually control and operate a complete line from Philadelphia to Pittsburg on its own tracks with its own trains.

The mills of Philadelphia grind exceedingly slow, but in this case, fine. As the Civil War proved Baldwin, so it proved the Pennsylvania Railroad. It was right in the middle, between East and West and North and South. From then on till the age of the automobile there was little question as to the stability of the Railroad.

There was also not much question, at the beginning, of its being a private money-making adventure. It was thought of as a public service, a state-chartered, though privately administered, attempt to "save the city." The first two presidents, Merrick and William

C. Patterson, were in no sense railroad tycoons. They were active gentlemen in other fields who presided over the board, and who went back to their real affairs as soon as they could.

This short era of Public Benevolence lasted only until 1852. It was followed by a thirty-year-long and very different era of Hard-Boiled Railroading. The next two presidents, surveyor Thomson and his friend and occasional assistant, plunger and politician, Tom Scott, took this rather discouraging noble experiment and built it into a giant corporation. Thomson the Great reigned from 1852 to 1872 — never made the Web. Scott the Glorious reigned from 1874 to 1880 — definitely did make the Web; he was, in fact, the first of the socially rewarded Pennsylvania Railroad presidents. Pattersons and Merricks and Copes and Tolands, of course, had meanwhile been getting along satisfactorily without benefit of railroads, except as stockholders. Not until the very late 'fifties, just before the Civil War, when the names of a George Rosengarten, a Wistar Morris and a Dr. Horatio C. Wood appear on the board, do really familiar Old Philadelphians begin to crop up there again.

After the Civil War, when the Railroad was obviously here to stay, the Oligarchy began to close in. Not only on the board of directors, where the first Biddle, an Alexander, appeared in 1874, but even in the presidency itself. Through another thirty-year period, during the tenures of George Roberts (1880–97) and Alexander Cassatt (1899–1906) and the years immediately following, the board began to achieve something of the choiceness of the Hand-in-Hand or the PSFS. It became one of Philadelphia's best clubs.

The Railroad's Golden, or more aptly, Iron Age, which was also that Old Philadelphia age of banking dominated by Effingham Morris, and of insurance dominated by Benjamin Rush, had as its railroad representatives two very different members of the Oligarchy. George Roberts was indisputably Old Philadelphian. Alexander Cassatt was not even from Philadelphia, but, perish the thought, from Allegheny, Pennsylvania, near Pittsburgh. This doesn't mean that he was not immediately and enthusiastically absorbed. Both, as is fitting, came in more or less from the top. Though they both had had long experience at the bottom, they neither of them climbed the ladder of corporative achievement rung by rung in quite the same fashion as did Thomas Scott, who ascended from country storekeeper, to toll collector, to supervisor of inclined planes (the Allegheny Portage Railroad), to director of the Western Division at Pittsburgh, and on up.

The Roberts family, far more than any of the families mentioned so far, even the Cadwaladers, represent the Welsh Barony. The marriage in 1683 of John Roberts the maltster to Gainor Roberts, daughter of Robert Pugh (ap Hugh) and Elizabeth Owen of Llwyndedwydd near Bala was the first wedding celebrated, if one can describe a Quaker wedding as being "celebrated," in the Merion meeting. Roberts settled on his acres called Pencoyd in one of the Barony's first stone houses, along the west bank of the Schuylkill, on what is now City Line. There the Robertses have been ever since (though most of their acreage has been sold off in the last few years), and there George Brooke (distant relation of the Birdsboro group) Roberts, the fifth generation from John the maltster, was born in 1833.

By that time the Robertses had shifted from malting to iron-making, another one of the Schuylkill valley establishments. George was educated as an engineer and, after a varied experience as a railroad consultant, came into the Pennsylvania as a thirty-year-old assistant to the president, then the great J. Edgar Thomson. From thence he moved up the vice presidencies to first, and finally, when Scott retired in 1880 after a stormy term which included the depression of 1873 and the great and bloody Pittsburgh riots of the 1877 strike, Roberts made president.

A small-boned, quiet, refined man with a sober moustache, he was properly devoted to good works. He was a director of the Free Library and vice president of the Fairmount Park Art Association. He encouraged the work of the YMCA among the employees of the Railroad, and was much interested in bettering their condition. He was a devout Episcopalian, the Robertses having long slid from Quakerism, and in Bala he built the

Church of St. Asaph, dedicated, as the saying goes, to the Glory of God and the convenience of the Roberts family. It was decorated with murals by cousin Elizabeth Roberts, for, like the Cassatts, the Robertses too had their lady artists.

Elizabeth was never as famous as her counterpart Mary Cassatt. As for Alexander himself, he was a very different make of railroad president. Son of a banker from western Pennsylvania whose business took him to Europe, Alexander and his talented sister were schooled abroad. Like Roberts, Cassatt worked as an engineer before becoming, in 1874, the Pennsylvania's third vice president in charge of transportation. He rose to first vice president. In 1882 however, at the early age of forty-two, he abruptly and casually retired from the Railroad and devoted himself to horse raising. There was talk that he was miffed because he wasn't made president instead of Roberts. He continued with the company as a director, and had a few other railroad connections, but for a full seventeen years his real interest was sports — huntin', coachin', racin', cricket. He settled on the Main Line, was involved in local affairs, and as bon viveur and connoisseur of horseflesh was embraced by society with open arms.

When in 1899 he strolled into the office of the presidency, a commanding figure whom one always pictures in gray topper, with boutonniere and field glasses, he was, if anything, already condescending to his new honors. He was a model of the kind of out-of-towner Philadelphians love. It is ironic that he is now generally remembered as the brother of painter Mary. Things were certainly the other way about in 1900.

Two buildings aptly symbolize the careers and personalities of these two great gentlemen of the Pennsylvania Railroad. The old Broad Street Station, in Philadelphia itself, might stand for George Roberts, although it was planned and partially executed before him. Pennsylvania Station in New York might similarly stand for Cassatt, though not opened till after his death. The two buildings, like the two men, represent two contrasting Old Philadelphia attitudes, two approaches on the part of the Oligarchy to the problem of Philadelphia versus the outside world.

Roberts can be made to stand, perhaps, for the stay-at-home, inbred, parochial view of Philadelphia as center of the universe; Cassatt for the much less typical, but still perennial aspect of Philadelphia measuring itself against the world, keeping up with whatever Joneses it chooses to recognize, once England, but sometimes, in later days, New York, at least culturally and economically. Roberts should have been painted by Eakins (but wasn't) ; Cassatt by Sargent. (He was. "Have you seen that thing he did of my brother Alec?" Mary said. "And did you know the price he charged? I call it dishonesty. I told Alec he ought not to allow that thing in his house." It's true that Mary herself did Alec much better.) Roberts should have gone to the University; Cassatt, particularly as an outlander, to Yale or Harvard. Actually most Robertses have been Princetonians, right far, yet not too far. Cassatts actually have gone to Harvard.

Broad Street Station was opened in 1881. The completed building with its great arched train shed and Mooro-Gothic ten-story corner tower was not done till 1894, so that although the plan was a product of the Scott era, the execution covered the whole span of the Roberts presidency. At the very center of town, facing City Hall itself, this great brick castle, which housed the general offices of the company, stood for fifty years as the Bastille of the Railroad's power. The original station had been in West Philadelphia, where the main station once again stands. To get trains from the main tracks there into the center of town, a massive elevated stone causeway was built, cutting the city in two between Market and Arch. Cross streets were permitted to go under it through gloomy dripping tunnels. This was the Chinese Wall; it was always called that, and it looked just like a Chinese Wall. What of course made it humorous was the reference to the Forbidden City; for south of Philadelphia's Chinese Wall, below Market Street, lay Rittenhouse Square and Old Philadelphia's sacred social center, while north of the wall lay the great unknown and unwashed, the Mongolia of "North of Market" where Nobody Lived. If the wall had been built not for the railroad but merely for protection against the barbarians, nobody would have been much surprised. The causeway was almost a solid block wide, and stretched from the Schuylkill to the center of the city at Penn Square. The degree of arrogance of this gesture on the part of a supposedly private corporation, even in the public interest, can be measured by the total destruction of one side of Filbert Street, a thoroughfare of "respectable residences," all of which were obliterated by the building of the causeway. Of course, "nobody lived" on Filbert Street. What would have happened if this had been tried on Walnut Street, where "people" certainly did live?

For years, getting grimmer and grimier, the Moorish mass of Broad Street Station was everyone's first introduction, or last farewell to Philadelphia. Even by 1886, in one record month alone, a million passengers passed through it. Lined up in a row, west to east, like a trio of dinosaurs, stood Broad Street Station, City Hall and Wanamaker's. If ever a city had a Hub, Philadelphia was the city.

Broad Street Station was in the fantastic style of the Centennial Exposition, exemplified at its best-worst in the works of its architect the Old Philadelphian Frank Furness, in the "new" library of the University out in West Philadelphia, in the "new" building of the Pennsylvania Academy of Art on Broad Street. Cassatt's monument, the Pennsylvania Station in New York, was a creation in the neo-Roman style of Chicago's Columbian Exposition of 1893, exemplified at its best-worst in the works of McKim, Mead and White of New York — the buildings of the "new" campus of Columbia University, or, in Philadelphia, Effingham Morris's Girard Trust building. Whereas the first style was closely identified with Philadelphia, the second was essentially non-Philadelphian. Modeled not on the Pantheon like the Girard Trust, but supposedly on the even bigger Baths of Caracalla, the Pennsylvania Station's echoing main hall revived effectively the Grandeur that was Rome, and enclosed an augustly impressive interior space. The immense columns, the vault, lit with the smoky radiance of a winter afternoon and filled with a subdued roar of travelers, provided moments of odd aesthetic and historical gratification. The Baths of Caracalla have no more to do with railroads than the Pantheon has with banks, but the effect was certainly impressive. Of all Philadelphia's Grand Gestures, the Pennsylvania Station was one of the grandest; but of course made in New York, to impress "foreigners." As such, it represents something of a defeat.

Even under Roberts, Broad Street Station and all, it became obvious that the primary purpose of the Pennsylvania Railroad, the channeling of the riches of the West into the port of Philadelphia, was not fulfilling itself. Riches got channeled, but despite all sorts of local efforts in Philadelphia, they got channeled into New York. The Pennsylvania Railroad acquired the tracks through New Jersey and the tracks up from Baltimore, and could rival and even surpass the New York Central, heir of the Erie Canal, as a funnel; but it had to stop dead at the Hudson, whereas the Central could, and did, go right down the middle of Manhattan, as the Pennsylvania could go right into City Hall in Philadelphia. Cassatt, giving up the thought of making Philadelphia the final terminus of his railroad, planned to take over, as much as possible, New York itself.

The building of the tunnel under the Hudson was a tremendous feat; the archaic and expensive ferries were eliminated, passengers and freight could go direct from Chicago to New York and north to Boston, all without changing. The opening of the Pennsylvania Station in 1910 was a glory for Philadelphia, a Trojan horse right there on the island, a massive insult to the Vanderbilts.

Though Cassatt, standing like Moses on the New Jersey shore of the river, had not lived to see his conquest of Canaan, the Station remained his great monument. It is due to be torn down in 1963, in what is one of the most wanton and barbarous acts of architectural vandalism in the history of America. Cassatt and McKim must be swiveling in their expensive graves.*

Broad Street and Pennsylvania Stations had still another parallel: they were great commuting centers. The Main Line traffic

* See Appendix.

was a creation of George Roberts, the Long Island Railroad an acquisition of Cassatt. The absentee mismanagement of the latter had long been a source of humor and despair. The Paoli Local, however, Philadelphia's Main Line suburban train, has been a source of pride, affection and convenience. Christopher Morley intimated that after his death one would find the words "Paoli Local" engraved on his heart.

The Main Line, Philadelphia's most famous suburban district, was deliberately conceived in the 1870's and 1880's by the Railroad, which built high-toned housing developments, ran hotels, more or less forced its executives to plunk their estates out there, and created a whole series of somewhat spuriously Welsh towns along the railroad tracks. The name "Main Line" is derived of course from that "Main Line of Public Works," the gaggle of rails, canals and inclined planes the state originally created to connect Philadelphia and Pittsburgh. Some of the station names — Haverford and Merion for instance — were original, and genuinely Welsh. Others, Bryn Mawr and Wynnewood, were brandnew as place names, being derived from the names of former nearby estates. George Roberts himself Welshed things up by changing the names of such stations as West Haverford, Elm and Morgan's Corner to Rosemont, Narberth and Radnor respectively.* Now everybody assumes these all date from 1682, like the Robertses; but as Chestnut Hill people like to say, "nobody but Welsh peasants lived on the Main Line till the Railroad built it up."

However, it was Roberts and the Railroad that began the process of mass suburbanization which soon gutted the city of Philadelphia. The automobile completed the process, and in turn gutted the railroad. Now the commuters who are left have become the Railroad's greatest headache, and the automobile suburbs are defeating themselves by overcrowding, cheap build-

* The mnemonic device for remembering the first stations on the Main Line is: "Old Maids Never Wed And Have Babies Period." (Overbrook, Merion, Narberth, Wynnewood, Ardmore, Haverford, Bryn Mawr; the "P" is for Paoli, the end of the line.)

[196]

ing and jammed traffic. No city has been more victimized by its ruthless transportation than Philadelphia.

Certainly no system of transportation was more sublimely ruthless, if still always respectable, than the Pennsylvania Railroad in its great years; but its great years have been over for some time. In 1952 Broad Street Station was torn down. The closing of the station was a sentimental occasion. As the last train pulled out, the Philadelphia Orchestra, crammed onto the observation platform, played "Auld Lang Syne" and there was not a dry eye in the concourse. The indignity of the Chinese Wall was gradually removed — where is poor Filbert Street? — and in its place extends that nasty, new, big, bare esplanade, Pennsylvania Boulevard, culminating in the Corinthian pillars of the new neoclassic 30th Street Station. On the site of the Old Broad Street Station sits Penn Center, largest, if most mistaken, effort of the Philadelphia Renaissance.

Roberts's memorial is gone. Its only souvenir is a big sculptured relief mural, symbolizing "Transportation," which used to be in the waiting room on Broad Street, now in 30th Street Station. It is full of lavishly bosomed figures riding in chariots and bearing wheels. In the far right-hand corner are several cupids holding models of the New Era: a steam locomotive, a paddlewheel river boat. The smallest cherub carries an old dirigible with wings. No cherub carries a model of the gasoline engine, but that's what wrecked this particular pageant. Trucks ride noisily over highways paid for and paid for by you and me, bearing the riches of the West over the mountains, while railroads maintain their expensive rights of way and then pay taxes on them. The board of directors of the Railroad is still rather Old Philadelphian, but laced with Midwesterners, though the balance of power still rests in the Right Hands. Later presidents, like Martin Clement or Walter Franklin, or like the forward-looking James Symes, are still accepted by all the clubs and all the boards, but are no longer social leviathans like Cassatt. Lots of Old Philadelphians don't even quite know how "Symes" is pronounced ("Sims" as in *the* Sims). Though the Pennsylvania Railroad is still a going concern, still Number One, and still officially centered in Philadelphia, things are certainly not what they were in the Iron Age. The empty marble reaches of 30th Street Station are full of the echoes of vanished power.

iii.   *The Iron Triangle III: Coal*

THINGS TEND TO COME in twos in Philadelphia. There are two rivers, the Delaware and the Schuylkill; two principal suburban districts, Chestnut Hill and the Main Line; two really acceptable men's clubs, the Philadelphia and the Rittenhouse; two old insurance companies, the Hand-in-Hand and the Green Tree; two really acceptable jewelers, Bailey, Banks & Biddle (no relation!) * and Caldwell's; two undertakers, Bringhurst and Bair. There are also two railroads.

The Pennsylvania Railroad is of course the Great Railroad, *the* Railroad. The other Philadelphia railroad is the Reading. The Reading is a rival of the Pennsylvania Railroad as a commuting line to Chestnut Hill, and connoisseurs take it nowadays to New York as being far more pleasant and convenient for Wall Streeters, at least. It has acquired somewhat the same detached, superior and slightly intellectual prestige as Chestnut Hill itself, and partisans of the Reading regard the Pennsylvania Railroad as distinctly middle-class.

This was not always true, and the Reading was once a very rowdy road indeed. In the old days nice young Philadelphia girls were permitted to travel unescorted on Mr. Roberts's railroad, but not on the Reading. It was and still is par excellence the coal road. Its main artery runs due north into the mountains and the mines. In its heyday it represented capitalism and absentee landlordism in its most brutal form. The story of the Reading is, in fact, the story of Coal, third side of Pennsylvania's and Philadelphia's Iron Triangle.

* One sometimes ponders on the fate, in Philadelphia, of being a socially respectable Biddle who is *no relation.*

Though coal, hard coal, has tone, it doesn't have quite as much tone as iron or railroads. It's considerably younger than iron, and considerably smaller scale than railroading, though a trifle older. It has been a dirty business in every sense of the word; yet it also involved in its earlier phases some fine pioneering courage and inventiveness. The history of the Reading Railroad takes in most of the dirtier aspects of coal. The cleanest and oldest aspects of mining history are summed up in the chronicle of the Lehigh Coal and Navigation Company, nicknamed The Old Company. Founded about 1792, it is the first and oldest corporation of its kind, and one of the older existing corporations of any kind in the country. In its great days, beginning about 1820 and ending about 1920, it was a formidable institution.

Coal has always been used. Even in America where wood was so plentiful, some Virginia coal was mined commercially before the Revolution. This was soft coal, and was not popular, at least domestically, because of its smoke and smell. Industrially, in the making of iron, charcoal was still preferred. As for anthracite, or "stone coal" as it was called, it couldn't be burned in an ordinary fireplace, and "practical men" didn't seem to catch on to the grate, though it had been used successfully throughout the later eighteenth century here and there.

The Old Company was the first coal-producing organization to break down the resistance of "practical men," and women, to the use of anthracite in Philadelphia. During those expansive and speculative years after the Revolution, a Colonel Jacob Weiss hopefully acquired land up in the mountains along the Lehigh River. One day coal was discovered there by accident. Weiss brought the accidental specimen to Philadelphia, showed it to friends, and a professor at the University certified that it was not only anthracite, but that, contrary to popular belief, it was burnable. Various friends of Weiss's interested themselves in coal promotion. Among them was John Nicholson, who had been comptroller of the finances of the state of Pennsylvania and a Revolutionary money hero, and who in turn interested Robert Morris and even a cautious contemporary Anthony Morris, in the project. They bought several thousand acres in what had been derisively if poetically nicknamed the "Wilderness of St. Anthony"; and in 1792 the Lehigh Coal Company saw the light.

Things looked good; but unfortunately just about that time most of the principal backers went bankrupt. Nicholson joined Morris in debtors' prison, and died there leaving eight children and four million dollars' worth of debts, a tidy sum in any age. Only Colonel Weiss kept the company going, at least in name and ownership of lands.

Various efforts to bring the coal downriver had been made, but even when they succeeded in getting it down, nobody would buy the stuff. Unburnable. Josiah White was the man who proved to Philadelphia that stone coal *was* burnable. White was a typical early nineteenth-century "energetic Yankee" (from New Jersey). He began with an interest in canals, and his original venture in 1810 was a dam and lock at the Falls of the Schuylkill. Until then navigation had been obstructed there by the rapids. This was the first such taming of a major river in the United States, and Josiah not only made money out of the lock, charging tolls on barge traffic, but he also created a small rolling mill there.

The dam, now right in the middle of the city between 30th Street Station and the Art Museum, had a tremendous effect on Philadelphia. For one thing, it opened the Schuylkill and all its rich commerce to river traffic, and was the first step in the eventually important Schuylkill canal system. For another, the backed-up water bred mosquitoes. This made the country estates along the banks of the river unsalubrious. The rich owners deserted them, the derelict estates were bought by the city, and Fairmount Park is the result. Still another effect was the use of the still water by sportsmen — skaters and oarsmen — who thus created, thanks indirectly to White, one of the most characteristically pleasant aspects of Philadelphia life. The dam, or its successor, remains.

Josiah White's rolling mill however got into trouble. Desperate for fuel during the embargo of 1812, White bought some of the "unburnable" stone coal for use in his little factory. But this particular load of Old Company coal seemed, as everyone said, to be unburnable. The workmen stoked all night, and were finally sent home. One workman however, who had returned for a forgotten jacket, discovered what he thought was a fire at the mill. It turned out to be the furnace, red-hot at last with the steady long-lasting blaze of anthracite.

This fortunate demonstration turned White's interest permanently away from canals and iron to coal. He sold off his interests at the Falls of the Schuylkill, and went up to the Lehigh River. There, with a younger partner called Erskine Hazard, he took over the Old Company's workings and tamed the rapids of the Lehigh as he had tamed the Falls of the Schuylkill. Soon he was able to send downstream all the coal anybody wanted. But still nobody wanted it.

His two chief enemies were the reluctant Philadelphia capitalist and the reluctant Philadelphia public, both just chock-full of Quaker caution. He and Hazard went to town to drum up some backing, and White has left a succinct account of what it was, even still is, like to raise money in Philadelphia:

> Joshua Longstreth appointed an evening for us to explain the subject to him. In the evening we called to see him but he was gone next door to a party to have some fun (magnanimous interest thought I and worthy the man).
>
> Benj. Stillé was polite eno. to allow of some general remarks, but said he was unable to appreciate them.
>
> John Stillé sd. politely how do do sires, how do you come on with the Lehigh? and before we could give him an answer he proceeded to read his newspaper and was so engaged at reading the chitchat of the day, he no longer had time to bid us good night.

Stephen Girard, and Napoleon's brother Joseph Bonaparte living at Bordentown, New Jersey, both turned the Lehigh down. Nobody nibbled. At last, however, this dam of Philadelphia reserve and condescension broke; a man called Shoemaker said he would raise fifty thousand dollars in return for twenty shares of Lehigh stock. In one day he managed what the boys had been unable to do in months. The third subscriber was jaunty Condy Raguet, founder of the PSFS. August, 1818, saw the creation of the Lehigh Navigation Company as a subsidiary of the Lehigh Coal Company.

They now had the coal, the transportation facilities, even the capital. The public remained to be convinced. The person who finally broke down their resistance was not a capitalist, but a woman. Josiah White's wife, a shy Quaker bluestocking, launched a sales campaign among the ladies of the city, and to her is really due the final success of anthracite in America during the nineteenth century.

She set up a burning grate, visible from the street, and an advertisement in the paper stated that "orders will be taken for Lehigh coal at 172 Mulberry st. It may be seen burning at the above address." And in another, "Stone coal . . . is free of all smoke . . . and consequently the chimney never gets foul. Its beauty in an open grate exceeds any other fuel known." Ironmakers began to design grates for the parlor, suitably ornamental. Friends of Mrs. White joined in her crusade. "Some patriotic ladies are exhibiting sample fires in their grates, among them the Widow Guest of Sansom Street." The power of women, even then not to be underestimated, turned the tide. In 1823 Josiah risked sending nine thousand tons downriver. The whole cargo sold. By 1826 thirty-one thousand tons went. The nineteenth-century coal boom was on, and for fifty years, until central heating finally displaced it, the coal grate superseded the wood fireplace as the proper hearth fire.

On the strength of new prosperity, White built a mansion in Mauch Chunk, center of his operations on the Lehigh, surrounded, like Mark Bird's of an earlier time, by parks, pleasances and even peacocks. The curious flocked in summer to see the new wonders and enjoy the salubrious mountain air. A "Mansion House" was built for the hundreds of genteel visitors, and Mauch Chunk became a spa and a local rival to Saratoga or the Catskills. The chief wonder was one of America's first operating railroads, a gravity affair, which switchbacked down from the mines to the river at the mad pace of sixteen miles per hour, carrying alternate loads of coal, shrieking ladies and mules. The mules rode down, calmly chomping hay, and then pulled the cars back up again. It was said that a decent Mauch Chunk mule could not be got to walk downhill after growing used to rail travel.

This Utopian picture of contented workmen, gay tourists and peacock-surrounded manor house, which led an enthusiast of the 1830's to describe Mauch Chunk as "a Paradise, the truth of a Socialist's dream, a patriarchal community in modern times," gradually changed as the century wore on. The surface mines, where rosy- if dirty-faced children gathered nuggets while their parents merrily plied the pick, gave way to underground works, manned by more professional but surlier types. Labor trouble, which began as early as 1833 elsewhere, finally came to Mauch Chunk in the 'forties, and from then on the atmosphere of a patriarchal paradise evaporated.

The Old Company, like the P.R.R., eventually fell like a ripe plum into the hands of its board of directors and Old Philadelphia. An Edward W. Clark of the banking family was one of its most successful later presidents, and Philadelphia clans of considerable modern position like the Leisenrings and the Rileys owe that position to fortunes made in the Lehigh Coal and Navigation Company.

The Old Company, around the time of White's retirement, ceased to be the only operation in the coal fields. For one thing, there came into being the rival Lehigh Valley Railroad, started by a shrewd Yankee called Asa Packer. He became the richest man in Pennsylvania and founded Lehigh College. To the southwest, in the Schuylkill Valley, the industry was dominated not so much by any one individual pioneer as by one pioneer company — the Reading Railroad.

The Reading, chartered in 1833, well before the Pennsy, carried traffic between Philadelphia and Reading by 1839, and reached the coal country at Mount Carbon in 1842. Eventually it absorbed its rival, the Schuylkill Canal, and after the Civil War gradually came to dominate the whole anthracite business.

Moncure Robinson, who began to lay out his masterpiece, the

tracks of the Reading, as early as 1834, differed in various ways from the typical J. Edgar Thomson–Josiah White–John Wanamaker figure of a Founder. He was for one thing of a well-bred Virginia family, a student at William and Mary in 1817 (alma mater of his wife's cousin Thomas Jefferson), and had traveled much abroad. He was essentially an intellectual engineer, rather than a railroad man, and his interests were as much theoretical as practical; and always more professional than financial (though he did all right that way too). He began, like George Washington, as a surveyor and more or less taught himself by study and observation the infant art of railroad building.

Like Josiah White, he found the Philadelphia capitalists a laggard group. Unlike Josiah, he had connections; when Philadelphia refused to support the building of his railroad, he simply went to England and there found the backing he needed. From a design he picked up there, with a few improvements of his own, he had constructed in Philadelphia a revolutionary locomotive, which he named the "Gowan and Marx" in honor of his English backers. Considering the later lurid history of the Reading, it was a sinisterly prophetic name. The Gowan and Marx made such a sensation that its fame spread back to England. The Russian Ambassador there heard about it, got in touch with the English backers and finally sent a delegation over to Philadelphia to look at the engine and to persuade Robinson to come to Russia and build railroads and locomotives for the Czar. Robinson refused. One George Whistler took on the job in his stead; and it was there in St. Petersburg that the engineer's son James first got his taste for painting and residence in foreign parts.

Robinson stayed home in America, and after safely launching the Reading, retired to Philadelphia at the age of forty-five, raised a family of ten children, and cultivated his investments. He had married a kin of the Virginia Randolphs, and as his grandson George Biddle remarks in his autobiography, the Moncure Robinsons "considered themselves something like royalty, and looked down on all Philadelphians as rather middle class and stuffy."

Robinson lived to be ninety, by which time his Reading Railroad had gone through some of its stormier episodes. There was no question here of a "Socialist's dream of Paradise." The coal business of the Schuylkill Valley, on which the Reading Railroad depended, was run by competing hardfisted types who were not in the least interested in socialist dreams or patriarchial communities. They treated their immigrant mine workers accordingly. Most thoroughly exploited and resentful were the Irish, who after 1848 began to displace the native English and German-speaking miners of the earlier and easier days of surface mining. Attempts at unionism had failed. A Bates Union of 1850 collapsed when Mr. Bates, the president, absconded with the funds. No more successful, but violently effective in stirring up trouble, was a later organization after the Civil War, known as the Molly Maguires. As might be deduced from the jolly name, they were Irish, but they were not very jolly; they were, in fact, a terrorist secret organization, like the Sicilian Mafia, who devoted themselves to assassinating the opposition. Mine superintendents died like flies, and so did any workers that crossed the mob. The local *Miner's Journal* of Pottsville listed some fifty murders between 1863 and 1867.

The man who broke up the Molly Maguires was a bright lad named Franklin B. Gowen, himself the son of an Irish immigrant to Philadelphia, but of a less violent and more affluent breed. Gowen, no relation to the Gowan of the Gowan and Marx, became a lawyer, after some experience in the coal world, and in 1870 became president of the Reading, after being their legal counsel for several years. He broke the Molly Maguires by hiring a Pinkerton detective, James McParlan, also an Irishman, who under an assumed name joined the inner circles and who, in the famous trial of 1875, in which Gowen was the prosecutor, exposed and identified the ringleaders. All twenty-four were found guilty, ten were hanged and the rest sentenced to jail. The Molly Maguires, as sad local folk ballads testify, were finished.

Franklin Gowen, on the strength of this spectacular victory, went on as president of the Reading to an attempt to corner the anthracite for the railroad. The Reading bought up all the coal lands available and became, as it continued to be for years, the dominant single influence in the world of hard coal; but not under Gowen. He was, it seems, a bit ahead of his time. He was caught short in mid-expansion, the company broke in 1880 and went into a long series of receiverships. Gowen resigned, returned to the practice of law, and in 1889 shot himself in a hotel in Washington. Rumors that he was murdered by revengeful surviving Molly Maguires seem to have no real basis.* Gowens have persisted in Philadelphia respectability ever since. James E. Gowen, retired chairman of the Girard Trust and onetime president of the Philadelphia Club, is of the same family.

It is at this point presumably that the Philadelphia Oligarchy should have, and probably would have, stepped in as they did in the case of the Pennsylvania Railroad and the Old Company. That is, the Reading was ripe enough, and should have been safe. They were prevented, however, by an even bigger Oligarch, J. P. Morgan the elder. The story is one of those complicated and fantastic bits of grandiose brigandage so craggily characteristic of the age of the robber barons.

Gowen, who was after all a fairly small herring in this world of big sharks, had had the presumptuous idea of making the Reading a rival of the great Pennsylvania Railroad, largely through his control of coal and various smaller northern and western railroads. After his debacle, the idea continued to please Vanderbilt and the New York Central interests. The Pennsylvania Railroad, equally aggressive, was out to challenge the Central in turn by building its own line up the west side of the Hudson River. The Central retaliated by getting hold of the Reading in one of its periods of reorganization, and beginning something called the Southern Pennsylvania Railroad as a parallel line west to Pittsburgh. It was the Battle of the Century. Vanderbilt and Carnegie between them chipped in some ten million, and the

---

* A. Conan Doyle, who dearly loved secret terrorist organizations, dearly loved the Molly Maguires. His book *The Valley of Fear* is laid partly in the Pennsylvania mine fields and concerns such a murder of retribution.

line of the Southern Pennsylvania Railroad was surveyed and tunnels were dug through the Alleghenies.

J. P. Morgan, however, had financial interests in both camps, and besides was disturbed at his Hudson River summer place, Cragston, by the blasting on the Pennsy's new West Shore Line. He decided that enough was enough. He invited George Roberts of the Pennsylvania Railroad and Chauncey Depew of the Central to his yacht, so felicitously called the *Corsair*. Holding them more or less prisoners on his floating pirate palace, he told them to make peace — or else. For hours the *Corsair* steamed through New York Bay as the two railroad titans fought it out. Roberts refused to give in till the very last minute. As he stepped ashore in New Jersey to take his private car back to Philadelphia, he agreed to Morgan's simple plan: the Pennsylvania Railroad would give up its West Shore line if the Central would give up its Southern Pennsylvania line. And it was done. Of course this ruined the poor little Reading once more, which had been counting on the new line west to make it important. In the new bankruptcy that followed, J. P. Morgan quietly slipped in and found himself a Hard Coal King, as well as king of various other aspects of American economic life. Perhaps this had been his real idea all along. The roadbed of the Southern Pennsylvania Railroad with its expensive tunnels lay idle and overgrown for years until, in 1938, it became the route of the Pennsylvania Turnpike, first of its kind, and herald of a new world of semi-socialized automobile transportation that was and is a far more deadly threat to the Pennsylvania Railroad than Vanderbilt ever thought of being. In a delayed and oblique way, the Reading has had its revenge.

The Reading, though now financially stable, was not to enjoy Morgan's Peace for long. In 1901 Morgan had installed as president of the Reading George Frederick Baer, a lawyer and newspaperman from Reading, early identified as Morgan's local representative, who had first made his reputation as a conductor of successful damage suits *against* the Reading. The year after, in 1902, occurred the first important successful strike in the history of anthracite, that of the United Mine Workers, 150,000 strong under the leadership of John Mitchell. Morgan would not involve himself, and so as his delegate, Baer immediately became the leader of the operators.

He simply refused to recognize or deal with the strikers at all. During the controversy, he carried on a correspondence with a soft-hearted gentleman of Wilkes Barre who appealed to him to end the strike in the name of Christian charity. At one point Baer was moved to answer: "The rights and interests of the laboring man will be protected and cared for . . . not by the labor agitators, but by the Christian men whom God in his infinite wisdom has given control of the property interests of the country." Unfortunately for Baer this ineffable pronunciamento got into the hands of the press, and soon the country, already emerging into the era of Teddy Roosevelt and the muckrakers, was convulsed with derision and denunciation. Despite Baer's further ukase that "we will give no consideration to any plan of arbitration or mediation or to any interference on the part of any outside party," Teddy Roosevelt stepped in with his big stick and the strike was settled in favor of the strikers. It was a great victory not only for unionism, but for the principle of government interference, and the beginning of the end of total "freedom of enterprise," so aptly caricatured by "Divine Right" Baer's arrogant words, invariably quoted as a pure gem of that specious identification of Christianity and money-making so popular at that time with John Wanamaker and others.

Since then the Reading has had a slightly more peaceful existence, captained or controlled by such Morgan men as Edward Stotesbury, and at present headed by a typical self-made "hired man," Revelle Brown, now chairman of the board, a native of Illinois who by merit and skill raised himself up the ladder from laborer to president of the Lehigh Valley Railroad and then president of the Reading. As such he has made important boards like the PSFS and John Wanamaker's, and is a member of the Racquet, but not the Philadelphia Club. Old Philadelphia is represented on the Reading board by J. Hamilton Chetson, the Chestons having, not surprisingly, Morgan connections.

iv. Petty Kings

THE DESCENDANTS of the coal families — Hazard, Leisenring, Clark, Gowen, Baer, everybody in fact except White — are still very much about in Philadelphia, and their present general acceptability, clubbability and connection by marriage has done much to maintain and enrich the "tone" which coal, especially hard coal, especially in Philadelphia, does have. This tone, however, does not have to depend for its final luster on such worthy if comparatively recent family connections. After all, even the Clarks are only nineteenth-century bankers ("not really Old Philadelphians"), and Robinson was not even a real Philadelphian of any vintage. What Roberts did for railroads was done for coal by the Coxes.

> Morris, Norris, Rush and Chew,
> Drinker, Dallas, Coxe and Pugh . . .

runs the Philadelphia Rosary, and though never quite as prominent either as a family or in its individual members as many of these other families, the Coxes have managed to preserve themselves for two and a half centuries and to maintain a certain quirky family resemblance, a trait of individualistic oddity that marks them from the beginning and on down to the present.

The first of the line was certainly an odd one. He was not an American, since he never set foot on the soil, but he had great interests here. He was a Dr. Daniel Coxe who as a physician to King Charles II and his successors flourished in London for many decades at the end of the seventeenth and well into the eighteenth centuries. He was a graduate of Cambridge, a member of the Royal Society, a writer on chemistry, and an avid land speculator. At one time he bought New Jersey; or at least half of it, and as owner of it was technically Governor of West Jersey from 1687 to 1692, though he never even saw it. He then unloaded Jersey in favor of lands farther west, specifically a tract called misleadingly "Caro*lana*," which was the western extension of Virginia and the Caro*linas* over towards the Mississippi. He sent two vessels up the river to explore it, and conceived elaborate plans for creating an ideal commonwealth or settling refugee Huguenots there, all of which came to nothing. For one thing, a lot of the land was claimed by France or Spain. He wrote and published a good deal in the way of accounts and advertisements of these tracts of his, in one of which he says that he had "made greate discoveryes towards the greate Lake . . . and contracted Friendship with diverse petty Kings" — all in his fancy of course since he never left London.

He sent his son Daniel, Jr., to check into the great "discoveryes" and "petty Kings," and Daniel settled, becoming progenitor of all the American Coxes. This "fine, flaunting gentleman" eloped with a Quaker, Miss Eckley, and eventually got himself expelled from Jersey for political reasons, surely one of the few men in history to earn that peculiar distinction. He was also the first appointed Grand Master of Masons in the colonies.

From him descended an extensive family, some of them remaining in New Jersey, others removing to Philadelphia. Later Coxes have been characterized by some of the crotchets and odd interests of the Doctor, their progenitor. John Redman Coxe for instance, an outstanding nineteenth-century figure, wrote all sorts of pamphlets with titles like *Considerations Respecting the Recognition of Friends in Another World* and *Soul in Brutes*. A William Coxe in New Jersey became a world-famous pomologist (apples). Not many of us are pomologists. Arthur Middleton Young, a modern descendant on the distaff side, is one of America's experts not only on vertical flight (helicopters) but also on astrology (astrology, not astronomy).

As far as coal is concerned, the link is Tench Coxe, Revolutionary figure, merchant, politician, economist, Assistant Secretary of the Treasury and, like his ancestors and his friends Robert Morris, James Wilson and John Nicholson, land speculator. In

politics he was famous for sudden conversions; from Tory to
Patriot during the Revolution, from Federalist to Republican
after it. In economics he continues that line of Philadelphia
protectionists beginning with Francis Rawle and extending up
through Mathew and Henry Carey.

As a land speculator he had better luck than Morris, Wilson
and Nicholson. As early as the 1780's, he bought great tracts of
mountain land in the Wilderness of St. Anthony, and unlike
Morris and Nicholson, managed to leave these lands to his heirs.

One of Tench's grandsons, Eckley, was trained as an engineer,
and in 1865 founded the Cross Creek Coal Company, with thirty-
five thousand acres near Drifton in the mountains, and its own
railroad. In 1906 the Coxes sold out their mining rights to Asa
Packer's Lehigh Valley Railroad for nineteen million dollars, but
kept the land, and the family still divides itself into Drifton and
Philadelphia dwellers. Eckley's brothers, Brinton, Alexander,
Henry and Charles, all mined and married well, and the result
has been to tie the Coxes pretty firmly and prosperously to the
center of the Web.

It is a temptation here to indulge in a sunset burst of genealogy; for though it might take a bit of work to get Leisenrings
and Baers enwebbed, it would be no trouble at all as far as the
Coxes are concerned. They're *related*. Eckley himself married
a Fisher, cousin of Sidney. Tench Coxe got his first name by
descent from Tench Francis (Chew, Shippen). A New Jersey
branch married the McMurtries, who in turn married McCalls
and Biddles. Algernon Biddle, whose mother was a McMurtrie,
married the daughter of Moncure Robinson of the Reading. And
so forth, quite endlessly.

As for anthracite itself nowadays, that is another and sadder
story. Soft coal has superseded it industrially, fuel oil has taken
over the domestic furnaces.* The big companies, though still
owners and controllers, do comparatively little business. Just in
1960 the Old Company shut down its last mine in Panther Valley, where White began his operations. Stone coal is not quite

* See John O'Hara's *Appointment in Samarra*.

dead yet, but it has been steadily dying ever since the First War. Fewer and fewer Philadelphia family fortunes are made or sustained by it.

v. Whither?

THERE IS, in fact, a dying fall to most of this recital of the Philadelphia Oligarchy's economic roots, and the manure around Philadelphia's family trees is unquestionably bleached out. However, life does go on. Banking may not be what it was in the time of Biddle, but most Old Philadelphia banks weathered the great depression of the 'thirties and they are still there. Family concerns fold up like flowers in frost, but some still persist. The Pennsylvania Railroad and the Reading have faced bankruptcy and the competition of the truck, but they are still running. Coal is no longer the universal fuel, but it is not completely outmoded. Iron and steel may have moved to Pittsburgh, but there are steel mills yet along the Schuylkill. The Iron Triangle is a frail, worn thing nowadays, and is still weakening, but fortunately for Philadelphia it does not support the whole city. From the earliest times Philadelphia's prosperity has been various. The diversification of the city's early family firms, the Morris breweries, the Rittenhouse paper mills, has its modern equivalent.

In fact, next to New York, Chicago and Pittsburgh, the Philadelphia area (and this does *not* include Wilmington) is still headquarters for more of America's largest corporations (and this does *not* include the Pennsylvania Railroad) than any other city (and this *does* include Boston, Los Angeles and Detroit) in America. Unfortunately for the Oligarchy, the particular boom areas of the modern Philadelphia economy, electronics, aircraft and chain supermarkets, are not in the hands of the Right People. Such newfangled industries seem to be controlled either by great national companies like General Electric that have no appreciable Philadelphia connections or, as in the case of Vertol helicopters, by local non-U self-made men, whose boards are not even remotely Old Philadelphian.

Still, the Pew Oil empire, the Dorrance's Campbell Soup and the Scott Paper Company in Chester do manage to pour a good deal of revenue, one way or another, sometimes by marriage, into Old Philadelphia pockets (a present Israel Wistar Morris is married to a Pew; a Charlotte Dorrance of Campbell Soup is married to William Coxe Wright). The families that still control these companies have not only married in, and made places for Old Philadelphians on their boards, but have essentially, particularly in the case of the Pews, gone a long way towards becoming Old Philadelphian themselves. In a couple of generations, with luck, they will be pillars of the establishment. All is not lost, though in general most Old Philadelphians, exercising their privileges of disparagement, will tell you that all is.

Philadelphia is still prosperous; but the decline and the threat of further decline is obvious. Not only is there a general decline, but there is a particular decline in the dominance by the Oligarchy. They had concentrated their wealth and interests in just those areas of the Iron Triangle that have declined most. As in every other American city, the large impersonal corporation has tended to take over the economy more and more, leaving Philadelphia and the Philadelphians behind.

The question is now: whither? Will some new opportunity, some unexpected bonanza come to the city's rescue as coal and the steam locomotive did a century ago? Will, for instance, the city's political and civic Renaissance somehow be able to stop the obsolescence of the city's real estate by the revitalizing shock of progressive political projects and plans?

Perhaps the future lies not in Philadelphia itself, but in Philadelphia's position at the center of something known as the Delaware Valley Development. There is a great amount of to-do about this Delaware Valley Development, and while Philadelphia itself has not been flourishing, the region around it, from Trenton to Wilmington, certainly has. Philadelphia and its banks and its workers and its stores and its transportation services are right in the middle of all this.

Philadelphia is the only regional center of social and cultural prestige. The Du Ponts for instance are not Philadelphian. They have never permitted themselves to be in the least influenced or absorbed by the Philadelphia Oligarchy. Comparatively few Du Pont marriages have been made with Philadelphians, considering propinquity and the number of available Du Ponts. Nonetheless, the neighborhood *is* close. The Philadelphia fox hunters south in Unionville are mixed inevitably with the horsy owners of northerly Wilmington estates. Marriages *are* made, such as the recent one between a Biddle of Andalusia and the daughter of L. Du Pont Copeland. Crawford Greenewalt, the recent chairman of the board of Du Pont, is on the board of the Philadelphia Orchestra. Du Ponts and their relations are listed in the Philadelphia Social Register. The Philadelphia Web is there, it centers about City Hall; it will be interesting to observe whether it will be able to extend itself, catch and hold the very big new flies of the big new Delaware Valley boom. Perhaps by extension, the walls of the Forbidden City can be enlarged to include further reaches and further riches, and Philadelphia's new economic salvation will come not this time from the hills with their coal and iron but from the closer riverbanks.

vi. The List

LAW, MEDICINE, banking, insurance, iron, railroads, coal — all this, however, to an Old Philadelphian is not so much important in itself, as because it has provided a basis for *Families*. In Philadelphia the feeling is not so much that the law has made Biddles and Cadwaladers important as that Biddles and Cadwaladers have condescended to honor the law — and that must mean that law is worthwhile. Banking did not so much make Effingham Morris and Benjamin Rush significant; it was, if anything, the other way round. To talk or even think of the Robertses as being a "railroad family" or the Coxes as being "in coal" or the Whartons "in nickel" would naturally be a gross indelicacy. Law and medicine are, of course, on another plane, so that with

Ingersolls, Rawles and Pepper it is somewhat different; but even so, it's just a tiny bit better to be really above it all, like the Biddles and Cadwaladers, than to be too exclusively identified. As for a family like the Wanamakers whose actual name is still in business, so to speak, it will be a good many generations before they can really stand on their own feet as a family, divorced from economic considerations, in the way that a real Old Philadelphia family should stand.

This consideration of Philadelphia's somewhat exhausted "working world" has had then a hidden motive: to introduce, in some reasonable context, a few of the endless number of names that an Old Philadelphian knows, has to know, assumes that everyone else knows; the List which all Old Philadelphians carry around with them. Nobody knows, or has to know for instance, what any given Morris *does*. Nobody much in fact cares. But everyone has to know who the Morrises *are*. All families of course get into Position because somebody did something; not the act but the fact counts now.

The names on this List, many of which have been mentioned under law or banking, as well as many others which just won't get mentioned, form the basis of most Old Philadelphia thought, talk and interest. Rawle, Coxe, Norris, McKean, Roberts, Hopkinson, Cassatt, Drexel and all the hundreds of others — in Philadelphia everybody assumes that everybody knows all that. Not one single solitary day during the entire year passes without at least one of the newspapers somewhere mentioning one, or many more, of the names on the List — in the Society pages; in the obituaries, where the Names always get more comparative space that others; in connection with good works, where an Old Philadelphian is usually presenting a medal or an award to a non–Old Philadelphian; even occasionally in the news, as when Thomas Gates, definitely a Web member, gets to be Secretary of Defense or when Senator Clark advocates something disturbing. This Rosary, this permanent index, this List, far more than any mere *Who's Who* or *Social Register*, is Old Philadelphia's permanent and favorite biographical and social dictionary.

1

i. Boards

PHILADELPHIANS, *the* Philadelphians, do not live by bread alone; they live by boards. Beyond "work," beyond the Railroad, beyond Family Concerns, beyond even banking and medicine and law, the ultimate goal, the ultimate reward of every good Old Philadelphian is — a chair; to be seated on, and as final accolade, chairman of, a board. This is the perfect expression in Philadelphia of the Sedentary, and the real rulers of Philadelphia are not its presidents, who can be hired ("You don't want to bother with people like that"), but its chairmen, who are usually, like poets, born not made. To be on a good board is reward, recognition, goal. That's where the real prestige and power are, and every aspect of Philadelphia life is securely boarded.

Though usually the importance of the board has something to do with the importance of the activity, this is not alway so. The Pennsylvania Railroad is obviously important, but in Philadelphia the Historical Society is important too. The PSFS is not the very largest of its kind, but to be on the Board of Managers is to be a member of a very good club indeed. Nobody would call the two old insurance companies, the Contributionship and the Mutual, economic giants, but membership on their boards, as we have seen, is one of Philadelphia's highest social distinctions.

For an active and prominent Old Philadelphian, such business boards are only a beginning; springboards to other boards, more definitely altruistic, with even more prestige, if perhaps less real power. There are worthwhile boards: charities, institutions. There are ornamental boards: clubs, hunts, artistic and cultural enterprises. A well-rounded hereditary boardsman will play the field.

Frequently this board life is, and more and more becomes with increasing years, a man's real career, and professional or business success a mere prelude to this final enthronement.

ii. Boards: Worthwhile

NOWHERE HAS the Quaker influence in Philadelphia been so strong and so lasting as in the quiet determined emphasis upon good works. As a result, charitable boards proliferate beyond conception. There are altogether over six hundred recognized charitable activities, and obviously there is room somewhere for anybody who has the heart, purse, energy or conscience to involve himself.

But also obviously some of these institutions are preeminent, and most obviously preeminent is the Pennsylvania Hospital. From the point of view of literary style, variety and general relief, it might be nice to omit what follows; but alas this cannot be done. The sad truth of the matter is that not only was the Pennsylvania Hospital founded by Benjamin Franklin, but it is also the First and Oldest in the country, both as an institution and as a building. The East Wing, the oldest part, built in 1755, is still in use, and always has been, as a ward. A few changes have been made, fortunately, but the ensemble of East Wing, with a central block and West Wing, both added in 1796, following the original design of builder, boardsman and Mayor of Philadelphia, Samuel Rhoads, still presents one of the noblest eighteenth-century monuments in America, comparable to Independence Hall itself.

The Hospital occupies the entire square between 8th and 9th Streets and Spruce and Pine, and various adjuncts spill over the edges, redeeming with medical respectability the fairly rundown antiquity of that area of upper "Society Hill." The principal façade, old brick with white pilasters and facings, looks on Pine Street, stretching the length of the square and dominating a

garden space and curved driveway with that benign combination
of cosy and elegant majesty achieved by the best American eighteenth-century architecture. On the warm walls are the plaques
of the Hand-in-Hand and the Green Tree. The driveway leads
up from two ironwork gates towards a beautiful fanlit doorway;
but it is never used except by pedestrians, and the gates are
never opened. They were traditionally used only for state occasions, and the last occasion considered sufficiently "state" was
supposed to have been the visit of Lafayette in 1824. A century
later, after the First World War, they were to have been opened
once again to welcome Marshal Foch, another touring Frenchman; but Philadelphia was disappointed. Foch never came.
Lord knows what will get them open again.

The modern entrance is around the corner, off 8th Street, into
a courtyard and up steps to the entrance hall. As you go in, a
somewhat baleful expanse of painting fills the back wall, "Christ
Healing the Sick," by Benjamin West. One turns south, from
West, to get to the old hospital proper with its grand double
staircase rising gracefully from the tile floor of the hall. A great
brass chandelier hangs in the stair well and the hall culminates
in that elegant front door through which no VIP now enters.
Flanking the door are an office, and the managers' boardroom,
a beautifully chaste affair full of chairs and portraits. There is
even a clock, though time at board meetings is traditionally supposed to be told by the bells of the "Town Clock" (if any) or
the watch of the "oldest manager present." Any manager who
missed a meeting was to be fined one shilling. Franklin built
up quite a tidy debt that way. The fine is still in effect, at fifty
cents per absence.

Up the stairs is the library, one of the most ancient and valuable collections of medical lore in the New World, a curious
and pleasant room of carved wooden bookcases. Above that, on
the third floor and in a dome, is the tiny blue-painted operating
amphitheatre, first in America. On its walls are little brass tickets
with the names of every intern from the first in 1773 up to 1955,
when they ran out of space. It is a poor Philadelphia medical

family that doesn't have at least one ancestral name up there. There is a proliferation of Morrises, Wistars, Wisters, Meigses, Woods, Hewsons, Norrises, Peppers and all the other dynasties, a John Rodman Paul of 1825 and another John Rodman Paul of 1920.

A clock built by David Rittenhouse guards the door of the library; above its face, instead of the conventional smiling moon, is a little orrery of revolving planets. And of course there are the portraits. Best of all is Eakin's picture of Jacob Da Costa, the weary, sensitive brown figure, definitely exotic for all the Victorianism, against an equally exotic burnt-orange background. Notable are two big Sullys on the second floor. One is a magnificent pale gray full-length picture of pale gray Samuel Coates, a manager, the very embodiment of the Quaker merchant, calm, fresh-faced, cautious, the cool outer light from the window back of him reflecting and symbolizing the cool inner light of his religious conviction. On the other side is its companion piece, an equally interesting portrait, though not quite as good a painting: Dr. Benjamin Rush.

In fact, the souvenir of Philadelphia's three great Benjamins — Franklin, West, Rush — faces you everywhere. They represent the three historic aspects of Old Philadelphia that have gone into the making of Philadelphia and its Hospital — boardsmanship, taste and the professions. On the basis of Franklin, at least, the greatest of these would seem to be boardsmanship.

Though Franklin is credited as its founder, the hospital was, in fact, the brainchild of Dr. Thomas Bond, who, wrote Franklin, in 1751

conceived the idea of . . . a hospital in Philadelphia (a very beneficient design, which has been ascribed to me, but was originally and truly his). The proposal being a novelty in America . . . he met with but little success. At length he came to me with the compliment that he found there was no such thing as carrying a public-spirited project through without my being concerned in it.

Bond was quite right, and once Franklin began to apply his sweet arts of persuasion and publicity, the future of the Hospital was assured. Franklin even managed to get money from the tight-fisted State Assembly; enough for building the East Wing, but not enough for a medical staff. Three doctors generously offered their services free for three years. They were Drs. Thomas Bond, his brother Phineas Bond, and Lloyd Zachary, who thus formed the first real hospital staff in the United States.

The medical "lines" founded by this first staff, and recorded as such, descend, through the eighteenth and nineteenth centuries, in a succession of names nearly all of which have Old Philadelphia connections, medical or otherwise. Line number one, which originates with Dr. Zachary, goes down through the William Shippens, Senior and Junior, to James Hutchinson, first secretary of the College of Physicians, then to Caspar Wistar, and on through names less famous but equally Philadelphian.

Nowadays things are very different. The staff, of course, is in the hundreds, many times the total of the seventy-three who served the Hospital during its first hundred and fifty years. For the present-day gleaner of Old Philadelphia names the roster makes slim pickings. The venerable Dr. George W. Norris is the dean of consulting physicians, and adviser to the board. Dr. Alexander Rush continues the ancestral pattern, and there are a few other such; but Drs. Wendkos, Principato, Economides and Kirshbaum represent the emergence into Philadelphia medicine of national groups not dreamed of by Thomas Bond as inheritors of his practice.

This is certainly not true of Franklin's board of managers, where similar "lines" in many cases, at least for some periods, have been actual lines of descent. They have increased in number too over the years, from an original twelve to a present sixteen, so that some of the "lines" are fairly young. As late as 1959 a new chair was added to make room for a G. Willing Pepper.

Morrises and Biddles have abounded here as in the Hand-in-Hand and the Green Tree (more Morris than Biddle), but as in the case of most Philadelphia institutions one family, the Lewises (later of Pennsalt), are peculiarly identified with the Hospital. Their tenure of office is reminiscent of that of the

James Somers Smiths as treasurers of the Contributionship. Mordecai Lewis, rich in the China trade, was treasurer from 1780 to 1799. He was succeeded by two sons, Joseph S. and Samuel N., and Samuel N. was in turn succeeded by his son John T. When John T. resigned as treasurer in 1881 he was elected a manager. He was followed on the board by his nephew John T., Jr., and when Junior resigned as manager in 1927, John Lewis Evans, a grandson of John T. Lewis, Sr., was elected treasurer, a post he held till 1948. This kind of continuity makes Philadelphians very happy.

Just to confuse matters, no Lewises are now on the board, but a James Somers Smith is; in fact, until very recently he was secretary (of the *Hospital,* that is, not the Hand-in-Hand). There are and always have been other overlappings of the Hospital and insurance. Dr. George Norris, senior member of the staff, is chairman of the Mutual; T. Truxtun Hare, president of the Hospital, is a director of the Contributionship; a Horatio Gates Lloyd is another director, whereas Horatio Gates Lloyd III is now secretary of the Hospital, succeeding Smith. Morris Cheston is chairman of the board of the Hospital; J. Hamilton Cheston is on the board of the Mutual; and so it goes. It remains, that is to say, a fairly small world.

A vast amount of lore, medical and incidental, clusters about the venerable Hospital, none of it more quaint than the connections with that other Philadelphia Benjamin, the expatriated Benjamin West. In 1800 the board of the Hospital wrote to him in London and, stressing the ties of home, asked for a picture. He painted for them a "Christ Healing the Sick." However the picture raised such a furore of admiration in England that noblemen and gentlemen, "solicitous that it should be considered as attached to the country," begged him not to send it to America. Instead, he more or less sold it to them for a purse of three thousand guineas, a good price in any age, and they used West's picture as the commencement and cornerstone of the National Gallery, where such was its popularity that "thousands of people of all descriptions" crowded "weekly into the gallery to have a

sight of it." One wonders if the British Public are today sufficiently grateful to West and the board of the Pennsylvania Hospital for giving their Gallery such an initial boost.

West was more gratified by all this than the managers of the
Hospital, though they perforce made allowances for "the dilemma
into which the most celebrated historical painter of the age has
been placed, by a powerful appeal of the principal patrons of
the art, in a country where his genius has been fostered." West,
however, had promised them a copy, an even better version, he
thought, since "my exertions are more complete . . . as I have
introduced a demoniac with his attendent relations." In 1817
it finally arrived, with its demoniac bonus, and a special house,
after suggestions made by West himself, was built for it on the
Hospital grounds. There in the so-called Picture House the painting was exhibited until 1843, earning for the Hospital over the
years some twenty-five thousand dollars in entrance fees. This
time the managers were more gratified than West, who rather
objected to the design of the Picture House; it had been done
Gothick, at least to the extent of pointed windows. This in the
opinion of the artist was

a misapplication . . . to a Place where the Refinement of Science is
to be inculcated, and which in my humble opinion ought to have been
founded on those clear and self evident Principles adopted by the
Greeks [*i.e.,* columns]. It is the Gothic Taste I combat with, as inapplicable to the Building in question, for that Architecture is the
Insignia of a Period, when the civilized World had passed away, Science
had fled and the Mind of Man lay in Darkness. Then arose monkish
superstition and monkish taste — but now that Science has arisen, let
the Cities of America in their streets and in their Highways proclaim
its Ascendency by every visible Mark of its eternal Truth. . . .

Washington, D.C., at least has obliged.

The picture now greets the visitor as he comes in the main
entrance. The Gothic picture house itself was used by the College
of Physicians and later by the Historical Society and was finally
torn down in the 1890's to make room for more wards.

A chair belonging to William Penn, from Pennsbury, his

manor on the Delaware, two vivid busts by William Rush of fierce cousin Dr. Rush and sternly handsome Dr. Wistar, a punch bowl made in China about 1800 with a picture of the Hospital on it, presented by Joseph Lewis of the China trading family and then presented back to his nephew in 1873 — all these and other souvenirs in or associated with the Hospital make for a rich aromatic Philadelphia atmosphere. The ancient edifice rests firmly upon its cornerstone, inscribed by Dr. Franklin himself:

> In the year of Christ
> MDCCLV
> George the Second Happily Reigning
> (For he sought the Happiness of His People)
> Philadelphia Flourishing
> (For its Inhabitants were Publick Spirited)
> This Building
> By the Bounty of the Government
> and of many Private Persons
> was Piously Founded
> For the Relief of the Sick and Miserable:
> May the God of Mercies
> Bless the Undertaking

Laid in 1755 with Masonic rites, the cornerstone holds up a great medical superstructure of wards and laboratories staffed by a group whose members represent a total spectrum of the modern world of medical science. Guiding the destinies of it all presides the board of sixteen men, descended from and connected in numberless ways to the flourishing Philadelphia of George the Second — happily, it would sometimes seem, still reigning.

In a pecking order based on the antiquity of Old Philadelphianism, but all below the Hospital, come the rest of Philadelphia's charitable boards. Some are very old, like the board that administers the Friends Hospital, where the same names — Emlen, Cope, Matlack, Scattergood — are liable to appear nowadays as they appeared in the 1750's. Even older, but definitely not better, is the board of the Philadelphia General Hospital. This is a huge municipal hospital which can trace its ancestry back even further than the Pennsylvania Hospital, to an almshouse of 1732 which was the first place in the United States where public medical service was available. As a result learned old gentlemen have been bickering for years over the firstness of the two hospitals, Pennsylvania and Philadelphia. But, after all, the Philadelphia was an almshouse, not strictly a hospital; and besides the history of the Philadelphia and its board has been so disgraceful over the years that most Philadelphians just don't like to think about it.

The trouble with the Philadelphia was that same board, the so-called Guardians of the Poor. Instead of being an hereditary succession of gentlemen of property and probity like the board of the Pennsylvania, it was a board appointed by the city fathers, or even, God save us, publicly elected. The result is that it was always more interested in its quarterly wine dinners than in the Poor, and has periodically disgraced itself. In the nineteenth century it was nicknamed the "Board of Buzzards." No respectable Philadelphian would have anything to do with it. Quarrels with the medical staff, always the best that the city could provide, exploded at intervals, so that the hospital was frequently without doctors. Relations were so strained that the slightest incident could lead to a debacle of this sort. Once in 1845, for instance, a cockroach walked across the interns' dining table. The quarrel that developed from the interns' complaints became so nasty that all the doctors resigned and the hospital remained virtually unattended for nine years. The insane ward, with its macabre balls and its "tranquillizing chair" (the obstreperous patient was strapped to a chair with a bladder full of ice on his shaved head until he was "tranquillized" into unconsciousness) presented scenes worthy of Dickens or Hogarth.

In modern times all has been reformed and "tranquillized," and even the board is fairly genteel, if scarcely fashionable. But the moral has certainly not been lost on Philadelphians: An institution is known by the board it keeps.

Other hospitals like the University, the Jefferson and the Bryn Mawr bask, then, in the glory of their boards. The Bryn Mawr derives further éclat from its sponsorship of the Devon Horse

[227]

Show, an appropriate way for a Main Line organization to make its money. In a similar fashion the University and the Jefferson look to a big, old, annual Charity Ball, whose board is superlative, for aid and comfort. Sectarian hospitals reflect in their boards the social status of the sect. Thus the Episcopal Hospital has always had a lovely board replete with Coxes, Ingersolls and McCalls. The others have to struggle along without this particular form of prestige.

iii. Facts & Things

ONE PHILADELPHIA CHARITY which has not had to depend on its board for its prestige, and which is probably the most virulently non-sectarian charity in the United States, is Girard College. Franklin's enterprises were merely non-sectarian. Girard College is actively anti-sectarian.

Girard College, now up among the row-houses of North Philadelphia on Girard Avenue, was the creation of Stephen Girard's will, and his principal beneficiary, much to the fury of his relations. This will is certainly one of the oddest documents ever written; it was, and still is, a continual source of income to lawyers, but was and still continues to be legally impervious. Girard drew it himself, with help from a Franklin-in-law, William J. Duane. It leaves, along with some other bequests, some two million dollars to the city of Philadelphia for the establishment of a school for "poor white male orphans."

What's odd about the will is that it first of all leaves so much money, the largest bequest in America up to that time, not to a person, or family, or church, or institution, but to a city; and secondly, that it specifies in such obsessive detail how the city shall run the school, and above all how the school building itself shall actually be built.

The specifications for admittance are: poor, white, male orphans between six and ten, their orphanship duly investigated, priority given to Philadelphian-born, then to Pennsylvanians, then to those born in New York ("that being the first port on the continent of North America at which I arrived") and lastly, those born in New Orleans, "the first port at which I traded."

Those orphans admitted to the College, "shall be there fed with plain but wholesome food, clothed with plain but decent apparel (no distinctive dress ever to be worn) and lodged in a plain but safe manner." The course of study was to be practical. *"I would have them taught facts and things, rather than words or signs.* I do not forbid, but I do not recommend, the Greek and Latin languages." This is right down the educational path so often advised by Benjamin Franklin and at the root of some of Philadelphia's resistance to belles-lettres.

The scholars are to remain in the College till they arrive at eighteen years of age (or graduate) and then shall be "bound out by the Mayor . . . to suitable occupations, as those of agriculture, navigation, arts, mechanical trades and manufactures. . . ."

It was a further provision that caused so much controversy:

I enjoin and require that no ecclesiastic, missionary or minister of any sect whatsoever shall ever hold or exercise any station or duty whatever in the said college: nor shall any such person ever be admitted for any purpose, or as a visitor within the premises. . . . In making this restriction I do not mean to cast any reflection upon any sect or person whatsoever; but as there is such a multitude of sects, and such a diversity of opinion amongst them, I desire to keep the tender minds of the orphans . . . free from the excitements which clashing doctrines . . . are so apt to produce.

However, "all the teachers in the college shall take pains to instill . . . the purest principles of moraliy . . ." so that when the students grow up, they can adopt "such religious tenets as their matured reason may enable them to prefer."

It can be imagined how that essentially rationalist eighteenth-century codicil went down in religiose early-Victorian Philadelphia.

But even more odd than all this is the incredibly minute description of the structure to be built as the "main hall" of his orphans' school. God's instructions for building the Ark were as nothing compared to these.

It shall be at least one hundred and ten feet east and west, and one hundred and sixty feet north and south . . . the sashes should open inside on hinges like doors and there should be strong iron bars outside each window . . . the steps of the stairs to be made of smooth white marble with plain square edges, each step not to exceed nine inches in the rise, nor to be less than ten inches in the tread . . . a chain, composed of bars of inch-square iron, each bar about ten feet long and linked together by hooks formed of the ends of the bars, shall be laid straitly and horizontally along the several walls.

These endless pernickety commands made legally binding by the terms of a bequest should, presumably, have made the work of an architect quite hopeless, and the result a monstrosity. This is far from the case. The winner of the architectural competition, sponsored and it would seem judged by Nicholas Biddle, was Thomas Walter, remodeler not only of the United States Capitol in Washington, but of Biddle's own Andalusia. He did a splendid job, and the enormous marbled and columned Greek temple erected, presumably embodying all of Girard's crotchets, is a really quite awe-inspiring edifice, in its severe way. It cost well over a million, and in the last days of his disgrace, this expensiveness of the then only half-finished Girard building was one of the many things that was brought up to discredit Biddle.

A room in the main building houses, again as his will directs, Girard's books, furniture and papers. The names of the side buildings also reflect him in the queerest way. They have names such as Bordeaux Hall (for the city where he was born), Mariner Hall, Merchant Hall, Banker Hall and even one called Good Friends; surprising that a building wasn't labeled One-eyed Hall.

Girard's whole plan for the College was threatened, however, by those disappointed relations. Their suit to break the will reached the Supreme Court, where the final argument took place before Justice Story and his colleagues in 1844. On one side stood Horace Binney and John Sergeant, pillars of the Philadelphia law defending their city; on the other side, Daniel Webster, most eloquent man in America, hired by the relations for fifty thousand dollars. The argument was reduced to fairly simple, and thoroughly emotional terms. Binney and Sergeant argued that a will was a will, un-Christian or not. When Webster, in an impassioned oration that went on for three days, shouted that "To argue upon the merits of such a will is an insult to the understanding of every man . . . it opposes all that is in heaven and all on earth that is worth being on earth," the audience broke into frenzied applause, courtroom or no courtroom.

The case was decided unanimously in favor of Girard and against Christianity and Webster's fifty thousand dollars.

This victory of course put the crown on the careers of Binney and Sergeant. President Tyler at once offered a vacancy on the Supreme Court bench to Sergeant. He declined, good Philadelphian that he was, but suggested that Tyler offer it to Binney, making sure that Binney should not even suspect that it had been offered first to Sergeant. Tyler then offered it to Binney, who, good Philadelphian that he was, declined and suggested that Tyler offer it to Sergeant, making sure that Sergeant should not even suspect that it had been offered first to Binney.

Webster seems to have remained content with his fifty thousand dollars.

The school was built, the endowment secured, and in 1869 a special board was created called the Board of Directors of City Trusts, which administered, evidently to everyone's satisfaction, the vastly increasing Girard Estate and many other smaller bequests left to the city for charitable purposes. It was never, of course, a really first-class board, since it was appointed by the city, like that of the Philadelphia Hospital, but up to very recent times at least, it always contained a leading Old Philadelphian or two — a Biddle or a Morris. The appointments since the depression have been more generally self-made presidents of things, though Morris Wolf, Philadelphia's most honored Old Philadelphian Jewish citizen, has been a member for nearly three decades, and John Diemand, already president of the Insurance Company of North America, not an Old Philadelphian but an Old Girardian, is now president of the board — an appointment which would have made Girard happy.

[231]

The excellence of the board has not prevented Girard from having desperate board trouble, however, again in the form of lawsuits, and again over the issue of morality. It is interesting to observe the change in the moral pattern and the issues involved from mid-nineteenth to mid-twentieth century. Once again all "right thinking people" are hepped up about an "immoral" provision in Girard's will. Once again the issue has been taken up through the courts to the Supreme Court. Once again, Girard's self-made will seems to be unshakable.

The trouble this time is not over clergymen, but over the phrase "poor *white* male orphans." From a humanitarian point of view it is most unfortunate that this fine free institution should be denied deserving Negro boys because of one word. Nor is it at all clear, as it is in the case of the clergymen, why Girard specifically excludes them. However, he does. Negro boys having been denied entrance, suits were brought on the ground that Girard College, as a public institution — its board being appointed by the city — had no legal right to discriminate. In order to get around this, the board had to be reorganized and a new board, specifically and privately attached to Girard College alone, instituted. The case, however, is still being agitated; and the morality of this age has been flouted by Girard as was that of an earlier age. In what way will he be offending the twenty-first century? By the word "poor" perhaps; or "male."

Although the Girard bequest, now worth almost a hundred million dollars in total assets, is no longer under its jurisdiction, the Board of Directors of City Trusts has many, many other, lesser trusts. Most important and extensive is that which supports the Wills Eye Hospital; but there are many smaller bequests. The oldest is the William Carter Fund, left to the city in 1734, whose income, "for ye use and service of ye alms houses belonging to ye sd. city," now amounts to an annual $51.15. The Roberts School Fund of 1763 is a miserable $12.65 a year; it is designed to help found a Public School in Bristol Township, or to support any other "meeting in said Township . . . provided it don't interfere or interrupt the said school." In 1956 the Board offered the John

Marshall School in Frankford $6.25 out of the Roberts Fund to buy magazines; they failed to use it.

Other older funds are a very different matter. The largest of these is the Benjamin Franklin Fund, created by his own will in 1790. Its capital amounts to a quarter of a million, its net income is around ten thousand dollars. The Fund is supposed to be "loaned to an amount not exceeding sixty pounds sterling to young married artificers under the age of thirty five years, who have served an apprenticeship in Philadelphia." This poses some problems for the Board, but they continue to make loans to whatever corresponds nowadays to "young married artificers." In 1956, they lent out nearly forty thousand dollars secured by Philadelphia real estate as collateral.

One of the largest funds is the Thomas D. Grover Fuel Fund of 1849, which distributes nearly $7,000 annually. Most of it has to go, whether anybody likes it or not, for fuel "among white widows of respectable character, who are housekeepers or room-keepers, born within the limits of the United States of America, whose husbands shall have died within the present defined boundaries of the district of Southwark." It is perhaps a steady influx of eager women with ailing husbands into the landlady business of South Philadelphia that makes it possible for the board to get rid of most of the income.

The smallest fund, and the most recent, is the Gertrude J. Mieterer Fund for Charity, established 1954. Its annual income of $1.74 remains undistributed.

Besides these city trusts, there are plenty of private foundations. There are also hundreds of miscellaneous good works, some peculiarly under the protection of Old Philadelphia. The Ladies Depository, or Woman's Exchange, has the best matrons for salesladies in its small shop on 18th Street. The Morris Animal Refuge takes care of some six thousand stray cats and dogs a year. The Octavia Hill Association devotes itself to fixing up slum houses and renting them cheap to the deserving poor. The Pennsylvania Society to Protect Children from Cruelty, usually just referred to as the "Cruelty" (I had two maiden great-aunts who always talked about "going down to the Cruelty" for board meetings), the Indigent Widows and Single Women's Society of Philadelphia — all these and so many others exist under the benign protection and cover of the Web. This edifice of good works, though it has queer corners, large lacunae and stuffy prospects, acts as a perpetual bond with Philadelphia's Quaker foundations and the otherwise lost ideal of Penn's Utopia in the wilderness.

iv. *F. B. F. F. &O.*

CHARITABLE PHILADELPHIA might be considered a basically Quaker legacy, but institutional Philadelphia is certainly the legacy of her great man Franklin. Though for the Hospital he was more advertising agent than originator, some other ancient Philadelphia worthinesses he actually originated and began himself, and they really express his own personal interests and skills.

The most distinguished of these Franklin-inspired institutions, and the one that represents Franklin at his most significant, Franklin as world figure, is the Philosophical Society. The name does not relate to philosophy in the sense of Plato or Dewey, but its literal meaning, love of wisdom, and refers, in actual fact, to science. The Philosophical Society as it is now constituted is an organization of "lovers of wisdom"; but its primary emphasis is especially on physics and related disciplines. Einstein has been its most famous modern member.

To say that, exactly like the Hospital, it was Founded by Benjamin Franklin and is the First and Oldest such society in the country is not so very distinguished in a city where everything was either founded by Franklin, is First, or Oldest, or all three together. (The Hand-in-Hand, Hospital and Library Company are all F.B.F.F.&O. The University is F.B.F. but *not* F.&O. The Philadelphia Club, Assembly, City Troop and Fish House are F.&O. but *not* F.B.F.) The position of the Philosophical Society, now grown to national eminence, rests on other things. However, it is F.B.F.F.&O. all right.

Its official date of foundation has been established, after a deal of backing and filling, at 1743. There was quibbling over the date, of course, and in true Philadelphia fashion a committee of nine in 1914 decided to push the founding back to 1727, when Franklin started his Junto, that discussion club of educated mechanics; but common sense prevailed — it was academic anyway, since the only rival, the American Academy of Arts and Sciences of Boston, didn't get going till 1780 — and in 1948 the date was switched back again to the original 1743. That was when Franklin "proposed . . . that one society be formed of Virtuosi or ingenious Men residing in the several colonies to be called the American Philosophical Society," and that "Philadelphia being the city nearest the Center of the Continent-Colonies . . . be the Center of the Society." It was obviously modeled on the Royal Society of 1662, in London, and was to concern itself with similar interests: the observational experimental sciences. It was another example of Franklin's and Philadelphia's bent toward the "useful and practical," for "facts and things," not "words and signs." Later on, in the nineteenth century, History, Moral Science and General Literature crept in, and by now all that goes under the term "Humanities" is included; but the essential concern of the Society remains physical science.

Like that other Franklin-sponsored institution, the Hand-in-Hand, the Society also had its doldrums and its schisms. "The members of our Society here are very idle gentlemen, they will take no pains," sighed the Founder as early as 1745; and as the Contributionship developed a rival in the Mutual, so the Philosophical had to contend with an "American Society for Promoting and Propagating Useful Knowledge Held at Philadelphia." The two societies opposed each other along political and personal rather than scientific lines. The "American" was liberal, the "Philosophical" conservative. Dr. John Morgan was active in one; so Dr. William Shippen became active in the other. Eventually, though not without considerable social and poltical stress and strain, these two rivals coalesced. They were brought together in fact by Venus. That is, the planet passed before the face of the sun in 1769, and caused so much scientific excitement in Philadelphia that the two societies forgot their feuds and pooled their resources. The result was union under the name of the American Philosophical Society. Franklin was first president of the new combine, and from that time to this there have been no more feuds or schisms.

The constitution and color of the Society has changed through the years to match the character of the various ages. During Philadelphia's great period as capital after the Revolution, the Society included just about everybody of significance in America whether they were scientific or not. All the foremost founding fathers for instance: Franklin was president till his death in 1790, Rittenhouse succeeded him, and he in turn was succeeded by Jefferson. Washington was, of course, a member, also John Adams, Alexander Hamilton, James Madison. Altogether thirteen Presidents have been members, including such later philosophers as J. Q. Adams, Buchanan, Grant, Cleveland, Teddy Roosevelt, Taft and Wilson. There were Revolutionary generals, foreign and domestic, Wayne, von Steuben, Lafayette, Kosciusko, and other Revolutionary figures like pamphleteer Thomas Paine and economist Albert Gallatin. Charles Willson Peale and his family and Benjamin West represented art. Later on there were Samuel Morse, portraitist and telegrapher, and Thomas Sully.

Above all there were Philadelphians. During the nineteenth century they more or less took over. Famous figures, of course, were always on the rolls, Darwin, Emerson, Pasteur, Gladstone, Louis Philippe, but in general the membership was pretty solidly Old Philadelphian. In the fullness of time sixteen Biddles belonged, few of them famous for significant contributions to thermodynamics or paleontology. At least a dozen Morrises, eight Whartons, seven Shippens, Cadwaladers, Wistar–Wisters and Rhoadses, six Tilghmans, Rawles, Meigses, Baches and Bartons, five Coxes, Woods and Thayers. Nearly all the chancellors of the Bar Association; the doctors on the staff of the Pennsylvania Hospital; Thomas Willing, Robert Morris, Stephen Girard, Nicholas Biddle among the bankers; railroad presidents Samuel Vaughn Merrick, George Brooke Roberts and Alexander Cassatt — in fact, not

to have been in the Philosophical Society in the nineteenth century was not to have arrived in Philadelphia.

In 1902, largely under the influence of Dr. Isaac Hays, the
Society reorganized itself. Before then the business of the Society
had been carried on in fortnightly meetings. Obviously Emerson
and Pasteur could not attend, but Biddles and Baches could. A
new program of annual three-day gatherings brought the out-of-
town members, and gradually the character of the Society changed
from that of an Old Philadelphian family club to that of a national
society of scientists. Presidencies still often went to Philadelphians — the lawyer Roland Morris was president from 1932 to
1942, Thomas D. Gates, banker and president of the University
of Pennsylvania, came after him from 1945 to 1948 — but the
last few presidents have been New Yorkers.

Nowadays the board and the membership are almost entirely
professorial; but there still does remain a small, hardy group of
plain old-fashioned Philadelphia boardsmen. All of them are
distinguished in their own personal right, some even "philosoph-
ically." However, in the whole range of the by now overwhelmingly degreed and honored and doctored and published and decorated membership, they do represent the only stand, with a few
other similar exceptions from other cities, of the amateur. Most
of them serve on the financial committees. All of them succeed
a long line of Philosophical Society ancestors.

Of these, most appropriately a member is Dr. George W. Norris, who belongs anyway on the strength of a distinguished medical career, but also has six Norris ancestor-members back of him.
Dr. Oliver Hazard Perry Pepper was another of the same, joined
by his cousin George Wharton and their four Pepper forebears.
There are R. Sturgis Ingersoll and Edward Hopkinson, Jr. (four
ancestors each), Henry Drinker, the third Drinker in line, and
Morris Duane, the third Duane (Franklin being another ancestor, and all those innumerable Morrises). Horace Howard Furness Jayne (his wife is a Bache descended from Franklin) of the
Philadelphia Museum of Art certainly belongs in his own right
as an archaelogist, but also is backed up by two dead Jaynes and

four Furnesses. Samuel Price Wetherill (listed merely as "man of affairs") can cite three former Wetherill members. Though most of these men would be ready enough to admit that their membership is not quite on the same footing as that of members J. Robert Oppenheimer and Robert Frost, they certainly can keep company with members John D. Rockefeller, Jr., of New York or Crawford Greenewalt of Wilmington.

Thus although the Society is no longer a significantly Biddle–Morris-run affair, in fact at present does without either Biddles or Morrises, Old Philadelphia still manages to keep its hand in. It keeps its hand particularly on the moneys, which are considerable. The Society's some twenty million dollars in endowments and real estate is a substanial contribution to the Philadelphia Nest Egg. Most of the income is used for research grants on almost any conceivable subject — Arapaho Indians, the psychophysiology of sugar preference, an edition of the postcards and notes of Walt Whitman, the political thought of Remigio de Girolami, and such. The rest goes for programs, prizes and buildings. The first of the Society's prizes, the Magellanic award for an "improvement in Navigation," was won in 1790 by Francis Hopkinson, of whom we shall hear again and again.

The Society is now the proud possessor of two buildings. One is their old original home, Philosophical Hall, snuggled up to the State House. This dates from 1789. The other is their brandnew Library, opened in 1959, with impressive ceremonies and the attendance of just about every important librarian in the world. This stands on the site and duplicates the looks of the original building, also of 1789, of the Library Company, Philadelphia's oldest subscription library.

Philosophical Hall, one of those antiques that stud the decaying fruitcake of the old city like plums, has recently been freshly done up as part of the Philadelphia Renaissance. Still, the effect both inside and out is somehow more one of worth than of aesthetic charm. There is a beautiful entrance hall and grand staircase, but otherwise the building is rather severely practical.

The trinity of chair, clock and portrait here reaches its apotheosis in Franklin's own chair, Rittenhouse's own clocks, and a fine portrait collection, including Sully's elegant study of the aged Jefferson, among many others. There is also a room full of fascinating models of inventions — a patented cheese presser, a wind-driven carriage of 1785, eighteenth-century rotary plows and pile-drivers.

The final Philadelphia touch is supplied to the Society by something called the Wistar Parties, which involve food. They were instituted in 1787 by Dr. Caspar Wistar, he of wistaria. As president of the Society he used to ask members to his house (the one now part of the offices of the Green Tree) every Sunday. There they regularly indulged in menus of deliberately rather restricted and simple nature. As Philosophers, they were supposed to be above anything beyond oysters and still wines. After Dr. Wistar's death the parties were continued in his memory by his Philadelphia friends, and with lapses, have continued down to the present. After 1842 the parties were conventionally restricted to members of the Society and their guests, and somewhere along the line sumptuary laws about food, almost Bostonian in their rigor, were codified to nip luxurious tendencies in the bud. The menus were to be limited to croquettes and oysters in one style, or oysters in two styles without croquettes, supported by one kind of salad, ices and fruits; only two kinds of wine permitted, sparkling wines strictly forbidden. The rules were occasionally breached by legally trained hosts, such as the man who served raw oysters, escalloped oysters *and* croquettes, arguing that raw oysters were in "no style."

v. The First Library

THE PHILOSOPHICAL SOCIETY along with Franklin himself (and the Pennsylvania Railroad) is one of the few indigenously Philadelphian phenomena that has transcended the local and become national. There is therefore some doubt among Philadelphians as to whether it can really be considered genuinely Philadelphian any more. There are no such doubts about the Library Company.

It is older than the Society and equally distinguished in its way, but it has always remained a thoroughly and even acidulously Old Philadelphian crustacean.

Founded in 1731, it sprang out of Franklin's Junto in a much more direct way that the Society and, if it wanted to lower itself, it too could fuss about pushing its date back; but again, like the Society, it has no competition to circumvent anyway. The Junto was a club of eager young artisans, led by their friend Franklin, who assembled to air their opinions on what they had read and thought. They continually needed more books than they could afford individually, so they decided to chip in and get themselves a library. As this idea matured, it was transformed by Franklin into a plan for a subscription library. There were to be twenty-five shareholders, there was to be a basic collection bought in England, and this was to be housed in a room with a librarian where the general public could get at it, though only shareholders could take the books out. Franklin's library is thus not only the ancestor of such later private libraries as the Society Library in New York and the Boston and Philadelphia Athenaeums, but it is also the first "public" library in the country.

The Company's first librarian, a Swiss called Louis Timothée, soon resigned and moved to South Carolina, and Franklin himself had to take over the job for three months. The first man to really stick at it was Robert Greenway, who held the post from 1746 to 1760, and he was succeeded by none other than Francis Hopkinson, who, along with all his other curious claims to repute, can add that of being one of America's first librarians.

The position of librarian became more onerous as time went on. Any person who "hath to be awakened twice . . . shall be requested to leave," and any books lost or damaged had to be paid for by the librarian. Then there were the Curiosities, of which the librarian became somewhat unwilling curator. The library began to acquire odds and ends over the years, usually in payment for shares: stuffed snakes, a set of skins made into robes for Indian chiefs, an antique sword hilt dug up on a farm. There were a set of fossils, a Microscope and Telescope (always capitalized), and crowning glory, "a noble present of a costly Air Pump" presented by Proprietor John Penn himself. The Indian robes began to smell and disintegrate and had to be disposed of, but the Microscope and Telescope were much in demand by Rittenhouse and others.

The Library moved from place to place, its premises becoming each time larger and more affluent, beginning in Pewter Platter Alley, and working up to Carpenter's Hall where it served during the Revolution as first Library of Congress. Finally, in 1790, it moved into its beautiful new building on 5th Street, right opposite Philosophical Hall. Franklin himself died just before the building came into use, but he lived long enough to write another of his inscriptions:

Be it remembered
in Honor of the *Philadelphian* Youth
(then chiefly Artificers)
that in MDCCXXXI
They cheerfully
at the Instance of *Benjamin Franklin*
One of their Number
Instituted the *Philadelphia Library*
which though small at first
Is become highly valuable
and extensively useful:
and which the Walls of this Edifice
are now destined to contain and preserve:
The first *Stone* of whose *Foundation*
was here placed
The thirty-first Day of August
An: Dom: MDCCLXXXIX

There the Library remained in peace for nearly a century.

There it brought together a collection of books, assembled sometimes at the direct instance of Franklin, sometimes by odd chance, that remains one of the treasure troves of the curious and rare in America. Its foundation was laid personally not so much by Franklin as by James Logan.

James Logan is the representative Philadelphian of the first half of the eighteenth century as Nicholas Biddle is of the nineteenth, or perhaps Senator Pepper of the twentieth. Like these other men, he remains more of a Philadelphia personage than a famous American, though he was certainly one of a handful of great colonials. He was born the son of a poor but learned schoolteacher in Ireland, came over with Penn as his secretary on one of his later trips, and stayed in Pennsylvania to become rich and to be Penn's most faithful steward in the New World. For all his varied successes as fur trader, politician, Quaker, architect, botanist, and linguist, he is probably best remembered as a book collector. His library at Stenton was always open to "ingenious young men," and later on he built a little building in the city and stored his books there where people could get at them. When he died in 1751 he left this Loganian Library, as he named it, to the "public" of Philadelphia. The oldest living Logan son in the male, or by default, the female line was always to be librarian; however, he must qualify as a classical scholar. The office devolved onto a family of the Smiths, descendants of one of Logan's daughters, and was held by them for generations. Logan Pearsall Smith, twentieth-century dilettante, expatriate, friend of Max Beerbohm, and writer of aphorisms, describes in his autobiography, *Unforgotten Years,* the delightfully musty atmosphere produced in his family by this hereditary librarianship. The Library Company took over the trusteeship of the Loganian Library, always with the stipulation of a Logan as a special trustee, and now superintends it as part of its collection. Nowadays the Logan representative on the Library Company's board is Treasurer William Logan Fox.

Logan's influence on the Library Company was direct. Though a political enemy of Franklin (he once called the Junto a bunch of "base and lying lackeys") , he was Franklin's scientific friend, and he was glad not only to become one of the first patrons of the Library, but to prepare for it an initial book list.

Logan's list is a formidable document, a short compendium of universal knowledge: Puffendorf's *Introduction* and his *Laws of Nature*; Dr. Howel's *History of ye World* in three volumes; twelve volumes of Rapin's *History of England*; grammars; books on architecture by Palladio and others; Perkinson's *Herball*; L'Hospital's *Conic Sections*. Homer and Vergil are the only poets; the essays in the *Spectator* and *Tatler* the only belles-lettres. It is for serious readers. "Facts and things, rather than words and signs." What is however most remarkable about the list, for its time, is the total absence of any religious books. No sermons, or apologies or commentaries or controversies. The Library thus was spared by the Quaker Logan, as Girard College was by the deist Girard, from the futile ruckus of sectarian controversy. Logan's book list indicated exactly the path the Philadelphia mind was to pursue for two centuries: history, nature, practical techniques and no fooling about with God and the Fancy.

For years the books slumbered picturesquely in their handsome Federal edifice on 5th Street. Then the calm was shattered in 1869 by a bequest. Dr. James Rush, a younger son of the great Dr. Benjamin, left the Library Company a million dollars — under certain conditions. The million dollars was, of course, immensely acceptable. Not so the conditions.

The money had come not from Dr. Rush, one of the most non-practicing of all Philadelphia's non-practicing doctors, but from his wife Phoebe, the famous hostess, whose father Jacob Ridgeway had been one of Girard's most successful rivals as merchant banker, and was left as a memorial to her. Dr. James Rush was a melancholy man, who carried his father's cantankerous and speculative tendencies one step further. He had no truck with his wife's elaborate social life, but buried himself among oddities. He studied Napoleon, the Negro and Egyptian antiquity, and wrote books. He wrote a *Philosophy of the Human Voice,* and a vast and verbose *Analysis of the Human Intellect.* He even wrote *Hamlet, a Dramatic Prelude in Five Acts* — a work, as former librarian and historian Austin Gray put it, "not to be confused with a play of similar title by another author."

Rush's original bequest to the Library was succinct and simple, but unfortunately, as the years went on, the childless widower kept adding codicils, some of which merely aired prejudices against newspapers, "mind-tainting reviews," "scribblings of poetry and prose" and "lounging readers." In the end it was a will as fantastically detailed but far less organized than Girard's. Like Girard's will it, too, provided a field day for lawyers.

Did the words about "mind-tainting reviews" mean that no magazines were hereafter to be permitted in the Library? And how about those "lounging readers"? Much graver was the distinct injunction that a new building must be built. A Mr. Williams, Dr. Rush's brother-in-law, had been named executor with powers to buy land and build. He said that Dr. Rush on his deathbed had told him to build on South Broad Street, between Catharine and Carpenter. This was, and is, way down south. None of the readers, subscribers or directors ever went, or in fact ever go, that far south. But Mr. Williams insisted; in fact he had already bought the site. The shareholders voted on the matter, and decided by a very slim margin to accept the bequest and the building; but they voted down a proposal to express gratitude to Dr. Rush.

The details of the bequest were fought through all the courts for a decade, but in the end Williams had his way. The beautiful old building on 5th Street was sold to a bank and outrageously torn down. The Library Company reluctantly moved into the vast gray neoclassic pile of the Ridgeway Branch on South Broad Street in 1878. As the board had predicted, "nobody" went there and "nobody" goes there, but there, in rather gloomy splendor, are housed the Library's treasures and there sits the occasionally chilblained librarian. There are buried Phoebe and James, side by side under a rather dreadful stained-glass window.

Like Girard's dream house, the Ridgeway Branch was projected by its benefactor, and whereas the Girard College building is stern but benevolent, like Girard himself, the Ridgeway is odd and gloomy, like the Doctor. It fairly radiates darkness. It occupies a whole square, surrounded by a moth-eaten park misused by local slum children as a playground. Inside it is probably the worst building for its purpose ever built. The whole center block is occupied by a great two-story peristyle, a pillared dusky hall topped by a skylight which has leaked ever since it was installed and cannot be mended. Around the hall runs a balcony designed to house the Loganian. The hall can't be properly heated and the temperature in winter remains a cosy 50°F. As this is the only reading room, the few brave researchers keep their coats on. The South wing is devoted to stately meeting rooms, some now converted into stacks for the rarer books. Though the building was built entirely of fireproof gray granite at enormous cost, the actual stacks are all wooden, the whole making a perfect firetrap.

In the hall are the Curiosities, or what's left of them. The Microscope and Telescope are gone, victims to the casual penchant of shareholders for just taking things; but the case, at least, of John Penn's famous Air Pump is still intact. The rather amputated original of the statue of Benjamin Franklin, donated by William Bingham, that used to stand over the door of the building on 5th Street,* and the Franklin cornerstone are both stored in the Ridgeway. The new imitation library of the Philosophical Society has to get along with copies. The principal Curiosities now are various rather curious pictures. One, painted by a minor English eighteenth-century artist especially for the Library, "shews" a female, presumably representing the Library, feeding knowledge to black slaves, presumably the shareholders. One of Sully's very best portraits in his gray vein, that of librarian Zachariah Poulsen, is there — all this despite the fact that Rush specifically codiciled that no picture collection should be acquired or exhibitions held. It may even be illegal for the Library to exhibit books; but they do it.

The Library now is becoming recognized not so much as a lending library but as a rare book collection. Nothing is rarer, however, than its board, which of all Philadelphia non-working boards is perhaps the most thoroughly Old Philadelphian. The board has stirred up plans and hopes of moving to a new and

---

* The old statue was supposed to descend from its niche at five o'clock, when the work day ended, and head for the nearest saloon.

more efficient site and building farther uptown, where "people go." However, the shareholders, not a group to encourage changes, must vote and the courts must permit. Meanwhile shareholders withdraw their detective stories from a small "uptown branch" in the Fidelity Trust Building. An older branch library built on Locust Street and architected by Frank Furness had to be torn down, but the Library is rich again from the proceeds of a parking lot on the site. And the Ridgeway Memorial remains, in its desolate way, one of the principal monuments of Old Philadelphia, and one of its hidden treasures.

These two grand old parties, the American Philosophical Society and the Library Company, dominate the historical skyline of the city, if not of the nation. They also illustrate one of Philadelphia's institutional problems. Either the institution becomes so great that it loses its Philadelphia accent (Pennsylvania Railroad, Philosophical Society) or it retains its full Philadelphianism, but gets into a state approaching decadence (Contributionship, Library Company). Then you have the University of Pennsylvania, which can never quite make up its mind.

vi. Offspring

As BASIC INSTITUTIONS, the Society and the Company have fathered other later Franklin-like, Franklin-inspired offshoots; Benjamin's intellectual grandchildren so to speak. The Library Company was followed by other private libraries. The Athenaeum is the most prominent of the surviving ones, always more private and clublike in its atmosphere than the Library Company, but also perhaps just a shade less distinguished in the Old Philadelphianism of its board. There was also, until very recently, a fine mid-Victorian Mercantile Library, with shareholders, chess players and an old building, but it has now succumbed. Not until comparatively late did Philadelphia get around to a real city-supported library system; today the huge Free Library, appropriately on Logan Square, is one of the country's best and biggest, and its board is one of Philadelphia's most noteworthy and generally "liberalized Old Philadelphian."

The offshoots of the Philosophical Society date from the same period as the Athenaeum, the early nineteenth century. This, after the blossoming of the mid-eighteenth century, seemed to be a sort of Silver Age of Philadelphia institutions. Like the Athenaeum of 1814, the Academy of Natural Sciences was started in 1812, the Franklin Institute and the Pennsylvania Historical Society both in 1824. All these were founded by Philosophical members who thought some special aspect of things needed more emphasis. The Academy of Natural Sciences was to collect and exhibit specimens, the Franklin Institute was to provide instruction in the mechanical arts and encourage and display new inventions, the Historical Society to investigate local as opposed to general history. Each was founded by a group of gentlemen gathering in someone's house and "proposing." Each is now housed in a comparatively fine, large, modern building, run by specialists and supervised by Old Philadelphians. Some of their boards are by now as flavorful as that of the Library Company itself.

They are all private, not public like the Free Library, and each in turn has given birth to even more specialized societies and boards, the Academy of Natural Sciences to the Geographical Society; the Historical Society to the Genealogical. When the Franklin Institute moved out of its fine small Haviland-designed building on 7th Street into a domed Roman affair on Logan Square, its old home was bought by the late Atwater Kent and endowed as the Atwater Kent Museum of local crafts and manufactures; so that it too can be considered a descendant. Thus institutions reproduce themselves like families in each generation. All the lines go back to Franklin; much more legitimately, in fact, than his own actual family lines.

The Franklin Institute — a museum of mechanical science, full of push buttons and models, and the small boy's delight — may be rather especially Philadelphian, but institutions like the Academy of Natural Sciences are certainly not peculiar to the city. Every respectable city has one, and those of Chicago and New

York are far more exciting. Even the Historical Society is not particularly or peculiarly Philadelphian. In fact, it is both amusing and significant to observe that far from being First and Oldest, the Pennsylvania Historical Society is a notorious latecomer. Historical societies had already been founded in Massachusetts, New York, Maine, Rhode Island and even, believe it or not, in Ohio (O shame!), before Philadelphia ever got around to the business. This is, in fact, very typical of Philadelphia's essential lack of "conservatism" — applauding the sentiment but neglecting the act. The Pennsylvania Historical Society has, however, made up for lost time by becoming one of the most active and useful historical societies in the country, and its magazine one of the most interesting and best edited.

Much more could be written about these institutions: their genuine contributions; their odd crotchets; their boards (in speaking of the election of the first Dr. George W. Norris as fourth president of the Historical Society, the historian Carson writes, "In accounting for the selection by the Society of a man as president whose name appeared but seldom in the minutes, . . . it is highly probable that his associates were largely influenced by the unusual representative value of his ancestral relationships. His colleagues . . . were excellent genealogists"; this being about as Old Philadelphian as one can get); their banquets (like the memorable one given to all the one hundred and some members of the Academy of Natural Sciences in 1854, for no particular reason, at the instance of Dr. Ruschenberger: two fish dishes, four boiled meats, ten side dishes, five roasts, pheasant, prairie grouse, partridge, terrapin, fried oysters, six pastries, ten desserts, Madeira, champagne, pale sherry, claret, brown sherry, Schwarzberger, Steinberger, Liebfraumilch, brandy, whisky — and punch); the Philadelphia touches (that moose shot by a Biddle and stuffed by a Cadwalader in the Academy, that Duane family Bible at the Franklin Institute); the especially Philadelphia difficulties encountered in an attempt to merge the Historical and Genealogical Societies (they operate in the same building, with widely overlapping membership and officers; but the Genealogical has women on the board, and the Historical doesn't; what can you do?). Then there are the other lesser organizations, such as the Numismatic and Antiquarian Society of Philadelphia, limited to seventy-five members, which owns one of the great coin collections, housed in a bank vault. For the 100th anniversary dinner (1857–1957, F.&O. in America need we say) a special medal was struck off bearing a Latin motto which translates "During a century, traditions form." After a meal of Maryland terrapin and squab stuffed with wild rice, the speaker of the evening, Dr. Gladfelter, Provost of Temple University, got up to talk on the effect of the Sputnik on education; he was, however, easily persuaded to change his topic to boyhood memories of York County (Pennsylvania).

vii. "Speed the Plough"

A CONTEMPORARY OF most of these institutions is the Horticultural Society, which first saw the light in 1827. It too began as a serious offshoot of the Philosophical Society, created by men, Nicholas Biddle among them, especially rapt over plants. Since its very beginning, it has given or sponsored an annual flower show, for a time in its own monstrosity, Horticultural Hall on South Broad Street, a white elephant if there ever was one. Nowadays it sponsors, but does not actually give, the annual Philadelphia Flower Show, held in Convention Hall, which brings out not only all the local florists, but also all the local garden clubs, which means nearly every woman in suburban and even central Philadelphia. They work like dogs in blue jeans transforming Convention Hall into a bower of premature tulips and azaleas. Although the board and officers of the Horticultural Society are still predominantly male, women have crept in even here, and the rank and file of interested members are no longer gentlemen amateurs of the herb and tree, but garden club ladies.

The annual Flower Show itself is one of the big events of the Philadelphia year, along with the Devon Horse Show and the Charity Ball. "Everybody" goes to the show which, along with the similar and simultaneous shows in New York and Boston, is a famous floral free-for-all as well as an informal social gathering. Less sophisticated and commercially glamorous than New York, but more opulent if less individual than Boston, it is best in the creation of conservatively lavish mock-ups of possible real gardens full of pools, rocks, holly trees, and flagstones, less successful in its attempts at the orchidaceous and exotic, things which New York really does with chic. When safe within the orbit of "Philadelphia Taste" — bosky suburban retreats, brick-paved city gardens, table settings for formal dinners — it is probably unsurpassed; when venturing into the Striking, Philadelphia is liable to be a bit corny. The city is not always at its best when it strives to be up-to-date; yet it always tries, and always has tried. Then "up-to-date" suddenly becomes "Philadelphia taste" and ceases to be awkward any more. As yet the Modern in Philadelphia remains "Moderne," and Philadelphia taste has yet to assimilate it or be assimilated, horticulturally, architecturally or culturally.

The Pennsylvania Horticultural Society is of course F.&O., but there is another group, considerably older, called the Philadelphia Society for Promoting Agriculture. It, too, is F.&O. of its kind; just, however. It was founded in February, 1785, and a similar society was founded in Charleston, South Carolina, in August of the same year. A close shave that one; you've got to watch Charleston. F.&O. but not quite F.B.F. Its founders were distinguished (and Old Philadelphia familiar) nonetheless: of the twenty-three original members who met at the "Sign of the Cock" to institute themselves, four were Signers of the Declaration (George Clymer, Robert Morris, James Wilson, Benjamin Rush; one wonders how they had time) and among the others were John and Lambert Cadwalader, Philemon Dickinson, Thomas Willing, Samuel Powel, Edward Shippen, Tench Francis and Adam Kuhn; George Washington, always one for promoting agriculture, was an active honorary member. They moved into Carpenters' Hall, more or less as the Library Company moved out, and adopted the motto "Venerate the Plough." In 1788 Washington thanked the Society for sending him their *Annals*, and wrote, "The more I am acquainted with agricultural affairs, the better I am pleased with them. . . . I am led to reflect how much more delightful to an undebauched mind is the task of making improvements on the earth, than all the vain glory which can be acquired from ravaging it." Oh, written like the Father of his Country!

The two leading figures in the Society's early life were ubiquitous Nicholas Biddle and John Hare Powel, "handsomest man ever seen" and evidently one of the most difficult. He fulfilled the Philadelphia pattern by causing a schism and founding a short-lived anti-body called the *Pennsylvania* Agricultural Society. Note that whenever there are two rival groups like this, one of them usually lumps for Philadelphia in the title, the other for Pennsylvania. It is impossible to make out what the Agricultural schism involved, except for a rhubarb about premiums at the cattle show of 1822, and the fact that the show itself was notorious for drunken rowdyism. In any case, Powel kept right on as a member of the *Philadelphia* Society, where he could heckle at meetings to his heart's content, and in fact was its president in 1829 just before Biddle.

As the years went by gentlemen, even Philadelphia gentlemen, grew more interested in making money than in raising sheep. After the Civil War the Agricultural Society became obsolescent, but was revived again in the early twentieth century and still continues, if no longer with its pristine dash.

It is typical of Philadelphia that an offshoot of the Society for Promoting Agriculture, something called the Farmer's Club, should have kept on flourishing on a scale and in a fashion that would have astounded, and probably appalled, its founders. The reason for this is a typically Philadelphian one: the Farmer's Club, which began as a serious agricultural group discussion of pigs and their urine, turned into a dining club, the most exclusive in Philadelphia.

The Farmer's Club was organized around 1847. The members got together once a month, on the first Thursday before the full of the moon (to facilitate night driving; and also following immemorial English country custom), dined, and read papers. They limited themselves to twelve. They were supposed to be actual owners and workers of country estates in the environs of Philadelphia. Each member in rotation would entertain the others, plus a few guests. It was considered a sort of "Laboratory Research Group" in the interests of the Society for Promoting Agriculture, to which all the Farmers belonged. Very sober and Philosophical. Few of the original twelve were really Old Philadelphian. Algernon Sidney Roberts, kin of Pennsylvania Railroad president George, was an exception. More typical were James Gowen, successful immigrant father of Franklin of the Reading, or David Landreth of the famous Philadelphia seed company. Sidney Fisher was a guest, and approved, though he never became a member.

It was obviously not long before an organization offering such ideal conditions for the practice of exclusiveness and country gentlemanliness should become as Old Philadelphian as possible. Before the Civil War Craig Biddle, John Biddle and Harry Ingersoll had all joined up; and also, it must be admitted, Samuel Vaughn Merrick, first president of The Railroad. Both the Biddle–Ingersoll and the Merrick–Railroad strains continued and exist to this day. In later years, however, after the Civil War, the emphasis grew more and more P.R.R. The membership of such Farmers as George Brooke Roberts and Alexander Cassatt of the Pennsylvania, George "Divine Right" Baer of the Reading, George W. Childs, publisher of the *Ledger* and his perennial guest, though never member, Anthony J. Drexel, gave a plutocratic and indeed sometimes fantastic aspect to the moonlit proceedings.

Expeditions to the farms of out-of-town members were always made by private railroad car, or even by private train. Colonel Duffy, an exuberant Irish politician, who lived up the Susquehanna at Marietta, always had thirty or forty guests for the occasion. An especially big bust was the dinner of 1884. A reporter from the New York *Sun* went along and was suitably impressed, though quizzical. The members rode up there in George Roberts's new $20,000 palace car, complete with brass cornices, mirrors with ormolu frames, chandeliers, sofas covered with sky-blue velvet, sky-blue velvet fauteuils, ottomans, rugs, mats and other such Sidney Fishery elegances. "The attire of the farmers is worth description," says the awed reporter. "Farmer Childs wore a diamond stud, patent leather shoes and a tight buttoned Prince Albert coat; Farmer Griscom wore kid gloves and an English cutaway. They talked not of crops . . . but of the relative value of gold and silver."

When they reached Marietta and joined forces with two other private trains, the guests were taken by carriage to Duffy's large fish pond. There Negroes in livery baited the hooks, and huge fish, trained for the occasion, avidly permitted themselves to be caught. Then on to late-afternoon dinner, where "the menu was printed in English, as very few American farmers understand French." Usual spread: clams, turtle soup, trout (caught by the guests), capon, lamb, chicken with truffles, turkey, deviled crab, ice cream with strawberries and the familiar array of wines. The Farmer's Club at that time had the custom of adopting as honorary member any daughter born to a member, and on this particular occasion the infant Miss Mary Agnes Duffy was honored. She was brought forth by her nurse and a silver cup was presented to her, engraved with the names of the twelve members and the motto of the Club, "Speed the Plough." Guest Senators could not be restrained from making speeches until it was almost time for the full moon to appear.

A choice dinner given by Farmer Childs next year at his lavish Tudor chalet Wootton developed the railroad theme to its ultimate. Among the guests were Chauncey Depew and Cornelius Vanderbilt, president and vice-president of the New York Central, respectively, George Roberts (a Farmer) and Frank Thomson of the Pennsylvania, Robert Garret of the Baltimore and Ohio, the bankers J. S. Morgan of London, J. P. Morgan of New York, J. C. Rogers of Boston and A. J. Drexel of Philadelphia. On this occasion several of the guests planted trees on the grounds of Wootton, and United States Attorney General

Wayne MacVeagh suggested that they come over to his place and pull up stumps, since they were, after all, farmers every one.

A new burst of opulence, paralleling that of the 'eighties, occurred in the late 'twenties, after Farmer Edward Stotesbury had built Whitemarsh Hall and Farmer Pierre Du Pont had created Longwood. By that time George Wharton Pepper was writing the minutes, and was not one to miss the incongruities. "In response to the summons of the host," he records a meeting at Whitemarsh Hall in May, 1928, "the Farmers . . . went into executive session in an apartment . . . which as respects paneling, pictures and furniture was as seemly a meeting place as any company of dirt farmers has ever assembled in." Or apropos a meeting at Longwood: "The Club met the other evening at Pierre Du Pont's general store down Kennett Square way. As we was a-settin' round the stove. . . ." When Pepper entertained on his own, it was usually only members and one or two others, at his tucked-away town house on Panama Street.

At Longwood, on the other hand, the dinners were usually for sixty at least, and were held in the conservatory. Another Secretary, Effingham Morris, writing the minutes as of 1936, describes the scene in loving detail. "Mrs. Du Pont received the members and guests on the esplanade outside the greenhouses, which overlooks the sunken gardens and the fountains. These were playing in part before dinner and in full force after dinner with the nearly full moon shining through them." The fountains displaced, he noted, 12,000 gallons of water a minute. During dinner, music was provided by the great pipe organ in the conservatory. Morris, always one for a classical or historical comparison, couldn't help wondering what Louis XIV would have thought of this modern Versailles, created by a descendant of a compatriot. Some might have wondered, as of the 1930's, what other farmers in Oklahoma and such dusty places would have thought of those 12,000 gallons of water per minute.

The members of course had very definite thoughts about such subjects, as reflected in the minutes. "The seemingly destructive experiments of the AAA occupied the mind of all members of the Club. The policy of artificially producing economic scarcity was recognized by everybody as in tragic contrast to the wisdom of permitting natural economic law to take its course."

The Farmers continue to meet as usual, although perhaps not in quite such magnificence. However, the present owner of Andalusia still entertains the Club there annually as did Farmer Craig Biddle from 1859 to 1907; C. J. Ingersoll has them at Warriston as his father did at Forest Hill.

Although the custom of adopting daughters as honorary members seems to have lapsed, the custom of giving a special dinner to any member who reaches ninety awaits the fortunate event. At such a dinner given to Frederick Fraley, onetime president of the Philosophical Society, at the Union League in 1904, Judge Biddle, quoting as his motto, "Weak with toil, yet strong in appetite," from Shakespeare's Cymbeline, discussed the efforts over the years by the Club to determine the proper diet for farmers. Should terrapin be prepared à la Philadelphia or à la Baltimore? What should the farmer take with him to the fields in his kettle — sweet or dry champagne? Biddle confessed that no decision had been reached. The issue still remains in doubt, but the Farmers continue to meet on the first Thursday before the full moon, and to debate these and other ways to promote agriculture and to "Speed the Plough."

2

i. Boards: Ornamental

"IN MY FATHER'S HOUSE are many mansions" might be amended in Philadelphia to "In my grandfather's house are many board-rooms"; boardrooms like clubs, clubs like boardrooms, and to these the young Old Philadelphian has the key. In fact, rather than comparing the Philadelphia princeling's gift at birth to a blank check, one might rather describe his dowry as a keyring. On this ring are hereditary keys to various doors in this great rambling edifice of institutions — insurance companies, banks, hospitals, libraries — to the boards of which he is born with an entree. This doesn't mean necessarily that he will be given a seat at the table; that requires evidence of merit.* But at least the doors will open.

The effect of this Grandfather's House on the Old Philadelphia young is various. Some enter it with pride, jangling their keys and getting into as many chairs as they can. Others, with a sigh of duty, do what is expected of them, oppressed by the whole thing but accepting it as a part of Philadelphia life. Many try to ignore it, filling their lives with business, suburbs, country club, family life or drink. And some just run like rabbits. These spend their lives in New York or some other place where the battlements of Grandfather's House aren't visible, where the shadows of its crenellations and mansards cannot fall, or the boom of its black bell (like that of City Hall) cannot penetrate.

---

* The Mutual Assurance Company, in fact, once gave a dinner for some dozen sons of former board members. The idea was to look them over as possible trustees; but they wouldn't do, and none of them was elected.

Later on, exposed to a shelterless world, they can grow homesick for that roomy, cosy, tyrannous bastille. As for those Philadelphians who don't have keys . . .

One of the largest and most actively inhabited wings of Grandfather's House, a great Steinbergian pile of treasure vaults, ballrooms, tucked-away cabinets of curiosities and neglected tower chambers, is that occupied by Old Philadelphians during so-called off hours; for beyond business and charity lies the world of Leisure, and in Philadelphia, Old Philadelphia at least, Leisure is as formally organized and boarded and clubbed as Work or Good Works.

This area of the Ornamental might be divided roughly into a Man's World of clubs and sports, a Woman's World of clubs and hobbies, and the World of Art, dominated by a few powerful men and supported by a horde of willing women.

For the Old Philadelphian the world of clubs and sports is immeasurably the most important of the three, and indeed it is impossible to exaggerate the desperate seriousness of this world in the minds of older generations. Now, as in all things, one has to use again that sad phrase "used to be," for though the younger generation is athletic and clubbable, it tends to be casual; it can take these things or leave them. Such was definitely not the case when the Oligarchy was in one of its finest flowers, say about 1900.

ii. Clubs

ALONG WITH THE FAMILY, and the Board, the Club is Philadelphia's most characteristic form of organization, ranging from gangs of juvenile delinquents (always prevalent in the city and just as active and deadly in 1850 under names such as "The Killers" and "The Bouncers" as in the 1960's) up to the Fish House or State in Schuylkill, which Philadelphians claim is the oldest and most select in the entire world.

There are the innumerable clubs of Mummers in South Philadelphia who parade up Broad Street for hours on New Year's

Day in fancy costumes with string bands. Nobody is really sure just why they do it, including the Mummers, despite much learned research and debate on the subject. The Mummers' Parade is one of Philadelphia's oldest and proudest traditions; but not at all Old Philadelphian.

There is the Pyramid Club, the American Negro world's most elite. There is Carpenters' Hall, which is really a labor union; the Carpenters' Company, which built and uses the hall, is an ancient craft guild (1724) and still has dinners upstairs, though the diners are no longer carpenters. The suburbs are dotted with country clubs, some run by companies for their employees, like the Philadelphia Electric Company's golf club in Darby, others exclusively Jewish like the Philmont. The women are organized into a vast network of garden clubs, and shading off from the clubs proper one gets into purely sporting organizations, such as the various fox hunts, or into patriotic societies, the Sons and Lords of this and Dames and Daughters of that.

There are clubs, as there are charitable boards, for all, or almost all; but they are organized into a strict hierarchy too, and firmly and finally at the top of all Philadelphia club life are its two oldest ones, the State in Schuylkill, nicknamed the Fish House, and the Philadelphia Club.

A fine example of Philadelphia's passion for collecting Firsts is the claim that the Fish House is the oldest club in the world; that is, the oldest formally organized men's social club in the Anglo-Saxon world; obviously only the Anglo-Saxon world counts anyway. The great London clubs, White's, St. James's, Boodle's, would all seem to be older, but you failed to read the fine print: "formally organized." These London clubs were all public coffeehouses, and did not become private in the usual sense of a club until White's "formally organized" itself in 1736. Thus the Philadelphia lawyers have been able to exercise their proverbial ingenuity in bolstering Philadelphia's sense of primacy, for the Fish House was "formally organized" in 1732.

It is appropriate that this oldest of Philadelphia's clubs should be mainly concerned with food. It is a cooking club, and important old gentlemen who wouldn't dream of touching the stove at home, or even looking into the kitchen, have for many generations donned wide aprons, peculiar straw hats called boaters, shaped like high muffins with broad brims, and planked the shad.

It is also appropriate that all this should have begun with the Welsh. The Welsh, who naturally celebrated St. David's Day, March 1, with leeks, sermons and banquets, formed into a company (1729) called the Society of Ancient Britons. For amusement on holidays they created a "Fishing Company" on the Schuylkill River, with a "fort" at the falls. This was the first of many such fishing companies, each characterized by some such slightly fantastical idiosyncracy, but the "Colony in Schuylkill" was the most fantastical of all. It had and has, not a "fort," but a "castle," and pretended (and pretends) to consider itself a separate government, originally a Colony complete with Governor, Counsellors, Sheriff and even a Coroner. Like Pennsylvania itself, it had its Proprietor or "Baron," William Warner, who owned the land on which the Castle stood. He was paid annual rent, the first perch caught at the opening of the season.

As the motto of the Numismatic Society says, "During a century, traditions form." After two centuries, the Fish House is a crusty coagulate mass of traditions. Limited to thirty members, plus five or ten apprentices, who may hope to be members someday when a vacancy occurs by death, the Fish House still continues its fiction of independent sovereignty, now with Secretaries of State and Treasury, and still with Governor, Counsellors, Sheriff and Coroner. Of its own volition in 1781 it joined the United States, and no longer a Colony, is now the State in Schuylkill. A dinner was given to Washington to celebrate the happy event, and a toast to Washington remains, as in the case of the Mutual Assurance Company, one of the prescribed rituals. However, fearing the encroachment on states' rights, the State never endorsed the Constitution; a powerful argument in the 1920's against adopting prohibition within the Castle walls.

The State in Schuylkill is now not only no longer a Colony, but it is not in Schuylkill. When Josiah White's dam at the

Falls backed up the water and made the region insalubrious, it also prevented the running of shad. The State moved downriver to a place called Rambo's Rock in 1822, and when that situation became too foul with industry, it deserted the Schuylkill entirely, without however changing its name, and in 1888 moved its Castle and all up to the shore of the Delaware. There it remains, near Nicholas Biddle's Andalusia.

There are thirteen appointed "fishing days" — now devoted to cooking — from May to October. One can get some idea of the kind of thing that goes on from a description of the entertainment given by the Fish House to the Farmer's Club in 1924. The notes of Farmer Effingham Morris are fairly detailed:

Upon arriving in the territory of the State in Schuylkill, situated on the bank of the Delaware . . . the guests were greeted at the "Clock House" by J. Somers Smith, High Sheriff, and served with aprons and straw hats worn by the citizens. These hats are of a pattern brought from China by a citizen early in the last century, and were worn by a high mandarin caste.

The Farmers were then assigned each one to the cooking of a separate dish. Edward Stotesbury drew the clam soup; Ingersoll, tomato salad; Roberts, boiled potatoes; Morris himself, lima beans.

The bell in the cupola of the Castle was tolled by apprentice Thomas Hart and at 5:30 the Sheriff appeared with his baton crowned by a carved fish tipped with silver, and made proclamation: "Oyez, Oyez, Oyez! All persons having aught to do with the Honorable the Farmer's Club will now attend in the Castle, by order of His Excellency Isaac W. Roberts, President."

As a precaution against fire a "state ordinance" forbids lights in the Castle, the original having burned down; so at six o'clock dinner was served in the Clock House.

"Pursuant to the custom followed for 192 years, each person by whom the dish was prepared served it with the assistance of the apprentices," proceeds Morris. At the end of dinner the first regular toast, "To the memory of Washington," was proposed by the Governor, followed by a second toast proposed by the

Counsellor, "To the memory of Governor Morris." (Christian Sam of course, member from 1748, Governor from 1765 for forty-six years.)

"The duties of the apprentices being terminated, an invitation was extended by the Governor for them to join the company at the table"; and not before, the apprentices usually being mere lads of forty or fifty. From then on joy could be more or less unconfined. Now in their 230th year, the program of the club has not varied, though then apprentice Thomas Hart is by now Second Counsellor.

Toasts, of course, are as important as fish, and drinks as shad. The most famous product of the club is its punch. Fish House Punch has by now become part of the national culture, and hosts are felling their guests all over the country with the soothing but deadly recipe. Few are aware, as they gently slip to the floor, of the background of what's hitting them. For years the punch was a secret. Around 1900 it was unwarily released to the "public" at a debutante tea. The ladies, never permitted in those days into the Castle, of course, dropped like flies and the night was hideous with dowagers roaring and hiccuping. One formidable maiden lady, whose red wig was also a carefully guarded secret, staggered home with it well down over her nose.

Following the Rule of Two, there is a junior cooking club, the Rabbit, much younger (*ca.* 1861), less exclusive (eighty to a hundred members), less formal, but equally "good." The name derives not from Welsh Rabbit, but from the site of the original clubhouse on Rabbit Lane on the Main Line.

The Rabbit is a winter club. It holds its meetings on alternate Saturdays and its sessions go on from morning, through lunch, prepared by the club servants, and dinner, prepared as at the Fish House by the club members. Here again toasts are offered to "Mr. Washington" and to the President of the United States, after which one can settle down to serious drinking. The Rabbit differs from the Fish House in that its punch, a hot one brewed for twenty-four hours in leather firkins, still remains secret. As opposed to Fish House Punch, its effect is sociable but not fatal, and it is meant to be drunk in quantity and continuously throughout the day.

Most of the members of the Fish House belong to the Rabbit; the members are nearly all descendants and kin of other members past and present, and of course are nearly all also members of all the other right clubs, boards and institutions. It is, as has been indicated, a Small World.

More normally "clubs" in the sense of men's city social clubs, are the Philadelphia and *its* junior, the Rittenhouse. The Philadelphia Club can't claim to be the oldest such club in the world, but it can and does claim to be the oldest in America (started in 1834, Union of New York dates from 1836, and the Century 1847; Somerset of Boston, 1851). It sits in a fine high handsome red-brick building, early Victorian but still classic, on the corner of 13th and Walnut Streets, in a district of shabby businesses and dubious real estate values. This was once the house of Thomas Butler, kin of the Pierce Butler who married and divorced the actress Fanny Kemble.

The Club is a very handsome affair, and full of handsome members; but it rather lacks the *Gemütlichkeit* associated with most Philadelphia enterprises. It is not, like, say, the Rabbit, cosy. Crotchety, however, it and its members are and have been. Metaphorically, at least, bits of broken hearts litter the pavement in front of the chaste fanlit door on Walnut Street, memorial to those who tried to get in and couldn't. More than any other single institution except the Dancing Assembly the Philadelphia Club has stood and still stands as the Gibraltar of social order, defending the purity of Philadelphia bloodlines against the nouveaux riches, and keeping up the tone of things. Even in modern days ambition has been nipped, as George and Mary Roberts recall in their book on Fiske Kimball. Kimball, director of the Philadelphia Museum of Art and one of Philadelphia's most famous and remarkable citizens, was a member of various other clubs, but still hankered after the Philadelphia. He had the boldness one time to suggest to a friend that the friend put him up. After some time had passed, and hearing nothing about the matter, Kimball asked his friend, "What about it?" The friend answered, "I have tried"; and that was the end of that.

It is not even so very easy to get in as a guest. There is still on the books a rule which limits non-member residents of the city to one visit a year. As late as 1910 a member "received a letter" from the board for introducing a "citizen" more than once and not registering him. Before 1867 resident non-members weren't allowed in at all. Whereas Boston's Somerset Club had a ladies' dining room from very early times, women, up to the grand reception given in 1934 to celebrate the centenary, had only been admitted to the Philadelphia Club on two previous occasions. Now they can come in most evenings for dinner.

Even when in, members have been subject to considerable discipline. Pipe-smoking was not permitted till 1921, and then not in the dining room. Business is still not supposed to be discussed there, and one of Philadelphia's senior citizens, a director himself of the Club, was asked to leave the room because he brought his briefcase to the table. In 1870 set back euchre was prohibited as gambling and detrimental to the morals of members. A motion to do likewise with Boston was laid on the table; the game, one presumes, not the city.

One should not get the impression, however, that there is anything puritan about the doings inside the Club. Most Club stories concern various sporting, betting, drinking and eating exploits. Photographs of cricket teams and of coaches-and-four hang in the bar. A typical old Club discussion between two antique members, as quoted by Owen Wister, ran something like this: "They should be planked on the left side," said the one; and the other, "I am not sure of that." Four hours later the first one was heard to observe, "Notwithstanding, I repeat that they should be planked on the left side." They were speaking, of course, of shad. Another member made a reputation by being able to drink a glass of Madiera standing on his head. The Club has its own private game called sniff, a form of dominoes. The authority is the book *Chew on Sniff*. On the whole, the billiard room has generally been a good deal more active than the library, which has now,

in fact, been converted into the ladies' cocktail room. The quintessence of Philadelphia Clubism, or even of a sort of Old Philadelphianism, was the beautifully dressed older member observed
playing billiards by himself, shod in a pair of sneakers. This
could have happened in Boston too; what made it Philadelphian
was the fact that they were handsome blue brand-new sneakers.

The presidency of the Club has been occupied by the same
names familiar in every other department of Old Philadelphian
life: Three Cadwaladers have been president, and two others secretary. Two Markoes had the presidency, as well as a Borie, a Wilcocks, a Hutchinson, a Vaux, a Meade, a Coxe, a Newbold and
a Keith (but not the husband of the lady with the hat). As for
membership, there have been about forty Biddles, surely an
American club record of some kind, twenty-five Morrises, twenty
Coxes, Norrises, Fishers, a dozen or more Whartons, Willings,
Wisters (only a couple of Wistars; they were more scientific than
social), Ingersolls, Peppers, Hutchinsons, Townsends, Newbolds
and all the rest of them.

Since the membership in general has never been famous for
either social tolerance or intellectual tastes, it is remarkable that
a number of old Jewish families have been members from the
very beginning, and that not one but two authors have been president of the Club. A half dozen Gratzes and Ettings, as well as
such less specifically and religiously Jewish families as Rosengarten and Horwitz have been more or less continuously on the
rolls. The authors were the poetic dramatist George H. Boker,
twice president in the nineteenth century, and the novelist Owen
Wister, president in 1934 when the Club's hundredth anniversary was celebrated; Wister in fact wrote the text for the centennial volume. S. Weir Mitchell, Old Philadelphia's other
famous nineteenth-century novelist, never made president, but
he was a prominent member for forty years. The chances of a
Jew or an author as such getting in at present are absolutely
minimal; but it really all depends on Family.

As for the great parvenus, most of them had to sit through
several generations. The Wideners finally made it in the present

generation with George, who belongs to the popular or non-Lynnewood branch of the family anyway; the Wanamakers only briefly with dashing Rodman II. Strawbridges and Elkinses made it early, Clothiers later. The Cassatts walked right in, of course, and indeed the president of The Railroad is almost automatically a sort of honorary member. The great professionals, too, like Dr. Samuel Gross and lawyer John G. Johnson were elevated, though Da Costas had to wait till the second generation.

At one time in the early 1900's the pressure to belong was so great that the membership limit was raised first to 500, then to 550, and the waiting list was well over a hundred. The First World War, prohibition, the automobile and suburban living, the general apathy of young generations, all have taken their toll. The limit is now back down to 400 resident members, and the Club, like all clubs, serves principally as a place for men at lunch and for mixed evening meals before the theater or concerts. The days when one walked from one's place of business and filled in with a few drinks and games before strolling home late to dinner have been made obsolete by modern life, and no doubt the modern wife.

A prime example of Philadelphia's essential lack of conservatism has been the effort at various times, always fortunately abortive, to move the Club from its splendid old building. The most nearly successful of these efforts occurred in 1927 when the members voted to sell and move to the Parkway, opposite the Roman Catholic cathedral on Logan Square. Plans by New York architects were drawn up, protests by a few diehards were applauded and ignored (the *sentiment* of conservatism is always admired) and the Club was only prevented from committing suicide by the timely intervention of a Cardinal who opposed the sale of the Parkway property to what he evidently considered undesirable neighbors for his cathedral. Otherwise the Club would have moved in October, 1929, and probably moved out for good shortly thereafter. The membership seems pretty generally content now to stay put.

As the Rabbit is less distinguished than the Fish House, but perhaps more fun, so the Rittenhouse compares with the Philadelphia Club; though one can't really describe the Rittenhouse Club as "fun," it is certainly less distinguished than the Philadelphia, but more genial. It was started in the 'seventies by a group, heavily Peppered, with more literary and less sporting tastes than the Philadelphia Club members, and its original and unfortunate name was the Social Art Club, luckily changed later to suit its location, on Walnut Street facing Rittenhouse Square. The tone of "social art" and literature has not survived very well, though the library itself is a magnificent cave of black leather, bronze statuettes and silence. It enshrines the books left by George Pepper; the classics are all there, but on a small shelf marked "new books" the very latest dates from 1947.

At the turn of the century the Rittenhouse was considered rather fast, and known to hoi polloi as Philadelphia's "junior ultra swell club." Now it is a little more professional and less hereditary than the Philadelphia, though still hereditary enough. A certain number of people (about forty, in fact) belong to both, but the membership of the Rittenhouse is more mixed, though actually smaller. The atmosphere is quite different. Whereas the Philadelphia Club is definitely stately, not to say austere, with high ceilings, white woodwork, dark portraits and discreet soft-footed servitors, the prevailing color scheme of the Rittenhouse is black and brown, late McKinley or early Teddy Roosevelt, and before a rather misguided effort at brightening the place up neutralized the effect a decade ago, it closely resembled the inside of a buffalo's mouth.* The staff, some of whom have been there for sixty years, are inclined to be friendly and familiar, the food still is good, though not as good as it was, lunch is crowded and at dinnertime, when women are allowed in as they are in most clubs nowadays, the atmosphere is extremely intime, with toasts between the tables.

There do not seem to be stories of hearts being broken be-

---

* A story, told of other clubs, might apply here. Two members on entering observed the hall decked in black crepe. "What's that for?" said one. "Don't know; but it certainly brightens the old place up."

cause of a failure to get into the Rittenhouse Club; nonetheless, those that are in it are sufficiently pleased. These two clubs are the only city clubs in Philadelphia that are accepted by Old Philadelphians as being absolutely beyond reproach. But there are other clubs.

The most conspicuous of these is the Union League; just that and not Union League Club. In Old Philadelphia circles it is understood that though the Union League is very honorable and important, it is not really socially flawless. A great many Old Philadelphians belong to it; for some it is their only club. It is grandly affluent and crusty, full of a rich Civil War fug, long portraits, gilt ceilings, marble floors, paneled banquet halls, thick carpets and curtains; but there is an undoubted tinge of boodle and smoke-filled rooms about it. One seems to sense the absence of spittoons. It is a distinctly political club; once only those who had voted straight Republican could be members, and a good many figures, important politically but not very proper morally or socially, have in the past lounged in the corridors and dozed in the wide chairs. The aroma of Philadelphia's old "corrupt and contented" is very pervasive.

The clubhouse is a wonderfully typical General Grant red-brick mansarded building smack on Broad Street, within a stone's throw, or a cigar ring's blow, of City Hall, which was for years merely the Union League's baser annex. It used to be said that any important member could stand at the head of the League's curving front steps and whistle, and the Mayor would come running. Nowadays things have changed. When Joseph S. Clark, Philadelphia's first Democratic mayor since 1881, was elected, Jack Kelly, who was one of the Democratic party's biggest backers, organized a private parade down Broad Street to the Union League, where he personally climbed up and tore down the club flag.*

* Even if the story isn't true, it should be, and I give it as I first heard it, without any nice qualifying "it is said," or "there is a story." Later, however I came across another version: Kelly, when running for mayor, thought himself elected. He then organized a private parade, climbed up on the Union League steps and delivered an oration. I told both these versions to a man who had actu-

The conspicuous position and venerable appearance of the clubhouse, the political power and civic influence of the members have given the Union League a popular reputation far beyond that of the Philadelphia or the Rittenhouse Clubs. For everyone except those who know better, it is commonly thought of as *the* club — which of course suits Philadelphians (Old Philadelphians) perfectly.

The case of the Racquet Club is more anomalous; it is a very respectable social club, with a splendid modern neo-Georgian clubhouse in the center of the business district close to the Union League, and with a large membership (over 1,000) studded with Old Philadelphians. "Everybody" belongs; a whole group of the Philadelphia Club's most indigenous members prefers to lunch there, though the food is not quite as good nor the surroundings quite as elegant. Most of the city's eligible younger men belong to it and use it, and of course as its name implies, it has special sporting facilities, squash courts and the city's only court tennis court. Nonetheless, it has, compared to the older clubs, less social standing, or what it has is "middle class." Though it is by far the best appointed, most frequented and prosperous * of all Philadelphia's clubs, for the Old Philadelphian (who is probably a member) it is a bit outside his Inner City.

The Penn Athletic Club, now occupying the former Van Rensselaer house close to the Rittenhouse Club, fails the Philadelphia Rule of Two by being number two, all right, but definitely "nonexistent" for Old Philadelphia. It did what the Philadelphia Club just failed to do; built a wonderfully extravagant clubhouse just before the Crash and suffered accordingly. The new club-

---

ally been there. According to him the incident took place in 1936 when Roosevelt was re-elected. Those in Democratic headquarters, including Kelly, the Francis Biddles and others, surged forth and danced arm in arm down Broad Street. When they got to the Union League, it was all dark and disconsolate. Kelly went up and peered through the glass door, frightening a lone attendant. This may be true; but it is not an anecdote.

* However, here too things are not as they were. The club has depended heavily in the past on revenue from its bars. Just lately, this has been declining, which worries the house committee. What's the younger generation coming to, anyway? It's a crisis.

house was on Rittenhouse Square, a skyscraper of orange brick, and had just about everything. It was able to accommodate the whole membership of the Horticultural Society at its hundredth anniversary dinner in 1927. Then came the Crash; the clubhouse was sold, and now contains in bleak functionalism various government agencies. The top-story icing of penthouses was shaved off. There have been many examples of skyscrapers *torn* down to make way for others, but only in Philadelphia, I'm sure, has a skyscraper been *cut* down just to make it lower.

The Franklin Inn is the one men's club which manages to combine Old Philadelphia and non–Old Philadelphia without perceptible loss of face. It was founded in 1902 by the doctor-novelist S. Weir Mitchell and his friends as a club for writers; but when it became obvious that Philadelphia didn't have enough writers to fill up a club, artists were asked in too and eventually persons "contributing notably to the literary, artistic or intellectual life of the community," a category which might well account for a sizeable minority, at least, of the members. At present the roster is dominated to a large extent by Philadelphia's more educated newspapermen and by professors at the University of Pennsylvania; nevertheless the hereditary strain is pretty evident here as elsewhere in Philadelphia's institutional life.

Then there are, naturally, women's clubs, and at least two of them are just as important socially as any of the men's clubs. The Acorn Club, that moved recently to an opulent smallish new clubhouse of its own on Locust Street within walking distance of the Academy of Music, is preeminent socially; the more modest Cosmopolitan Club is more intellectual. The Acorn would not be true to Philadelphia type if it were not, like the Philadelphia Club, the oldest of its kind in the country (1890) and equally hard to get into. And like the Philadelphia Club, it is full of handsome old furniture and handsome old members. The Cosmopolitan Club goes in more for lectures.

Philadelphia's only respectable bisexual club is the Art Alliance, which brings together men, women, rich, poor, Old Philadelphia and non–Old Philadelphia, artists and patrons, all in support of all the arts. It gives exhibitions of paintings, wonderful modern jewelry, hand-created pots. It gives concerts and lectures. Its clubhouse has a delightful bar with a famous bartender called Archie, and a pleasing restaurant. This being Philadelphia, you have to belong to use these; but the exhibitions are open to the public.

iii. Sons and Daughters

CLOSE IN SPIRIT to Philadelphia's clubs and overlapping in membership are the Societies, in which the emphasis is patriotic, hereditary, or both. The odd fact of the matter is that Philadelphia has not, as compared with New York, been especially interested in this sort of thing until very recently. After all, everybody in Philadelphia knew whose ancestors were whose; and a good many hadn't been very patriotic anyway. A very Old Philadelphia woman was approached by the DAR, who wanted her to join. With somewhat malicious pleasure she had to inform them that she was not eligible, since all her important ancestors had been either non-participating Quakers, or American Loyalists. Some were even thrown in jail.

A few of these National Societies, however, are very choice in Philadelphia nowadays; the Colonial Society of Pennsylvania for instance, not to be confused with the Pennsylvanian Society of Colonial Wars, equally good. Or the Sons of the Revolution; definitely not to be confused with the Sons of the *American* Revolution, which is out. Or the Welcome Society, local variant of the Mayflower Society, the Society of the War of 1812 and some others. They are particularly Old Philadelphian, especially when, like the Colonial Society, they have the forethought to limit their membership to 225. Their dinners are all rich and well-attended.

More essentially Philadelphian than any of these is something for the ladies called the National Society of the Colonial Dames of America, which is *not* to be confused with the Colonial Dames. It is, in true Philadelphia fashion, the result of a schism. An important Philadelphia dowager applied for membership in the Philadelphia branch (Chapter II) of the Dames, on the basis of her descent from Benjamin Franklin. She was turned down because all of Franklin's children were more or less bastards. With fury in her breast she rallied her friends around her and they started their own Colonial Dames (the National Society etc.).* Far from being a really National society, it is a very parochial one. Everywhere else the regular Colonial Dames is paramount. In Philadelphia, the "bastard society" holds the regulars in contempt, referring to them disdainfully as "Chapter Two's" and thinking of themselves definitely as Number One. They have a lovely clubhouse and gardens in town and though just as many Old Philadelphiennes do belong to Chapter II, it isn't quite the same.

Another nationally famous organization that is likewise somewhat déclassé in Philadelphia is the Society of the Cincinnati, which was formed by officers after the Revolution. They were accused of trying to establish a new American nobility, for only eldest sons of member fathers are eligible, and it's all very august; but not in Philadelphia. For one thing, it's dominated by New York. For another thing, most of Philadelphia's blue blood — Cadwaladers and Morrises for instance — officered militia organizations like the City Troop and were not with the regular Continentals; hence ineligible. Most Old Philadelphians who do belong to the Cincinnati belong as the Delaware branch.

Groups such as the Netherlands Society, the Swedish-American Society, the Alliance Française and the English-Speaking Union have little real Philadelphia ancestral or patriotic background, but in Philadelphia they seem to have a disproportionate amount of social distinction. They offer, of course, many opportunities for dinners and exhibitions and concerts and "openings," all of which Philadelphia society loves; they also give hostesses a chance to lionize visiting foreigners, and Philadelphians just as good an

---

* Here too the truth is a bit complicated by details which make the story less pointed; but . . .

excuse to dress up as more indigenous affairs. Since there is no night life, it is only on occasions like these that Philadelphians can be seen dressed up in public, or semi-public.

The reason for this interest in such hands-across-the-sea organizations is probably historical. In Philadelphia the foreign consuls, especially the British and French, have always had a distinguished social position. An active and attractive consul, such as one recent incumbent of the British office, the witty Geoffrey Aldington, can have an enormous influence in spreading good will about. It is all a faint remnant of the time when Philadelphia was the capital, favorite place of retreat for foreign refugees; of the days when Louis Philippe, future — and last — King of France, painted miniatures of local ladies, or later on Joseph Bonaparte, Napoleon's oldest brother and former King of Spain, wintered in town and was a bosom friend of Charles Ingersoll and Joseph Hopkinson.

The French emigration provided Philadelphia with some of its most curious characters, worthy citizens and amusing incidents. For instance, while in Philadelphia Louis Philippe paid court to one of the Miss Willings. Her father was discouraging, however. "If you are returned to your rights," he told Louis, "it will be too great a match for her; and if you aren't, it will be too great a match for you." The Willings knew just where they stood. (A parallel to this is the equally famous story of the Philadelphia Quaker mother whose son danced with Queen Victoria at some court function. When his mother heard of it she was worried. "I hope thee will not marry out of meeting," she wrote him.)

The two most romantic émigré settlements during the post-Revolutionary period were not in Philadelphia — though they both used Philadelphia as headquarters — but at the Azilum, way up north on the Susquehanna, and at Point Breeze, on the Delaware at Bordentown, New Jersey. The so-called Azilum, evidently a French idea of a Latin version of the word "asylum," was a colony of escaped Royalists who built a log-cabin community in the wilderness on land belonging to Robert Morris and John

Nicholson. They expected Marie Antoinette to come and join them, and with that in mind erected a huge house all of log with salons and many fireplaces. She didn't come, of course; Morris and Nicholson went bankrupt, and after a few years the colony dispersed, but it made an elegant footnote to American history while it lasted.

Point Breeze, the Bonaparte estate on the Delaware, came after, when the Royalists had returned to France and the Bonapartes were now exiles in their turn. It was a magnificent place of some 1,800 acres, with a mansion stuffed full of Empire furniture and a hundred and fifty old masters, including a Raphael and a da Vinci; undoubtedly the best art collection in America at that time. During the 1820's, the Bonapartes and their kin cut a large swathe in Philadelphia social and intellectual life. Like the Royalists before them, they all went home when the chance came. However a few Frenchmen were left behind, such as the Du Barrys, who came with Joseph Bonaparte (active now is Joseph Napoleon Du Barry IV) ; the Bories, who fled from slave rebellions in the West Indies; or such enterprising citizens as Condy Raguet, Peter du Ponceau and Stephen Girard, all of whom made their permanent mark on the city.

Along with the French and English, Philadelphians are particularly fond of the Swedes, who were the first settlers on the Delaware, contributed some notable characters to local history, introduced the log cabin to the continent, and even founded families. Such present-day Old Philadelphia names as Morton (Marten), Sinnickson and Nielson go back to that log-cabin Swedish settlement, and it is a point of pride on the part of any descendants of the Swedes that they were the ones who were here to welcome the *Welcome* when Penn and all the other Philadelphians arrived on it. Since this Delaware settlement was the only Swedish colonial adventure in the western hemisphere, there is the kind of cosy specialness about it that Philadelphians most admire.

All this must not be confused, however, with an avid interest in other cultures and world affairs. It is rather ancestor worship,

and a memory of those days when Philadelphia entertained foreigners as the capital of the United States; memory rather than
awareness is involved here, as so often in Philadelphia.

iv. *City Troop*

IT IS SOMETIMES HARD to know just where the world of clubs and
societies really ends. The City Troop, for instance, is not precisely a club, nor a society, but it might as well be. It is, in fact,
America's First and Oldest (1774; how this phrase can become
monotonous when dealing with Philadelphia!) volunteer cavalry
corps. It was founded not by Benjamin Franklin, but largely by
Christian Sam Morris and his fox-hunting friends of the Gloucester Hunt, who transposed their chase from red foxes to red coats.
The first captain was the exotic Abraham Markoe of St. Croix,
and Sam himself was the second. The Troop's full name of course,
is not City Troop, but the First Troop, Philadelphia City Cavalry,
and its hour of greatest glory was appropriately enough the Battle
of Princeton, to the University of which so many of the Troop
members past and present have gone.

The Troop hasn't really done very much since, at least as a
unit. It stood on guard below Philadelphia to prevent an inva-
sion of the British from Washington in 1812. It skirmished during the Civil War as a body, and many of its members achieved
honor, and some of them, such as Captain Joseph Penrose Ash,
graves in action. It also furnished two major generals and nine
brigadiers to the Union cause. The Spanish–American War saw
the Troop as far as Puerto Rico; but just as the members were
preparing for battle a messenger galloped up to tell them the war
was off, and they had to go home. Aggravating.

The Troop's in-between peacetime record is a rather dreary
one of breaking up Native American riots in South Philadelphia
and strikes in the Pennsylvania mines and railyards. In 1918,
however, it saw action, or its individual members did. "No National Guard organization in the country did more relatively in
the War than the 1st troop Philadelphia City Cavalry," said

General John J. Pershing afterward, in a pleasing if somewhat qualified statement, and here too, the Troop had its heroic casualties such as Harry Ingersoll and Richard Stockton Bullitt. This last war, of course, again involved everyone in the Troop as individuals, and such Troop members as Secretary of Defense Thomas Gates and others had all the war experience they wanted.

The picture entitled "Pistol Charge" in the beautifully gotten-up memorial volume of 1948, catches the Troop roaring fiercely into the camera, brandishing pistols, wide-brimmed hats blown backward like so many Remington cowboys, or Rough Riders charging up San Juan Hill. The date of the picture is 1941; and since then the Troop has been mechanized — so much so, in fact, that there has been a steady decline in general horsemanship and even lately an heretical movement in the ranks to do away with horses altogether. Most hard-working Troopers have less time to practice horsemanship, and opportunities for public display do not, perhaps fortunately, occur often. When they do the result can be disturbing, as when recently a Trooper's horse ran away with him on parade, in the middle of the city, dashing through traffic and finally leaping a taxicab in a grand final debacle. Besides his bruises, the Trooper suffered considerable financial loss. He had to treat the entire Troop to champagne, that being the traditional fine for such mishaps.

Aside from strike-breaking, the peacetime history of the Troop seems to have been one long picnic of rigorous but jolly training periods in camps, parades, usually to escort Presidents through the city streets, and a perpetual round of dinners and dances. Balls, dinners, escort duty or, in fact, any occasions when the Troop can get into its uniform are very dashing and gorgeous occasions indeed,* for the City Troop's uniform is *full*. Knee-high black jack boots, spurred of course and flaring at the top, tight white breeches, a wonderfully befrogged and medaled and

---

* A Philadelphian away from home at a stuffy party found himself rather desperately describing to a deaf partner the glories of the City Troop. He enlarged on their customs and costumes, their helmets, their tight pants. "And," he found himself shouting during a sudden lapse in the conversation elsewhere, "they have the most magnificent *balls*."

[275]

ribboned and epauleted black jacket or blouse, and all crowned by a stupendous silver-mounted helmet with a bushy black bearskin curving over it after the model of ancient Greece. Sword and sabretache clank alongside to complete the ensemble. It takes a good deal of physical presence to carry off this sort of thing, and it is certainly to the credit of Philadelphia upper-class heredity that on the whole the Troopers do manage to live up to their uniforms, none more successfully, as a rule, than the Captains. Recent Captain William Stokes, in particular, occupied during his incumbency the position of "Handsomest Man ever Seen," which remains, before and after John Hare Powel, one of the perennial Philadelphia roles. In fact the City Troop's real function in Philadelphia is to nourish the ideal of a Philadelphia Chivalry, a hard-riding, hard-drinking American version of the Guardsman, heroic in war and horsy in peace.

The Troop also serves, like most Philadelphia organizations, as an excuse for genial social gatherings, and what the Fish House and the Rabbit are to an older, the Troop is to a younger generation of Old Philadelphians: a club. Rituals and uniforms serve here too to keep up esprit de corps and memorialize the past, and as at the Fish House, fine points of etiquette have to be observed with care. One Trooper at a party was scandalized at the uniform of a fellow member. "Look at that fellow!" he snorted. "Active blouse and inactive trousers!" But esprit de corps does remain high, if horsemanship may have slipped. A former Captain died, most embarrassingly, in the bed of his best friend's wife; all was forgiven though, since the husband too was a loyal member of the First Troop, Philadelphia City Cavalry.

There is the usual umbilical connection between the Troop and other old Philadelphia organizations. The bond with the Fish House is especially close. They have in common, for instance, Christian Sam, and as he is still toasted in the Castle up on the Delaware, so he is still toasted in the Troop's Armory on South 23rd Street. The same old names — Morris, Coxe, Ingersoll, Cadwalader — turn up here too. Every now and then there is an offbeat accent; none more offbeat for such a masculine organization than the name of a nineteenth-century trooper called Violet Primrose. Modern troopers choose to think this is a malicious joke on the part of some ancient roll-keeper.

There seems to be an irresistible temptation, even among Old Philadelphians, to make fun of the Troop, at least among non-Troopers; and there is undoubtedly something a bit anachronistic about a lot of young bankers all dressed up in jack boots and helmets riding through the traffic-clogged streets of America's third largest city (ex-third anyway). Still the Troop does stand for a long and honorable tradition of military dash and glory, and keeps alive the memory of a day when personal gallantry was still an important factor in war, and in peace too.

v. "It Is Proposed . . ."

IN A SPECIAL POSITION by itself, also neither quite a Club nor a Society, is Philadelphia's Assembly, not a debutante affair, despite the presence of those few chosen buds, but, as stated before, a grown-up dance. It is held now only once a year, but is still referred to sometimes in the plural as "The Assemblies," a reminiscence of the day when there were two or more during the winter. It is of all Philadelphia's many institutions the most socially venerable and the most venerated, and combines in a fine bouquet almost everything characteristic of the city. It is both a club and a family occasion, and though a dance, involves food and drink, and a good deal of sitting.

It is needless to say First and Oldest, having been started in 1748, though decidedly not by Benjamin Franklin, who at that period was definitely inadmissible. When Washington attended as President in the 1790's it was already a well-established hereditary institution. Its only rivals in antiquity and prestige are the St. Cecilia in Charleston (1762) and the Baltimore Cotillion, a newcomer from 1796. Boston's Assembly, a parvenu affair of the 1840's, has withered away and New York's Junior Assembly, a purely debutante dance of the twentieth century, is still as fresh as paint.

Admission to the Assembly is, or is supposed to be, strictly hereditary in the male line. That is, sons and daughters of members are eligible, though not automatically, when they reach a proper age. If a daughter marries out of the Assembly, she stays out. A son however can marry anybody and stay in. "A man can bring his cook, if she's his wife," is the usual way of putting it. He can't bring her if she has been divorced, however, or come himself if he has been. In older days this hard and fast rule was said to have kept many Philadelphia marriages together, but now it just means the continual weeding out of possible subscribers. Archaic as the rule seems to outsiders, in as tight a world as this, most divorced members of the Assembly immediately remarry other divorced members of the Assembly, and if they all got together in the same room it might be deuced awkward.

Subscribers now number about 1,800, of whom two-thirds actually attend in any one year. Older people these days are full of horrified comment about "letting down the bars," which usually means admitting the ineligible husbands of once eligible wives. But what with divorce and even plain lack of interest (young people tend to think of it as "stuffy") the Assemblies could hardly continue to exist if they held rigidly to the hereditary principle. Nonetheless the subscribers still represent a pretty homogeneous group, most of them firmly caught in the Philadelphia Web, and more or less related to all the others.

The position, particularly the former position of the Assembly in the world of Old Philadelphia (and if one is a sufficiently hereditary member of the Assembly, one is ipso facto Old Philadelphian), is demonstrated again and again in novels about Philadelphia, particularly those of the period between the World Wars. Most of the important ones, such as Morley's *Kitty Foyle*, at least mention it prominently, though few actually describe it. Typical are the remarks in William Bullitt's *It's Not Done*. A returning former Philadelphian, long married to an Englishman, and home in the earlier 1900's, says,

"It can't be twenty years since I left! Nothing's changed. Not a new house. Yes! There's a tram." "Trolley." "Tram or trolley, you should never have allowed it, Randall! Chesterbridge [Philadelphia] ought to have been embalmed just as it was. And I suppose," [she continues] "the privilege of dancing at the Concourse [Assembly] is still the *summum bonum*." "More than ever." "And that you still refuse to admit the existence of New York." "Except as a convenience; a place to keep theatrical troupes and ladies who are no better than they should be."

They go on to discuss the weekly visits of an elderly relative to his lady, no better than she should be, in New York.

Non-fiction works, too, like Dixon Wecter's *The Saga of American Society* or John Gunther's *Inside U.S.A.*, give the Assembly its proper place in the Philadelphia scheme of things. But a measure of change in things is the fact that later Philadelphia novels, such as Livingston Biddle's *Main Line* and Richard Powell's *The Philadelphian*, seem to get along without any "Assembly scene" at all.

"Like the old gray mare and Society in general," says Frank Brookhouser in his *Our Philadelphia*, "the Assembly balls ain't what they used to be. They do not prompt the awesome esteem of half a century ago." Such esteem as the Assembly still prompts is pretty awesome, however, at least among Old and especially among would-be Old Philadelphians. The newspapers continue to give it a full-page Sunday spread, and the gulf between those Philadelphians who can go to the Assembly and those who cannot remains quite a giddy chasm. Principally, along with all these other institutions, it serves two functions: that of a club of "congenial" insiders excluding "uncongenial" outsiders, and that of a historical reminder, another annual plowing and reseeding of hereditary memories.

As in the case of all these other storied relics, "traditions gather," and anecdotes too. Henry Savage, Philadelphia's favorite eccentric, about whom so many other stories are told, would be less eccentric and less favorite without his Assembly story. He was said to have appeared annually in full dress, except for sneakers and a very long red cummerbund. Once on the dance floor he would simply hand one end of the cummerbund to the

nearest male, put the other end around his waist and roll himself up. This toilet completed, he would dance all night with
the best of them.

Some traditions go back to the days of Washington, who proposed a toast at the Assembly given in honor of his birthday in
1793. "The Dancing Assembly of Philadelphia: may the members
thereof and the Fair who honour it with their presence, long
continue in the enjoyment of an amusement so innocent and
agreeable." That too, like his letter to the Society for Promoting Agriculture, has the true Washington ring. For several years
thereafter similar Assemblies were given especially in honor of
his birthday.

Other out-of-towners were not as favored as Washington.
Moreau de St. Mery, French exile of just that period, couldn't
get it. He had been reduced to keeping a bookstore. "There
is a great deal of snobbery in Philadelphia," he writes in his
American Journey,

where classes are sharply divided. This is particularly noticeable at
balls. There are some balls where no one is admitted unless his professional standing is up to a certain mark. To one of the balls held on
February 23rd 1795 . . . I begged Mr. Vaughan, my dear neighbor and
my colleague in the Philosophical Society, to buy me one of the tickets
of admission. But he replied that since I was a "storekeeper" I could
not aspire to this honor.

Though St. Mery was not allowed in after the Revolution, a
King of the Mohawks, before the Revolution, was. He made his
appearance on the ballroom floor in 1755, where his followers
"danced the scalping dance, with all its horrors" and almost ter-
rified the company out of their wits.*

Stories about the Assembly usually seem to concern people
who either were or weren't let in, that presumably being really
more important than the occasion itself. A White Russian émigré

* The account of this occasion proceeds, "They brought with them a beautiful
young lady, who in public made the Indian compliment, a Tender of her Person
to the Governor; as gallant a Man as he is, he was quite confounded at the time.
I know not if he accepted her."

couple, distinguished but untitled and of course poor, were much taken up by Philadelphians in the 'twenties. They had a daughter they thought should go to the Assembly. Letters were written, but there was considerable doubt. Finally, however, the girl was admitted; it was discovered that her mother was a descendant of Genghis Khan. Now the chief problem facing the Assembly of the future is whether or not Princess Caroline of Monaco will be invited. Actually there should be no problem, since Caroline is from Out of Town; the barriers against guests from Out of Town being comparatively relaxed. They have even been known to have been divorced. Caroline's mother, Princess Grace, was of course never asked. When a younger Clothier, at one time very attentive, wanted to bring her, he was informed succinctly, "You'll have to marry her first."

The feelings of some of those who weren't invited are rather unashamedly revealed in the autobiography of the younger Peter Widener, *Without Drums*. This Peter was in the third generation of a family that had followed the Quaker formula faithfully, but not with complete success. Grandfather Peter had done well, certainly, by cornering the market in streetcars, and rising from actual participating butcher, through supplier of meat to the Union Army in the Civil War, to Traction King, along with his partner Elkins. Son Joseph E. Widener had married well, the beautiful and charming Ella Pancoast, whose family, of nineteenth-century medical renown, had been natural members of the Assembly for some time. The rule stuck, however; Ella Pancoast had married out and she stayed out. "As Mrs. Joseph E. Widener, she was never again invited to the Assembly Ball." She didn't much care, but her husband did. In 1919 daughter Fifi had one of the grandest of Philadelphia debuts; everybody went, but Fifi nonetheless was one of the debutantes not asked to the Assemblies that year. Father Joseph was furious. He tried the kind of blackmail possible in such circumstances; he balked at serving on a civic committee where his presence and above all his money were essential, unless Fifi got her invitation. Since the Wideners had now moved from their impossible address on

North Broad Street to a pillared château called Lynnewood Hall outside the city, the legal minds of the Assembly's Board of Managers found the solution. Fifi was asked as an "out-of-town" guest, still without her mother.

After making their appearance, Fifi and her escort Peter left because they were "bored." Whether one is bored or not by the Assembly depends pretty much not on one's social status, but on one's age. Like so much in Philadelphia it is really designed to cater to a "middle" — the middle-aged. The young people are there as décor and to be seen by their parents' friends. It's an honor for them and whether they have a "good time" or not is somewhat immaterial. The Assembly seems to be one last vestige of a world run for and by adults rather than adolescents. As such it aims to be pleasant rather than exhilarating. Champagne flows as continuously and immemorially as Meyer Davis's music, and the supper is rather elaborate, though no longer of terrapin supplied by the Rittenhouse Club, as of yore; in those days a guest from out of town could be identified by the difficulty he had disposing of his terrapin bones. Unless he came from Baltimore of course.

The dance is held, as it has been since 1904, in the Bellevue-Stratford Hotel, not otherwise so very chic any more, but still a thoroughly appropriate background, with its marble stairs and gilt ceilings. White tie is required of the men, and white gloves for both men and women. The receiving line of patronesses greets each arrival with a curtsey and the guests bow and curtsey back. These patronesses are always married women, symbols of the chaperone. Each year one recently married youngster is a sort of "Bride of the Year." Miss Anna Ingersoll broke all precedents when she was nominated by the Managers as the Assembly's only unmarried patroness.

Despite the essential atmosphere of "nothing having changed," the Assemblies are not quite as immovable a feast as they seem. For one thing, they have changed location many times, from their original not very fancy headquarters down at Hamilton's Stores on the wharf on Water Street; there ladies in full eighteenth-century ball dress had been known to ride on horseback. There were even a good many years when they were not held. Sidney Fisher speaks of a "revival" in 1838. "Went to a ball, a revival of the old assembly at the Masonic Hall. I like a public ball — I mean a select one. It is a pity that the old assembly has been suffered to fall into disuse. The reason has been, the great increase in private parties."

Young Francis S. Lewis on the other hand seems to consider the Assemblies of 1850 a routine, if glorious, fact of life. "Last night the 2nd Assembly came off at the Musical Fund Hall. It was the most magnificent Ball ever given in this city. The room was decorated with red flowers, Breiter's band was engaged. There were a great number of strangers there from Boston, New York and Baltimore." So evidently they had been thoroughly revived by then. The dances moved from the Musical Fund Hall to the Academy of Music foyer, and finally to the Bellevue. There were wartime lapses, the longest of these being the five-year gap caused by the last war from 1941 to 1946. The assembly was then reborn in time to celebrate its bicentennial in 1948.

As an instance of Philadelphia's being a "man's town" even this affair is run by men, a self-perpetuating board of six managers, most of them sons of fathers who were themselves managers. The board in 1849 included a Rush, a Cadwalader, an Ingersoll, and a Biddle — a list that has been practically permanent since. Of all Philadelphia's boards this one is perhaps the most socially exalted, though unlike other boards, some of the members are usually young men, active in the City Troop and such.

The list of managers is complete and continuous only from 1869; but the names of the fifty-nine original subscribers as of 1748–49 are on record. Many of the names are unfamiliar. Have the descendants of James Polyceen or Benjamin Frill (surely the beau of the ball) survived? Certainly not in the male line as Old Philadelphians, despite the supposedly strict heredity of attendance. There is also an inevitable lack of all sorts of family names, famous then and familiar now, but still Quaker in 1748. No Morrises, Biddles, Cadwaladers, Logans, Whartons, Rawles,

Norrises here; this was a party exclusively for the Anglican gentry and their Jewish and Scotch friends. There is a Hamilton (law) and Kearsley (medicine); David Franks, then leader of Philadelphia's Jewish community, and Dr. Phineas Bond are there too. There is a Willing, a Shippen, a Wilcocks and no less than four McCalls, no doubt all suabacious. No Ingersolls yet of course; they were still in New England, making Salem ghosts for Hawthorne.

As in all Philadelphia institutions, there is one family in particular which has been peculiarly associated with the Assembly down through the years. This is the family of Sims. A Joseph Sims and a Buckridge Sims were on the original Assembly list, a Joseph Sims was on the board of Managers in 1948, two hundred years later, and himself wrote the 200th anniversary account; though actually the Sims name does not obtrude much in between. Still Sims and White are the only names common to the boards of 1748–60 and 1948–60. All this can be evidenced in powerful support of still another Philadelphia, or Quaker Philadelphia, law, the Survival of the Quietest. The families in Philadelphia that seem to have lasted longest are not those of the dashing Anglican leaders of fashion, but of the well-established Quakers. Even when these became Episcopalians and Assembly-goers, they seem to have retained a certain subdued ability to keep going.

"It is proposed to give an Assembly," is the way invitations to the affair still read, rather as though the splendid idea had just occurred to the Managers and they were asking one to approve of the novel venture. There seems every reason to believe the Assembly will meet as proposed at least once a year for some time to come, and though it may no longer prompt awesome esteem, it is certainly proposed to keep it pretty hard to get into. Anything that's over two hundred years old and is hard to get into is liable to prompt quite a bit of esteem, at least in Philadelphia.

These old worthies, the State in Schuylkill, the Dancing Assemblies and their like, have become almost too familiar to Old Philadelphians. Those who write about Philadelphia go from one to another like pilgrims to shrines, doing obeisance to the quaintness and venerableness of it all, and the route of their devotions has become rather dusty and well worn. Most Old Philadelphians, of a younger generation especially, are really quite fed up. Nonetheless, the fact is that they do all exist, and of course they *are* quaint, venerable, awfully Philadelphian, and in their way a vital part of the "American Heritage" about which Americans are increasingly concerned. And a surprising number of non-Philadelphians, and even Philadelphians, still don't seem to know about them.

vi. *Sports: "The Unspeakable and the Uneatable"*

FAMILY IS IMPORTANT, work is important, food, drink, boards and clubs, the Troop and the Assemblies are all of them important; and sports are *very* important. Sports are no more an individual affair in Philadelphia than any other aspect of life, since to indulge in most of Philadelphia's most characteristic sports one has to belong to some sort of club, and then often to a team within a club. This of course involves being eligible, preferably of course by heredity, and involves too the boards and committees and officers, the banquets and dances without which no Old Philadelphian activity can be properly undertaken.

Nonetheless, sport does differ from other Philadelphia activities in that active participation and skill is really more significant than boardsmanship. It is better to be a director than a president of a bank or a business or an institution, but it is as important to be a good horseman oneself as a Master of Foxhounds. It is odd, too, that both of Philadelphia's chief native sports, riding and rowing, involve sitting down — the Sedentary Principle again.

First and foremost in the regard, mythology and history of Philadelphia sports are its fox hunts. It is quite characteristic that an Elder Statesman, giving me inside information on who would be most apt to know most about the city, should begin his list not with experts on hunting in general, but with those who knew most about each individual fox hunt in particular.

The Gloucester Hunt (America's-first-formally-organized-fox-hunt-1766) is no more, and the country it once hunted over is a melancholy wilderness of suburban New Jersey slums about Camden; but it is Philadelphia's claim to primacy in this particular field. The members led by Christian Sam Morris, the Club's first Master of Foxhounds, were all Philadelphia city men.

Although formal fox hunting died off in the 1820's and 1830's, it persisted as an informal country pastime, and in 1859 a revival began with the founding of the Rose Tree, which remains Philadelphia's oldest, and the oldest now in existence in the United States. Benjamin Franklin had nothing whatever to do with either of these. He swam.

One of Philadelphia's most famous hunting personalities was the late J. Stanley Reeve. Not only was he conspicuous for fifty years of active devotion to the sport, and for his meticulous but striking get-ups, involving a pale derby hat and tweed coats "the colour of scrambled eggs" (not on the hunting field, of course), but he is known and loved in all American hunting circles for his writings These books of J. Stanley Reeve are curious documents; hunting diaries most of them, detailed yearly accounts of each individual sporting day either with the Radnor Hunt, or later with Mr. Plunket Stewart's Cheshire Foxhounds. They provide a record, probably unique in America at least, of spills and hounds and foxes, and who was there, plus a bit of gossip. This is all interlarded with the kind of rollicking if lachrymose poetry much cultivated by fox hunters, especially by English ones; as a captious critic put it, "dolorous doggerel about dead dogs." There's no sentimentalist like a sporting sentimentalist.

The preface to the first of the Reeve books, *Radnor Reminiscences* pretty well establishes the Philadelphia attitude towards it all. Written by a latter-day Benjamin Chew, who was M.F.H. of Radnor around the First War, the preface recalls that:

the members of the Gloucester Foxhunting Club, most of whom were members of the old State in Schuylkill, the oldest club in the world with a continuous existence, formed, in the early days of the Revolution, the now famous First Troop, Philadelphia City Cavalry, which has distinguished itself in every war in which this country has ever engaged. A great majority of its members have been good foxhunters, and the lessons of the hunting-field have been useful without doubt in camp and field of battle.

As the English like to claim that Waterloo was won on the playing fields of Eton, so Philadelphians seem to claim that American victories were won on the hunting fields of Radnor.

Of the really large American cities, certainly Philadelphia is still and always has been, the most fox-conscious. Baltimore would be the only other contender. William Penn himself hunted over his Irish acres; such early and prosperous emigrants as the Farmers, ancestors of the Brookes of Birdsboro, who first settled the area of Whitemarsh where Stotesbury's Whitemarsh Hall was later situate, brought over in the seventeenth century, along with their twenty servants, a pack of hounds. Not all our first settlers were felons, indentured or peasants. The Gloucester Foxhunting Club was merely a crystallization of several generations of informal private hunting, and when the Club suspended operations in 1818, that by no means meant the end of such informal private hunting.

Philadelphia's really expansive fox-hunting days, however, coincide with its industrial and social expansiveness after the Civil War. From then till the First World War Philadelphia and its surrounding countryside contained more packs and more hunts, private or organized, outlaw or official, than any other section of the country. At the turn of the century the landscape was crawling with hunters; it was not uncommon for a combined meet of some dozen of these clubs to put into the field well over a hundred riders and three hundred hounds.

Since then things have simmered down considerably. Although Benjamin Chew's gloomy predictions of 1921 have still not quite come to pass: "The increase of the motor . . . seems to indicate the gradual elimination of the horse, and it may well be . . . that in another generation or so the breeding of horses, especially in this part of the country . . . will be abandoned and foxhunting will become a thing of the past," there is no use pretending that things are as they were. From a disorganized fifty or so, the number of

[287]

hunts in the area settled down after about 1910 to an organized dozen.

Until recently the city was still totally surrounded by a ring of hunts from the banks of the Delaware north down around to the banks of the Delaware south. North were the Huntington Valley and the Whitemarsh, next, in the Penllyn area, Mr. Newbold Ely's Welsh Hounds; across the Schuylkill the Pickering and Eagle Farms, then Radnor and Rose Tree back of the Main Line. South of the ring, Mr. Plunket Stewart's, the Brandywine and Mr. Jefford's completed the circle towards Wilmington, where the Vicmead of that city took up the cry. Of these, as of 1960, only half were left in active existence: Pickering, Radnor, Rose Tree, Stewart's and Jefford's. Radnor has had to move away from Radnor itself and farther out from the city. The others have been victims of postwar taxes and postwar developments. There are still a few other lesser hunts even farther out in the country, and quite a few unrecognized, informal or "farmers'" hunts, so that altogether one could probably still count a dozen, or even more, packs of one kind or another in the general environs of Philadelphia; but it has been a slow retreat.

Nevertheless, on a brisk weekend in late fall a motor drive on the back roads of Chester County is almost bound to take you through a mess of hounds and horses somewhere along the way. Beyond West Chester, around Unionville, in the southernmost reaches of Philadelphia suburbia, where it comes into contact with the Du Pontland of northern Wilmington, congregates a group of hunting fanatics comparable in America only to the Green Spring Valley in Maryland or Piedmont Virginia. Most of them are Philadelphians, driven out of their ancient haunts on the Main Line by over-building. There is also a sprinkling of Du Ponts and some foreign horse lovers, notably the Texas Klebergs of the King Ranch. They live mostly in the kind of remodeled stone farmhouse that is the peculiar charm of such farther reaches of Philadelphia, but many also in somewhat grander and more pretentious manors, surrounded by fields and patches of woodland and post-and-rail fences, with wide grass horse-trails along both sides of the roads, "set-backs," a sure sign that one is in hunting country. It is a most beautiful and beautifully kept landscape, groomed and curried, and a powerful argument for ownership of the land by fox-hunting gentry. This is certainly the way God and nature meant a cultivated countryside to look.

The reason for most of these gentry being there is Mr. W. Plunket Stewart's Cheshire Foxhounds. Mr. W. Plunket was not a Philadelphian, but a Baltimorean, whose brother Redmond was onetime MFH of the famous Green Spring Valley Hunt. Plunket devoted his life and fortune, beginning in 1913, to developing his pack and the hunting in Chester County around his country place Brooklawn. As Master of his own hunt he was something of a dictator and was particularly offended by sloppy dressing in the field. When one member of the hunt turned up several times in succession in what he considered inappropriate costume, he spoke to him sharply and requested him to appear henceforth in uniform. "You owe it to the hounds," he said.*

East of West Chester towards Philadelphia and north and south of the West Chester Pike is still the playground of Philadelphia's two most famous hunts, the Rose Tree and the Radnor. They sometimes interfere with each other, which has caused a good deal of bad feeling in the past, always happily ending in reconciliation, brotherly love and lots of drinking. This is nothing, however, to the bad feeling caused by the intrusion into the sacred precincts of various so-called "outlaw packs" — groups of sportsmen recognized neither officially nor as a rule socially, who invade a field without permission, causing untold confusion, especially if the paths of two hunts happen to cross.

Sometimes these bootleg organizations have gone to great lengths to attract publicity; the most spectacular feat, which made the front pages of the local papers, being a fox hunt by airplane. A fox was let out of a bag with a white streak painted from his head to his tail, and was followed by a field of airplanes, each flown by a war ace and containing one socially prominent lady.

---

* As a purist what he undoubtedly said was, "You owe it to hounds." One doesn't use "the" in front of "hounds."

[289]

There is no record of the casualties of this particular run, but considering that it took place in 1919 and that those involved — Miss Constance Drexel, Miss Isabelle Wanamaker and her sister Mrs. Warburton, Mrs. William Du Pont and others — survived for many long years, one can presume that God was definitely on the side of the outlaws that day.

Actually the routine of non-outlaw hunts, as recorded day after day from 1912 to 1940 by J. Stanley Reeve, contains no such excrescences as plane-hunts. It is a sober record of runs, weathers, broken collarbones, and of course surrounding gaieties. For there is a good deal of extracurricular social life connected with these hunts. In certain cases one feels that tail, or cocktail, wags hound. There are such well-earned banquets as the Hunt Breakfasts after the hunt itself, and balls, annual meetings, dinners of all kinds and endless intramural drinking bouts. Pink coats liven up the usually drab stag line at a dance considerably; and in Philadelphia the various Hunt Balls, especially those of the Radnor and Rose Tree, are among the Main Line's most cherished and bibulous functions, culminating in such events as the great quadrille of 1917, four figures danced to hunting songs like "John Peel" and performed by twenty-four couples of Philadelphia's best of breed. The committee included Chew of the preface, Horace Binney Hare, who married that ardent huntswoman Ellen Mary Cassatt, one of her Aunt Mary's favorite subjects, and W. Plunket Stewart himself, who was as famous for his lavish social activities as he was for his hounds. It has been through their participation in occasions like these that both Strawbridges and Clothiers, fox hunters all, have been so thoroughly absorbed by the Main Line strands of the Philadelphia Web.

Then there are, or more exactly were, dinners. The Rose Tree gave thirteen "moon dinners" a year, somewhat like the Farmer's Club. The Radnor was given an annual breakfast by a real farmer over whose land the hunt rode, and in turn gave a dinner to the farmers. The members of the hunt would annually cook and wait on the farmers à la Fish House; the farmers, singly or jointly, would entertain all the members of the hunt. These festively democratic events died out not from any lack of good will but from a lack of farmers in the hunting areas; but the grave of old farmer Jesse Russell, who was buried at his request on Hunting Hill, so that the "cry of the hounds might ring in his ears until the end of time," is a monument to this earlier and more really native era of Philadelphia fox hunting, when the chase was more important than the dress.

There are other monuments also: to animals, such as horses and hounds. J. Howard Lewis of the Rose Tree buried his fourteen-year-old hound Slasher with ceremonies and a Latin inscription. At the funeral poems were read, tears shed and toasts drunk. The wake lasted for three riotous days. Oddest of these memorials was a dinner given in memory of Pandora, famous and favorite mount of Dr. Rush Huidekoper of the Rose Tree. Pandora, who had survived unscathed a betting jump over a barrier of bayonets, finally rode for the last time and had to be put away. A memorial banquet in Pandora's honor was given at the Philadelphia Club — where Pandora was served up to old friends in the form of steaks.

The world of the fox hunter is a special world all right. There is, for one thing, the enormous emphasis on the "right thing" — the right clothes, the etiquette and traditions, the use of hunting horns and ancient cries such as "Gone away." J. Stanley Reeve is, of course, an encyclopedia of such matters, and in his works, particularly his *Foxhunting Formalities,* indicates how careful one must be. Apropos of clothing (one owes it to hounds) he writes, "It is just as inappropriate to appear at covertside in ratting kit after November first as it is to wear a dinner coat to a ball." This might puzzle some, but a fox hunter knows it means: don't wear ordinary tweeds astride when the real hunting season begins. The uniform is either black coat and hard hat, preferably topper, bowler at least, or pinks for members of the hunt. "When the Master . . . walks past you, lift your hat to him as you do to a lady or when passing a coach and four. It's part of the etiquette of fox hunting and a tradition hundreds of years old." So is everything else, such as "Never smoke a pipe until you are hacking home. Cigars, cigarettes, yes, but not a pipe," or if you sight a fox, say "Yonder he goes," don't say "There it goes." "The servant riding in front of the pack is the first whipper-in; mind you say 'whipper-in' not 'whip.'" Imagine a boor, blatant in November tweeds, pointing his pipe at a fox and yelling "Hey, Whip, there it goes!"

Then there is the strong atmosphere of social exclusiveness, partly based on just sheer money. It takes sheer money to keep a pack going in the first place, then even more money to maintain a stable and to afford the time, for those with city professions, to actually hunt enough to make it worthwhile.

Behind all this is the extraordinary psychological obsession with "courage." Bravery in the face of danger is, of course, always very admirable, but many fox hunters go to extremes. One prominent Philadelphia sportswoman, for instance, having completely smashed her knee when her mount ran away with her into a concrete post, now rides strapped to the saddle. In all probability her next spill will be her last; but that doesn't stop her for a minute. This all seems at once quite fine and quite foolish. As a way for an otherwise idle aristrocracy to keep itself in tune between frequent and cavalry wars all this had its uses, but one suspects that in the days of the Gloucester or the early Rose Tree things were tough enough without going to such extremes as riding strapped to the saddle.

Another part of the mystique of fox hunting is the sheer beauty of it all, often given literary form. Two of Philadelphia's nineteenth-century writers, George Boker and Bayard Taylor, are remembered by the gentry, the first for his ballad of "The Legend of the Hounds" and the second for his novel, *The Story of Kennett,* which opens with a description of an eighteenth-century fox hunt over the same Chester County country now ridden by Mr. Plunket Stewart's stalwarts. This literary fox hunt has been commemorated several times by real fox hunts following the same general course. The latest was in 1940 and started off from Pierre Du Pont's Longwood. Nearly 550 riders participated in this one, the largest field in the history of American fox hunting.

There have been other ties between hunting and art. The Philadelphia artist Charles C. Young (who married a Coxe), now a ninety-year-old veteran of the brush and the chase, painted many views of the Radnor Hunt and its countryside when both were at their best, and was an active rider himself. His paintings of meets were so realistic that not only the riders but the individual hounds could be identified.* Arthur Meigs, Philadelphia's favorite twentieth-century architect of country houses, lived and hunted in Chester County and there built himself a beautiful mansion. And then there is that poetry, perpetrated by Philadelphians too.

This worship of the horse, fox and hound is nowadays increasingly centered south toward Media and West Chester. The Main Line is not as hunt-conscious as it was and other regions are far from enthusiastic. The general Philadelphia attitude towards fox hunting, in fact, is not as unanimously idolatrous as others, or even some Philadelphians, seem to think. Opinions are divided. The Main Liner still tends to regard it with proper reverence; others either pooh-pooh the whole significance of the horse in Philadelphia life or regard it as a curse, rather than a blessing. That "the horse is the enemy of the book" is one Philadelphia attitude that follows the equally old English tradition of anti-fox-hunting, which culminates in Oscar Wilde's notorious definition of a hunt as "The Unspeakable in pursuit of the Uneatable." Chestnut Hill tends to look on hunting as a rather minor fact of life, and the old city residents and those descendants who follow that tradition still think of hunting as a convenient way for Main Line parvenus to crash in because they can afford to keep horses. There is a considerable lack of interest among younger people, particularly younger men. At the debutante age one estimate is that about one girl in four is interested in horses, but only about one in ten of the boys. The boys simply don't have time or opportunity

---

* The paintings were much in demand in hunting circles. One testy gent bought a Young, but couldn't recognize all the people in the rear of the picture. When the various figures were pointed out to him, he realized his worst enemy was among them. Turning purple he roared, "I'll be goddamned if I'll pay ten thousand dollars to have a picture of that son-of-a-bitch in my house!" and turned it back to the artist.

or even the money for horses any more. Certainly the caustic observations made by old-timers on the riding of the City Troop
nowadays would seem to indicate a chaotic falling off in youthful
horsemanship.

Despite all this, Philadelphia is still a comparatively horsy city,
and the hunting tradition is still strong. The fantastic doings
pictured in such Broadway farces as *Happy Hunting* where the
rich Ethel Merman just "gives a Hunt" the way one gives a fancy
dress ball, made even non-hunting Philadelphians hoot with contempt, whereas on Broadway itself nobody knew the difference.

There are of course many other horsy and houndy experiences
open to Philadelphians besides fox hunting. There are hound
shows (Bryn Mawr Hound Show) and races (Radnor Hunt
Races) all attended by parties and sometimes by balls. There is
beagling, which might be described as fox hunting on foot. Here
the hare, not the fox, is hunted by the popular beagle hound and
by people in green, not pink, coats. Though considered a low
sport by fox hunters, it is still socially acceptable. Beaglers too
give balls, and look pretty snappy in their *greens*.

Biggest and most famous of all Philadelphia horse events is the
annual Devon Horse Show. For sixty-odd years this and its immediate predecessors over in Chestnut Hill have dominated the
spring social season. Horses and owners and trainers come from
all over. The booths that sell everything from lipsticks to lemon-
sticks (a Philadelphia favorite consisting of a lemon with a piece
of candy cane stuck in it for a straw) and the general decor reflect a charming sort of church-fair version of Philadelphia Taste,
and it is all very jolly and exciting. As in many Philadelphia en-
deavors, the tense competitiveness, both in the ring and in the
booths around it, is veiled by an atmosphere of cosy casualness and
intimate jollity. Even if you compete, you must pretend not to.
Everybody seems to know everybody. Children are all over the
place and those crops of beautiful adolescents that Philadelphia
produces each year, along with the flowers and strawberries,
gangle about on their own hilarious errands. It is such a suburban-
community-family kind of business that it is hard to realize how

vital an occasion it is in the hard-boiled world of international horse, and in the fairly hard-boiled world of local female social competition.

At the 1957 Devon Horse Show one of the events, the coaching, had to be called off for lack of entries. This seems to be the sad demise of one of Philadelphia's most elegant pastimes. Thomas Eakins in his pictures of the Fairman Rogers four-in-hand has memorialized the sport in its heyday. Rogers was the most formidable and famous of Philadelphia coaching enthusiasts. He was actually a well-known engineer, but found time to be a manager of the Academy of Fine Arts and one of the first to introduce polo into this country. His two greatest passions were his coach-and-four and the paintings of Eakins, which he happily combined by having the former painted by the latter. He wrote the definitive book on coaching, and died in Vienna.

The walls of the Philadelphia Club are a mosaic of photographs of the great coach run between New York and Philadelphia in 1888. However, coaching persisted long A.A. (after the automobile). It has not been very many years since Isaac Clothier's annual Christmas-card-calendar bore the picture of his coach-and-four "bowling along" the roads of the Main Line; only a couple of years back the author John O'Hara drove up in style to the Playhouse in Fairmount Park in the equipage of a friend. These are but remnants of the days when such figures as Alexander Cassatt and Rodman Wanamaker could make a genteel splash with their outfits.

One would ordinarily expect, under these horsy circumstances, that racing and polo would also flourish; but not particularly in Philadelphia. The real capital of these two sports is New York, where going fast and beating somebody else out are the breath of life. Philadelphia prefers the hunt, where no matter how fast one may go, one is not competing. Also the Pennsylvania blue laws have tended to discourage racing and betting in Pennsylvania and consequently have exiled such activities to New Jersey, Delaware and Maryland. This has not prevented Philadelphians from owning, breeding and racing horses but somehow, compared to

Kentucky or Maryland or Long Island, racing doesn't seem, despite George Cadwalader and his trotter Ned Forrest, to be a very essential Old Philadelphian avocation.

The exception to all this is the Widener family, who have been racing's devoted patrons for decades. Joseph was boss of both Belmont and Hialeah race tracks, and his nephew George follows in his footsteps. This is merely another indication of the Wideners' lavish non-Philadelphianism which has only been lived down in the present generation. Philadelphia does not fail, however, to lay claim to a first, if not an oldest, in this line too. There was a Jockey Club in Philadelphia in the eighteenth century. It has not survived.

vii. The Schuylkill Navy

NEXT TO HUNTING, Philadelphia's indigenous upper-class sport is rowing, immortalized like coaching by Eakins, and also, like riding, a strenuous but still sedentary activity. Hunting is eighteenth century, country, Main Line and expensive. Rowing is nineteenth century, bound of necessity to the Schuylkill and hence urban, and connected umbilically with the University of Pennsylvania. Though not necessarily a poor man's sport, it does not have the slight edge of conspicuous consumption that makes hunting a bit contemptible in some quarters. But like hunting, rowing is also a matter of clubs, known in this case as barge clubs. As the train from New York crosses the Schuylkill and runs down the west side of the river into 30th Street Station, the barge clubs are lined up for inspection across the way, shabbily quaint Victorian wood structures with towers and curlicues and the flat sloping docks characteristic of such rowing boathouses.

There are now nine or ten of these barge clubs (the number varies almost annually as old clubs fold up and new ones take their place), bound together in an ancient league called, originally somewhat humorously, the Schuylkill Navy. The Bachelors, Undine, University, Malta, Vesper and College are the old core of surviving nineteenth-century barge clubs; such clubs as the

Fairmount, La Salle and Penn Athletic rowing associations are additions to the League in the twentieth century. With the exception of the college clubs (*i.e.*, Penn and La Salle), the members are mostly middle-aged amateurs who row for the fun of it, usually in inter-club regattas and sometimes against the similar boat clubs of other cities. Occasionally, however, and notably in the case of the Kellys of Vesper, the Schuylkill Navy breaks into the Olympics and the headlines.

As in the case of all these clubbed Philadelphia sports, there exists a curious combination of athletic democracy and social exclusiveness. Fox hunting is half chic and half farmer. No one is more socially exalted than the active member of a good hunt; but at the same time the field is supposed to be open to anyone who can ride in it, and the sport itself has real roots in the rural dirt. In the same way, the membership of the Navy covers a wide social spectrum; but as far as Old Philadelphia is concerned, there is really only one barge club left, which is the University Barge Club. The crews of the University seldom win any races in the regattas these days, but they do row; and of course indulge in all the social activities proper to clubs and especially Old Philadelphia clubs. For sheer, solid, unmitigated Old Philadelphianism the roster of the Club has been equalled only by the Assembly itself. Over the years since its founding in 1854 (neither First nor Oldest, so we'll just pass over that),* there have been twenty-one Biddles and fifteen Morrises, seven Penroses, six Peppers (including the Senator) and a full quota of Chews, Coxes, Drinkers, Fishers, Hutchinsons, Ingersolls, Kuhns, Lewises of various species, Markoes, McCalls, McKeans, Meigses, Mitchells, Newbolds, Norrises, Packards, Pauls, Platts, Rawles, Robertses, Rushes, Savages, Sinklers, Thayers, Wetherills, Whartons, Winsors, Wister–Wistars, Woods, Wrights, Wurtses and Van Pelts. No Zantzingers, and only one Cadwalader. Odd. Even the winners

* The first, or at least oldest, rowing club is actually the Detroit (ugh) Boat Club of 1839. Who was way out there then? Probably exiled Philadelphians. The Bachelors (1853) is older in Philadelphia. The University, however, is the oldest member of the Navy. The "University" refers to Penn, students of which made up the original membership.

of rowing cups — Savage, Drinker, Cheston, Winsor, McCall — manage to bear the right names. Concentrating more on endurance than vulgar speed, the club's choicest trophy is one called the President's Cup, awarded annually since 1893 to the member who rows the greatest number of miles on the Schuylkill during a given year. Mileages of well over a thousand are the rule nowadays, but the all-time Club record was achieved by J. Elliot Newlin in 1946 when he rowed 2,059 miles. He was sixty-two at the time. The total long-distance record of something like twenty-five thousand miles over a period of thirty years is held by another University Barge Club septuagenarian, Lindley Johnson, Jr.

From 1887, when the club arranged to lease a broken-down old house from the Fairmount Park Commission, the club's social activities have been concentrated in The Lilacs, as the place was named, rather than in their actual boathouse. Beloved and beautified over the years, the handsome eighteenth-century farmhouse with low ceilings, wide fireplaces and shuffleboard tables * was one of Old Philadelphia's favorite gathering places, center for summer festivals on the river, or the winter dinners of the Pickwick Club, as well as anniversary dinner-dances and meetings of the Club's various select boards. Old-timers get all choked up over past merriments, especially the boating parties with ladies in boats and mellow evenings on or along the water. Young people seem to remember The Lilacs more in terms of fairly riotous drinking bouts.

In 1920 the same long-distance J. Elliot Newlin, then Commodore of the Schuylkill Navy, presented, as head of a committee, the gold Philadelphia Challenge Cup to its first winner, John B. Kelly of the Vesper Barge Club. This cup, created by a popular subscription of more than $2,500, was to be for rowing what the Davis Cup is for tennis. It was designed as a reward for the winner of the Single Sculls Championship in Olympic competition. Three other members of the Schuylkill Navy won it later; but none with as much attendant glamour and publicity as Kelly.

---

* Shuffleboard in Philadelphia is played not on decks, but on long tables, down which one pushes round wooden counters. It is a connection of the English shove ha'penny.

This was a climatic moment for Philadelphia rowing and for the career of Philadelphia's greatest oarsman and all-around Fighting Irishman. It followed his winning the Olympic Championship at Antwerp in August, 1920, and his *not* winning the Diamond Sculls at Henley in England a few months before. The reason for his not winning the Diamond Sculls created one of the finest rhubarbs of rowing history, and is a story so famous by now that it has acquired the quality of a myth. In order to keep the Henley strictly amateur, and also to avoid competition between gentlemen and laborers, whose professions might theoretically give them an unfair advantage in brawn and condition, there is a rule that no one who has "worked with his hands" is eligible to row in England's most famous boat race. In 1910, when Kelly was starting out in the world as the son of an immigrant, but by no means impoverished, Irishman, he worked for a while as a bricklayer for a firm owned by Patrick, one of his numberless brothers. By 1920 he was already head of his own company, John B. Kelly, Inc., that later, as largest brick contracting firm in America, made him a millionaire. Nonetheless, almost at the last minute, the Henley officials turned Kelly's application down on the grounds that because he had once worked as a bricklayer he "wasn't a gentleman."

Behind this unfortunate decision lay a previous fight between the Henley officials and Kelly's Vesper Club. Kelly devoted most of his pugnacious years to evening that score. First he went on to win his first Olympics at Antwerp, beating that year's Henley champion, the Englishman Jack Beresford, in the process. He also took the doubles sculling title, rowing with his cousin Paul Costello, just to keep it in the family. He then repeated the process at the next Olympics in 1924 by winning the doubles again, still teamed with cousin Paul. In 1926 he retired from rowing as the world's acknowledged undefeated champion oarsman. During the years 1919–20 alone he had won 126 consecutive races of one kind or another.

This was by no means the end of his revenges. He brought up his son to win the Henley Regatta, and win it he did. Jack Jr. or

"Kell" won the Diamond Sculls at Henley in 1947, wearing his father's old green sculling cap. John Sr. sent the sweaty old cap to the King of England, George VI, as a booby prize. Jack Jr. proceeded to win the Diamond Sculls again in 1949, just to rub it in. *Erin go bragh.*

Kelly Sr. was, needless to say, Commodore of the Schuylkill Navy for a term beginning in 1935, and patron saint of Philadelphia rowing for the rest of his life. He continued to row five miles a day for pleasure, and to keep in shape the physique that earned him the nickname of the "Rowing Adonis" when he was at the height of his career. His only disappointment was Jack Jr.'s failure to win the Olympic Championship too. "Kell," now in his thirties, has given up singles, but is still trying for the doubles title.

Kelly Sr. was certainly one of Philadelphia's most popular idols. Before his sudden death at seventy he was well on his way to becoming a foremost Senior Citizen. Whether in earlier days he was ever made aware of any "not a gentleman" stuff at home in Philadelphia is generally not recorded. The Kellys' Club, the Vesper, though antique (1865) and unquestionably the foremost club of the Schuylkill Navy as far as rowing ability is concerned, is not and never seems to have been up to much from a purely social point of view. It is hard to say what underwater tension these class distinctions have caused over the years.

Other clubs — the Bachelors and Undine in particular, both of them (though not to compare to the University) old and socially eligible, especially the Bachelors — still have their extra-curricular hideouts, reminiscent of the old Schuylkill fishing clubs with their "forts" and "castles." The Bachelors has one called The Button and the Undine a Castle Ringstetten. But The Lilacs is no more. Victim to the kind of decay that so often afflicts Old Philadelphia institutions — lack of youthful participation, rising costs — The Lilacs lease was given up and the old house turned back to the Park, which now uses it to house its employees. This is a blow from which the social standing of Philadelphia rowing may not recover.

Rowing does not have its mystique in quite the same way as fox hunting, but it does have its aesthetic connections. One of the most famous pictures in America, Thomas Eakins's "Max Schmitt in a Single Scull," shows an earlier hero of the Schuylkill Navy in his proper habitat on the river. He was a member of a once famous but now defunct Pennsylvania Barge Club, and in 1866 and 1867 won the Navy's first races for single scull. As such, he is a direct sporting ancestor of the Kellys. Who remembers Schmitt now? He was not even an Old Philadelphian. But Max rows for eternity through the halls of the Metropolitan Museum in New York, carrying the Schuylkill Navy and Philadelphia on to another sort of glory.

Some of Eakins's most charming pictures are of sailboats skimming over the muddy Delaware, and boat life along that river has been one of the chief pastimes of Philadelphians of all times and classes. More exclusively upper-class boating centers about the Corinthian Yacht Club; this is Philadelphia's only socially recognized local concession to yachting, and one hears of it more often in connection with society than with boats. It lies downriver from the city, at a spot once occupied by the palace of Governor Printz, tub-size governor of New Sweden. Sidney Fisher's son Sydney (he changed the *i* to *y*), an eccentric bachelor and historian, died there, and there were discovered the volumes of his father's diary.

viii. Sticky Wickets

ACTUALLY MOST upper-class Philadelphians are yachtsmen more by adoption, in New England summer resorts or West Indian winter ones, than by nature. Philadelphia is after all not on the ocean, and boat enthusiasm is a bit acquired there, as horsiness is in Boston. The kind of big-scale yachting that goes on around New York, or the salty monomaniac small boating of the New Englander are neither of them quite native to Philadelphia.

Much more native are those sports that require well-clipped lawns, and of these, of course, the most conspicuous has been that aggravatedly Anglican pastime, cricket, and in more recent times lawn tennis and bowling on the green. All these involve clubs and teams of course, and all require room and greenery. If not sedentary like riding and rowing, cricket has at least been described by ignorant partisans of more violent sports as being as near to sitting as you can get and still play ball.

Bowling on the green is certainly not a violent game either, and has always been at home on Philadelphia lawns. In the last few decades there has been a remarkable revival of the game, beginning in Philadelphia cricket clubs and spreading all over the country. There are public greens in Fairmount Park, and national tournaments at Buck Hill Falls in the Poconos, and altogether Rip Van Winkle would feel quite at home.

Archery too, another antique pastime, has Philadelphia origins, as far as non-Indian America is concerned. A club called the United Bowmen of Philadelphia was formed there in 1828 — First-and-Oldest-in-America — much under the influence of two of the sons of the artist Charles Willson Peale. Franklin and Titian Peale, along with a Morris, a Griff*itts* and a Griff*ith*, banded themselves together, created a picturesque uniform and developed all sorts of quaint customs, besides shooting the country's first amateur arrows at a target. Among the customs of the club was and is the "mark." Each member, when he is elected, receives or inherits his "mark," a sort of device on a shield — arrowhead, wreath, crossed bones — each with appropriate or humorous motto. That of Crossbones for instance, originally belonging to founder Dr. Griffiths, is "Bonis omnia bona." When the club gathers for its banquets, nowadays in a great remodeled barn called Bowman's Hall in suburban Horsham, each member finds his seat by his shield placed at it. After the blessing by the Chaplain the shields are rehung over the seats, each in order of seniority, and very important to everybody is the line of descent of each "mark" from the original possessor. It goes without saying that the club has its own punch, called the Hail Storm, and that there should have been a gap, between 1888 and 1932, when it was more or less inactive. During this time its souvenirs, including a priceless great silver prize bowl, were deposited in the Historical Society, where they are still on exhibit. The Annual Prize meetings and dinners have taken place, since 1936, at the Corinthian Yacht Club. (Everything in Philadelphia connects up.)

Cricket, however, is the one sport most usually identified with Philadelphia, and during its great period, the second half of the nineteenth century, it was immensely popular there. Philadelphia's three oldest country clubs were originated as cricket clubs, the Merion, the Germantown and the Philadelphia; in fact, cricket might well have been not only Philadelphia's favorite sport, but our national game. During that great ferment of interest in sports which from 1830 to 1850 converted the average American male into a games enthusiast and athlete,* cricket ran neck-in-neck with baseball as a bat-and-ball favorite. Before 1830 all games were for schoolboys, and rowdy ones at that. They were frowned on by good society as being low, rough, ungenteel and probably immoral. Colleges deplored them and tried to prevent them. Even as late as the Civil War, old President Johnny Maclean of Princeton declared that baseball was "base in more ways than one." Schoolboys, of course, paid no attention to all this. They played a makeshift form of cricket all over the country, just as they played a makeshift form of baseball.

Just about the time that baseball's final form crystallized in Cooperstown under the auspices of Abner Doubleday, and that the Knickerbocker Baseball Club in New York made itself the first and lordliest of amateur baseball teams, so an already crystallized English cricket was introduced into Haverford College, and the first well-organized amateur upper-class cricket teams of Americans were started in Philadelphia. Up to the Civil War, in fact, there was very little difference in the popularity, social tone and general backwardness of the two rival games. The first really expert players here were English.

Textile workers from Nottingham, who had become England's best cricket players, brought the game to Philadelphia with them,

---

* Adult American males have always been sportsmen, but not, like the English, players of games.

in the early 1800's, and played it all over North Philadelphia, and the Germantown area in particular. An English landscape gardener named William Carvill, who worked at Haverford College, in the 1830's, introduced the game there, and various cricket enthusiasts emerged among the graduates. In college they belonged to cricket leagues called the Delian, Lycaean and Dorian, and afterwards they joined in with the mill workers, organizing various teams around Germantown. This combination of Haverfordians and Nottinghamites created a cricket-conscious world there, and the influence spread to schools such as Germantown Academy, and to other colleges, particularly the University.

Most notable of the Germantown residents to be infected were the young Wisters. There were six of them, all cricketers, but the most notable of all was William Rotch Wister, who saw his first game on the Old York Road about 1842, played by a group of hosiery workers at Wakefield Mills who had formed a club under the leadership of Lindley Fisher.* Soon all six Wisters were hard at it, despite the distinct disapproval of their father, who called cricket "that most monstrous of games," and the united clucking of all female relatives. Cricket was low, there was no doubt about it. As played by the mill workers it was closely associated with taverns, Saturday-night brawls and especially wild betting. Hardly a Quaker atmosphere. One of the captains of a famous mill worker's team was mine host of the Star Tavern, and many of the Regency abuses of English cricket had been imported into sedate little Germantown. (In the 1817 match, for instance, between the famous English Marylebone Cricket Club and Nottingham, both teams had been simultaneously bribed to throw the game.)

The Wisters changed all that. William Rotch himself was involved in the foundation of three of the first clubs, the most notable being the still very much existent Philadelphia Cricket

---

* "Wakefield" was the name of the old Fisher place where Sidney so admired the inherited good manners of his Quaker kin. One wonders what Sidney thought of his cousin Lindley's low sporting associations. Not much, one presumes.

Club, which saw the light in his office in 1854. In the same year, the rival Germantown Cricket Club was founded.

Under the thoroughly Old Philadelphian auspices of such clubs, cricket became respectable. No betting or swearing was allowed, and the presence of ladies assured a proper deportment. When the All England team ventured over in 1859, the first such team ever to leave England, they were surprised to find things so well developed, even if the local competition wasn't very strong. They played on the grounds of the Camac estate, and initiated a series of cross-Atlantic tours, in both directions, which kept up actively till the 1920's.

Before the Civil War, the game was dominated by Wisters; afterwards by Newhalls. Of all Philadelphia cricketing families, the Newhalls are the most famous. Three things really established cricket in Philadelphia after the Civil War in this Newhall era: the clubs, the foreign tours and international matches, and the immense popular support and interest. The clubs, particularly the Great Three, Germantown, Philadelphia and the somewhat later Merion (1865) became huge, rich, immensely social affairs, and grew by 1900 to over one thousand members apiece; and all on the basis of cricket. Besides these still existent and noble clubs, there was another important but a bit less socially elegant club, the Belmont, on the way out to Media and West Chester, and there were innumerable lesser clubs, some for working men, some for gents. Over the years there were hundreds of these clubs, and in the great days from 1890 to 1910, Philadelphia kept at least fifty going at once. Well over three hundred formal matches, or "fixtures" were recorded annually in good years. The landscape was as cluttered with cricketers as it was with fox hunters.

There were inter-club rivalries, and competitions with the rest of the United States and with Canada, in which Philadelphia nearly always won. Something called the Halifax Cup was fought for each year, after the first winning of it in Nova Scotia in 1874 by a Philadelphia team of three Newhalls, Spencer

Meade, son of the General, the elder Edward Hopkinson and other Old Philadelphians. The cup itself disappeared almost as soon as it was brought to Philadelphia, but even as a myth it served the purpose of stimulating local rivalry.

But what really gave spice to the game, and brought out the crowds, were the international competitions with England and Australia. The first of these really to cause a stir in Philadelphia was the visit of the first Australian team on its way to victory in England. The Australians stopped by in 1878, and in their tour of the United States, their match in Philadelphia was the only one they didn't easily win. Actually they might have been officially defeated if in pique over an umpire's decision the Aussie captain had not called his team off the field. Threats to stop payment on the $2,500 check (cheque) guaranteed them for their appearance in Philadelphia induced them to play ball again, but by then it was too late to finish the match properly. The Philadelphians were considered to have won a thorough "moral victory," being ahead when the game was stopped; at least the fans, some fifteen thousand strong on the third day of the match, thought so, and so did the newspapers, who made a big thing of it. Altogether the match established Philadelphia cricket both at home and abroad as a serious affair.

The things that strike one about the flowering of cricket in Philadelphia are: the tremendous popular support and interest, the dominance in actual competition of the Oldest Philadelphians, and the incredible success, by any reasonable standards, of the "Gentlemen of Philadelphia" in England at the turn of the century. The latter is probably the most amazing. It is rather as though a nine of Earls should come over from England, take on the Boston Red Sox, the Dodgers and such, and average out ahead. Of course even the best teams in England are, or were in those days, at least half gentleman-amateur, and the Gentlemen of Philadelphia never actually met All England. Nonetheless, they held their own with the lesser country teams they played. Philadelphia's greatest player, J. Barton King, originally of Belmont, was acknowledged as one of the "very best

Mayor, now Senator, Joseph S. Clark, by Franklin Watkins.
The portrait hangs in City Hall.

Edward Hopkinson, Jr. in the Philadelphia Club.

The menu board reads:

A.D. 1752 YEAR 225
STATE IN SCHUYLKILL
Wright 2 pm
Lunch
Boola-Boola Soup
Lamb Chops
Mint Jelly
Corn off-the Cob
Carrots
Lettuce & Tomatoes
Cheese & Crackers
Coffee
HOSPITALITY · ALL HANDS

E. Shippen Willing at the State in Schuylkill, with boater and utensils.
The Castle is in the background.

Samuel Chew in front of Cliveden.
The statue was decapitated in the Revolution.

Captain William S. Stokes in the Troop uniform.
The silver tankard on the table belonged to "Christian Sam" Morris.

R. Sturgis Ingersoll in the Museum.
Behind him is C. W. Peale's trompe l'oeil portrait of
two of his painter sons, the famous "Staircase Group."

Sidney Fisher, by Sully.
Sidney's diary was discovered and preserved by Sturgis Ingersoll.

Nicholas Biddle's Andalusia.

(*Left*) Nicholas Biddle as a youth. (*Right*) A modern Nicholas Biddle, Jr. on the steps of the Bank. He is not a banker, but a partner in the insurance firm of Biddle, Townsend and Company, member of the board of the Athenaeum, and Commander of the Military Order of Foreign Wars of the United States, Pennsylvania Commandery.

John Hare Powel's Powelton.

Girard College.

"The Fairman Rogers Four-in-hand" by Thomas Eakins.

Henry S. Drinker on the steps of the Art Museum.
In the background are City Hall, the PSFS and the bastions of the Nest Egg.

"Max Schmitt in a Single Scull" by Thomas Eakins.
The rower in the near background is supposed to be Eakins himself.

View of Fairmount Dam and Josiah White's lock seen from the present site of the Art Museum. The small building on the bank below the lock is probably White's foundry where the usefulness of anthracite was first demonstrated to Philadelphia.

C. W. Peale's self-portrait with his Museum,
complete with mastodons and Founding Fathers in the background.

"Christ Healing the Sick in the Temple" by Benjamin West. Note demoniac.

The facade of Frank Furness's Pennsylvania Academy of the Fine Arts.
The drawing was made by Joseph P. Sims, architect, President of the Orpheus Club,
memorialist of the Assembly.

Bust of Dr. Benjamin West by sculptor and cousin William Rush.

Eakins's picture of William Rush using a nude model while carving his
allegorical figure of the Schuylkill. Directors of the Academy were to take note.

"Gross Clinic" by Thomas Eakins.

Mrs. Bingham. Gilbert Stuart refused to finish the picture after a fight with William Bingham over a financial matter.

Fanny Kemble, by Thomas Sully.

Mrs. Harry Ingersoll, by Sully at his Sully-est. It was Mrs. Harry with whom Sidney Fisher conversed so pleasantly at the Hutchinson's elaborate party.

bowlers in the world" (*Encyclopaedia Britannica*) of his time, and other members of these invading American teams, now active in their seventies and eighties, such as C. C. Morris, W. P. O'Neill, Percy Clark and Dr. J. A. Lester were in their prime equal to all but the very best cricketers of England and Australia, and better than the run of Canadians, South Africans and the Irish, either amateur or professional.

In those great days before World War I the *Public Ledger* gave two full pages to cricket scores, and crowds of from five to ten thousand watched from "behind the ropes" at Merion, Germantown and Philadelphia through three days of long drawn out play. The games would start each day about eleven and stop when the light failed before six. The fashionables appeared in their coaches-and-four, and watched from under parasols and awnings while they ate their elaborate picnic lunches. Later on there would be tea on the Club veranda. The common herd were brought out from town by special trains supplied by the thoughtful Railroad. The Pennsylvania even had a station called Cricket in North Philadelphia, as well as their own team which competed with that of the Reading. It was all very delightful and characteristic and a bit baffling.

A far cry from today, when the Fairmount Cricket Club, and the somewhat inelegantly named General Electric Club (British research workers at a local laboratory) are the only two elevens active in the area. They play all summer long in Fairmount Park and keep the flag feebly flying. Haverford continues as ever to man a team which plays whatever turns up. Every fall the Orpheus Club, Old Philadelphia's male chorus, plays a game at the Merion Cricket Club with a clutch of members. Old-timers scornfully consider this somewhat of a mockery, with the interest much more in the singing and drinking that goes on after the game. Despite a few promising auspices, the fact is that at the moment, cricket in Philadelphia is just about dead.

The reasons for its collapse are complex and mysterious. Everyone has tried to explain it. "Lack of gentlemen" is one forthright suggestion. "Cricket is too slow for the American Temperament" is another. Presumably the American Temperament was lying dormant in Philadelphia between 1830 and 1930. John Gunther in *Inside U.S.A.* has this bit: "I asked a gentleman who might have stepped out of the ruins of Persepolis why cricket had declined. 'Because,' he answered dryly, 'America consists today of people who want to bat *all* the time.' "

Baseball was certainly partly responsible for the diminishing interest of the Americanized children of the Nottingham mill workers. But what really killed cricket among the upper classes was — tennis. Lawn tennis. It was tennis that stole the younger generation of sportsmen away from the game of their fathers and uncles, tennis that allowed women to participate rather than merely watch — ladies could play it, according to Henry James, either with or without parasols — and tennis that finally crowded the elevens off their beautiful turfed "creases" at Merion, Germantown and Philadelphia. The cricket clubs of Philadelphia became American centers of lawn tennis, produced the "world's greatest tennis player," and still possess more beautiful grass courts than any other city in the country. The upstart tennis, like the cuckoo, took over the nest, and finally killed off cricket, the unwary foster parent.

ix. The Cuckoo

LAWN TENNIS WAS INVENTED in England. In 1873, a certain English Army man, Major Walter C. Wingfield, having nothing better to do in those halcyon days, made up out of his own head a game he laboriously called Sphairistike. This is Greek meaning "the art of ball-handling," pronounced, one supposes, real Greek, or *Sphaïristikē*. This was a lawn game which consisted of an hourglass-shaped court, with a high net at the waist, and a scoring system modeled after that of the ancient and honorable game of court tennis. Besides this unfortunate scoring system, full of "loves" and "advantages," the only other bond was the fact that a ball was indeed batted over a net by players holding rackets or racquets. The Major's new game stirred up quite a bit of interest in polite circles, and soon came under the notice of the august Marylebone (Marlybone) Cricket Club, or MCC, which is to English cricket what the Bank of England is to English finance. The Club took up Sphairistike, and in no time at all did away with most of the Major's whims, including the name. The court was straightened out into the present oblong shape, and the name was changed to the more discreet and descriptive "lawn tennis."

Lawn tennis struck the East Coast of America about 1874 in a three-pronged beachhead which beautifully characterizes the attitudes of three cities, Boston, New York and Philadelphia. In Boston it was adopted more or less as a Cause, at Nahant in particular, by two very Proper Bostonians, Dr. Dwight and Mr. Sears. Dr. Dwight and Mr. Sears seemed to believe that tennis was Good for People, and that Everybody ought to play it. They devoted years to propaganda and exhibition, in the process becoming America's first doubles and singles champions. In New York, as represented at Newport, it beame the Thing to Do. Very expensive grass courts were created in the middle of the Newport Casino, where they still are, and ladies went to fancy dress balls decked out in nets as "Tennis." It was fashionable. In Philadelphia anything approved of by the MCC was of course of vital interest to the various local cricket clubs, and so they all dutifully laid out lawn tennis courts, off to the side where they wouldn't interfere with the serious business of cricket, and very soon the Philadelphia cricket clubs began to produce champions of their own.

The Lawn Tennis Association was formed in 1881. Already in that year C. M. Clark and Frederick Taylor of the Young America Cricket Club of Philadelphia beat the perennial Sears and Dwight in the brand-new National Doubles Championship. In 1883, Joseph Sill Clark, Sr., a member of the Philadelphia Cricket Club, won the first intercollegiate singles representing Harvard, and in 1885, with Richard Sears himself as partner, won the National Doubles Championship at Newport, thus uniting all three aspects of early American Lawn Tennis in one triumph.

Both Clarks were of course of the banking Clark family, Joseph being the father of the present Senator.

It was in a later generation, however, that Philadelphia tennis really emerged from the background of the cricket clubs and took over nationally in the persons of R. Norris Williams II (Philadelphia Cricket Club), William Clothier (Merion Cricket Club), and finally the great William Tatum Tilden II, or Tooth, as he liked to call himself (Germantown Cricket Club).

R. Norris Williams, who was United States Singles Champion in both 1914 and 1916, was less famous for his victories than for his tennis form. He was the "tennis player's tennis player," and old-timers who saw him in action consider him at his best the greatest of them all; the only man really capable of beating Tilden at *his* best. Clothier, although he was American singles champion too in 1906, was not in the same league. He was more the golden ideal of the Philadelphia sportsman-gentleman, equally adept at tennis or foxhunting. As for William Tatum Tilden II, he was, of course, Big Bill, "greatest tennis player in the world," and perhaps the first to inject a dubious note of professionalism into the game. Whether he really was the greatest tennis player of all time or not, Tilden has been enshrined in that curious imaginary Pantheon erected to the great American sportsmen of the 'twenties, when America first emerged as winner of world championships. Along with Babe Ruth, Bobby Jones, Red Grange and Jack Dempsey, Tilden is one of the Immortals, and whatever the facts, he has a good chance of retaining his perhaps spurious world title down through the ages.

Actually Tilden was United States Singles Champion straight through from 1920 to 1925 inclusive, and then again in 1929. He was men's singles champion at Wimbledon in 1920, 1921 and 1930. He was a doubles champ there in 1927, and with Vincent Richards, three times United States men's doubles champion, in 1918, 1923 and 1927. These of course are only the most conspicuous of his victories. What Jack Kelly was to rowing in the same period, Tilden was to tennis. In these two men Philadelphia achieved her summit of amateur athletic prowess.

Kelly was, according to Henley, "not a gentleman." Tilden, on the other hand, was a "gentleman" by those standards, if hardly by certain other standards. The Tildens if not famously Old Philadelphian were at least respectable; "people knew them," and they were members as a family of the Germantown Cricket Club. It was there in Germantown that Bill and his older brother Herbert were brought up, as orphans, by elderly relatives, and where Herbert taught William all about tennis. William's devotion to his older brother was absolute. In any tennis crisis he would ask himself "What would Herbert do?" and then do it.

As a person Tilden had charm and color — some of it off. He was decidedly not in the conventional Germantown mold. Quite aside from his later notorious sexual irregularities, he was recognized by people who knew him best as almost a psychopath, full of hallucinations, persecution complexes and other quirks. Despite all this, people were fond of him; his irregularities were known but ignored. Unlike the genial, upright Kelly, Tilden was hardly suitable as a Sporting Ideal for American Youth. He was, however, especially for a champion, a curious and complex character. If and when it can be written, his life should make an interesting story.

Nowadays Old Philadelphia, or even just Philadelphia, doesn't produce tennis champions. Victor Seixas seems to have been the last. Tennis has become much too professional a racket, or racquet, for gentlemen. Its place, for them, has been taken by squash, and in this much less publicized area Old Philadelphia still sets up a few winners. In fact, since about 1935, they've had a near monopoly. Diehl Mateer of the Merion Cricket Club and several junior Heckshers still get their names, briefly, in the papers. Even Seixas now specializes in squash.

This is the game of squash *racquets* which is not to be confused with squash *tennis* or racquets (plain) or lawn tennis or above all court tennis.

Court tennis, the ancestor of the whole brood, which in court-tennis circles is always carefully referred to as just plain "tennis," is the sport of medieval French kings, and requires a fairly literal indoor reproduction of the original palace courtyard, with all sorts of antique penthouses, windows at odd intervals and such. Obviously tennis courts of this kind are not to be built casually, and the one at the Philadelphia Racquet Club is one of only seven in the United States.

Court tennis was brought over to New York in the Gilded Age, about 1900, as a piece of extremely conspicuous consumption, and for years its most notable American and indeed world exponent was the millionaire Jay Gould. This Jay Gould was the grandson of the extremely conspicuous Jay Gould who tried to corner gold and might have gone to jail for it. He was certainly not a Philadelphian. George Jay, son of the original Jay, had built a vast palace at Lakewood, New Jersey. This palace, called Georgian Court, had a bed worth $25,000 in it, a shooting gallery, a Turkish bath — and a "tennis court." Here George's son young Jay learned his art; when the palace vanished, he transferred his activities to the Philadelphia Racquet Club, and from 1907, when the club moved into its new building on 16th Street, through 1925, Gould held the National Tennis Singles Championship in the name of the P.R.C. The first such singles champion was, incidentally, redoubtable Mr. Sears of Boston, father of American lawn tennis. When Gould retired, the championship returned to New York and has been held by New Yorkers like Ogden Phipps ever since; but Gould is usually acknowledged to have been the greatest court tennis player the world has ever known.

Now that cricket is pretty well defunct, and that champion tennis players no longer come from Philadelphia, Old Philadelphia is content with the usual country-club routine of strictly "fun" tennis and golf.

Philadelphia does not seem to have produced male Old Philadelphian golf champions to match the tennis ones; but there are some females. In fact, the sporting woman has been a fairly consistent modern product. There is, for instance, the famous Glenna Collet Vare, seven times United States women's amateur champion, who still plays out of the Philadelphia Country (not Cricket) Club. Mrs. Harrison Flippen, wife of one of Philadelphia's best-known physicians (these doctors keep their wives healthy) in 1959 won the United States senior golf title for the fifth time in succession by a large margin, and there were a good many other healthy Philadelphia matrons in competition with her. Nor can one fail to mention Helen Sigel Wilson, socially prominent golf champion, mentioned before as owner of one of Philadelphia's few good restaurants.

Most peculiarly Old Philadelphian of women's sports has been field hockey. One is accustomed to the field hockey played by schoolgirls, but not to field hockey pursued as a serious sport by grown-up women; but in Philadelphia it is so pursued. It was, like tennis, introduced into the cricket clubs, in 1903, about the same time as squash. Since then there have been international matches, a United States Hockey Association, and gates of thousands of spectators (really and truly). Teams for the Merion and the Philadelphia Cricket Clubs still seem to have the last word nationally. Mrs. Edward R. Krumbhaar of the Philadelphia and Miss Anne Townsend of the Merion have been outstanding players and patronesses. An athletic dynastic union of some sort was celebrated when Barbara Newhall, champion hockey player and daughter of the cricket clan, married John Elliot Newlin, Jr., son of the Commodore of the Schuylkill Navy. Their children certainly ought to be good at something; though with the continental change of emphasis in Philadelphia sport, one wonders at what.

The cricket clubs are now devoted to everything except cricket; a very young member of one of them was even heard recently to inquire what the old club had to do with insects anyway. They are rivaled by a whole set of later clubs of social standing, such as the Gulph Mills or the Huntingdon Valley, more especially and originally devoted to golf. Nonetheless, in the hierarchy of the country club in Philadelphia, the Merion, Philadelphia and Germantown still hold first place socially, and their present prestige derives from their former association with Philadelphia's "peculiar pastime."

x. *Humane and Eccentric*

WHEN JOSIAH WHITE started taming the Falls of the Schuylkill, and when the dam was built there, the effects may have been disastrous for real estate, but they were good for sport. The calm backwater that bred mosquitoes and drove away the owners of country houses encouraged boating in summer and skating in winter. All during the nineteenth century this was Philadelphia's favorite skating ground for all sorts and conditions, as prints of the animated scene testify. It was not particularly safe ground, however. Not only did people drown themselves individually, but there were collective disasters when the whole ice covering broke loose and took everyone over the dam.

To mitigate these disasters, a Philadelphia Skating Club and Humane Society was formed in the mid-nineteenth century. The members not only encouraged the art, but went around with ropes tied to their backs to rescue unfortunates. The Humane aspect has pretty well worn off, but the Society goes on, and remains as Philadelphia's foremost skating club. A rival Wissahickon Skating Club is of recent date, and teams of ex-college hockey stars play each other, Humane versus Wissahickon.

Considerably less Humane is one of Philadelphia's oddest sports, Cat Hunting. Cat hunting was supposed to have originated in a fight between the late John Sergeant Price and two maiden neighbors of his in Chestnut Hill. The ladies were inordinately charitable to stray cats, and the yowling of toms at night became too much for Price. His complaints had no effect, so he invited a group of equally afflicted neighbors to dinner and afterward they all went out shooting cats. The cats were skinned and each participant eventually received a catskin vest as a souvenir. The event proved so popular that it became an annual affair, and spread to other parts of the suburbs. Still today occasional forays of cat hunting take place. I have heard a debutante of the 'thirties describing the difficulties of hunting cats by moonlight in a ball gown from the rumble seat of a car.

Although the sport of cat hunting might seem eccentric, and even disagreeable, to some, among Old Philadelphians there is, on the contrary, something a bit eccentric about a fervid interest in proletarian sports like boxing or baseball. At least, the two most famous Old Philadelphian patrons of these sports happen to be Old Philadelphia's two most famous eccentrics, the boxer Anthony Drexel Biddle and the baseball fan Henry Savage. Biddle loved nothing better than to square off with visiting champs in his living room, and his favorite avocation, of many, was that Bible Class, in which Scripture and fisticuffs were blended. Henry Savage was a familiar spectacle, dressed in dingy clothes and wearing a battered straw hat, on the trolley to the ball park, during the great days long gone when Connie Mack's Athletics ruled America's baseball roost. Although a Yale man, Savage spent the spring afternoons out at the University fields with his favorite willow bat, swatting flies for the members of the Penn team to catch. These activities, however, were all part of the benign "eccentricity" of Philadelphia's favorite individualist, and certainly could not be considered very typically Old Philadelphian. Perhaps most unusual of all Philadelphia's present-day ball fans is Maximilien de Schauensee, who also happens to be Philadelphia's one really nationally known music critic. Not only is he an avid rooter for the home team but he keeps on file, along with his comprehensive collection of operatic letters and autographs, another comprehensive collection of photographs of famous ball players.

It is a permanent illusion, transferred ritually from generation to generation, that the past was more "characteristic," "original" and full of flavor" than the present. Each new generation, especially one might say in Philadelphia, goes on believing this, though logic and probability are against there being a perfectly even continual process of de-flavorization right down through the ages. But certainly looking upon the Philadelphia scene of sports, not to mention clubs and businesses, one can't help but remark on a lamentable decline in individuality and local oddities. Cricket and coaching have almost vanished, fox hunting is certainly hard pressed by the modern realities, and a sort of bland suburban country-clubbism with conventional winter excursions into squash, or skiing in the Poconos, seems to follow the trend in business toward the vast impersonal monopoly or in social life towards a universal standardized American-middle-middle-class-country-club-and-cocktail-party melting pot.* Actually this all really may be an illusion; cricket and coaching were after all popular in their day in other places besides Philadelphia. It was merely that Philadelphia kept on with them longer than most places. This is a perennial Philadelphia trick, and gives to Philadelphia a sort of perpetual feeling of loss. Philadelphians are always just now getting rid of things that are picturesque, like those gas lamps on the streets, only because everybody else got rid of them long ago.

Just the same, it does seem hard to believe that the present era of supremacy in squash will ever seem to have the sporting glamour of the Iron Age: the Gentlemen of Philadelphia taking on England, the Rogers four-in-hand dashing through Fairmount Park, the regattas on the river beginning and ending with parties at The Lilacs or even the more modern-seeming triumphs of Williams and Clothier, of the less Old Philadelphian Kelly and Tilden. Sports in Philadelphia, among the upper classes especially, are in a sort of decay. Nearly Everybody plays games, for fun and exercise, but Hardly Anybody takes the trouble either to cultivate difficult ones, like cricket and fox hunting, or to become champions at others, like tennis. It is probably all just a phase of the national *Zeitgeist,* the taking over by the public of what used to be a preserve for the private. Even collegiate football, once full of Old Philadelphia champions, particularly

---

* Digby Baltzell, in his *Philadelphia Gentlemen,* even views with some alarm the formation of a sort of standardized "national upper class" of more or less interchangeable mass production "Ivy League" parts, which he feels is increasingly displacing the older more local and indigenous upper classes, including that of Philadelphia. The alarm was grossly misinterpreted by Vance Packard in his *The Status Seekers;* he seemed to think Baltzell meant to indicate a modern "hardening of class lines." Just the opposite, in fact.

at Penn and Princeton, no longer produces winning teams composed almost exclusively, like the famous Princeton team of 1936, of gents, and Old Philadelphia gents at that.

Even proletarian sport ain't, like society or the old gray mare, what it used to be. Philadelphia's remaining baseball team rests securely on the bottom.* Kelly and Tilden, Philadelphia's chief contributions to the gallery of Great Sports Figures of All Time, are both dead and have no real successors. Philadelphians have, in fact, every opportunity of indulging in their favorite emotions, regretful nostalgia and disparagement of the present, as they contemplate the field of sports. And, as said before, there's no sentimentalist like a sporting sentimentalist.

---

* It must be admitted, however, that professional football and Philadelphia's Eagles do better. They were national champions in 1960; but in the cellar in 1962. Perhaps an increasing interest in the sport by Old Philadelphians accounts for the decline.

1

i. Boeotia

As A CENTER OF ART, letters and intellect, Philadelphia has enjoyed the dubious distinction of being called the Boeotia of
America. The tag seems to have been attached early, as witness
S. Fisher's remarks about politicians from "our Boeotian State"
of Pennsylvania. Boeotia was a northerly province of Greece
which was looked upon by Athenians as the home of boors and
numbskulls. Philadelphia is said to be in exactly the same geographical latitude, and to be equally numb to all areas of higher
sensibility. Actually about all that one is likely to know about
Boeotia nowadays is that Hesiod and Pindar, two of the Greeks'
best poets, were natives, and that later on the Boeotian city of
Tanagra made and exported little figurines which are models
of grace. It was also the locale of a family marriage even closer
than those of the Biddles: that of Oedipus, who married his
mother, much to Freud's satisfaction.

Boeotia may have been no Athens but what does survive of it
is its art (and its tradition of family Togetherness). Philadelphia is obviously no Paris, but its only really world-famous citizens, Benjamin Franklin, Thomas Eakins and Marian Anderson,
have been artists, its most famous export these days is its Orchestra, and, despite unfriendly or unsympathetic atmospherics, the
arts have persisted throughout the history of Philadelphia in a
quiet but determined fashion.

Most of this persistence, and most of the Boeotian atmosphere
too, is the direct result of the Oligarchy's somewhat condescend-

ing patronage of the Muses. Franklin, Eakins and Anderson were none of them Old Philadelphians; still it was a world of letters, painting and music supported, created and maintained largely by Old Philadelphians, with vital help from the German and Jewish bourgeoisie, that made it possible for artists to exist in Philadelphia at all. There are few if any American cities where the connections between art and the aristocrat have been so close, not always to their mutual benefit. Yet in general, there is no place where the arts are or have been generally regarded with less real esteem.

In Old Philadelphia sports are very important, and active participation is required. In Old Philadelphia arts are very unimportant, participation is slightly suspicious, but patronage is more or less a duty. If you must be an idler, a sporty idleness may be forgiven. The sign of decadence in a Philadelphia family is not usually an increasing anemia, dilettantism or feebleness, but the relapse into a large, handsome, healthy boorishness, and it is common to run across the grandsons of men famous for their professional acumen, classic learning and intelligent appreciation of art, whose strong bodies and weak heads contain nothing but the points of horses, women and liquor.

The only really respectable approach to art is by way of the boards of institutions. Less respectable, but permitted, is a flagrant amateurism. Every now and then a youngster born to the purple shows signs of real aesthetic talent and ambition, and this in the past has always caused great concern in the Family. Nowadays people care less, but in the Oligarchy's heyday a career as a serious artist was about as shocking as an open irregular liaison; that is, all right as a secret vice, unpardonable in public. This did not prevent many Old Philadelphians from breaking loose, but there was usually a note of rebellious bitterness in their attitude towards their class and their city.

The peculiarly Philadelphian paradox, however, is that the higher you get into the echelons of Old Philadelphia, the more at home art is. The innermost shrine of the hidden core of the Hidden City might be symbolized as a dusty altar to a thwarted creative talent. From Francis Hopkinson, Nicholas Biddle and Charles Ingersoll down to Ingersolls and Biddles of today that strain of aesthetic sensibility, usually undeveloped or dilettant-ized, and however disapproved of publicly, keeps popping out. The figure of the dilettante-gentleman who, often at the expense of his talents, occupies a place at the center of the Philadelphia Web is so common, recurs so frequently, that he might be taken as one of the Ideal Prototypes of Philadelphianism. Hopkinson, Nicholas Biddle, Charles J. Ingersoll, George Boker, Owen Wis-ter, William Bullitt, George and Francis Biddle were only the more prominent of these gentlemen artists. Sidney Fisher or John Hare Powel have a strong dash of the disappointed-gentleman-dilettante in them too, and even today in the city's civic life the type is often seen — the man blessed with every gift, handsome, rich, active, charming, talented, who out of a career of disap-pointed ambition, dissipated achievement and disguised frustra-tion manages to be only one thing really successfully — a Phila-delphian.

ii. *Bishop's Length and Kit-cat**

YET THERE IS NO BRANCH of the fine arts to which Philadelphians or at least artists practicing in Philadelphia, have not made fairly significant contributions. The aesthetic temperature of Phila-delphia has been a steady simmer, which seldom comes to a boil, but which never quite grows cold, and there has been a remark-able continuity, a tradition, in some cases almost a fatality, a special permanent tone to each art individually.

Painting is the art which has flourished best and longest there. One explanation has been that having no ideas in them, paint-ings are not controversial; but the history of Philadelphia paint-ing does not seem to support this (witness the stormy career of Thomas Eakins or the reactions of George Biddle). Whatever the cause, the reputation of Philadelphia's Great Tradition, from

---

* "Bishop's Length" and "Kit-cat" were nineteenth-century artists' trade names for specified sizes of portraits.

Peale and his family to Eakins and on, has never been higher and shows no signs of diminishing. It is a tradition tied firmly, through the portrait, to patronage by the upper classes; and whenever an artist tends away from this tradition he usually suffers for it or leaves town. Sometimes it would have been better for various artists (Benjamin West is a striking example) if they had stuck to the tradition and stayed home. Eakins, the greatest of them all, did stick to the tradition and did stay home, though being original he suffered for it. Still, he might serve as an object lesson to future Philadelphia artists. One wonders, for instance, if George Biddle's portraits (such as the splendid picture of Van Wyck Brooks which hangs rather mysteriously in the rare-book room of the University of Pennsylvania Library) may not end up being considered his most powerful and even original works; and whether he does not succeed as an artist to the very extent that he comes close to the Philadelphia tradition that he so obstreperously despises.

The tradition is there at any rate; and in the person of Franklin Watkins, Philadelphia's present First Portraitist, the apostolic succession continues.

There were various competent enough painters in Philadelphia from the early eighteenth century on, despite a strong Quaker bias against any sort of worldly show, even portraits. Most notable of these were the Swede Gustavus Hesselius, a cousin of Swedenborg, who arrived in America in 1711, and his son John. But Philadelphia's real artistic history begins later, with Benjamin West (1738–1820) and Charles Willson Peale (1741–1827), who in themselves symbolize pretty neatly the double bias of Philadelphian, and indeed American, culture, one the essentially colonial tradition looking to Europe for values and approval (Fancy?), even to the extent of expatriation, the other the essential native who stays at home and tries to see for himself (Plain?).

West was probably, at his zenith around the end of the eighteenth century, the most famous, popular and respectable painter of the Anglo-Saxon world; which is a rather damning comment on the tastes of the Anglo-Saxon world. He was a good portrait painter led astray by ambition and royal encouragement into the field of grandiose allegory for which he was technically not very well equipped; but, in its excitement over his subject matter, his public never seemed to notice this. Two of his great absurd phantasies, "Death on a Pale Horse" and "Christ Rejected," still adorn the Moorish walls of the Pennsylvania Academy. There they have been a "terror to generations of Philadelphia children," and have had "a very somber effect on the Philadelphia imagination." Then there is that "Christ Healing the Sick," with demoniac and relations, which greets the visitor at the Pennsylvania Hospital. If one can forget the almost laughable impression of the dramatics and the higgledy-piggledy way the figures come together, and concentrate on the individual faces, one finds the precise thing so often missing in other, better executed big pictures of the sort: each face has life and character. If he'd been forced to stay in Philadelphia and grind out likenesses of worthies, Philadelphia might have had a gallery equal to Copley's in Boston.

West was so famous in his time that everything turned to myth, as it tends to do with great figures. His birth and childhood are haloed by tales of prodigy: how his pregnant mother was so stricken at Meeting by the hell-fire of a visiting Quaker saint that she nearly had him there and then, and it was assumed from the start that he had been chosen by God for great things; or how, when he was out in the woods as a little boy sketching for pleasure, Indians appeared and taught him the use of color — red and yellow clay. His mother supplemented this limited palette by lending him some of her indigo dye. Having heard that paintbrushes were to be made of camel's hair, and there being no camels available, he took the fur from the tip of the cat's tail. Gradually the cat began to look very patchy. His mother thought the animal had the mange; but Benjamin could not tell a lie. His mother, always encouraging, kissed him for his ingenuity.

He was already a journeyman painter at sixteen, and was called to Philadelphia shortly thereafter by Provost Smith of the College to be his personal scholarship pupil there. At college he became fast friends with Francis Hopkinson, future Signer, Thomas Godfrey, Jr., future dramatist, and others of that early blossoming of the College's intellect. His poetic friends celebrated the genius of West with many a limpid verse in the local newspapers, and they all fished, strolled and recited poetry to each other on the banks of the salubrious Schuylkill.

But destiny called. A New York and a Philadelphia patron together sent him to Italy, "nurse of the gentler arts," where his myth-making ability did not desert him. Taken before the Apollo Belvedere by an escort of cognoscenti anxious to see how a savage from the howling wilderness of Philadelphia would react, he reacted perfectly. "My God, how like a Mohawk warrior!" he exclaimed, and West was a made man. He absorbed the last decadence of the Grand Manner during his Italian stay, then went to London — supposedly for a brief visit on his way home — and there fame and fortune trapped him. He never returned to America. First coming to the attention of London's great world as an accomplished skater, he soon made his way as a painter too. Such was his rapid success that in three years he was a popular idol. Given a commission by the Archbishop of York to do "Agrippina with the Ashes of Germanicus," he was taken up by King George III himself, then a young patron of art, and asked to paint "The Departure of Regulus from Rome." This was the beginning of one of the most curious of friendships between the democratic Quaker colonial painter of historical pageants and the German ruler of the British Empire whose policy of timid despotism caused the Americans to rebel. The friendship was blighted by West's patriotism and George's madness, but nothing blighted the career of West himself.

One of the founders of the Royal Academy, and twice serving as its president, West was able to refuse a proffered knighthood on the grounds that it could not possibly add to his reputation; though he did hint that a peerage might help. He didn't get the peerage, but his death in 1820 was considered a national calamity, and though he was not a proper communicant of the Church of England, and in fact had never been baptized, he was buried with pomp in St. Paul's next to Sir Joshua Reynolds. No American painter before or since, with the exception of that other expatriated Philadelphian, John Sargent, has ever done better in England than the Quaker Prodigy.

Not the least among the myths that cling to him is that surrounding his marriage. Before he left for Europe he had been engaged to a Philadelphia girl, Elizabeth Shewell, kin of still another Philadelphia expatriate, Leigh Hunt. The family disapproved of a low painter. When West, established in England, sent for his fiancée, her brother refused to let her go, and shut her up, a prisoner in the family house. Three of West's Philadelphia friends however spirited her away at night, out of her bedroom window, and put her on board a waiting ship; an elopement by proxy, so to speak. The three friends were Francis Hopkinson, William White, later on first Episcopal Bishop of Pennsylvania, and — (you guessed it) Benjamin Franklin.

Whatever the judgment of West as a painter, there can be no question about his influence as a teacher. Despised for a century after his death, his art is now suddenly being reappraised. Nobody likes the religious pictures that made him most famous, but his essays in neoclassicism and romanticism make him a forerunner of the most important currents of art in the early nineteenth century. As a teacher of art he can claim, along with Washington, to be a Father of his Country. Everyone studied with him, and benefited from his kindness, discipline and patronage. All the early American masters, Peale, Copley, Stuart, Trumbull, did time with him, as well as a later generation of Sully, Morse, Allston and Leslie. Whether his influence was universally beneficent is a question; but there is no question that it was overwhelmingly pervasive.

Charles Willson Peale, who stayed at home, was one of those crotchety, curious-minded, many-faceted individualists that Philadelphia seems to have nursed so willingly in its great days, and so grudgingly later on. Like his literary-scientific counterpart Franklin, Peale was not a Philadelphian originally; unlike Franklin, he was not always well treated in Philadelphia; but he stayed, and by his staying really established painting as something native to the city.

He was a Marylander born, brought up in Annapolis, where he began as a saddle-maker, watch-maker and anything-maker, and gradually turned himself into a sign-and-portrait-maker. He preserved the character of that great Revolutionary age in an endless series of portraits, large and small, many of them now housed in Independence Hall. More and more his full-length portraits of Washington as a young, strong, energetic general have come to be regarded as truer to the subject than Stuart's far more famous, old, heavy-jawed icon.

He studied in London with Benjamin West, like everyone else, but it did not take. He refined his technique a bit, but rejected the suavities learned by Stuart or the Grand Manner of the master himself. His eye remained clear, native and not too flattering. He served actively and gallantly in the Revolution — "painted and fit, fit and painted" — and did miniatures of officers during the dreadful winter in camp at Valley Forge. Afterwards he helped celebrate victory by creating, like Leonardo da Vinci, illuminated displays and triumphal arches. One of these burned while he was working on it, nearly killing him with exploding firecrackers; from another a laurel wreath was ingeniously dropped plunk on the head of Washington as he rode under it and into Philadelphia to take his place as President.

The great hobby and profession of Peale's vigorous old age was his Museum, which contained portraits of Revolutionary heroes and stuffed animals in about equal proportion. Eventually the animals outnumbered the portraits, and Peale invented for their display the "habitat group" — a natural background for them such as is now common in all good natural history museums. His greatest coup was the excavation and assembly of the skeletons of two prehistoric mastodons. He not only painted a picture of the process of excavation, but at eighty-three did a fine full-length picture of himself lifting a curtain to disclose the wonders of his Museum, mastodons and all. He also tinkered with windmills, stoves, velocipedes and false teeth. Finally, on his deathbed at eighty-six, Peale asked one of his daughters to feel his pulse. She failed to feel any. He nodded, "No, I thought not," and quietly died.

Not only was Peale the first really competent Philadelphia portrait painter, but he is generally considered the creator of the Pennsylvania Academy of Fine Arts, first to be actually chartered and officially established in the country. He also sired or taught a whole clan of other Peales. His brother James became during his long life not only America's foremost painter of still life, but also in his turn sire and teacher of painters. James in turn had as a follower his nephew, Charles's talented but unfortunate son Raphaelle, who before his early drunkard's death surpassed his uncle as a still-life artist. This tradition of the still life became a peculiarly Philadelphian one, and reached its final flowering in Harnett, Peto and other "illusionists" of the late nineteenth century, who painted with a vengeance "facts and things." Once confined to barrooms, their pictures now hang in the best museums. "Facts and things," sober though they may be, wear well.

Rembrandt, another son of Charles, carried on his father's tradition of head-hunting, and made a good thing out of mass-producing pictures of Washington for patriotic homes. Peale's son Titian was a painter of birds, and still another son, Rubens, also did still life. The boys carried on the Museum, and branched out on their own in Baltimore and elsewhere. Altogether seventeen Peales painted in one way or another, and the last of them, a maiden granddaughter of Charles named Mary Jane who did miniatures, did not die till 1902.

Longevity, in fact, was another of the Peale talents. What killed off Charles in his eighty-sixth year was overexertion in his efforts to find himself a fourth wife. Brother James lived on till 1831 and was still working in his eighty-second year. By this time Thomas Sully, successor in the line of Philadelphia's "First Portraitists," had been established for over a decade.

Though Charles and James Peale were born in Maryland, nothing could be more thoroughly Philadelphian than this Peale familyness. In their limited but seemingly durable competence, in their concentration on portraiture and still life, family faces and the edible, and in their handing down of tradition from one generation to the next, the Peales certainly can stand as Philadelphia's representative artistic family. Philadelphia's heart, however, remains with the next dispensation, the era of Sully and Neagle.

Thomas Sully was everything the Philadelphia upper classes wanted a portrait painter to be. He was English-born, though reared in the South, he studied with Benjamin West and learned the fashionable Lawrence manner in London, he painted the Queen, and he did Biddle after Biddle. Whatever his faults, and however variable his technique, he nearly always succeeded in one principal aim: his subjects looked like ladies and gentlemen. This was the sine qua non of English portrait painting, and it became that of Philadelphia portrait painting.

Sully was very prolific; though many of his pictures are mere brownish hack work. His most characteristic style is one of glowing, grenadine-soaked flattery, charming, a bit silly in its unctuousness, a bit cloying in its blatant superficiality and eternal pink-and-white-and-red-all-over. There is another, better vein of Sully though, a grayer vein, in which he shows a more refined touch than his master Lawrence, is in fact perhaps in "better taste," somewhat as the eighteenth-century Philadelphia cabinetmakers were in "better taste" than the English virtuosi just because, probably out of pure necessity, their handiwork was more simple and more restrained. In pictures such as those of Major Biddle the duelist and his wife in the Metropolitan, of the Penn–Gaskells in the Philadelphia Historical Society, or of Zachariah Poulsen at the Library Company, he captures not the surface but the essence of breeding, a sensitive, quiet, completely natural elegance, without pomp and sham, which is certainly the Philadelphia aristocracy's very best face.

In true Philadelphia fashion, Sully's younger coadjutor and pupil, John Neagle, whom he outlived, was a member of his family, having married his niece. Neagle represents a sort of transition towards Eakins. He is more bourgeois than Sully, more forceful, and less refined. Certainly less elegant. Where Sully painted the families established during the Revolution, Biddles and Ingersolls, Neagle painted more the doctors and lawyers and professors, or the newer Victorian man of wealth whose families came to seem Old Philadelphian only by contrast with the robber barons after the Civil War. Nowadays families can be graded according to their portraits, as Peale, Sully or Neagle families.

Neagle, like Sully, has suffered for the things he did most flamboyantly — the famous one for instance of Pat Lyon the blacksmith in his leather apron which has even made *Life*. This kind of drama has, like Sully's pink-pearl-and-raspberry Queen Victoria, tended to overshadow his more serious, sensitive, strong portraits: of John Kintzing Kane for instance in the Princeton University Museum, or his substantial Thomas Cope, who presided at that meeting in the Chinese Museum when the Pennsylvania Railroad was born, full of color, phlegm, authority, character, a less intellectual forerunner of the kind of thing Eakins did later with just this sort of Philadelphia professional personage. Sully and Neagle really stopped painting in the 'fifties, and the Civil War years were filled only by the Pennsylvania Academy and the last efforts of the Peales.

Thomas Eakins, next in the succession, did not study with West or Sully. He studied rather at the Jefferson Medical College, where he undoubtedly learned more than he ever did in any studio or at the Pennsylvania Academy. His anatomical and medical bent influenced him all the rest of his life.

Eakins's interest in medicine was as characteristically Philadelphian as his interest in sports, particularly rowing and coaching. His serious amateur musicians playing in the gloom their Bach, Beethoven and surely Brahms are the essence of Philadelphia's Germanic-amateur musical culture. Brahms in fact is exactly the musician one thinks of. The effects of sobriety of color and almost stifled richness of feeling, the deliberate conservatism, the general air of sumptuous, earnest, large-scale Nordic gloom — these are as close a parallel as two such different mediums, painting and music, and two such different cultures, Germanic and American, can produce.

Philadelphia, but *not* Old Philadelphia. Eakins's world was an intellectual professional upper-middle class. Even when Eakins does the Fairman Rogers coach-and-four one misses the Sargent dash and suavity and glitter that would no doubt have been preferred. Eakins was too serious for the subject, and he was much too serious for the Philadelphia upper classes of his time. Brought up on Sully, Old Philadelphians were quite unwilling not to be flattered. They hated Eakins's honesty, his middle-class plainness. A gentleman in Chestnut Hill had Eakins do himself and his wife. When the pictures were done he sent his check, the pictures were carefully packed and carted to Chestnut Hill, the butler met them at the door, took them down to the cellar and burned them in the furnace. This was in general the Philadelphia upper-class comment on an artist who violated the appearances.

His "Gross Clinic" was not permitted to be hung in the Fine Arts exhibit of the 1876 Centennial. People were outraged by the blood on Dr. Gross's hands. It was hung in the medical section instead.

Eakins taught for ten years at the Pennsylvania Academy, completely reforming and revitalizing the course of study. When in the interests of accurate anatomy he insisted on having a nude male model pose for a class of women, Philadelphia was outraged again. Daughters of directors of the Academy were in the class, and those directors saw to it that Eakins was forced to resign. He did not starve. Like any good Philadelphian he "had money," even if it wasn't exactly Old Philadelphia money. He lived and died where he was born, in a substantial house — still standing, though without a marker — on Mount Vernon Street, north of Market and therefore déclassé.

Philadelphia did not treat its greatest artist well, but it *had* Eakins, and in a very definite way. Few American artists of accomplishment have been so very local, so very native, so very representative. All his scenes are Philadelphian, except for a few done in the Far West. To come from the contemporary and so completely antagonistic world of French Impressionism, all grace, color, worldly pleasure and perhaps wearisome sunlight, into the world of Eakins is like coming from a summer picnic into a big black-walnut-paneled late Victorian library where a concert of serious music is going on. The contrast is shocking, but not un-refreshing, and though one might not want to live in it, this world of sober tragedy and muted honest grandeur is very com-pelling.

To think of John Singer Sargent as the expatriate counterpart of Eakins, as West was of Peale, is rather farfetched. He did very little work in Philadelphia; perhaps his prices were too high for the residual Quaker thrift of his possible Philadelphia patrons. Perhaps he was too dashing, a bit risqué for them. Nonetheless he was a Philadelphian — though Philadelphia Fancy, as Eakins was Philadelphia Plain. His father, born in New England, studied and practiced medicine in Philadelphia. His mother — well, who *were* the Singers, anyway?* They were Philadelphian, and they seemed to have money. In any case, the Sargents had enough in 1854 to settle more or less permanently in Florence.

When on a visit to his cousins, the Newbolds, Sargent did carica-tures of the family in the form of animals. When these turned up at a later date, the family burned them, as being what Phila-delphians like to call "unnecessary." The blood that Eakins pic-tured on the hands of Dr. Gross, the nude male model were "un-necessary." It is hard to believe Sargent was ever guilty of being "unnecessary"; but evidently in this one case he was. Perhaps a feeling of being "unnecessary" among his relatives is what kept him from being more closely identified with his native city.

"Miss Mary Cassatt, sister of Mr. Cassatt, president of the Pennsylvania Railroad, returned from Europe yesterday. She has been studying painting in Paris, and owns the smallest Pekinese dog in the world." This, one of Philadelphia's most trenchant pieces of art criticism, appeared in the Philadelphia *Ledger* when Mary had already an established reputation abroad. It reflects

* A family of German descent. Mrs. Sargent's father had married a Newbold.

rather adequately Philadelphia's appreciation of its other most internationally famous native painter. Miss Cassatt was born near Pittsburgh and died near Paris, but she remained all her life the epitome of Philadelphia spinsterhood, upright, caustic, severely dressed, serving tea to friends with the help of starched maids. Degas's picture of her from the back (she wouldn't let him paint her face), now owned by Philadelphia's Henry McIlhenny, shows a rigid, uncompromising elegance which is certainly neither Pittsburgh nor Paris. Her pictures, nearly always of pastel women, or women and children, are quite contained in the tradition of Degas and French Impressionism, but she never lost her native accent. The firm outline, the delicate prettiness of the colors, the simple maternal tenderness, the scrubbed healthy soap-and-water fairness of her children are American; rather more specifically American Philadelphia feminine upper class.

Philadelphia's other woman artist, the one to counterbalance Cassatt's expatriatism, who stayed at home, is Cecilia Beaux, also a Philadelphia spinster. Her paintings, nearly all portraits, have what Mary Cassatt's lack: force, vigor, enthusiasm. They also lack what Cassatt has: style, particularly individual style. A good Beaux portrait immediately makes its impression of power and warmth, but does not immediately sign itself as a Beaux. Yet a roomful of her paintings, such as that gathered by the Academy for its 150th anniversary show in 1955, is wonderfully striking; rich, broad, exhilarating, a sort of fine human dazzle.

Oddly feminine and Philadelphian, both these artists excelled in portraits of their own families. Mary's pictures of Cassatts, Cecilia's of Drinkers are still in family hands, still among the most charming of their works. Not many artists have found their patrons and models so extensively among their own kinfolk; and there is something awfully Philadelphian, as well as feminine, about this.

iii. Illustrators

PHILADELPHIA PRODUCED, often only for export, enough other painters of some merit during this particular artistic heyday, from 1880 to the first World War, that it *could* have been the center of American painting, if it had somehow managed to transcend its native limitations, acknowledged Eakins and Cassatt, patronized more lavishly Sargent and Beaux — and kept hold of the Ash Can School. This group of artists — Henri, Glackens, Sloan, Shinn, Luks — the self-appointed liberators of American art before the wave of French modernism struck American painting in 1913, began in Philadelphia, studied there, worked there — and left.

New York was the obvious setting for painters who wanted to bust up the genteel world of John Sargent and William Merritt Chase by their slashing brushwork and "sordid" subjects — barrooms, ferries, slums and their inhabitants. Still most of them learned their profession at the Pennsylvania Academy under Thomas Anshutz, disciple and successor there of Eakins, and got their feeling for city life working as illustrators for the Philadelphia Press.

Much more characteristic of Philadelphia at the turn of the century than the Ash Canners, however, were the Illustrators. They too divide into Patriots and Loyalists, stay-at-homes and go-abroads; but no matter how far they went, they remained, unlike the Ash Canners, essentially Philadelphian.

From the mid-nineteenth century up to the very recent past, most of America's famous book illustrators — Felix Darley, Edwin Abbey, Arthur Frost, Joseph Pennell, Howard Pyle and his pupils N. C. Wyeth, Maxfield Parrish and Jessie Willcox Smith, the Oakleys, Thornton and Violet — have either been native Philadelphians or have studied and taught there, though many of them had to go to New York or London for their markets; certainly there is something awfully Philadelphian, and indeed Old Philadelphian, about this ripe, indeed overripe friendship between books and drawing. Felix Darley, generally thought of as America's first important humorous illustrator, was Philadelphia-born, though he moved to New York as early as 1848. By the time he died in 1889 he was surrounded by a new crop of competitors, also from

Philadelphia, who had also moved to New York. Some of them, like Frost, at least stayed in America. Others, like Pennell and Abbey, moved to England, and, like West, on to fame and fortune.

Of these certainly the most Philadelphian were the Pennells. Joseph, already a well-known sketcher of Philadelphia scenes, married Elizabeth Robins, daughter of a banker and schoolgirl friend of writer Agnes Repplier. She was also a niece of writer Charles Godfrey Leland, and was a writer herself. The Pennells bicycled about Europe and wrote travel books together, with her text and his pictures. *Two Pilgrims' Progress from Fair Florence to the Eternal City of Rome* was the flossy title of one of these. Their most notable effort in this field was the non-bicycling *Our Philadelphia,* which, with many complaints on the barbarism of "modernity," combines autobiography and a fine picture of Old Philadelphia before the First World War. The Pennells settled in London and were among the best friends of Whistler, and wrote the official biography of him. Pennell went on to a career of triumph as an etcher of modern industrialism, his dramatic studies of the Panama Canal, of smoky factories and the clutter of sky-scrapers the first pictures to reveal to his rather reluctant contemporaries that there was possibly beauty in such things.

It was Howard Pyle (1853–1911) of the stay-at-homes who had the greatest influence in Philadelphia and is most identified with the city — for all the fact that he was born and lived and worked for most of his life in or near Wilmington. He did teach in Phila-delphia, and there, largely at the Drexel Institute, he founded a sort of dynasty of pupils, and pupils of pupils, and even children of pupils that goes right on to this day. He was himself not only a classic illustrator of classics, but a writer of them. Much of his work in a naturalist vein is rather drab, or rather corny; he is at his best in the medievally pen-and-ink, quasi-woodcut drawings for his own famous *Robin Hood.* The influences of Dürer and the pre-Raphaelites and William Morris are dominant; but for sheer visual charm and matching literary quaintness no American or English books are better in their kind than his lovely *Wonder Clock* and *Otto of the Silver Hand.*

Among Pyle's most famous Philadelphia students were Jessie Willcox Smith, hollyhock illustrator of Stevenson's *Child's Garden of Verses;* Maxfield Parrish, son of a Philadelphia marine painter, whose incredible technique was at its best also in a fairy story world; and N. C. Wyeth, who illustrated just about every boy's classic ever written, very much in the tradition of his master's *Men of Iron,* but with more verve and color. Wyeth, who settled near Pyle and near Wilmington, at Chadds Ford on the Brandywine River, taught or sired a whole clutch of artists: his distinguished son Andrew Wyeth, most famous of today's younger realist painters; his equally distinguished son-in-law Peter Hurd of New Mexico, first really native painter of the Southwest; and another son-in-law John McCoy, a most sensitive and interesting painter in a shyer vein.

The Oakleys, another family constellation of writer-artists, lived in Philadelphia and have become thoroughly absorbed in the Web. Violet did murals for the state capitol at Harrisburg, and her brother Thornton, famous as an etcher, did, with his wife Amy, attractive travel books exactly in the tradition of the bicycling Pennells. As for the tradition of Pyle and his children's books, it is ably and profitably continued in Philadelphia today by Marguerite de Angeli, an adopted daughter of the city, whose more than a dozen books, written and illustrated by her, adorn the bookshelves of Nearly Everybody — (and not just readers of the *Bulletin*) — who is or has a child in the house.

iv. *A.A. (After the Armory)*

THE ARMORY SHOW of 1913, engineered by those ex-Philadelphians of the Ash Can School, completely overwhelmed native, and above all Philadelphia native, painting with the intoxicating impact of French art, post-Impressionist and Cubist. The two men who best represent Philadelphia painting around the First World War, and the results of this French influence, are George Biddle and Adolph Borie.

Though Beaux and Cassatt were both of the upper class, the

significant male painters of Philadelphia had up to that time, belonged to a class that is somewhere between artisan and professional, and thus can be safely patronized. There was none of this safeness about either Biddle or Borie. Each came from one of Philadelphia's very best families, not only of the same circle, but of families that were close personal friends. The Biddles have been mentioned; the Bories only as representative of one of Philadelphia's more exotic strains, that of the French West Indies. The Bories, originally refugees from slave rebellions, had by the end of the Civil War abjured their native Catholicism, remade their fortunes, and had Position. This position was fortified when a senior Adolph Borie, already one of Philadelphia's first citizens, somewhat humorously condescended to be Grant's Secretary of the Navy for a few months in 1869. He admitted he knew nothing about the Navy, and let the Admirals do all the work; still it was an honor of sorts.

The fact that both the younger Biddle and Borie insisted on being professional painters was, even as late as this, a shock. George Biddle compounded the initial shock by further behavior and statements. Perhaps because by birth he was so far in, he had to make so much the greater effort to get out. He left in high dudgeon and went not to England, where nineteenth-century painters went, but to New York, where twentieth-century painters go.

I was glad to identify my professional name with New York [he wrote in his autobiography of 1939]. Philadelphia has its own brand of integrity. It believes in itself; although there is nothing much any longer worth believing in. It respects its own standards, although these standards are inconceivably shallow and antedate in great measure the birth of our nation. It has the logic and the courage to love what it likes, and almost always to mistrust or to dislike anything worth achieving — anything as a rule that is not Philadelphian. For a century with its tremendous inertia Philadelphia has relentlessly hated ideas and consequently disliked artists. Artists have in the main reciprocated and have run away. Benjamin West, Mary Cassatt, Cecilia Beaux, George Luks, Robert Henri, William J. Glackens, John Sloan and myself escaped Philadelphia.

A.A. (After the Armory)

New York, though an infinitely healthier climate for the artist, was not Athens nor even Paris. It never, of course, wanted the best; it only aspired to the latest. Yet New York had qualities for which the American artist must always remain grateful. In short, one harbored a little love and some respect for Philadelphia; but one loathed it.

Specific rejection could go no further. But Biddle compounded the judgment with political and social rejection as well. He was, like his brother Francis, an ardent supporter of his fellow Grotonian F.D.R., and through his acquaintance with Roosevelt, did as much as anyone to create the WPA artists' program, the first and only large-scale government patronage of the arts in our history. Naturally all this was not populai in the Philadelphia of Senator Pepper and the Farmer's Club. George Biddle was accused, like Roosevelt, of being a "traitor to his class," to which he retorted;

If *my class* means such American citizens as are eligible to the Somerset, Knickerbocker, Philadelphia or Baltimore [i.e., Maryland] Clubs and to the various Assemblies, then it is a completely negligible fraction of America, either numerically, politically, intellectually, financially or socially. . . . *my class* is without any clear-cut meaning — unless it be a large and somewhat amorphous classification of all those whose political, social, artistic and moral habits, minds and tastes are thoroughly repugnant to me.

Adolph Borie, older than Biddle, was a very different man, and his charm, verve and gentleness overcame whatever residual family or Philadelphia opposition there might have been to his becoming a painter. He settled eventually with his family in a rather Frenchified Tuscan villa in West Philadelphia, with matting on the floor and a walled garden. He and his wife Edith belonged to the small but shining Philadelphia upper-intelligentsia that gathered about Philadelphia's two famous salonières of the 'twenties, Caroline Sinkler and Emily Balch. Along with the Stokowskis and the Hergesheimers, the Biddles, Francis and occasionally George, various Ingersolls and Fiske Kimball, the Bories helped create a gay, brilliant, sometimes even a bit rowdy circle that dominated and illuminated Philadelphia's artistic and aristocratic avant-garde between the wars.*

Where Biddle's painting was, and is, nervy, bitter and intensely individual, Borie's was subdued, well-bred and rather frankly imitative of Renoir and Cézanne. He painted exactly the kind of pictures that one would expect an American gentleman who had studied the French too thoroughly to paint. They are in that same vein of almost withdrawn good breeding that one finds in the best (only the best) of Sully. As with so many Philadelphia painters, Borie excels in still life; and of course, portraits. But the "public Bories" which still hang on all the right institutional walls are comparatively styleless and academic, compared with his private, personal work in which he showed the French flair and taste which was his real charm as a painter.

v. The Royal Succession

THERE WERE OTHER arts practiced all through the history of art in Philadelphia. Sculpture for one. William Rush, carver of figureheads, who tried to follow the lead of Benjamin West into noble allegory, can in true Philadelphia fashion lay claim to being America's first serious sulptor. An incident in his life is also memorialized in one of Eakins's best pictures. Rush asked a debutante of the time to pose for him in the nude as a model for his statue of the Schuylkill River. Eakins took the incident to heart; he had had trouble about nude models with later debutantes and their fathers, and his staging of the incident, with a respectable old chaperone knitting in the shadows, must have been designed to make Old Philadelphians of the 'eighties feel ashamed of themselves.

Typically Philadelphian has been the production through three generations of a family of respected, if not always respectable, sculptors, the Alexander Calders. Alexander the First was most respectable, and most Philadelphian, though born in Scotland. He emigrated and lived to do General Meade, Philadelphia's hero

* Francis Biddle's *A Casual Past* has some nice glimpses of this group and period.

of Gettysburg, in Fairmount Park, and as his literally crowning achievement, the gigantic William Penn on top of the tower of City Hall. His son Alexander II, more imaginative and eclectic, whose statues bore names like "Primeval Discontent" and "The Man Cub," obviously had to move to New York. Nobody who did statues called "Primeval Discontent" was going to pass his days in Philadelphia. He is represented in Philadelphia however by the beautiful Leda and the Swan fountain in Logan Circle, a monumental pun, since the fountain is a memorial to a Dr. Swann, by a legacy of his widow.

The last and third Alexander is rather removed from the Philadelphia orbit, but has become more famous than either of his forebears by inventing mobiles, moving sculptures of wires and bangles that change with the breeze. It's a shame the Philadelphia Museum can't put an Alexander the Third somewhere on their front steps. One would then have an impressive summary of the three generations: William Penn dominating the skyline at the end of the Benjamin Franklin Parkway, Leda's fountain visible in the middle of it, and a mobile in front of the Museum at the end, all in one *coup d'oeil* from the Museum's front windows.

Charles Grafly was perhaps the best-known of all the turn-of-the-century native sculptors, and was in true Philadelphia style, a master of the portrait bust. His daughter Dorothy Grafly is now Philadelphia's best-known art critic. Grafly's most famous work, so to speak, is not by Grafly. This is the Goat in Rittenhouse Square, beloved by generations of children as a safe mount, and celebrated by much sentimental amateur Old Philadelphian prose and poetry. It was made, exactly in Grafly's best style, by a pupil of his, Albert Laeslle, and remains probably the one piece, of all Philadelphia's enormous forest of statuary, which *every* Old Philadelphian knows and loves.

One can't really say that painting in Philadelphia flourished between the World Wars. Still, exiled Philadelphia painters, notably Charles Sheeler and Charles Demuth, and painters who studied in Philadelphia like John Marin — all of the so-called "Stieglitz School" — were leaders of modern art in that period.

Of the exiles, it is probably Sheeler, with his breathlessly photographic studies of factories or furniture, who best represents the Philadelphia still-life tradition and its emphasis on "facts and things."

At home in Philadelphia modernism was championed by Arthur Carles, pioneer abstractionist, a dynamic fellow with a rippling beard who knew Everybody, and married various maidens of high degree. All good Philadelphia collections of that period contain several of his powerful bruise-colored flower studies, brutal for all their delicate subject matter. Conservative painting, as blessed by the Academy, might best be represented by the pictures of Daniel Garber, little influenced by even Impressionism, but glowing with their own rich warm life. Carles died comparatively early of drink and madness; Garber at a good age fell while gardening.

Philadelphia is crawling with painters nowadays, but the two acknowledged leaders are Walter Stuempfig and Franklin Watkins. Stuempfig is the chief representative of the Manayunk School, Philadelphia's first real school of landscape, though he has certainly gone far beyond the absorption in the picturesque stone mill town on the Schuylkill from which the school gets its name. He is a realist and romantic painter of rather gloomy or even sordid landscapes shot with an electric menace. The strange and often beautiful figures who stand about like ballet dancers off duty on Stuempfig's ravaged shores don't do anything. They seem to be waiting for some dreadful storm to break, or to be mourning some dreadful storm that has passed. Occasionally the gray walls and breakneck streets of Manayunk are involved, but often enough it is the wide melancholy of the Jersey shore or the parking-lot-battered brick slums of Philadelphia itself that are depicted.

If Stuempfig's world is rather German in its weight of brooding nostalgia, Watkins's is one of French elegance, a nervous, spidery, rather overbred world, formed after Matisse and colored like Degas. He made his first reputation as a painter of chicly shocking figure pieces, "Suicide in Costume" and "The Fire Eater," with a macabre circus background. Lately he has come to be acknowledged as Philadelphia's, if not the nation's, leading painter of likenesses. One of his latest, a picture of Mayor — later Senator — Clark, when publicly exhibited at the elite Negro Pyramid Club soon after it was painted, caused considerable rumpus. The portrait, with its informal pose and bright coloring, was obviously quite different from the darkly pompous effigies of previous mayors. Though it hangs now in City Hall, it does in fact stand out as a light in darkness.

It is significant that both Stuempfig and Watkins are realists, both paint portraits and that nowhere yet in Philadelphia has there been any significant acceptance of the New York School of abstract expressionism. Unlike New York, where painting seems to develop in sudden "schools" like the Ash Can or Stieglitz groups, the Philadelphia pattern, an individual apostolic succession of portraitists, still goes along continuously and calmly, close to its traditions of the real and the personal, rather subdued, rather sensitive and stylish, always in the front of whatever is behind, representative of the conservative, though not necessarily old-fashioned or academic, leadership of the times, as witnessed now by the realists Watkins, Wyeth and Stuempfig.

vi. Boards: Aesthetic

PAINTING IS MADE by painters of course, but Philadelphia's painters have been sheltered, and sometimes stifled, by its institutions, the three most prominent being the Pennsylvania Academy of the Fine Arts, the University of Pennsylvania Museum, and the Philadelphia Museum of Art.

The Academy covers American art, the University Museum ancient art, and the Philadelphia anything after about 1000 A.D., but mostly European. Of the three the Academy is the most venerable, being a true Philadelphian First and Oldest (1805) and if not founded by B.F., at least started by Charles W. Peale. The Academy is primarily an art school, but from the beginning it has held exhibitions. Among the earliest exhibits were casts after the antique collected in Europe by young Nicholas Biddle. Philadelphians were dubious about their nudity. The statues were kept covered most of the time, and ladies and gentlemen only allowed in separately, on different days.

The boards of all three museums are today beyond reproach; but the Philadelphia Art Museum, though latest of the three, seems to come first these days because of its size, commanding position and general glamour. It began during the Centennial Exhibition of 1876 as a sort of mixed-up collection of industrial exhibits and curiosities (a panorama of Pompeii was one), as well as art, in a great gray building called Memorial Hall. For years the cluttered gloom of Memorial Hall contained such European art as the city of Philadelphia had, most of it a large collection left by the Wilstach family which was the foundation of the Museum's present collection. The Wilstach taste ran heavily to French Salon pictures of Arabs, and not startlingly authentic Italian Old Masters, but there were plenty of good pictures in the collection — Rubens, El Greco, Courbet and others — besides a sizable fund for new purchases.

One of Philadelphia's grandest Old Men, Eli Kirk Price II, during the 1920's wheedled and threatened the city fathers into building the great Benjamin Franklin Parkway, and into putting the new Museum at the end of the vista, crowning an acropolis where once a reservoir had been. Of all Philadelphia's Grand Gestures, this has been the grandest. Price planned to have all Philadelphia's major institutions line this esplanade in huge buildings bristling with columns, but only a few, like the Free Library and the Franklin Institute, succumbed; others, like the Philadelphia Club, didn't budge, and in the end the Parkway failed to become the grandiose Via Romana of cultural splendor Price envisioned. For years most of it was lined by humps of rubble, mercifully concealed back of trees.

The Museum, too, was for a while a magnificent shell. When the new building was opened in 1928, though hardly finished or filled, Philadelphia's "instinct of disparagement" had a field day. Modernists despised it because it was classic, classicists criticized it because it was yellow instead of white, and Old Philadelphians in general considered it a desecration of the pretty little old waterworks buildings on the bank of the Schuylkill below; the museum was so "over-powering" and out of scale. Henry McCarter, pioneer modernist teacher at the Academy, referred to it as "the Greek garage." Joseph and Elizabeth Pennell, those bicycling custodians of Philadelphia culture, went wild with fury.

The Museum is, in fact, probably the most beautiful neoclassic building in America, certainly the only one to overcome the usual heavy rigidity of large-scale neoclassicism by following the subtle curves of wall and pillar that make Greek buildings light and graceful instead of stiff and squat. The tawny orange of the stone mellows with age, and the building's spectacular site provides the grandest possible climax to the majestic vista made by the tree-lined Benjamin Franklin Parkway as it sweeps out from City Hall. When the azaleas in the forecourt are blooming in the spring, the flowers, the building itself, the fountains and the broad views all make for a visual experience not to be excelled anywhere in the world, a triumph of Philadelphia Taste; and this is only the outside of the museum.

Though one of the most conspicuous buildings in Philadelphia, it is actually one of the least well-known, since it is almost impossible to get to it except by car from the suburbs. Cut off from human contact by the endless swirl of traffic along the Parkway at its feet, remote from the center of town, it sits beautiful and inviolable. Taxis will take you out, but you can't find one to take you back.* As a result there are afternoons when nobody is in the Museum except the staff and a few students. It is, despite its flagrant situation, one of the most successfully hidden of all Philadelphia's hidden delights.

I once asked a trolley conductor on Market Street how to get to it. He not only did not know that, but did not know where or even what it was, though since his route took him by City Hall he could hardly fail to see it every time he passed that way. A

---

* A bus service to and from the Museum and the center of the city has at last been inaugurated. High time.

Philadelphia acquaintance of mine, descendant of a family famous for beneficence to museums, was giving me some help on a question of genealogy. "I'm just a huntin' shootin' man myself," he said, "I don't know much about things like that; but I have a cousin, he's head of one of those things — you know," he snapped his fingers, "that big thing as you come out on the Parkway."

The Philadelphians who don't go to their Museum are missing one of the best collections in the country. Although obviously not as comprehensive and overwhelming as the Metropolitan in New York or the National Gallery in Washington, it ranks next, along with the museums of Boston, Chicago and Cleveland, as one of the best, some think the very best, of America's big city museums. Much of the credit must go to Fiske Kimball, its first director.

The stories of fabulous Fiske Kimball's brilliant reign at the Art Museum and his tragic end as a lunatic have been brilliantly told in *Triumph on Fairmount*, by Mary and George Brooke Roberts (grandson of the George Brooke who was president of The Railroad). Kimball was to the Museum what Leopold Stokowski was to the Orchestra, and like Stokowski not only a master at his job but a flamboyant showman. Dinner parties still devote themselves to talking about him and his sometimes outrageous quips and oddities; but again, like Stokowski, his very non-Philadelphianism, his extravagant talk and gestures, his ribald jokes, even his occasional rudeness, all seemed to delight people who never would have taken these things from their relations. Other museum directors complained that he got more money by a few well-placed insults than they had by years of flattery. He and his wife lived at Lemon Hill, Robert Morris's old summer mansion in Fairmount Park, and during the 'twenties and 'thirties were, again like the Stokowskis, leaders of Old Philadelphia's very small but very lively aristocratic intelligentsia.

Though Kimball was not Philadelphian, the Museum he put on the map could hardly be more so. The interior has, for one thing, that slightly unfinished look of the Philadelphia not-quite-fulfilled Grand Gesture; the ceiling of the entrance hall remains

incomplete, a clerestory of bare brickwork and exposed planking.*
Down underneath there are the same echoing deserted passage-
ways that one finds in 30th Street Station. On a day when nobody
else is in the museum one wanders about, whistling "I dreamt I
dwelt in marble halls," like a visitor in an enormous country
house, tenanted only by footmen and a few family ghosts. The
illusion is strengthened not only by the views of the trees of
Fairmount Park, but by the planning of the exhibits themselves.
The whole second floor is devoted to period rooms, English,
American, Dutch, French, Gothic, even Chinese, with appropriate
furnishings and pictures. Again and again the Philadelphia
trinity of chair, clock and portrait occurs. There are close to
three hundred chairs, sofas, benches, stools or sittables of one
kind or another, perhaps the largest exhibition of the Sedentary in
the world, although actual resting places for the weary-footed are
not very frequent.

There is even an actual ghost story, sort of. The late Miss
Sarah Lowrie, one of Old Philadelphia's more famous spinsters,
walked into a newly installed Pennsylvania Dutch room. She was
describing some of the room's characteristic features to an out-of-
town guest when she found herself unconsciously saying ". . .
and out that window is where the milldam used to be." She
suddenly realized that she had no idea whether there had been
a milldam outside the room in its original site; but when she
investigated, she found, sure enough, that not only had there
been a dam, but the house had been built and lived in by one
of her own ancestors. So at least the story goes, giving to a somewhat impersonal place the homey and family touches dear to
Philadelphians.

The rest of the collection has its local character and family
touches too. There is a gallery devoted entirely to Philadelphia
and Pennsylvania furniture, and a charming small fashion gallery,
with tableaux of elegantly dressed ladies of various periods, from
gray eighteenth-century Quakers up to flappers in the knee-length,

---

* They are fixing it. High time.

heavily beaded tubes worn to the Assembly during the 'twenties. Each dress has been given by a descendant of the well-known Philadelphian who wore the original, the walls of the imaginary rooms have a few choice portraits on them (nice chairs nearby, too) and after ball gowns of the 1930's and 1940's, the exhibit culminates in the wedding dress of Her Highness, the Princess of Monaco.

There are just plain pictures too, among them good Eakinses and Cassatts; but the main collection of pictures is, in true Philadelphia fashion, not one designed to overwhelm you at first sight. Conspicuous by their absence, and for the most Philadelphian reasons, are batteries of High Renaissance masters — of Rembrandts and Van Dycks, for instance, or any inordinate number of Cézannes or Renoirs. Their lack can be accounted for by the absence from the Museum of two of Philadelphia's greatest collections, significantly missing for somewhat the same reason: the real or imaginary pique on the part of *nouveau riche* collectors at what they considered, with some justice, to be the slights of Old Philadelphia.

vii. Art and Argyrol

THE ART INSTITUTIONS of Philadelphia have been dominated by Old Philadelphian autocrats such as Eli Kirk Price or John F. Lewis, Sr., great patron of the Academy of Arts. The actual art in Philadelphia was largely collected by three non–Old Philadelphian autocrats, the lawyer John G. Johnson, the traction king Peter A. B. Widener, and the lord of Argyrol, Dr. Albert C. Barnes. All three of these men rose from a background of poverty, Johnson the son of a blacksmith, Widener himself a practicing butcher, Barnes the son of a jobless one-armed Civil War veteran. All went to that famous, but also very non–Old Philadelphian, Central High School, an all-male public school for selected good students, as did also the artists Eakins, Glackens and Sloan. All three made fortunes, in law, trolleys and medicine (sort of) respectively. Johnson and Widener were contemporaries and close friends. Barnes was of a later generation.

Of the three, only Johnson was accepted, indeed embraced by Old Philadelphia. Just being a leader of the bar was an asset. Then he was the legal savior of Big Business. Besides this, he married well — one of the last of the Powels, Ida, of the same one "l" Powels as elegant Samuel III, patriot mayor and fancier of art. Like Samuel in this respect, if no other, Johnson, too, was an art fancier. He did not buy the big black old masters that were the backbone of most of his millionaire clients' collections. He wasn't that rich, for one thing. For another, he objected to being milked by art dealers; and then he developed taste on his own. He started acquiring small jewel-colored Flemish paintings, not yet really fashionable, and peculiar Italian and other primitives by the "Master of This" and the "Master of That." As a result, before he died in 1917, he had a collection unrivaled in America for rarity, oddity and stylistic interest. He had no children and cared little for social life and boardsmanship. His one passion was his art, and he made his city his heir, like Girard. Tucked away in an ugly big house on South Broad Street (Nobody lived on South Broad Street), a house for all its size much too small for the collection, his pictures were stuck in closets and hung in bathrooms.* His will, however, instructed that they remain there, unless "some extraordinary situation should arise," making it necessary to move them. The city accepted the gift, for all the ambiguities and difficulties of the will, which has provided lawyers with considerable opportunity for "forensic eloquence," and the trustees gradually proceeded, over a period of years, to violate Johnson's intent, until the collection found itself in the new Art Museum. It is obvious that, though Johnson wanted the pictures to stay in his house, it would have been ruinous both aesthetically and financially to have tried to keep them there. In 1958, after two years of deliberation, the court

* Francis Biddle has a nice story of Johnson's asking the maid to run upstairs and fetch the Botticelli leaning on the bathtub.

gave permission for the house to be torn down, and for the
pictures to stay in the Museum for another ten years. The judge
was pretty unhappy about the legality of the whole thing, however, and said so. In 1968 it all goes to court again.

Meanwhile Johnson's wonderful collection is in Philadelphia
and visible to those citizens willing to climb up to the acropolis.
This is not true, alas, of the equally and differently wonderful
Widener and Barnes collections. The trouble between Philadelphia and the Wideners had to do not with the Founder, Peter,
but with his son Joseph. Joseph, as previously indicated, put on
the Second Generation act with tremendous bravado. He married a Pancoast, he built a palace, he refined his father's art collection, he gave lavish parties; but he lacked one essential talent
for the role — charm. He was haughty, ugly, diffident and generally unlovable. Philadelphia would certainly have taken him in
if he'd been at all ingratiating. They did take in his brother's
family, and his nephew George Widener is safely ensconced in
Philadelphia affections and clubs; he is, in fact, the Chairman of
the Board of the Museum. Not so Joseph. But he had his
revenge. When a Philadelphia parvenu feels snubbed, he appeals
to a higher court. Stotesbury cut a social swathe in Palm Beach
he couldn't quite manage at home. Widener, after all sorts of
dickering and dangling and coyness with the Museum in Philadelphia, and despite efforts by the Pennsylvania Legislature to
restrain him, in the end gave his great masters to the National
Gallery in Washington.

The Barnes collection is still right in Philadelphia, or at least
in Merion, one of the closer Main Line suburbs. But though you
can see the Johnson collection in Philadelphia and the Widener
in Washington, up to very recently you couldn't see the Barnes
collection; not easily, at any rate,* and not if you were an old
Philadelphian. For of all Philadelphia's snubbed parvenus, Dr.
Barnes reacted most violently. As a boy who spent much of his
bitter childhood among the shacks and garbage dumps of the

---

* As a result of the latest suit, the Barnes Foundation has planned to open itself
to the Public for a few hours a day, a few days a week.

Neck in southmost Philadelphia, he seemed to have developed a very special and indeed psychotic combination of brilliance and truculence. After Central High, he went to the University of Pennsylvania, where he joined a mediocre fraternity and studied medicine. He then went to Germany. Some time after he came back, he began producing a medicine called Argyrol. Argyrol, a rust-colored bitter fluid, was once very popular for sore throats. It seemed to burn out the infection in a nice disagreeable, therapeutic fashion, and Barnes, dropping a German partner along the way, became enormously rich. He moved to the Main Line and took up fox hunting. As a member of the Rose Tree, he was conspicuous for his falls. His courage may have been admired, but his style and manners were not. He gave up hunting. A close friend of the Ash Canner Glackens at Central High School, and always interested in painting, he took up art seriously. First he tried painting himself, but realized he was no good, and destroyed over a hundred of his own works. He turned to collecting and theorizing instead.

It was Glackens who first led him toward modern French art. He began to collect well before the Armory Show gave Modernism so much publicity, and he soon became a famous personage in Paris. In 1923 he discovered the Russo-French artist Soutine, then unsold and unknown, and bought all the pictures Soutine's dealer had on hand, somewhere between sixty and a hundred of them, for three thousand dollars. Soutine blew it all on a single cab ride to the Riviera. Barnes was also one of the first to buy Modigliani's pictures, and his acquisitions not only "made" Soutine and Modigliani (already dead), but also made Barnes. A special exhibition of his purchases was held in Paris which was "international news."

Barnes could hardly wait to share the excitement with Philadelphia. Next year he and his Philadelphia artist friends Arthur Carles and Henry McCarter arranged to bring the Paris exhibition over to the staid Pennsylvania Academy. Philadelphia and indeed America were not ready for it. The local critics frothed at the mouth. Words like "unmentionable," "infectious scourge," "unclean things" flapped about and a group of psychologists declared in a public manifesto that "the artists who painted such things were either crazy or moral degenerates." Barnes was rabid with fury, as though he had created the works himself. He wrote ferocious personal letters to the critics, suggesting to a female one that she would never be a real critic until she had relations with the ice man, this being typical of the Barnes approach to an enemy. He couldn't, however, do much to the critics except insult them; but he, like Widener, had his revenge on Philadelphia, and it took him the rest of his life.

He had been long interested in housing and showing off his paintings properly. To that end a Barnes Foundation was created, and a marble gallery built in Merion which was also to be a school, where a way of looking at art derived from various sources, but developed by Barnes himself and his disciple-master the philosopher John Dewey, would be taught. Cutting out all the historical and descriptive detail he considered irrevelant, Barnes believed one should look at paintings purely as structures of mass, color, line, space ("Facts and things, not words and signs"). His pictures were to be used as examples in teaching this method. Whether anybody beside the pupils saw them or not he considered as irrelevant as the subject matter of the pictures.

But, of course, Nearly Everybody wanted to see the pictures, and Almost Nobody could get in. The stories of people who tried and failed are as numberless as the stories of people who tried and failed to get into the Assemblies, the difference being that anybody who danced at the Assemblies was sure *not* to get into the Barnes Collection. Anybody connected with the Academy or the Museum would be, if possible, forcibly kicked out. For years and years the Battle of the Barnes raged. Insulting letters to Fiske Kimball and Sturgis Ingersoll, press releases and letters to the editor, all just carefully non-libelous, an attempt to sabotage the WPA art project in Philadelphia because those who ran it had Museum connections, battles with the University's school of Fine Arts — fact was as fantastic as legend, and it is still impos-

sible to be quite sure which is which. Examples: An Old Philadelphian art patron finally arranged a special visit on a Sunday,
when the Gallery was usually closed. He arrived at the appointed
time and was refused admittance. Furious, he insisted on trying
to come in and was thrown bodily out the door and down the
steps. A very worthy older woman wrote a humble letter asking
to be admitted. Barnes refused and added, "the last woman I let
in gave me the clap." The outraged lady took the letter to her
lawyer, who explained how carefully Barnes had avoided legal
difficulties: he hadn't said *she* had given him the clap. There are
dozens of stories of this sort, some obviously true, some false, but
all of them to the same effect. It was Revenge all right on a
grandly protracted scale.

The most celebrated affair was his fight with the English
philosopher Bertrand Russell, who, though not an Old Philadelphian, comes close. He is an Earl. An enormous admirer of
philosophers in general and Russell in particular, Barnes hired
Russell to lecture at the Foundation in the early 1940's. Russell,
persecuted in England and New York for his heretical opinions,
was in a bad way financially and accepted with gratitude. Barnes
gave him a salary and arranged a place for him to live. Russell
arrived with his third and much younger wife. Then the trouble
began. Lady Russell, as she preferred to call herself, and Barnes
did not get on. The smoldering feud at last broke out over a
question of knitting. Lady Russell liked to attend her husband's
lectures and knit. Barnes approved of neither her presence nor
her pastime. Lady Russell was amazed. "Why, I always knit in
Bertie's clahsses," she said, but was happy enough not to, if
Barnes insisted. Barnes insisted. Russell considered his wife had
been insulted. Barnes eventually fired Russell. Russell sued —
and collected twenty thousand dollars. Barnes was considered to
have met his match at last, and people are still talking about it.

In 1951 Barnes drove through a stop sign and was killed by a
truck; again, as people said, he had met his match. His Foundation carries on along the lines laid down by the Master. Classes
are held daily during the week, and those who take them are

often enthusiastic converts to the Method. Christine Cadwalader Scull, daughter of Dr. Williams of the Zoo, is a noted one, and has begun a small collection of her own under the Barnes influence. This particular collection, in fact, became rather notorious in Philadelphia. It contained a statue of considerable erotic interest. Mrs. Scull, no doubt innocently, put it up on her roof where everybody going past on the road could see it. Traffic was jammed for days at this particular place, until she had to take the statue down.

Not only pupils but many others are impressed by Barnes's theories, and everybody admits the collection containing hundreds (I mean hundreds) of the world's best Cézannes and Renoirs,* together with all the other later French masters, and a small selection of earlier masters, to be superlative. John Dewey and Irwin Edman liked and admired Barnes as a person. Most Old Philadelphians still loathe him, however, and laugh at him, and they still tell incredible stories of his incredible rudenesses, obscenities and reported lecheries and drunkennesses.

Two recent books, the Robertses' *Triumph on Fairmount* and and William Schack's *Art and Argyrol*, give various versions of his stormy career and his fights with that "whore house on the Parkway," which was one characteristic way he had of describing the Museum. The Barnes pictures are not, never have been and probably never will be in it, even as loans. If they were, and if the Museum also had the Rembrandts and Van Dycks of the Widener collection, it just might be at the bottom of the country's best museums of the first order, instead of at the top of those of the second order. But that would have meant surrender to the bad manners of Barnes and the arrogance of Widener. It is Philadelphia's virtue, her insistence on proper conformance to the rules of good breeding on the part of her new millionaires, that has cost her a place among the foremost centers of art in the nation. But the price for first place, in this as in so many things,

---

* At present inflated prices, when good Cézannes and Renoirs go for $100,000, the value of the Barnes collection must be incalculable. 100 Cézannes @ $100,000 . . .

was too high. Philadelphia preferred here, as elsewhere, to be herself.

There are no collections being formed in Philadelphia nowadays quite like Widener's, and the lively doings of the Barnes controversy are no more; but there are still collectors, and the artistic life of Philadelphia still centers around a few Old Philadelphians and a few artists, and carries on the tradition of a sophisticated "aristocratic bohemia" established in the 'twenties. The Ingersolls are not "collectors" in the sense of Johnson, but their various houses are full of paintings and their gardens contain statues ranging from Courbet and Maillol up to Picasso and beyond. The Carrol Tyson collection, a soberly expensive sampling of the best French art, is perhaps the closest thing to an old-fashioned Great Collection now in the city and in private hands. Other collectors on a smallish scale are the H. Gates Lloyds, the James Magills, and a whole group of Jewish art patrons, of whom the late Raymond Speiser was perhaps the best known.

Most famous of current Philadelphia collections is the very personal one of Henry McIlhenny. Housed in a Victorian mansion on Rittenhouse Square, almost the last private residence there, the pictures are frequently on view at the Museum. McIlhenny has concentrated on French art too, from before the Romantics to the present, and the collection reflects an extraordinary flair for the unusual on the part of the collector. Such items as the Degas portrait of Mary Cassatt from the back, or Van Gogh's particularly wet picture of rain in Provence, a relief from his usual sun-tortured landscapes, illustrate aspects of the artists not usually seen elsewhere. Henry McIlhenny himself, as an opulent bachelor who maintains a castle in Ireland as well as his collection in Philadelphia, along with the artist Emlen Etting and his dynamic wife Gloria, née Braggiotti, create a sort of chic, rather international set for themselves in town which seems a bit outré to other suburban Philadelphians, but which is certainly right in the tradition of the salons before the last War of

Emily Balch and Caroline Sinkler, and those gay days of the Stokowskis, Hergesheimers and Kimballs.

Nowadays this world is almost entirely centered around painting, however; and there is no comparable literary or even musical set. McIlhenny works for the Museum as Curator of Decorative Arts; his sister, Mrs. Wintersteen, is one of the city's most amiable art patrons and Chairwoman of the Museum's Board of Governors. Other "Museum people," the Horace Jaynes, the Ingersolls, the Henry Cliffords, the architect George Roberts and his wife, as both professionals and Old Philadelphians, keep things lively and fashionable. This "art world" in Philadelphia, though small and limited, has a tradition and a tone, which combines Old Philadelphia and New Movements in a judicious balance, unmatched anywhere in the country, except perhaps in Boston and San Francisco, and is of course quite different from the great international shark-tank of New York. Of the artists, only Watkins and Stuempfig seem to move in it quite as a matter of course, and it has a reputation of being a "snobbish" and a bit precious clique; a very stylish clique in any case, and one that does more to keep taste and intellect alive in Philadelphia than any other single factor.

viii. Monuments

PAINTING IS FIRST among the arts in Philadelphia; but architecture too has a long, honorable and continuous history, and is equally bound to the upper classes by the same links of taste and patronage. The total effect however of architecture in the city seems somehow less fortunate. After all, the great mass of undistinguished painting sinks with time below the waves, but the work of undistinguished architects is still right there. Also, a few people in Chestnut Hill burned their Eakinses, but more good pictures survive than good buildings, for Philadelphia with characteristic lack of conservatism has never hesitated to tear down any building that failed to pay its immediate way. Even Independence Hall was threatened in the nineteenth century.

Here at least Philadelphians did object. The Philadelphia Club was only saved by the depression. The drive to destroy City Hall is still very much alive. Luckily the construction of the building seems to have been so wastefully solid that the cost of destruction would, it is hoped, be prohibitive. This is sometimes all that saves important Philadelphia buildings.

It is pretty hard not to be angry with what Philadelphians, and Old Philadelphians especially as owners and leaders and administrators, have done in the past to Penn's "greene country towne." Not only has most of it been as wantonly destroyed as if it had been bombed, "shell-raked" as Cornelius Weygandt was able to call it even in the 1930's, with gap-toothed parking lots breaking up the symmetry and solidity of every old block; and glaring asphalt surrounding every old landmark left; but nearly everything new that has been built is pretty bad. Not bad with a flamboyant nastiness, true enough, but bad in the sense of timid, anonymous drabness — drab monumentality in the business cen-ter, with skyscrapers of crouching neo-colonial or moderne, afraid to soar, drab elsewhere with grimy warehouses and miserable shops and depressing institutions and schools. Not to mention of course the slums and row-houses, the worst in America.

The summation, the payoff, the veritable jackpot of Phila-delphia's architectural stupidity has been the proudest achieve-ment of the Philadelphia Renaissance, Penn Center, which in-stead of being turned over to the guidance of any one of several imaginative local architects was handed on a silver platter to architects and contractors of no distinction or imagination, who have put up buildings so lacking in character that they might just as well not be there at all, and surrounded the whole with blank white concrete pavement, an open space freezing in wind-swept winter, frying in unshaded summer, a great civic grave-yard for the hopes and missed opportunities of what could have been one of America's finest civic efforts. One of its few saving graces is that various vistas of the incongruous richness of City Hall façade have been opened up, and that the whole is still rather clean and neat — so far.

In the vast desert of sheer dumbness that the physical plant of Philadelphia city represents, there are, however, numberless exceptions, and by concentrating on these and forgetting all the rest, Philadelphians, especially Old Philadelphians, manage to salve their consciences and bolster their civic egos. There are throughout the center of the city those back streets, those oases of charm and gentility that still somehow manage to exist: Clinton Street, Camac Street, Delancey, Panama, Ringgold, and the blocks of Locust beyond Rittenhouse Square. These oases are actually increasing, since more and more old houses on such streets are being bought up by intelligent entrepreneurs and converted into charm and respectability. Fawn Court, for instance, once a slum fearsome enough for Dickens, is now a little nook of tranquillity, and all sorts of things are going on in the really old part of town near the Delaware River.

There are of course still many monuments, though as a rule these have no geographical connection with the oases of gentility, being usually isolated in already ravaged parts of the city. Actually Philadelphia contains at least one, sometimes two or three, superlative examples of each historical American style, often produced by the preeminent architect of that style, and often the best example of the style in the country. Independence Hall, often locally called the State House, remains the finest original group of eighteenth-century civic buildings in the nation, and is now a National Park, and the core and cause of a whole revivifying and restoring movement to preserve what is left of Philadelphia's antiquity. Christ Church too must be the most elegant of America's colonial churches, and the Pennsylvania that of hospitals. These famous three were all designed by amateurs: the State House supposedly by lawyer Andrew Hamilton, Christ Church by Dr. John Kearsley, the Hospital by Mayor Samuel Rhoads. These amateurs have never been surpassed as architects, but Philadelphia's age of professional glory belongs to the later Jeffersonian, neoclassic period of around 1800.

To this period, from 1785 to 1830 or so, belong Philadelphia's best architectural names, and some of its best architectural remains. Of the names, those of John Haviland, William Strickland and Thomas Walter are the most famous. Benjamin Latrobe, though not a native, practiced in Philadelphia, and to him and his pupils is dubiously credited the design of the pretty little waterworks, still standing, by Josiah White's dam on the Schuylkill. Considering how famous and active these architects were, there's precious little left of their work. The buildings of the Second Bank of the United States, Biddle's bank, by Strickland, and of the old Franklin Institute, by Haviland, are among the few vestiges of this noble period in Philadelphia. The Girard College buildings, too, form one of the largest and most complete statements of this style, once so very dear to Philadelphia hearts.

The sponsor, inspirer and patron of neoclassicism in Philadelphia was Nicholas Biddle himself, who, among his many tastes and talents, had a yen for the glory that was Greece. He personally hired and superintended the work of Walter in the building of Girard College, and his own columned mansion at Andalusia is one of the grandest of our templed country seats. It was certainly Biddle who fixed the style upon banks, and the neo-Biddle bank style has persisted, perhaps a bit ironically, as the very symbol of powerful financial respectability in bank façades ever since. The style reaches its final grimly monumental statement in the Ridgeway Library on South Broad Street, and of course revives again in the not very interesting buildings about Logan Square, in 30th Street Station, and in the wonderful Museum of Art.

Neo-Gothic in Philadelphia does not seem to fare as well. St. Mark's Church on Locust above 17th (this rather casual way of placing addresses in town is universal in Philadelphia) remains one of the few really successful Romantic Gothic buildings extant there. Its rich crumbly brownstone gables and pinnacles have exactly the Olde Worlde, Cruikshank-illustration picturesqueness that the nineteenth-century architects wanted, and so seldom achieved. The architect, John Notman, was more famous for another transitional, essentially more classic style, that of the Tuscan villa, tall brownstone residences with flat-topped towers and rounded windows. There are none in town, and few even in the suburbs, though West Philadelphia row-houses show the influence of this fad. One of the most famous of Notman's villas, Alverthorpe, built by Sidney's cousin Joshua Fisher, was inexplicably torn down by the otherwise exceptionally sensitive Lessing Rosenwald. Actually the best and most of Notman is in Princeton, New Jersey, where he not only remodeled Nassau Hall, after a fire in 1855, but designed the president's house, Prospect, and other mansions.

Real screwball Late Victorian had a short, but hectic and flowery, heyday in Philadelphia around the time of the great Exposition of 1876. This was not a style one feels that really suited or expressed Philadelphia, which came to it late, and left it early when, already in the 'eighties, the best people began to turn to the more indigenous and sympathetic neo-colonial. While the orgy lasted, however, it produced as fantastic a riot of imaginative archaeological non sequiturs as you will find anywhere in the world. The leader in this witches' Sabbath was Frank Furness, brother of the Shakespearean scholar Horace Howard Furness, and the only one of Philadelphia's architects, up to that time, who could himself claim to be an Old Philadelphian. One suspects he was a rebellious Old Philadelphian, for certainly the Arabian Nightmares of his buildings have a restless, strained exoticism that is as far as possible from the calm orderliness of Philadelphia's usual temperament. He built the Pennsylvania Academy's "new" building in 1872, an indescribable example of Masonic Moorish, grotesque but compelling, and the equally distorted old Library of the University of Pennsylvania. They are very hard to take, but there is no denying their originality. His influence is demonstrated in the rows of embellished insurance offices in the Independence Hall region, many of them now torn down, where into each narrow city façade have been crowded more interrupted Egyptian columns, Venetian windows and doorways from Babylon than would seem humanly possible. Furness is revered nowadays as a grandfather of modern American architecture; Louis Sullivan of Chicago sat at his feet, and Frank Lloyd Wright sat at Sullivan's.

The most splendid of Philadelphia's Victorian buildings, probably the most splendid, again, in the country, if most maligned, is City Hall itself; but it is neither the Gothic or Tuscan of Notman nor the Arabian of Furness. It belongs to the Empress Eugénie Neo-Louvre which swept America with its mansard roofs in the 'seventies and 'eighties. In New England, where every boardinghouse boasts one, they are called "French roofs"; elsewhere the style is usually referred to as "General Grant." City Hall is the apotheosis of General Grant, as the Union League's clubhouse is the quintessence. It is not a pretty, graceful building, and has no vestiges of "Philadelphia taste." It is not, in fact, an upper-class building at all. It represents the Philadelphia of robber barons and robber bosses, a crude but vigorous and richly charactered group of rogues, and City Hall is a crude but richly charactered building. Upper-class Philadelphians have united in detesting it from the day it was built. "Enormous ugly raw buildings," said Elizabeth Pennell, that combined, according to Agnes Repplier, "bulk" with "sterling insignificance" and "squalid paltriness." But City Hall is the grandest of all the city's public monuments, and sits exposed at the axis of immense vistas, Broad Street and Market Street and the Benjamin Franklin Parkway, with the same craggy complacency with which the Republican party during the period of its greatest power and corruption faced the continual exposure of reformers. It has something of the somber bourgeois grandeur of Eakins, without his intelligence. City Hall might be referred to, somewhat exaggeratedly, as frozen Brahms. In any hour of the day or night it is impressive and romantic. Inside are tucked away great gilded official chambers full of portraits, and soaring over everything is the totally out of proportion tower, crowned with Calder's William Penn, who faces, with hand outstretched, what was once the red-light district. This outstretched hand is so placed at hip level that sailors coming up Broad Street from the

Navy Yard have reveled for years in the obscenely phallic effect. The tower itself, finished about 1894, so haughty and dominant and removed from its crude rich base, might very aptly stand as the symbol of the Philadelphia Oligarchy and its relation to the political forces it chose to encourage and to ignore. William Penn looks out serenely towards the country, and pays no attention to what has been going on right under his nose. The tower, like the Oligarchy, remains the highest thing in town despite all modern encroachments. A sort of gentlemen's agreement (and City Hall control over licenses) insures that this shall be so.

The fever of Victorianism, that is, exotic eclecticism, abated and the long reign of neo-colonial began, first in chaste and often still delightful town houses, such as the Markoe house dating from 1900 or earlier, or in numberless suburban houses. The style, of course, was most suitable to country houses, and there it flourished and flourishes to this day; its most native and most beautiful form being that of the remodeled Pennsylvania stone farmhouse, or imitation thereof, rambling, gabled, set with careful informality among orchards and lawns. These remain as the loveliest modern expression of "Philadelphia Taste," unostentatious, roomy, traditional, informal, yet luxurious, indigenous yet essentially romantic. Unfortunately also imitative, uncreative, eclectic, reactionary, increasingly now "old-fashioned"; still, it is the best that Philadelphia has produced in modern domestic architecture, and at its height, during the 1920's and 1930's, neo-Colonialism did serve to control the taste of domestic architecture, in the Eastern United States, anyway. Even to the cheapest developments the style lent some measure of taste and decorum. The breakdown of this taste in favor of Italian contractor pseudo-Californian "rancher" has been an absolutely unmitigated disaster as far as Philadelphia is concerned.*

In town the pseudo-colonial was only really successful for resi-

* But there has been, in the last few years, a decided reaction among developers, towards "Colonial-type" houses again; their conception of "Colonial-type" is peculiar to say the least, though just lately a curious return to a 1930 sort of authenticity seems to be taking place. What does this mean?

dences and small business buildings. Even with buildings no larger than the Racquet Club (1907) and the Historical Society's "new" home (1909), a sort of heavy incongruous blankness results. When applied to twenty-story office buildings of course the result is simply ludicrous without being interesting. At best a sort of dignified and well-proportioned stuffiness is achieved, like George Page's Insurance Company of North America building. At worst, as in the buildings of the Curtis Publishing Company on Washington Square, right next to Independence Hall itself, the result is simply a warehouse plainness.

Along with suburban neo-colonial various other eclectic suburban neo's flourished, one of the pleasantest being the Norman farmhouse developed by Arthur Meigs, another distinctly Old Philadelphia architect of this century. He built a not very chic perhaps but awfully well-bred and "nice" kind of house of native stone with steep roofs, graceful, cosy, rambling, roomy, one that adapted itself to the hilly sites, terraces, walled gardens, cobbled forecourts and other nostalgic Europeanized details for which the cultivated and traveled patrons of the past Philadelphia generation yearned. At their best these houses are still attractive and livable and not disastrously old-fashioned, which is a severe test for any building that falls under the Fifty Year Shadow, the time lag that comes after things are in style and before they start becoming curious, then quaint, then suddenly historic monuments. Very little, however, can be said (by me at least) in favor of the vast white wedding-cake châteaux constructed by parvenus like the Wideners, Stotesburys and Elkinses. They imitated New York and Newport, and were generally looked on in Philadelphia as exotic and ostentatious — which they were.

At the other extreme were the brave modernisms put over with such bravura by Arthur Meigs's onetime partner George Howe; they were very characteristic of the nervous, somewhat overbred taste of those Philadelphians so Old that they have a permanent perverse itch for anything they think is non–Old Philadelphian. This usually is a refined version of something that has just ceased to be very modern in Europe. George Howe was the darling of these people; he implied that he sneaked his more modern plans through the office when his partner Meigs was on vacation, but Howe was obviously a born *épateur* of the Philadelphia bourgeois. A New Englander with Philadelphia connections, he is still remembered and loved in Philadelphia for his personal style, charm and wit — and also for his seemingly irrestible charm and dash, which cut a swathe through the local females. His principal works were built in Philadelphia, but later on as Professor of Architecture at Yale he was a powerful influence among younger architects. His masterpiece is the PSFS building, one of the very first skyscrapers in America to be built (along with his partner Lescaze) on the pernicious assumption that a skyscraper doesn't go up, but is merely a directionless steel framework. Since this has become the norm nowadays, as witness the miserable packing boxes of Penn Center, the building is a landmark, a progenitor. But even on its own it is a very elegant construction, full of "Philadelphia taste," though of a somewhat exotic sort. It is in fact a very famous building, still the tallest and most beautiful skyscraper in Philadelphia, though built in 1932, still a monument and model of "modernism," although thirty years old. Its boardrooms, where the august PSFS board gathers, are regarded as the most chic in America. Howe's worst effort is the *Bulletin* building opposite 30th Street Station, a gray slab of the monotonous set off by a vicious little gray cobbled courtyard, treeless and desolate, like a landing field for midget spaceships and decorated with saucer-shaped tin bat-catchers. For sheer deliberate, rather than merely acquired, drabness nothing can equal this except the editorial policy of the *Bulletin* itself. Yet advanced Philadelphians have been unanimous in their affection for this strictly old-fashioned mousetrap; it represents an explicit rejection of any possible Old Philadelphia charm and cosiness, and therefore seems very daring and novel and brittle to them.

Modernism in Philadelphia may be said to have stuck at Howe and then gone downhill. There is, however, great hope among

the city's architects. The University of Pennsylvania has a re-
furbished School of Architecture, under the direction of Holmes
Perkins; and there are new buildings going up, designed by
Saarinen, the local Louis Kahn, and others, which promise to
redeem the cause, though they also all seem to be holding to the
all-glass, no-fun, no-charm cereal-box line.*

Domestic and suburban architecture is now completely in the
doldrums. No one seems to have been able to find an acceptable
working synthesis of modern techniques and indigenous traditions
and sentiments. Old Philadelphians seldom build now anyway;
they remodel, or cling to a sort of nineteen-thirtyish, Anglicized
stripped-colonial or French provincial. Meanwhile developers
are destroying the amenities of the suburbs without reference to
any taste or gentility, reproducing ad nauseam whatever the
contractor thinks, without benefit of architect, the emigrant from
North or South or West Philadelphia will buy. Since anything
looks better than the row-houses he is used to, the emigrant takes
what he gets and likes it.

If the suburbs are on the skids aesthetically, as the center of
the city was in 1900, in the center of the city things are now
improving. The Independence Hall restoration has churned up
a ferment of proposed conservation and development in the old
section, especially that part known as Society Hill. If even half
the dreams for transforming Society Hill into an urban paradise
of preserved old houses, gardens and malls and walks and brand-
new wonders can be carried out, the old part of Philadelphia will
become a model for other cities of civic self-salvation. Actually
only a few old houses in the area have been bought and restored
thus far; but since they have been bought and restored by Ingersolls and their kind, it has been considered a "movement." It is
certainly a reversal — the only such trek inwards in Philadelphia's
history, which has heretofore always been exploding and evacu-
ating outwards. Despite the general decay there is an awful lot

* The new Bell Telephone building on the Parkway, opposite the ICNA, all of
burnished, brownish metal, is as chic and fetching as a Nan Duskin ballgown.
There *is* hope.

of specific hope in architectural Philadelphia these days; though perhaps only a small straw in a faint breeze, this revolutionary trend into, rather than away from, town may have the most momentous effect on the future of Philadelphia and of American cities in general. Perhaps, led by the stalwart advance guard of Old Philadelphia pioneers, the American city can once more be recaptured for human beings.

2

i. *Killed by Kindness*

PHILADELPHIA has always been a bookish place, and its upper classes in particular have always had "literary tastes." There have always been libraries, and book fanciers and publishers of books and magazines, and a host of dilettantes. Celebrities have been birds of passage. Freneau, America's first poet, was a journalist there, Poe an editor. Thomas Moore visited, and for years a shack on an island in the Schuylkill, that went by the un-Mooreish name of The Pig's Eye, was pointed out to travelers on the Reading as being Moore's cottage. Most famous, of course, was Whitman, who settled during his last decade across the river in Camden, took daily tours down Chestnut Street, and after whom a Camden hotel and a huge bridge have been named.

When it comes to actual native literary production, Philadelphians themselves tend to be rather apologetic. Admittedly Philadelphia has produced no Great Writer — which is to say, no Emerson, Thoreau, Dickinson, or Hawthorne, no Melville, Whitman or James. But the standards for measuring literary worth among lesser figures than these are open to question. As Arthur Mizener says, speaking of Scott Fitzgerald's eclipse in the 'thirties, the American critic tends to think of writers as "Great, with a very large G, or something to be condescended to with all the force of one's own uncertainty." Philadelphia writers have been victims not only of this, but of their own fellow Philadelphians' "instinct of disparagement," and above all lack of conservatism; that is, lack of memory, lack of pride and lack of interest.

They have not on the whole been victims of lack of success or opportunity. There seems indeed to be a certain curious recurrence in Philadelphia's literary history of boom and bust, of distracted dilettantism and forgotten fame. There has never been a time when Philadelphia has not possessed a native writer of considerable contemporary reputation, or several persons of obvious native gifts; but the reputations seem to wither after death, and the native gifts to be diverted into other fields. Literature is a plant that evidently requires an acid and stony soil to produce the durable. The soil of Philadelphia is too fertile, words grow too easily and go to seed too quickly there. Or so, at least, one must judge by the record.

Literature began in Philadelphia with Penn, who was no mean word handler. He published at least half a hundred pamphlets of varying length and importance, and at his best commanded a rich seventeenth-century English. Both James Logan and Provost Smith of the College, though not exactly "writers," wrote and wrote and were definitely "literary men." But Philadelphia's first real writer, and most famous one was Benjamin Franklin. Who else?

Franklin was an amateur soldier and diplomat, an amateur scientist, an amateur politician, but as journalist, printer, editor and all-around propagandist he was very much a professional. His mind was essentially a writer's mind, imaginative, curious, eclectic, superficial in scholarship but deeply intuitive. His *Autobiography* belongs with *Robinson Crusoe, The Vicar of Wakefield* and *Gulliver's Travels* among those few prose works of the eighteenth century written in English which have had a continuous popular as well as a scholarly or special audience. No book has had a greater and perhaps more pernicious effect on generations of ambitious young Anglo-Saxons. No one could deny that it is a Great Book, yet no one seems to want to think of Franklin as a Great Writer. His supreme work of fiction was Poor Richard, that picture of himself as he was not, the cautious, parsimonius, canny epitome of common sense. Seldom has a fictional char-

acter been so successful, or so successfully obscured the real "I"
of his creator.

The Revolutionary and post-Revolutionary periods present two
separate and almost simon-pure representatives of the Philadelphia fate in Francis Hopkinson and Charles Brockden Brown.
Nobody could better exemplify the distracted amateur than Hopkinson, or the forgotten professional than Brown.

There was nothing Hopkinson couldn't do; he played a nice
harpsichord, signed a nice Declaration, helped design a nice Constitution, founded a nice family and wrote reams of nice poetry.
He was so busy, in fact, with such a number of things that he
never really settled down to perfect himself in any one. His verse
was almost entirely occasional, gallant sentiments addressed to
the local fair, polished political satires or rough squibs. His most
famous work, a mock epic called *The Battle of the Kegs,* about
the naval blockade of Philadelphia, was extremely popular in his
own day, but none of Hopkinson's literary works, unlike those
of his contemporary Freneau, have passed the censorship of time.

Charles Brockden Brown (1771–1810) of the next generation
has a more somber history than Hopkinson's and comes closest
among Philadelphia writers to the stereotype of the "forgotten
genius starving in a garret." He was another Philadelphia first,
America's first serious novelist, and his Gothic romances with
their somewhat incongruously Philadelphian background, *Arthur
Mervyn* for example, were known at least among intellectuals.
In England Shelley and his circle admired them, and Mary Godwin Shelley copied them in her now far more famous *Frankenstein,* as Brown in turn had copied her father's novels. Like many
native Philadelphia writers he did most of his serious writing in
New York. But his half dozen novels did not sell enough, despite
his international reputation, for him to support himself, and he
returned to Philadelphia and a humdrum, short, not even financially rewarding editorial and business career.

Hopkinson was remembered, though not usually as a writer.
Brown was more or less forgotten, though his work left its mark

on Hawthorne * and Poe, at least, until his revival in the twentieth century by students of Americana. Hopkinson the dilettante was very much of the Philadelphia upper classes. Brown, the professional, was rather respectable middle class, though descendants of a brother, Armitt Brown, were bigshots of a later period; this too tends to be a pattern.

Charles Jared Ingersoll and Nicholas Biddle, both friends and clubmates of Brown in Joseph Dennie's Circle, carried on the tradition of the upper-class literary dilettante with conspicuous éclat. These somewhat over-talented Princetonians, perfect models of the Sully fine young gentleman, spent their energies largely in affairs. Biddle's literary production is almost negligible: a few articles on the fine arts, the charming "Ode to Bogle," the offhand editorship of the *Port Folio* (1812–1814) (this is rather as though the young J. P. Morgan had taken over the *Atlantic Monthly* for a while just to help out), a eulogy of Jefferson which must have annoyed his conservative Philadelphia friends (again somewhat as though the same J.P. had written a eulogy of F.D.R.), another editorial job on the first history of the Lewis and Clark expedition.

Charles Ingersoll, whose career as non-practicing lawyer and political intransigent has been covered above, actually produced a good deal more than Biddle. His precocious tragedy, *Edwy and Elgiva*, was played professionally in Philadelphia, with some success, in 1801, before he was twenty. Later on, in 1810, already deep in politics as an anti-British Republican, he published a satirical pamphlet called *Inchiquin* that purported to be a translation of a French Jesuit's descriptions of America, and though it fooled nobody, it pleased many, and was read all over America as a forceful statement of American independence from British thought, manners, letters and morality. Charles was Sidney Fisher's father-in-law, but as one can imagine, they did not see eye to eye.

Towards the end of his life, after he had retired from active political strife to his Philadelphia estates, he wrote some more;

---

* Hawthorne gives him credit in his poetic essay "The Hall of Phantasy."

another verse tragedy *Julian,* one more in that tradition of Philadelphia poetic dramas by lawyers, and a *History of the War of 1812.* This is a disjointed affair, but full of firsthand material. Finally he wrote his *Memoirs.*

In the end, like Hopkinson or any other good Old Philadelphian, Ingersoll was a gentleman first and a writer and politician second. He was an Ingersoll who wrote, not a writer called Ingersoll. He was a century ahead of his time in his views on the Civil War and far more in the great American tradition of Franklin than the hotheads who tore the Union to pieces between them; but a prophet without honor at home. He has left no permanent mark as either a writer or politician.

The one significant local professional of the post-Revolutionary period was the cantankerous emigrant from Vermont, Joseph Dennie. He was, with the patronage, assistance and support of young Philadelphians which included both Biddle and Ingersoll, the founder and editor of the *Port Folio,* which became the country's leading intellectual organ. Under the sobriquet "Oliver Oldschool" Dennie inaugurated the Philadelphia tradition of the reactionary but benign Addisonian familiar essay which culminated a century later in Agnes Repplier. However, he was more influential as an editor and literary focus than as a writer.

ii.   *The Three B's*

AFTER THE DECLINE of the *Port Folio* in the 1820's, Philadelphia lost for good and all its dubious position as "Athens of America." First New York, in the days and person of Washington Irving, then finally Boston took over, and from that day to this Philadelphia has remained a literary backwater; but an active one.

During the mid-nineteenth century Philadelphia's principal literary output was poetic dramas. These were not written by professionals; most of them were fruits of leisure in the careers of lawyers like Charles Jared Ingersoll. Of a dozen such amateur playwrights, the most successful were three rather romantic gents whose names began with B.

James Barker (1784–1858) was a politician, a Mayor of Philadelphia whose father had been Mayor before him, and who was as famous for his duels and club life as for his writings. He ended up as Comptroller of the United States Treasury in Washington, but meanwhile fathered a dramatization of Scott's *Marmion* that went through years of performances, and a play called *Superstition* about the gloomier aspects of New England. This anticipated Hawthorne and Arthur Miller, and still has power.

Marmion was popular, but *Spartacus, or the Gladiators* by Robert Montgomery Bird was nothing short of sensational. First produced in 1831 as one of the plays solicited by the actor Edwin Forrest in his effort to encourage the native American drama, it played over a thousand performances during the comparatively short life of its author, and was the first serious American drama to run successfully in London. Bird would have been rich if Forrest, who played the part of Spartacus for years both in America and England, had not managed to keep all the money the play made himself. The hero's oration to his gladiators became famous, not to say infamous, as a schoolboy recitation, making perhaps its final appearance in *The Solid Gold Cadillac*, where it still resounds through the night of summer theaters, to extremely humorous effect. ("Ye call me chief, and ye do well to call me chief.") The original was not so intended, of course.

Bird wrote other plays, notably *The Broker of Bogota*, which had some success, but he couldn't make a go of it, and supported himself meanwhile by teaching at a Philadelphia medical school, since he had really trained as a doctor. Finally he gave up playwriting and turned to novels. His anti-Cooper romance called *Nick of the Woods*, which presented the Indian not as the noble red man but rather as a marauding savage, swept both this country and Europe, especially Germany, where it went into four editions and was the childhood reading of innumerable notable Teutons.

The third and by far the most significant of these three B's, another successful but nearly forgotten dramatist, was George Henry Boker. Boker, after the manner of Nicholas Biddle, was

an almost too-perfect prototype of the Philadelphia princeling.
He was very rich, the son of a bank president. He was very
handsome, a superb horseman, described by his friends as an
Apollo and by N. P. Willis as "the handsomest man in America."
He was very intelligent and talented, he was evidently a man of
charm and character if the lifelong devotion of his friends and
his social prominence means anything. He had only one thing
wrong with him; he wanted to be a poet. Like Biddle he went
to Princeton, where he engaged in "refined dissipation" and
helped to start the still fluttering *Nassau Literary Magazine,* usually called the *Lit.* He went back to Philadelphia, married a
Washingtonian and devoted himself to the Drama — grand romantic poetical tragedies on the Elizabethan scale, of which he
wrote a series. Most of them were produced in Philadelphia, one
even in London. They had considerable critical success, but not
the popular esteem for which he hoped. Nonetheless, by the time
his *Poems and Plays* were published in two fat volumes in 1856,
he had become a respectable, if not a famous, national literary
figure.

Boker's father died, and for fifteen years abandoning the Drama,
he was involved in one of Philadelphia's favorite occupations, a
lawsuit with a bank. His father was accused of having embezzled
his millions from the Girard Bank (not to be confused with
Stephen Girard's own bank, or with the Girard Trust of today)
while an officer of it. Boker finally won the suit, cleared his
father's name, and secured his inheritance, a victory which he
celebrated by writing a long poem called "The Book of the Dead"
devoted to the memory of his father, and excoriating his enemies.
Discreetly, he did not publish it till the 'eighties, when everybody it attacked was safely dead.

The Civil War again distracted him from literature. Violently
pro-Northern, Boker was one of the original founders, in fact probably *the* founder, of the Union League, as a protest against the
Copperheadism of the Philadelphia Club, the Wistar Parties and
Philadelphia in general, and he published war ballads which were
popular at the time. After the war Grant appointed him Min-

ister to Turkey, and then to Russia, where he became an intimate of the Czar. But his diplomatic, like his dramatic, career
came to an end prematurely with the end of Grant's term of
office, and the rest of his life was spent in Philadelphia leisure.
In a big house on Walnut Street near Rittenhouse Square, he
entertained visiting notables and died, in 1890, a disappointed
man, but revered as an Important Philadelphian. Philadelphia
conferred on him her highest honors, the presidencies of the
Union League and the Philadelphia Club; did everything, in fact,
but recognize him as a poet.

He published a few more things before he died. Another
collection of poems and dramas is distinguished for the "Legend
of the Hounds," about one of the early feudal ironmasters, Peter
Grubb of Cornwall, who in a fit of anger drove his faithful foxhounds into his furnace because they lost the scent one day in
the field. As a result he was haunted to death by them. Boker
does a fine job with this piece of extremely local lore, yet demonstrates a weakness typical of the residual colonialism of the place
and time when he transfers the locale to a sort of vague England,
probably to make it "more romantic."

Long after he had given up any serious attempt to be a poetic
dramatist, he did at last achieve the success he desired. In 1882
Lawrence Barrett, then considered second only to Booth as an
American Shakespearean actor, revived in New York Boker's
Francesca da Rimini. It was a smash hit, running on to what was
then the remarkable span of nine consecutive weeks. This for
an already old-fashioned American poetic drama was fabulous.
It would still be pretty good today. Barrett played it off and
on all through his active life, and in 1901 Otis Skinner, who had
played in it with Barrett, revived it with himself in the lead. But
this recognition came too late.

The First War and the literary revolution that followed it
swept away the whole world of what came to be called the "Genteel Tradition," and Boker's name disappeared along with so
many others. In the 1920's, however, Scully Bradley, later the
Vice Provost of the University of Pennsylvania, but then a grad-

uate student, writing his thesis on Boker, made a discovery. The younger Mrs. Boker, Boker's daughter-in-law, had given Bradley the run of her house on 13th near Walnut Street, and in the library, in one of the cabinets below bookcases, he came on a sheaf of manuscript. It was poetry. It was obviously in Boker's hand. It was a collection of sonnets. Pinned to the front of it was a final draft of a dedicatory sonnet, dashed off evidently in a white heat of sudden inspiration — on a single sheet of old-fashioned golden toilet paper. (The Sedentary Principle with a vengeance.)

Bradley published the sonnets in 1929, hardly a propitious moment for the introduction of a mess of Victorian sonnets. They received no critical attention, but were variously anthologized, notably by Mark Van Doren in his magnificent *American Poets* of 1932. They represent one of the most curious and impressive monuments of American literature. The bulk of them is a more or less consecutive sonnet sequence written to a mistress of long standing, what was obviously an extremely passionate affair, evidently well-known in Philadelphia at that time, as such affairs usually were, but carried on with the usual discretion so as to avoid public scandal. The affair went through all the amorous stages, but ended disastrously, if we are to believe the sonnets themselves. There are 313 in the posthumous collection; together with those he published in his lifetime, Boker left nearly four hundred sonnets. This of course does not rival the thirteen thousand so-called sonnets of Dr. Merrill Moore of Tennessee and Boston, or the thousand of Petrarch himself, but it does come close to the Wordsworthian record, and far outstrips such comparative lazybones as Shakespeare and Spenser. The sonnets are all Petrarchan too, in itself a more difficult form than the more native Shakespearean sonnet.

What counts of course is quality, not quantity; in the case of Boker, the quality is hard to assess. Almost everything can be said against his sonnets. They are imitative, they are stuffy. There is about his poetic handling an amateur clumsiness, his lines are frequently harsh and lumpy. In his forms, diction and attitudes, he is always conventional. Even at his most frenzied he wears his language like a frock coat, a bit formal, elevated, ponderous. He is a very unsympathetic artist, especially to our time, and almost bound to repel at first.

Yet under the frock coat, in his grand images, the telling simplicity of an occasional line, he reveals a virility, a passion, a dark seriousness that becomes compelling and moving. He has a way of making most of his contemporaries seem frivolous and false by comparison. Critics in writing of Eakins speak of "honesty" and "gravity." Though Boker is in many ways very different from Eakins in generation and in style — elaborate and romantic where Eakins is plain and realist — they do have in common this Roman *"gravitas,"* and this sort of Brahmsian, City Hall scale and somberness; and, of course, a complete Philadelphianism.

If Boker is hard to estimate, it is because one measures him against something of a vacuum. He is certainly the greatest poet of Philadelphia; but so what, who else? He is the greatest American dramatist of the nineteenth century, but again, who else? He is, in fact, quite probably the best poetic dramatist in English of the nineteenth century, but even here competition is pretty slim: Shelley's *Cenci,* the *Virginius* of Sheridan Knowles, Bulwer Lytton's effective but corny *Richelieu,* Browning and Tennyson at their acknowledged worst. He is certainly one of the significant sonneteers of his period; but his mid-century period is not one of significant sonnets.

It is as a counterbalance to Whitman perhaps that Boker can best be appreciated. They were almost exact contemporaries and lived for a long time close to each other. They must have met. What they thought of each other, if so, does not seem to be recorded. They are an exact antithesis, personally and poetically; Whitman the radical, democratic nonconformist, Boker the conservative, colonialized traditional; Whitman making up an entire new poetic apparatus of his own, Boker sticking to nineteenth-century English imitations of sixteenth-century forms, the sonnet, the ballad, the poetic tragedy. Whitman (Plain) represents in its extreme the native, anti-colonial, anti-European, and so was of course immediately appreciated in Europe. Boker (Fancy) represents the old stock, upper-class respecter of Old World upper-class culture, and has never been appreciated anywhere.

However he is evaluated today, Boker is certainly the perfect representative of the Philadelphia fatality, universally favored in his outward fortunes, utterly forgotten, after a modest lifetime reputation, both by America in general and Philadelphia in particular. Along with Nicholas Biddle, he remains among the largest of the Hidden City's hidden figures; and the best hidden.

iii.   *Brandywiners — and Others*

Two OTHER MEN, along with Boker, more or less sum up serious literary effort by Philadelphians in the period from 1850 to 1890, the "Civil War generation." Like Boker, these two were also rather glamorous as persons, but unlike him, they were both tremendously famous during their lifetimes. Bayard Taylor was the great traveler, the Lowell Thomas of his time, as well as the poet laureate of the Genteel Era. Charles Godfrey Leland was famous for his humorous ballads. Both of them were bosom friends of Boker and of each other.

Leland combines the Philadelphian character of dispersed talents and vanished reputation. Though he published a book a year, more or less, from 1855 to 1900, nothing remains of him except the ghost of two lines of dialect poetry, "Hans Breitmann gife a barty, Vhere ish dot barty now?" These were from his once famous Hans Breitmann ballads, German-American spoofs popular in his day even in Germany. They were, however, a mere by-blow of a career of literary and artistic-professional dabbling. Leland did serious poetry, travel sketches, translations, mostly from the German, investigations into the ways and languages of the Gypsies and the Italian witches, a book of memoirs which might have been better if it had been less offhand; above all he had a devotion to handicraft, work in metal and wood, which he propagandized by books and introduced himself by talk and example into the public schools of Philadelphia and eventually of America in general. He is the father of what is now known in the world of education as "manual training."

Leland was a man of curious learning, had married a Fisher (cousin of Sidney's), and was a striking-looking fellow, tall, bearded, dynamic. His picturesque figure was familiar in Philadelphia during his middle years when he was a prominent editor and columnist there, and in his old age along the streets of Florence, where he retired after inheriting some money. He knew everybody famous, and everybody knew him, but Vhere ish Leland now? The Victorian thank offering to him is a biography by his niece Elizabeth Robins Pennell. He was lucky in that it was better written than most of its kind.

Boker was a real talent, but an amateur; Leland a professional dilettante; Boker's other dear Philadelphia friend, Bayard Taylor, was grindingly and fatally a professional. He was not by birth a Philadelphian, like Boker and Leland, certainly not an Old Philadelphian — he was the son of a Quaker farmer — and most of his professional activity in America was centered about New York. Nonetheless he remained faithful to his native Kennett near the Brandywine River in Chester County, where after he made his money he maintained a typically Philadelphian big country place called Cedarcroft, an elaborate Gothic-Tuscan villa surrounded by lawns and bowers.

Few writers in America have been better known for a larger variety of things than Bayard Taylor. Of a dark, strong-featured, exotic good looks described as "oriental but frank," he built his original reputation by travel books and above all by lectures as the Traveler from Far Countries, the sunburned friend of sheikhs and Lapps. His picture in lithograph form, exotically dressed, was a familiar parlor ornament from coast to coast. In between he did editorial work in New York and spent his hard-earned dollars on Cedarcroft. When he turned to fiction, his first novel, *Hannah Thurston,* a satire on reformers, transcendentalists and eager females, raised a profitable storm, and his *The Story of Kennett* (1866), laid in his own Brandywine country, remains still a local classic, celebrated by that memorial fox hunt of 1940 around Taylor's own Kennett Square. This must certainly be the only book in America to receive this peculiar and peculiarly Philadelphian accolade.

His real vocation however was poetry, at which he was very serious, very expert, and quite prolific. Unfortunately he made a reputation too soon and too specifically. His first poems were Oriental, in that especially spurious Turkish-corner-and-hookah pseudo-Byronic way. People loved them, especially his famous "Bedouin Love Song," with its rather grand refrain of love that shall not die ". . . Till the sun grows cold, And the stars are old. And the leaves of the Judgment Book unfold." Unfortunately, his later poetry, though some of it is much better, was not so appealing. Nonetheless, he was during his lifetime, perhaps the most reputable poet of the post–Civil War generation; and he is now best, in fact only, remembered for poetry, his verse translation of Goethe's *Faust,* which even yet remains the standard English version despite its old-fashioned air. A great admirer of Goethe and the Germans, his life culminated with his appointment as minister to Germany in 1878. He had in mind a combined biography of Goethe and Schiller and sailed to Germany after banquets, honors and torchlight parades, only to die within a few months, worn out by work and success.

He had had eventually to give up ruinous Cedarcroft, but some of his best poetry, the honest and bitter "Home Pastorals," was written there, and set in the Chester County that he loved, but that did not love him. His great house, lavish hospitality, bohemian or worldly friends, the champagne and the high doings offended his old Quaker neighbors and relations, and he was hurt. Hankering after Old World Romance, he could not really adjust his vision to an American landscape; but he tried, and the "Home Pastorals" reflect the state of mind of the traveled and sensitive American, one feels especially Philadelphian, of that so-called Genteel Period trying to see America through a haze of poetry as one saw the Rhine.

He wrote good verse too in his later "Lyrics," a distillation of light, high, dry poetic wine, delicate and without much body or flavor, but really elevated in its pseudo-Goethean way. It is "genteel poetry" at its best and beyond the limitations, and along with Boker's sonnets it deserves much, much better than oblivion and academic scorn.

Two other Brandywiners from the mid-nineteenth century became adopted Philadelphians. One was Thomas Buchanan Read, Philadelphia's only really popular serious poet, the other the fantastic George Lippard, Philadelphia's most popular low-down novelist. Read was once famous for his epic "The Wagoner of the Alleghenies," and his ballad "Sheridan's Ride," as well as the deliciously Victorian "The Bay of Naples." Lippard was never famous, but his lurid novels sold like fury, and he founded a sort of fascist secret society called the Brotherhood of the Union, with himself as Supreme Washington, that survived into the twentieth century. Both Read and Lippard were quaint characters, but had little to do with Old Philadelphia.

iv. The Mitchell Coterie

THOUGH THE Philadelphia Civil War generation of Boker, Taylor and Leland has grown remote, the next Philadelphia literary generation, the group of Mitchell, Lea, Furness, Wister, Repplier, is still current enough in its names at least, even if works by these writers are not much read. The Boker–Taylor–Leland constellation was only somewhat peripherally Old Philadelphian, and their careers were spent partly away from Philadelphia. Not so the later dispensation. They were not only born and bred Philadelphians, they were most of them Old Philadelphians, or close to it, connected by all sorts of family ties to each other — Wister and Mitchell were cousins — as well as to Everybody. That is, enmeshed in the Web.

Weir Mitchell, Horace Howard Furness and Henry Lea were actually contemporaries of Boker and Taylor, and Mitchell went to school with Leland. What puts Mitchell in a later literary generation is the postponement of his writing career. He was first and even foremost a doctor, and is recognized as an American pioneer in psychiatry. Like his father, also a doctor, before him, he had always written poetry, but it was not until he took up the writing of novels (his first was published in 1885) that he became known.

Hugh Wynne, the nation's biggest best seller in 1897, made Mitchell famous. This large slow historical novel of Philadelphia Quakers during the Revolution, a mixture of good sober realism and bad tepid romance, sold over a million copies, and is still on school reading lists. It is not, actually, his best book. *The Red City,* his novel about Philadelphia during the plague of 1793, has a more interesting background, and his modern novels, especially the rambling, anecdotal, *Characteristics* and its sequel *Dr. North and His Friends,* are far more sophisticated and palatable. They also give a pleasant picture of the Mitchell–Furness–Lea circle. One of his later psychological novels, *Constance Trescott,* is still pretty gripping. His poetry is correct, and had some reputation at the time.

Mitchell was a trustee of the University of Pennsylvania, chairman of the board of the Mutual Assurance, founder and first president of the Franklin Inn, twice president of the College of Physicians. For his second wife he married a Cadwalader. This combination of medical renown, social connection, boardsmanship, and as an added grace note, literary éclat, was of course irresistible to Philadelphians. Mitchell's Saturday evening receptions in town were obligatory, and during his lifetime he was considered a modern rival to Franklin himself.

Horace Howard Furness, Mitchell's good friend and contemporary, was not so much a writer as a scholar. However, he and Mitchell were the kingpins of Philadelphia's late-nineteenth-century literary flourishing, and the Sunday afternoons at his country place Lindenshade were companions and rivals to Mitchell's Saturday evenings in town. Furness had the inestimable advantage from the Philadelphia point of view of being Second Generation in what had already become a definite Family, though not quite a really Old Philadelphian one. His father, a Bostonian, had come down in the 1820's as pastor of Philadelphia's first

Unitarian Church. Though Unitarianism never really caught on in Philadelphia, Furness did. He was a splendid preacher, and one of Philadelphia's leading clerical intellectuals. One son, William H., Jr., was a talented though short-lived portrait painter. Another was Frank, the architect. Horace Howard, the third son, devoted his life to a definitive edition of Shakespeare, editing a play a year from 1871 till his death in 1912, after which, in hereditary Philadelphia fashion, the work was carried on and finished by his son Horace Howard, Jr. A son of Horace Howard, Sr., William H. III, became a distinguished ethnologist (*Homelife of Borneo Headhunters* and the like) and the Furnesses soon became established as Philadelphia's premier social-scholarly family. Horace Howard's sister became Mrs. Caspar Wister, and was well known as a translator of German novels. This helped too.

Henry Lea, also of the older generation, and also of Family, if not quite as elegant a one, was also a late bloomer. He followed his father Isaac Lea and his grandfather Matthew Cary in the publishing business, but retired to devote himself to history. He ran a sort of transatlantic research industry, with people working for him all over Europe digging out facts from monasteries and museums. His monumental four-volume *History of the Inquisition* is still considered to be definitive — both impartial and objective. Perhaps his divided heritage, Quaker father, Catholic mother, balanced out. He himself was a Furness-Unitarian.

These older men did not achieve their fame until the 'eighties or 'nineties, and all lived and worked and produced into the twentieth century. (Lea died in 1909, Furness in 1912, Mitchell in 1914.) Thus Owen Wister and Agnes Repplier, though they were actually much younger, began to publish at the same time, and by around 1900 they could all consider themselves literary equals and personal friends despite the great differences in years.

The Furnesses were already a Family, but not strictly Old Philadelphian. The Wisters, as we have seen, were both. The Wisters, though no very close relation to the Wistaria, were grafted onto the Morris family tree, and like the Morrises, or the plant Wis*t*aria itself, began overrunning Philadelphia. This Welsh–German genealogical creeper clambered to the Philadelphia heights when Owen's father, Dr. Owen Jones Wister, married the intellectual daughter of wicked Pierce Butler and the dashing English actress Fanny Kemble. Owen was thus born under propitiously Philadelphian stars, brought up either in Europe or at Butler Place, his grandfather's country estate, landscaped by Fanny Kemble herself. He went to the fairly recently established St. Paul's School in Concord and then on to Harvard, the Porcellian, Harvard's ultimate social club, and friendship with Proper Bostonians and Teddy Roosevelt; he began to write almost immediately.

His first "published work" was a story for his St. Paul's School magazine. In an essay he wrote for the same magazine he describes a visit to the seashore, and a hotel where "the boarders are of such a low class, with one or two exceptions, that it is impossible to distinguish between master and man without noticing which of the two waits on the other"; evidence of a rather appalling sort of social precocity. His book about Harvard called *Philosophy Four,* involving a couple of gay swells who hire a greasy grind to tutor them for an examination, created an equally unfortunate impression. It has blasted Wister's reputation permanently among a later generation of Harvard men. One can see why the Wild West seemed so very, very different to Wister.

Like any other good young Old Philadelphian he was more or less forced to study law and join the bar, though his real interest at this time was music, and he had studied composition in Paris and had played for, and been praised by, Liszt. Though he hated the law, he began well; and one would have thought with all this in his background he would have been fairly contented. In fact, however, like his friend Teddy Roosevelt, his health declined, and following Roosevelt's example and Dr. Weir Mitchell's advice, he went West for his health. This was just what the doctor ordered; the West, free, wild and wide-open, was a revelation after what seemed to him the oppressively gray hothouse world he had been brought up in.

He started to write about it, at first short stories in the 'nineties, as dramatic and real as the pictures of his new-made acquaintance Frederic Remington, and then finally his chief work, in 1902, the novel *The Virginian*. This was an instant, overwhelming success, outstripping even that of Mitchell's *Hugh Wynne* of a few years previously. It sold millions of copies and continued to sell for decades — over three million copies have been printed all told. Next to Franklin's *Autobiography* it is certainly the most widely read book ever written by a Philadelphian, and its influence as the first "western" has of course been enormous, as the movies and television demonstrate ad nauseam day by day, week by week, year by year. The book has been so imitated that it is hard to get back to seeing it freshly again. Probably only those who know the West well to start with can judge today just how and where it is authentic. As in *Hugh Wynne* sober realism is compounded with tepid romance. When the Virginian is not pursuing his obnoxious chit of a New England schoolmarm (even Wister admitted she was "the failure . . . without personality"), the incidents, atmosphere, conversation and psychology are as true to the West as anything ever written about it, except Wister's own excellent short stories. The plot, however, and the "love interest," are pretty weak affairs now. Unfortunately these were just the things that the readers of 1902 found slightly shocking and therefore delicious. The book was popular for the wrong reasons, and that hurt its reputation later on.

Many authors are one-book men; none more so than Wister, as he may have realized himself. Even so, literary history does not often present the picture of an author writing his one book and then more or less just stopping, to lead a long afterlife of conventional leisure. Especially not an author as dedicated and excited and hugely successful as Wister. He did write one more novel, *Lady Baltimore,* about Charleston, which was very well thought of. But after that appeared in 1906 he wrote no more novels, and very little else. Why?

One reason certainly was that he felt his Western experience had been exhausted, and nothing else interested him enough.

He fell victim to the fallacy that catches all those who discover the West — the idea that the "Old West," the really authentic West, is gone. For Wister the Old West, *his* West, died before 1900. The "Old West" is always the West people know when they are young, and doubtless there are college boys right now discovering a West that in twenty years will be to them the vanished "Old West."

Another and more curious reason for Wister's premature literary silence might be a strange incident that occurred in the summer of 1912. He had been out in Wyoming at a ranch in Jackson's Hole, then quite out of reach of anything but two-weeks-old mail. His father-in-law, also named Wister, had died in Maine. (In good Philadelphia style Owen had married a Wister, a first cousin.) The newspapers somehow made the mistake of thinking this was Owen Wister the writer. There were lengthy obituaries and criticisms, but unlike Mark Twain, who in a similar circumstance could remark that the reports of his death were greatly exaggerated, Owen Wister could not easily laugh at himself. The critics more or less united in faint praise; one in fact referred to him as a "first rate second rate writer." For a man so sensitive to the opinions of others, who had been tutored by Howells and Henry James, to whom Teddy Roosevelt as President found time to write a five-thousand-word letter of literary advice, this must have been a fairly crushing blow.

In any case, whatever the reason, his literary career was almost ended. The projected novel about a Philadelphia which he called "Monopolis" never progressed. He spent the rest of his life, until his death in 1938, as an Old Philadelphian should, in boardsmanship and travel and club life. He was, like Weir Mitchell, chairman of the board of the Mutual Assurance Company, the Green Tree. The First War excited him into several volumes of violently pro-English propaganda. How Philadelphian that the possessor of a German name should have been by this time so utterly Anglicized! He published a series of light poems with illustrations by George Howe, the architect of the PSFS. He wrote the centennial history of the Philadelphia Club in 1934 and was subsequently its president. The parallels to Boker's career are obvious.

Wister's contemporary Agnes Repplier, though equally Philadelphian, came from a very different background and had a very different life. The Reppliers were not only almost middle-class, they were poor, and what is worse, Roman Catholic. Agnes attended Eden Hall, a famous and still very much existent Catholic girls' school in Torresdale, where she knew Charles Leland's niece, and the artist Joseph Pennell's future wife, Elizabeth Robins. She found herself, her medium and her publisher early, and in 1886 began to contribute the kind of dry, witty and bookish essay to the *Atlantic Monthly* that was to occupy her for the rest of her long life. Besides nearly a hundred such essays, she wrote three biographies of Catholic New World religious figures, a rather casual short history of Philadelphia in 1898, and a book of memoirs of her life as a student at Eden Hall.

Though often caustic about her city, she remained an indigenous and faithful Philadelphian, a member of the literary circle of Mitchell and Furness, and for years Philadelphia's Grand Old Lady of letters. She was more at home in the literary atmosphere of the time before the First War than at any time afterward, and even more at home in what she called the "happy half century" — England between 1775 and 1825. But she never lost her sharp way with words, her interest in English literary history and her not entirely uncritical Catholic faith. Her essays on Byron's illegitimate daughter Allegra and on foolish Regency bluestockings, on cats and on tea are likely to be good more or less forever. She supported her family for years, outliving all but the youngest generations. She was still writing in 1940, and did not die until 1950.

The sort of essay she wrote — sherry-flavored, chuckling, learned, somewhat reactionary and at once objective and personal — reached its top form in the work of Agnes Repplier. Deriving obviously from Addison, it was instituted in Philadelphia probably by Dennie as "Oliver Oldschool" in his *Port Folio,* though before him Franklin's witty bagatelles are in the same tradition, with a French accent. The tradition has been carried on in the present day by Christopher Morley, A. Edward Newton and Cornelius Weygandt, and is still carried on by the columnists for the *Evening Bulletin,* Morley Cassidy, Paul Jones and Don Rose.

That Agnes Repplier seems to have suffered also the Philadelphia fate of being more or less forgotten is certainly an oversight that outside-of-Philadelphia barbarity and inside-of-Philadelphia stupidity will have to correct. It's a small still voice, but perfectly true and clear, spinsterish but incisive, and American literature has nothing better in this vein. She is, or ought to be, a classic in all senses of the word; a "non-fiction Austen."

Other writers with Philadelphia backgrounds were tremendously popular in that pre-war period to which Agnes Repplier belongs. There was Richard Harding Davis, who carried on the tradition of Taylor as traveler, and of John Hare Powel as "handsomest man ever seen"; he was the original Gibson Man. There was James Gibbons Huneker, America's first really sophisticated writer on music, and well known too as an advanced novelist. Frank Stockton pushed Philadelphia aplomb to deliberate fictional absurdity. In his characters Mrs. Lecks and Mrs. Aleshine, who were "cast away" on a desert island, the Lady from Philadelphia who meets the wildest circumstances with practical sense achieves her apotheosis. His story "The Lady or the Tiger?" is a classic; but does anyone read Stockton now? Perhaps, since Mrs. Lecks and Mrs. Aleshine are now available in paperback form. Francis Hopkinson Smith, though a Baltimorean, has obvious Philadelphia connections, and was equally well known as an illustrator and a sentimental novelist. All these people went to New York to make their fortune. They all made it. They all now gather dust in libraries.

v. *Postwar*

THE FIRST WORLD WAR saw the end of the Mitchell–Wister coterie, most representative of Philadelphia and of Old Philadelphia. Postwar Philadelphia writing was, obviously, quite different in atmosphere, and is best represented by three writers, Joseph Hergesheimer, Christopher Morley and Struthers Burt, and by the yet-continuing phenomenon of the "Philadelphia Novel."

In the Philadelphia Novel, whatever the backgrounds of the hero and heroine may be, the real protagonist is always the Philadelphia Oligarchy, brooding and dominant as City Hall and the boom of the bell from its tower,* Old Philadelphia rich and cruel, subtle and conventional, gracious and hypocritical, cultured, uncreative, churchly and intensely worldly; not so different, in fact, from its Edwardian counterparts elsewhere, a smaller and simpler London, without the garish élan of Paris and New York but still very lush, much more opulent than Boston, more civilized than Chicago and points West, more prosperous than the reconstruction South. Two dominant, though contradictory, themes almost invariably run through the fabric of the Philadelphia Novel: one is elegaic and nostalgic, a lament for the decline in modern days of the form and glitter, the code and taste and manners and art of living, the food and houses and horses and wine and conversation destroyed either by cheap modern money, or by the lack of it. The other theme is rebellious, the struggle of the young idealist, male or female, inside or outside, to preserve his love and his convictions against the pressure of the past, the sacrifice of the individual to the Family, the oppressive weight of convention and keeping up of appearances, the timidity in the face of ideas or passion or creative power.

Hergesheimer, Morley and Burt, though they all wrote many other things, write characteristic specimens, in fact *the* characteristic specimens of the Philadelphia Novel.

Joseph Hergesheimer, though a Philadelphian by birth, was of the three perhaps the least Old Philadelphian. However, he was the only one who really settled in the city. His first solid success, *The Three Black Pennys,* in 1917 might be considered the first of the Philadelphia Novels. It presents the recurrence of a certain family strain in three individuals, and in three centuries;

---

* Livingston Biddle, in his *Main Line,* actually uses this bell in an interesting and modestly symbolical way.

the "black Penny" that is supposed to crop up occasionally in an otherwise solidly conventional blond family of ironmasters named Penny. One of those feudal ironmaster families like the Brookes of Birdsboro, the Pennys begin as pioneers in the wilderness and end as sophisticated Old Philadelphia rentiers, their works finally absorbed by Big Steel from Pittsburgh. The final Penny, an exquisitely cultivated Edwardian of the old school, watches his world of form and elegance break up under the impact of the early Jazz Age of 1917, whereas his favorite niece, who really represents the modern strain of black Penny, defies convention to run off with her rebellious steelworker lover. Not only the action, but the rather elaborate style of the book, the concern with beautiful things and textures, clothes and furniture and houses, the intense awareness of gentility and the lack of it, is characteristic of later Philadelphia Novels.

Hergesheimer wrote other successful books, notably *Java Head,* but none so specifically Philadelphian. He made a lot of money, had a beautiful house outside of Philadelphia near West Chester, gave lavish parties and was very much a celebrity, local and national. A dip into critical writers of the 'twenties (Rascoe, Mencken, Lewisohn) gives some idea of how seriously he was taken. All this success unfortunately did not help his work, which declined with time, drink and a rather cheap interest in movie queens, who even began to obtrude their spurious presence into his novels. By the 1930's his reputation had much fallen off; he stopped writing in the middle of that decade and as yet no appreciable resurgence has set in. His works are perhaps not quite old enough to escape from the shadow of old-fashionedness. They are not Jazz Age, nor yet late Victorian. When they do come out of the shadow, the style and color of the best ones should certainly keep them alive, and *The Three Black Pennys* will always have to be recognized at least as an important piece of Philadelphiana (the very word is like a bell).

Christopher Morley was more definitely an Old Philadelphian, at least by association, than Hergesheimer, but with the exception of *Kitty Foyle* most of his long list of books — like Leland or

Taylor, he produced almost a book a year — have nothing to do with Philadelphia at all. Morley was a product of Haverford, that small, excellent Quaker men's college on the Main Line where his father taught and of which in later years his brother Felix, a Philadelphia newspaperman, was president; but there is certainly nothing particularly Quaker about him. Philadelphian, however, is certainly the extreme quixotic bookishness and the penchant for the occasional essay. One of his earliest books in fact is a collection of newspaper sketches called *Travels in Philadelphia* which he wrote when he worked for the Philadelphia *Record* in 1919–20. These are typically casual explorations of Philadelphia's odd corners and queer characters, the sort of Watsonian poking around in the attic which is almost a local vice. But shortly after that he migrated to New York, rather in the footsteps of and looking for the same sort of lowlife as the Ash Can School painters. He discovered rather than New York itself, the more-like-Philadelphia boroughs of old Brooklyn and run-down Hoboken, where he created a special sort of Morleyesque Philadelphia-away-from-Philadelphia, a city of quaint learning, fantastical coincidence and whimsical Rabelaisianism. His most typical books in this vein are the early *Parnassus on Wheels* and *The Haunted Book Shop,* the later fantasies *Thunder on the Left* and *Where the Blue Begins* (all the characters in this are dogs).

Kitty Foyle, his one Philadelphia novel, is quite unlike his other books. It is also, oddly enough, by far the most popular of all his popular books, a great best seller when it came out in 1939, a very popular movie, and has even, God help us every one, been spun out into a sort of television soap opera. The theme of the typical Philadelphia Novel is here presented in primary but effective colors: Kitty Foyle is the beautiful, intelligent, tough and warm-hearted daughter of an old-time North Philadelphia cricketer. She falls in love with the handsome Princeton-cum-Main Line Wynnewood Strafford VI (both names, and most others in the book, are derived from stations along the Main Line itself, in this case Wynnewood and Strafford). Needless to say his Family breaks it up and she goes off to New York in a huff and to a very conspicuously non–Old Philadelphia beau called Mark. Meanwhile we've had reminiscences of the days of cricketing, some discussion about the Assembly, thought we don't actually get there, and a good cry. The twin themes of glamorous upper-crustness and independent rebellion have been handled with gusto. The fact that its chief character is the heroine, and definitely from outside, rather than the hero from within, the Web perhaps helps account for *Kitty Foyle*'s singular success. But there is a sort of beery tough-sentimentalism about it that dates it and takes the edge off of much of its irony and observation.

Old Philadelphians are inclined to sniff at *Kitty Foyle,* as indeed they are apt to sniff at any book about Philadelphia, as the work of an outsider, or one who "didn't know." Morley's acquaintance with the world of Wynn Strafford VI was perhaps not very intimate. Struthers Burt's *Along These Streets* has along these lines a good deal more authenticity, and though it has no central character as vividly realized as Kitty herself, the book presents a much richer and subtler portrait of Philadelphia and of Old Philadelphia especially. It is based on the perennially intriguing notion of a poor man going to a strange city to claim a fortune he has inherited. In this case the man is a youngish professor, son of a Philadelphia misalliance, and the city is, of course, Philadelphia, where he has not been since childhood. Here again the two themes, nostalgia for the past as represented by the beautiful old house that is part of his inheritance, and rebellion against the conventions, as represented by the hero in his relations with three different heroines, develop leisurely. Here is the scene at the Assembly, the lovingly described texture of furniture and food and houses, and again, as in *Kitty Foyle,* the final defeat of the idealist by the massed forces of the conventional.

It is all done with the solidity and the authority of a writer who was not only a professional, like Morley, but an insider too, who had actually been to Assemblies. Born in a poor branch of a rich family, Burt was able to observe, if not always to participate in, the creamy luxury of turn-of-the-century Philadelphia social life. Though never as fortunately favored as Owen Wister, he still found the native atmosphere oppressive, and he too escaped to Wyoming, where he knew Wister, but where, unlike him, he actually settled. For many years he ran a successful dude ranch in Jackson's Hole, where Wister had gone hunting in the 'nineties. Beginning with a real animus against his native city, Burt gradually returned to it more and more in his writing. His last two, and perhaps most durable books, *Along These Streets* and the informal history of the city, *Philadelphia, Holy Experiment,* were written with love, despite a prevailing tone of irony.

These three professionals, all now dead, were not the only ones to mine the ores of Philadelphia. Two brilliant amateurs, William C. Bullitt and Francis Biddle, both even more definitely Old Philadelphia insiders, wrote novels (every well-educated Philadelphia princeling should write a novel, to prove he can do it — in the nineteenth century, it was a poetic drama) which caused considerable furore in their day.

In Bullitt's extravagant *It's Not Done,* published in 1926, the protagonist is an insider, a rebellious idealist of good family who has an affair with a young woman artist of incredible earthiness and humanity, but deserts her for a conventionally approved marriage. This leads to no good, naturally, and he ends up at once lamenting the decline of Old Philadelphia and rejecting what's left of it. Though he never does get the girl, he has rebelliously Come to Realize, and presumably is off to Russia, where Bullitt himself actually went later, to rediscover life from a fresh, non–Old Philadelphia angle. What made the book exciting to Philadelphians was not only the frank sex and inside knowledge of the highest echelons of the Oligarchy, but also its obvious characterization of real people, especially the acid portraits of such parvenus as Widener and Wanamaker. The story is that William's more conservative brother Orville hurried around to all the local bookstores trying to buy up every available copy, but since the book was selling rapidly in Philadelphia, this effort was not enough. It remains the book about Philadelphia that the oldest Old Philadelphians invariably still mention. They certainly didn't like it, but they remember it.

Philadelphians didn't like Francis Biddle's book *The Llanfear Pattern* either, but as it was not as spectacular, it was more easily dismissed. Its story is really the same as that of the Bullitt book: idealistic young Harvard man returns home, makes an unsuccessful marriage, is stifled by convention, has a frustrated affair with a Real Woman, and ends disillusioned. The characters are not as jazzily alive as Bullitt's, but they are far more credible, and the book is, what Bullitt's is not, a really serious work of fiction and art. Very suave and full of brocaded Edwardianism that, when it appeared in 1927, probably just seemed old-fashioned, it now takes on a very Henry James attractiveness. It perhaps rather defeats its purpose, however, since upper-class Philadelphia life is presented in such seductive colors that it somewhat diminishes one's sympathy for the rebel.

Neither Bullitt nor Biddle wrote any more novels. Both were led away from literature by public affairs, Bullitt into diplomacy as Roosevelt's Ambassador to Russia (like Boker), Biddle into the New Deal as Roosevelt's Attorney General. Their careers in the first half of the twentieth century strikingly parallel those of Charles Jared Ingersoll and Nicholas Biddle in the first half of the nineteenth: the same talent and taste for literature, the same liberal politics (though Bullitt seems to have strayed to the Right), the same background of good family. Francis Biddle is, of course, a Biddle, though not of the Nicholas branch. Bullitt, though not actually an Ingersoll himself, comes close; at least, his brother Orville married one. Neither one lives in Philadelphia now. Biddle is in Washington and Bullitt seems to be as far away as Formosa.

This by no means ends the list of Philadelphia Novels, of course. Henry Hart, in *The Great One* (1934), applied the formula of the disillusioned Harvard man to the career of Philadelphia's great upper-class political scoundrel Boies Penrose, with considerable effectiveness. (In the early novels of this genre the hero is usually a Harvard man; later on almost invariably a Princetonian.) Walter Gilkyson's *Toward What Bright Land* (1947) is a thoughtful and picturesque panorama of a Philadelphia boy

growing up in the 1870's (this boy, for a change, goes to Penn).
Livingston Biddle, nephew of apoplectic Anthony, had a best
seller in 1950 with his soberly realistic *Main Line*. Macready Huston has made the formula a standardized recipe for rather civilized popular fiction, in a series of novels of varying merit.

The latest, and by no means least known, entry has been Richard Powell's *The Philadelphian* (1956). An immensely readable,
though hardly well constructed book, it traces the history of a
family of Irish immigrants in their advance through the female
line to respectability, and finally in the person of the (illegitimate) male fourth generation, to the ultimate Philadelphia moun-
taintops. The hero as a young lawyer wins a dubious legal case
and marries a girl who is named Grace Shippen, but who is described as looking exactly like Grace Kelly. The hero decides in
the end that he *will* run for Mayor, on a sort of neo-conservative
platform which is meant to signify idealistic rebellion. The story
is full of outrageous absurdities, and is hardly an inside job from
the Old Philadelphian point of view. But it is certainly lively,
and is full of very penetrating side comments on Philadelphia.

Old Philadelphians seem to have read *The Philadelphian*, but
are fairly universal in their condemnation. The book's most
lurid scene, in which the heroine of the third generation leaves
her uninteresting bridegroom on their wedding night at the
Bellevue-Stratford Hotel in order to become pregnant by a late-
working contractor, was deemed implausible by Philadelphians.
"Who ever heard of anyone spending their wedding night at the
Bellevue?" was one comment. The author, a personable native
who at the time worked for the N. W. Ayer advertising firm, was
described on the book jacket as being of a family resident in
Philadelphia for seven generations. A Chestnut Hill woman having a literary discussion with a friend naturally asked if he were
related to *the* Powels. "No," said the friend, "he has two l's." The
lady from Chestnut Hill was amazed. "But how can any family
stay in Philadelphia for seven generations and still be so undistinguished?"

Not a novelist, but the unquestioned Queen of present-day

Philadelphia writing, is Catherine Drinker Bowen. As the author of five famous biographies, two of musicians. (Tchaikowsky, the Rubinsteins) and three of lawyers (Adams, Holmes, Coke), she has not only done well popularly but has been showered with official honors. In fact, when a member of her family is asked where she is, the answer is usually "Oh, Kitty's off somewhere getting another prize." In good Philadelphia fashion she has another talent, and is an accomplished violinist. She, like Owen Wister, also began by studying music for a career. One of her principal non-biographical works is a delightful account of her life as ensemble player in quartets called *Friends and Fiddlers,* and she performed fairly regularly in the orchestra that accompanied her brother Henry Drinker's famous Sunday night amateur choral sings. The painter Cecilia Beaux was her aunt, and her brother Henry, besides being one of Philadelphia's leading lawyers, and one of the country's most formidable amateur musicologists, has also been president of the Pennsylvania Academy of Fine Arts.

The writer of biographies that are both authoritative and readable would seem to have a fairly secure position, so one can hope Mrs. Bowen has broken the Philadelphia jinx. The causes of this jinx are, however, not entirely inscrutable. Among the reasons for Philadelphia's forgotten authors are simply Philadelphia's own capacity for forgetfulness, and the lack of real concern of all but a few Philadelphians for literature in general and Philadelphia literature in particular. This is partly colonialism. Philadelphians were slobbering over Tennyson and Thackeray while they condescended to Emerson and Hawthorne. (Sidney Fisher is, incidentally, a surprising exception.) Whitman and Melville of course were considered rude barbarians. In later years colonialism became provincialism, and Philadelphians waited for the accolade from Boston or New York. "Philadelphia is extremely proud of its sons, once they have been approved of by New York," as Struthers Burt said of Richard Harding Davis; but the same thing is true today.

This sort of provincialism accounts for the lack of appreciation Philadelphia authors receive at home. Elsewhere it is Philadelphia artistic conservatism, the attachment of all the earlier Philadelphia figures from Boker through Repplier to the "Genteel Tradition," that has placed them, since the Great Revolution of the 'twenties, in a critical eclipse.

Basically, however, one has to recognize a weakness in the Philadelphia Tradition itself. Even at its best, Philadelphia literature has not fostered originality, pioneering, a fresh viewpoint. Like Philadelphia itself, Philadelphia writing is apt to be well-padded, luxurious, a bit easy and very conventional. These happen to be qualities not now, in the mid-twentieth century, very much in fashion. If fashion should change, Boker, Taylor, Mitchell, Repplier, Hergesheimer and all the rest may find themselves posthumously more esteemed than they are now. Historically at least, the Philadelphia Tradition of Brown, Boker, Wister, Repplier and on to Bowen is certainly of some importance. It is a cinch, however, that as in the case of Eakins, the change of fashion, the rediscovery, will have to come from outside, since Philadelphia itself still does not seem to have the assurance, or the interest, intelligently to defend its own.

CHAPTER

3

i. God Helps Those . . .

PHILADELPHIA may not have done well by writers, but it has
certainly done well by its printers and publishers. Nowhere have
they reaped more honor and fortune, and it is appropriate that
its greatest citizen, Franklin, and some of its most conspicuous
by now Old Philadelphian families, Duanes, Baches, Leas, Lippincotts and others, should have been publishers. Franklin heads the
list, of course, but he was only prince among peers.

Franklin is the only citizen in the entire history of Philadelphia
that everybody acknowledges as a Great Man, a great national
figure. This does not mean that there is not a small group of
ultra Old Philadelphians who don't still dislike him as a parvenu,
and an out-of-town parvenu at that. They also don't approve of
his laxity in matters of religion and sex. To tell the truth, Philadelphians have been trying for a century and a half to camouflage
the fact that Franklin represents just about everything Old Philadelphia doesn't approve of. He was not a Philadelphian by birth,
he was not an hereditary gentleman, he wanted to get ahead and
wanted everyone else to get ahead too, he was intensely curious
and disliked the conventional and the taken-for-granted, he believed in starting new things and reform rather than in merely
letting old things slide gracefully downhill and in not upsetting
the applecart. He was a radical, not a conservative, and in modern
days would undoubtedly have been fighting Old Philadelphians
tooth and nail in politics, in the realm of ideas, and socially, just
as he fought with them then. The whole early history of the

University of Pennsylvania, for instance, was nothing but a struggle between forward-looking Franklin and backward-looking Old Philadelphian trustees. Nonetheless, since he is Great, and can't be ignored, Old Philadelphians have done their best to hide him under a pile of laurels, to make everyone think he was a cautious, worthy, quasi-Quaker busybody, to honor his name and ignore his reality. They have almost succeeded. Unfortunately Franklin himself helped them by writing and printing his *Poor Richard's Almanac*, with its pithy proverbs, and the *Autobiography*. He did the one to make money and the other to help young mechanics like himself move up in the world, but in so doing he failed to present Franklin the intellectual, the wit, the bon viveur and darling of the ladies, the Franklin that risked his life in military enterprises and his life, fortune and "sacred honor" in the Revolution. The Franklin that was the American disciple of Voltaire and the French Encyclopedists is another Franklin from the man on the masthead of that Bible of the bourgeois, the *Saturday Evening Post*. Its readers would probably have loathed the man himself and everything he stood and fought for.

However, Franklin does serve a vital Philadelphia purpose. As has been suggested earlier, he is, appropriately enough, a sort of lightning rod. If you want a great Philadelphian, says Philadelphia, well there he is. Who could ask for a greater? Meanwhile we can go about our business of being just plain Philadelphians. Let tourists and historians and other such annoying people from out of town gawk and stare at the State House (which they persist in calling Independence Hall) and Franklin, and keep their noses out of Delancey Place, or rather nowadays Ithan, Ambler and Chester County. We'll throw them a Biddle or two if they insist on a First Family. Otherwise, hang out the sign "Please do not disturb." This, at least, has been the local philosophy for a century; but now, with the new Democratic reform, the redevelopment of the city, the resurgence of hope and energy, the spirit of Franklin is abroad again, and there's no telling what may happen.

Franklin is the unique Great Philadelphian, but as a printer, publisher and editor he had many worthy competitors and collaborators, predecessors and successors. In fact, few other fields of activity have produced more, or more interesting, or more durable family successions — as witness the Bradfords, the Franklin–Bache–Duane complex, the Carey–Lea–Bairds; or the Lippincotts, of later date, and the Curtis–Bok–Lorimer group in this century. In most of these cases the family founder began as a radical, like Franklin, despised and feared by the Oligarchy, and later descendants have married into and been accepted by that same Oligarchy. There is a long road from William Bradford imprisoned and exiled in the seventeenth century; from Franklin, leader of that Junto which James Logan called a set of "base and lying lackeys"; from Benjamin Franklin Bache, who suggested that the nation jubilantly celebrate the happy day when George Washington relieved the country of his repressive presence as President; from Mathew Carey, kicked out of Ireland for subversion; from all of these down to present-day Morris Duane, partner of one of Philadelphia's most Old Philadelphia law firms, director of the Hand-in-Hand and of the Girard Trust, a road that, incidentally, from the arrival of Bradford to the present, almost exactly covers the whole history of the city, now lumbering towards its 300th anniversary.

The first of these august printing families was that of the Bradfords. William, the first of them, started printing in Philadelphia as early as 1685; but he was involved in the Keithian Schism, along with ironmaster Thomas Rutter, printed incautious things, and was thrown into jail. He left Philadelphia in high dudgeon, removed to New York, and became the first printer there.

His son Andrew came back to Philadelphia and prospered, and Andrew's son William, known as the "Patriot Printer" for his Revolutionary zeal, was even better known. Not more prosperous, however, as the Revolution ruined him. He had the generosity to tell his children that he thought the new Republic was worth it.

In their day the Bradfords were the greatest publishing family in America. The reason that Franklin came to Philadelphia in the first place was to get a job with Andrew Bradford. The job was gone when he got there, and he lived to become Bradford's most successful competitor and bitterest enemy. Franklin considered his rival illiterate. The Bradfords and Franklin were *not* friends.

The last conspicuous Bradford was another William, great grandson of William the First. He became second Attorney General of the United States, and very rich. He would undoubtedly have established the Bradfords in the very topmost Philadelphia echelons if only he had lived longer and had children. As it was, the Bradfords gradually declined through several less interesting generations, and are now nonexistent, at least as being an important Old Philadelphia family.

The Baches and Duanes — Franklin's own descendants — have survived, although they were originally far more controversial than the Bradfords ever thought of being. "We consider Mr. Franklin to have been of a somewhat shady family," is another of those gems quoted by the not very friendly John Gunther in examining the City of Friends for his *Inside U.S.A.*, which is to say that the Great Doctor's own personal family group was put together in a fairly haphazard fashion.

Arriving in Philadelphia from Boston, Benjamin entered upon a sensible engagement of marriage with a Miss Deborah Read. No relation to *the* Reads of New Castle; she was Nobody, the daughter of his first Philadelphia landlady. She was an amiable girl, too amiable perhaps, by whom Franklin apparently had an illegitimate son. They suited each other, and Franklin decided he preferred the economies of wedded life to irregular liaisons. It was certainly no Great Romance. However, after becoming engaged, Franklin went to England, and while he was there Deborah showed deplorably bad sense by marrying one Rogers. Rogers immediately deserted her, disappeared and never was heard from again. All this failed to deter Franklin from his plans, except to make him sorry for Deborah. They set up housekeeping as man and wife, but of course could not be legally married, since she was still Mrs. Rogers until the statute of limitations should take effect. Franklin's household thus consisted of (1) Deborah, his common-law wife, (2) William, his "natural son" as we genealogists always put it, he being presumably also Deborah's natural son, (3) their quasi-legal daughter Sarah. There were other children, natural and unnatural, but they did not survive.

Franklin's son William was a handsome and sociable lad, made powerful friends when in England with his father, and ended up as the last Royal Governor of New Jersey. He also ended up a strong Loyalist, and broke with his father. His final days were spent in England as a pensioner of the British government. Though legally married himself, he, too, had a natural son, William Temple Franklin, who was his grandfather's secretary in France, and died there in Paris at an advanced age.

The true Franklin line in Philadelphia comes down through quasi-legal Sarah, not through William. She married Richard Bache, a merchant, who succeeded his father-in-law as Postmaster General of the nation. The son of Richard and Sarah however was very much in Franklin's line. He was Benjamin Franklin Bache, a journalist, and a firebrand.

This journalist Bache founded and edited what conservatives would nowadays call a "pink sheet." It was named the *Aurora* and supported Jefferson and the French and Jacobinism to the hilt, as opposed to Washington, Adams, the English and Fenno's *United States Gazette.* The two papers slung mud back and forth at each other, and sidewise onto the Founding Fathers. Absolutely no holds were barred. Bache even printed a suggestion that Washington had overdrawn his salary as President and was nothing but a common thief. Thanks to such outspokenness, Bache's life and property were frequently in danger. He was beaten up, and arrested under the Sedition laws; it was in fact all pretty much like the Bradfords a hundred years earlier, but this time politics, not religion, was at issue.

Bache's fiery career was cut short by yellow fever in 1798, when he was still in his twenties. His paper was taken over by his associate, William Duane; he also took over Bache's widow, who had been none other than a Margaret Hartman Markoe before she was married. One wonders how a pair of subversives like Bache and Duane ever came to marry into the Markoes, even then very high-toned. Willam Duane had been born of a good Irish Catholic emigrant family in New York state; when his father died, his mother took her brood back to Ireland. There William took up the printer's trade, and eventually landed in India, where he started a paper called the *Indian World*, in Calcutta, and soon made a fortune, being then twenty-seven years old. However, he could not resist controversy. He attacked the East India Company, and in no time found himself on board a ship bound for England, under arrest, his paper and fortune confiscated without trial. He spent some time in London trying to obtain justice, then finally in disgust emigrated to Philadelphia.

The *Aurora* was obviously Duane's niche. He took over where Bache left off and carried mudslinging to such a length that even some Democrats blanched. He "exposed" all sorts of Federalist misdoings, fought the autocratic Alien and Sedition laws, by which John Adams, his particular enemy, hoped to deport him, and did more than any other journalist to elect Thomas Jefferson. He too, like Bache, was physically attacked, and his house saved from being destroyed by a mob of Federalists only by the timely intervention of a mob of Democrats. Those were stirring times. After Jefferson as President left Philadelphia for Washington, and Philadelphia was no longer the political cockpit, both these families, Baches and Duanes, simmered down politically and moved up socially. It was William's son William John who actually connected up with Franklin by marrying a Deborah Bache, the latter's granddaughter. All during the nineteenth century Baches distinguished themselves mildly in a scientific-military-professional sort of way, Two Baches, a chemist and a geographer, followed their ancestor Franklin as president of the Philosophical Society. Baches married the right people, like the Dallases, and they exist still in the highest social sanctity and in the persons of a gradually diminishing number of Misses Bache.

The Duanes headed for Law, and in the fourth generation

after the fiery William, a Russell Duane did well by becoming one of Philadelphia's most prosperous lawyers, and the first Duane in the firm of Duane, Morris and Heckscher. The Morris was Roland Morris, Democrat, Ambassador to Japan and, along with Effingham of the Girard, leading Morris of the twentieth century. Russell Duane also married well — Roland's sister Mary, usually called May, who created a special reputation as a poetess by reading her works to friends and printing them herself. This is a very Philadelphian sort of way to become a poet, and about the only really respectable way.

Final offshoot of all this has been Morris Duane, son of Russell. With the exception that he went to Harvard ('23) instead of to the University, he has followed, one might almost say created, the Old Philadelphian pattern for the middle-aged generation of the present day. Not enough that he has Benjamin on one side and Christian Sam on the other; he must also go to Episcopal and St. George's, and redeem himself after that escapade in New England (but after all, Horace Binney went to Harvard too) by returning to the Law School, then by joining the family law firm, where he has served with distinction. His taste in boards has been excellent; he's been on the Finance Committee of the Philosophical Society, concerned with the American Lawn Tennis Association, and needless to say, member of the Philadelphia Club. He married a Harrison. When Philadelphians refer to Franklin's "somewhat shady family" they certainly do not mean to include his most conspicuous descendant in Philadelphia today.

ii. *Carey and Lea*

THE BRADFORDS and Franklin–Bache–Duanes began as printers and newspapermen, but quit the business. Two other later families, the Carey–Leas and the Lippincotts, still extant and become equally Old Philadelphian, began as book publishers, and are both still at it.

The Leas are the older, as a family foundation, and for real determined intellectual contribution continued through several generations and in several members, they and the Careys (as a complex) probably can't be beat in Philadelphia's history. It's typical of course that nobody much outside has ever heard of them. A quite literally incalculable influence on American thought and affairs has been exercised by the Careys in particular as principal exponents of an economic theory, or group of theories, which has at various times and in various disguises dominated the policy and practice of both of our political parties, and of our general economic life.

Mathew Carey, who founded the American branch of the family, was an Irish Catholic who, like any good Irishman, got into trouble and had to skip the old sod; in this case, disguised as a woman. He had started as the son of a Dublin baker, become a printer, been kicked out of Ireland once, to France, and then had returned to be kicked out once more. During his exile in France he had worked in Franklin's press at Passy; so that it was natural for him to emigrate to Franklin's own town in America. In Philadelphia he immediately engaged in politics again, but for all his revolutionary instincts he lived to become one of the city's most respected and richest citizens. In addition to being a printer, he edited newspapers and magazines, sold books, wrote pamphlets and became an economist, chief theorist and propagandist for what he liked to call his "protecting system." But his real career was in book publishing, and his major achievement the founding of the publishing company that still exists as Lea and Febiger.

Given Carey's background, it was inevitable that, no matter how much money he made, he would become a Democrat (or Republican, then) and join the battle royal alongside Bache and Duane. He fought a duel with one Oswald, who put a bullet through his leg — he was already lame from childhood — that kept him out of action for months. During the Great Plague of 1793, he was one of the few who stayed to help, rather than running away. He joined Girard in his efforts to found a hospital at Bush Hill and afterwards wrote an account of the dire event that became a local classic. His publishing prospered; he was active in philanthropy, and Catholic though he remained to the end, as well as Democrat, Philadelphia was forced to accept this success- ful Fighting Irishman as it has been forced to accept others since.

Carey might have been speedily forgotten after his death in 1839 if it had not been for his descendants. His sons, notably Henry the economist, and Edward, carried on their father's pub- lishing business with great profit, joined by his son-in-law, Isaac Lea, whose name was added to the firm. (Lea was of a Wilming- ton Quaker family, but little conflict seems to have been caused by his marrying a Catholic — he had already been turned out of meeting anyway for once enlisting in the army.) The firm eventually became Lea and Febiger, now one of America's most respectable publishers of medical books. But a century or more ago, under Henry Carey, it was the largest, richest and most enterprising publisher of fiction in the country. Scott, Dickens, Cooper and Irving were all "Carey authors" and glad of it. Henry's nephew and Mathew's grandson, Henry Carey Baird, ran a very successful publishing firm of his own, as well as writing, speaking and otherwise publishing the Carey economic theories, so that the Carey line of economists and publishers lasted down to his death in 1912.

The Leas were not economic, like the Careys, but scientific, like the Baches. Isaac Lea was a noted malacologist, that is, he collected the shells of fresh-water, and other, mollusks, and wrote some 279 articles and books on the subject. His son Mathew Carey Lea was a chemist, who in his secretive laboratory in Chest- nut Hill did all sorts of ingenious things with photo-chemistry. And Henry Charles Lea, another son, as the historian of the Inquisition became one of America's first scientific, as opposed to romantic, writers of history (Facts and Things). This Scientific Lea line extended to Henry's death in 1909.

Henry Charles Lea was, and is, an important historian; but Henry Charles Carey was not *a*, but *the* important American economist of the nineteenth century. He was the culmination of a Philadelphia line of economists, of sorts, that goes back to

Francis Rawle and his advice on how the inhabitants of Delaware could become rich. The line extends through Benjamin Franklin (of course), and Tench Coxe, "Father" of both manufacturing and cotton, as well as Nicholas Biddle, with his ideas on banking, and Mathew Carey himself. The most significant non-Philadelphian in this line is Alexander Hamilton; but unlike him, most of the Philadelphians, including Biddle, were of the party of Jefferson, and included that Great Beast, the People, in their economic calculations.

The "Carey Theory" seems to go something like this: "Classical Economics," the English School of Adam Smith, David Ricardo, John Stuart Mill, likes to think of the economy as something static, say a pie. There is only so much wealth available at any given moment. It is obviously then a "natural law" that the bigger the slice of pie that goes to profits, the less there will be left for wages. The laborer and the capitalist are thus natural enemies — more wages, less profits; more profits, less wages. This can be interpreted in two ways. Reactionary: Since the economy only functions when the opportunity to make profits is high and hence the incentive great, keep profits high and wages at subsistence level, or at least not so high that they destroy the incentive of high profits. Society then is in equilibrium and "natural laws" like those of Supply and Demand can get to work properly. Radical: Since the workers really create the pie by the sweat of their brows, give them the whole pie. On the one hand, then, laissez-faire free-trade capitalism; on the other hand, socialism.

Henry Carey, as both an Irishman and an American, spent his life fighting Classical Economics. His theory was dynamic, not static. Economics is a process, not a state of being, a spiral, not a pie. In any healthy nation, where techniques are improving and inventions are encouraged, labor and capital are partners, boosting each other up the spiral, not enemies quarreling over pie. The more active the economy, the more it produces. The more it produces, the more labor it hires. The more labor it hires, the higher wages go. The higher wages go, the more the workingman consumes. The higher the consumption, the more production, the more employment, the higher the wages, the more consumption, etc., etc., etc.

Carey's theory too can be interpreted differently. Conservative (McKinley): Stimulate and protect production and industry in every possible way (tariffs), and the rest will take care of itself. Liberal (F.D.R.): Keep up the buying power of the consumer, by artificial means if necessary — relief, government spending, etc. This will in turn stimulate consumption, and thus production. Around and around we go again. J.F.K's tax plan would seem to combine both right and left wings of this "spiral" theory.

It can easily be seen from this rudimentary outline how Marx, following a principle of economic scarcity and of "natural law," gave the Soviet Union its economic rationale; and how the United States, constantly expanding, bases its economics however indirectly on Carey. Republican policy after the Civil War, including the McKinley tariff, was consciously and directly based on Carey's theories, and he was honored as their creator. Henry Ford, not a thinker but a doer, by mass production, lowering the price of cars and raising wages, put Carey's spiral into practical operation. Carey's connection with Franklin Roosevelt can also be traced through his principal disciples, two professors at the University of Pennsylvania, William Elder and then, around the 'twenties, Simon Patten. Patten's most famous pupils there were Rexford G. Tugwell, Leon Henderson and Frances Perkins — generally acknowledged as the three chief architects of the New Deal. Thus the "dynamic spiral" which seems to be the core of the Carey theory, though he never expressed it that way himself, accounts for such seemingly contradictory results as the Tariff, the Tin Lizzie and the WPA.

As for Carey himself, he was a thoroughly crotchety and indigenous example of the Old Philadelphia gentleman-amateur intellectual. A big handsome Irish-looking man, he was forthright, thoroughly anti-British in his sympathies, but thoroughly pro-Philadelphian in his taste for Madeiras and dinners. He had no formal education, but his father's conversation and his own reading made him one of the most widely, if sometimes erratically, knowledgeable men of his time. He is supposed to have been put to work in the Baltimore branch of his father's bookstore at the advanced age of twelve; certainly he was active in the business as a teen-ager, and very successfully so. Like Franklin, however, he regarded making money merely as a means to an end, and retired as soon as he thought he had enough. For the rest of his life he lived well and wrote about economics.

Carey was social and talkative, and livened his conversation with curses. Every winter Sunday afternoon, from four to six, he entertained the intellectuals of the city at his big dark mansion at 1102 Walnut. The "Carey Vespers," as they were called, got to be one of Philadelphia's institutions after the Civil War, as the Wistar Parties had been before it. The Vespers in fact are right in the tradition of a long series of such affairs in Philadelphia: Franklin's Junto, the bluestocking Elizabeth Graeme's pre-Revolutionary Saturday Evenings, Dennie's Tuesday Club, the Catholic publicist Robert Walsh's Soirées of that same *Port Folio* period, where Biddles mingled with Bishop White and the local Catholic hierarchy, then the Wistar Party, its post–Civil War successor the Saturday Club, and finally the Franklin Inn and the revived Wistar Parties of the present day.

For all his economic radicalism, for so his attack on British economic theory was considered, Carey himself became a typical Old Philadelphia "things-were-better-in-the-old-days" codger. Dr. Gross the famous surgeon played cards with him. After a regular Tuesday evening game of euchre on New Year's Day 1878, as he recounts in his autobiography, Gross asked Carey who he thought had been, in his lifetime, Philadelphia's "great women." Carey was in a good humor, having come out even in twelve games; he got surly if he lost. He expanded: "I can recall only three of any celebrity in their day . . . Mrs. Meredith, Mrs. Rush" (Phoebe) "and Mrs. Gilpin. There are no such women now. The present race is frivolous and insipid. The men are no

better. There is no literary talent among them; they are tradesmen and shopkeepers" (there speaks America's greatest economist). "The Wistar party comprised men of distinction. The
Saturday Club which succeeded that party is made up of all sorts
of men. The Binneys, the Ingersolls, the Duponceaus, the Whartons, the Merediths . . . have disappeared and there are none
to fill their places. There is no one to take my place at my
Sunday evening reunions. We have no historians" (nephew
Henry had not yet followed his uncle's example and retired from
publishing), "no poets" (Boker, a friend of Carey's, was writing
his sonnets in secret), "no novelists" (Mitchell was still a doctor),
"— no writers, in short, of any great merit in any branch of
literature. Philadelphia has gone to the devil!"

Ah, shades of Sidney! It is no wonder that a character like
that, so rich in Philadelphia prejudices, should have been looked
at askance in his own time, as in ours. Those who are not
offended by his originality have been offended by his quixoticism.
Though a firm advocate of really scientific, as opposed to merely
philosophic system in economics, he himself took untenable positions, indulged in strong prejudices and confused writing. Liberal economic historians like Joseph Dorfman have tended to
scorn him for being a protectionist and connected with Republican politics, conservative writers for being against laissez-faire
and England. The gentlemen of the Farmer's Club, as they sat
about at Longwood in the moonlight watching the fountains displace 12,000 gallons of water a minute while they discussed the
Dust Bowl, were as much anti-Carey as a historian like Arthur
Schlesinger, Jr., in retrospect a partisan of Jackson and the "people" against Biddle and the bank. The Farmers talked about
how wrong it was for the AAA to interfere with "natural law,"
and Schlesinger speaks of the Bank as an oligarchic incubus on
free democratic development, but they both really talk Adam
Smith or at least laissez-faire.

Nevertheless, Carey was terribly respected, during his lifetime,
as the "Father of Protectionism." As early as 1859 he made a

sort of triumphal tour through Pennsylvania, along with his disciple Elder. In Scranton, Wilkes-Barre and Mauch Chunk, processions of miners, factory workers, fire companies and brass bands followed his carriage through the streets, and he dined with Simon Cameron, boss absolute of Pennsylvania, and other notables. And though Marx and Engels dismissed his theories as being based on peculiar and transitory American conditions and inapplicable to Europe and the real world, Marx himself wrote of Carey as "the only American economist of importance." But economics is not a popular science, and a euchre-playing, Madeira-drinking economist is as far from the popular pattern of American heroism as a verse-writing banker, or a poet who was president of two clubs. The position of Carey in the Pantheon, like those of Boker and Biddle, remains equivocal, to be championed as a cause rather than asserted as a fact.

Obviously Henry Carey thought of himself as a "literary" man, and the members of these famous publishing families dealt with the printed word throughout their lives, writing, publishing, editing. Yet not a single one of them — Bradfords, Franklin, Baches, Duanes, Careys, Leas — ever became what we would call an "author"; that is, a professional writer of belles-lettres, of novels or poetry or even general essays, of literary criticism, of a picturesque, as opposed to a scientific, history. (Though Henry Lea comes closest.) None of them, in other words, had anything to do with the "fancy." Facts and things, facts and things: economics, electricity, law, politics, shells, chemistry. They, more than any other Philadelphians, spent their time from childhood surrounded by other people's imaginations, yet their own imaginations and avocations turned to the verifiable and the concrete. If Philadelphia was, during the nineteenth century in particular, the American center of medicine, natural science and economics, as Boston was of literature and philosophy, this was certainly no accident, but an innate characteristic of the place and the people, reflected and determined by the attitudes of its ruling Oligarchy, and surely by their Quaker ancestry. For all the seducement of intellectual Old Philadelphians into literature (Biddle, Boker, Wister), the pull towards science has been far greater, has helped make science and medicine far more important in Philadelphia's intellectual history than its generally inhibited tradition of letters has been.

iii. *1792 and All That*

THE OTHER GREAT book-publishing family in Philadelphia has been that of the Lippincotts. Joshua, the first of them to make his mark in Philadelphia, came over from New Jersey in mid-nineteenth century, and practically in his teens, like Henry Carey, established himself in the book business. He became one of the most successful men in it; he began strongly with Bibles, but published fiction and technical books too, and the firm remains one of the few important well-established old publishing firms not located in New York; also one of the few in America still actually owned and run by the founding family. From the 1880's to the First War Lippincott also put out a fine literary magazine that upheld the tradition of the *Port Folio,* or at least rivaled in taste and interest such magazines as *Scribner's, Harper's* and the *Atlantic.* A son of Joshua married a daughter of Joseph Wharton, and the fourth generation, in the person of a Joseph Wharton Lippincott, Jr., now sits in the president's chair.

J. W., Senior, grandson of the founder, has rather bruised the Philadelphia tradition of being himself a successful author of fiction. His books are basically studies of natural history for young people, and his interests more scientific than fictional; but *Old Bill: The Whooping Crane* and others are stories just the same, not just "facts and things." Mr. Lippincott has done more to save the whooping crane than almost anyone else, and knows all the surviving specimens personally. His books have gone into many editions and have been translated into many languages; an exception being the language of the crows. The crows (the birds, not the Indians) speak a fairly complicated language of some hundred cricks and caws, and Mr. Lippincott speaks it too. He can carry on a considerable conversation with any crow you care to name, and make him do things he shouldn't, such as coming around to be shot by Mr. Lippincott while marauding in the Lippincott fields in Bethayres. For Mr. Lippincott is not only a famous naturalist but a famous sportsman, a hunter of birds, game and foxes, long the M.F.H. of the Huntington Valley hunt, and deep-sea fishing companion of the late Ernest Hemingway. He is also a trustee of the University, though Joseph Jr. went to Princeton; a lapse only too common in Philadelphia families, like that from Quakerism to Episcopalianism.

Lippincott however was an old Quaker name around Philadelphia long before Joshua crossed the river to fame and fortune. It still remains one of the most extensively represented in the *Social Register,* where there are over a score of listings. Like the Wisters and Wistars, there are really two families of Lippincotts, or more, descended from an original New Jersey Richard, who antedated Penn; but since then they have split into various increasingly distant branches. However, they all more or less warily eye one another as "cousins." The kinship is considered close enough so that, according to one of them, "if we see a Lippincott drunk on the street, we help him home."

As Philadelphia publishing families go, Lippincott is fairly recent, since Joshua did not really set up on his own till 1836. (There's a certain business about having started in 1792; however . . .) * Philadelphia's latest and most gaudily successful publishing family is at least two generations younger. The Curtis–Boks, like the Wanamakers, are really hardly out of the woods yet socially speaking, from an Old Philadelphia point of view, but the Curtis Publishing Company has been so overwhelmingly prosperous in the last seventy years,† and the original

---

* A plaque on the front of the building states that the company was "founded in Philadelphia and developed from an unbroken publishing history beginning in 1792." This does not mean that J. B. Lippincott was actually founded in 1792, but merely that it brought up, in mid-nineteenth-century, another old bookselling-publishing company that really did go back to 1792. But in Philadelphia this is good enough.

† Up to now, at least

Curtis and Bok so overwhelmingly civic-minded that the aroma of Old Philadelphianism has gathered fast about the whole business and the whole family.

iv. Sacred Few

PHILADELPHIA has been a center for magazines, often *the* center in America, from the mid-eighteenth century on. It has been F.&O. & F.B.F., but each separately. "First" was Andrew Bradford's *American Magazine* of February 1741; "F.B.F." was a long-titled, short-lived *General Magazine and Historical Chronicle for All the British Plantations in America* published by Bradford's deadly rival Franklin, which came out three days later. "Oldest" really and truly is the *Saturday Evening Post* but it was *not*, as the masthead claims, "founded by Benjamin Franklin," and not in 1728. This is the classic example, for all time, of semi-fictitious Philadelphia pre-dating; worse even than the University's 1740. The real date of the *S.E.P.*'s founding is 1821, and it was started not by Franklin but by a couple of very obscure people indeed; even so it is the oldest magazine in general circulation in America, though the *North American Review*, which hardly counts, as it has become a sort of subsidized vehicle for neo-conservative propaganda, can claim 1815. Then there are various technical and religious journals, many of those also published in Philadelphia. However, even though not F.B.F., the *Saturday Evening Post* really is Oldest.

Back of the *Post* there was a whole history of Philadelphia magazines, each "best in America" of its time and of its kind. The two little first sprouts of 1741 died quickly, but William Bradford, "patriot printer," started another *American Magazine* in 1757 (up to now, there always seems to have been some *American Magazine* afloat somewhere since the first one of 1741). This one, of 1757, which managed to run for a year, good going then, was edited by Provost Smith of the University, and printed poetry by Francis Hopkinson, Thomas Godfrey, Jr., Nathaniel Evans and Smith himself. They formed themselves into a sort of clublike group, and represented Philadelphia's first attack on beautiful letters. A *Pennsylvania Magazine* of 1775 was edited by the great Thomas Paine, with the liberal help of brandy bottles, and had poetry in it too. It also had scientific articles by Rittenhouse, Rush and others, and reached an unprecedented circulation of 1,500. The Revolution killed it.

The two best and first really established American magazines after the Revolution, in the 'eighties and 'nineties, were the *Columbian* and *American Museum,* the latter edited by Mathew Carey, the former for a while by Francis Hopkinson (editor, librarian, judge) and by Alexander Dallas. The name of the *Columbian* was finally changed to the *Universal Asylum.* Asylum did not suggest then what is suggests now. The Post Office Department did for both of these by making postal rates too high; thus began its long warfare with literacy which continues down to the present day.

Philadelphia's real preeminence in the world of the magazine began — and ended — with Dennie's *Port Folio,* which saw the light in 1801. For the first quarter of the century it was what the *Atlantic* became later, the principal literary journal of the time and the country. Dennie was certainly the best magazine editor America had seen up to then. His chief talent to the purpose was his ability to make and keep friends, mostly literary young gentlemen who would take the trouble to contribute, for there were no professional writers then with the lonely sad exception of struggling Charles Brown. Dennie collected in his Tuesday Club not only the most literary, but the most Old Philadelphian group of young gentlemen ever gathered, like a choir of angels, about any magazine. They all actually wrote too — Hopkinson (this was Joseph) on Shakespeare, Biddle on art, Cadwalader on Horace, Ingersoll, Wharton, Rush, Coxe, Binney — one is flabbergasted. And never has editorship by club been more successful. Dennie's delightfully foppish and convivial personality, and the fact that most of the contributors were cousins, helped keep up the morale and cohesiveness of the little group.

Thomas Moore, in his otherwise scathing poetic criticism of America, wrote:

> . . . oh you sacred few
> Whom late by Delaware's green banks I knew;
> Whom, known and loved through many a social eve,
> 'Twas bliss to live with and 'twas pain to leave.

It was the only company in America in which he felt at home. Sidney, too, one felt might have tolerated it, but he was born too late, and Agnes Repplier, though a woman and born much too late, belongs in spirit to the group that gathered about caustic "Oliver Oldschool," and she transferred much of the spirit of the *Port Folio* into the pages of the more serious *Atlantic*.

Dennie died in 1812, but the *Port Folio* continued until 1825. Just as it closed up in 1826, a man called Atkinson launched a monthly venture called the *Casket*. This was the beginning of a new phase in Philadelphia's periodical life — that of the Family and Female Journal. He had already started, five years before, a weedy weekly called the *Saturday Evening Post*. It would have been immoral to print and distribute a newspaper on the Sabbath of course, hence the "Saturday Evening." It corresponded very closely to the present-day Sunday magazine supplement, on the order of *This Week* or the *American Weekly* and was similarly innocuous. No politics; verse by local females. Stories clipped out of other and better magazines, a few essays and tales by ye editor. A serial, "Guilt Triumphant over Innocence; or the Story of Emma Somerton," ran through the *S.E.P.* issues of 1822 in a chain of tears. The *Casket* was actually just a monthly digest of material from the *Saturday Evening Post* and hence doubly digested.

In 1839 a young Philadelphian, George Graham, then only twenty-six, took over both these feeble shoots from Atkinson, and renaming the *Casket* after himself, made things hum. With the help of his editor, Charles J. Peterson, he transformed his new magazine into the liveliest journal in the country. The two men also ran the *Post* at first, but then turned it over to a cousin of

Charles, one Henry Peterson, to keep it in the family. The *Post* under this Peterson was a success, but nothing to compare with the giddy popularity of *Graham's* during the 'forties when it became America's first nationally distributed magazine of importance.

Graham's combined fashion plates and fiction, poetry (lots of poetry; our ancestors did like poetry, especially if it was bad) and pictures. Poe, who was a contributing editor for a while, though he loathed the magazine and felt degraded by working for it, published his *Murders in the Rue Morgue,* America's first detective story, in *Graham's* and his poem "To Helen." William Cullen Bryant, Henry Wadsworth Longfellow and James Fenimore Cooper joined Poe in its pages, along with many others less known to fame. But literature was not really what Graham had in mind; it was circulation. *Graham's* 40,000 circulation — a world record for its time — was based on best-selling names as contributors, and energetic advertising of the magazine itself. The editors collected the names by paying unheard-of prices. For the first time also in American history, writers could make a real living by writing for magazines, especially when *Graham's* competitors were forced to follow suit.

For a decade, Graham, and his authors too, rode high. He bought a fine house on Arch Street, gave elaborate dinners, and drove around in a carriage. But he could not resist that besetting vice of expansive magazine publishers — newspapers. Fancying himself a molder and elevator of public opinion, he sank all his money into the *North American* and the *Evening Bulletin* and by 1848 he was bankrupt. The magazine had to be sold, and though Graham later managed to get it back, neither he nor his magazine ever recovered. The competition in Philadelphia of *Godey's* and in New York of *Harper's* was too much for *Graham's.* It sank for good in 1858, and Graham himself was supported by jobs and charity till he died, forgotten, in 1894.

Graham's was the ancestor of Lorimer's *Post,* and *Godey's Lady's Book* the ancestor of Bok's *Ladies' Home Journal.* The guiding genius of *Godey's* was not so much that deliciously fruity and gallant New Yorker, Louis Godey, who so loved his "fair readers" one and all, but a New Hampshire girl, Sarah Hale. Mrs. Hale, a self-supporting literary widow, was made of sterner stuff. She was a devout believer in woman's education and general improvement, and wrote "Mary had a Little Lamb," immortal poem if there ever was one. She also put the holiday of Thanksgiving upon a sound national basis. She made her magazine, from the time she took over in 1837 till her retirement in 1877 at the age of eighty-nine a bastion of feminine delicacy and self-righteousness. After her rule, though the magazine actually continued into the 'nineties, overlapping the *Ladies' Home Journal*, things were never the same.

Godey and Graham and even redoubtable Sarah Hale did not found Philadelphia families. They did, however, found a pattern of Philadelphia magazine publishing which in the end founded families. Graham also helped start off on its career the Peterson family that dominated a large section of Philadelphia publishing during the rest of the nineteenth century. There were no less than six Petersons, all active in editing, publishing and even writing in Philadelphia from 1840 on. Charles, who was Graham's partner, went off on his own to edit a very successful ladies' magazine, rival of *Godey's*, called *Peterson's*. The *Saturday Evening Post* saw its first years of real prosperity under cousin Henry Peterson. Theophilus and two brothers ran a publishing house. Finally there was Robert, who distinguished himself by marrying a Bouvier, like another later non-Philadelphian called Kennedy. (The Kennedys were from Boston and in Politics.) The Bouviers were Provençal Quakers, if one can conceive of such a thing ("Dance, and Provençal song, and sunburnt mirth"), who had settled in Philadelphia. Then Peterson's daughter Emma married George W. Childs, her father's partner and destined to become Philadelphia's greatest newspaper publisher. Thus the Petersons form a tenuous link between the Age of Graham and the Age of Childs.

Peterson, in becoming the partner and father-in-law of George William Childs, certainly picked the right man. Childs was a bastard; that is to say, he too, like some later Franklins, was "a natural son," in his case of an unidentified but prominent Baltimorean. He did his best to shroud his early life in shadow, with the result that nobody knows much about it; but his Philadelphia career, which began at fifteen with his sweeping off the sidewalk in front of a bookstore while Graham flashed by in his carriage, is flooded with light, a light which he continually did his best to increase. Before he was thirty, he was a full-fledged partner with Peterson. They made a killing off Elisha Kane's *Arctic Exploration* in 1856, largely due to Childs's genius for exploiting all that was picturesque about the author and the subject. Kane himself made seventy thousand dollars out of the book; think what Childs and Peterson must have made. Before the firm dissolved in 1860, both partners had made their fortunes, but Childs's career had not even begun.

Early in his hardworking youth Childs had become a friend of Anthony Drexel, son of Francis the painter and chief Philadelphia inheritor of his father's bank. It was one of those Victorian Damon-and-Pythias, David-and-Jonathan affairs, like that of Boker and Bayard Taylor, which nowadays might cause a certain twitching of the Freudian eyebrow, but were then most highly esteemed. There is a quaint daguerreotype of the two serious boys, side by side on the photographer's bench and hand in hand, with solemn faces, long hair and constrictive waistcoats, that is both funny and touching. They grew, hand in hand in business as well, to be two of the greatest of Philadelphia bigwigs as partners in their newspaper, the *Public Ledger*. The *Ledger* had existed before Childs took it over in 1864, but under him it soon became *the* Philadelphia paper. It came to occupy the position in Philadelphia that the *Times* does in New York, or that the *Transcript* did in Boston. It was the only possible Philadelphia paper for the respectable household. It was chaste and solid. Its print was dignified. It printed pages of cricket scores. The breath of scandal seldom, if ever, brought a blush to its pages. It made Childs one of Philadelphia's richest men.

He built a mansion that was most extravagantly admired at

the time, out in the then brand-new suburb of Bryn Mawr where it would stimulate interest in friend George Roberts's effort to settle the elite along the tracks of The Railroad. It was called Wootton and was (and is, now in religious hands) a red-brick jumble of gables, turrets, frets, Gothic and late Victorian fancy. It was very famous. A large staff, as many as fifty of them, kept it up, inside and out. The grounds were as famous as the house itself; the more special guests were led to plant trees there, as on that occasion when Childs entertained the Farmer's Club and most of the railroad presidents of the eastern seaboard. Those were the days, and Childs lived up to them. His great sorrow however was his childlessness, and to make up for it his pal Drexel named his own son George William Childs Drexel. Childs made the boy his heir, so that a Drexel lived in Wootton after his death. It is a later but also magnificent George William Childs Drexel mansion on Rittenhouse Square that now houses the Curtis Institute of Music; another odd link between two of Philadelphia's grandest gentlemen of the press.

v. *1728 and All* THAT

WITH CHILDS'S DEATH in 1894 (the same year that his model, poor forgotten Graham, also died), the Peterson–Childs lineage and empire came to an end; but already the succession was secure in Cyrus Hermann Kotzschmar Curtis. Curtis had traveled down from Portland, Maine, via Boston, and had, as of 1883, started his *Ladies' Home Journal.* Once he took a special trip down to Philadelphia just to look as Childs's splendid new mansarded *Ledger* building on Chestnut Street. The vision stayed with him like that of the Grail. He chose Philadelphia because he liked it better than New York, because he admired Childs so much and because printing costs were so much cheaper. Perhaps the traditions of Godey and Peterson and Graham had something to do with it too.

Curtis derived his awesomely Teutonic name not, as one might suspect, from a Pennsylvania Dutch ancestor: he was pure Yank.

He got it from his parents' love for music. The senior Curtises were modestly prosperous in Portland, and they had patronized a worthy emigrant German organist. They were such admirers, in fact, that they named their son after him; the name and the influence of Kotzschmar have borne fateful fruit in Philadelphia, as the Curtis Institute today testifies.

Before Cyrus could get around to building a mansion in Wyncote about an organ, on which he played and improvised the "simple airs that he loved," he made his pile during years of incredibly profitable journalism. He built his *Ladies' Home Journal* into what has been probably the most continuously successful woman's magazine the world has ever known, and then transformed the *Saturday Evening Post* from a relic to America's favorite popular reading. Curtis, like Graham, knew and cared rather little about either women or literature. He was a financial and advertising genius; and he knew how to pick editors. He picked two, Edward Bok for the *Journal* and eventually George Horace Lorimer for the *Post,* financed them, turned them loose, and himself concentrated on building circulation.

Bok, a bachelor, knew nothing much about women either; yet he knew just how to edit for them. From an already amazing circulation of 700,000 in 1889, the *Journal* reached a stupendous, record-breaking, earth-shaking million in 1903. Graham and Godey would have gasped. Like Graham, Bok paid the best writers the highest prices. Mark Twain, Bret Harte, Conan Doyle — anybody who was a "name" saw it printed in the *Journal.* Like Godey, Bok kept his "fair readers" amused, instructed and protected. No liquor or tobacco ads in the *Journal!* Like John Wanamaker in his store, Curtis in his magazine frowned on playing cards. Authors weren't even allowed to mention liquor in their tales, which caused contributors like Kipling alternately to splutter and snicker. Like Sarah Hale before him, Bok was a reformer, and though most of his reforms, like John Wanamaker's, came to very little (Paris fashions and billboards are still with us, alas) — it was such good publicity! There are those who think Bok did more to elevate taste in America than any other single man in the twentieth century. There are those who don't. Whatever his influence, there was no doubt about his success. Curtis made millions; Bok, soon a partner of the Curtis Publishing Company, also made millions.

As a bachelor editor of a woman's magazine, he was long the butt of coarse humor. One rival magazine even ran a whole series of false announcements engaging him to various inappropriate ladies. He stopped that sort of thing by following in George W. Childs's footsteps: he married his partner's daughter. So, oddly enough, this particular "figure in the carpet" repeated itself; the Bok and Curtis strains united as did the Childs and Peterson (Mrs. Hale did *not* marry Mr. Godey). The line continued however; and the late Curtis Bok in particular has been in a different way as distinguished as his parents — as lawyer, judge, witty essayist, novelist and exposer of the follies of capital punishment.

As for the *Saturday Evening Post,* that was deliberately designed by Curtis to be a masculine counterpart to the excessively feminine *Journal.* Not that men didn't, and don't, read the *Journal.* Everybody was amazed at the number of copies that went into the camps and trenches during the First and Second World Wars; just as *Godey's* was read by Civil War soldiers, also much to everyone's surprise. Mr. Godey was so pleased, and remarked that the Northerners, at least, must compose a very "refined and well-conducted army."

The *Post,* by the time Curtis bought it for a song (a thousand dollars) in 1897, had long passed its Henry Peterson prime. It was a miserable, sickly, more or less local Philadelphia weekly proud of nothing but being "the oldest literary and family paper in the United States. Founded A.D. 1821." Curtis followed the same policy with it that he did with the *Journal.* He found, after various mistakes, and several million dollars of lost investment, a genius for an editor, turned the policy of the magazine entirely over to him, and concentrated on building up circulation by advertising. By 1908 the *Post* too had its first million subscribers, and more important, its proper quota of full-page advertisements. Under the editorship of George Horace Lorimer, it was on its way.

The secret of the success of both magazines lay in two things: a firmly, richly and relentlessly all-Amurrican middle-class point of view, male and/or female, and a sort of application of the Carey–Ford "spiral of prosperity" to the world of letters. That is, cheap price (the *Post* began at a nickel), vast distribution, the highest rewards to the workers (in this case, the writers), and a resulting vast profit for the producer. There was one special element in the Curtis formula that was new however, the use of advertising as a major source of revenue. It was Curtis who first let the genie out of its bottle. In its happier, earlier days the *Post* was a real organ of its subscribers, progressive, reformist, thoroughly back of T.R. in his attack on entrenched privilege. It was only after Wilson, and the return to "normalcy" that the *Post* began to seem reactionary, and to represent more and more not its subscribers, or its writers, but its advertisers. After F.D.R., of course, the split was permanent, and led, upon the death of Lorimer, to a whole shift of policy. Neither the *Post* nor the *Journal* now speak for the middle class with their former complete assurance.

The question about all this is just how Philadelphian are and were the Curtis publications? There can be no doubt that the pattern of Curtis journalism was evolved in Philadelphia, and by Philadelphians originally — Graham, the Petersons. The great figures, however, have all been from "out of town." Childs, although he always considered himself a Philadelphian, was born in Baltimore. Mrs. Hale and Curtis were New Englanders, Bok from Holland via Brooklyn, Lorimer from the Midwest, as much as from any one place. Bruce and Beatrice Gould, long-time editors of the *Journal*, were not only from Iowa, but lived in New Jersey, and had no real social or personal or institutional ties with Philadelphia.

The Boks and the Lorimers, however, are now both pretty safely wedged into satisfactorily Old Philadelphian niches. The board of directors of the Curtis Publishing Company is certainly thoroughly Philadelphian, if not overwhelmingly Old Philadelphian.*

The rich, plushy, safe-and-sound, upholstered, anti-intellectual-but-more-intellectual-than-you'd-think quality that still breathes through the increasingly glossy pages of the magazines, the arch-conservative politics, the suspicion of anything offbeat or bizarre or egghead or advanced in thought or action or art — this may be Philadelphian enough; but still, more essentially middle-class than upper-class Philadelphian. Watson and his "solid comfort," a certain Quaker love of the "plain but rich," might feel at home on Independence Square, but never the esprit de Nicholas Biddle, with one hand on a Greek bust and the other on the country's finances, or of Francis Hopkinson, trustee of the University at his harpsichord, or Sidney Fisher riding through the woods with Fanny Kemble. The Curtis ban on liquor was just as abhorrent to the Madeira-drinking directors of the Hand-in-Hand as it was to Kipling. Philadelphia, the "most American of cities" as some are fond of calling it, Philadelphia the home of respectability and the city of respectable homes, Philadelphia keystone of the Grand Old Party, of Safe and Sound perhaps; but never Philadelphia as a city of champagne-drinking, terrapin-eating, French-novel-reading non-practicing doctors.

One small example indicates the world of difference between the tone of the *Post* and the attitudes of Old Philadelphia. During the earlier 1900's the *Post* waged a small war against what it liked to call the "snob private schools" as opposed to the public schools. These were of course the church schools like St. Paul's and St. George's, the very ones to which Old Philadelphians preferably sent their sons. The *Post* had editorials and articles on the subject. One article in particular, in an early "College Man's Number" excoriated an alien atmosphere where the teachers were called "masters" and the principal the "Head," where, O shame! honest Amurrican boys were restrained from playing "America's national game" baseball and forced to play — cricket. The article

* See Appendix.

may have been published, but could hardly have been written, in the cricket-mad Philadelphia of 1905. The attitudes of the magazine that published it may have been Philadelphian, but they certainly weren't Old Philadelphian.

As for that Spirit of Benjamin Franklin that is supposed, as Founder, to hover over the destinies of the *Post;* the magazine still carries the information that it was founded in 1728, and has ever since the idea first struck Curtis in 1898 (about the time the idea first struck the Trustees of the University that they were founded in 1740). The claim was based on a tradition which Curtis bought with the paper, and which was certainly one of the reasons he bought it; but it's a pretty tenuous one. The facts go like this. Keimer, Franklin's original Philadelphia boss, founded the *Pennsylvania Gazette* in 1728, and turned it over next year to his employee. Franklin later on took in a partner called David Hall, and when Franklin got out of the *Gazette* entirely in the 1760's, David Hall became sole owner. His descendants published it till 1815, when it quietly expired. However a David Hall III, grandson of the first Hall, kept on in business as a printer, taking in a partner called Charles Alexander. Hall died in 1821. When Atkinson started his *Saturday Evening Post*, Charles Alexander was *his* partner. They used the Hall–Alexander shop to print their paper in, the same shop where the *Gazette* had drawn its last breath. That's the connection, and the only connection between the *Post* and 1728 and Franklin. Nor does the real spirit of B.F. himself, intellectual, Deist, radical, man of affairs in every sense of the word, have much to do with *Post*'s early-twentieth-century Babbittism. However, it does breathe a kind of Independence Hall, Poor Richard aroma, synthetically Philadelphian; Philadelphian after the fashion of the décor of the new Stouffer restaurant in Penn Center, a New York decorator's idea of Philadelphia.

The two big chunks of Curtis office building in neo-colonial-warehouse style dominate the West side of Independence Square. In the main hall a mosaic mural by Philadelphian Maxfield Parrish reflects its imaginary landscape in a real pool. Peculiar, very slow electric trucks creep about the Philadelphia streets delivering tons of Curtis publications, obstructing traffic but costing virtually nothing in fuel or upkeep. Curtis's daughter, now Mrs. Zimbalist, reigns over the Curtis Institute and is a Philadelphia Queen of Music. The names of Bok and Lorimer, added to the rolls of Old Philadelphia, are the fine flower of two centuries of Philadelphia magazine publishing. As compared with the newspaper Duanes or the book-publishing Leas and Lippincotts, they are latecomers; but the history of the magazines is certainly a Philadelphia story, and has even become at last a Philadelphia family story.

vi. Nearly Everybody

THE HISTORY of newspapers in Philadelphia is full and rich and complicated and not to be gone into. It is also one of those areas which is decidedly more Greater Philadelphian than Old Philadelphian. Only one paper, the *Ledger,* ever seemed to have become a really Old Philadelphian institution. One cannot quite think of the readers of the *Ledger* swaying in the wind "like a field of ripe corn," as T. S. Eliot described the readers of the Boston *Transcript.* They didn't sway; they *sat.* Nor was the *Ledger* ever quite so queerly local, but the two papers did have quite a lot in common. The *Ledger* was sedate, social, and full of letters in the spring about the first robin. There is no paper like it at present.

After he'd made his pile in magazines, Curtis, like Graham before him, had a hankering for newspapers. He bought Childs's old *Ledger,* which had been sold by the Drexel estate to Ochs of the New York *Times,* and attempted to revive it. His intentions were impeccable. He thought Philadelphia should have a really good newspaper and he poured millions and millions into the *Ledger* in his attempt. Unfortunately he didn't seem to know quite how to go about it. The *Ledger,* like the *Transcript,* succumbed finally to modernism and the depression.

There are now three newspapers in Philadelphia for a city of four million, and one active Old Philadelphian newspaper family; but even Philadelphians, who Nearly All read the *Inquirer* in the morning and the *Bulletin* in the evening are not too happy about the situation. The third paper, a tabloid, the *Daily News,* hardly competes as yet with the Big Two. These Big Two are quite separate, but they are so alike that only careful scrutiny reveals any differences. They are another example of that often beneficial Philadelphia law, "the survival of the quietest," whose backside is a generally malevolent tradition which might be called "the persistence of the drabbest." In the past Philadelphia papers have been full of vim, opinion and color. With the demise of the Democratic *Record* under Stern, all vim, opinion and color seems to have departed too. The *Inquirer* and the *Bulletin* are edited so as to offend nobody. As a result, a pervading dullness infects every page of both of them. The *Bulletin,* as a caustic letter-writer once put it, is the only paper in the United States whose editorials are written on milk-toast. They come out strong against crime.

There are advantages of course. Both papers are infinitely more serious and respectable than the shocking rags of Boston, or the lascivious tabloids of New York or the snarling Hearst papers. They are decent, and that's something. They have respectable (dull) type faces and respectable (dull) news coverage; and they certainly canvass the local scene. Like small-town papers, they aim to get *everybody* in the metropolitan area mentioned in print at least once a year. List after list of all the graduates of all the high schools appear. No local football team is so obscure that its career is not lovingly chronicled and its baby stars described in feature articles. Janitors have their obituaries, every bride has her day, and even the suits for divorce are discreetly listed. Each substantial will filed in Philadelphia is discussed; if it's sizable, it's estimated as "$200,000 for probate purposes," which means really about $2,000,000. It's pretty hard not to get your name in the paper if you live in Philadelphia.

And there's always Society. Society of course "ain't what it used to be." The daily *Inquirer* has a few paragraphs and the

Bulletin confines itself to something called "Evening Chat," a half-page of weddings, births and "back from the West Indies." The days when the *North American* published a genealogical account of an Old Philadelphia family every single week, for years and years, have passed. On Sundays, however, Society still gets pages and pages in both papers. This is not, as in New York, a sort of queer, spurious newspaper columnist society, or just brides and charitable committees, but real Old Philadelphia, huntin', dancin', marryin', with of course a good many spectacular new recruits; but before the Assembly or on the opening night of the Opera or on any good ritual occasion the people in the pictures are the Right People, and no mistake about it.

The two papers are alike in this, but once you get used to them there are significant differences. The *Bulletin* is really quite a lot more Old Philadelphian, and somewhat more interesting, than the *Inquirer*. The *Inquirer* aims to be "livelier" but its liveliness seems to consist entirely of syndicated columns, including so-called "social" ones of the Cholly Knickerbocker and the Hedda Hopper sort. The *Bulletin* has syndicated columns too, but its chief interest and glory is a whole stable of local columnists, who give the paper what quality it has. There are a round dozen of them, Rose, Brookhouser, Cassidy, Jones, Livingston, Page and many others, most of whom concentrate on the local scene, though a few write on national affairs. A good many of them are really excellent in their quiet way. Rose, Jones and Cassidy in particular keep up the tradition of the humorous occasional essay; Brookhouser covers night life. The Sunday social columnist is a handsome indefatigable woman called Ruth Seltzer who manages to get to, and report on, everything from meetings of the Numismatic Society to Fernanda Wanamaker's latest party for her chimpanzees. Nobody knows how she does it. These columns really provide what Philadelphia atmosphere Philadelphia journalism still has; not terribly exciting perhaps, and awfully, awfully local, but often humorous, generally kind and sometimes acute and learned — a series of small oases in what otherwise tends to seem like a waste of Wanamaker ads. What's left of the tradition of Childs and of the *Ledger* survives in the *Bulletin,* hidden away in its columns.

The *Bulletin* has for several generations been owned by the McLeans, the *Inquirer* by the Annenbergs. The McLeans are "nice people" whom "Everybody knows," and have become thoroughly absorbed. The Annenbergs can't somehow quite be called "nice people"; but despite the elder Annenberg's period in jail (income tax trouble), "Everybody knows" and likes them, and they are pretty glamorous. Their *Inquirer* has a typical tortuous claim to being America's First and Oldest Daily Paper (1771).

Unfortunately the family personalities do not seem to affect the editorial policies, which are neither "nice" nor "glamorous." Safe and sane and determinedly lower-middle-class and row-house both papers remain. A rival, that perky tabloid the *Daily News,* has attempted to break in on the duet. Like New York's *News* and *Mirror* it aims to substitute murder and sex for news; but in Philadelphia somehow it all comes out rather innocent and innocuous. Just no news, that's all. So far the newcomer has not seemed to unsettle the position of the Big Two, even among morons. Nearly Everybody continues to read both of them; educated people supplement the bland diet with the out-of-town spice of the New York *Times* or *Tribune.* Yet, and still, and on the other hand . . . the *Inquirer* and the *Bulletin* are so much better than so many other papers! The *Bulletin,* in fact, though it hardly bears thinking of, may just possibly be the best evening paper published, not just in America, but in English.

V

C H A P T E R

1

i. Theatre

THE ARTS of painting and literature, though they cannot be said exactly to have been blessed by the Quakers and Philadelphia, at least were early and easily tolerated; as long as they minded their manners. But not the stage. The stage in any form, no matter how noble, was an agent of the devil, and that was that. Quaker toleration did not extend so far, and the whole early history of the theatre in Philadelphia is one of surreptitious ducking around laws and censorships, of being outlawed and sneaking back into town.

Pressure on the part of Anglican high society overcame puritanism in the 1750's, and the Hallam Company was asked down from New York. It was not till 1766, however, that the company became a permanent fixture. The Hallams erected a new theatre in Southwark and there they produced America's first drama, *The Prince of Parthia,* by Philadelphia's own Thomas Godfrey. A stiff but not unworthy eighteenth-century poetic drama, it was written, in true Philadelphia fashion, by somebody's son, Thomas Jr. being the precocious but short-lived offshoot of an already famous Philadelphia character, Thomas Godfrey, self-educated glazier, amateur scientist, inventor of the quadrant, friend of Franklin. *The Prince of Parthia* was also the first in that long tradition of Philadelphia poetic dramas, many of them by upper-class Philadelphia amateurs, of which Boker's *Francesca da Rimini* is the climax.

The Revolution more or less put an end to all stage activities for the duration, but Hallam returned cautiously when the fighting stopped. Though plays were once again outlawed, for a time, in the name of wartime economy, in 1784 Hallam began his "moral lectures" and edifying "readings." He billed ballad operas as "concerts" and the Southwark Theatre was renamed the "Opera House" (first of that familiar designation in the country) and everything was given for the benefit of American captives in Algiers or some other worthy cause. People came to hear an instructive dissertation on "Filial Piety" and remained to see *Hamlet*. Finally, spearheaded by a committee of doctors and Angelicans, including Dr. John Redman and William Temple Franklin, the Doctor's illegitimate grandson, counter-petitions to the Assembly and endless newspaper controversy caused the Assembly to change its mind. In 1789 all restrictions were removed, just in time to welcome that confirmed theatre-goer, George Washington.

The last stage box of the Southwark Theatre was fitted up as a Presidential box, with the national coat of arms and red drapery. The director, Thomas Wignell, in full dress with white wig, carrying two silver candlesticks, would await Washington's arrival at the door of the box and conduct him, with many a courtly bow, to his seat. Soldiers were posted about strategically, and when the President was there people *behaved,* which was far from common in those rowdy days.

Theatre in Philadelphia had arrived, and though the old Southwark soon succumbed to its newer rivals, the grander Chestnut, Walnut and Arch Street Theatres, Philadelphia was never again without drama.

During the nineteenth century Philadelphia rivaled New York as a theatrical center, and had its own creative theatrical tradition, both comic and tragic, as exemplified by Barker, Bird and Boker. Later, when the theatre moved definitely to New York in the twentieth century, two other Philadelphians, with otherwise distinguished family names, made names for themselves as playwrights.

Before the First War, Langdon Mitchell, son of Weir Mitchell the novelist, achieved two great successes. One was his adaptation of Thackeray's *Vanity Fair*, called *Becky Sharp*, starring Mrs. Fiske. The other was his original play, *The New York Idea*. This was considered very chic and risqué at the time it was produced in 1906 because it was all about divorce in smart circles. It concerned an independent divorcée just about to marry a very important but stuffy man, who falls in with her ex-husband, a sporty type, and finds she has much more in common with him than with her new husband-to-be. So they run off and get remarried. What's odd about this still amusing soufflé is that it has approximately the same plot as Philip Barry's *Philadelphia Story* of thirty years later. The irony being that *The New York Idea* was written by a Philadelphian, *The Philadelphia Story* by a New Yorker. Langdon Mitchell followed in the footsteps of Owen Wister and just stopped writing. Though he lived well beyond the First War, he never wrote, or at least never had produced, any more plays, except for another and not so successful adaptation from Thackeray, *Pendennis*.

After the War, George Kelly, brother of John the oarsman and uncle of Grace the Princess, won the Pulitzer Prize in 1926 for his *Craig's Wife*, later a movie with Rosalind Russell, and was the author of *The Show Off* and other good plays. His satire on Little Theatre, *The Torchbearers*, continues to be played by little theatres.

There were other successes: Owen Wister and a collaborator turned *The Virginian* into a hit of 1904. John Luther Long's *Madame Butterfly* ended up, via Belasco, as Puccini's *Madama Butterfly* and maintains, I suppose, Philadelphia's reputation in some way as being the only successful libretto of American origin in the world's standard operatic repertoire.* Long wrote other

---

* Another, sort of, is the libretto of *Tosca*. This was written originally by Maurice Barrymore for Modjeska and called *Nadjezda*. He sent it to Bernhardt, who had the drama rewritten by Sardou for herself, and produced it as *Tosca*. When Barrymore had the effrontery to complain, the Bernhardt answered, "An idea sometimes is suggested to a dramatist by an obscure source. Sardou is a master; the man who accuses him insignificant." Puccini made his opera out of Sardou's *Tosca*, not *Nadjezda*, of course, and Barrymore wasn't exactly a Philadelphian, or even really an American; but still . . .

plays also. Richard Harding Davis wrote plays which did well,
Edward Childs Carpenter, a Philadelphian, was during the 'twenties one of Broadway's chief writers of comedies (*The Bachelor
Father* still gets revived in various forms). Clifford Odets, at
least born in Philadelphia, was the pink-haired boy of the proletarian 'thirties. The last two decades seem to have done without much help from Penn's godchild, and no Philadelphian is
now a conspicuous dramatist. Still, plays *about* Philadelphia —
Philip Barry's famous and unforgotten *Philadelphia Story* and
the more easily forgettable *Happy Hunting* and *Happiest Millionaire* — have given Philadelphia, even Old Philadelphia, a few
tenuous connections with the modern theatre.

ii. Poor Players

ACTUALLY a more picturesque bond has been not with plays but
with players. The person and career of Edwin Forrest may seem
the antithesis of Philadelphianism — although in contemplating
the careers of other such Philadelphians as Robert Morris, Boies
Penrose and Albert Barnes, one wonders if Philadelphia really
does inhibit flamboyance after all — but this powerful, selfish,
dynamic ham was born in Philadelphia, began to act there, and
lived and died there; and he was especially a Philadelphian in at
least one notable respect — he was a First: America's first serious
successful internationally recognized tragedian. Muscular and belligerent, he was type-cast for his roles as Othello and Macbeth, and
above all his most famous characterization as Spartacus in Robert
Montgomery Bird's *The Gladiators*, where he could display his
massive physique and roaring mannerisms to perfect advantage.

The career of Forrest is in itself the most rip-roaring melodrama of the American, or perhaps any other, stage, and would
do well on the wide screen, in color. Equipped with a magnificent voice, great animal magnetism (Mrs. Drew remembered
young Forrest as the handsomest man she ever saw; one more
in the particular Philadelphia line), he soon shook off the lower-
middle-class respectability of his family, and became in his teens

a wandering player. He traveled all over the pioneer Midwest in the Mrs. Trollope period, doing blackface, circus acts and anything else, and finally landed, still not twenty, in New Orleans. There he learned about knives from his friend Colonel Bowie, about the noble redman from his pal Push-ma-ta-ha the Choctaw chief, and about Life. He returned to Philadelphia in 1825, broke but experienced, and began to lay the foundations of his extraordinarily successful career.

He made his first impression in Albany, where he was allowed to co-star with the great Edmund Kean. He modeled himself upon Kean not only in acting style — thunderous climaxes of passion being the specialty of both of them — but in misconduct of private life and of public relations. Kean at that time had just been hissed out of Boston for his rudeness to an audience he thought too scanty, and in England an alderman had just won a criminal suit against him involving Mrs. Alderman. Forrest later on did pretty much the same thing.

Against everyone's advice, Forrest made his debut in New York as Othello, in the Bowery Theatre, and from 1826 till after the Civil War, he held securely the place of America's Greatest Actor.

As a grandly patriotic gesture, and with an eye to securing feasible vehicles for his peculiar talents, Forrest offered more or less annual prizes for the best "new American drama." Nine of these prizes were actually awarded, nearly all of them to Philadelphians, but only four of the plays survived in Forrest's repertoire. These were *Metamora* by the non-Philadelphian John Augustus Stone, the first of the litter, *The Gladiator* and *The Broker of Bogota* by long-suffering Robert Montgomery Bird, and *Jack Cade* by Judge, then Mayor of Philadelphia, Robert T. Conrad. Although Forrest was much criticized for his financial meanness, his enterprise did stir up a sort of tiny flowering of the drama in Philadelphia in the nineteenth century.

In 1834 Forrest made his boldest move, and one as yet unprecedented in stage history. He decided to go to England, and to open in London in Bird's *Gladiator,* an American tragic actor

[435]

in an American tragic play. How the Eagle screamed! A patriotic banquet was given to send him off, organized by Washington Irving, James Monroe and J. Fenimore Cooper, at which Forrest sat next to the Mayor of New York and answered to eight formal toasts beginning with "The Drama: the mirror in which life, like Narcissus, delights to contemplate its own image," and working through Shakespeare and Garrick to "the Dramatic Genius of our country: the ruddy brightness of its rise gives token of a goodly day." It probably would have meant war if Forrest had been less than a hit in his London debut. But he took London by storm too. London critics didn't think too much of *The Gladiator,* though it was certainly not much worse than Englishman Sheridan Knowles's popular *Virginius,* but with one conspicuous exception, they all praised Forrest the actor.

The exception was unfortunate. A critic called Forster handed in a sarcastic and condescending minority report. Unluckily, as it turned out, John Forster was well known to be a close friend and ardent critical supporter of William Macready, already crowned as greatest tragic actor of England. Though Macready in person bent over backward to be nice to Forrest, "everybody" knew that Forster's barbs at Forrest were really a defense of Macready; and no one knew it better than Forrest and Macready.

Nevertheless, on the whole Forrest was overwhelmed and elated at his reception. A dinner was given him at the Garrick Club, and Macready was there, gracious as all get out and drinking a special toast together with his rival. Forrest was full of gratitude and collected as mementos of the occasion three swords that had once belonged to the actors Kean, John Kemble and Talma. The Drury Lane Company gave him a golden snuffbox; and last but by no means least of his trophies, he brought back a wife, the beautiful Catherine Sinclair, of an acting family of course. They were married in London, and "never was seen a more beautiful pair."

Forrest returned to America for his great decade. Secure in his position now as America's first actor, rivaled only by Macready as chief actor of the English-speaking stage, married to a lovely well-bred and talented wife, lionized by society everywhere, even in Philadelphia, friend of everybody worth knowing in the country, doubling his already sizable fortune, still young, handsome and vigorous, he was obviously a ripe subject for the sport of the Grim Sisters — as he no doubt might have expressed it himself.

The first and most conspicuous of his disasters began with his second trip to England in 1845. His rival but still supposed friend Macready had toured America in 1843–44, and Forrest saw no reason why the compliment should not be returned. He opened *Othello* in London, as he had twenty years before in New York, and though the London audience as a whole was well disposed, little knots of hissers here and there about the house gave strong evidence that an organized clique was out to get him. The critic of *The Times* praised his later performance of *Lear* as "masterly"; but Mr. Forster, that friend of Macready, called it a "roaring pantaloon." The hisses, Forster's criticism and various other incidents gave Forrest to think that it was Macready himself who was out to get him. When Forrest in person hissed Macready in person in Edinburgh, war was declared.

So began the most famous and bloody feud between actors in modern stage history. Its climax was the celebrated Astor Place riot, when on the night of May 10, 1849, over thirty people were killed and one hundred and fifty injured. Forrest partisans, afire with Americanism and whisky, broke up Macready's performance of *Macbeth,* as well as the Astor Place Opera House. When the smoke of battle cleared, Macready had left the United States never to return, and Forrest was left alone as unrivaled king of the American stage; but most nice people held the riot against him, and his reputation was tarnished.

Forrest, having played Macbeth, now proceeded to do Othello; in real life, but still very much in public. No sooner had the corpses of the Astor Place riot been interred and decently forgotten than the Forrest Divorce Case rocked the newspapers. It began by Forrest finding an incriminating love letter from an actor called Jamieson addressed to his wife. It was, at least by

Victorian standards, moderately hot stuff. Forrest sued her for divorce in Pennsylvania. Mrs. Forrest countersued in New York. Mrs. Forrest won her suit, and in the process proved conclusively that whatever she may have been doing, Forrest was doing it in a far more active way. The papers loved and printed every single detail, daily, and summed up later in pamphlet form. Sales were not inhibited when Forrest, meeting on the street by chance the poetaster N. P. Willis, friend of his wife and one of his most vicious public detractors, beat him to a pulp. Willis sued for assault and battery, Forrest sued for libel. It was, in other words, a journalistic field day. All the "better element," the people who had given him banquets and medals, already put off by the Astor Place riots, turned against him for good. He abandoned Fonthill, his half-built castle on the Hudson, and retired to Philadelphia, where he built a big house on North Broad Street all for himself, and began to appeal his divorce case. After five tries and the expenditure of seventy thousand dollars he gave up. He gave up the role of Othello too, and now took on that of Lear.

Alone in his gloomy mansion, surrounded by ghosts and luxury, he brooded. Every now and then he would burst forth, make a whirlwind tour of the country, still triumphant, return with lots of money and once more retire into seclusion. Surrounded by a few worshipping disciples and yes-men, he grew old and sick, and even, at the very end, no longer popular with the public. In 1872 he made a last appearance, reading, but no longer able to act, Othello. A few days later he was found dead, alone in his somber rooms. He left all his money and property to create a Forrest Home for Actors in Philadelphia, which still exists, the last living memorial to the first of America's great actors. Poor Ned.

Forrest left no family, but his theatrical tradition at least carried on for awhile among Philadelphia theatrical descendants. John McCullough in particular, a local boy, was chosen and trained by the Master to inherit the mantle, and for a decade after Forrest's death, McCullough too toured the country satisfactorily, tearing passion to tatters in *Metamora* and the other

Forrest roles. Finally, in the middle of a performance of *The Gladiator* in Chicago, he went crazy. He was taken home to die in Philadelphia, and he, too, was buried there. With him died *The Gladiator, Metamora* and the whole tradition of the Forrest–Philadelphia drama, except as it may be said to have continued and fulfilled itself, refined and chastened, in Boker's *Francesca*.

Forrest's personal melodrama opened and closed in his native Philadelphia, but the eruptions of riot and passion took place elsewhere, New York, London, Edinburgh. The upper-class psychological novel (small-screen, black-and-white) which was the career of Fanny Kemble began and ended in London, but its muted climax took place in Philadelphia, and in fact in the very inmost bosom of Old Philadelphia. Forrest's life was in the style of Robert Montgomery Bird himself; Fanny Kemble's life was pure Henry James. (He was one of her best friends, later on.)

The Kemble theatrical background was as different from the Forrest theatrical background as can be imagined. Forrest was the epitome of the self-made man. Fanny Kemble was the last important member of England's greatest theatrical family. Only Philadelphia's own Drew–Barrymores compare. From 1721 when the first acting Kemble, Roger, was born, right down to the very present, Kembles of one sort or another have been on the boards. Fanny's aunt Mrs. Siddons was queen of the tragic stage as her uncle John Philip Kemble was king of it. Her father Charles shone in gallant rather than pompous parts, and spent a good deal of his time rather unsuccessfully trying to make a go of Covent Garden Theatre. His lovely older daughter Fanny had no intention of being an actress. But, to help rescue her father's faltering fortunes, she appeared under his direction and often opposite him, as Juliet, beginning in 1829 when she was nineteen. Her beauty and electric personality immediately made her the toast of London, her father was saved from bankruptcy, and Fanny was stuck with a career.

She and her father, now favorites of all England, came to America in 1832, opened in New York, repeating their success, and then went on to Philadelphia. There Fanny met Pierce Butler, of Philadelphia and South Carolina, perhaps at Mrs. Willing's party, the first ball she went to in Philadelphia. It was hot and crowded and she didn't care for stewed oysters and terrapin. After a traveling courtship, in which Butler followed her to Niagara on a tour of waterfalls (for Fanny had a thoroughly Freudian passion for waterfalls), she succumbed, and Pierce and she were married, in 1834, by Bishop White in Christ Church. This was intended to be her permanent retirement from the stage; she chose to become a conventional housewife, mother and hostess in Philadelphia. Why?

The answer must be that Pierce Butler, universally maligned by all historians of Fanny, and with some justice, for his extravagance, immorality and meanness to her, had something; something, that is, besides a large fortune. Though usually referred to as a "Southern planter," he was actually a Philadelphian, born Pierce Mease, who inherited the great fortune in plantations and slaves of his South Carolina maternal grandfather, Pierce Butler, and like John Powel Hare, changed his name to suit his inheritance. Mease was not much more than respectable as a Philadelphia name (medical), but Butler was a name to conjure with in South Carolina, where grandfather Butler had been the first senator from the state, and Butlers were definitely first citizens.

Fanny Kemble gave up her career with relief, and settled back to become Mrs. Butler. Unfortunately, she had had no experience of ordinary domestic life, especially in Victorian Philadelphia. Pierce put her out in his country house Butler Place, which she did over tastefully, inside and out, and went on about his business, which was drinking, gambling, and keeping up with a very fast set to which his wife was evidently not introduced. Fanny stayed out at Butler Place and was bored to insanity. "You can form no idea, none, none, of the intellectual dearth and drought in which I am existing," she wrote in despair. Her marriage very soon began to split at the seams.

Various little incidents helped hasten the split. In 1835 she published a *Journal* of her American visit. It was not anti-Amer-

ican in intention, as so many Tory English travel books of the
period were, but it did poke fun, called Americans vulgar and,
in a word, was tactless. The American publishers were Carey
and Lea of Philadelphia, and Pierce insisted on "editing" it for
them. This made Fanny furious. When the book came out it
was something of a sensation, which was nice for Carey and Lea,
but made Pierce furious. Then Fanny paid a visit to her husband's Southern plantations. She was appalled at what she saw,
and became an outspoken abolitionist. This, in the foreign wife
of one of the country's richest slaveowners, was also tactless;
honest and good-spirited perhaps, but not tactful.

Later on, in 1844, Pierce was involved in a scandal with some
of his fast friends. They'd all gone to New York for a fling, very
much as fast Philadelphians do today, leaving Fanny behind. One
of the husbands in the party got jealous, beat his wife and challenged Pierce to a duel. They fought, and no one was hurt
except Fanny, who was not pleased, and the wife, who sued her
husband for divorce.

The Butlers were not, in other words, compatible. Fanny was
a highly charged intellectual, who liked stimulation; Pierce was
a conventional man of pleasure who like stimulants. They were
both dashing and charming perhaps, but in an entirely different
way. "The death I should prefer would be to break my neck
off the back of a good horse at a full gallop on a fine day," wrote
Fanny. Pierce might do the same for a bet while drunk, but the
motives would be quite different; in one case Romanticism, in
the other swagger.

Their ways became increasingly separated. While Pierce was in
town having his idea of a good time, Fanny filled in by bearing
and raising two daughters, going to parties where she met Sidney
Fisher, and riding about all by herself, then considered a somewhat daring thing for a lady to do.

Fisher tells of a call at Butler Place in 1839.

We staid an hour and had a warm discussion on the nature of true
art etc. Butler is extremely gentleman-like in manner and has I think
many excellent traits of character. They are rich and live in hand-

some style. The place tho' it possesses no advantages of situation is surrounded by fine trees and the grounds are admirably kept.

As for Fanny herself, he was at first much smitten. He speaks of her at parties, "looking very beautiful." He met her out riding alone. "She is very independent and rides about constantly unattended. Had some agreeable talk and accompanied her home. Never saw her look so well. Her costume was becoming and peculiar, a green cloth riding habit. . . ." which he then describes and itemizes; trust Sidney for the minutely irrelevant detail that is the sure sign of a born diarist.

But he began to be offended by her.

Mrs. B. is an agreeable companion, but does not interest me. She is too prononcée, wants delicacy and refinement, and is the reverse of feminine in her manners and conversation. She is also guilty of the imprudence and bad taste of alluding constantly to her domestic troubles, which I believe are brought about by her own want of tact and temper. She has talent however and converses well. She has seen the best English society and her descriptions of men and manners are very interesting. What a different and superior existence do they exhibit. . . .

Sic semper Sidney. "Mrs. B. has published a volume of poems for the purpose, as she told me, of paying for the horse she rode." This book of poems was a prime example of her "bad taste" and "want of tact," since it dwelt heavily and in melancholy terms on her own present and domestic misery.

Finally she couldn't stand it any longer and after ten years went off to England, leaving her husband and children. She returned briefly to the stage. Pierce sued her for divorce on the grounds of desertion and won the case and custody of the children. Philadelphia sided with him, although definitely disapproving of both his personal extravagance and his meanness to Fanny. In 1859 — just in time — he sold all his slaves and slaveholdings to pay his debts.

Fanny took back her maiden name and was henceforward known as Mrs. Kemble. She turned from acting to readings from Shakespeare, and there found her real vocation. With the proceeds she bought a cottage in Lenox, Massachusetts, which she first established as a literary and fashionable summer resort. One of her two daughters married a clergyman in England, the other became Mrs. Owen Jones Wister, mother of Owen Wister, and lived, after the death of Pierce in the 'sixties, in Butler Place. Though never again really accepted by Sidney Fisher's circle in Philadelphia, Fanny Kemble had very good Philadelphia friends, notably the Fox family of nearby Champlost, and spent some quiet years back in the Philadelphia area, having become a good deal less "prononcée" as time went on. In the decade before her death in 1893 she returned to London for good, kept a salon where Henry James was a familiar, and published her autobiography in a series of *Journals*. By the time of her death her grandson Owen Wister was already making a name for himself as a writer, and her kinsman Henry Kemble was doing well in London as a popular actor. It was a pleasantly autumnal end to a rather stormy life, but somehow a dying fall for the last of the great Kembles.

There is a touching little footnote to Fanny's later years in Philadelphia. Weir Mitchell had been to visit her at Butler Place; when he got up to leave she detained him. "No, don't go yet. I am old and lonely, and never again will you have these chances to talk with a woman who has sat at dinner alongside of Byron, who has heard Tom Moore sing, and calls Tennyson 'Alfred.' "

iii. *"It's Good To Be Home"*

THE FORREST AND KEMBLE sagas are only partially Philadelphian. The Jeffersons and Drew–Barrymores, however, are firmly rooted there, though both families originated in England. All the important members of both families were either natives, or spent their active lives in the city. Philadelphia can thus pretty well lay claim to two of America's greatest acting tribes. But their stories, for all the family fame, do not make neat drama as do the stories of Forrest and Kemble.

Both families began humbly and emigrated in the second generation to America. The original American Jefferson, Joseph the First, reached Philadelphia in 1803, and for thirty years was a pillar of the Chestnut Street Company. It was his grandson, Joseph the Third, who was the famous Jefferson, "Rip Van Winkle," America's favorite comic actor. Though he too was born in Philadelphia, he left as a child, carried all over the country by his wandering parents, and his later career was made in New York and London, not Philadelphia.

In a similar fashion the Drew–Barrymore family story begins in eighteenth-century England, takes root in Philadelphia and more or less explodes elsewhere, in New York and in Hollywood. The chief progenitor of this clan was a woman, born Louisa Lane, who got to Philadelphia as a girl with her widowed actress mother, in 1827. As the elder Jefferson was a pillar of the Chestnut Street Theatre, so she was of the Arch Street, which flourished in the 1830's while the Chestnut Street declined.

Louisa was put to work at once. At the age of eight she appeared in a skit called *Twelve Precisely*. In this she impersonated five midget characters, a midget soldier, a midget Irish girl and other midgets, all to immense Philadelphia applause. From then on she was acting and managing and marrying all her long busy life till she dropped in 1897. Though Philadelphia was always the center of operations, she wandered over the hemisphere, was shipwrecked at eleven on the shores of Santo Domingo, where she lived like the Swiss Family Robinson in shelters of old crates and bits of driftwood, played at the new St. Charles in New Orleans, Peale's Museum in Baltimore, opened the first theatre in Chicago, and went on to Nova Scotia. She acted everything and with everybody: Macready, whom she hated; Forrest, whom she admired for all his "moroseness"; Junius Brutus Booth, the original Tyrone Power.

Her marriages were brief interludes, always in the circle of the Profession as a matter of course. Unfortunate Mr. Hunt, even more unfortunate Mr. Mossop, played their brief parts and made their swift exits. The third of them, that handsome, affable actor of Irish parts and Irish origins, John Drew, Sr., lasted a while longer. He managed to sire four children by her (there was some question about one of them) before he too, worn out by a trip around the world, succumbed to the inevitable fate of Louisa's husbands.

Before he died in 1862 Drew had undertaken the management of the Arch Street Theatre. His determined widow took over his duties and for a decade under her, the Arch Street Company was the most respected on the American continent. Everybody who was anybody acted with them, and there innumerable young actors and actresses got their start. Of these, none got a better start than Louisa's own children, John and Georgiana.

It was John who best carried on the family traditions. He was brought up not to be an actor, but to be a Philadelphia gentleman. Taken regularly to St. Stephens, his mother's church, and schooled at Episcopal, he was fashioned, like Grace Kelly in a later age, into an almost too-perfect, once-for-all-time model of that favorite Philadelphia character, so often prominent in real life, the second-generation Philadelphia princeling. Charming, gifted, athletic, mildly intellectual, clubbable, he played cricket and rowed with the Malta Barge Club, dressed to perfection and drank gallantly, was mad about horses and lowlife and highlife; and wherever he was, whatever he did, nothing ever disturbed his easy, natural, genial Philadelphia aplomb.

For lack of anything better to do, he thought he might as well try the stage. His mother put him on as a cool young man in *Cool as a Cucumber.* He took it all so coolly that she was furious with him. No one must trifle with the Drama. She adlibbed the lines "What a dreadful young man! I wonder what he will be like when he grows up." The audience, who thought of the Drews as members of the Philadelphia family (theatrically of course, not socially), roared with appreciative amusement. She gave it to him proper afterwards, and he never again approached the Fane with such lack of trepidation. Louisa took her son in hand, disabusing him of his Philadelphia accent and his idea that acting was a cinch; but whether because the offers were better, or because he wanted to get out from under, he went to New York and Augustin Daly's company the next year.

In New York he stayed, taking on some of the more brittle arrogance of a Manhattan "swell," always urbane, always success-ful, for the rest of his long life; King of Hearts, First Gentleman of the Stage, fashion plate, profile, the most socially eligible of actors, who belonged to clubs to which no other actor had ever before aspired.

With him the fortunes of the family shifted to New York. The children of his fascinating but short-lived sister Georgiana, the famous Barrymores, Ethel, Lionel and John, were all brought up in Philadelphia by their grandmother Mrs. Drew in her gloomy house there, nicknamed the "Tomb of the Capulets." But the Arch Street Theatre failed, Mrs. Drew in her old age had to join her son in New York, and there the younger Barrymores began their unwilling stage careers. Still, they always thought of them-selves as Philadelphians, and no one who heard it can forget Ethel's curtain calls, when in town on tour, and the effect of her baritone voice saying to the Philadelphia audience, "It's good to be home!"

It would seem, in looking at these often sad but vivid tales of the theatrical great, as though Philadelphia served the somewhat odd function of an incubator, or a "ground" in the hunting sense. In Philadelphia Forrest began and ended his stormy days, retiring there like a savage old bear to count his money and lick his wounds. There the saga of the great Kembles came to its real close, for though there were Kembles afterward, Fanny was the last of the Royal line, and her stage career stopped when she vol-untarily buried herself out in Butler Place. There, almost as though literally under earth, were planted the roots of the Jef-fersons and the Barrymores, to flower later and elsewhere, but starting in Philadelphia, as the Kembles stopped there.

All these Poor Players had a definite relationship to Old Phila-delphia itself, as distinguished from Philadelphia in general.

Forrest of course was never admitted as an Old Philadelphian, and after the Riot and the Divorce was socially ostracized there. Before that, however, he had his moments. Not only was he given testimonial dinners at the Merchant's Hotel, Nicholas Biddle presiding, but he was actually asked to dinner in private by the Ingersolls. He got as far as the front door, but was so panic-stricken that he tried to cut and run. His manager Wikoff was with him, however, and persuaded him to see it through. The Cadwaladers, Biddles and Rushes were there. They were charming, charming and of course everything went off beautifully. Forrest was elated. He said to Wikoff, "This is the proudest day of my life, for I have met on terms of social equality many of the conspicuous men of my native city whose names have been familiar to me from my boyhood, and whom I never aspired to know." Forrest was always at heart a Philadelphian. Poor Ned.

Fanny was different. She came to condescend. She lived to regret it. In the end, not for herself, but in her children, she was accepted. Her daughter Mrs. Wister and her grandchildren Owen and Fanny were great figures in Old Philadelphia, and their lives very much part of the mythology of the nineteenth and twentieth centuries in its more elegant phases. As an ancestress, at least, Fanny has been made at home. Her personal reactions were more ambiguous. She obviously hated Philadelphia, yet she lived there a good deal, over a long period, years of married life, and many odd years later as a mother. She had dear friends there, and she certainly left her mark.

The Jeffersons never had any real relationship to Old Philadelphia. Like any other craftsmen they were respected there for their craft, but not involved socially. With the Drews it was somehow a bit different. They too were respected for their craft, and not involved too much socially, but Mrs. Drew's connections with St. Stephens, and John Drew's attendance at Episcopal gave them friends and acquaintances on the right side of Market Street. If not exactly Old Philadelphian, the Drews, of all Philadelphia's acting families, were the most Old Philadelphianized.

The influence carried on into the Barrymores, especially in Ethel who doted on society, from the Winston Churchills to the Boston Searses and Philadelphia Griscoms and Rosengartens. They were not so much *of* as modeled *after,* and John Drew represented a type of Old Philadelphia to his age as Grace Kelly does for hers.

iv. *Philadelphia Story*

THERE WERE OF COURSE, always have been, and still are numberless other Philadelphia-born actresses and actors; W. C. Fields, for instance, deadpan genius of the twisted billiard cue, drinking friend of John Barrymore, hater of children, and if we are to believe his reputed "epitaph," hater of Philadelphia (On his tombstone he wanted to have inscribed: "I'd almost rather be in Philadelphia"). Ed Wynn is another; his grandson has been a student at Penn and has been seen at the right Philadelphia parties. There are many others. It might be possible to worry out something very Philadelphian about all these; but merely being born in Philadelphia doesn't make one a Philadelphian, much less a Philadelphia actor, unless this birthright in some way carries over, determines to some extent the character and the career.

Really Philadelphian then in that sense has been Grace Kelly, Princess of Monaco. There are few actresses, in fact, whose characters and careers have been so totally determined by their birthplace and heredity. The ramifications of the Kelly family are so numerous that it is hard to determine where the Kelly story really belongs. Through Philadelphia sports, politics, business, religion, the stage, the Kelly name and influence weave in colorful and sometimes cross-grained strands, and the story ends (up to this point) in a fairy-story blaze, another Philadelphia first: the first American girl to marry an actual reigning Prince and become his actual reigning consort. Baltimore came close with Elizabeth Patterson Bonaparte and Wallis Warfield Windsor (the big ones that got away). New York has Peggy Greene, Princess of Denmark's cosy kingly family. But none of them has actually worn a crown, even such a diminutive crown as that of the Principality of Monaco. Though Grace may not have made the *Social Register* at home, much less the Assembly, she has made the *Almanach de Gotha* and the ranks, albeit the lowest ranks, of the monarchy.

In 1958 there was revived, at Philadelphia's biggest movie theatre, a movie with the somehow quaint and antiquated title, *High Society*. The revival was in honor of Princess Grace and her visit home. The movie, made before the marriage, just missed being the sociological document of our times; it was a remake of Philip Barry's *Philadelphia Story* and the heroine was played by Grace Kelly. The paradoxes of this particular mixture are very involved and very Philadelphian.

The Philadelphia Story, as a play, is intended as a picture, and a pretty sympathetic one, of upper-class Main Line Philadelphia life. It is a generalized rather than a particular portrait, and though the old jokes, about the Drexels and the Biddles and the qu'est-ce que c'est Cassatts are quoted, it could with the adjustment of a few details be laid anywhere from Providence to San Francisco. Still, one of the morals of the piece, and actually its chief theme, is a defense of just the sort of rather unambitious, taken-for-granted gentryism on which Philadelphia does pride itself. The heroine, a haughty heiress, with stiff ideals about male accomplishment and virtue, winds up (just like her original prototype in Mitchell's *New York Idea*) by marrying again her first husband, a rather worthless but extremely amiable sportsman whom she divorced precisely because of his lack of ambition, instead of the stuffy but ambitious rags-to-riches Horatio Alger coal millionaire to whom she is engaged, or the unworldly reporter who makes love to her on the eve of her second wedding. In the end, having been humbled by drink and indiscretion, she is ready to appreciate the qualities of kindness and being at ease which attracted her to her first husband originally. The play is, in other words, despite its humorous and graceful persiflage, a fairly strong plea, in terms of character, for the virtues of the Arrivé, as opposed to the Arriviste; the essential virtues possible, at least, to the inheriting classes of relaxed, unstriving gentleness, of Maintenance as opposed to the more often celebrated virtues of striving Achievement.

The paradox lies in Hollywood's casting Grace Kelly in this particular role. The heroine of the play is represented as the epitome of secure heredity who eventually comes to realize the values of just such secure heredity. The Philadelphia Kellys in real life represent the epitome of successful, ambitious heredity, a family most spectacularly on the make, and Grace in an almost incredible way is the projection of the ambitious Kelly family ideal. That is to say, she is the perfect, almost too-perfect simulacrum, on the order of John Drew, of just the sort of secure hereditary Philadelphia heiress that the heroine of *The Philadelphia Story* is *supposed* to be, but which, of course, Grace Kelly emphatically isn't.

The movie spoiled the whole point, or at least added another sociological complication, not only by the very title *High Society* which just by itself indicates a way of thinking in complete conflict with Old Philadelphia, but by laying the scene in Newport, which is also an exact contradiction to everything *The Philadelphia Story* meant to celebrate. Newport is par excellence the graveyard of parvenuism, of the ostentatious, essentially vulgar but certainly imaginative New York millionairism of the last few generations — which was, of course, precisely the thing Philip Barry *wasn't* talking about. The movie makers then added insult to injury by casting Bing Crosby, who can wear a blazer so that it looks like an old sweater, as the husband. He's amiable and relaxed all right; but they couldn't have picked anybody, except Will Rogers who is dead, who more calmly embodies American Classlessness, and a triumphant and assured Californian Non-U-ness.

Nobody could say the same of Grace Kelly; and in fact there can be few more conspicuous examples of the effect of parental ambition and devotion to very specific class standards and ideals in the molding of a personality. Grace Kelly may not in fact, or in Philadelphia, be or be considered the Perfect Philadelphia

Lady that she was considered to be in Movieland, but there can be no doubt that she gives the right effect. Of course few real Philadelphia belles ever achieve quite such chiseled perfection. Indeed to do so would be rather suspect; sort of New York. In real life the type is inclined to be softer, heartier, a little more countrified and less exact. But Grace Kelly is an exaggeratedly flawless realization of a type, almost *the* type, of traditional Philadelphia upper-class belle, tall, cool, neat, very blonde, and just off-classic. Sully painted her, family photographs enshrine her, and such clans as the Ingersolls seem to produce her or acquire her by marriage down through the generations.*

It has been amusing to see how the influence of Grace Kelly has spread and worked, in a sort of reverse English (or Irish). Now anybody who writes a play or a best seller about Philadelphia seems automatically to cast Grace as his Old Philadelphian heroine. Most notable and flagrant has been Powell's Grace Shippen in his novel *The Philadelphian*. Even more wildly paradoxical, the young heroine of *The Happiest Millionaire,* the play about the real Biddles, was played by a lovely thing who not only in looks but in manner obviously recalled no one but her Highness. Since this heroine was meant to be Cordelia Biddle, a perfectly real Biddle, confusion as you see has been compounded. Miss Biddle, now Mrs. T. Markoe Robertson, is and was a charming woman, but she does not, and never did, look like Grace Kelly. I need hardly add that the ingenue who played Ethel Merman's daughter in *Happy Hunting* was a pocket edition of the same thing.

Despite all these conspicuous Philadelphia theatrical connections, past and present, and Philadelphia's antique theatrical tradition (the Walnut Street Theatre is still the oldest American theatre building in actual professional use), theatre in Philadelphia is defunct, and has been since the turn of the century. Like night life in general, like restaurants, the Theatre belongs essentially to the world of "entertainment" and public "good times," and in this line Philadelphia has long ago given up trying. Pro-

* See Mrs. Harry Ingersoll.

fessional theatre in Philadelphia is now in the hands of New York road companies, and the try-out companies, and though it does as well as any other of the theatrically provincial cities of America, it does little better.

Repertory and especially amateur theatre has flourished, however, and there are now over forty different groups active in the city or the suburbs. Oldest and most distinguished of Philadelphia Little Theatres are the Hedgerow and the Plays and Players. The Hedgerow in particular, a suburban repertory company out Media way, has the longest history of any such little theatre in America. It is *not* an amateur group however, but a professional stock company on the order of the numerous summer theatres now sprung up everywhere. The Hedgerow goes all year. The leading spirit of it has been Jasper Deeter, and it has concentrated since 1923 on "serious theatre" — O'Neill, Shaw, Chekhov, Pirandello — and is a remarkable, if not always properly supported, Philadelphia phenomenon.

The Plays and Players, on the other hand, is in town and definitely amateur. It is merely First and Oldest, and most Old Philadelphian in a whole proliferating world of Philadelphia stage amateurism. This is not the same, though, as Mrs. Drew and the old Arch Street; if Minneapolis and Dallas and other newer towns can have a real municipal city-supported repertory, why not Philadelphia? The answer is probably, as it has been in opera — New York is too close.

2

i. Music

MUSIC, unlike the theatre, flourishes in Philadelphia today, and like the other fine arts, painting and literature, is and has been tied to the Oligarchy by patronage and by institutions. It differs from painting and literature somewhat in that, with a few very notable exceptions, the Oligarchy does not seem to have thought of music at all creatively; it remains for them essentially an art of performance only. Philadelphia music, in fact, resembles insurance, rather than banking; it seems a history of institutions rather than of men, and groups of venerable bodies, all still in being, have been founded at various times which have served as the center for the musical arts in the city. They all, it goes without saying, have boards.

Musical Philadelphia falls into five chronological periods, a Quaker or no-music period (1682–1750), an English period (1750–1830), an Italian period (1830–Civil War), a German period (Civil War–1912) and a Modern period (Stokowski on). The dates are approximate, to put it mildly. Each of these periods was determined by the attitudes of the upper classes, as leaders of fashion, and each period except the very first, culminated in a still-existent characteristic institution or two: the Musical Fund Society of 1820, the Academy of Music of 1857, the Orpheus Club of 1872, the Philadelphia Orchestra of 1901, and the Curtis Institute of 1924.

Music got off to a slow start in Philadelphia. It's a wonder it got started at all when one remembers that Philadelphia was

founded and at first dominated by the one sect that not only disapproved of worldly music but in fact of any music at all. However, Quaker tolerance did permit non-Quakers to practice private flute-playing and public hymn-singing. As a result of this
semi-tolerance, there was some music in Philadelphia from its first
years; Anglican and German music of a quite high order in fact,
and the plainer music of the plainer churches.

The mysteriously romantic Hermits of the Wissahickon, or the
"Society of the Woman in the Wilderness," who arrived in 1694,
when they weren't indulging in contemplation in caves, peculiar
fire ceremonies, casting horoscopes and the like (there is a distinct
whiff of the Black Arts about the Hermits), were building organs
and playing musick on the hautboy, viol and sackbut. Their
leader, Kelpius, was a skilled musician. In the first half of the
eighteenth century there was an enormous amount of chorale
composing and trombone playing among Germans in Philadelphia
and the Moravian colonies of Bethlehem and elsewhere. By the
second half of the century there existed a real school of chamber
music composing à la Haydn which was quite beyond the capaci-
ties of the rest of the Americans. But this all existed shut away in
small German-speaking communities, of which Germantown was
one, and it seems to have had no effect on anybody else. Conrad
Beissel, founder of the Ephrata Cloisters near Lancaster, is one of
the claimants as "America's first composer" on the strength of
his hundreds of peculiar hymns. Actually Kelpius of the Hermits
may have beaten him to it by several decades as a hymn writer,
which does keep the title in Philadelphia; but this German
music-making as a whole is Pennsylvanian, not Philadelphian.

Real Philadelphia music begins later. Philadelphia's first theatrical company, Murray and Kean, gave ballad operas as well as
spoken plays, over the dead bodies of the Quakers in 1749. Those
that followed, the Hallam Company and its successors, were really
just as much opera companies as they were drama companies.
When the rebuilt Southwark Theatre opened in 1766 as America's
first designated "Opera House," the devil's music established a
foothold in Penn's godly city, and was there to stay. Its character-

istic form was ballad opera on the order of *The Beggar's Opera,*
spoken text and songs thrown in, most of these being new words
set to old tunes like "Yankee Doodle."

The first recorded serious concerts in Philadelphia were given
by one John Palma in 1757. George Washington went to the
second of them and listed the price of the tickets in his ledger, but
nothing about the music. It's his first recorded concert too. From
then on there were other occasional concerts by immigrant teachers and performers, and of course there was music in churches,
notably St. Joseph's Catholic Church and the Anglican Christ
Church; but the really important and interesting music in Philadelphia before and during the Revolution was amateur upper-
class music, and this pre-Revolutionary amateur upper-class music
is dominated and represented by one already familiar and very
Old Philadelphian name. It comes up in law and insurance, in the
annals of the Philosophical Society and of the Library Company,
of literature and of cricket. The name is Hopkinson.

Of all the bewildering variety of interests that characterized
Francis Hopkinson — politics, law, shipping (he was the first to
occupy the position later designated as Secretary of the Navy),
art (there is a claim that he designed the American flag), invention, poetry — music claims first place, and if he can't quite stand
as America's First Composer (there are all those Germans) he is
still America's first native-born secular composer. He was just as
versatile a musician as he was a man. He was a competent harpsichordist and organist, he directed and trained Christ Church choir
for a while, edited a book of hymns and wrote on the subject of
church music. He was interested in acoustics and the improvement of instruments, and he composed not only the songs on
which his claims as "first composer" are based, but various other
choral works and cantatas. It was above all as an enthusiast and
connoisseur, a chamber music player and organizer of concerts
that he was really important. He introduced music into Philadelphia society.

He was a fine specimen of the "second generation," but his
father was not really a self-made man. Thomas Hopkinson was

an immigrant of some family; one of his wife's brothers, for instance, was a Lord Bishop of Worcester living in Hartlebury castle, where Francis visited, and from their Philadelphia beginnings the Hopkinsons were *in*. However Francis did the right thing anyway. Born in 1737, he went to the College of Philadelphia; after graduating in 1757, he studied law with Benjamin Chew and was barred in 1761. He then fulfilled his obligations, after a trip to England, by marrying Anne Borden, heiress of the first family of Bordentown, New Jersey. From then on he followed the career appropriate to his station and to his patriotism — Continental Congress, Signer of the Declaration, Secretary of the Naval Commission. After the Revolution he was a Judge, Trustee of the College, etc. He died prematurely in 1791, but very much a town father.

Francis knew everybody of course, not only other Old Philadelphians, but also the Founding Fathers. Washington, Jefferson and Franklin were his particular friends, but he met all the others. John Adams first saw him at Charles Willson Peale's studio. He wrote of him to Abigail, "He is one of your pretty, little, curious ingenious men. His head is not bigger than a large apple. I have not met with anything in natural history more amusing and entertaining than his personal appearance, yet he is genteel and wellbred, and is very social." Jefferson took him more seriously, and they had a long correspondence.

He began his musical career as early as 1757, while still an undergraduate, making his debut in public at an Oratorial Entertainment put on at the College. He played the harpsichord at this one. In 1761 he not only played, but wrote the music for a "Commencement Ode" in memory of George II, unhappily no longer reigning. Even during the Revolution, when he was busy with so many other things, he kept up with his music. In 1781 he put on another Grand Oratorial Entertainment, a sort of Masque, for which Francis wrote the words and the music, involving the Genius of France, the Genius of America and Minerva. George Washington and his lady attended the performance at the Hôtel of the French Minister, and were no doubt pleased and edified.

In between Hopkinson kept music going in Philadelphia by sponsoring subscription concerts during the 1760's. There were programs of chamber music, *concerti grossi* of the best modern masters, in which Francis on the harpsichord, and Governor John Penn, grandson of the Founder, on the violin, joined with the local professionals to make public and private music. Penn had Sunday soirees at his house on 3rd Street, where Hopkinson and Dr. Adam Kuhn, another amateur, attended and performed.

All the more ambitious music of Hopkinson is gone. His fame, such as it is, is due entirely to his songs. The first, dated 1759, is also the first one composed by an American, and is the comparatively well-known air "My days have been so wondrous free." Appropriate words for the First American Song, and well-known because the song is liable to be dragged in on occasions when a piece of genuine colonial music is called for. It is quite pretty. Hopkinson published, much later, a set of eight other songs, dedicated to Washington, for which the Father of our Country wrote him a nice letter of thanks. Jefferson recorded how one of these ditties, a pathetical one, made a younger daughter of his cry when an older daughter played it.

Besides all this, Hopkinson found time to invent a new method of quilling the harpsichord which earned him some reputation abroad, where his name is buried in histories of the instrument, without anyone seeming to know who he really was. Jefferson and he wrote each other on the subject of harpsichord quilling.

Though not a commanding figure as a composer, Hopkinson is a most engaging one of a gentleman amateur of the period, active about his music as he was about his politics, and unquestionably the founder of music in Philadelphia. His career throws such a curious sidelight on eighteenth-century American life — those grandiose Oratorial Entertainments, those musical soirees with Penn and Kuhn, above all that musical correspondence with the other Founding Fathers. Was there ever a group of men so cultivated, curious, reckless, determined, witty, contentious, farsighted, universal — and successful! Their really acute, if not very profound, interest in music makes the dreary Philistinism of most later American politicos especially obnoxious. It is hard to think of a modern Secretary of the Navy, or Judge of the Admiralty, writing, like Hopkinson:

> Oh! I would die with music melting round
> And float to bliss upon a sea of sound!

Oft thought; but where so well expressed?

Washington, though not a practitioner, never missed a chance to hear good music. Jefferson, though not creative in this field, was a connoisseur; and then there was Franklin.

It is hard to believe it, but perhaps one of the principal reasons for Franklin's fame all over Europe, outside France, was a musical one. He was not a composer* and certainly not a concert performer, though he played the guitar, the harp, the violin and something called the Sticcado-Pastorale, made out of glass rods. However, he did perfect, though he did not invent, an instrument called the Glassychord, or Armonica, which thanks to his improvements became the rage all over Europe. It was a set of musical glasses, with a Franklin mechanism attached which made it possible for a performer to play quite complicated music on it. As early as 1762 Franklin's version of the instrument was famous in England, where a Miss Davies took it on tour, and by the 1780's musical Germany, in particular, was enthralled by it. Many well-known composers of the time wrote music for it, including Beethoven. Mozart wrote a beautiful quintet (K. 617) for harmonica, flute, oboe, viola and cello; Schumann was fascinated too, and Goethe and Schiller were full of enthusiasm. It evidently had a weird other-worldly sound which drove performers mad, including poor Miss Davies, and was used most effectively by Mesmer, father of hypnotism, in his séances. Franklin called it the "ar-

---

* However, the manuscript of a funny little string quartet, supposedly by him, was found in Paris in the 1940's. It is a sort of musical joke, or puzzle, playable entirely on the open strings of a specially tuned quartet of three violins and a cello. It's cute.

monica" in "Honor of the Italian language": it probably picked up the "h" on its way through h'England, and though the instrument has vanished from the concert stage, Franklin's name for it survives, attached to a quite different instrument, the mouth organ. That Franklin!

Along with Hopkinson, there was another pioneer musician-composer active in Philadelphia in the early years. This was the hymn composer and editor James Lyon. He vies with Hopkinson for the title of "first composer," as writer of some Princeton commencement music, also in 1759. Lyon edited in 1761 a collection of psalmody called *Urania*. Included among hymns and anthems from the best hands were several of his own. *Urania* was not the first hymn collection published in America, though by far the most elegant and sophisticated; but James Lyon *is* the first authenticated native-born hymn writer. Though he was not a Philadelphian, *Urania* was published there. Lyon left shortly afterward, and ended as a respected pastor in Machias, Maine. No later music of his is extant, and he did not become Maine's foremost musician. That distinction fell to another — Supply Belcher, "the Handel of Maine," as he was called.

ii. Philanthropy

MUSIC IN PHILADELPHIA before the Revolution was largely a Hopkinson affair. Afterwards he was still around as a patron, but music-making was now in the hands of various professionals, mostly English, who settled in the city when the war was over and for half a century made of Philadelphia a neat, pretty provincial center of British musical taste, with emphasis on the ballad opera, Anglican church music and the works of Handel and Haydn. Philadelphia was, during that period, the chief musical metropolis of the country, especially when it was the capital, and had a well-rounded, sober, indigenous Anglo-American musical culture not matched elsewhere in America. Well-rounded, but definitely stuffy.

There were many professional musicians involved in this little

Philadelphia musical flowering, but chief of them were Alexander Reinagle, an Austro-Englishman, who worked in Philadelphia from 1786 to 1800, his teacher but contemporary, Raynor Taylor, who outlived his pupil by many years, and Benjamin Carr (1768–1831) a younger man who was called, if not Handel, at least the Haydn of Philadelphia (every musician apparently had to be one or the other). These men became, like Sully, whom Carr in particular resembles, thoroughly identified with the city, and turned their hands to any musical ventures that came along. They all composed.

Reinagle began by running a series called the "City Concerts" which as early as 1783 had given Philadelphia high-minded chamber music. He then went on to found and direct the music of the new Chestnut Street Theatre. Little of his "popular music" for ballad operas remains, but a set of piano sonatas in the style of his good friend and correspondent "the Great Bach" exists — not Johann Sebastian, but his then much more famous son Karl Philip Emmanuel.

Taylor, Reinagle's teacher, was the organist of St. Peter's Episcopal Church and famous both as an improvisor and as a musical clown. His take-offs on Italian opera were considered to be a scream. He was associated with Carr in the foundation of that English period's most typical institution, the Musical Fund Society.

Carr was also an all-around musician, a church organist and choir director, a conductor and a composer for theater orchestras, a pianist, a singer, a successful publisher and editor of a magazine, first of its kind in America, called the *Musical Journal* — in fact, the Bernstein of his day, except that any competent musician then was expected to be as versatile. Carr left a good deal of music, now unperformed, about which one is curious; he was the most proficient composer active in America in his period, and perhaps the first really serious professional one.

The Musical Fund Society (1820) was, like the PSFS, a child of benevolence. Unlike the PSFS, it was also the child of the

Muses. Carr knew his Philadelphians well enough to know that just plain music wasn't enough. What was needed was philanthropy, and a *board.* It was the ingenious thought of combining concerts and good works that made of the Fund Philadelphia's most enduring institution, though not, however, F. or O. or F.B.F. Charleston's St. Cecelia was originally musical (1762) and Boston's famous Handel and Haydn Society beat out the M.F.S. by five years (1815).

A group of music lovers, notably Dr. William De Wees, Dr. Robert Patterson and John Kintzing Kane, all of the Philosophical Society (Patterson and Kane were Presidents), had the habit of meeting in each other's houses to listen to string quartets. The quartet gradually grew into a larger ensemble that rehearsed in Sully's painting gallery near 5th and Chestnut, and the idea arose that it might be well to keep the group together and give public concerts. But how? Auditors and performers held a meeting and decided that Philanthropy was the answer. The concerts could be given for the benefit of "decayed Musicians." The society was organized, with officers, a board of twelve managers and with eighty-five members.

The aim of the Society was also to perform the works of Handel and Haydn, but it took several years before they could muster up enough courage and performers. The first concert of 1821 was pretty miscellaneous, but in 1822 a grand presentation of *The Creation* established the Fund as Philadelphia's foremost musical organization. Up to a hundred musicians took part, the trombonists were brought all the way down from Bethlehem, and Mrs. French, a pupil of Carr's, brought down the house. (The lady, in fact, on another occasion literally brought down the house when the ceiling of the hall where she was singing collapsed.) Nearly two thousand people turned out for the concert and, as a cautious Philadelphian critic put it, they "appeared to be more pleased than it was expected they would be."

The Society went on to do *The Messiah* and Handel's *Dettingen Te Deum,* and made so much money that they decided to build a hall. It was, and is, located at Locust and 8th, out in the sticks then, down in the slums now, and the Society gave their first concert there in 1824. It was a handsome building in the rather severe style of William Strickland, and until the opening of the Academy of Music in 1857, nearly every important concert, opera and public meeting took place there. The building paid for itself in no time, and the Society's annual concerts remained "the thing."

Membership in the Society and on the board was "the thing" too. About half were musicians and half were Old Philadelphians. The musical board members included of course Carr and Taylor, Reinagle's nephew George Schetky and early members of the Cross family. The plain membership however, from 1820 to 1858, consisted of the same Old Philadelphians who belonged to all the other institutions of that Silver Age of institutions: Nicholas Biddle, Horace Binney, Samuel Vaughn Merrick and anyone else you care to mention from Bayard to Zantzinger. Sidney Fisher belonged as well as naughty Pierce Butler (he played the flute). There was a Drinker then as there is a Drinker now; six Pattersons belonged all told, and of course four Hopkinsons. The only expected name in fact that's absent is Ingersoll. In all these Philadelphia memberships one always notices at least one name that is specially associated and one name that is conspicuously missing; in this case Patterson, and Ingersoll. Biddles are universal.

Though the Society's concerts were "the thing" for nearly forty years, with the deaths of Taylor and Carr, the day of the gentleman musician of British tastes and training, of the competent local composer who drew inspiration from Handel and Haydn, was over. Madame Malibran, first of the visiting divas and precursor of that wave of Italian melody which was to intoxicate the populace, appeared, a warning sympton, in 1827. Mr. and Mrs. Wood, for years the leading local operatic favorites, gave a performance in 1835 of Bellini's new opera *La Sonnambula* and that was the end of the popularity of the old English ballad operas

like *The Beggar's Opera* and *Love in a Village*, which had been
Philadelphia's musical fare all through the reigns of Reinagle and
Carr. Opera, real Italian Grand Opera, struck the city and swept
all before it.

iii. The Academy

FROM 1830 and on after the Civil War, the record of music in
Philadelphia is just one long superlative of sensations — prima
donnas, the Jenny Linds and Adelina Pattis,* Madame Sontags
and twenty others, each the "world's greatest singer" of her particular year. At first they appeared in Musical Fund Hall, though
they had precious little to do with the Society, but the Hall was
not suited to grand opera, not big enough. In 1857 a new hall,
specifically designed for opera, was opened and called the Academy of Music. It had, and has, red plush, boxes, gilt, paintings
on the ceiling, a large stage and perfect acoustics. Old Philadelphia lost interest in the Musical Fund orchestra and their old
Haydn and Handel. The orchestra was given up in 1857, and the
Society did nothing much of interest until the end of the nineteenth century saw the beginnings of a revival. Nowadays it is
active in a quiet way, still presents concerts for the benefit of
decayed musicians, and still has a board and membership of the
best people, but scarcely dominates the Philadelphia scene, either
musically or socially, as it once did.

The Hall itself exists too, but no longer as a concert hall.
After a rather humorous "Jenny Lind" centennial concert in
1920, with the musicians in costume and Henry Drinker playing
the part of P. T. Barnum, Jenny's manager, the Hall relapsed
into silence, and before the Second World War was sold to a
tobacco wholesaler. A hideous brown façade had been tacked
onto it in 1891, and the surroundings remain slums, but the shell
is still there. Philadelphia does desperately need a good small
public chamber music auditorium, and perhaps with the re-

* Patti gave her first coloratura concert in Philadelphia when she was only seven!

development of Society Hill and the area around Washington Square, Musical Fund Hill could be restored and made to sound again.

Its successful rival, the Academy of Music, despite its disreputable exterior, is in fine shape. It remains the oldest large concert hall still in use as such in America, and the handsomest. It is Philadelphia's musical center, and one of its civic prides, and is classed by Philadelphians along with the State House as an historical monument and an architectural gem (inside). Its acoustics are famous, and are generally ascribed to the fact that it was modeled by architect Napoleon Le Brun on Milan's La Scala, and that it was "seasoned" — that is, the shell was allowed to stand for a year in the weather without a roof, so that no shrinkage or dampness or dryness has ever bothered the Old Lady of Locust Street since.

The quarter of a million dollars required to build was raised by a board which included a George Pepper and Fairman Rogers, of coach-and-four fame, and shares were sold. The shareholders had certain hereditary rights to seats, and to be a shareholder of the Academy became one of the marks of Philadelphia prestige. Eventually the largest of these shareholders was John Frederick Lewis, Sr., autocrat of the Pennsylvania Academy of the Fine Arts, who evidently liked to collect Academies. He virtually owned it. Unfortunately, Lewis's sons, who inherited the Academy, didn't care for music — a Philadelphia sort of paradox. They kept it up for years out of a sense of duty, losing twenty-five thousand dollars a year or so on it, but the Old Lady was getting a bit shabby. Eventually the Philadelphia Orchestra bought it, the city waived its taxes, and it is now managed by an Association, with a board and committees and all the usual Philadelphia paraphernalia. They even give a party; not a dinner, but a ball, a benefit affair following a special concert, which in the few years of its existence has become one of the great social events of the season.

Thanks to the proceeds, the interior of the Academy is all prettied up, and after enough Balls, perhaps something can even be done to the exterior, which looks like a deserted brewery. It remains the permanent home of the Philadelphia Orchestra, and was that of the Metropolitan Opera for many years on its Philadelphia visits. Its walls are studded with plaques memorial to older Philadelphian musicians, most of them now forgotten, and to patrons. It even has a legendary bat, which has struck terror into the hearts of old ladies who remember it, or its ancestor, from the days of their youth. They are really quite fond of it; it is a part of the Academy's tradition.

The period of Italian opera in Philadelphia managed to produce another Philadelphia musical first. William Henry Fry's opera *Leonora*, produced in Philadelphia in 1845, was the first real genuine grand opera written by a real genuine native American to be really genuinely performed in America. Fry was the son of a well-to-do and respectable, if not exactly Old Philadelphian, newspaper publisher. Encouraged at home in both music and literature, he began to write orchestral overtures as a boy, and composed an opera called *Aurelia*, set to a libretto by one of his brothers, Joseph. It was never produced, but *Leonora*, with a libretto also by Joseph, was; though Fry had to pay for it himself, which he seems to have been able to afford to do. In 1840 he launched a widely acclaimed American premiere of Bellini's *Norma*. His own *Leonora* was considered to bear only too much resemblance to *Norma*, but it ran nearly two weeks (in English), and was presented in 1858 in New York (in Italian). Fry also wrote four symphonies with "programs" — *Childe Harold, A Day in the Country, Hagar* and a *Santa Claus Symphony* — all of which were performed, as well as a tone poem called *Niagara*. He had big ideas. His last work was another opera, *Esmeralda*, also produced in Philadelphia, after his death.

Fry was actually a musical amateur, but he was a professional journalist. In 1844, for instance, he was the editor of the Philadelphia *Ledger*. In 1846 he went to Europe as a correspondent for the New York *Tribune* and there became a friend of Berlioz and other famous people. When he returned he settled in New York as a music critic for the *Tribune*, and became famous as a lecturer on what is now called "Music Appreciation." He was a forthright, not to say violent, champion of American music. Unfortunately his own works were better known for their length and Italianism than for their Americanism, and he is remembered now chiefly for his firstness, his journalism and his Americanism. A curious figure, apt product of the Italian Age of Philadelphia music, he also reminds one of Boker; but Boker showed a real mastery of his foreign forms, whereas Fry evidently did not. He died, like Boker a somewhat disappointed man, as a diplomat in the West Indies in 1864.

iv. Brown Velvet

THE GERMAN INFLUENCE which dominated Philadelphia after the Civil War was also an imported, not a domestic one. The old Wissahickon and Moravian "Pennsylvania Dutch" music had long been forgotten. It was the new German music of Mendelssohn, brought over by the émigrés of 1848, along with lager beer, the Turnverein and funny German accents, that began to rival the Italian prima donna for favor, and introduced the symphony orchestra, the male chorus and Wagner as substitutes. The rivalry continues right down to the present; but Philadelphia's important musical institutions of the post–Civil War period were definitely founded under German influences.

It all began, appropriately enough, in 1848, when a traveling Germania Orchestra struck town and was ignored. Nobody wanted to hear all that awful cold intellectual Mendelssohn when they could hear *Norma*. Evenutally the Germania Orchestra disbanded, scattering its musicians all over the country, like spores. Some settled in Philadelphia, and in 1856 they had sufficiently recovered to start a new Germania Orchestra of their own in Philadelphia, thus taking over just as the Musical Fund's Orchestra stopped, and presumably with some of the same performers. The Germania lasted till 1895, many of the Germania players then being absorbed into the picturesquely named Thunder

Orchestra (the conductor was Henry G. Thunder). All Thunder's men were taken into the Philadelphia Orchestra when it was organized in 1900; a handful of them were still in it as late as 1940, so that the Germania Orchestra was very definitely the ancestor of the Philadelphia Orchestra. Philadelphia in other words has not been without a resident symphonic group since 1820, when the Musical Fund Society started. (Fund, Germania, Thunder, Philadelphia).

The male chorus club was another especially German institution, and dozens of these were started in the 1840's and 1850's. A Männerchor was founded, in fact, as early as 1835, and lived to celebrate its centenary, as the oldest German singing group in America, there was also a Jünger Männerchor (1850), the Arion Singing Society (1854) and the Harmonie (1855). A later such group was the Abt Male Chorus, named after a prolific and once popular German choral composer. In 1872 the conductor of the Abt, Michael Cross (*not* a German) led the group in a performance of Vogel's "Walz." The words of this so shocked the Board that "serious differences" with the conductor resulted, and Cross resigned to found his own chorus, taking five members of the Abt with him. Another Philadelphia schism. His new chorus was called the Orpheus Club, and though the Abt has gone, the Orpheus is still very much with us, and is Old Philadelphia's principal amateur glee club.

The Orchestra and the Orpheus are then the two surviving monuments of the German Period, and are unrivaled in prestige today in their very different fields. Their German origin is quite clear.

Despite all this foreign influence there was a curious revival of native-born Philadelphia music during the Iron Age, after the Civil War, before the First World War. Its principal figures were all Philadelphia-born musician sons of Philadelphia-settled musician fathers, and despite the generally German tone of their musical activities, they were all of British stock. Like Carr and his contemporaries, they were competent at almost anything musical, but unlike Carr they eschewed "ballad opera," which had by this time become "operetta," and was no longer quite respectable. These musical gentlemen were nothing if not respectable.

Their names were Cross, Jarvis, à Becket and Thunder, all active and prominent locally in two, or even more, generations. Michael Cross, besides directing the Orpheus, was a fine pianist, organist and chamber music performer. His Philadelphia-born father Benjamin had been the last conductor of the Fund's orchestra, after the death of his teacher, Benjamin Carr. The Jarvises, father and son, were pianists too, and Charles Jr. rivaled Cross as a chamber-music man with his Classical Soirees which took place for thirty years over a swimming tank, in the Natatorium, where Elizabeth Pennell's august Dancing Classes (that "always have been") were also held. Henry G. Thunder, who conducted the Thunder Orchestra, was the son of a musician, brother of another — all Irish and organists. The à Beckets were English and pianists. Both Thomas Sr. and Thomas Jr. played the accompaniments for the Orpheus, and in addition Thomas Jr. ran the music at Girard College for forty-five years.

None of these men shook the earth, even when alive, but they are examples of the tradition of quiet competence and versatility that persisted as a legacy of the English period. Like their predecessors, they were also "gentlemen" socially, though naturally not In Society, or considered really Old Philadelphian. However, all musical Old Philadelphians knew them and studied with them and patronized them as their fathers had known and patronized their fathers. Music in Philadelphia, despite Italy and Germany, remained, in other words, still pretty much a family affair.

Into the ranks of these natives were adopted a few talented outsiders. There was David Wood, a blind organist, and one of the greatest exponents of Bach of his time. He was the teacher and main inspiration of J. F. Wolle, who made famous the Bach Festival at Bethlehem. Hugh Clarke has the distinction of being, along with Paine of Harvard, the first collegiate professor of music in the United States (both from 1875). He was still teaching at the University of Pennsylvania and conducting at eighty. His pupil William Gilchrist (1838–1916) was Philadelphia's foremost composer during that period. He is best remembered for winning prizes. He played tennis and cricket and even studied law, so that he was almost considered a Philadelphian, although born in Jersey City Like most American compositions of this time his are dismissed as "genteel" and "academic," and his symphony, his chamber music, his songs and choruses are never performed. Philadelphia seems not to have shown much posthumous interest in its foremost late-nineteenth-century composer.

By the 'nineties Philadelphia was something of a provincial musical backwater. It was behind the times particularly in the matters of orchestras. London had had its Philharmonic since 1813, New York hers since 1842. The Boston Symphony was created, as by the wave of a wand, by Colonel Higginson in 1881. Theodore Thomas, after a life of heartbreak, some of it in Philadelphia, had finally arrived in Chicago and started a symphony there in 1891. Cincinnati had just started one too. People began to feel that Philadelphia should have a really first-class band of its own. The Thunder group wasn't enough. Local pride began to smart.

Various attempts were made to get Thomas or Damrosch to come, but nothing worked. Finally, however, a conductor was found, a board was formed, money was raised, and a "Philadelphia Orchestra" at last gave its first concert in the fall of 1900. The conductor was an earnest, high-minded, hard-working German martinet called Fritz Scheel. He had been discovered conducting an orchestra out at Woodside, an amusement park, and persuaded to stay in Philadelphia for a year as conductor of the amateur Philadelphia Symphony Society while a professional orchestra was gathered together for him.

The first thing to do, naturally, was to build up a board. A. J. Cassatt, Eckley B. Coxe, C. Hartman Kuhn, Clement Newbold, Thomas McKean, James W. Paul, and Mrs. F. H. Rosengarten were asked to serve on it, as well as William Elkins and P. A. B. Widener himself; Alexander Van Rensselaer was made president of it and remained so for years. Despite his New York name, he was, like Nicholas Roosevelt, very much a Philadelphian. He was with Drexel and Company and married to a Drexel, and his marble mansion on Rittenhouse Square, now the Penn Athletic Club, was one of Philadelphia's great social centers.

The board builders built well, and it still remains the best board, or one of them, though its job — to raise money — wasn't exactly easy, particularly at the beginning, since many of the boardsmen themselves had no interest in orchestral music. When Van Rensselaer was called on to be president, he laughed and laughed. He said he'd never heard a note of straight orchestral music in his life; opera of course, but. . . . He was president of the board till 1935 and is considered one of the principal Founders.

Fritz Scheel built up an efficient ensemble, the board collected enough money to get started, but nobody came to the concerts. There were often as few as six hundred subscribers in the roomy spaces of the old Academy. For a time it looked as if the Orchestra was done for —until the formation of a Women's Committee. Led by indomitable Miss Fanny Wister, sister of writer Owen, and namesake of her grandmother Fanny Kemble, the ladies saved the day, alerted not only the city but the surrounding regions, and since their organization in 1904 have done a lot to keep the Orchestra afloat. Miss Wister did not die till 1956, active to the end, and presided annually at a ritual presentation of a gold watch to any Orchestra player who had completed twenty-five years of service. Nobody has quite taken her place since, though Miss Gertrude Ely comes pretty close despite her "advantages" in "not being an Old Philadelphian."

Later on financial problems loomed again, but were solved for some time when an Anonymous Donor announced in 1916 that he'd pay the deficits for five years if the board would raise an endowment fund of half a million. They did and more. In 1920 the masked marvel was revealed as none other than Edward Bok, editor of the *Ladies' Home Journal*. By that time, however, the reputation of the Orchestra had been made not by Old Philadelphia but by the new conductor — Leopold Stokowski.

Scheel died of overwork in 1907. He was succeeded by a seemingly colorless German, Carl Pohlig, who kept the band in shape but did nothing to increase its prestige. In fact the Orchestra and Philadelphia both suffered a blow when Pohlig attempted a foray to New York in 1907 and the critics came down hard. The New York *World* said, "Provincial was writ large over the whole proceeding; and one felt tempted to inquire, why Herr Pohlig, why the Philadelphia Orchestra . . . at any rate in New York?" Philadelphia editorial writers seethed in print. "The smug self-sufficiency . . . of people who reside . . . on Manhattan Island is comical to witness. . . . We are above any need of the endorsement of . . . New York. . . . A spirit of selfish commercialism rules its affairs," etc. Pohlig had not done well as an ambassador and Philadelphia's cultural stock was certainly at a new low.

All this was altered when a young semi-Pole, then conducting in Cincinnati, was hired to replace Pohlig in 1912. It was Leopold Stokowski who made the Orchestra famous, who gave Philadelphia back its musical position, gone since the days of Carr, and who is the real founder of modern music in Philadelphia. In his personal flamboyance and belligerent approach to Philadelphia, he reminds one somewhat of his contemporary Fiske Kimball of the Art Museum; but he was far more glamorous and famous, a national figure in fact, rivaled only as "world's greatest conductor" by Toscanini of the New York Philharmonic and Koussevitzky of Boston. The three of them established the conductor, in America at least, as a figure of romance and temperament equal to the operatic diva, and fixed the symphony orchestra in favor as the biggest expression of American musicality. In 1912 "serious music" for most Americans meant Caruso and Opera. By 1960 for most of them it meant the local symphony orchestra and its soloists.

Stokowski was born, according to legend, as Stokes, an accident easily remedied later on; and not in Warsaw but in London. Though his mother was Irish, his father was a legitimate enough Pole; to adopt a vaguely international accent was no throuble at all at all for his Oxford-educated son. Leopold wore his golden curls in an un-English halo and capitalized on a svelte back and expressive hands by conducting without a baton. He was poetry itself. He also was a conductor who could extract the most lush and luminous sounds from his already thoroughly disciplined Philadelphia instrument; and he was a genius, like Wanamaker, at publicity.

He succeeded where Pohlig failed; he conquered New York. In 1916 he held up the reluctant board of the Orchestra for $14,000 to put on an American premiere of Mahler's enormous, mushy, mystical Eighth Symphony, "Symphony of a Thousand," which requires not only an augmented orchestra but seven soloists, who sing the parts of Una Poenitentium, Mulier Samaritans, Pater Ecstaticus and other somewhat curiously sinister Faustian characters, as well as three separate choruses, one of them of children's voices. All Stokowski needed was chariots.

Excited rumor in Philadelphia had sold every seat in the Academy two weeks in advance. Dozens of musical celebrities came down from New York to fill the boxes. Fifteen minutes before the concert started, a fanfare of horns in the lobby drove the customers to their seats after the manner of the Wagner performances at Bayreuth, and there stood the great chorus, all 958 singers banked twenty-four tiers high, with the Orchestra at their feet. After the concert the whole house stood up, whistling, cheering, clapping; Mr. Van Rensselaer presented a wreath — and the New York visitors took note. The whole kit and kaboodle, well over a thousand strong, was then shipped to New York, where before another packed house and such celebrities as Paderewski, Casals, Alma Gluck, Mischa Elman and Fritz Kreisler, Stokowski repeated his triumph.

From then on until he left in 1936, Stokowski had Philadelphia where he wanted it; under foot. He bullied and posed and experimented and scolded and pronounced, and despite considerable outrage, Philadelphians, especially Philadelphia women, loved it. He was just the way a musician should be, beautiful, temperamental, scandalous, colorful. And, of course, a good musician. Gunther quotes a Philadelphian at dinner as saying, "The trouble with Stokowski is that he *is* a damned good musician." Even those, especially Philadelphia men, who found his phony accent, golden curls and swooning hands hard to take, had to admit it. He made many transcriptions of Bach organ works, now considered a somewhat dubious musical practice. He introduced many dissonant novelties, most of them now forgotten, kept moving the choirs of the orchestra about, and on several occasions doused all the lights so that the men played in the dark with little lamps fastened to their desks, while a Pentecostal spotlight played on the Leader himself. All these things were not only good publicity (like the reforms of Wanamaker and Bok), they also served to keep the audience in a state of expectant turmoil. What would happen next? When old ladies stomped out in protest against Modern Music, he scolded them from the podium. Sometimes they scolded back. After one of his tirades a dowager countered, "Young man, you're hired to lead the band. Play on!" The result was not only a pleasurable excitement at the time, but in the end a thoroughly devoted, not to say cowed, public, which will take stuff that makes older New York Philharmonic subscribers rattle their jets and thump their canes. A wistful remark during intermissions to the effect of "Why do we have to listen to that when there's so much beautiful music in the world?" is about as far as Philadelphians dare go, even to this day.

Stokowski's real contribution, besides the devoted local following was the special tone color he gave to the Orchestra, most often described as "rich, lush, opulent." Many, especially those who don't know Philadelphia, are inclined to consider this Philadelphia quality an anomaly in what they think of as a drab Quaker town. But the critic-composer Virgil Thomson, comparing the "tone" of say Boston and Philadelphia, writes:

Boston is tougher, more independent. Nothing ever happens that isn't clear. The Philadelphia sonorities are less transparent . . . rounder and deeper and more human. They have a tactile quality too, like a skin you might touch . . . Nowhere else is there such a string choir, one would like to stroke its tone . . . like pinky brown velvet.

Locale is as important in creating this tone as the nationality of the respective conductors, he says, and contrasts "Boston, the intellectually elegant and urbane" with "Philadelphia, where everything, even intellectual achievement and moral pride, turns into luxury, into a sort of sensuous awareness of social differences."* The rich silks of eighteenth-century Quakeresses, the rich minks of modern Main Line matrons, the very "pinky brown velvet" in which the lushest of Philadelphia drawing rooms are still upholstered (one thinks of the "rich fawn-colored stuff" admired by Sidney Fisher in the Hutchinson house parlor) — this is the rather feminine Philadelphia which Thomson sees reflected in Philadelphia's Orchestra.

As for Stokowski himself, he has become a legend of his own, quite apart from Philadelphia and its Orchestra; but, as in the case of a good many other people, it was only during his Philadelphia stay that he achieved a proper balance between flair and solid achievement. Since he left, his career has been first an increasingly Hollywood story of movie-making, the fabulous lapses of taste of the Walt Disney *Fantasia*, in which, of course, the orchestra was also involved, the odd peripatetic romance with Greta Garbo; and then a sort of decline into "Youth Orchestras" and guest conductorships. But then and now he made and makes good copy.

His successor Eugene Ormandy is a very different sort of person and conductor. Having celebrated in 1961 his twenty-fifth anniversary on the Philadelphia podium, he remains a short, dynamic, bouncy, cheerful man, full of energy and good humor. Despite an easily felt force of character, there is nothing of the prima donna or poseur about him. Where Stokowski was striking,

* The Kennedys versus the Kellys?

Ormandy is confident. He has taken the legacy of Scheel's soundness and Stokowski's brilliance and added to it a stylishness of his own. Philadelphians are generally content in the assurance that under him their Orchestra is the "greatest in the world."

Philadelphians subscribe en masse and in three different groups. Most Old Philadelphian is the Friday afternoon, obligatory for matrons. These matrons differ from the similar Friday afternoon matrons of the Philharmonic in their chummy homogeneousness and general tweediness, and from the equally tweedy Boston Friday group in their less obvious "character." The Philadelphia ladies maintain a curious look of having dropped their trowels in the flower bed and just made the Paoli Local (where they forgot their glasses). They are all awfully glad to see each other again at intermission, having all just had lunch with each other at the Acorn Club. Saturday night is intellectual, students and young musicians upstairs, Jewish society downstairs. A few Old Philadelphia ladies used to cling to their Saturday night seats in memory of days when Saturday night was the right night; but now Nobody goes. Monday night has become the night for Old Philadelphian connoisseurs, and is when Old Philadelphia men go, scorning Friday as being much too garden club. It is on Monday that one sees the male members of the musical boards and the doctors and lawyers and professors who make up a sizable chunk of Philadelphia's music-loving population. There is also a new Thursday night, quasi-rehearsal series, which does not yet seem to have developed its special cachet. Philadelphians don't push and shove to get in to Ormandy as New Yorkers now push and shove to get in to Bernstein and Lincoln Center; but they are faithful, and like the Academy, the Orchestra is one of the pillars of Philadelphia and Old Philadelphia pride.

The Orchestra is par excellence *the* Philadelphia musical institution; but the special product of the Modern Period in Philadelphia's music is the Curtis Institute, which ranks with Juilliard and Eastman at the top of American conservatories. It was founded in 1924 by Mary Louise Curtis Bok, and is housed on Rittenhouse Square at Locust Street in the former George

William Childs Drexel mansion. It is an endowed scholarship affair and its pupils are chosen from the most talented applicants. Probably more than any other single institution it has maintained Philadelphia's reputation as a serious musical city, though neither its graduates nor its teachers are Old Philadelphians, with, however a few exceptions here too. Its most famous resident teacher is probably the pianist Rudolf Serkin. The former Mrs. Bok married Efrem Zimbalist, violin virtuoso, once married to singer Alma Gluck, and between them they act as Queen and Consort of the Curtis. It is said that at concerts there one waits for the Zimbalists to clap first. What with the memory of Bok's subsidy of the Orchestra and Mrs. Bok's of the Curtis Institute and her gift of the magnificent new organ to the Academy, the ghost of Hermann Kotzschmar has been kind to Philadelphia music: indirectly anyway.

CHAPTER

3

i. Opera

ALL THIS "abstract" music is very well, but far more dear to the Philadelphia music lover's heart has always been the human voice on stage. Until recently Philadelphia has always managed to support a fuller season of Metropolitan Opera visits than any other American city, as well as two rival opera companies of its own. But essentially the story of opera in Philadelphia and Old Philadelphia is one of significant failure; in particular the failure to establish a permanent resident opera company all its own.

The reason is quite simple: the continual success of visiting companies. After the days of Reinagle and Carr, who composed their own "operas," Philadelphia never again produced a real school of native song. Potential composers like Fry never had a chance against Bellini, and local companies never had a chance against the Metropolitan. Philadelphia has heard the best singers in the best operas for the past century and a quarter, and upperclass Philadelphians have been able to chat about opera at dinner tables with the best of them. There has, since 1930, always been opera in Philadelphia; never Philadelphia opera.

The operatic staples, all during the nineteenth century, were *Norma*, introduced by Fry, *La Sonnambula*, *Ernani*, *Lucia* and then, as they came along, *Trovatore*, *Traviata*, *Rigoletto* and at last *Aïda*. *Don Giovanni* and *Fidelio*, *La Serva Padrona* and a few other older operas survived. *Der Freischütz* (as early as 1827, in French) was about the only German piece in the repertoire, but French operas were only somewhat less popular than Italian

[477]

operas, as the century moved along, starting with *La Juive* and *Les Huguenots* and culminating in *Faust*. The English composer Balfe, with his *Bohemian Girl* and others, had his constant admirers. Nothing Russian; and, of course, nothing American. Though Fry's *Leonora* and *Esmeralda* never became fixtures in the repertoire, it is a distinction of sorts that at least one Philadelphia composer did manage to squeeze in performances of two of his works among the innumerable renditions of *Norma* and *Faust*.

It must be remembered that at the beginning especially, these were all brand-new operas, hot off the Italian and French griddles. Philadelphia heard Bellini and Verdi and Meyerbeer very soon after the premieres abroad. From half a dozen operas a year presented in the 1830's to almost weekly performances during the winters of the 1870's and 1880's, there is a steady increase in number and also a steady hardening of the programs into more or less the "standard repertory" of today. All this is really quite impressive, especially when one considers that there was no local company, no municipal support or grand-scale patronage. Opera in Philadelphia has always depended on just plain box-office, plus a modest amount of backing.

The Metropolitan Opera Company, founded in New York in 1883, began its Philadelphia tours in 1885. This finally sealed the fate of any possible competing local rival. New York was too close, and in those days the Metropolitan too generous. For many years, up to 1930 in fact, they gave weekly performances in season, sometimes as many as twenty-five operas a year. No one could survive that sort of competition from the world's most expensive operatic troupe. It's surprising that so many tried, and still try.

Most spectacular of these tries was that of the Oscar Hammerstein company in 1908. Hammerstein built an enormous theatre way up North on Broad Street. He named it, just to confuse everybody, the "Metropolitan Opera House." He opened with *Carmen* and gave Philadelphia four operas a week for a twenty-week season during two winters, 1908–9, 1909–10, years which marked the floodtide of opera in Philadelphia. During these

years there were as many as a hundred and twenty opera produc-
tions a year, of one kind or another, Hammerstein, Metropolitan
or local; four continuous months of singing. It gives one pause;
and let's incidentally hear no more about the "innate unmusi-
cality" of the American public, or "opera is an exotic" or anything else of that sort. All this opera was supported by ticket-
buyers.

The new Hammerstein opera house, a direct challenge to the
Old Academy of Music and the commuting company of the
Metropolitan, was a magnificent affair. There were boxes for the
elite and a special foyer for them, and there was room for four
thousand downstairs and in the single balcony above. There was
only one thing wrong with it; it was north of Market. Cartoonists
of the times had a field day, picturing Old Philadelphians leaving
Rittenhouse Square in sleds, bundled in furs as for a trip to the
North Pole, with weeping relatives and servants saying farewell
forever as they set out for Hammerstein's opera house. The cartoonists were right, in fact. Hammerstein's attempt at a resident
company with rotating national stars failed. For fifteen years
after his company evacuated the opera house, the Metropolitan
gave its performances there, and Old Philadelphia religiously
traipsed to the North Pole. At last in 1925 the Met returned
to the Academy, where it belonged.

Hammerstein's grand theatre gradually declined, and now
houses Negro evangelists; the Met's Philadelphia performances
too have declined, in frequency. Each year they have given fewer
and fewer. In 1960–61 they gave only six, and announced at
the end of the season that they wouldn't come the next year at
all. This is the end (perhaps only temporary) of a long association; but one that has now left Philadelphia high and dry, without a socially respectable program of opera. For years the first
night of the Met in Philadelphia has been as much a social celebration as the first night of the Met in New York. Of late years
in fact a great deal more socially significant. Real people still
turn out for the Philadelphia first night, as opposed to the largely
synthetic "celebrities," models, clothes designers and entrepren-

eurs that now catch the photographer's eye in New York. The Met's last First Night of 1960 was a poor one, hampered by rain, but it was Ingersolls and others in jewels and white tie that braved the storm to celebrate the seventy-sixth, and last, anniversary of one of Philadelphia's great social traditions. What now?

Only the Met has been able to capture permanently the vital support of Old Philadelphia and of society. But there *are* local companies, despite the fact that "Nobody goes," which keep afloat and often present very good opera. They tend to be a bit timid in their repertoire, but encourage local talent, of which there is a lot, mostly Italian. The two present companies are the Philadelphia Grand Opera Company, up to now conducted by Maestro Giuseppe Bamboschek, and the Philadelphia Lyric Opera Company. Both of these give about a dozen performances a year, largely Italian works, and belong generally to what in New York used to be called the "spumoni circuit" — opera produced largely for and by Italian–Americans for their own delight, and more or less shunned by the Diamond Horseshoe crowd. Opinions as to which of the two Philadelphia companies is better vary. Bamboschek was generally regarded as one of opera's most competent conductors, once assistant to Toscanini. The rival company, run by Signor Fabiani, a concert promoter, gets bigger stars. Passions run high among the rivals; stilettos, plots and character assassination are the order of the day and each group would cheerfully cut the others' throats. Such local stars as the beautiful young Anna Moffo of Wayne appear with the Philadelphia Grand Opera or the Lyric, to great acclaim; and all the Old Philadelphians, though Max de Schauensee scolds them regularly in his column in the *Bulletin,* stay away. To them "opera" has meant the Met and nothing but the Met for years. That's where they saw their friends, and no amount of mere good music will get them to an opera under any other conditions.*

Philadelphia's long tradition of operatic sophistication is represented today in various odd ways. De Schauensee, the *Bulletin* music critic, is one of America's foremost opera experts, and has

* See Appendix.

often been heard during the intermissions of the Metropolitan broadcasts on the Opera Quiz. Samuel Barber and Gian Carlo Menotti, both important opera composers, are Curtis graduates and more or less local boys. Yet in Philadelphia, a city whose culture, led always by the somewhat suspect passion of the upper classes for the operatic form, has been saturated with vocal music for a century, to a greater degree than any other American city except New York itself, opera has remained a spoiled foreign visitor, not a citizen.

ii. Why, Why?

OPERA HAS, however, had one indirect effect upon the city; Philadelphia, even Old Philadelphia, has produced singers of a somewhat bewildering variety. Most famous of these was David Scull Bispham. George Tucker Bispham, one of the last of the nineteenth-century Chancellors of the Law Association, has been mentioned. (Bisphams married McKeans, McKeans married Whartons, Whartons married Peppers, Peppers married Norrises, Norrises married Logans, Logans married Fishers, Fishers married Ingersolls, Ingersolls married Bullitts, Bullitts married Horwitzes, Horwitzes married Grosses, Stop! Stop! Catherine Drinker Bowen's late husband was Thomas McKean Downs, Henry Drinker's wife is a Hutchinson, Rhoda Morris's last husband was a Hutchinson, her first was a George Clymer Brooke. . . .) David Scull Bispham was of the same family as George Tucker Bispham (Sculls married Biddles, Biddles married Biddles married Biddles married . . .), but David's family were strict "dry" Quakers who lived on Arch Street.

For all the grave disadvantages of his background, David Bispham eventually became the greatest Wagnerian baritone of his time, and after success in London and on the Continent, was even asked to the Metropolitan; the first American male singer to receive that accolade, always reserved then exclusively for foreigners. He was not only the first Quaker opera star, and the first American man at the Met; he was also probably the first singer to go into opera at the behest of a ouija board. At the time he received this directive, he had already appeared in concerts and comic opera in London, but had made no serious artistic impression. He could not make up his mind whether he should confine himself to concert and oratorio, or go against his Quaker mother's wishes and into opera. In London he had met a Swede, the Baron Rudbeck, who was supposed to have "powers." One evening in Bispham's presence Rudbeck sat at a table in front of a great sheet of paper with a "planchette" and attached pencil under his hands. Almost immediately, although no one had spoken, and no questions had been asked, the planchette wrote in large letters, "Opera, by all means." Bispham of course realized that this was addressed to him, and he asked, "What operas shall I study?" "The operas of Verdi and Wagner." "Which of these operas?" "*Aïda, Tannhäuser, Tristan* and *Meistersinger.*" "What roles?" "Amonasro, Wolfram, Kurwenal and Beckmesser." "When shall I be engaged?" "In a couple of months you will know."

Bispham was far from being convinced, but he decided to take no chances and for two months slaved at these four difficult roles. A "couple of months" after the séance he gave a concert of Wagnerian music at a private house. Sir Augustus Harris, impresario of opera at Covent Garden, was one of the guests. He was so struck with Bispham's singing that he engaged him immediately to take the part of Beckmesser in a forthcoming performance of *Meistersinger.* One of the stars however caught cold, the performance was put off, and Bispham was asked if he could, with no further preparation, switch to the role of Kurwenal in *Tristan.* He could. With one day's notice he made his operatic debut, and from then on was recognized as one of the great Wagnerian baritones. His chances to sing Amonasro and Wolfram came soon enough afterward. Incidentally, all these roles, even the Wagnerian ones, were sung in England in Italian, a policy of Covent Garden in those days which Bispham himself was one of the first to fight against, with eventual success.

Bispham is the only genuine Old Philadelphian to achieve real renown as a singer, in fact probably the only male Old American anything to be a first-class operatic performer. There have been however dozens of Philadelphia-born singers; especially Marian Anderson. A television show about her has even been dubbed "The Lady from Philadelphia." She is probably the most famous native citizen of Philadelphia in this century, and she has, partly perhaps on account of her troubles in Washington with the Daughters of the Revolution, become a, almost *the,* symbol of the serious Negro artist, and as such a member of that hagiocracy, the P.H.B. or Professional Human Beings, of modern saints which includes Helen Keller and Albert Schweitzer. She had no connections with Old Philadelphia, even as patrons, on the way up, though she has been met and recognized by Old Philadelphians in her later triumphant years.

Miss Anderson is far from being the only South Philadelphian to sing her way to fame; in fact South Philadelphia, that red-brick monotony ranging from the desperate Negro bandbox slums near Lombard Street, just below Old Philadelphia's last thin red line on Pine Street, down into increasing Italian respectability, has become a veritable hotbed of warblers. These flock in two species, large Negro women with powerful voices and personalities à la Anderson, such as Dorothy Maynor, who was patronized by Old Philadelphia in the persons of the late Miss Winsors, and Ethel Waters; and bushy-haired boys, usually Italian.

As a specialist journal called *Teen* puts it (September, 1960), "Why? Why is Philly * such a talent-teeming town which seems to breed more pop personalities per square mile than any place in the world?" First of these pop personalities were Mario Lanza and Eddie Fisher, who began their careers back in the 'forties and 'fifties when the readers of *Teen* were babes. More recently there have been a Fabian, a Frankie Avalon, a Bobby Rydell who sings and a Jimmy Darren (not to be confused with a Bobby Darin) who acts. Fabian, now almost grown-up, was once a real-life sixteen-year-old called Fabiano Forte, spotted lounging around

* In Philadelphia itself "Philly" has much the same lack of status that "Frisco" has in San Francisco, or "Saint Looie" in St. Louis.

the streets by a hep manager who said to himself, "That boy looks like a teen-age idol." Overnight the renamed Fabian stampeded them at the Steel Pier in Atlantic City, and fans everywhere have tried to tear the clothes off him. Jimmy Darren (Ercolani) and Bobby Rydell (Ridarelli) and Frankie Avalon (Avallone), all pals, neighbors and high-school contemporaries of "Fabe's," have also rocketed into international fame, familiar to billions from Calcutta to Moscow and back round again. Few Philadelphians of any kind, even Franklin, have ever been so famous. Most startling newcomer to these ranks is the non-Italian Chubby Checker (Ernest Evans), who popularized the Twist. Yes, the Twist too comes from South Philadelphia. Shades of William Penn!

But we were talking about Old Philadelphia; and if the American Philosophical Society, say, or the Directors of the Library Company ever run into Fabian or vice versa, one would indeed be surprised. However an answer to the question "Why? Why is Philly such a talent-teeming town?" probably is: opera. All this frenzy of vocalism in modern times is the oddest offshoot of Philadelphia's long devotion to bel canto. It has, in this generation of Italian–Americans, certainly changed into something rich and strange.

The South Philadelphia singers are not the only ones today to make money off music in Philadelphia. Don't forget that the Victor Talking Machine Company still exists across the river in Camden, now the R.C.A. Victor Corporation. Theodore Presser and Philco Radio prosper, as did once Atwater Kent Radios. No "families" have been produced by all this wealth, however, except the Kents, who in this generation are known, liked, and "in Society" in the person of Atwater Kent, Jr.

iii. Amateurs

ACTUALLY much more indigenously Old Philadelphian than any of these performers or conductors or musical businessmen have been the amateurs. This of course is the preferred direction of Old Philadelphia music-making, and there have been some conspicuous family lines and names — Kuhn, Hopkinson, Wister, Drinker — and some conspicuous institutions, like the Orpheus Club and the Savoy.

This amateur musicianship has been a familiar part of non-Quaker family life from a very early period. Hopkinson is the prime example from the eighteenth century. Dr. Adam Kuhn was another, and the two families kept right at it. Joseph Hopkinson, son of Francis, was a patron of music, and achieved fame by writing the words of "Hail Columbia," which all through the nineteenth century was one of our two unofficial national anthems. It was only because Admiral Dewey, at the time of the Spanish–American War, preferred "The Star-Spangled Banner" that this became traditional in the Army and Navy. Not till 1931, when President Hoover signed a bill on his last day in office, was "The Star-Spangled Banner" legally proclaimed our one real National Anthem. Philadelphia lost out again. Later Hopkinsons kept going as prominent amateurs into the twentieth century.

Performing organizations, too, have always been important in the city's life. Amateurs played in the Musical Fund Orchestra, and in such organizations as the Philharmonic Society and a Philadelphia Symphony Society. An entry in the diary of that man-about-town Francis Lewis shows how easily musical amateurism fitted in with the life of a Philadelphia gay blade in the nineteenth century, along with dances, clubs and fire-fighting. He indicates, as of 1849,

The way I pass my time.
I am:
   Pres. of the board of the Phoenix Hose Company
   Pres. of the Firkonian Association (numbering 187 members)
   Pres. of the Gipsy Club
   Director of the Philharmonic Soc. of Phila. — also a performer in
   the orchestra on violin.
   Clubs: member of 'Cornet Club,' 'Amphion' (performer on cornet), 'Washington Greys,' Franklin Institute
   Take French lessons of M. Drouin and music of R. Breiter.

Have *no* wife or its substitute, drink a *little*, chew a *little*, smoke a *little* and partake of all the pleasures of this life in a *moderate* way — and I don't know who has a better right.

A thoroughly sound Philadelphia attitude on the subject.

That November of 1849 as Lewis records it was a busy month. The Philharmonic concert on the first, which Lewis had helped arrange, was a success; Tedesco in costume sang *La Colepa* and took the house by storm. Lewis was so busy with his musical arrangements that he failed on the same day to run to a fire with the Phoenix. "They have almost given me up as one of their *certain* men. Well, I have run for 3 years and never missed *hardly* a fire, and I think it is some excuse for not turning out so regular now. . . . I will run again — not dash headlong however as heretofore, as if I thought and wished for nothing but a fire." Next evening "Serenade by the Amphion to R. Penrose. After playing 6 pieces we were asked in to supper." The next February he notes, "Had a very good rehearsal at Amphion last night. Jared Ingersoll was there to play 3rd cornet." Evidently the absence of Ingersolls as members of the Fund was not due entirely to lack of interest in music.

The casual interweaving of music with Philadelphia club life continues down to the present. The Philharmonic and the Amphion do not survive, but certainly the Orpheus Club assumes pretty much the same role in the life of pretty much the same sort of person right at the present.

It would be of course inconceivable for members of any good Old Philadelphia organization not to surround themselves with all sorts of traditional jollity. In some places perhaps people who belong to choruses go to rehearsals, give concerts, and then go home, thinking no more of it. Not the members of the Orpheus Club. For years the formal concerts have been only a sort of excuse, a core about which cluster skits, dinners, outings, cricket games and all the paraphernalia of a Philadelphia social life, carrying into maturity the atmosphere of the 1910 or pre-Bach-and-madrigal college glee club.

The seriousness of the performance at the concerts is genuine, and the conductors, over the years, beginning with Michael Cross, have included such notable musical figures as Frank Damrosch and Horatio Parker. To present-day tastes the repertoire seems pretty corny. But the problem of what to do with glee club males in their more soulful moments has not really been solved by a resort, as in most college clubs nowadays, to Palestrina and Hindemith. It certainly hasn't been solved, either, by the Orpheus Club's traditional adherence to, say, the "Thanatopsis" of J. Mosenthal, who died in 1896, none too soon, and whose fame as a composer rests on the fact that he was a brother-in-law of the Damrosches. But in all this world there is absolutely nothing that better exemplifies the expression "warming the cockles of the heart" than the Orpheus in a lighter vein — sentimental or silly — before an audience of its friends. When they really let down and dig into such things as "We Never Speak of Aunt Clara" or their repertoire of pre–First War ballads, they are hard to beat. If you want to get a taste of Philadelphia *Gemütlichkeit* distilled, one of those occasions when the Orpheus sings for fun — after the annual cricket game at the Merion Cricket Club, for instance, or above all inside their own memento-crowded clubhouse — will give you the best possible opportunity; but of course you have to be *invited*. Like nearly everything else good in Philadelphia this is not for the "public." The Orpheus, in fact, never sings in "public," even though their three annual concerts fill the Academy of Music. Everybody is a guest; and on gala evenings everybody is in evening dress too.

The Club is divided into two sections. There are the Active members, less than seventy of them, who actually sing, and then there are the Associate members, some five hundred of them, who are privileged to go to the annual concerts, with their guests. The Active list is Old Philadelphian enough, but after all one has to be able to sing, rather than merely be a Biddle. Only two Biddles have made the Active list; but the Associate list is something else again, and Everybody is on that. Theoretically of course, almost Anybody might be on either list, but as Dr. Chance writes in his description of "Orpheus Traditions and Trophies," "The membership of the Orpheus Club has been closely identified with the social life of Philadelphia and the policy of the Club . . . has been to seek as prospective members only those who have been associated in polite and artistic circles." As for those Traditions and Trophies, most of them have to do not with music but with athletics and horseplay.

Since the first Orpheus cricket teams were formed in the 'eighties, the Club has been playing games either with itself (tenors *vs.* basses) or with outsiders. An Annual Outing of some sort, involving a day of golf, tennis, baseball, cricket, eating, drinking — and singing, has been traditional since the 'nineties. Now there is an annual cricket game at the Merion Cricket Club between Orpheus and Merion, on the old cricket grounds, the lawn tennis paraphernalia having been removed for the occasion. The best play is inevitably provided by the seventy- or eighty-year-old veterans of Philadelphia's great days. This remains the last upper-class cricket game played in Philadelphia, at least outside of Haverford College and its occasional opponents.

Alexander Van Rensselaer, or Alex Van, as he was nicknamed, was an Active member of the Orpheus for fifty-nine years; in his day the Club's outings were much concerned with the Corinthian Yacht Club, of which he was Commodore. While the Farmers were being wafted upstream to Andalusia or the State in Schuylkill, the Orpheus was yachting downriver to the Corinthian; when Alex Van got a new yacht in 1913, the Club participated in a body at the launching, and presented the yacht with a chronometer — although Van Rensselaer himself was in Europe at the time. There is something about a choral society presenting a chronometer to a yacht (while the owner is away) . . . . Anyway, one of the high sentimental points in Club history was the occasion, at the Twelfth Night Revels of 1932, when Van Rensselaer gave back to the Club the silver loving cup which the Club had given him on his wedding day in 1898; somewhat on the order, in reverse direction, of the Lewis bowl, presented by a Lewis to the Pennsylvania Hospital managers and later presented back by them to the Lewises. A cup in Philadelphia has not acquired patina until it has been presented back and forth in this fashion.

The Twelfth Night Revels have more usually been associated with satire than with sentiment, and every year since 1897 have involved the members in stage production of buffoonery, thick with "puns of the genuine Philadelphia stamp." George Wharton Pepper distinguished himself for years at these Revels as a humorously dictatorial and bumbling "property man." For a greatly revised version of *Uncle Tom's Cabin* in 1927, Pepper had failed to supply ice for Eliza's escape from the bloodhounds. A member rose in outraged protest from the audience, and the distinguished Senator was forced to tear up large pieces of cardboard and toss them in front of the fleeing heroine.

These Outings and Revels are annual, but there are all sorts of other random activities — Round Table sings and dinners at the Club House, concerts for prisoners and sick people and at funerals ("Absence," the club song, and Sullivan's "The Long Day Closes" are appropriate), memorial services such as that arranged for the recently deceased Edward VII, the welcome to General Joffre, who was *not* asked to go through the gates of the Philadelphia Hospital, like Generals Foch and Lafayette (Joffre of course is not to be confused with Foch), and hundreds of other such miscellaneous events.

There has to be one particular Old Philadelphia family associated with the Orpheus as there is with each other Old Philadelphia antique. In this case it is the Sims family, the same Simses that are so entangled with the history of the Assembly. A John C. Sims was the first Orpheus president, his brother James succeeded him in the 1870's, his son Joseph Patterson, chronicler of the Assembly, was president in 1932, and Joseph's son Joe Jr. is an active singing member right now. Except for a decade between the death of John C. and the debut of Joseph P., there has always been a Sims singing in the Orpheus.

Two other amateur organizations, without whose perennial efforts Philadelphia would not be what it is, are the Savoy Company and the Mask and Wig. The Savoy is America's longest continuing amateur Gilbert and Sullivan troupe. They have been

[489]

at it since 1901, and have produced all the available operas, most of them many times. The approach is on the whole reverent. This means that the singing is superb, the leads being, in fact, most of them local professionals, but that the action and the sets are "authentic," which is to say, a bit stuffy and shabby. During their annual production, the jollity of the evening is a bit dimmed by all that reverence, but not the group's esprit de corps, which is maintained in a fine Philadelphia way by outings and rehearsal parties and all the rest.

Somewhat the same atmosphere of reverence has tended to hover over the efforts of the Mask and Wig Club, but without the same legitimate excuse. Actually the Mask and Wig is (or was) merely the annual transvestite musical show of the men's college of Pennsylvania, corresponding exactly to the Triangle Club of Princeton and the Hasty Pudding of Harvard. It is equally antique, famous and carefully produced; but whereas the graduates of Princeton and Harvard sometimes go away, and out into life or even Hollywood, the graduates of Penn and the Mask and Wig graduate to a clubhouse in town and stay right there in Philadelphia. The result has been a tendency to confuse the Mask and Wig with an Old Philadelphia institution, which has not necessarily been good for its collegiate joie de vivre. The Orpheus, the Savoy and the Mask and Wig give parties to each other, and Trophies and Traditions are preserved intact. In late years the Mask and Wig members have confined themselves to really undergraduate shows for the local undergraduates, without much interference by Old Philadelphia graduates. The clubhouse still exists though and the doings there are noticed in the Society pages along with the Devon Horse Show and the Assembly. It remains another instance of that curious and not always fortunate tug of war between the University and Old Philadelphia. Typically Philadelphia-P.R.R. is the Pullman coach car named the "Mask and Wig." Presumably the New Haven or the Boston and Maine may sport one called the "Hasty Pudding"; but I haven't seen it.

A modern Philadelphia musical institution which perhaps more strikingly than any other such illuminates the relationship between Old Philadelphia and music is the Drinker Sing (or are the Drinker Sings, usually referred to in the plural). The real name is the Accademia dei Dilettanti di Musica; the creation of Henry and Sophia Drinker, it is a chorus of a hundred or more amateurs that meets every so often in the Drinker house in Merion. It is unusual in that it never gives concerts, and never rehearses, but just sings for its own pleasure. It sings just about everything in the classic choral repertoire, the core of this being the Bach Cantatas; the chorus is accompanied by an organ and by a string orchestra, and Henry Drinker conducts it himself. One has to be invited of course, as to the concerts of the Orpheus. The criterion is the ability to sing a good part; and to have met or be introduced to the Drinkers. The result, considering the almost totally amateur nature of the event, is amazingly satisfactory.

The Drinkers not only supply the hall for the get-togethers — that is, a special room in their house in Merion designed for the purpose, lined with some of Aunt Cecilia Beaux's best pictures, all of Drinkers of course — and the conductor, Henry himself; they also supply quite a few of the musicians. Mrs. Drinker, herself a choral conductor, gives leadership to the women's voices and Henry's sister Catherine Drinker Bowen does the same for the string group. The Drinkers also supply the food and drink during the intermission. Above all, Drinker has provided the sheet music for the singers; for one of his most amazing contributions has been the editing of a Drinker Library of Choral Music. He has taken authoritative musical texts, translated the words into English, and had the whole printed up for use by choruses. This library includes 212 Bach cantatas, all the Brahms vocal works, and a quantity of other choral and vocal works by Bach, Palestrina, Schubert, Schütz and so forth, most of which the Accademia has sung through in its time.

The Accademia, now thirty years old, is obviously the end product of a long background of musical amateurism, not only in Philadelphia generally, but in the Drinker family in particular. Catherine Bowen's book *Friends and Fiddlers* and Cecilia Beaux's autobiography both give graphic pictures of how the family background was saturated with music during the growth of both these enterprising members. The net result, in its somewhat specialized and rather narcissistic way, is certainly a fine flower of American culture; a roomful of good sight readers, many of them Oldest Philadelphians, and most of these related to the Drinkers, singing with competence the highest efforts of choral music, conducted by one of the city's great lawyers, who incidentally also edited the texts used for the performance, the string section led by a member of the family, who also happens to be the city's foremost author and one of the foremost in the country, while from the walls look down the warm family portraits painted by a member of the family who also happened to be one of Philadelphia's, and America's best portrait painters. It is nice to think that such things can go on nowadays in much the same way that they did in the days of Francis Hopkinson.*

iv. Professionals

IT MUST BE emphasized, though, that nowadays Philadelphia is a booming professional musical city. It maintains and has maintained for half a century, since Stokowski, one of America's recognizably great orchestras; in fact Philadelphia is probably better known for its orchestra nowadays than for anything else. It is also, with the Curtis Institute and many other good conservatories, such as the Academy of Vocal Arts, a center of professional education. And two of Philadelphia's composers are now in the forefront of modern America's serious music, though neither is really native to Philadelphia, or particularly reflects Philadelphia

---

* No sooner written than the Drinkers sent out word that the Accademia has celebrated its thirtieth anniversary by closing down. Philadelphia musical life without the Drinker Sings is inconceivable; perhaps they can be continued by disciples, after the manner of the Wistar Parties, in grateful remembrance of the happy musical evenings in Merion. The fabulous Drinker Library has been deposited, meanwhile, at the Philadelphia Free Library.

(whatever that would mean, musically) in his work, or lives in Philadelphia now. They both, however, in a curious way do represent the Philadelphia tradition of opera, and it is perhaps not too absurd to consider them as artistic descendants and justifiers of William Fry.

Samuel Barber is the closest to being a native. He was born of well-to-do parents in West Chester, which is not Philadelphia, or even a suburb, but certainly comes close. He was one of the Curtis Institute's prize pupils, gifted in other musical ways as a pianist and singer. He resembles Gilchrist, too, in his ability to win prizes, and resembles so many other Philadelphians in having a traditional family background. The singer Louise Homer, also a settler in West Chester, was his aunt. He won the American Prix de Rome in 1935, the Bearns Prize in 1928 and 1933, and he twice won the Pulitzer Prize (1935, 1936). He is famous largely for his neo-romantic orchestral works, but his most notable recent venture has been the opera *Vanessa,* put on by the Metropolitan in 1957 and written to the libretto of his friend and fellow student at Curtis, Gian Carlo Menotti.

Menotti is considerably less of a Philadelphian, having been born in 1911, a year after Barber, in Milan. He did not leave Italy for Philadelphia until he was seventeen, and he came to study with the famous Italian theorist Scalero, then head of the composition department at Curtis, and has been in America ever since. He is certainly America's best-known living operatic composer; if such a very Italian composer can be called really American. His first success, put on by the Met in 1938, was the opéra bouffe *Amelia Goes to the Ball;* but his reputation was made by his short opera *The Medium.* This macabre essay was followed by a larger work, *The Consul,* which established the remarkable record of ninety-three performances on Broadway, something unheard of for a serious opera in English, in America or anywhere. His television opera *Amahl and the Night Visitors* has already become a Christmas classic. Nothing he has done since *The Consul* has been as unashamedly a hit; but certainly his success, even as partial as it is, has done a lot to make up for poor William Fry's life of aggravated frustration.

Vanessa, which employed the talents of both of these semi-Philadelphians, contains an awful lot of the tradition not only of Fry, but of Barker–Bird–Boker in it; a tradition of grand-scale, gloomy, poetical, nostalgic, Europeanized drama, looking backwards yet by no means either old-fashioned or imitative. It is not certain that *Vanessa* will be kept in the repertoire, as it should be; yet one can't help feeling that for all its faults, it remains the one really viable Grand Grand Opera, in the traditional sense, that has yet been written by an American.

As for a "musical world" in Philadelphia today, correspondent to the active and lively artistic-museum world, it is difficult to find positive traces of it. There are lots of musical people and musical circles, but they don't seem to coalesce under the leadership of Old Philadelphia in at all the same way. The Zimbalists rule one sector, the world of the Curtis. The late Mrs. Clarence Warden and Mrs. Herbert Morris, neither of them Old Philadelphians (this Morris is one of the very few in the *Register* that's not a Christian Sam Morris) have given fantastically beautiful musical parties in courtyards and gardens, and Everybody goes. There is the world of the Orchestra, with Ormandy representing music and Orville Bullitt boards, or the world of Opera; Henry McIlhenny, the art collector, is the Philadelphia member of the board of the Metropolitan, and Margot (Mrs. Alexander) Biddle is an ardent patroness. But somehow this doesn't all add up, the way the art world "adds up." There are even composers besides Barber and Menotti, good ones and native ones, even Old Philadelphia ones, of whom André Constant Vauclain is the most conspicuous. Vauclain is an expert composer and a famous local teacher of theory and counterpoint, both at the Curtis and the University. His works, however, do not seem to get played very often. There are other composers; two Italian–Americans, Vincent Persichetti and Vittorio Giannini, carry on Philadelphia's Italian–American tradition on a considerably higher plane than does

Fabian. But they don't appear everywhere at functions and represent music to the Philadelphia world in the same way their painter colleagues Watkins and Stuempfig seem to do. Somehow music, except in the one direction of amateurism, seems not quite wholly acclimated in the Quaker city. Perhaps the ghosts of the Founders still disapprove.

As for the final answer to the question, "Why? Why is Philly such a talent-teeming town?" you will have to look elsewhere. Try *Teen*.

v. The Dance

BALLET LIVES perhaps somewhere on the fringes of music, since it has usually flourished in the past as an ornament to opera; one would imagine that a section on Philadelphia ballet would be a short one, would one not? As far as its connections with Old Philadelphia are concerned one would be right enough, for except for a brief flowering in the 1930's, when two ladies named Mary Binney Montgomery and Catherine Littlefield ran ballet companies in the city, there has been no direct contact at all between Old Philadelphia and Terpsichore, save that between audience and performer; and perhaps some less publicized ones between ballerina and bachelor.

With this general assumption in mind I had dashed off a confident paragraph, dismissing ballet in Philadelphia with offhand "of courses" and references to Fanny Elssler. But incredible as it might seem, Philadelphia turns out, on the contrary, to be one of the fountainheads of the art of the dance in America. It has a whole string of the usual Firsts to its credit: the first native-born male performer, choreographer and dance director, John Durang, who made his debut right after the Revolution doing a peasant dance at one of Hallam's "lectures," and whose sons Charles, Ferdinand and Augustus were all well-known theatrical figures who danced, did acrobatics on horseback and sang the first performance of the "Star-Spangled Banner"; two of the first

American prima ballerinas, La Maywood and La Lee; and the very first American premier danseur noble, Le George Washington Smith (sic).

I shall forbear to chronicle the career of funny little moustached Le George Washington Smith, who looked somewhat like Chester Conklin of the old silent movies, and who supported, quite literally, all the famous ballerinas who came to America in the nineteenth century from Fanny Elssler to the notorious Lola Montez. Smith toured with her, and once had to spank her to get her under control. He staged the first Philadelphia production of *The Black Crook* and opened a dancing school in Philadelphia in 1881, where he lived in high respectability with his Philadelphia wife and ten children. One of these, in proper Philadelphia fashion, also became a dancer. His name was Joseph, and though he was trained classical by his father, he introduced into America both the Apache Dance and the Turkey Trot ("Everybody's doing it. Doing what? The Turkey Trot"), the latter of which he invented.

I shall even forbear to give the history of lovely Mary Anne Lee, first American Giselle, who made her bow at the Chestnut Street Theatre at the tender age of fourteen in 1837, and after a short, brilliant career, touring all over the country, retired to leave the spotlights to her New York rival Julia Turnbull.

I cannot however forbear to say a few words about Augusta Maywood, another Philadelphia girl who made good. She made so good in fact, that she became and remains America's one and only *prima ballerina assoluta* in history. She first appeared in that same performance at the Chestnut Street with Mary Lee; Maywood was only twelve, and the city of Philadelphia was torn apart by the jealousy of the adherents of the two infant stars. Maywood was shortly taken to Europe by her ambitious father and never returned. Her conduct later on was considered so shocking that her native city (well, sort of native; nobody was sure just which theatrical trunk she actually was born in) frowned upon her. She should care. Like Aunt Clara, whose picture was turned to the wall, Maywood wound up as one of the Toasts of Europe.

First came Paris. There her debut was reviewed by Théophile Gautier in unmistakably Parisian fashion. "It is something abrupt, unexpected, bizarre which sets her completely apart," he wrote of her in 1839.

Daughter of a New York or Philadelphia theatre manager, we aren't too certain which, she created a furore in America. She came in search of Parisian sanction, for the opinion of Paris agitates even United States barbarians in the world of railroads and steamboats; for a prodigy, Mlle. Maywood is truly quite something.

The costume she wore the day of her first debut was in rather American taste; a toilette to enchant a rope dancer (this is not a term of scorn; we adore rope dancers!).

Ah, Paris toujours!

Unfortunately Maywood eloped with a miserable Parisian dancer. This seemed for some reason to be an international scandal. The pair fled to Lisbon, she abandoned him; or did she? They, or she, went to Vienna, and at last in 1848 she (not they) danced at La Scala and took over Italy as her special province for the rest of her active life. She retired, full of honors in 1862. In Italy she shared, with Fanny Elssler, that most coveted title Italia, nurse of the gentler arts, bestows — the resounding appellation of *prima ballerina e prima mima assoluta*. No European historians of the ballet, particularly English ones, have paid any attention to her, it seems, since she was after all only an American, but she was nonetheless one of the three or four great figures in the ballet of the mid-century, and undeniably the queen of the dance in her adopted country.

As far as Old Philadelphia is concerned, its connection with ballet begins and ends with those two modern ladies, La Montgomery and La Littlefield. Mary Binney Montgomery seems to have been a rebellious, brilliant girl, who was probably a better pianist that she was a dancer; she had a "group" and the group was very stark and modern, if amateur. It and she became something of a local sensation in the 'thirties; after all, nobody with the name of Binney had ever done anything at all like that. Combined with a fairly flagrant flirtation with Stokowski, these activities shook up Binney-loving circles in Philadelphia considerably.

Catherine Littlefield was another matter. Her actual personal Old Philadelphianism seems to be suspect or even nonexistent, but during the 'thirties, she and her company were the darlings of aesthetic Old Philadelphia, and made a real and significant contribution to the American ballet renaissance. It was the period when native American ballet first began to shake off its Russian influences and strike out on its own; and Old Philadelphia found it very exciting and fashionable — for a while. Littlefield was a native Philadelphian, born there in 1908 and trained there by her dancer mother. She danced in New York, under Le Ziegfeld, then became première danseuse of one of Philadelphia's now defunct local opera groups, the Philadelphia Civic Opera Company. In 1934 she formed her own Catherine Littlefield Ballet Company, and also under the patronage of Stokowski, like Mary Montgomery, she performed regularly with the Orchestra as the Philadelphia Ballet Company. In 1937 the Company toured Europe — another Philadelphia First, for it was the first American ballet company to be seen abroad. It stressed American themes, as exemplified in *Barn Dance,* set to American music and founded on American square dances. This enchanted everyone in Paris, especially as coming from the barbarous *pays* of steamboats and railroads.

The Littlefield ballets continued to cultivate this vein, and were considered very good at it, though lacking in "daring, breadth and keen contemporary feeling." That is to say, quite Philadelphian. However, Miss Littlefield got seduced by the New York World's Fair, where she choreographed ice shows, and since her departure and Mary Binney Mongomery's marriage, the brief liaison between Old Philadelphia and the ballet has never been resumed.

Nowadays not Stokowski, but the Art Alliance is the only effective patron of ballet in Philadelphia. The Art Alliance is, in fact, the one clearing house for all such artistic and intellectual activities. Its clubhouse is one of the few Philadelphia town houses that might, like the present home of the Curtis Institute, or the Van Rensselaer house, be called a "mansion." This formerly belonged to an Old Philadelphian full of art in all its forms, called Christine Wetherill. Her first and chief love was the theatre. She founded Philadelphia's most Old Philadelphian amateur group, the Plays and Players, and kept on presenting herself as star in various grandiose pageants, all either translated or written by herself, bearing titles like *The Flight of Time.* Such large and gauzy ideas were obviously more at home in California, where she settled at the end of her life, and there she had her fling producing *The Light of Asia* with Walter Hampden and Ruth St. Denis. Finally she bought a canyon out there and closed her career with a production of *The Life of Christ.* In her memory a lighted cross glows nightly over the City of the Angels. As can be seen, she drifted right far from Rittenhouse Square. Her memory lingers on in the Art Alliance, which is usually still referred to as "the old Wetherill house." A relation of Christine Wetherill, Christine Wetherill Shillard-Smith, has become a well-known dress designer. She changed her name to Tina Leser, for business reasons.

vi. Exordium

IT IS HARD TO KNOW what all this art in Philadelphia does prove about the city. There can be no doubt of a few things: there has been an awful lot of it, a good deal of it has been good, and all of it has been simultaneously nursed and stifled, encouraged and limited by the steady patronage and persistent amateurism of the Old Philadelphians. Philadelphia art in any form would hardly have been what it has been without them; but whether this is a good thing or a bad thing it's hard to say. A few, like George

Biddle, come out swinging for the negative. The affirmative has never been properly put.

Philadelphia may be the Boeotia of America; its aesthetic limits are obvious, and these are too the aesthetic limits of its patronizing upper class: lack of curiosity, failure to appreciate new talent or new trends, a provincial cuddling of ingratiating little talents like Buchanan Read while disapproving of big ones like Poe or Eakins. On the other hand, few cities anywhere show such a steady conservative cultivation of a steady conservative local tradition, supported by institutions as honorable as the Academy of the Fine Arts or the Orchestra, still both among the first of their kind. One is continually affronted in Philadelphia social life by a forthright Philistinism, and then surprised by a hidden connoisseurship. The Philistinism at least is honest; such people are not pretending to be "up on things" for which they obviously care nothing, although there is some of this in smarter Philadelphia circles. Still, Philistines needn't be so all-fired satisfied with their ignorance as they are in Philadelphia. In those best Philadelphia circles where arts are genuinely appreciated, art is more quietly at home than in any other American milieu as part of the pleasures of life, not merely as a form of chic or conspicuous consumption.

One can look at art in Philadelphia in two ways. On the one hand, for such an old rich large city, with so much education and so many advantages and such a long prosperity, Philadelphia may not have lived up to its expectations as a cultural center, certainly let slip or snubbed many talents that it might have helped and cherished. On the other hand, as a really quite new provincial city in a quite new continent just carved from the wilderness, not a capital, only a metropolis in the last hundred years, without royal or state patronage, founded and extraordinarily influenced by a religious sect that positively hated art, Philadelphia has been an aesthetic miracle, in a small way. How do Marseilles and Lyon, Turin and Hamburg, Birmingham and Glasgow really compare? After a thousand years of culture, has Vienna really produced a painter of as much force and weight as Eakins? For all its thousands of years as capital of Europe, has Paris been home to a more civilized mind than that most French of Americans, Franklin? We are not remembered, as nations or cities, by our talents, who are many, but by our geniuses, who are extraordinarily few.

All Philadelphia needs then is another great man or two, to match her Franklin and her Eakins, and she is set for the centuries; one durable good composer for instance, or a poet, somewhere in the twentieth century would be enough. Failing that, perhaps the Boeotian label will have to stick. Whether Philadelphia at present might be capable of producing and sustaining such greatness is, like the question "Why? Why is Philly such a talent-teeming town?" a hard one to answer. It must be admitted that Old Philadelphia never asks the question, and never bothers to try to answer it. It remains perfectly content with what it already patronizes and has always patronized. "To thyself be enough," is the troll's motto in *Peer Gynt,* in place of "To thyself be true."

vii. The Sciences

THOUGH THE CONTRIBUTIONS of Philadelphia, above all Old Philadelphia, to the arts are sufficiently impressive, there has been a certain coolness between Old Philadelphia and the Muses which has not existed between Old Philadelphia and the sciences. Science as an avocation has always been more respectable than dabbling in the arts, and for generations Philadelphia gentlemen have been puttering around their laboratories, or observing species in the field. The way to be a man of letters in Philadelphia was first of all to become a lawyer, and then, as non-practicing lawyer, to write. The way to become a man of science was to become a doctor, and then as professor, preferably in a Chair at the University, devote oneself to experiment or observation. There are whole families of these scientific Chairmen, of whom the Bartons were the most famous. But here again "facts and things" have been predominant. The marvels of Visible Nature — birds, electricity, fossils, shells, plants — took the mind of Philadelphia first and last. Philadelphians have been cataloguers and experimenters rather than creative thinkers.

The names and contributions of these Philadelphia-born or Philadelphia-settled scientists have been more important than those of her artists. The Bartrams, the Bartons, Franklin, Rittenhouse, Wilson and Audubon, Leidy and Cope — all these are "Fathers" of some aspect of science in America, botany, physics, astronomy, ornithology, paleontology. Through their genius and diligence most of these sciences were first acclimated here. There is no doubt that in them Philadelphia really holds an unchallenged first place among American cities as an early scientific center.

Actually, then, a full-bodied history or evaluation of Philadelphia, even of Old Philadelphia, should devote more time and room to science than to art. However, descriptions of exploits in malacology, photo-chemistry and vertebrate paleontology will not be found here, and if the reader wants to find out just what Isaac Lea and Edward Drinker Cope really did he will have to look elsewhere. Since publicity is written by writers, it's no wonder that the bards of Cambridge are better known than the botanists of Philadelphia. As Richard Shryock put it for good twenty years ago, "Boston once excelled in cultural achievement by the simple device of defining culture in terms of those things in which Boston once excelled."

Still, there are some pretty picturesque specimens among these Philadelphia scientists, and the whole group of them hangs together in a remarkably Philadelphian way, either by blood or by discipleship. In fact, like other Philadelphia things, science has been more or less a family affair.

All the important early men cluster about three principal family groups, Bartram, Rittenhouse and Franklin, as kin or as pupils. The one great original founder of Philadelphia's scientific life is not, as one might suspect, Franklin, but James Logan, who as a scientific amateur himself, writer, experimenter in cross-fertilization of plants, owner of America's greatest scientific library of the time, was the patron and educator of the whole later generation, including Franklin himself.

John Bartram was the earliest and the most ingratiating of these "Logan men." He seems more a mythological figure or a character out of a sentimental eighteenth-century fable à la Rousseau than a real person. He is the very paragon of the patriarchal Friend and the "natural philosopher" of French Encyclopedic dreams. He was born in the last year of the seventeenth century, and lived into the Revolution, so spanning all those more idyllic-seeming years of early Pennsylvania history. Son of a Quaker farmer, he was almost entirely self-educated. Perhaps it is more correct to say "Logan-educated," for it was under Logan's patronage and by his help that he was first exposed to formal scientific knowledge. Bartram got Parkinson's *Herbal* out of the library at Stenton and Logan taught him Latin and the use of the microscope, and introduced him to the Linnaean system of classification. Logan probably got him in touch with that other curious, botanical Quaker, Peter Collinson of Gracious Street in London. Collinson arranged for Bartram to send specimens of Americana to various English collectors like Lord Petre, so that eventually Bartram was able to make a good living out of his botany. He and Collinson had a long friendship by mail, trading seeds and advice, and quarreling over the qualities of the "sensitive Tippiti-wichet" and the relative merits of the narcissus and the daffodil. They never met.

Bartram's garden in Kingsessing down along the Schuylkill became famous all over the world. From it he corresponded with aristocratic and learned persons wherever botany was pursued, and wrote to Dillenius of Oxford, Grovenius of Holland, Linnaeus and his patron Queen Ulrica of Sweden. Linnaeus, greatest botanist in the world, is said to have called Bartram the greatest *natural* botanist in the world. His correspondents sent him rare plants for his garden. In the middle of it, as in the middle of Eden, he built with his own hands a fine graystone house. Over the windows he carved:

It is God alone, Almyty Lord,
The Holy One by me adored
John Bartram 1770.

House, garden and inscription still exist.

Here visitors came from everywhere to see garden and gardener, and to marvel at this re-creation of a pastoral antiquity. There the Frenchman Michaux and the Swede Peter Kalm found Bartram seated at table with his Negro servants, whom in detestation of slavery he had freed, dispensing the simple but bountiful hospitality of the New World, and they took back to Europe with them accounts of saintliness and science which justified all the fateful visions of what society might be if freed from aristocratic artificialities and oppressions.

There in this dream garden Bartram brought up his children, and none of them better justified their upbringing than the poetic William. Whereas John was saintly and patriarchal, William was adventurous and romantic. Although, like his father, a botanist, he was really renowned as a travel writer. His *Travels* through the South, published in 1791, was reprinted in London, translated into German, Dutch and French, and the descriptions of lushly exotic southern swamps and savannahs had an almost explosive impact upon the budding Romanticism of literary Europe. Coleridge and Wordsworth in England, Chateaubriand in France not only read him but adapted him; the most famous of these literary borrowings is Coleridge's dream-poem "Kubla Khan," where the images of Bartram lodged in Coleridge's subconscious are reproduced in one of Romanticism's greatest poems. William lived well into his eighties. His last years were spent maintaining his father's garden. There he died suddenly, just after writing a description of a plant, just before setting out for a garden stroll.

There were other scientists in the family, notably Humphry Marshall who followed his Bartram cousin's example by studying plants and creating a botanical garden in Chester county; but the Bartram line continues most notably in a disciple of William Bartram, America's first and foremost ornithologist, Alexander Wilson.

There was nothing very saintly about Wilson. He was born in Paisley, Scotland, of a family of weavers and apprenticed to the trade at thirteen. He did not like weaving. He liked poetry. In 1790 he managed to get a slim volume of it published and his poetry eventually got him into trouble. A bitter satire on some local mill owner put him in jail, where he had to publicly burn the offensive squib himself. When he got out he emigrated to America, and made his living as a poor schoolmaster in the environs of Philadelphia. He finally came to roost down the Schuylkill at Gray's Ferry, which was next to Bartram's garden. William Bartram met him, took an interest in him, and revealed to him that his real talent was not poetry but birds. Alexander studied up in the Bartram library and devoted the rest of his not very long life to discovering, drawing and describing the native songsters in his *American Ornithology*. This massive work appeared from 1808 in volume after volume; as the eighth was in press, Wilson died. His work was carried on and completed by a disciple called George Ord, and several extra volumes were added by Charles Bonaparte, nephew of Napoleon and son-in-law of Joseph Bonaparte of Bordentown, so that the whole work is now properly called *The Wilson–Ord–Bonaparte Book of American Birds*.

Ord is probably more famous for his feud with Audubon than for anything else. Audubon, the rather ne'er-do-well West Indian bastard of a prosperous French trader and landowner, started his American career outside of Philadelphia. Among the lands his father owned was a lovely, and still existent, farm called Mill Grove up the Schuylkill. There Jean Jacques lived for a few years, and there he began his long romance with the American wilderness, hunting and shooting and stuffing specimens, dressing up in fancy pumps and frills and successfully wooing Lucy Bakewell, daughter of a neighboring landowner. With his bride he soon took off for the center of the country, and after years of business failure and ornithological observation and drawing, he returned to Philadelphia in the 1820's to get his bird plates printed up.

It was then that Ord's jealousy of anything that might compete with his master Wilson's book broke out. He organized a cabal to prevent Audubon from being printed. Charles Bonaparte advised the discouraged young man to try Europe. Audubon did, and so ended not only his connection with Philadelphia but Philadelphia's chance at claiming all for her own both of America's great early ornithologists.

George Ord lived till 1866 and well beyond the Golden Age of Philadelphia science. The last really important scientific Bache died in 1867; he marks the end of a second family group of Philadelphia scientists that also began under the wing of Logan — the Franklin group. Every child in the world has a picture in his mind of a fat old Quaker running through the fields after a kite, in some mysterious way generating electricity with a key. Actually it is not always appreciated that as John Bartram was the greatest natural botanist of his century, so Franklin was the greatest natural physicist. He remained always an amateur, busy about so many other things; but science was his real love and luxury. He had an insight into the nature of things far in advance of most men of his time. Probably nobody really did know more about electricity than he did. The fact that our basic electrical terms "positive" and "negative" were coined by him is some indication of his primacy in the field.

It is also not always appreciated that he was by no means alone in Philadelphia as an outstanding "natural scientist." In the Franklin group, as members of the Junto, or just as fellow experimenters, were Godfrey, glazier and mathematician, Scull, mathematician and surveyor, Owen Biddle, watchmaker and astronomer, Ebenezer Kinnersly, who knew as much as Franklin did about the mysterious "vital fluid," and several others. These "mechanical persons" were all patronized and assisted not only by Logan but by the Shippens and the Bonds, Thomas Hopkinson and a whole group of gentlemen amateurs. The atmosphere of the city in the eighteenth century was saturated with science.

Then there was a third group around Rittenhouse, by trade an instrument maker, who was America's first important astronomer.

His sister married a clergyman called Barton, and from them descended a family of Philadelphia scientists, doctors only a shade less famous than the Bartrams. Actually the Bartons don't seem to have done much really; but they were well to do, well connected (the legal Sergeant family got in with them, which meant by extension Nearly Everybody) and there were a whole pack of them. From Benjamin Barton, nephew of Rittenhouse born in 1766, down through John Rhea Barton, who died in 1871, the Bartons were *the* hereditary Old Philadelphia scientific family-in-chief. Baches and Leas were better as *families*, you understand, but not just as *scientific* families. It's like the difference between Chews and Rawles, or Biddles and anybody else. Chews may be better family, but Rawles are better *legal* family. Subtle. The Bartons tended to be practicing doctors, but they also botanized, held down Chairs at the University, collected, wrote, patronized and had disciples.

The fruit of all this botanizing and collecting was the Academy of Natural Sciences, first of its kind. One of the oddest of its founders was Thomas Say. All the elements of Philadelphia's hereditary science might be said to have merged and then been dissipated in him. He was a Quaker cousin of the Bartrams, born rich but peculiar. His great-uncle William Bartram got him started on nature, and, though he had a stab at the drug business, where he lost all his money, and was a member of the City Troop, he soon settled down to entomology. He became the "father of descriptive entomology" for America, as John Bartram was the "father of botany" or Rittenhouse of astronomy or Wilson of ornithology. When Say wasn't off on long nature trips South and West, he not only worked but actually lived in the rooms of the recently established (1812) Academy of Natural Sciences. There he cooked his own frugal meals and existed on seventy-five cents a week, wholly absorbed in insects.

For about fifteen years Say was one of a curious coterie of scientists from many lands — which included the Dutchman Gerard Troost, the Scotch geologist William Maclure, and the Frenchman Charles Lesueur — that created and dominated the

Academy. Suddenly, in 1825, the whole group, inspired to a fine frenzy by William Maclure, who had the money, decamped and went out to the wilderness of Indiana, there to found a community based on Ideal Scientific Communistic Principles, as outlined by Robert Owen, the English social experimenter. In New Harmony they built some charming if silly neo-Oriental Victorian villas, and in no time the whole thing collapsed. The town of New Harmony, as it was named, remains, still full of odd houses and rare trees, and though most of the scientists left, Say stuck on there, completed his monumental *American Entomology,* and died there in 1834. The New Harmony experiment and its curious connection with Philadelphia makes a pretty story; but not really a Philadelphia story, alas.

The greatest figures of nineteenth-century Philadelphia science, and among the greatest figures of nineteenth-century American science, were Joseph Leidy and Edward Drinker Cope. They were of a later generation than any of the others mentioned so far, and were not either descendants or disciples of the three early scientific "families." Leidy, it may be remembered, was the member of the board of the Hand-in-Hand who was too busy to make money, which obviously qualified him as an insurance executive. Cope, as might easily be deduced, was related to the Drinkers, the Copes and most other people; People who were Anybody, that is. The two of them, along with residual Leas, Baches and Bartons, pretty well sustained the Old Philadelphia reputation of the city as an outstanding scientific center up to the twentieth century.

Both Leidy, American "father of vertebrate paleontology," and his pupil Cope were fossil collectors. Cope more or less specialized. Leidy was interested in everything from snails to parasites; but in proper Philadelphia fashion, he was interested only in facts, not theories. A man of immense industry, he covered the world of zoology in his research from microbes to man. He taught for over thirty years at the University, was President of the Academy, and though his father had been a hat maker, he was accepted everywhere in Old Philadelphia. When he died in 1891 he was acknowledged as perhaps the greatest natural scientist in America;

last of the country's universal scientists, as Franklin was its first universal man.

The problem of advertising Philadelphia's postion as an intellectual center is perfectly illustrated in Leidy. He was great all right; but he made no one electrifying discovery or revolutionary invention. He just knew more about shells and fossils and things than anyone else. When you've said that, you've said about all that can be said outside of a technical journal. Yet along with Nicholas Biddle or George Boker, or Henry Carey, though not quite so obscurely, he can join that procession of Philadelphia's hidden, or half-forgotten, great men.

His younger friend Weir Mitchell writes of him as a delightful companion on a woodland walk. He could stand and "call by name every living thing, and the stones beneath your feet also. Turn over a bit of rock, and as the queer tiny menagerie . . . scuttles out, he knows them one and all — their lives, their marriages, what they eat, their ways, their deaths." Mitchell further remarks that Leidy did not really care a "sixpence for all the poetry from Homer to Longfellow." Facts and things.

Cope was more limited in his surveys. Also his position as foremost paleontologist was challenged by Marsh of Yale. A famously bitter feud developed between the two men that enlivened many a scientific journal with invective, and was as notorious in a later time as the Audubon–Ord feud had once been. When Cope died young in 1897, Philadelphia did not replace him with any more scientific "fathers." In fact, though science is worthily pursued in all Philadelphia's various universities and hospitals and industrial research centers, it would be difficult to characterize the city any longer as *the* scientific metropolis of America. It remains, through the American Philosophical Society, something of a national center, as far as meetings and publications are concerned. If there is a center in the area famous for its science, it is not Philadelphia but Princeton, "right far from Philadelphia." The college that Charles Godfrey Leland characterized as an "infant arithmetic school," like Philadelphia also emphasized science at the expense of letters. It also maintained a tradition in the great Joseph Henry (first real inventor of the telegraph), and others. The tradition now flowers in the neighbor Institute of Advanced Study, the laboratories of the Forrestal and in all sorts of research projects, scholastic and commercial roundabout. The place is a warren of physicists and mathematicians. This is of course not Philadelphia; but at least one might say that a certain historically regional emphasis may have borne fruit there. Facts and things, though, have been pretty well superseded there by words and above all by signs, as a glance at brisk periodicals like the *Annals of Mathematics* awesomely demonstrates.

BOOK

VI

1

i. Living

WORKS, GOOD WORKS, Play and Patronage, sports, arts and sciences frame and form the life of the actively retired Old Philadelphian — of any age. The center of life, the fine flower and best fruit of any system of Maintenance however is always not Doing but Being, not achievement but existence. In general, and in a specialized sort of way, an almost unconscious way really, Philadelphians have a fairly firm grip on a basic principle of life that often evades the citizens of more enterprising communities: that the goal of living is to live, and that most activities are merely means to that end. They are much too Quaker still for idleness, but they achieve a good life first of all by making work, good works and other duties as relaxed, amiable and intimate as is possible under sometimes adverse circumstances, and by not letting any of these things interfere too extensively with life at home. A young lawyer comparing New York to Philadelphia legal life put the differences clearly. In New York, money and excitement; in Philadelphia, the whole weekend off without paper work. The Philadelphia climate is not encouraging to those who want to sit about enow with a book of verse, jug of wine and thou. Philadelphians don't read much verse anyway. However they do try to see that their insurance companies serve good dinners, and that good dinners are served at home. As for restaurants, who wants to sit around with a lot of strangers anyway?

Thus the real, steady-beating heart of Philadelphia is not visible in public; for the heart of Philadelphia is at Home, that most hidden part of any city, and the essence of Philadelphia life is its home life. The rest is really surface or substructure or super-structure.

Philadelphians don't go in as a rule for the pernickety little class indices which seem to make English life so variegated — the importance of tying one's shoelaces correctly, saying "glass" for "mirror," or vice-versa, having the right kind of note paper. Philadelphians are too casual for that; but if they are snobs, that is, if they do tend to evaluate and "place" people by externals, it is by houses. Philadelphians are house snobs. They are almost universally, man, woman and child, rich and poor, U and Non-U, interested in house and garden, furniture and flower. If this is materialism, then they are wholehearted materialists. If this is aesthetics, then they are all would-be artists. Not necessarily suc-cessful ones, for bad taste luxuriates in Philadelphia with a fear-some bourgeois splendor, and parvenu monstrosity in houses is a flagrant fact of the Philadelphia prospect. It's just that Old Philadelphians, much more generally than, say, Old New Yorkers or Bostonians, are acutely conscious of all the nuances of this kind of thing. They can spot and damn a solecism in curtains or chairs as surely as an Oxford grammarian can smell out the mis-usages of "which" and "shall."

In a word, houses and gardens, like sports, are very important, and Old Philadelphians often have lovely ones; of their kind, and within their limitations as lovely as any in the world. These houses come, or at least came, in two kinds, town houses and so-called "country places" which are often as not really suburban. The town houses are all over sixty years old. The country houses are anywhere from three hundred to three years old, but actually seldom as recent. Most Philadelphian country places are at least thirty years old, except for remodeling. Old Philadelphians do not care to live in really new houses, much less modern ones, if they can avoid it. Apartments are only for the aged.

The town house for the last thirty years has been pretty much of an anachronism in Philadelphia. Of the some eight thousand listings in the Philadelphia *Social Register,* less than three hundred give "Center City" addresses. "Nobody lives in town" is the local cliché. Those few that still do, and manage to keep up town houses in the old way, like the John F. Lewises or the Leonard Beales, consider themselves the last of the Mohicans. Until this past decade the tide set relentlessly out, away from the city and toward the suburbs.

Nevertheless, firmly at the back of the Old Philadelphian's mind is the atavistic memory of the family town house. Such a town house, if established before the twentieth century in some proper location, is, in fact, a sort of necessary patent of gentility. The house may have been a piece of parvenu ostentation when built, but reality by now is lost in a nostalgic haze of memory of past family grandeur and "Philadelphia taste." The house itself is usually gone, or turned to base uses. The land, as like as not, may still be controlled by the Estate, and the Estate by the Girard, somewhat to the disadvantage of everybody. To have had no genuine town house (which, of course, is a bit different from just having a house somewhere in the city) or to have had a genuine town house in the wrong place, such as North of Market, remains forever a sort of bar sinister on the family escutcheon.

These town houses at their best were, in fact, the quintessence of Philadelphia Taste. They resemble, of course, the town houses characteristic of other big Atlantic seaboard cities of the same period, solid blockfronts of brick, with marble steps and classical doorways, giving way at the end of the nineteenth century to brownstone. They differed from Boston in being far more uniform ("we" not "I"). They differed from New York in being far more modest-seeming, without the high stoops and lofty façades of Washington Square; in Philadelphia there remained a residual Quakerism. There were notable exceptions, of course, like the "folly" of Robert Morris; but there was never anything in Philadelphia like the Vanderbilt-château efflorescence of Fifth Avenue, or even the brown piles of Commonwealth Avenue in Boston.

Outside, in fact, the Philadelphia town houses tended to be rather uninteresting, and numberless travelers remarked on the monotonous conformity of Philadelphia in the nineteenth century, like Baltimore still in the twentieth; rows and rows of identical brick houses with glistening marble steps, white shutters downstairs, green shutters on the windows of the floors above. Usually there was a "busybody," a small mirrored box, at one of the second-floor windows, which enabled the housewife to see who was at the door without poking her head out. Breaking up this monotony were churches, and the more lavish spreads of the especially elegant, full of restrained architectural fancy and surrounded by large walled gardens. Such was the palace of the Binghams, with its marble staircase, or the house built by John Hare Powel where the Historical Society now stands, or the great mansion of Phoebe Rush near Rittenhouse Square. These were houses of people who could either afford to be swank, in their position, or who didn't know any better, and often suffered for it.

The average person of quality lived alongside others of his kind in his more modest and conformist brick mansion, built usually according to that nice Philadelphia plan, the original split level. Downstairs was the parlor, a formidable double room running the full length of the house, and usually empty except for large gloomy furniture and pictures. I met for the first time at a lunch an old gentlemen who as a boy helped to appraise estates. He said to me, "I remember your Great-greataunt Mary's house. Whatever happened to the picture of Niagara over the fireplace?" Whatever indeed! This picture was in the parlor, of course, and the statement not only gives a hint of the atmospherics of the Victorian Philadelphia parlor, but also of the tenaciousness of the Philadelphia memory.

The staircase curled up through the gloom from a hall alongside the parlor. At the turn of the stairs, at the half landing, began the split-level design. Out to the back was the dining room, with a semi-basement kitchen under it. Up the stairs at the front of the house was either a master bedroom, or in a really civilized establishment, a library. Then on up the stairs off another half-landing was the real heart of the house, the sitting room, over the dining room. These half-landing rooms in the back buildings had, in a well planned house lot, all sorts of advantages. They were off the street and therefore quiet. They took up only half the lot, and so had sunshine and looked out on a garden. All these things in a nineteenth-century city house were rare blessings. The plan compares very favorably with the narrow, dark, straight-through aspect of the average New York brownstone. The real charm of the Philadelphia house lay in these back sitting rooms. Wistaria, like as not, clambered up the walls from the garden, perhaps over a small iron-laced balcony. Out back was a big rustling tree. The furnishings were intimate and comfortable, and frequently exhibited more real "Philadelphia taste" than the more august purlieus downstairs. Family portraits and maiden aunt samplers and watercolors, rather than paintings of Niagara, cluttered the walls. Above and beyond were the bedrooms, with servants squeezed into not very spacious dormer rooms in the attic. The air of sober solemnity was reinforced by the ticking and striking of clocks, the rustling and whispering of starchy maids, usually Irish, the glow of furniture polish on dark mahogany, and the residual fragrance of rich food and Madeira.

Another perpetual Philadelphia cliché has been the "English look" of such houses, a cliché perpetuated as often as not by the English visitor himself. The brick façade and the Palladian doorway, the impression of a clutter of well-kept inherited furniture inside are like enough no doubt. Whether or not the "pervading comfort" of which Sidney Fisher speaks is so characteristically British as he seemed to think, certainly the Philadelphia town house was full of Watson's "solid comfort," with coal grates and central heating introduced in the 1820's and bathrooms not long afterward.

English visitors often tend to react in a somewhat similar way to the Philadelphia countryside. The touring graduate student who responded to the reaches of Penllyn with a mock-sentimental " 'Ome!" reflects a similarity which is hereditary rather than imitative, like fox hunting and a general tendency to squirishness. The Philadelphia country places however have always been essentially suburban, that is, the country seats of city men, not the headquarters of people who really supported themselves off the land. Penn planned this union of town and country, and it persists, with the odd paradox that now very few city people live in the city at all.

Though the Philadelphia town house has usually been characterized by a certain demureness, as well as uniformity, in the country the Sense of the Meeting seemed less effective. Grandeur began with William Penn's Pennsbury, up the Delaware. Mount Pleasant and Cliveden, or later on Powelton or Andalusia were as fancy as any Southern plantation house or Hudson patroonery of the same dates. Indeed, a sort of city-country double standard of "ostentation" seemed to exist; the lavish turn-of-the-century suburban pleasure domes of Wideners, Stotesburys and Elkinses, though considered definitely ostentatious, were still admired, while similar city houses of these same people were considered contemptible.

Whereas the town house, partly out of necessity, sticks pretty close to its heritage, the country house in later days wandered far afield architecturally. Lynnewood Hall, the Widener chalet, and Stenton, the house Logan built, have nothing in common except that they are both "country houses." Logan's more or less self-architected retreat up in the Northern Liberties, built in 1728, while not the most elegant or elaborate of such houses, epitomizes the real heritage of the Philadelphia country house.

It is a fairly small, quite simple foursquare brick house with high-pitched roof and back buildings. It is surrounded now by a few acres of old garden, but was once the center of a great and prosperous plantation. There is nothing about it, inside or out, of the palace or château, nothing in the least ostentatious; yet it is not a farmhouse or a cottage. The simple architectural dignity stamps it inevitably as a "gentleman's seat," a small manor. The brick is mellow, the proportions just. It is, above all, exactly the right *size*: large enough for dignity, spaciousness, generosity, elbow room, small enough for comfort, easy keeping, modesty. Large enough to be a significant architectural monument, small enough to be the living quarters of a purely private person. Large enough for aristocracy, small enough for democracy. This is exactly what the human shell is meant to be, the final and ideal shape of any one man's house. The house keeps itself without postulating a class of serfs or servants to hold it up. Yet it takes for granted the full leisure of library, garden, dining room and parlor. It is impressive without the slightest hint of cumbrousness, elegant without the least affectation.

There Stenton still sits, maintained now by civic organizations and protected by the city, an oasis of the human past in the desperate inhuman jungles of the present. All around it for miles the once matching and smiling richness of country has been transformed forever into a hell of faceless row-houses, the degenerate offspring of the Philadelphia town house, mile after mile of semi-respectable dreadfulness. Far off the suburban descendants of Stenton still flourish, swollen into fatuousness like Wootton and Lynnewood Hall, reduced to squalid meanness in the "Estates" and "Manors" of the developer.

We can see in Stenton what, with a bit of intelligence, America might have been and should be; in North Philadelphia, what it has, at least in the recent past, become. There are many houses like Stenton still standing around Philadelphia, some preserved as museums, some lived in privately. A few, like Cliveden, are in the hands of the families that built them. More than any other single thing, the history, fact and continuing tradition of these country places buttresses the sort of class-conscious romanticism which so pervades Old Philadelphia. They are evidence that Philadelphia began to have taste, a gentry and good living almost as soon as people scrambled off the *Welcome*. Pont Reading, begun in 1683, is also still in the hands of descendants of the builder. So is Pencoyd, of the same date, homestead of the Robertses. That's about as early as you can get in Philadelphia without being Swedish.

Town houses come and go, but Pont Reading and Pencoyd, Stenton and Cliveden, Belfield and Andalusia remain, public or private memorials to the good old days. And they were good; no shameful memories of slavery or serfdom, of "gloomy wrongs" and insufferable privilege shadow them. Though some of the men that built them may not have been quite the hereditary gentlemen, nor the money always quite so spotlessly come by, as their descendants would prefer to believe, still these ancestors were not the reckless financial brigands and exploiters of a later age, glorying in rapine, oppression, corruption and illiteracy. They knew what an honest gentleman of education and taste was supposed to be like, and they each hoped to pass for one.

ii. The World of Eberlein

THE CHIEF AUTHORITY on all this world of "places" ("a country place" is the correct way of putting it not an "estate" or a "plantation" or a "suburban villa") is an active octogenarian called Harold Eberlein. He has devoted his lifetime to cataloguing, and almost in a way creating, this Philadelphia outside of Philadelphia, so full of charm, so full of snobbery. In the process, he himself has become a sort of Philadelphia legend. In book after book he has described in scholarly and knowing detail the pediments and pedigrees of these houses, their gardens and ghosts (for every good house must have both), the furniture and silver and coats of arms appertaining to each recognized occupying family. He has carried almost to absurdity that vision of Philadelphia as the high tide of the South, where a man is automatically coupled with the name of his place (John Smith of Smithside). The Philadelphia he celebrates in his more informal book *Philadelphia Scrapple,* where he gives full rein to his fancies in chapters headed "Of Great Ladies," "Of Heraldry," may be of the past all right, but it carries on with a surprising amount of vigor into the present. The society page of the *Bulletin* chronicles with affection the doings at Cliveden and The Highlands, and Ruth Seltzer cultivates the pride of "place" as assiduously in her very up-to-date columns as Eberlein, in his by now rather quaintly cotillion-leader way, did in his beautiful books.

The world of Eberlein involves far more than the mere architectural shell of houses. It swims in a rich sauce of good living, for houses are only containers after all, and what they chiefly contain, in this Eberlein world of Old Philadelphia, is dinner parties.

The fine flower of what the Old Philadelphia house is for, town or country, is entertaining, and the fine flower of Philadelphia entertainment is the dinner party. The suburban dinner party is the principal reason why Philadelphians so seldom get to town, or out of Philadelphia and its atmosphere. Bound in a chain of social obligation absolutely unbroken since the seventeenth century, Philadelphians have for generations been shuttling back and forth from beautiful house to beautiful house, eating creamy food, drinking rich wines, talking about each other and never seeing anyone else at all. Out-of-town guests do occasionally break things up a bit, but once the machine of the dinner party gets going it proceeds relentlessly: one has people by whom one has been had, one is had by people whom one has. A woman who actually kept count found that of the forty-odd dinners she went to in the shank of the season, she saw not one face that she hadn't seen before, usually at other dinner parties. There is very little room for people who can neither regularly have or be had. Couples inevitably settle down to a routine of other couples, plus a stray bachelor and spinster or two, both of these being antique and venerable positions around the Philadelphia dinner table. The bachelor traditionally sports a white moustache, a taste in wines and a muted, blighted "affair" with some social queen. The spinster smokes, drinks, reads esoteric books and is shockingly independent.* Individuals of either species are liable to be the best of Old Philadelphia products. That all these people are more or less kin is taken for granted.

Charles Leland accused Philadelphians of being much more concerned with what was on the table than with what was about it. This is the inevitable result when the dinner guests are inevitable. The concentration on the accouterments becomes intense, and extends not only to food, but to china, silver, furniture, décor and everything else. As there are famous Old Phila-

---

* Two nice modern versions of these in Livingston Biddle's *Sam Bentley's Island* (1961).

delphia eatables (scrapple, cinnamon buns, terrapin), there are famous Old Philadelphia furniture makers (Randolph, Aphleck, Savery), silversmiths (Syng, Richardson), glass blowers (Wistar, Steigel), and china makers (Tucker), and it behooves the Old Philadelphian to have a bit of their work on hand, preferably inherited. Pride comes to its crest if one can casually stick away in the living room a highboy with a plate on it authenticating authorship and one's continuous family ownership. There are famous pieces with family names, such as the Wister–Wistar Desk in the Metropolitan Museum, and some of these are even still in original Philadelphia hands.

The quality of Philadelphia buildings and furnishings and silver somewhat resembles the quality of Philadelphia food: rich and smooth, as in creamed oysters, chicken or seafood croquettes, white mountain cake and Philadelphia ice cream. Furniture follows English models, with fairly sumptuous fidelity, always a few decades behind the times. It is, however, simpler and less elaborate than its models, less virtuoso or creative, but gives an effect of better taste in being less showy and ornate and pompous. The Philadelphia style remains the high style in American colonial craftsmanship. The New England style compared in skill and exceeded Philadelphia's in delicacy and imagination, but was much more provincial. It is more appealing now because of that very provincialism, which gives to New England work a prim piquant originality lacking in things from Philadelphia; but it is obviously less genteel and sophisticated of its period.

In the nineteenth century Philadelphia lost its primacy as a setter of styles, and has never regained it. Nowadays the only really proper style for a Philadelphia house is eclectic, a mixture of the beautiful old and the convenient or interesting new, uncontaminated by the rude hand of the decorator. A few fashionables can still afford the modern counterpart of the Hutchinsons' plate glass firescreen; white brocade sofas, "frescoes by Monachesi," and other Fishery delights. The livelier Biddles and Cadwaladers may have their places done modern or Baroque or Oriental; but this has to be done right and by the right people and as a sort of gesture of self-indulgent extravagance. Otherwise most really good modern houses in Philadelphia are owned by what the more reactionary Old Philadelphians like to dismiss as "Jews and artists" and other outsiders. Most Old Philadelphians prefer to live with the furniture that God, abetted by will and testament, gave them in houses approximating as closely as possible the Old Family Place.

iii. With the Sun

IN THE GOOD old days the climax of the dinner party was the Madeira ceremony that followed it. The ladies left, the table was cleared, as it still is at the Green Tree dinners, and around the mahogany the decanters slid in their coasters clockwise, "with the sun," from connoisseur to connoisseur. To send the wine to the right was believed to be fatal to its bouquet. The diners' palates were so exquisite that the slightest taint of cork was anathema, and Philadelphia wines were never permitted to be bottled as they were in such barbarous places as Charleston and Boston. One man could detect, as he drank, in which of two glasses an egg had been broken the day before. Not only corks, but women were dangerous. It was believed that if a woman went into the wine room the wine would be permanently soured. Sent around Cape Horn to be seasoned by a long sea voyage, the "Capeturned" vintage would be stored down cellar (or up attic) in five-gallon demijohns, each wine labeled with its own name — *Juno,* after the ship on which it had been seasoned, *Butler* or *Willing* after the man who had first imported it. If the wine showed signs of cloudiness it was "fined" by the addition of the powder of an eggshell stirred into white of egg. According to an ancient precept, this medicine had to be administered to the demijohn in the wane of the moon, otherwise it wouldn't work.

Nowadays sherry with the soup, Madeira and port after the meal are still a traditional part of the more stately Philadelphia dinner, but the ceremonies of clearing and clockwise passing have disappeared except among a few men's club dinners. The tradition of punches still flourishes, however. One doesn't mix, one "builds" a proper punch, and every good organization has its own, like the Fish House or the Rabbit or the United Bowmen with their Hail Storm.

Drink still remains the prerogative of the male, but most of the rest of the world of Eberlein has devolved, rather by default, into the hands of the female. This was by no means the case in earlier days. Not only did Philadelphia men themselves order and frequently design their houses, furniture and plate, but they did the marketing. It was a familiar sight, even up to a few years ago, for the paterfamilias of the most august Philadelphia families to walk or be driven, once by coachman then by chauffeur, down to the market with a basket in hand. Nobody else could be trusted to pick the proper roasts and fowl, and nobody else at table could be trusted to mix the salad.

This was true of gardening, too, and it was the founders of the Horticultural Society, men like Nicholas Biddle and John Hare Powel, not their wives, who planned and supervised their gardens. In these Degenerate Days, however, When We Are All Lower Middle Class, women have taken over. This coincides to a remarkable extent with the disappearance of hired labor; though men don't seem to think of suggesting this to their hard-troweling wives. In any case, Old Philadelphia womanhood has a firm grip on gardens now, and through the Garden Club of America, Philadelphia strongly influences, if it does not control, the world of the American garden. Representatives of the twelve original chapters of the Club met originally in Philadelphia in 1913 to organize themselves, and of the whole proliferating universe of American lady diggers, arrangers and exhibitors, these twelve remain socially and horticulturally elect. Three of the twelve were Philadelphia branches, the Garden Club of Philadelphia, the Gardeners and the Weeders. The Weeders were originally a group of girls, most of them now in their eighties, who got tired of waiting to get into the Gardeners and started their own branch. The name was considered a great joke, but it's taken pretty seriously now.

Philadelphia, like London, is definitely a man's town, as Paris and New York are women's towns, and most of Philadelphia's characteristic phenomena, customs, institutions or even arts, are male dominated. However, unlike Boston, whose women have been more famous for their books than their looks (unfairly of course), Philadelphia has been famous for its belles. Generation after generation has produced reigning beauties; some of these have been social queens as well. For one role in which woman, even in Philadelphia and in the past, has always been supreme is the role of hostess, and again almost from the beginning there have been salons and salonieres, fashionable, intellectual or both.

Philadelphia's most famous pre-Revolutionary salon-keeper was lovely Elizabeth Graeme of Graeme Hall. She dabbled in verse, corresponded with poets, translated from the French and kept an elegant house; but during the Revolution she was suspected of Toryism and lost both her social leadership and Graeme Hall.

Poor Peggy Shippen, the wife of Benedict Arnold, never had a chance at a salon; but she was one of Philadelphia's most famous belles of Revolutionary times, and participated in Philadelphia's most curiously extravagant party, that Meschianza put on by British officers of the Occupation at staid Quaker Joseph Wharton's Walnut Grove. It was a most un-Quakerish affair.

The party, largely gotten up by the charming, ill-fated André, lasted during the day and on till four o'clock in the morning. First there was a water pageant. Then there was a joust of fourteen "knights," young British officers in fancy costumes, with fancy names like the "Knights of the Blended Rose." Each knight had a lady — a Chew, a Bond, a Shippen — as well as black slaves in Oriental garb, and esquires. The Knights of the Blended Rose jousted on horseback with the Knights of the Burning Mountain, and afterwards everyone danced and ate and gambled and drank till dawn. Philadelphia had never seen anything like it, up to that point.

However, the Meschianza seems to have started something, for from that day to this Philadelphia has continued to be famous for the lavishness of its parties. Not a year goes by, except during wartime, without some quietly awe-inspiring spectacle of this kind, big or little. A recent one I remember as typical was a "barn dance." Sixty people in full dress sat down to a many-coursed champagne dinner, with dancing to a small orchestra. It was, sure enough, actually given in a barn; nobody thought it anything special. As for really big splashes, nothing in the way of bands, marquees, décor and drinks is too much. The results are not always fortunate, as in the case of a famous Paul party of a good many years ago. Exotic butterflies were supposed to fly out of cages in the ceiling; but when the cages were opened, all the butterflies had died and merely fell into everyone's champagne.

As for Peggy Shippen, when she married General Benedict Arnold, he gave her Mount Pleasant, one of the fine houses on the Schuylkill, as a wedding present. But she never had a chance to occupy it, much less have a party or salon there. Arnold turned traitor, and Peggy went with him into exile, where in London she was much admired. Mount Pleasant remains as one of that chain of houses preserved as museums in Fairmount Park. Queen of the Republican Court after the Revolution was Anne Bingham. She was not at all literary. She was just very beautiful, very fascinating and very rich. She tended to be fast and fancy. Philadelphia remained in a constant but delighted state of shock at her dinners where guests were announced by footmen, and at her dresses.

Abigail Adams turned a very cold New England eye upon such high doings. She speaks of "one continued scene of Parties upon Parties, Balls and entertainments equal to any European city." However, "the Publick Amusements 'tis true are few." Things really haven't changed so much.

As for the Binghams themselves and their dresses, Abigail found them outrageous. There was, for instance, the unfortunate Comtesse de Tilly, nee Bingham, whose secret marriage to a profligate Frenchman at the age of fifteen and consequent divorce after a cash settlement were the scandal of the Republican Court. This did not prevent the Comtesse from showing up in society, where according to Abigail "she has all the appearance and dress of a Real French woman, rouged up to the ears. Mrs. Bingham did not appear to feel any embarrassment at introducing her, tho' I cannot say she did not create one in me." And as for those dresses,

. . . really an outrage upon all decency — a sattin petticoat, nothing beneath but a chemise . . . and without staye or Bodice. A tight girdle round the waist and the "rich luxuriance of nature's charms," without a handkerchief, richly displayed. The face, a la mode de Paris, red as a brick hearth. Not content with the show which nature bestows, they borrow from art, and literally look like Nursing Mothers.

(So much for John Watson's solid and sober days of our forefathers.)

The mid-nineteenth century was dominated less scandalously by Phoebe Rush — wife of gloomy Dr. James Rush — from her palace on Chestnut at 19th Street. This palace seems to be the very first known example of the neo-colonial, a style later so dear to the Philadelphian heart. Though large, it was deliberately built "old-fashioned and quaint," brick, with a Palladian doorway approached by curving double steps, and the idea was to suggest eighteenth-century hospitality of the Bingham sort. Inside things were a bit different. Parties for eight hundred filled the stately chambers, illuminated by six thousand candles, and enlivened by recherché suppers, music and dancing. Famous were Phoebe's Saturday morning levees, to which an invitation was a command; not to be included meant social disaster. She had a way of promenading up and down Chestnut Street, dressed to kill in "blue or crimson silk or velvet of the last Parisian cut," and holding court there. Everyone stopped and spoke to her, even Sidney Fisher. He was fond of her, and defended her against her detractors, who were many. She was *not* a belle, but was stout, florid and, according to her enemies, raucous and crude. She was, however, in the Graeme tradition, intelligent, well-read and acquainted with the ways of the great world after many years abroad. The Library Company's Ridgeway Memorial is her inappropriate monument. A movie theatre stands on the site of her mansion.

The tradition of the salon has been maintained best in this century by two Southerners, Caroline Sinkler and Emily Balch. The Sinklers, though South Carolinians, had become thoroughly domesticated in Philadelphia, like the Butlers, and there are still quite a few of them there. Miss Sinkler had a lovely town house near Rittenhouse Square, and she bought and restored one of Philadelphia's loveliest old country places, The Highlands, now owned by her niece Mrs. Nicholas Roosevelt. It was at her parties that the Stokowskis and the Ingersolls, the Hergesheimers and the Biddles got together. Miss Sinkler provided for them on the basis of South Carolina charm, Philadelphia food and drink, and a special rather expansive atmosphere all her own.

Emily Balch, a Virginian who married an Older Philadelphian, was more decidedly literary. An editor, as Emily Clark, of one of the first "little magazines" in the South, she knew most of the important writers of her period, and as a well-to-do Philadelphia widow she ran a sort of chain of salons, one in Richmond, one in her Philadelphia town house on Spruce Street, with more or less the same clientele as Caroline Sinkler, and one in New York. Her friendships and feuds with people like James Branch Cabell, Henry Mencken, Joseph Hergesheimer and Thomas Wolfe were staples of literary gossip. She had a genius for loosening the tongues and breaking down the reserve of her guests, and during the 'thirties in particular her parties came closer to the salons of older days, if a bit less decorous, than anything else of the sort in America.

Nobody has quite taken the place of these two charmers, in Philadelphia or even in New York. Perhaps closest in Philadelphia comes Gloria Braggiotti Etting. A magnificent-looking Italian-Bostonian, with a flair for clothes, conversation, writing and genteel publicity, she comes nearer than anyone else in Philadelphia to filling the role of saloniere-in-chief. True, she functions perhaps more actively as a guest than as a hostess; she is the key figure of Philadelphia's art-and-museum society. Her husband Emlen Etting is a painter, as well as an Etting and hence related to everybody, and in their house on Panama Street or by their presence at most of the important artistic do's they provide a focus for the smart artistic world.

iv. *"North of Market"*

PHILADELPHIANS are house snobs in more ways than one; in the old days when Everybody lived in town, at least in winter, not only *how* one lived, but *where*, could mean the difference between social life and death. Market Street was the "tracks" and if you lived "North of Market" you were on the wrong side of them! "Nobody lived there." It took families such as the Wideners several generations and removals to live down the fact that they had not merely a house but a mansion on North Broad Street. The bigger the house the more flagrant the offense. Old Philadelphia gossip is full of not-very-nice stories about North-of-Marketers who first moved to the suburbs to cover their tracks, then sneaked back to Rittenhouse Square, hoping nobody would notice. Given the "Philadelphia memory," of course, everybody did notice, and continued to ignore the newcomers as only the right Philadelphians can ignore the wrong Philadelphians.

The right side of the tracks, the only area of the city that Old Philadelphians consider really Philadelphia, is that narrow belt that extends from the Delaware to the Schuylkill south of Market and north of Lombard. The rhyme "Chestnut, Walnut, Spruce and Pine, Market, Arch, Race and Vine" expressed the ultimate limits, north and south, of an Old Philadelphian's personal knowledge of the city — and Race and Vine Streets were only included because of the rhyme. A sort of strict Quaker ghetto occupied Arch Street. Market became early commercialized. Locust and Sansom were "too small" for inclusion in the rhyme. Below Pine began, and begins, the colored district; indeed this began with little alleys like Waverley Street that ran right behind the respectable doctors' houses on the south side of Pine.

Except for the more liberated spirits, or those for some reason not totally assimilated, Old Philadelphians when they say "Philadelphia" mean automatically this sacred zone, their somewhat limited Philadelphia, and not the sprawling jungles to the north, south, west and even east across the river in Camden, the Greater Philadelphia of Frankford and Kensington, Manayunk and Passyunk, the Greater Philadelphia of Connie Mack, the Mummers' Parade, of Marian Anderson and Father Divine and Ethel Waters. It is not that they don't know this Greater Philadelphia exists; in fact many of them, particularly historically-minded older gentlemen, have a sort of benevolent curiosity about it, the feeling a birdwatcher has for some particularly busy bog; they know *about* the people that live there, but they don't and won't actually know the odd specimens inhabiting this swamp that surrounds the walled bastion, the Inner, the Forbidden City, of *real* Philadelphia, their own narrow historical, hereditary waistland.

However, within this narrow band, containing nearly all of Philadelphia's historical monuments, public institutions, great businesses and stores, as well as whatever remains of residential quality and charm, Old Philadelphians have kept on the move. With typical lack of conservatism, they have never stayed in one area for more than one full generation. They have never built up a Beacon Hill, or a Battery, or even a French Quarter, like Boston, Charleston, and New Orleans, but have gradually forged west, like a snail's imitation of America's own continental migration, creating charming cosy neighborhoods and then abandoning them for newer or more fashionable quarters just as they begin to get really ripe. Fortunately, a few stubborn or impoverished old people always stayed behind, so that a residue remained, a tucked-away old street, a house here and there; but this was by accident.

The first good neighborhood was of course right along the Delaware, where the earliest settlers, then mostly Quakers, built simple but substantial small brick houses after the model of those in their native Lincolnshire. This original respectable neighborhood was more North than South of Market; so if you go back far enough in Philadelphia, you probably came, paradoxically enough, from North of Market (then High Street) and are proud of it. The earliest Quaker Meetings and Christ Church, Philadelphia's first, most famous, most fashionable Episcopal church, even the first synagogue, are all in this area. Christ Church and a miraculously preserved small street called Elfreth's Alley are all that now remain to indicate the character of this earliest of Philadelphia's fashionable neighborhoods.

Fashion soon began to trickle southward, and from the middle of the eighteenth century to the middle of the nineteenth occupied the area around Washington Square now vaguely known as "Society Hill." Though the name was appropriate enough, at least socially, it had nothing to do with High Society, as almost all who mention the name nowadays in connection with the Philadelphia Renaissance fall all over themselves in their eagerness to point out: as though the nickname were a disgrace. In fact, it was named for an early commercial group called the Society of Free Traders which owned property, including a now vanished hill, in the area before it was built up. It is in this area, and its extension west toward Broad Street, that most of Philadelphia's beautiful old houses were built. A few of them still remain there, the best extant example being Samuel Powel's house on 3rd Street.

By the 1850's Washington Square had become old-fashioned, and Old Philadelphia's brave pioneering venture westward had begun. Between the Civil War and the First World War, Rittenhouse Square and the streets off it from Chestnut to Pine and from Broad to about 22nd Street composed Old Philadelphia's Forbidden City, protected on the north by the ramparts of the Chinese Wall. Senator Pepper's picture of the Sunday parade on Walnut Street dates from this period, and Ingersolls and Cadwaladers left their beautiful houses on Fourth Street to build larger but less beautiful mansions near what became known as simply "The Square." "Nice old-fashioned people" continued in diminishing numbers to live on Clinton Street, alongside Agnes Repplier and the Pennsylvania Hospital; Drexels built gloomy monuments to themselves in West Philadelphia; the Irish had fine houses on South Broad and the Jews on North Broad; but Nearly Everybody lived on or near The Square.

v. Suburbia in Excelsis

Beginning, however, also as early as the 1850's, the trek even further west to the suburbs began. The first suburban areas evolved for Philadelphia in and about Germantown or in those Northern Liberties where country places like Wakefield and Stenton and Butler Place had already domesticated the country-side. Sidney Fisher, who himself moved permanently to the country after his marriage, writes approvingly as of the 1850's about this new world where "One may now have a villa 10, 20, 30 miles from town and yet go in half an hour and return after the work of the day is over to dinner. In consequence . . . cottages and country estates, some of them very beautiful and costly, are multiplying."

What was true of the 1850's was still true of the 1960's, though the facility of travel which Sidney admired grows every year less facile, and the cottages less beautiful. The railroads in those earlier years knew a good thing, and soon took an active hand in creating semi-rural paradises. The Germantown boom was fed largely by the Reading; the Main Line as we have seen was deliberately cultivated by the Pennsylvania, and so was Chestnut Hill in a less direct way. Chestnut Hill was more or less the personal creation of one man, Henry Houston. He made his in The Railroad, of which he was a director, and in real estate and mining. Houston owned most of the land on which the western side of Chestnut Hill now stands and could travel all day in that pre-automobile era without even setting foot off his own property. He laid out the streets, financed the relocation of the Philadelphia Cricket Club there in 1883, built a summer hotel which is now Chestnut Hill Academy, and like the Robertses erected for himself a family church, St. Martins-in-the-Fields, to the Glory of God and the Houstons. Most of his great real estate holdings were inherited by his daughter Mrs. George Woodward, and some two hundred houses in the town are still owned and rented out by the Houston–Woodward estate.

Chestnut Hill and the Main Line became the centers of expensive suburban living. The last Old Philadelphian town houses were built around 1900, and from then on fashionable city life was doomed. The 1920's saw the almost complete removal of upper- and middle-class Philadelphia from the city to the suburbs, and by the Second World War the Forbidden City was a gutted shell, a deserted memory.

The owners of the city abdicated. Safe beyond the range of city taxes and city politics, they lost all interest in city reform. Since they didn't have to see what was happening, they didn't care; Philadelphia became another demonstration of the dangers of absentee landlordship. The wholesale decay and destruction of old houses and consequent blight on city real estate values that followed were outward signs of inward corruption.

No other city suffered so early and so terribly from the impact of the automobile. Even before the First War, Elizabeth Pennell was able to see what was happening. However, the final stage of transportation decay, so familiar now everywhere in America, has been averted. The automobile has not yet succeeded in completely abolishing comfortable and convenient public transportation. Thanks largely to a Transport Plan worked out by the reform government of the city, the trains do pretty well and still serve most of the principal areas of the city, assisted by subways, buses and even residual trolleys. When there isn't a strike (as in January, 1963) few cities are as comparatively easy to get around in without a car. The good service on the P.R.R. and the Reading contribute notably to this happy situation.

Meanwhile in the bosky bumps and dells of the Pennsylvania countryside, up the rushy glens along the west bank of the Schuylkill as far as Valley Forge, out along the railroad tracks to Paoli, up the Wissahickon into Chestnut Hill, in the more flat and open reaches of Whitemarsh, Bryn Athyn, Ambler, Penllyn, Philadelphians from 1880 to 1930 built up their private dream world, a rural fantasy, first of vast estates surrounded by miles of walls, with miles of driveway leading to great craggy mansions, and then, later, a more modern Arcadia of remodeled stone farmhouses surrounded by pastures with post-and-rail fences. Along crooked lanes with picturesque names, tree-shaded and lined on each side with wide bridle paths for horses, the Old Philadelphians tucked themselves into an impenetrable green maze. Here in a new and even more successfully Forbidden City, Philadelphians within only a few miles of the slums of North and West Philadelphia were able to cultivate the illusion that they really were country folk, and forget the ugliness and contradictions of the industrial civilization that supported them.

It was nice while it lasted. In a landscape where every prospect pleased, Philadelphians rode horses, cultivated gardens, gave parties and ignored the rest of America. The First War was an aggravating incident, the 'twenties ruffled the amenities and threw up an unfortunate new crop of uncouth millionaires. The crash of 1929 brought down the house. People dismissed their second chauffeurs and assistant gardeners; some even closed up the big mansions and moved into gate lodges. The dream world began to grow fuzzy and unkempt. Then came the Second War; prosperity returned and that completed the business. Nobody now wanted to live in the big houses or keep up the big grounds. The great acreages were sold off, the houses torn down, and in their place conscienceless and tasteless postwar developers have erected their colonial-type split levels. The former owners of the acres moved further south and west.

As in town, where the more emphatic glories of Walnut Street and The Square have vanished, but the more retiring areas around Spruce and Pine survive, so in the suburbs the survival of the quietest has again been evident. The huge places have gone, but in the heavily settled townlike sections of suburbia, many pleasantly old-fashioned neighborhoods, nice houses surrounded by beautiful trees on quiet streets, remain as they were. The real flower of Philadelphia suburbs, the rural-seeming prosperity of rolling pastures and forests inhabited by only an occasional well-placed herd of black angus or a mansion with its gardens and stables, does still exist, tucked away here and there, but always with the question in mind, "How long?" A thoroughly Indian summer melancholy hangs over the few secluded sanctuaries of this old way of life.

vi. *Home Away from Home*

THE ODDEST ASPECT of Philadelphia suburbia, and one which often strikes observers from out of town, is the fact that no matter how far the Philadelphia suburbs spread beyond the official bounds of the city, the inhabitants always seem to think of themselves as Philadelphians. This is quite different from New York, of course, where dwellers in Greenwich, Connecticut, Morristown, New Jersey and Cedarhurst, Long Island, are citizens of these respective places and not "New Yorkers." Philadelphians, however, can live an hour away from the city without seeming to lose their identification in the slightest. Still further extensions of this elastic Philadelphianism are the various resorts that Philadelphians have made their very own.

Potentially, the Philadelphia climate could have been one of the most broadening of influences. The summers may be less overwhelming than those of New Orleans, but July and August are still to be avoided if possible, and from the eighteenth century on, Philadelphians have been avoiding them whenever they could afford it. To get to coolness, Philadelphians have to travel beyond their own suburbs, and travel far. They have no North Shore like Boston, or lake front like Chicago. This presumably should have forced Philadelphians to be less insular — in summer, at least; but it hasn't. They just swarm where other Philadelphians swarm.

Three resort areas in particular are recognized Philadelphia beehives. For the very upper class and Sidney Fishery Old Philadelphian, there is New England — Northeast Harbor in Maine, with a smaller but more intellectual enclave in Saunderstown, Rhode Island, across the water from Newport; for a more Quakerishly modest John Watson sort of Old Philadelphian, the Pocono

Mountains in northern Pennsylvania; and for the general average suburban well-to-do Philadelphian, the Jersey shore, in particular Bay Head and Mantoloking, and Cape May. Cape May, with its strong Baltimore influence, has a Catholic tinge to it.

None of these is an arch-original Philadelphia resort, for as Philadelphians moved from neighborhood to neighborhood in town, so they have moved, slowly, from one resort to anther. The first Jersey shore summer refuge was Long Branch, now long since deserted by them. It was there, according to crusty old Charles Biddle, father of Nicholas the Great, that occurred the archetypal confrontation of Quaker caution and the wild waves. John and James were about to take the plunge. "How does thee feel, John?" said James. "I feel very well," said John. "So do I; would thee feel any better for going into the water?" said James. "I doubt it," said John. "Nor would I. Let us then not go into the water, John," said James, and they retired landward.

Things were more reckless at Newport, which in the early nineteenth century, and especially after the advent of the railroad, became The Place. Sidney Fisher glowed at the very prospect of Newport in 1844:

> No other resort could exhibit a crowd so distinguished for refinement, wealth and fashion. The number of persons who were vlugar or underbred was so inconsiderable as to produce no appreciable effect. Far more recherché indeed than . . . our cities where society is rapidly losing its tone. Philadelphia was very well represented — Mrs. Ridgeway, the beauty of the season, Mrs. Jno. Butler, Mrs. Wilcocks, Miss Waln, Pierce Butler etc. We had two balls each week, and two fancy balls. Among the novelties was a new dance, the Polka, just introduced in this country. It is somewhat like a waltz. Ten years ago everyone would have been shocked by it, but we are improving.

The only trouble was getting to Newport and back in the plebeian cars, "crowded to excess with all sorts of people. . . . The masses in this as in everything else have destroyed all decency. In coming from New York there were 5 negroes in the same car with me. This I have never seen before."

But alas, Newport too succumbed to vulgarity, and Philadelphians could stand it no longer. In the 'eighties and 'nineties, led by vigorous Weir Mitchell, who craved a simpler, if by no means too simple, life, they shook the gold dust of Newport from their hiking boots and decamped to Mount Desert in Maine. There in a sort of Marie Antoinette rusticity, they passed summers of walking and talking nicely described by Mitchell himself in *Characteristics*. The fictional Dr. North and his friends went on tramps and picnics in the woods which seem really rustic enough until one reads, ". . . as the servant busied himself with the lunch, and put the wine to cool in the brook . . . ." Simplicity with a difference. At Bar Harbor, Philadelphia girls taught Boston boys how to flirt, and it was all recherché enough to have pleased even Sidney.

But here, too, nice people were driven out by rich people. First the acceptable but certainly not simple J. P. Morgan and Alexander Cassatt, and then, after the First War, the deluge. What happened is best illustrated by the story of the second Mrs. Stotesbury, she who taught her Edward to "play." She bought the Cassatt house, but it wasn't big enough. It had only fifteen servants' rooms. She needed forty, so she tore it down. She went over the plans of her new house with her architect, and ordered him to have it ready and furnished for her to move in when she came back next summer. It was ready and furnished sure enough. She walked all over it and said, "It won't do. Tear it down and build it over again; and this time I'll stay here and see that it's done properly." For decades houses like the Stotesbury and the Atwater Kent houses with their stalls for fifteen automobiles and their yachts at the dock were shows for passing tourists. The Old Philadelphians with lips acurl moved over to Northeast Harbor, and there they remain in comparative wine-cooled Mitchell "simplicity." As for Bar Harbor, hubris brought on nemesis, as it properly should. Never was the survival of the quietest and the downfall of pride more dramatically represented. In 1947 Bar Harbor was more or less wiped out by a great fire which destroyed all but a fringe of the by now semi-deserted mansions. The

Stotesbury house had been sold to a junk dealer for about five thousand dollars. He tore it down to salvage the lead in the plumbing and resold the land for a ferry dock, where very non-recherché trippers from Nova Scotia now debouch. Northeast Harbor sits back, rather smugly saying "I told you so," and supports a full summer quota of Chestons, Clarks, Coxes, Lippincotts, Madeiras, Morrises, Newbolds, Peppers, Robertses, Rosengartens, Thayers and Yarnalls.

There is no other summer place quite like Northeast for sheer concentrated Old Philadelphianism, and no winter resorts are really Philadelphian at all in that sense. Stotesbury and his like helped to get Palm Beach going, and a few more genuinely Old Philadelphian people have plantations in South Carolina or plantation houses on St. Croix in the Virgin Islands, but there is nothing in winter to correspond with Northeast, the Poconos and the Shore in summer. Of course in winter, what with hunting and balls and the Orchestra, one is kept pretty busy at home. And there are some other really exciting things going on there too these days; part of what is called the "Philadelphia Renaissance." Nearly Everybody is involved in it in some way.

2

i. C and C

IN 1956, on the east side of Washington Square in the old section
of the city, between the Athenaeum and the offices of J. B. Lippincott Company, Richardson Dilworth, already at that time
Mayor of Philadelphia, built a town house. It is somewhat pre-
ciously imitative of an eighteenth-century Philadelphia town
house of the Powel or Shippen sort, but certainly very pretty.
What is important about it is not its architecture but its location
and its date. The building of a new town house even by a mayor
might not seem so significant; but in Philadelphia it was and is.
No such town house had been built anywhere in Philadelphia
since about 1900. The Dilworth house was, however, no whim,
no eccentric and isolated "folly." It was a straw in a change of
wind, a wind of change blowing for the first time in Philadelphia's history from west to east, rather than from east to west.

The Dilworth house was a milestone in the renaissance of
Society Hill. Literally hundreds of houses in this most venerable
of Philadelphia's once fashionable neighborhoods have now been
bought and remodeled, a few of them by Old Philadelphians,
and for the first time since the Revolution real estate down there
is booming. The renaissance of Society Hill, however, is just one
piece in a gigantic jigsaw puzzle of reform and renewal which
has stirred Philadelphia from its hundred-year sleep, and prom-
ises to transform the city completely. This movement, of which
the return to Society Hill is a significant part, is generally known
as the Philadelphia Renaissance. People actually call it that; the

fact of this Renaissance does much to contradict and correct all that has been said so far about Philadelphia and Old Philadelphia. There really has been, even in the five years during which this book has been written, an extraordinary change — one of the most remarkable reversals of form, and rejuvenation, in the history of American cities. Just in time, too.

To understand the full meaning of the Philadelphia Renaissance, one has to go back not just into the history of real estate and fashionable neighborhoods, but into the history of politics. Half a century ago, in 1903, Lincoln Steffens, chief of the Muckrakers, wrote an article on Philadelphia which he called "Corrupt and Contented." The label was so exactly descriptive that it stuck, and for decades Philadelphians acknowledged the soft impeachment with indulgent chuckles. It was almost as if they were proud of it; many Philadelphians, but not all Philadelphians. There were of course degrees of contentment and varieties of corruption, but for seventy-odd years, from the end of the Civil War to the great depression, both Philadelphia and Pennsylvania lived under a one-party dictatorship kept in power by a benevolent if tyrannous prosperity. The corruption could not have existed without the contentment. Could the contentment have existed without what caused the corruption? Philadelphians never really dared to try to find out.

Between the two dates — 1903 and 1956, when the Dilworth house was built — there has been a complete upheaval, and Philadelphia is no longer either notably contented or notably corrupt. Naturally the contentment disappeared first. That contentment, based so firmly on the Iron Triangle with its steel and railroads, its Baldwin locomotives and Cramp ships, kept people of all degrees working, and prevented them from thinking. Conditions at the very bottom of the pile among miners and sweatshop workers may have been unbelievably dreadful; but most of these workers were recent immigrants who were used to even worse treatment at home, and who took a while to realize just how they were being exploited here. Meanwhile the majority of the native-born, the millions of respectable upper-echelon workers and craftsmen, the storekeepers and clerks, owned their own brick row-houses, enjoyed their cricket and baseball, drank their beer and voted religiously the ticket of the party to which presumably all these blessings were due — the Grand Old Party, the Republican Party, the party of the sacred Tariff that protected both labor and management from nefarious furrin competition.

In Philadelphia and in Pennsylvania there was only one party. There was no division along class or geographical or country-city lines. Everybody was a Republican, nobs and snobs, Old Philadelphians and new Philadelphians, Episcopalians and Catholics, farmers and manufacturers. A few scholarly and supercilious Biddles, Cadwaladers, Ingersolls and Whartons continued in their prewar and hopeless pro-Southern loyalty to the Democratic Party. This merely had the effect of making the Union League always just the least bit déclassé socially; and eventually it did produce a crop of Biddles and Ingersolls who in the twentieth century upset the Union League, as we shall see, by helping to elect a Democratic mayor. But except for this tiny Sidney Fishery dissent at the very top, the voting was pretty much unanimous. Nomination, as in the South today, was equivalent to election.

Nearly Everybody was Republican.

The reasons were various. First, Pennsylvania had been *invaded*; Philadelphians were scared pink by Gettysburg, and then wildly elated by the victory led by Philadelphia's own General Meade. The War, in the eyes of Boker and his like, became a sacred cause, and though Philadelphia took a long time converting, it converted hard. "Democrat" became tantamount to "traitor."

There was also the Philadelphia tradition of protectionism. After the Civil War the Republican Party became the unswerving champion of protectionism, high tariffs and help for the manufacturer, Pennsylvania being par excellence the manufacturing, rather than the commercial or trading, state. Not only did Pennsylvania and Philadelphia manufacturers benefit hugely from this policy as opposed to New York or the South, but this protectionism was the justification of a century of peculiarly Philadelphian economic thought, from the theories of Rawle on how the inhabitants of Delaware were to become rich through Tench Coxe, "father of manufacturing," to Henry Carey and his disciples.

Still another factor that helped Philadelphia to remain a one-party town was the somewhat less dense and less different quality of its immigration. The large German immigration of the mid-century was easily assimilated in a city already so early and so thoroughly Germanized. In any case, nowhere did ethnic groups get up an opposition to the ruling classes as the Irish did in Boston. All were Republicans; Irish, German, Jewish, Negro.

But what really made Pennsylvania a one-party state and kept it that way was the Organization. The Organization was first created by a somewhat unsavory character called Simon Cameron. He began political life in the 1830's as a western Pennsylvania Democrat, but switched early to the new Republican Party. His career, one of long and prosperous malfeasance, began with his defrauding the Winnebago Indians of their lands and moneys; when Lincoln was forced by a political deal to make him Secretary of War, Cameron used the post most advantageously for himself and contracting friends. What was good for Cameron was good for the country, he believed. The only way Lincoln could get rid of him was to appoint him minister to faraway Russia.*

From 1867 on Cameron was Senator from Pennsylvania, and absolute boss of the state. He saw to it that his Princeton-educated son James Donald took over as Senator when he retired in 1877. James was a chip off the block and for twenty more years he sat in the Senate and ruled Pennsylvania as his father had done. He was assisted in this pleasant occupation by a squint-eyed, Latin-reading son of a clergyman called Matthew Quay, a sinister personage whom Kipling considered the best-read man in America, and who kept a file, known as "Quay's Coffin," which furnished him with items for blackmail, at need, on anybody of

---

* Curiously enough Pennsylvania and Philadelphia seem to have specialized in producing ministers to Russia from Buchanan and Dallas in the 1830's, through Cameron and Boker, and finally to Bullitt and Bohlen in modern times.

political consequence in Pennsylvania. The Camerons and Quay served to justify Sidney Fisher's earlier opinions about the kind of men elected from the western part of "our Boeotian state." The axiom that no gentleman went into politics was thoroughly confirmed in them.

Boies Penrose, who succeeded the younger Cameron in the Senate, was something else again. He was an Old Philadelphian of the most unquestionable sort; but there was also no question at all about the ungentlemanliness of his politics. He is certainly one of the largest and oddest specimens of Old Philadelphia ever to appear on the local or the national scene.

As absolute ruler of Pennsylvania after the death of Quay in 1904, and therefore dominant figure in the Republican Party nationally, Penrose was in the early years of the twentieth century one of the most powerful men in the country. In a time when any Republican was pretty sure to get elected, and when the Senate and House were ruled by that party, Penrose made or approved of or vetoed all important nominations (it was he who by choosing T. R. as V.P. "kicked him upstairs"), collected and distributed all major contributions to the party, dominated all important Senate committees and hence all legislation, and kept the Pennsylvania Organization he inherited from the Camerons and Quay in prosperous and working order. The question is, why? The Camerons and Quay were in politics to make money and get ahead. They made money and got ahead. Penrose, however, being a Penrose, already had money and was ahead, facts which he was at no pains to conceal. Nor did he conceal his contempt for others less fortunate. He seemed to be in the business purely for pleasure; at once an amateur and the most professional of professionals.

The Penroses have already been mentioned as a family of shipbuilders in the early eighteenth century with the Penns as partners. By the later nineteenth century they were primarily doctors and scholars, affiliated with the Biddles and with the Philosophical Society (the Society is supported right now by a Penrose bequest). Boies went through the proper paces, Episcopal Academy, Harvard '81, law in the office of McVeagh and Bispham. At college he exhibited a literary bent, like his collegemates Theodore Roosevelt and Owen Wister. He wrote two plays, one a modern romance, the other a pseudo-Greek tragedy. He destroyed them. He majored in political economy, and after failing his exams out of sheer inertia, he was reinstated, through family pressure, and was graduated second in his class. His thesis on Martin Van Buren was pronounced "masterly."

There would seem to be evidence that, like the typical hero in the typical Philadelphia novel, he returned from Harvard determined to reform the city's politics, but became disillusioned.* Certainly his first successful political coup was the election of a reform candidate as city councilman over the objections of the ward boss. He also supported the new Bullitt city charter, one of the many reforms of that period, and saw it through over the opposition of local bosses. These symptoms of reform appear to be delusive, however. Everything that one knows of his character predisposes one against thinking of Penrose as a reformer, even a disillusioned reformer. He was born disillusioned.

Evidently to Penrose the only thing of real interest in life was the intricate game of party politics, which he played to win, as others play to win at poker. He had studied the game at college; afterward he practiced and perfected his skill at it, first on the local, later on the national level. The chips were power; but it was the game, not the chips, he loved. He disdained the People, the democratic process and other politicians. He cared less than nothing for popularity itself; in fact he loathed it and anyone who sought it. He respected only power and force and the clever use of force to maintain power. He had no desire to change the rules of this game he loved; he just wanted to win and keep on winning. In the end, the game won him, and left him bankrupt in every way except financially. He wound up with the one thing for which he cared nothing — money. When he died, he left a personal fortune of several millions. There was, however, nothing the least ascetic about this man who so disdained money. He was,

* See *The Great One* by Henry Hart.

[544]

in fact, something of a spendthrift, with a gargantuan and ruthless appetite for physical pleasure. He was a giant in size and strength, six feet four and powerful. The only thing that kept him from being a famous football player at Harvard was his equally giant inertia and his phobic distaste for physical contact. He couldn't stomach the thought of mingling with other smelly players, and later in life he never shook hands if he could help it. Many a minor politician lived to regret a moment of mistaken familiarity with Big Grizzly, and he especially disliked anyone who whispered to him.

Though he scorned any games except political ones, he was a fine rider and avid hunter. His favorite sport was, appropriately enough, hunting grizzlies out West. When he was about to be nominated to the state legislature, he spent the campaign with his older brother Charles, later a celebrated surgeon, in the Tetons of Wyoming, where Owen Wister also hunted. Penrose's brother was badly mauled by a wounded bear; scorning his local guides, Boies broke through across country, the shortest route to the nearest railroad, with his wounded brother slung to the saddle, and saw him to the hospital and safety. When he returned to Philadelphia, having been nominated without any effort on his part, he failed to mention the incident. Nobody's business.

His ability to gratify his tastes in liquor, food and women became a legend. There are awed accounts of his breakfasts — a dozen fried eggs, a half-inch slice of ham, a dozen rolls, a quart of coffee — or of his making a dinner of twenty-six reed birds, which he ate out of the chafing dish, elbows firmly planted on table and working on them with both hands alternately. He finished up by scraping the bed of wild rice from the bottom with a spoon and drinking down the bowl of gravy.

He was a handsome young man in the arrogant bull-headed fashion of the time — large head, curly hair, heavy regular features like Boker and Wister — but in the end his diet wrecked his spectacular physique. He grew immensely fat, almost three hundred pounds, but till the very end never lost his dignity, presence or appetite. As he grew fatter he gave up his horses for a series of fire-truck-red motorcars in which he indulged his love of country tours and botanizing. He was an expert amateur naturalist. "He knows more about nature than any man in Washington," said Teddy Roosevelt, "except me."

Penrose could absorb immense quantities of liquor too without showing it, but made no pretense at hiding either his occasional drunkenness or continued lecheries. "I do what I damn please," said Big Grizzly. "The masses like that." He had no patience with temperance advocates and made no bones about his hatred and flagrant violation of Prohibition when it came. "The best drinkers I know," he liked to say, "are Quakers. They are sober even when drunk." Penrose evidently inherited at least one quality from his Quaker ancestors.

He scorned marriage and his association with bawdy houses cost him his first and most bitter defeat. His chief ambition had always been to be Mayor of Philadelphia. Senator from Pennsylvania was second best. He stood for the nomination in 1895, supported by Quay but opposed by the city organization. The mayoralty was in the bag, however, until a picture of Boies coming out of a known whorehouse fell into the hands of the opposition. They threatened to put in on the front page of every Philadelphia newspaper, and for once in his life Penrose had to back down. He conceded the Republican nomination — that is to say, the election.

This had no effect on his later career, and he continued to scorn convention and hypocrisy in an age peculiarly devoted to both. In this he makes a nice contrast to his equally sincere antagonist, Pious John Wanamaker, whom he defeated for Senator in 1897. The life of Penrose, in fact, was one long insult to the sensibilities of nice people — "mice people," as he called them. He swore, he drank, he whored and he didn't care who knew it. The most famous of Penrose stories concerns an episode aboard his yacht *Betty*. In the middle of a mixed party the Grizzly appeared awesomely nude. As he was about to dive over the rail for a swim, one of the ladies, her face covered with confusion and fingers, let out a genteel scream. He turned on her.

"Madam," he said, "if you see anything you haven't seen before, you should be ashamed of yourself." (The story is told less appropriately of J. P. Morgan; Morgan was more massively respectable.) Once asked by an eager reporter if the Organization had picked a man qualified to be the next Republican candidate for President, Boies replied that they had indeed found just the man; a man of lofty ideals, familiar with world problems, of spotless character, an inspiration to all of us, on whom one might look as a national hero. "Who is it?" asked the reporter, breathless. "The late Buffalo Bill," answered Penrose. Usually he didn't bother to be satirical about his candidates. "Public office is the last refuge of the incompetent," he liked to say. He was no more tactful in social life. He never mixed in Old Philadelphian circles if he could help it, much preferring the company of ward heelers and whores. On one occasion, however, a cousin dragged him to a tea. Guest of honor was an august dowager who used a cane. "Glad to see you, madam," he bellowed. "What the hell's the matter with your leg?"

A character he magnificently was; but what did he do? Nothing. He was Senator from Pennsylvania continuously from 1897, third in the dynasty that began with Simon and James Cameron, till his death in 1922, and as Senator he did — nothing. Nothing except keep the Republican Party in complete control of Pennsylvania for three decades, and so by extension, the nation; and himself in complete and autocratic control of that party in Pennsylvania, and so by extension the nation. Any means that served that simple purpose served him. The wholesale graft and bribery and corruption that went on underneath him was no concern of his. He himself was above small dishonesties. Graft disgusted him. No money scandals ever dented his own hide. He had no master, but like John G. Johnson, he had clients and he served them well; for the six great traction kings — Widener, Elkins, Dolan of Philadelphia and Yerkes of Philadelphia and Chicago (the last memorialized by Theodore Dreiser in *The Titan*), Ryan and Whitney of New York — for Frick and Carnegie, lords of Pittsburgh and steel, Penrose supported tariffs and emasculated antitrust and labor laws. He laughed at "statesmanship" as he laughed at reform. Woodrow Wilson summed up everything he thoroughly disliked in politics; so much so that he remained resolutely opposed to American entry into the First War, regarding it throughout merely as a Democratic peccadillo and brainstorm of Wilson's. One will find no taint of statesmanship on the record of Penrose as Senator. He was a politician, nothing but a politician, and proud of it.

Like William Penn on top of City Hall, before mentioned as an appropriate symbol of the Oligarchy's attitude toward politics, Penrose stood alone and aloof, his hand extended in benediction over the red-light district, paying no attention to the small delinquencies of City Hall below. He was the Old Philadelphia figure of the Iron Age in politics, as Cassatt or Effingham Morris or Joseph Wharton were figures in business. But Penrose was not one of them. He was a rebel, in his way, an outcast of sorts, not really accepted. Though nine Penroses, past and present, have been members of the Philadelphia Club, this particular Boies was not. Nor was he active in the Philosophical Society, as was his brother Charles, nor did he play cricket or sit on charitable boards. His "mice people" were afraid of him, and he scorned them. Much like the later offbeat Philadelphia lawyer Chippy Paterson, he preferred low to high life, and functioned rather as as enemy than as an ally of the society that bred him.

He was, however, still a son of that society, another disappointed Philadelphia princeling like Biddle and Boker. Handsome, rich, intelligent, well-bred, he too wanted to play the game of his choice superbly, but with condescending ease, as a Prince should (Biddle running the Bank as one who "liked to be irresistible," a "young person good naturedly ordering the servants about"). Like them Penrose was brilliantly successful, yet in the end a disappointment. He would not wholly bend his neck, submit himself, sell his soul; he remained, like Biddle, superior to the game he played. But he lost it.

He cannot be regarded as a symbol of Old Philadelphia or, like George Pepper, of the Gentleman in Politics. Aristocrat he may have been and always remained; gentleman he was not. There is a difference between the man who says "I do as I please" and the man who says "I do as I ought." He is rather *the* symbol of the "corrupt" in "corrupt and contented." Ruthless, cynical, blind to any conception of an honorable commonwealth, he yet secured for the city, the state and the nation the kind of smoothly organized misgovernment they deserved. Nearly Everybody was contented with it.

ii. *Renaissance*

NEARLY EVERYBODY, but not everybody. All during this period a futile stir of reform splashed at the foot of City Hall and splattered the Organization with exposés. As early as 1871 a Municipal Reform Association composed of Better Citizens began to be active. The Bullitt Reform Charter was hailed as the dawn of a new day. A Committee of 100 in the 'eighties took up the good work and all sorts of glorious accomplishments were credited to them. A Democratic mayor was even elected for a term in 1881. In 1883 a book called *The Fall of Bossism* was written about Philadelphia, full of revelations and ending on the note of Virtue Triumphant. But the waters of pollution closed over the city once more, the Committee of 100 returned to private life, and the Gas Ring and the Organization and the Bosses and all the rest took over. Business as usual. Still, the Better Citizens continued to celebrate Virtue Triumphant about every ten years or so. In 1911, for instance, a jolly German-turned-Quaker, Rudolph Blankenburg, was elected Mayor on an independent ticket. Old Dutch Cleanser started to shake things up; but his councilmen betrayed him, and another reform was done for.

So it continued right down to the 1950's. In the 'twenties and 'thirties William Bullitt electioneered and campaigned, ran for Mayor — and was defeated. George Earle, an Old Philadelphian, made a controversial Democratic Governor — for a while. John Kelly ran for Mayor too. Everybody agreed he certainly would have won except for fraud at the polls; but officially he lost. The depression, which everywhere else induced reforms or Democratic triumphs, had no effect on Philadelphia. The Republican city fathers turned down nineteen million dollars of Federal aid rather than be beholden to Roosevelt. After the War, the Organization was still in power, and Philadelphia was still corrupt.

But hardly contented. A revolution, a really serious revolution, was in the making. Its leaders, a group always referred to as the Young Turks, had graduated from Harvard, Yale and Princeton, mostly, during the depression. At college they, like Boies Penrose, had studied political economy, but came out with very different ideas. Though some of them were Republicans, they were all at heart New Dealers. They believed that the city could be planned back to prosperity, and that politics could be radically and even permanently reformed; but not by Better Citizens and Committees and Amateur Gentlemen of the Bullitt sort, the "boutonniere candidates." The Young Turks meant business, and like Penrose, they meant to be professionals. Reforming professionals.

These Young Turks knew better than to tackle City Hall on their own. They in themselves represented nobody in particular. Some of them were rebellious Old Philadelphians; others were young intellectuals. Some were political theorists, others architects and town planners. They looked for more powerful allies, and they found them.

Of the older Old Philadelphians who had been carrying on the battle for reform in the old Committee way, rather ineffectively, as undeviating Republicans, the most important was Edward Hopkinson. As senior partner of Drexel and Company, he was successor to Stotesbury as leading financier of the city. As great-great-great-grandson of Francis the harpsichordist he was ineffably Old Philadelphian. The political leader and inspirer of the Turks, a more modestly young Old Philadelphian named Walter Phillips, converted Hopkinson to the revolution, and Hopkinson in turn converted or even coerced other reformist older Old Philadelphians to fall in line. One of the leading figures among these converts was C. Jared Ingersoll; led by the prestige of Hopkinson and Ingersoll all sorts of other Committeemen, despite their deep-seated Republicanism, joined up, and in desperation, and not without hesitancy, agreed to help, even if it meant the election of a Democrat.

There were also the older rebellious Old Philadelphians of the Biddle-and-Bullitt sort. They joined in with enthusiasm. Most effective of their organizations was the arch-liberal Americans for Democratic Action, the Philadelphia branch of which was largely founded and inspired by John F. Lewis, Jr., past owner of the Academy of Music and President of the Academy of the Fine Arts, and his wife Ada. Everyone said that the A.D.A. was named after her. This again was a mixture of rebellious Old Philadelphians and all sorts of very non-Old Philadelphians, equally rebellious.

The ethnic minority leaders who counted most in the struggle were John Kelly and Matthew McCloskey, contractors representing Ireland and Catholicism, and Albert Greenfield, real estate mogul and one of the most powerful men in the city, representing Greenfield and the Jewish community, along with box manufacturer and former concert pianist Frederic Mann. Kelly had already had his fling at reform; Greenfield, formerly a staunch Republican, had switched to the Democratic side under the New Deal.

The Democratic machine in Philadelphia was (and remains, unfortunately) as corrupt and obsolescent in its own way as the Republican machine. It too depended on ward heelers and patronage for its direction and sustenance. It had, however, picked up a bit of New Deal liberalism during the 'thirties, and some minority group support. And as it became obvious that this reform was going to be, for the first time in years, a Democratic, not an Independent or Republican reform, the Democratic organization also had to be brought into the movement.

Through the late 'thirties and 'forties the ground swell grew, and the somewhat motley alliance of Young Turks, Better Citizens, radical Democrats, minority leaders and Democratic ward heelers practiced working together. Republican Mayors kept on being elected with depressing regularity, but gradually even the People, always the last to know, and so long accustomed to corruption and contentment, began to realize that something was up.

In 1952 they were forced to take notice, for in that year, for the first time since that abortive reform of 1881, a Democrat was ensconced as Mayor. His name was Joseph Sill Clark, and when he went on to become Senator, the succession was continued by his good friend Richardson Dilworth. These two have been the active vote-getting leaders of the Renaissance, politically and personally united in a sometimes uneasy Damon-and-Pythias relationship.

Clark had become a lawyer in the family firm after graduation from Harvard in 1923 and law school at the University. When the depression more or less liquidated the family firm, Clark, already a Democrat despite a long family tradition of Republicanism, allied himself with the Young Turks. Though somewhat older than most of them, he was hand-picked as their "political front," a man to act as their office-holding spokesman. Aside from gifts of personality — energy, a somewhat brusque charm, and brains — he also satisfied what were still considered essential qualifications for any reform candidate; he was Protestant — Kelly's defeat was considered, correctly or not, an indication that though Catholics might run the politics of both parties, one could not be actually elected — and a Better Citizen himself.

Dilworth was (and is) to Clark somewhat as Cassatt was to Roberts. Like Cassatt, Dilworth is the kind of dashing and sporty Pittsburgher that Philadelphians take to their hearts. After schooling at St. Mark's and Yale, neither of them Philadelphia resorts, he married a Philadelphian and settled in Philadelphia as a lawyer. Both he and Clark emerged after active war careers, fed up with contented Philadelphia law and corrupt politics, and ready to lead the charge. Of the two, Clark is perhaps the more uncompromising idealist and reformer. Dilworth is the more easily popular and more expert politician.

Part of Clark's initial success was undoubtedly due to the fact

[552]

that he is, despite all his demurrers, very much an Old Philadelphian, if not an Oldest Philadelphian. Clarks have been presidents of the Old Company, and famous at cricket and tennis too. (It was Senator Clark's father, as before indicated, who won the national doubles championship with Mr. Sears in Newport in 1885.) Over thirty Clarks now hold down their page in the *Social Register* and nearly a dozen Clarks, dead or alive, their chairs past and present at the Philadelphia Club. Clarks may or may not consider themselves really Old Philadelphian, but Nearly Everybody else does. As a knight in shining armor Joseph Sill Clark would do very well. And he did.

One of the goals of the Young Turks had been a charter that would give greater power to the Mayor. With Clark's accession they got it, and Clark's first sweeping out of City Hall raised a tremendous dust. Abuses a century old were revealed and corrected. Half a dozen suicides, including that of the Chief of the Amusement Tax Office, who hanged himself, scores of indictments, impeachments and imprisonments for embezzlement and extortion livened things up and kept the newspapers happy. Besides the grand frauds, there were all sorts of picturesque peccadillos. For decades Philadelphia water had been pumped almost untouched out of the sewage-receiving Schuylkill, and was universally known to be undrinkable. One reason Philadelphians were supposed to be ancestor-conscious is that they absorbed so much of the run-off from the family bones in Laurel Hill Cemetery. To avoid contamination, judges in City Hall had been supplying themselves with bottled water and charging it to the taxpayers. Quill pens were still in use there, while elsewhere a prison chief ran a restaurant where he sold for his personal profit food canned by his prisoners. All this was due to be changed.

It was a glorious spree of housecleaning. In place of the malefactors Clark installed not so much Democratic machine men, as Young Turks and Old Philadelphians. Walter Phillips was made head of the Department of Commerce. Edward Hopkinson, Jared Ingersoll, Shippen Lewis, Morris Duane, Alfred Scattergood, Robert Yarnall, Stewart Rauch and others with Old Philadelphian names or connections were for the first time since the 1830's involved in the various branches of the city's public life. Mann and Greenfield and Kelly were also put effectively to work, and as a result pretty Nearly Everybody joined the parade, and submitted, on the local level at least, to Democratic rule.

Perhaps one of the most striking documents of Philadelphiana in modern times was a full-page advertisement that appeared in the papers in October 1959, when Richardson Dilworth, Clark's successor as Shining Knight, was running for reelection as mayor against the increasingly egregious Harold Stassen. In huge capitals the advertisement was headed, "If you believe in Philadelphia give RICHARDSON DILWORTH four more years to finish the job." Following an explanatory paragraph was a list of signers that looked pretty much like those of the Declaration of Independence, or at least the Constitution. Henry Drinker, Morris Duane, Leonard Beale, Radcliffe Cheston, Jared and Sturgis Ingersoll, Isaac Roberts, Nicholas Roosevelt and others were joined by Elias Wolf, D. Hays de Solis Cohen and Lessing Rosenwald in an array of names deliberately designed to be impressive; impressive you understand to the average newspaper-reading man-in-the-street. This was to be a consummate collection of Better Citizens for public consumption. Of the thirty-odd signatures, twenty at least were either flagrantly Old Philadelphian, including Jewish Old Philadelphian, or close connections thereto. None of them was an active Democrat of the John F. Lewis or Francis Biddle sort (no Biddles of any branch signed), or people like Hopkinson too closely allied with the administration.

Two things made the document memorable. One is that these people, some of them arch-Republicans, should finally have been brought to cross party lines so conspicuously (there was a disclaimer at the bottom making clear that they were not backing any *party*). The other is the clear evidence of the weight of Old Philadelphia and its names in the city. That these particular names, many of them two hundred years old, should so be used, considered to be politically effective in a modern American city, is itself fairly unusual. That they should be used to back a Democrat, even a reforming one, in Philadelphia is almost unbelievable; a real revolution in local political attitudes.

iii. Redevelopment

THE CLEAN SWEEP of political reform has had an influence far beyond City Hall. It has affected almost every aspect of Philadelphia life, as it was meant to. Most obvious result has been the physical change. Up to the beginnings of the Renaissance Philadelphia resembled nothing so much as a huge rusty complicated old machine sinking into the mud. The pretty brick-and-marble town of the 1820's, Philadelphia's Silver Age, had grown into a sooty late-nineteenth-century Iron Age monster of row-houses and warehouses. Then the depression and the automobile began to knock holes in the fabric. Buildings were torn down to make parking lots, or just torn down, and by 1950 the city looked much like London after the blitz.

Physical renovation began long before political renovation. For years a "crackpot dreamer" called Charles Abell Murphy had been besieging Better Citizens with a plan for clearing the area around Independence Hall of its shabby business buildings and giving that National Shrine a fit setting. Nobody listened to him; yet in the 1940's another, separate and more effective movement, initiated and led by Judge Edwin O. Lewis, prevailed upon the state to open up a Mall north of the building planted with grass and trees and making a grand vista (too grand, many think) before the façade of the State House.

This Mall was the first step in the resurrection of the whole lower and older part of the city. The National Park Service stepped in, took over the State House itself, and acquired the squares eastward down to the Delaware River. Here the government cleared away all the buildings, preserving a few monuments like Biddle's and Girard's neoclassic banks, and filled the space between with a series of charming brick-walled gardens. Then with the coming of the reform administration, the City Planning Commission, under the chairmanship of Edward Hopkinson and the direction of an Old Philadelphian town planner and original Young Turk, Edmund W. Bacon, took up the good work. It produced a scheme for the renovation of that whole area of the city, south to Lombard Street, west to 7th Street, in what is loosely called Society Hill. The plan, now actually being put into effect, is one of the most daring and most tasteful pieces of town planning ever conceived, an attempt to salvage what is good of the old, add what is needed of the new, and in general transform that part of the city into a sort of urban residential paradise without making a museum-fossil out of it.

A good deal of the land has already been cleared (some think too much and too ruthlessly) and modern town houses and a few very tall modern skyscraper apartments are being built. Eighteenth-century houses are being transformed from cheap rooming houses and small shops into beautiful places for people of means to live in. There will be a series of tree-shaded walkways through the middle of the blocks, small gardens and parks, and a sensibly controlled plan for traffic and parking. Along the river itself, beyond a projected Delaware Expressway, and on the now battered waterfront, will spread a grandiose marina with boat docks, restaurants, marine museums and whatnot (maybe). On the other side of Chestnut Street, northward from the State House and along the Mall, the Federal Government will build a series of fine new office buildings (maybe). Since the Mall itself now reaches all the way to Franklin Park this means that a great swathe of the city, about seven squares by seven (and Philadelphia squares are big) is actually right now in process of being rebuilt. Every month some old pretzel factory comes down and some block of old houses perks up, some park or garden emerges, some new apartment house begins to sprout.

This revival in the older part of the city is the single most attractive and exciting part of the Philadelphia Renaissance, and has most vitally intrigued Old Philadelphians. Remodeling old houses is, after all, one of Old Philadelphia's favorite indoor sports, and to be able to remodel and consciously serve the cause of civic revival all at once has gone to the heads of the upper classes like champagne. Hundreds of houses have been or are slated to be bought up down there, and following the example of Dilworth in his move to Washington Square, family after family has returned to its city roots. People who haven't owned a town house in sixty years are following the trek, led by the Jared Ingersolls and supported by a wave of euphoria and excitement. Nearly Everybody's either doing it or is excited about it. There's still a long way to go before the neighborhood is once more really pretty and respectable; but when and if it all does get done according to plan, Society Hill will be an American showplace of city restoration; not a Williamsburg, but a living, breathing modern example of what a city can do for itself.

The kind of remodeling of old houses characteristic of Society Hill and sponsored there by the city has been actually going on in Philadelphia for a long time. Little Panama Street, south of Rittenhouse Square, where Senator Pepper once lived and where the Emlen Ettings still do, was a restoration of the 'twenties; the southern squares of Camac Street, too. On these little alleys or mews running between the main streets were built small working-people's houses, where folk such as the Blizzards could enjoy the bells of St. Mark's, or carriage houses. When done up pretty they make ideal small town houses for modern households. The contagion of remodeling has passed through these streets like a fever, from Schulykill to Delaware, and what were slums a few years ago have blossomed into pink and pistachio plaster. One can walk the twenty-five or so squares across town without ever leaving the shelter of these delightful hidden purlieus, with the exception of a few crass commercial blocks near Broad Street.

Along the Schuylkill, too, a park has actually been created, for the first time in history, and eventually a tree-lined esplanade will connect northward with Fairmount Park. Beyond the river, in West Philadelphia, old neighborhoods of stately Tuscan villas flanked by old magnolias and surrounded by seedy hedges have brightened also into pink and pistachio, and similar activity goes on in the shabbier parts of Germantown and Chestnut Hill. Besides this predominantly upper- or middle-class activity, a wave of lower-class prinking, much of it under the guidance of an active garden expert called Mrs. Bush-Brown, has brightened a hundred slum or close-to-slum streets with window boxes and new trees and fresh paint.

And then there is Urban Redevelopment. Remodeling and prinking are characteristic Old Philadelphian approaches to fixing up the city; but the Planning Commission has much more grandiose projects. Acres and acres of the most hideous slums in the world have already been torn down and in their places have been erected decent and sometimes even pleasant-looking modern row-houses or low apartments or skyscrapers, surrounded by lawns and trees and walkways and playgrounds. There is even a plan for a city-within-a-city, called Eastwick, way down on the other side of the lower Schuylkill. This enclave will house some fifty thousand people and is to include commercial and industrial sections too — once the extremely resistant squatters and shanty dwellers have been evacuated.

Besides these projects for the non–Old-Philadelphian poor, there are projects for the non–Old Philadelphian rich. Along the Parkway, in a triangle of land planned no doubt as the site for some Roman Institution, but actually for years a slice of slum and then a rubble heap, there has now been built by private funds but with various forms of city and United States subsidy a set of shiny new apartment blocks called the Park Towne. Visible from every incoming train, they inject a note of feeble verticality into the horizontal classicism of the Benjamin Franklin Parkway. A veritable Shangri-La of light, air, greenery, peace and convenience only a few blocks from City Hall, the Park Towne is a dream; though at a price, for the apartments were deliberately designed by the planners as a lure to bring well-to-do suburbanites back to town (or towne). Another equally chic apartment house has now been erected on the new Pennsylvania Boulevard that runs so nakedly along the route of the old Chinese Wall; still another one is in process of building farther west. These buildings are fully rented as soon as advertised; but they have not quite fulfilled the planners' hopes of repatriating Old Philadelphia suburbanites. The fact is that "Nobody lives there." They have become very expensive ghettoes, almost entirely Jewish and quite segregated. One doubts somehow that this is what the Planning Commission had in mind.

This illustrates some of the problems planners have to cope with. Apartments, especially where surrounded by free space on all sides, as well as parks and gardens, certainly offer many advantages for city dwellers. They also provide greatly increased tax revenues per square foot; Park Towne has already repaid its various debts to city and county several times over. A few Old Philadelphians have always lived in rather moth-eaten older apartment houses along Rittenhouse Square or in such residential hotels as the Barclay, but these have usually been older or single people. Nearly Everybody else in Philadelphia wants a house, and the basic Philadelphia psychology for centuries has been oriented, like London, toward houses, not, like Paris, toward flats. As far as Old Philadelphia is concerned, remodeling houses in Society Hill is suitable; renting rooms in Park Towne is not. One is curious to see then what will happen to the immense new Hopkinson House on Washington Square, on land once owned by Greenfield, or to the tall fingers of concrete proposed by the Chinese-American architect Ieoh Ming Pei * for Society Hill. One must admit that everywhere a great boom in big elaborate apartment houses has suddenly struck the city, whether "anybody" lives in them yet or not.

The master planning for Philadelphia's rehabilitation extends far beyond mere slum clearance or the erection of apartment houses, however. In the office of the Planning Commission are two large maps: Philadelphia before and Philadelphia after. Different colors indicate areas of different use — residential, commercial, industrial, institutional, and an important aspect of the Renaissance has been the effort to increase and concentrate areas of commercial and industrial activity right in the city where they can pay taxes. Most majestic of these new commercial areas is Penn Center, on the site of old Broad Street Station and its at-

* Known as "Pei in the Sky."

tendant wall. Whatever it may be lacking as an architectural monument, as compared to the average car-congested, hemmed-in city business block, it is something of a revelation; and it's certainly better, even in its present unfinished state, than what was there before.

Then there is a magnificent Food Distribution Center way down in South Philadelphia somewhere, and the new University Center over in West Philadelphia, linking Penn and Drexel Institute. Professors gasp in alternate spasms of enthusiasm and fury as each new building is put up: most gasp-creating of all is the new Saarinen women's dormitory, which looks like a beleaguered prison outside and A Day in Old New Orleans inside. All very exciting. A minor spasm of the same sort is taking place about Temple University on North Broad Street.

Out of the city, now choked with traffic jams each evening, writhes the white concrete of the Schuylkill Expressway ("Sure-hill" is its nickname), destroying the rural effect for which Fairmount Park was once so famous. It is a valiant if unsuccessful effort of the planners to handle that monster Traffic. Evidently the only way of handling the traffic hydra is to kill it; that is, get rid of automobiles. However, the planners look forward to a day when one will be able to zip through and around Philadelphia without disturbing any Philadelphians, which is a nice thought, at least for Philadelphians.

Whatever its faults, or future, the Philadelphia Renaissance has certainly managed to capture the enthusiasm of most Philadelphians, including especially Old Philadelphians, even though their interest may be somewhat parochially engaged by Society Hill, whose name becomes more and more appropriate. A significant celebration of this interest took place in May of 1961 when the Athenaeum gave a ball. It must certainly be the first time in history that a library has given a ball; in the library too. The Boston Athenaeum does *not* give balls. The ostensible cause for celebration was the occupancy, for the first time, by the library of its ground floor, hitherto rented out to insurance companies. Actually the ball amounted to an official opening of Society Hill.

As well as being the first ball given in the Athenaeum or any other library, it was the first ball given in that part of town in the memory of living man; probably since the Civil War.

It was all done vaguely period, 1814 when the Athenaeum was founded. Girls in Empire dresses splitting at the seams * were driven up to the door in carriages and did a minuet, champagne flowed, terrapin was gobbled by dowagers who hadn't had much lately, two maidens strummed the harp during supper and Meyer Davis played and played. *Life* came and was hidden behind bushes, but since nobody did anything exotic or spectacular *Life* failed to use the pictures it took. The Committee that ran the dance was choice beyond measure, consisting largely of ladies whose immemorial right to the Assembly had been impaired by divorce, and fraught with Biddles, Duanes, Ingersolls, Lippincotts, Peppers, Coxes, Wolfs, Simses and what have you. What is really significant about the affair is the location. Society Hill had been introduced, in this generation, to Society again.

It is impossible not to be exhilarated, fascinated and impressed by the Philadelphia Renaissance, which is remaking the city physically and even spiritually, stirring up old institutions to give balls and generally wakening Philadelphia from its slumber into a new century of dazzling potential. But the ointment is not as flyless as most of the eager and dedicated planners would like to have one think. Latest and saddest fly has been a series of old-fashioned scandals in the city government, hardly comparable of course to the old days of total freebootery, but still a blot on the escutcheon. The corrupt wards that used to vote corrupt Republican now vote corrupt Democratic. Also, with the abdication of Dilworth, the Renaissance is more or less leaderless.†

Still, the Renaissance has given Philadelphia, in its middle age, something it desperately needed to keep it alive: hope, energy, purpose. If the bad habits of years don't overtake the city again, and Democratic boss rule doesn't manage to equal Republican

---

* The dresses split at the seams not because modern girls are fatter, though they are bigger, but because their rib cages are larger. The smallest segment of an Empire girl's anatomy was not her waist but her rib cage; hence consumption.

† See Appendix.

boss rule in nastiness, if the Better Citizens don't relapse into inertia, or become once more alienated from politics, if the money, governmental and city, doesn't run out, if . . . well, if all these things and many others don't happen, Philadelphia may some time find herself, if never again the capital or first city of the country, at least the only American city really fit to live and work in, the only city where educated taste and the requirements of ordinary human beings are considered along with commercial razzle-dazzle and real estate values, the only city where tradition is respected without destroying imaginative experiment, and where, in sum, Penn and Franklin might return to feel at least spiritually at home.

iv. Minorities

THE LEADERSHIP of the Philadelphia Renaissance is a scrapple of many ingredients, one of the prime ones being the so-called "minority groups," whose active participation accounted for much of the success of the New Deal nationally. In their progress from slum-dwelling immigrant to respectable Philadelphian these "minority groups" represent, as in most American cities, a distinct challenge to the previously dominant "old stock." In New York these groups are now dominant politically and culturally, in Boston they are dominant politically, but in Philadelphia they work in an uneasy alliance with the old stock and even Old Philadelphia and though their influence and power are enormous, they are still in the process of being taken in, rather than of taking over.

It is sometimes hard to tell exactly what really constitutes a "minority group"; but certainly in Philadelphia the Germans in the eighteenth century represented the typical alien "threat" to the English-speaking community which became so familiar to the nineteenth century, and the same reactions of distrust and distaste, exclusion or conversion were evident. Provost Smith, for instance, sponsored an attempt to found schools to teach the Germans English, and Franklin attempted a newspaper in German to influence their opinions. The Germans resisted these efforts strenuously; and actually of all our immigrant groups they have proved the most stubbornly unassimilable, many of them speaking and reading German or the half-breed Pennsylvania Dutch almost to the present. Yet assimilated most of them were, and Peppers, Wister–Wistars and a dozen other old Philadelphia names testify to the totality of that assimilation. Nobody could be more "old stock" now.

At present in Philadelphia the four principal minority groups, or large, easily distinguishable, compact ethnic groups which have not yet melted completely into the Philadelphia pepper pot as have the Germans, are the Negroes, the Italians, the Jews and the Irish Catholics. The impact of some of these groups on Old Philadelphia has been powerful, and the Old Philadelphia attitudes toward them special.

The Negroes and the Italians have as yet not got into such a position of power, political, financial, cultural, that Old Philadelphians have to be very much aware of them as potential peers and social competitors. The Negro community in Philadelphia is old, and in its continuity since the eighteenth century has managed to get itself pretty Old Philadelphianized at the top. There is the Pyramid Club, which has all the earmarks of social exclusiveness and artistic patronage. There is an annual ball called the Cotillion, white tie, with debutantes, ballets and awards to worthy Negroes. There are old families, such as that of the present Judge Alexander, who are as a rule descendants of free Negro religious and educational leaders of the late eighteenth and early nineteenth centuries, when the various Negro churches evolved, many of them in Philadelphia. A militantly Liberal Old Philadelphian described as "stuffy and snobbish" a dinner he attended at the house of such an old family, where the atmosphere of the Philadelphia town house was perfectly maintained — the rich food, the silver candelabra, and on the walls nineteenth-century family portraits not only of Negroes but by accomplished Negro portrait painters of the period. Henry Tanner, who made a reputation around 1900 as an exhibitor at the French Salon and painter of religious subjects, was one of these. His pictures occasionally turn up at the exhibitions of the Academy of the Fine Arts, where he studied, his father being a famous African Methodist Episcopal bishop based in Philadelphia.

These old family Negro leaders are occasionally visible at general gatherings of thanksgiving and praise, and sit on committees that are civically widespread. Politically liberal Old Philadelphians know them and bring them into causes such as the World Affairs Council; but they can scarcely be considered candidates yet for real acceptance into Philadelphia's social life. The Old Philadelphia Negroes themselves are a precariously tiny minority inside, if at the top of, Philadelphia's enormously increased Negro population, which since the war has grown by hundreds of thousands of penniless and near-illiterate sharecroppers from the South, who crowd into areas formerly occupied by other national groups, creating slums and delinquents as they go. Their presence as a good third of the city's population presents Philadelphia with one of its most staggering civic problems; and yet one that seems to be solving itself, as all these "minority group" problems have so far solved themselves — by that glacially slow move up in class and status, as Negroes seep into steady professional jobs with secure incomes and into better neighborhoods like Germantown where they own their own homes.

The Italian community scarcely compares with the Negro, it is so much superior financially, educationally and culturally. It is much smaller and historically much newer, though most youngsters are now Philadelphia-born. It has already acquired a thorough shellacking of Philadelphia respectability and nothing is really more like old nineteenth-century Philadelphia now than the brick-and-marble-step decency of the Italian community in South Philadelphia. The most noticeable influence of the Italians on Philadelphia, outside of politics and contracting, has been musical, both pop (Fabian) and opera (Fabiani).

The Jews and the Irish are something else again, and represent two very different formulas in this complicated chemistry of minority-majority acceptance and rejection. Negroes and Italians

have not played any particular role in the chronicle of Old Philadelphia because they have not been represented by any recognized
upper class. Whereas the history of the old Negro and the new
Italian community is one of very gradual emergence into middle
from lower class, the history of both the Jewish and the Irish
Catholic community has been one of a descent from the very
highest possible social position to the very lowest, and then pain-
fully back up again. It was of course in both cases a matter of
separate waves of immigration.

Of the two groups, the Jews were most completely accepted,
became the most completely rejected and now bid fair to be the
most thoroughly re-accepted. The first Jewish immigrants settled
in Philadelphia, made money, and almost immediately joined
the ranks of the highest existent society. The Frankses and their
cousins the Levys were chief of these social leaders. Both were
on the original list of the Assembly in 1748 (David Franks and
Samson Levy) and the Franks girls were unquestionably the belles
of the ball before the Revolution. Abigail Franks married the
son of Andrew Hamilton to whom Philadelphia lawyers "look
as their exemplar," and so her blood flows into the vast ocean
of Morris. Beautiful Becky, one of the stars along with Peggy
Shippen at the Meschianza during the British occupation, married one of her dashing British army officers, and her descendants
have carried on into modern times as Johnsons of Bath in Burke's
Peerage.

As business apprentices, though no real kin, of the Frankses
and Levys, the second group of these socially irreproachable Jews
emerged in the mid-eighteenth century and dominated the Jewish
community till the Civil War. The principal family names were
those of Gratz, Etting and Hays, all related. Unlike the David
Frankses and Samson Levys, who were soon seduced from Judaism
into Anglicanism, and hence lost touch with the Jewish community, the Gratzes in particular were the leading members of Philadelphia's first synagogue, Mikveh Israel, at the same time they
were leading members of the best Philadelphia society. Hyman
Gratz, already mentioned as president pro tem of the Philadelphia

Club, was the principal Jew around 1840. His cousins the Ettings were the principal Jews of Baltimore, where an Etting was the first Jew elected to public office. Before then a religious oath prevented Jews from being sworn in. Relatives of the Ettings, Isaac Hays and his son Isaac Minis Hays, were among the most distinguished doctors and medical writers of the nineteenth century, pillars of the College of Physicians and the Philosophical Society. Father and son, they edited the *American Journal of Medical Sciences,* oldest of its kind in the country and still published by Lea and Febiger.

The Ettings migrated back to Philadelphia in droves and up to 1900 no good Philadelphia organization or club was complete without its Gratz, Etting or Hays. The Philadelphia and the Rittenhouse Clubs, not to mention the Union League and the Racquet, the Rabbit and the City Troop, the Historical and Philosophical Societies, the Academies of Art and of Sciences, the Athenaeum were all membered and often officered by twigs of this family tree. It would be impossible to be more fully accepted without being physically eaten and digested. In the process, to be sure, as in the case of Methodists or Presbyterians,* Gratzes, Ettings and Hayes all became Episcopalians, like everybody else. If anybody during that period ever thought about "race" there is no record or evidence of it.

The bar to intermarriage was religious, but despite family reluctance, marriages were made. The Ettings in particular married just about everybody from Philadelphia Newbolds to New York Verplancks, and most of those who married Christians converted, or at least their children were brought up as Christians. Some women, however, were converted the other way to the religion of their Jewish husbands, and one famous Old Philadelphian, Warder Cresson, converted to Judaism out of pure conviction, and ended his days in Jerusalem with a new Jewish name, a would-be rabbi and student of the Talmud.

---

* "No Dissenter drives his coach for three generations without relapsing into the Establishment." — Emerson on England.

The most fascinating figure of this dispensation was Rebecca Gratz, sister of Hyman, a heroine of romance if there ever was one. There is an ineradicable legend that she was the model for Walter Scott's Rebecca in *Ivanhoe,* thanks to Washington Irving, close friend of them both, who described Rebecca to Scott. Samuel Ewing, son of the Presbyterian Provost of the University, paid court to her. He escorted her to the Assembly in 1802, and they fell in love. Though the fond attachment was mutual, they were both too sectarian to consider marrying out of the fold. Ewing, still in love with Rebecca, married a Redman, but died young. Rebecca, faithful to the end, never married. When Samuel lay in his coffin Rebecca appeared and silently placed over his heart a miniature of herself and three white roses. She devoted the rest of her life to Jewish charities, as the name Gratz on various charitable and educational institutions testifies to this day. Perky Becky Franks and poetic Rebecca Gratz remain two of the most enticing women in Philadelphia's social history.

There are no Gratzes, no male Hayses and only one male Etting (Emlen) left today, though descendants and relations in the female line abound, especially of the Ettings. The Jewish community of today has no real connection with this group. It is dominated by the leading families of the Second Wave, the German one usually associated with 1848, but which actually took place all through the 'thirties, 'forties and 'fifties. The Jews who emerged from this immigration, though they too began or became socially and intellectually cultivated as the older families of Mikveh Israel, were never accepted socially by the Christian community. The Gratzes evidently made no effort to include those newer parishioners in their social circles, with the result that for the first time there was an abrupt cleavage between Jew and Christian.

Again, however, the prejudice was not primarily religious or racial. It was class and national. Though a few of the new Germans, Jewish and Christian, were well educated "Forty-Eighters," most of them were simply poor immigrants — Krauts who talked mit funny agcentz and trunk lager peer, as portrayed in the Hans Breitmann Ballads. The fact that some were Jewish, some were Lutheran, and many were Catholics made little difference. They were all unacceptable as odd lower-class persons of foreign extraction. And besides, most of them, even the rich ones, lived North of Market. One will look just as vainly for the names of the descendants of German brewers and uniform makers of the Civil War period upon the roster of the Philadelphia Club, the Assembly and the City Troop as one will for the names of their German Jewish fellow immigrants. The social gates were closing against anybody who was not already in.

Various families took over the leadership of the Jewish community from the Gratzes, but never their Old Philadelphia social leadership. Abraham Hart, partner of Edward Carey in the firm of Carey and Hart, was a prominent figure, and there were others. But Old Philadelphia Jewry as it is now was the product of the various mid-century fortunes and mid-century marriages of the Binswanger, Rosenbach, Polock, De Solis-Cohen and Wolf families. Although these families were "Portuguesers" who followed the Sephardic religious rites of Mikveh Israel, they were all strictly German-speaking and German-oriented. They knew and mingled with the Christian upper class on boards and institutions and in intellectual affairs, to a slight extent they followed the same educational paths, but they belonged to their own clubs, supported their own charities and lived in their own residential area on North Broad Street; and married their own cousins.

A single family, the Wolfs, dominate the Philadelphia scene in the present century as the Biddles did the Christian scene in the last century. As there is, or was, a Biddle, so there is a Wolf for every occasion: sporty Wolfs,* scholarly Wolfs, artistic Wolfs, social Wolfs, legal and financial Wolfs. No genuine board is complete without the presence of Morris Wolf, senior member of the clan

---

* A Connie Wolf is America's foremost female balloonist. She skips all over the place, lighter than air, and just set the women's world record for solo flight. Said she got tired of hearing about Russian women winning things.

and senior member of the chief Old Philadelphia Jewish law firm, Wolf, De Solis-Cohen, etc. He is on boards that have not harbored a professing Jew since before the Civil War. No scholarly gathering is complete without Edwin Wolf II, librarian of the Library Company, no social occasion without the charming Elias Wolfs. Though Wolfs still do not belong to most Old Philadelphia clubs, they are otherwise pretty thoroughly absorbed. Not since the days of the Gratzes has a Jewish family held comparable position, distinction and respect of the Christian community.

Actually the member of this family complex to achieve more than local reputation was a cousin of the Wolfs in an older generation, Abraham Simon Wolf Rosenbach. Like Logan, he was famous as a book collector, but unlike Logan, he was *not* an amateur. He was the most famous bookseller in America. Already a bibliophile and scholar when he took his Ph.D. in 1901 from Penn, he got into business in Philadelphia through his eccentric bookselling uncle Moses Polock, and through his flamboyant non-bookselling brother Philip. Philip started a store for bric-a-brac financed by his mistress, a curvesome lady from Atlantic City, who was in turn financed by an aging and evidently not very demanding sugar tycoon. The Rosenbach bookstore was at first an adjunct of this emporium, but soon took wings. Rosenbach quickly soared to the top of the profession internationally, more or less creating the Henry Huntington collection in California and becoming well known to newspaper readers everywhere as the man who paid $106,000 for a Gutenberg Bible. Roly-poly, full of scabrous stories, a heavy drinker and late talker, Rosenbach either utterly charmed or utterly repelled those who knew him and dealt with him; the charm, as his fabulous success testifies, usually predominated. Edwin Wolf and John Fleming, who worked for him, give in their biography of him all the gory details of his fascinating and spectacular life.

Rosenbach, his friend the essayist and Philadelphia "character" A. Edward Newton, young Harry Widener, whose death on the

Titanic with a Bacon first edition in his pocket deprived America of its most knowledgeable connoisseur, his cousin William Elkins, along with a few others, made Philadelphia for a while around the First War the center of American book collecting. Widener's monument is in the ponderous Widener Library in the Yard at Harvard, an architectural monstrosity erected by his grieving mother in his honor. Elkins's memory is preserved by the transplantation of his complete library, paneling, furniture and all, into the Free Library on Logan Square. The illusion is fortified by photographs, outside each of the Elkins windows, of the original Elkins landscapes, lawns and orchards rather uncannily real. Rosenbach's memorial is the elegant Rosenbach Foundation headquarters on Delancey Street. In this fine example of a Philadelphia town house have been collected the Doctor's rarest books and brother Philip's rarest furniture and pictures, and under the care of the present able and enthusiastic director, William McCarthy, it is a fabulous cave of literary and aesthetic charm, without doubt the most beautiful of American book museums.

The interesting Old Philadelphia clan of which Rosenbach was the most famous member fans out into Gerstleys, Fleishers, Wassermanns, Gimbels and dozens of others. Several Jewish families have also been assimilated into Old Philadelphia, not from the Jewish community, like the Ettings, but as individuals. Dr. Da Costa, who married a Brinton, is one example. Another, by extension, is the original Horwitz, Jonas or Jonathan, who spent the years around 1812 in Philadelphia trying to promote the publication of a Hebrew Bible. Unsuccessful, he turned to medicine for a living, married a granddaughter of Haym Solomon, famous Philadelphia Jewish financier of the Revolution, and moved to Baltimore, where when he died, he was buried in an Episcopalian cemetery. His descendants, two of whom married daughters of Dr. Samuel Gross, were all brought up in the Christian faith. Today his line is once more practicing medicine in Philadelphia, though no longer trying to promote Hebrew Bibles, in the person of Dr. Orville Horwitz. A Bullitt married a Horwitz, so that now the only direct descendants of Haym Solomon are Dr. Horwitz and Orville and William Bullitt and their off-spring.

And then there is Albert Greenfield. The Jews that backed and financed the Philadelphia Renaissance were not Gratzes and Horwitzes, nor even so much Wolfs and Binswangers. The Jews were represented chiefly by Albert Greenfield, "Mr. Philadelphia," largest and richest real estate operator in the city.

Greenfield comes out of the third, latest, most numerous and most unpopular of the Jewish immigrations, that of the Eastern European Jews fleeing pogroms in Poland and Russia between 1880 and 1920. Different in class, physique, and culture from the first English migration or the second German one, the Jews of the Third Wave were received as charitable wards and co-religionists by the German Jews, but firmly rejected socially. Members of clubs like the Mercantile and synagogues like Mikveh Israel looked upon the newcomers in their Yiddish ghettoes with even more distaste than other Americans, since not only did they feel an obligation to help them, but they also could see that as these people came to typify "Jew" among Christians, so their own status would suffer; and they were quite right. The low ebb of Jewish fortunes in America was certainly that very period when Eastern Europeans were most numerous but least "Americanized." For the first time "race" began to become part of the issue. It was then that the now offensive nickname "kike" was first coined by German Jews to stigmatize these strangers whose names so often ended in "ki" (the "kikis" or "kikies"). They were definitely not asked to join the Mercantile Club.

On the other hand, the newer immigrants immediately and amazingly began to make money and acquire culture, if not yet Old Philadelphia patina. Not only by sheer numbers but by sheer energy they dominated the Jewish community. It was they who contributed the lion's share to Jewish charities, built new synagogues and produced a new crop of doctors and lawyers. The Germans could no longer keep them out. When, in the 1920's,

Albert Greenfield was admitted to the Mercantile Club in town and the Philmont Country Club up near Jenkintown, a shudder went through the whole Family, and Wolfs acknowledged the handwriting on the wall.

It was Greenfield, the immigrant from Kiev, who was sought out by Edward Hopkinson and converted to the Renaissance. Since then, as onetime chairman of the Planning Board, he has played an enormously prominent role in the new order. More prominent, one gathers, than popular. The fact is that powerful, intelligent and generous though Greenfield undoubtedly is, he remains a somewhat equivocal figure. Though many prominent Old Philadelphians admire him, he has been described by others as the kind of man, rather like Stotesbury, who would give himself a testimonial dinner and then clap at the speeches.

Until the Third Wave acculturates, as we sociologists say, generosity, intelligence and money will not be enough. Though the barriers and differences between Second Wave Germans and Third Wave grow less and less, the Philadelphia Jewish community is still led socially by that dwindling but distinguished group of German families whose American progenitors may not have been accepted either by Old Philadelphia, but many of whose descendants are.

Out of the few thousand people — thirty thousand at the very most, two or three thousand really — who determine "social acceptance" in Philadelphia, most of the oldest have some sort of "Jewish" blood — bleached out or Episcopalianized though it may be — or relationship, or have aboriginally Jewish names (Madeira? Hecksher?) or some sort of close connection to those who have. In addition, most Philadelphians who get about in civic and social life have one or more considerably less bleached-out Jewish friends, a Wolf or a Wassermann, an Annenberg or a Snellenburg, whom they see everywhere but at their clubs and their board meetings. Then out beyond, along of course with all the other four million Philadelphians of all kinds, are the ordinary Jews, who may live in apartments on Rittenhouse Square, subscribe to the Orchestra on Saturday night, buy houses and horses on the Main Line

(Merion Station is almost completely Jewish now) and go to Europe and Florida, but of whose existence Old Philadelphia remains firmly unaware.

v. Erin Go Up

WITH THE CATHOLICS it's a bit different; and by Catholics one really means nowadays Irish Catholics. Though they are not distinguished physically from the majority of Philadelphians except insofar as they are spectacularly handsome, as the Kelly (and Kennedy) families amply demonstrate, what keeps them separate is religion. Unlike the Italian or Polish Catholics, who remain Italian or Polish first, the Irish Catholics seem Catholic first and Irish second. Their religion not only keeps them apart, it keeps them together — though not, one feels, for very much longer. There is getting to be something rather sentimental and archaic about this "Irish identity."

The Irish too had their waves, a colonial first wave, whose well-to-do members were immediately acceptable and absorbed, and a second wave, whose members were not. There was, however, no third Irish wave. As with the Jews, it is from the second wave that the present leading families of Philadelphia Irish Catholicism come. There is no real social continuity between the two immigrations.

There is one great difference however: Jews of the second wave were segregated largely for social and national reasons. Irishmen of the Second Wave have suffered from a really *religious* prejudice.

To an old-fashioned Protestant, the Jewish religion seemed to be merely another form of Protestantism which emphasized even more the Old Testament, and had some quaintly barbaric customs. Not so Catholicism, Popery, Abomination, the Whore of Babylon. Among many Protestants, except oddly enough the Quakers, the great International Conspiracy, with its monks and nuns and Jesuits and Hierarchies, "spies and commissars," has been feared and hated as nowadays the Americans have learned to

[573]

fear and hate the organizationally (if not doctrinally) similar Communism. The difference in Old Philadelphia attitudes toward Catholicism and Judaism was beautifully illustrated by a beautiful Old Philadelphia lady with manners like Madeira and a mind like a dark wine cellar. Of Catholicism she always spoke in horrid whispers . . . the R.C.'s, whose churches were *dirty*. Of the Jews she merely remarked that she was sure some of them were charming, but that she had never happened to have met any. She was, of course, distantly connected with the Ettings herself, but that wasn't the same thing.

The eighteenth-century Philadelphia Protestants, particularly Anglicans, welcomed the Jews socially as soon as they divested themselves of peculiar habits; but they did their best to suppress Catholicism. Philadelphia was the only place in the British Empire where Mass could be publicly celebrated. It was a scandal to the righteous, and only the constant protection of the Quakers, who had suffered too from the righteous, kept the persecution at bay. On one occasion it is said weighty Quakers actually patrolled St. Joseph's themselves to prevent a mob from sacking it.

Though Catholicism was always suspect, well-bred Catholics like the Wilcoxes, Sands, Keatings and Meades, or the French Bories, or the later Austrian Drexels* were taken right in despite their religion; their Irishness or non-Irishness was of no particular moment, so long as they were gentry and substantial.

Representatives of such Irish Catholic Old Philadelphians were the Meades, perhaps the only truly military Old Philadelphia family. George Meade, second of his line in Philadelphia, and his brother-in-law and partner Thomas Fitzsimmons were both ardent patriots and fought in the Revolution (what Irishman wouldn't jump at the chance to beat the British?). Fitzsimmons, who has a statue to him, later went to Congress, was president of the Insurance Company of North America, trustee of the University and in every way a pillar of society. George

---

* Though most present-day Drexels are not Catholic, some have remained so; one even joined an order and was known as the "millionaire nun." She became a Mother Superior and established the first Catholic college for Negroes, Xavier in New Orleans.

Meade was the principal contributor to St. Mary's, Thomas Fitzsimmons to St. Augustine's. George's grandson George Gordon Meade, born in Cadiz where his father was permanent American representative and a famous collector of art, turned out to be the Hero of Gettysburg. He married Margaretta Sergeant, daughter of lawyer John. His brother Richard was a captain in the Navy, and of Richard's sons, one was an admiral, another a general in the Marines. They all displayed a fine reckless Irish gift for insubordination throughout their careers.

The reputation of citizens like Mathew Carey, or the deaf intellectual editor Robert Walsh, both Irish Catholics, helped enhance the high social position of rich Irish Catholicism in the earlier nineteenth century. Still the prejudice against Popery remained strong, and the intrusion of the vast potato famine immigration of the 1840's touched off Philadelphia's most famous and disgraceful incident, the Great Riots of 1844, which remain one of the few blotches of this sort on Philadelphia's otherwise fairly tolerant historical record.

William Bradford the pre-Revolutionary printer was persecuted, but by the upper-class authorities; the Great Riots were a strictly poor white trash affair. Back of them was, of course, just plain simple xenophobia, hatred of strangers. The particular issue that set them off, however, was religion in the public schools. The Catholics objected to having the King James Version of the Bible read to Catholic children there. This roused anti-Catholic feeling, and it all sounds quite familiar; except that in those days the Catholics objected to *wrong* religion in public schools, not to *no* religion. About this issue crystallized a whole body of anti-immigrant sentiment, and a Native American Party established itself in Germantown and drew up resolutions protesting the granting of citizenship to anyone not born in this country.

The Native American Party was only mildly successful, and nothing more might have been heard of it if the membership had not gathered in the Nanny Goat Market in North Philadelphia and in front of the Hibernia Hose Company. Hibernians, enraged at the Native American speeches, started to fire at them from the

Hose Company windows, and a battle was on that raged for a week. Before it was done a score of people were killed, and the Hibernia Hose Company's building and the Nanny Goat Market both were burned down, along with blocks of nearby tenements. Two churches, St. Michael's and St. Augustine's, were totally destroyed, together with attendant schools and libraries. Resolutions were passed by Horace Binney, and General George Cadwalader and his soldiers marched up the street and then marched down again, but the rioters, armed with muskets and even a cannon or two, did pretty much what they wanted to. Ironically, in the final free-for-all, the first man killed was an old Jew, Isaac Freed, and the last an anonymous German who stuck his head out of an attic window and had it blown off by a cannonball. It was a rough day for minority groups.

The Native American Party, which had been very obscure before the riots, now became very important; proving that there's no publicity like bad publicity. They staged an elegant Fourth of July parade, complete with banners and floats, and membership jumped from five hundred to four thousand almost overnight. It finally developed into Know-Nothingism in the 1850's and died a natural death during the Civil War — unless Ku-Klux-Klannism and general Jim Crowism might be considered its illegitimate offspring. But from the time of the Great Riots down to the present, anti-Catholic prejudice has been taken for granted in Philadelphia both by Catholics and non-Catholics. What had been merely a poor white trash emotion now became a universal conviction that no nice people were Catholics, that priests were sinister and their congregations superstitious. Most of these congregations were Irish, and the only Catholic Irish the upper classes now knew were servants and corrupt politicians. The Careys had turned Protestant. There were no more intellectual Walsh soirees where one might encounter a charming and erudite monsignor. The Riots effectively destroyed the social prestige of Catholicism in Philadelphia. The fact that the Hibernia Hose Company fired first was not forgotten.

From then on Irish Catholicism grew up in a South Philadelphia ghetto no less isolated and exclusive than that of the Jews in North Philadelphia. In time fortunes accumulated and families were founded. The legal Irish Gaffneys married the industrial German Horstmanns with just the same overlapping complications that characterized Shippens and Willings. The Catholic Philopatrian Literary Society changed from a debating society to a social club, the way any good Philadelphia organization should, and a thoroughly Philadelphian web of family connections and social distinctions evolved among the Irish as it did among the Jews.

There were still differences, however. The German Jews brought a tradition of intellectualism with them, and the best brains went into finance and law and stayed in Philadelphia. The Irish brought little of that sort along, and their best brains went into the Church, and so away from Philadelphia. The results are nicely illustrated by the two national figures of the 'twenties who emerged from these two groups. Jack Kelly was America's greatest oarsman. Dr. Rosenbach was its greatest bookseller.

Old Philadelphia Irish Catholicism is not now represented by Meades and Careys, any more than its Jewry is represented by Gratzes and Ettings, but by Kellys, McShains, McCloskeys and their like, rich from contracting, who are kept together "ethnically" only by religion, family feeling and a strong Irish patriotism. They are, in fact, more wilfully separatist than the Jews, make no effort to mingle in Philadelphia society, and as a consequence are really less identified with Old Philadelphia than the upper echelon of the Jewish community; though of course Everybody has known and admired the various Kellys in their various generations.

Obviously this separateness is a fragile thing. In the suburban melting pot, where religion is no longer an issue, most of the Irish Catholics are being absorbed into country clubs and car pools. In the old days, it was different, and many of those Irish who made money converted. This was, and remains, the greatest crime an Irishman can commit against the clan, and these new Episcopalians were venomously nicknamed "the Holy Eunuchs" by their bitter former coreligionists. Having converted, however, they were immediately lost in the mass of Philadelphians.

Few of these converts' names have been added to the lists of the Assembly, though as a matter of course descendants of Meades and Careys and Bories and Drexels dance there. "Will Princess Caroline dance at the Assembly?" is, in fact, not the real issue. "Will the great-grandchildren of Jack Kelly dance there?" is more to the point. If they and other such Irish Catholics convert and marry Old Philadelphians, there's not much question of it. To marry into Old Philadelphia without converting may prove difficult. To get into the Assembly without marrying into Old Philadelphia is almost impossible. Meanwhile there has certainly been no direct effort on the part of any of these Irish offspring to get to dance at the Assembly. They seem totally uninterested, so the question, burning as it may be, remains for the present purely academic.

C H A P T E R

3

i. Sine Nob

ALL THIS BUSINESS of Ins and Outs, who dances at the Assembly and who doesn't, comes generally nowadays under the heading of what is called Snobbery, and all Right Thinking People are against it; as they used to be against Girard's will, for instance. This is all part of the victory of Liberalism, and is probably a good thing; but this kind of Liberalism has by now become a syndicated, thoughtless prejudice, and as such no more intelligent than any other syndicated, thoughtless prejudice. "Anti-snobbery" is just a majority reaction, not a clear principle. Let the man, or especially woman, who doesn't practice "snobbery," or "exclusiveness," throw the first stone. We are all excluders and excludees.

"There is no country in the world where society is more exclusive than it is in America . . ." So wrote Nicholas Biddle *ca.* 1810, beginning an essay that in typically dilettante fashion he never finished. If he had, it would be among the most curious and valuable of the documents of Americana. As it is, it is curious enough. He goes on to express his distaste for English social life, where rank intrudes into the drawing room, and where a young pup precedes a distinguished statesman through the door merely because he is the son of an Earl. He then expresses his fondness for the French, who practice a true democracy of the salon; if one is a guest, one is presumed an equal. But unfortunately, after these intriguing comparisons, he never gets back to his main point: the ultimate exclusiveness of American Society.

He meant, of course, Philadelphia society, since that was the

[579]

society he knew best. He knew what he was talking about, and it would not be too difficult to finish his essay for him, using even modern Philadelphia society as a model. By "society" he meant the essentially family-bound, family-connected Philadelphia Web, no less cohesive in the 1960's than in the 1810's — and probably not much larger.

What Biddle no doubt intended was a comparison of an English society of fixed public rank, and a French society of wit and compatibility, with a Philadelphian society of pure birth and position. In England a Duke is a Duke, even if he's merely a Battenberg. In France, no one asked who Madame de Staël was before she was married. In Philadelphia a Biddle is a Biddle only by birth or marriage. One can't be created Biddle or achieve Biddledom by intelligence. Also, it must be stressed, just having the name Biddle, or being a Biddle in some remote New Jersey offshoot, doesn't make one qualify either; name *and* position, both are necessary.

This means, of course, that people who would like to be included, like to have position, and who have every right to think they should have it, nevertheless don't; and know they don't. These then are the victims of snobbery, and many of them are, and always have been, pretty sore about it. Millions more, who have no thought of inclusion, resent the whole idea of exclusiveness as being undemocratic, or out-of-date, or silly or just vaguely irritating. Biddle himself, incidentally, as a good Jeffersonian liberal, took satirical swipes at this Philadelphia exclusiveness in a fragment of a society novel, in which he describes a group of (presumably) Biddle ladies making out a list for a little party of four hundred. He pokes a good deal of fun at their arbitrary sniffs at summer acquaintances, country cousins and people in the wrong line of business, such as auctioneers.

Philadelphia has and always has had a fearsome reputation, probably justified, for this sort of exclusiveness. As the elaborate revenges of Joseph Widener and Dr. Barnes would indicate, resentment can burn long and high. To label this exclusiveness as snobbery and hence dismiss it as contemptible may be pleasant, giving one a small glow of self-congratulatory broad-mindedness, but it is a form of easy, and hence not necessarily accurate or acute, thinking.

In the first place, there's that word "snob." Hardly anyone seems to know what it really means, but everybody is pretty sure it's a nasty word, an epithet no less abusive than "son of a bitch." In fact snob is a wonderful example of how a word, particularly a slang word, can make a complete turnabout, come to mean almost the exact opposite of what it once meant, and yet still carry with it the atmosphere and stigma that it used to have.

In the arrogant eighteenth century when everybody, even confirmed radical democrats, believed in the virtue of class distinctions of some kind, the word snob was not in common parlance. In the schoolboy and collegiate world of England, snob was a contraction of the phrase *sine nobilitate,* without nobility (s. nob.), a term used to distinguish the commoner from the titled undergraduate on the rolls of Oxford and Cambridge.

In America it seems originally to have been used also as collegiate slang, and in the first half of the nineteenth century meant the toughs and townies with whom the young gentlemen of Princeton, Yale and Harvard carried on the kind of gang warfare that is now considered to be juvenile delinquency. "Snobs" were gangs of toughs, and the contempt was purely that of upper-class boys ("nobs") for lower-class boys, and no democratic equivocation. The contempt was, of course, returned in kind, and many a happy hour was spent in rumbles, mass mayhem between town and gown, the snobs and the nobs.

Meanwhile, largely under the influence of Thackeray, who knew one when he saw one (it takes a thief), "snob" emerged into the adult world, derived from the collegiate one, as a person who himself is not a member of the upper class, and desperately wants to be one. What used to be called in more recent schooldays "sucking a drag," or "brown-nosing," that is, buttering up a superior, toadying, making oneself familiar with the great for purposes of self-advancement — this was the essential activity of the snob. As one side product, "vulgar ostentation," the desire to impress others with one's virtues and status, became a snobbish attribute. As another side product of flattering the great, cutting or condescending or trying to impress the non-great also became established as part (though only part) of the snob's repertoire. All this was the very essence of the English nineteenth century when a rising mercantile Forsyte middle class found itself becoming in fact, despite the presence of an older feudal aristocracy, the ruling, controlling, that is to say, real upper class.

Of course the genuine gentleman, the born aristocrat, whatever he was could not be a snob. Arrogant, unkind, cruel, rude, boorish, yes, but snob, no. Lady de Bourgh, or Darcy himself, who so fearsomely condescend in *Pride and Prejudice,* are unpleasant, but not snobs. Mr. Collins, the cringing clergyman, fearsomely is. Becky Sharp, delightful and realistic as she may be, most certainly and wonderfully is another. There were of course all sorts of snobs, *Vanity Fair* is full of them — cynical, knowing snobs like Becky, stuffy conceited snobs like George Osborne. What they had in common was not arrogance, but a desire to be thought what they really were not quite — bona fide hereditary "gentlemen and ladies."

But O the heavy change. Now it is the Marquess of Steyne and Darcy and Lady de Bourgh who are snobs, and Becky Sharp is just a little girl who wants to get ahead, like Kitty Foyle.

The transmutation of the snob was, I suppose, a gradual thing. Thackeray himself helped. There was the fact that many snobs were arrogant, and did parade class associations and distinction. There was also the corollary fact that really sensitive (one can't say necessarily well-bred or high-born) gentlemen and ladies didn't. Noblesse oblige has certainly always contained the injunction that one must never make inferiors aware of or uncomfortable about their inferiority. A gentleman is a person who never proclaims he is a gentleman; those that don't know he is one degrade themselves. And so forth. This moves on to the concept that the very idea of making class distinctions is vulgar and ungentlemanly, a form of indirect boasting. These are the roots of that apologetic air, the statements beginning "I don't want to seem snobbish but . . ."

Things have, however, now reached such a point that the mere possession and demonstration of breeding is considered snobbish. Russell Lynes, who has done more to confuse the whole issue than any other living man, wrote an article in a mass magazine fairly recently, in which he demonstrated that among the younger generation the word "lady" is a term of abuse that indicates a hoity-toity, stiff, prudish attitude, as in the word "snobbery." That is, nowadays, to *be* a lady is to be a snob.

It all boils down, socially at least, to a fundamental issue: do upper classes exist, and if so, are they superior in any recognizable way to middle or other classes? If upper-classness, aristocracy, gen-tryness and gentility are pure figments of the imagination, mere pretensions and affectations on the part of people with money or power to keep down other people and build up their own egos, with artificial distinctions and so forth, then it would be absurd to consider breeding and being a social "lady" or "gentleman" a form of excellence. It is, or would be, a form of pretension and as such rightly considered contemptible. This would seem to be at the bottom of the modern use of the word snob — a real feeling that social superiorities do not really exist, that they are in them-selves pretensions; that the whole concept of hereditary breeding is pernicious nonsense.

If this is all so, then maybe it is proper for the new word "snob" to retain some of the stigma of the old word "snob." If not, how-ever, the word becomes more or less meaningless. In that case we might keep snob to mean arrogant class-conscious superiority, without reference to *validity;* and some other word — "climber," perhaps — might take over the role once given to snob. It's a commentary on a climbing world that no one now seems to find the climber ridiculous. He is just a "status seeker," and displays an amiable, largely psychological-sociological weakness.

[583]

ii. Gentry

THE UPPER CLASSES, meanwhile, or preferably the gentry, do emphatically exist in America. A little bit more so perhaps in Philadelphia than in some other places, but certainly not only in Philadelphia. They may or may not be superior to the middle or other classes; but they are different, and their difference is one of class.

They differ, that is to say, not in essential character, heart or brains, but in training and manners; also, to an extent, in physical characteristics. If they have a superiority to others, it lies in the superiority of this training, these manners and those physical characteristics.

The training involves being brought up to know and obey a whole code of conduct at various levels, derived from an antique feudal code of chivalry, modified for modern usage to conform to a later code of middle-class morality. From chivalry are derived the values of Honor; loyalty, sportsmanship, fair play, courtesy, modesty, reverence, dutifulness, integrity, courage, gallantry, reticence. If these virtues resemble the Boy Scout oath or the Laws of the Range as exhibited in the more non-adult western, that is, of course, no accident. The Boy Scout movement was intended by its gentleman founder Lord Baden-Powell as an education in the code for youth unfortunate enough not to be trained at Eton. The Law of the Range, the chivalric cowboy, was to a considerable extent the creation, based of course on reality, of that supremely honor-conscious Philadelphia gentleman Owen Wister.

From middle-class morality are derived the more practical virtues of Honesty: truthfulness, reliability, punctuality, neatness, a word that is as good as one's bond, sobriety, moderation, cleanliness, a strict observance of marriage vows and appearances, piety, support of worthy causes, etc. As Franklin and Washington said, "Honesty is the best policy." Nobody ever said that Honor was the best policy; but the modern Gentleman must be both honorable and honest.

The point here is that these codes are instilled into the better children at their better schools or by their better parents as being not just codes of general morality, but specifically as the codes proper to the gentlemen and ladies they are supposed to grow up to be.

It does not automatically follow, of course, that these children do grow up models of all these virtues. But it does pretty much follow that a real gentleman or lady is bound to know about these codes; to know what Honor and Honesty are.

Other crucial adjuncts to this code are manners and breeding. Good men and women after all have everywhere been observing the codes of honor and honesty without reference to class. One may have honor and honesty then and still not be a gentleman. One must also have manners and breeding. To have manners without honor is, of course, dreadful, and from Iago on down the stage villain has always been just that curly-mustached wretch with all the manners of a gentleman but no honor or honesty.

Essential manners according to the code of chivalry is noblesse oblige; that is, one must never abuse one's position at the top of the heap. Treat everybody as you would like to be treated yourself. "The essence of good manners is to be easy in oneself and easy to all about one" is a very eighteenth-century definition. A twentieth-century one might be "All self-assertion is apt to be vulgar." Oscar Wilde's seemingly flippant observation that a gentleman is someone who is never unintentionally rude has its sober side. A perfect gentleman would know almost instinctively what was polite and considerate in any possible situation. Rudeness would be reserved for the "proud and tyrannous"; or those who don't know their place.

Part of all this is etiquette, customs, mores, any conventions which make doing the right thing standard and easy. It is silly to have to waste time thinking about which fork to use or what color tie to wear with formal dress. Beyond this are vaguer but sometimes equally arbitrary rules, changing with the centuries or even the decades, that cover the gentleman's approach to clothes, words, and tastes in general. These, the Customs, aren't fixed like etiquette, and the gentleman can only get to know them by association with other gentlemen. In general they favor simplicity and inconspicuous consumption — saying "dead" for "passed on" or "rich" for "wealthy" and driving small or old cars. All these are not very important; but a gentleman *has* to know them.

There seems to be nowadays a great deal too much fuss about these customs — all that business in England about U and Non-U, in America about "snob" and "sophistication" and "status." One gets the impression that saying the "right word" is what really makes one a lady or a gentleman; or wearing old clothes well. In other words, just a form of chic. These things are, of course, only superficial indices. They can be a means of recognizing a species, but that's about all the value they have. No real lady or gentleman should be seriously concerned with them.

A far more important index of the gentleman and the lady is that other more or less undefined term, "breeding." Breeding is not a code, but a result. There might be distinguished two very different kinds of breeding: the breeding of training, and the breeding of blood. One approximates good manners, good form. What the French call a "jeune fille bien elevée" is a "well-bred young girl." What the French call "race" is the breeding of blood. This presumes that if gentlemen and ladies cohabit through the generations, certain effects not only of bone and sinew but of stamina and character will be produced. Gentlemen have spent a good many centuries breeding horses and dogs, and they are very apt to carry their experiences there over into the breeding of humans, where the applications are more dubious. Still, it is perfectly obvious that the upper classes do manifest, as often as not, certain physical characteristics — a tendency say to tall fine-boned leanness, with thin distinct features and prominent noses; a certain firm delicacy of outline which in overbreeding loses its firmness.

In the newspapers, on the occasion of Khrushchev's visit to America, there appeared a picture of three almost-first ladies,

Mesdames Khrushchev, Nixon and Rockefeller. It was a perfect demonstration of physical breeding in three stages — the matronly peasant stolidity, the upstanding but not too refined good looks of the middle class, and the almost over-emaciated elegance of the gentry. "Good bones," rather than just leanness, "character" rather than just elegance, are more along the line of breeding. Churchill, for all his fatness, is "well-bred." Old John D. Rockefeller, for all his leanness, wasn't; but his grandchildren are catching up.

Since a Lady's Honor (in her case peculiarly involved with chastity) and honesty are supposed to be taken care of by chivalrous males, the other two qualities, manners and breeding, are even more important to her than to the male. As the woman from Boston said, "Breeding is everything."

As the woman from Chicago said, "Breeding is lots of fun; but it's not everything." There are obvious holes in even the total code of the gentleman and lady. Critics past and present have not been loath to point them out. "Gentleman" does not, for instance, equal "Christian" or "scholar," despite their frequent past association. There is too much bloodshed, worldliness, power back of the codes of honor and honesty to qualify them for the Kingdom of Heaven. The very nature of a class code is bound to hamper the Genius, whether artistic or political. And the connection between the codes of the gentleman and the codes of maintenance are too obvious to need pointing out. A state of life which finds that all "self-assertion is apt to be vulgar" is for those who have arrived rather than for those on their way. Nonetheless it is on the basis of a possession of these qualities and virtues — honor, honesty, manners and breeding — that the superiority of gentleman and lady as members of a class is to be based. Money, talent, achievement, belong to a very different order of things; individual, as opposed to purely class, superiorities. It's obvious that throughout history money and achievement have put people in a position where they can acquire manners and breeding. Still, the figures of the well-bred, well-mannered lady and gentleman, with all that they imply in the way of codes, must remain a constant standard for any group pretending to be an upper class.

iii.   "Sacred Honor"

THE RELATIONSHIP between Democracy and the gentleman is particularly ambivalent. The gentleman is not an outlaw, but he is certainly a bit suspect. There are those who think the gentleman a nefarious anachronism. There are those on the contrary who see in Democracy the perfect expression of true gentility.

This ambivalence in the relationship of the gentry to Democracy begins with the beginnings of the United States. The very men who declared that "all men are created equal" were themselves gentlemen. Some of these founding fathers were gentlemen-born, others gentlemen-made; but all very much gentlemen. They pledged not only their lives and their fortunes but also, as gentlemen, their "sacred honor"; and don't forget it. "Sacred honor" is not a phrase that comes tripping to the tongue of shopkeepers and farmers.

The management of the country remained for several decades after the Revolution in the hands of the gentlemen, who evolved two opposing solutions to the problem of the existence of an aristocracy in a democracy. One solution, that might be called the Hamiltonian, envisaged America as a bureau dominated by its top drawer. Unlike the bureaus of Europe where the top drawer was shut and locked, the American top drawer was to be opened freely to men of talents, energies and taste (like Hamilton). The Republic was "democratic" then in that ability, rather than just heredity, was to populate the drawer. The system was established in Hamilton's home town, New York, where it flourished. At present the top drawer is crowded with talents, and the bureau is an immensely stylish affair, all chromium and glass. The only trouble is there are no gentlemen in it; those that are there have been forced to retreat into a secret compartment from which they seldom emerge and from which they definitely do not govern the nation, as Hamilton hoped they would.

The Jeffersonian formula was far more idealistic, if less practical. Jeffersonians looked forward to a Republic in which everybody — liberal planter or educated yeoman — would be a gentleman. Ideally, since a gentleman must treat everyone as an equal in order not to lower himself by servility or arrogance, the perfect expression of the gentleman in politics is not rule by aristocracy, which presupposes inferiors, but the self-rule of a corporation of free and equal gentlemen. The Jeffersonian hope was that if artificial barriers were removed, if no great differences in economic power existed between men, if the same education were available to all, then the ideal of a commonwealth of pure gentlemen would be realized, the sort of meeting of minds between gentlemen-born and gentlemen-made that did actually occur during the Revolution. Alas, the Jeffersonian ideal has been realized, and there partially, only in the country and especially the cattle-raising Far West, where the kind of classless self-respect of individuals for each other, with the consequent code of honor and good manners (but not necessarily honesty), does still exist.

However, everywhere, the figures of the aristocrat and the gentleman remain to haunt the conscience of Democracy. The code of the gentleman and the lady sets up a standard which cannot be ignored, especially when it is actually embodied in real people, and exemplified in large on the public stage in men like Washington, Lee, the Roosevelts, or Stevenson and Lodge in our own day. (Not to mention Mrs. Franklin Roosevelt or Mrs. John Kennedy.) One can either accept the standard and attempt to adjust it to democratic realities, or one can hope to supersede it with other presumably higher ideals.

An enormous number of Americans of course simply ignore the standard of the gentleman out of ignorance or perversity. They would pretend that gentlemen don't exist in America, or at least shouldn't exist. In fact, a good deal of propaganda is disseminated by publishers of middle-class magazines and by poli-

ticians, reassuring their readers or constituents that all Amurri-
cans are just ordinary folks like you'n me. This is the Procrustean
formula, which hopes to achieve Democracy simply by cutting
off the heads of superiors and the feet of inferiors, and positing
as an ideal a homogeneous mass of mediocrity. The home of this
sort of thinking is only too often the Midwest. It chief representative figure is not a real man, but a fictional character, George
Babbitt.* This is, of all the products of Democracy, the most
vile and the most dangerous in its tendencies towards tyranny.
De Tocqueville was properly suspicious of it. However it does
at least solve the problems of aristocracy by liquidating all forms
of difference or superiority.

Another and far nobler approach to the problem, if it is a problem, is what might be called the Whitmanesque ideal, the hope
not of avoiding or suppressing the standard of the gentleman, but
of surpassing it. America is to produce a wider, larger, freer,
grander sort of person, physically magnificent, mentally un-
hampered, heir to the wisdom of the ages, at one with nature, a
sort of human eagle, an incarnated bird of freedom. This all
might be dismissed as the vapors of a "neurotic poet" if, in fact,
America had not produced Lincoln. The Midwest may be the
land of Babbitt, but it is also the land of Lincoln, and this noble
ghost walks to confute and confuse mean conformity and mass-
man.

Meanwhile the class of gentlemen with all that it connotes,
good and bad, indisputably, unavoidably, irremediably continues
to exist in America. The class, as such, is not on the national
scene an aristocracy, since it does not rule. It is not everywhere
an upper class. In Detroit, for instance, the tycoons of automobile are unquestionably there the upper class; but they are not
gentlemen, as exhibited in the ineffable Charlie Wilson, or the
late great Henry Ford. Nor can the class of gentlemen be identified with the plutocracy. Some plutocrats are gentlemen and

---

* Actually, Sinclair Lewis's fictional Babbitt was a rebel against this very concept
of Universal Mediocrity.

ladies, and many more would like to think they are. But the American plutocracy as exhibited in New York and Newport during the Gilded Age was very far from being a gentry, and adopted, without much warrant, like Boies Penrose, the motto of the Ancien Régime, "I do as I please," rather than the chivalrous "I do as I ought." Aristocrats, maybe; oligarchs certainly; but not gentry. This "Society," that according to Cleveland Amory has been "killed," deserved to be.

It seems proper then to call the class of ladies and gentlemen in America a Gentry, which involves a consciousness of being such ladies and gentlemen, of having inherited manners and breeding, without any reference to political or economic dominance. Within the ranks of this class one can distinguish between gentry and patricians. The gentry exist all over, often far removed from their origins, and not essentially identified with their communities. The better New York suburbs for instance are full of them. The patricians on the other hand are those who by long heredity and tenure of position are established as "first families" of one given locale, city, county, state. They sometimes (Philadelphia) but not always (New York) function as a real ruling class, that is, an aristocracy. Mostly they don't.

The fact that a gentry and a patriciate have managed to survive the democratic erosion of two centuries is something of a miracle, black or white magic depending on your point of view. But the real questions today are: Is the existence of the gentry, with its inevitable assumption of class differences, a good thing in a democracy? If not, why not, and what standards are higher and better, and how formulated and propagated? If the existence of the gentry is a good thing, must it be an hereditary class? If so, can such an hereditary class exist without tenure of money and power?

Many generous and liberal Americans, especially it might be remarked rebellious hereditary gentlemen, have hoped for the world of Whitman, or at least of Jefferson. Happy indeed the civilization where all were at least gentlemen. Meanwhile, in the unregenerate real world of Hamilton and Babbitt, an hereditary

gentry certainly serves a vital function; that of a social brake.
It resists by its standards Standardization, the gospel of Get Ahead,
of Boom and Bust, of the Bonanza; of total turnover, of Majority
Tyranny, all those evils in fact of which De Tocqueville warned
us (many of his attitudes towards democracy being distorted because he didn't, or wouldn't, admit the existence of a gentry in
America).

The gentry provides a sort of school in decency for those who
manage to get ahead. It clings to history and the past in a world
too eager for the future, too careless of the present. It could
teach Babbitt, if he would learn, all sorts of things he ought to
know, like not wearing Hawaiian shirts out over his fat rump.
It could instruct the pullulating status seekers of Vance Packard's suburbs what status really is and what its proper symbols
are — not big cars and plate glass but modesty and reticence.
Reactionary as most, but not all, of the gentry are in their longing
for the Good Old Days, they do draw certain lines. As the tele-
vised portrait of Senator McCarthy flashed on the screen in the
Rittenhouse Club, gentlemen whose hearts had died with Mc-
Kinley rose and snorted: not a gentleman!

It does not seem likely that a democracy ever could or would or
should submit to the real *rule* of an aristocracy, no matter how
benevolent, any more than it should submit to a theocracy. The
separation of Church and State is a fixed, and most think beneficent, policy in America. Why not a similar conscious separation
of State and Class? Which actually exists in any case. The Philadelphia patriciate has again and again been stigmatized for its
lack of public spirit; but perhaps they had something. Certainly
the careers of neither cynical Penrose nor ineffectual Pepper serve
as very exhilarating examples of the gentleman in politics. Unless
they can rise to Jeffersonianism, or Washingtonianism, patricians
had best keep out of Washington.

The clergy tell us how to be good, but not how to be governed.
The gentry could raise standards "to which the wise and honest,"
the rich and successful at least, might repair, without necessarily
being given the reins of political power. By associations, tradi-

tions, institutions they can chasten the pride of those who are on the way up with the realization that others have been there before them.

iv. Madeira from Sour Grapes

THIS RATHER DIDACTIC and superficial digression may seem to take us right far from specifically Philadelphia. Nonetheless these conceptions involving the gentleman and his codes must be basic, overtly or tacitly, to any discussion whatsoever of "society" or "status" or "aristocracy" or "class," since for centuries in America the lady and gentleman have actually been considered the highest representatives of all these things, the standards in all these areas. There's a very strong suspicion, however, that a good many sociologists, journalists and novelists who write about such things nowadays don't have any such conceptions in mind; in fact, have never really heard of them. The concepts of the Lady and Gentleman were so familiar, nauseatingly familiar to our grandparents that they became embarrassed if they were even mentioned. Many of their grandchildren don't even seem to know the words. Philadelphians, even Philadelphian grandchildren, do by and large still understand what this is all about — gentleman and lady, codes, manners, breeding and all. They assume such things to be at the root of class pretensions, and that to be of "good family" means purely and simply to be of a family of ladies and gentlemen.

In fact, Philadelphia still thinks itself the sole repository of taste and gentility in the country, and could never be made to believe it makes up just one fragment of the total American patriciate, one variation of the species of gentry. Old Philadelphians think of themselves as *the* gentry; everyone else is a bit off. It may be true that at its very top and at its very best, Philadelphia does indeed produce the purest, most inevitable specimens of the American lady and gentleman. The run-of-the-mill upperclass Philadelphian, however, evidences some very obvious local failings. The obfuscated politics, the insular prejudices, the contented Philistinism, the Quakerish conformity, caution, plainness, a sort of tough ordinariness, are all, from the point of view of an ideal of gentility, illiberal or even déclassé.

In fact visitors are usually disappointed to discover that the Philadelphia gentry is so superficially ordinary. They expect to find the Republican Court in full swing complete with minuets and knee breeches, instead of which they find people in shorts playing golf, or even "gawlf." Important social events, as *Life* discovered at the Athenaeum Ball, turn out despite minuets to be nothing special; just rather nice people having a rather nice time. Philadelphians don't aim to be picturesque, and what's peculiar about them, and pretty peculiar it can be, does not appear on the surface. Only when you *know* that no divorced person is present at the Assembly does it begin to seem quaint. Perhaps it is just this surface anonymity which has protected Old Philadelphia through the centuries.

In any case, Philadelphians couldn't care less. As perhaps the only hereditary gentry outside of Kuwait, Afghanistan, Monaco and Tonga still seated, however shakily, in the saddle, they can afford to smile gently if complacently at those lovely charming impoverished Southerners, those dowdy or over-stylish disenfranchised New Yorkers, those odd bookish Irish-dominated Bostonians. Even the English nobility, groaning under the punitive yoke of the Welfare State, draws from the Philadelphia eye the sympathetic, but yet a bit condescending tear.

Perhaps the nearly three-hundred-year-old reign of this Philadelphia family group, this absolutely continuous Web which continually weaves in new strands, is coming to an end. A revolution has certainly occurred; but to a great extent, Old Philadelphia leads it. All sorts of new blood and new power has come up, but not yet to submerge Old Philadelphia in its financial, cultural or even basic political primacy. Certainly not in its social primacy.

In twenty years, in forty years, in a hundred years this rule and even the existence of Old Philadelphia may be at an end. There is certainly nothing in the current of modern affairs to

give encouragement to the persistence of any aristocracy anywhere, much less one of birth in America. In Philadelphia there
are all sorts of signs, perhaps misleading, of a slackening of grip.
There seem to be few replacements for the George Wharton Peppers, Henry Drinkers or Jared Ingersolls of an older generation.
Philadelphia is littered with youngish gentlemen of looks, charm,
talent and family who by any standard have done precious little
with themselves. Some of Philadelphia's grandest names, Norris
and Cadwalader for instance, seem on the edge of extinction.
There are younger McKeans and Willings, but no longer in Philadelphia. Biddles and Morrises, though God knows not extinct,
do not seem to be casting up candidates for the Philosophical
Society, or presidents of the Girard Trust. There is much wail-
ing and gnashing of teeth about this among Old Philadelphians;
which would be more convincing if one were not also convinced,
reading Sidney Fisher or listening to Henry Carey ("the present
race is frivolous and insipid"), that it has all been going on for
a long, long time. The Degeneracy of These Days is part of the
inevitable equipment of the Tory.

In any case, thar' she blows! One of America's largest cities,
and still pretty much characterized and dominated by her gentry.
Imagine (as John Watson might say) an unlikely scene; a Very
Oldest Philadelphian strolling around the edge of City Hall, and
connecting his Family with what he sees. City Hall itself might
have few such connections. A couple of ancestors in white wigs
hang inside as portraits of long-dead mayors. Others plaster the
walls of the Law Library there. Another more recent, less often
mentioned ancestor made his out of the marble of which City
Hall is built. Around the base of the pile are a few statues to
nineteenth-century connections, generals, reformers. North, up
Broad, he sees nothing but the Academy of the Fine Arts, where
more pictured ancestors hang, and of which innumerable forebears have been directors. The same is true of those pillared institutions along the Parkway; more portraits, more patrons. Espe-

cially the Art Museum, which his sisters and his cousins and his aunts are still all patronizing like mad, as donors and on committees.

Out there sits the equally neoclassic 30th Street Station for The Railroad, to which the Family contributed those Directors. Then southward, the world of Banks — the Girard, the Provident, the First Pennsylvania. His wife's grandfather was president of one, his brother-in-law's uncle is chairman of another. That skyscraper there bears the Family name (The Bowen Building; or ap Owen, as it once was in the Welsh Barony). This one here was designed by a cousin in love with the Colonial. The chaste shape of the PSFS looms; known all the directors since they were boys, or at least father and grandfather did. Further south comes the Union League (most of the family, except the most distinguished and Democratic branch, have been members from the beginning) and the Bellevue (no wedding nights there; but infinite balls and Assemblies) and the Academy of Music (every single woman in the Family has spent every single Friday afternoon there for every single winter). To the east spreads the Delaware, on the banks of which the Family had its first houses and warehouses; to the west, the Schuylkill, where in later generations bloomed their country seats (John Smith's Smithside, now a museum). As he looks about him and sees each landmark starred with conspicuous family associations, how can he help feeling identified, important, elevated into Position? This is His City.

It's been His City since 1682, and though the Oligarchy has had its ups and downs, it's never been down and out. In two great waves, the fortunes of Philadelphia and its gentry have risen and fallen together. A slow swell through the eighteenth century culminated in the Golden Age of the Revolution, the Age of Franklin. For the years before 1800 Philadelphia was Number One in every way. A slow decline through the early nineteenth century, when Philadelphia remained the "Athens of America," first still in finance, music and institutions, the Silver Age of Biddle, struck bottom under Jackson. Then another wave, rising through the Civil War, culminated in the ten years before

1900, the Iron Age. No longer either the Capital or the Athens of America, Philadelphia was then most securely third, most securely owned by its upper classes. Then boomed Iron and Railroads and Coal, Cramp and Baldwin. Then fox hunting and Eakins and cricket and the coach-and-four flourished together. Then began the Orchestra and the Curtis Publishing Company. Bottom was struck again under F.D.R.

Philadelphia and its Oligarchy stand now in the hope of a new wave. Will history repeat itself? In the ten years before 2000 will Philadelphia achieve another climax? Of what kind? And will this city of 1990 still be His City? These questions definitely ferment in the mind of the more intelligent Old Philadelphian. But most of the time he continues to jog along in the comfortable ruts laid down for him by his ancestors; no longer so comfortable, but still ruts. Law, medicine, insurance, banking, good works, institutions, clubs, sports — even arts.

Along these ruts there is much that is worthy, curious, even, in a smothered way, great. Great men, most of them now unknown, have made the ruts, created the institutions. Great things have been done in the city, most of them forgotten. Philadelphia is quite willing to have it that way, and stay Hidden. Who cares what other people think anyway? "To thyself be enough." But Philadelphia does know, in its bones, what many other cities don't; that Maintenance, that Philadelphia, is not the Past but the Future. Philadelphia is what cities *become* — all those other cities that once, too, hoped to be Number One, and find themselves growing older, like Philadelphia, as Number Two, Number Three, Number Four. Better, then, to be oneself than vulgar Number One.

Philadelphia is now hopeful again; but its inhabitants, perhaps more so than those of most American cities, are inclined to be skeptical. The ruts are comfortable and secure, but they do not lead to the stars, to the Bonanza, to the Championship Cup. Philadelphia had the Cup, and lost it, and is now used to making Madeira out of sour grapes. It's a fine vintage, warm, rich, flavorful; but there's a drop of bitterness in the bottom of the glass.

Philadelphia, has, after all, for all its prosperity, been a Disappointment; not the Holy City Penn had in mind, not the Enlightened Center of the Republic Franklin had in mind.

It's been something else, maybe worse, maybe better. It's been — well, Philadelphia.

Appendix

WITH FINGERS CROSSED, I have observed events since the "closing of the books" (of this book) on January 1, 1962, hoping I would not have to do too much rewriting. In general, I have been able to let things be; but a few conspicuous changes must be noted.

P.R.R. (page 195): The Pennsylvania Station in New York is indefinitely scheduled to be torn down. May the President and Board of Directors be blasted by the curse of all those who value American architectural monuments. May they go down in history as infamous. Equally important to Philadelphia is the proposed merger of the the Pennsy and the N. Y. Central. Union of these old rivals will probably mean the transfer of the main office of The Railroad to overswollen New York, and Philadelphia will lose another ripe old plum. There is an effort to somehow force or persuade The Railroad not to move. But . . .

CURTIS (page 423): Front-page news has been the earthquake in the Curtis Publications, and the actual removal of most of their editorial offices from Independence Square to New York. A new one-eyed president Matthew J. Culligan, fine flower of Madison Avenue and described as a "tiger of a competitor," has taken over. Though the Curtis family still owns stock, The Curtis Publishing Company can no longer be called a Philadelphia or a family concern. Television having assumed the role of mass-advertiser, the *Saturday Evening Post* and *Ladies' Home Journal* have been floundering financially despite their huge circulations (what are a dozen million among so many?). Tiger Culligan may be able to pull them through, but it won't do Philadelphia much good.

OPERA (page 480): The issue of Philadelphia's operatic quandary has been a most happy one. With some ludicrous aspects. When the Met pulled out, the Grand Opera Company, under the leadership of deaf boardsman H. Douglas Paxton, got Signor Fabiani's Lyric to merge with it, and secured the backing and patronage of most of the bewildered former habitués of the Metropolitan (Margot Biddle, Henry McIlhenny). Signor Fabiani's principal condition to the merger

[599]

was that the Grand change its name to his Lyric. The new Lyric has been putting on wonderful performances of a dozen operas from the standard repertoire, and Everybody has been going, all dressed up. It is a milestone in the history of opera in Philadelphia that at last Old Philadelphia and Society are willing to get behind a really local company, even in its embryo stage (the chorus and orchestra are resident, the stars still imported for the occasion). However, some disgruntled boardspeople split off, and decided to run their own rival company. They call it the Grand Opera Company. Confusion reigns. What was the Grand is now Lyric, and something that might have been the Lyric is the Grand. Philadelphia still has two rival opera groups, but it also is putting on and going to hear a lot of good opera all on its own.

POLITICS (page 561): The Renaissance proceeds, but without its Knights in Shining Armor. Clark continues in the United States Senate. Dilworth resigned from the office of Mayor to run for state Governor — and lost. Nobody knows quite what this will mean for reform government. Little scandals continue to bubble up involving little Democratic politicians, as they used to involve little (and big) Republican ones. The furore over Society Hill and redevelopment and slum clearance continues unabated; but a new Knight in Shining Armor does seem called for. Walter Phillips, running in the Democratic primaries in 1963 against machine candidate acting-Mayor Tate, might fill the bill. He has certainly served to emphasize the growing split between Reform Democrat and Machine Democrat, a split which threatens to sink the whole Renaissance.

Acknowledgments

Like any portrait that aspires to be genuine, I did not mean this picture of the Old Philadelphians to flatter or expose. I have not tried to tone down the warts, or underemphasize the wrinkles. On the other hand I have to confess to a somewhat unethical softening of the heart; perhaps of the brain. A less than strictly reportorial fondness on my part has been caused, often against my better judgment, by the Philadelphians I happened to have met. I looked forward so eagerly to meeting those philistine, parochial numbskulls that all Philadelphians in particular warned me about. I met certainly some very queer, very limited, very crotchety and sometimes very condescending and unresponsive people. But though often astounded and amused, and sometimes irritated, I can't honestly recall ever having been really offended or above all really bored.

I have been, in other words, as all sorts of people warned me, seduced by meeting the nicest Philadelphians first. This was largely due I think to the numberless people who introduced me to them, being themselves the nicest of Philadelphians. I can't possibly in print mention the names of everybody in Philadelphia who helped me — sometimes unconsciously. In the first place, some of them might not like it. I must, however, in all decency give thanks to a few who went out of their way. They are not, of course, to be held accountable in any way for the errors and lapses of this book; but they did help make it.

First there are the people to whom the book is, with considerable temerity, dedicated. Then there are a score of others who were equally kind and helpful along the often rugged way.

To both Joseph Wharton Lippincotts, Senior and Junior, I owe much in the way of help and hospitality.

My editors, Alan Williams, Corlies Smith and Catherine Carver wasted an enormous amount of valuable time on me and my manuscript.

Certain Philadelphia friends were in on the project from the beginning, with help, hints, arguments and even readings. Of these

Richard and Cintra Huber, George and Ann Clay and John and Charlotte Archer gave an immense amount of lore, suggestion, anecdote. Whole sections of the book indeed are derived solely from material to which they first introduced me.

An entire phalanx of Ingersolls, several Morrises by birth or marriage, and various Biddles were so nice to me that I feel guilty writing anything about their families at all. Unfortunately, I couldn't help it. I devoutly pray that nothing will offend people who have been so very kind. Among other friends, both the Arthur Youngs and the Arthur Pauls have opened vistas I should otherwise never have suspected. The John F. Lewises continued to be friends of the second generation as they were of the first. They already have a dedication, which is my only reason for not printing them in mine. Similarly, I couldn't in conscience call the Ralph Pages "Philadelphians"; but my warmest thanks to them here.

Two institutions in particular, both in Philadelphia, were invaluable, and I spent many laborious days in each, helped by all. To the directors, officers and staff of both the Pennsylvania Historical Society and the Athenæum I can never be sufficiently grateful, especially to Messrs. Nicholas B. Wainwright and R. Norris Williams of the former and to Mrs. Isabelle E. Meade and Mr. Francis James Dallett of the latter. To Mr. Edwin Wolf II of the Library Company I am grateful. In Princeton, too, my gratitude goes to all at the Princeton University Library, from the Chief Librarian Mr. William S. Dix on to the hardpressed ladies back of the desk; with a special note of thanks to Mr. Henry L. Savage, former archivist there.

I suppose it is irregular to make the same sort of acknowledgment to a club; but certainly the Franklin Inn and its members have contributed a lot over the years in a more informal way.

The diary of Francis Lewis, lent me by Mrs. Leonard Beale, and the diary of Charlotte Wilcocks, lent me by Mr. C. Jared Ingersoll, were treasures; as, of course, was that of Sidney Fisher, first introduced to me in typescript by Mrs. George Clay and then assimilated through the pages of the *Pennsylvania Magazine* as edited by Nicholas Wainwright. The whole typescript is in the Pennsylvania Historical Society; obviously it should be in book form.

To Mr. W. B. McDaniel of the College of Physicians, Mr. Anthony W. Ridgeway of Episcopal Academy, Mr. Martin P. Snyder of the Orpheus Club, Mr. Louis Santore of the Rittenhouse Club, Miss

Acknowledgments

Ellen Schaffer of the Free Library, Mr. William McCarthy of the Rosenbach Foundation, Major Bruce Payne of Wilkes-Barre, Mr. Alexander W. Williams of Boston, to Miss Anne S. Cooper (now Mrs. Philip N. Kniskern) and to Mrs. Donald A. J. Bohlen, who did research for me, and to many others I owe all sorts of assistance in special matters.

I am particularly indebted to Professor George Tatum of the University of Pennsylvania, for his help with the pictures, as well as to (again) Mr. Nicholas B. Wainwright, and Miss Jane Wilson of *Horizon* magazine.

And there are so many more. In a few cases I have left out their names for fear that favorable mention of them in the text might be construed as favoritism (which I suppose it is). If I have slighted the names of others, it is sheer unfortunate oversight or, in a few cases, false delicacy.

N.B.

A Reading List

This book, belonging squarely as it does in the area of "nonfiction," is meant not for students and scholars, but for the lay reader. It therefore deliberately dispenses with source footnotes, references to authorities and a bibliography. The sources have been in most cases the most ordinary and accessible ones — the *Dictionary of American Biography*, *Who's Who* and the *Social Register*. The anecdotage is in most cases verbal and at first hand. Anecdotes have a way of shaping themselves into pithy form without regard for nice nuances of truth. I have tried to indicate this by such phrases as "it is said"; but sometimes I've let them stand ungarnished.

I do include here a reading list, which actually gives most of my principal sources. I have included, however, only books that might conceivably be read or consulted by interested non-scholars.

Of these Scharf and Westcott's *History of Philadelphia* (1884) is the most unreadable, but it has just about everything in it. What it doesn't contain is lost somewhere in Watson's *Annals of Philadelphia* (1857). They are for *reference*; but Watson can be fun.

As for reading:

I. Information about Philadelphia in general:

1. *Philadelphia, Holy Experiment* by Struthers Burt (Doubleday, 1945). An atmospheric historical survey in one volume also for people, not scholars.

2. *Philadelphia Gentlemen* by E. Digby Baltzell (The Free Press, 1958). Not meant for people, but can be read by them profitably; ignore an occasional barrage of sociological terms.

3. *The Delaware* by Harry Emerson Wildes (Farrar and Rinehart, 1940). Meant to be the history of the river, but concentrates on Philadelphia.

4. *Philadelphia, the Place and the People* by Agnes Repplier (Macmillan, 1898). Graceful, witty and admired by many. I found it supercilious and sloppy; but anything Repplier writes has style.

5. *Philadelphia* by Horace Mather Lippincott (Macrae Smith, 1926). A well-organized pilgrimage to the Old Philadelphia shrines.

A Reading List

II. Special periods of Philadelphia history:

1. *Rebels and Gentlemen* by Carl and Jessica Bridenbaugh (Reynal and Hitchcock, 1942). A classic of social history; Philadelphia before the Revolution.
2. *Meeting House and Counting House* by F. B. Tolles (University of North Carolina Press, 1948). Another classic, an examination of the pull between Mammon and the Quaker conscience in the eighteenth century and later.
3. *Our Philadelphia* by Elizabeth Robins Pennell (Lippincott, 1914). A richly detailed and pictured memoir of the nineteenth-century Philadelphia girlhood.
4. *Lanternslides* by Mary Cadwalader Jones (Privately printed, 1937). Further quaint glimpses of the Pennell world.
5. *A Madeira Party* by S. Weir Mitchell (Century, 1895). Fictional account of a Madeira-tasting and its lore and customs.
6. *Portrait of a Colonial City* by Harold Eberlein and C. Van D. Hubbard (Lippincott, 1939). A beautiful book on beautiful old houses and what's in them.
7. *The Saga of American Society* by Dixon Wecter (Scribner, 1927). Not just about Philadelphia, of course, but the basic book on the general subject. Very readable; but anybody who starts with the meaningless word "Society" is bound to get into confusions.

III. Biographies and memoirs:

1. *Benjamin Franklin* by Carl Van Doren (Viking, 1958). Another classic, which gets far from Philadelphia without ever being irrelevant to it.
2. Biddle books:
   (a) *Nicholas Biddle* by Thomas Payne Govan (University of Chicago Press, 1959). The first attempt to dust off Biddle, and though technical, full of interest.
   (b) *An American Artist's Story* by George Biddle (Little Brown, 1939). Brilliantly written, and the early chapters full of Philadelphia interest.
   (c) *A Casual Past* by Francis Biddle (Doubleday, 1961). Covers the same Philadelphia ground in more detail and with more kindness, if less brilliance.

(d) *My Philadelphia Father* by Cordelia Drexel Biddle (Doubleday, 1955). Cheap but fun.

(e) *Autobiography of Charles Biddle* (Privately printed, 1883). A ragbag of striking incidents of the Revolutionary period.

3. *Autobiography of Benjamin Rush* edited by George A. Corner (Princeton University Press, 1948). An insight into America's greatest early man of medicine.

IV. Arts and Sciences:

Painting and Architecture:

1. *Mainstreams of Modern Art* by John Canaday (Simon and Schuster, 1959). Definitely not about Philadelphia; but such good reading, and ties in Philadelphia painting wherever it does connect with the Mainstream.

2. *The Proud Possessors* by Aline B. Saarinen (Random House, 1958). Gives the story of John G. Johnson, also of Mary Cassatt and her influence on American collecting. Good reading too.

3. *Triumph of Fairmount* by George and Mary Roberts (Lippincott, 1960). The story of Fiske Kimball in modern Philadelphia told with skill and affection.

4. *Art and Argyrol* by William Schack (Yoseloff, 1960). The story of Albert Barnes; impartial and amusing.

5. *Henry McCarter* by R. S. Ingersoll (Privately printed, 1944). This casual memoir of an interesting artist of the twentieth century gives a nice impression of Philadelphia's modern artistic life.

6. *Penn's Great Town* by George B. Tatum (University of Pennsylvania Press, 1961). Handsome picture-book coverage of Philadelphia architecture.

Writing and Books:

1. *George H. Boker* by Scully Bradley (University of Pennsylvania Press, 1927). The only biography.

2. *Representative American Plays* edited by A. H. Quinn (Century, 1917). Has dramas by Barker, Bird, Boker and others for those who are curious.

3. *S. Weir Mitchell* by Ernest Earnest (University of Pennsyl-

vania Press, 1950). A sober (and earnest) assessment of the subject.

4. *Owen Wister Out West* edited by Fanny K. W. Stokes (University of Chicago Press, 1958). A long-hidden journal of Wister's early Western trips.

5. *Agnes Repplier* by George Stewart Stokes (University of Pennsylvania Press, 1948). Nice short biography of a charming writer.

6. *Agnes Repplier* by Emma Witmer (Dorrance, 1957). Graceful reminiscences by her niece.

7. *The Confident Years* by Van Wyck Brooks (Dutton, 1952). Good chapter on the writers of the Mitchell era.

8. *Rosenbach* by Edwin Wolf 2nd with John F. Fleming (World, 1960). Rich, full biography of a rich, full bookseller.

Theatre, Ballet, Music:

1. *Fanny Kemble, a Passionate Victorian* by Margaret Armstrong (Macmillan, 1938). Lush but vivid picture of the lady and her times.

2. *Good Night, Sweet Prince* by Gene Fowler (Viking, 1944). Vivid picture of a lush and his times; also, the panorama of the Drew–Barrymores.

3. *Ballet in America* by George Amberg (Mentor Books, 1949). Contains the story of Philadelphia's dance pioneers.

4. *Music in Philadelphia* by Robert A. Gerson (Presser, 1940). Not for fun; but the complete musical history of the city.

Politics, Economics:

1. *Power and Glory* by Walter Davenport (Putnam, 1931). A roguish portrait of the great Senator Penrose.

2. *Image of America* by R. L. Bruckberger (Viking, 1959). Introduces Henry Carey to the general reader; witty and controversial and seen from a fresh French point of view.

Science:

1. *Alexander Wilson* by Robert Cantwell (Lippincott, 1961). A beautiful book about this queer duck.

V. Professions, Institutions, Businesses:

1. *Bring Out Your Dead* by J. H. Powell (University of Pennsylvania Press, 1944). Fine book on the plague of 1793 and hence on medicine under Rush.

2. *Blockley Days* by Arthur Ames Bliss (Privately printed, 1916). A nostalgic and horrifying journal of the Philadelphia General Hospital in the bad old days.
3. *Philadelphia Lawyer* by George Wharton Pepper (Lippincott, 1944). A candid and graceful self-portrait.
4. *Biography of a Business* by Marquis James (Bobbs-Merrill, 1942). The story of the Insurance Company of North America, and pretty sprightly as such things go.
5. *A Philadelphia Story* by Nicholas B. Wainwright (Private, by the Contributionship, 1952). The Contributionship and its barnacled career, rich in Philadelphia lore.
6. *Banks and Politics in America* by Bray Hammond (Princeton University Press, 1957). Heavy going for the uninitiated, despite the wit; but invaluable in the understanding of Willing, Biddle *et al.* and their role in history.
7. *Benjamin Franklin's Library* (printed as *The First American Library*, 1936) by Austin K. Gray (Macmillan, 1938). A charming short history of the Library Company.
8. The works of J. Stanley Reeve are gems of their kind, at least for anyone interested in American fox hunting. I have looked at:
   Radnor Reminiscences (Houghton Mifflin, 1921).
   Foxhunting Formalities (Derrydale, 1930).
   Red Coats in Chester County (Derrydale, 1940).

VI. As for novels about Philadelphia, I've mentioned in the text the good ones I've read. Novels *by* Philadelphians will have to be tracked down by the reader. I do recommend however *Lady Baltimore* by Owen Wister (despite what Wallace Stegner says in the *Dictionary of American Biography*), and *Constance Trescott* by S. Weir Mitchell.

As for essays: Repplier's *Essays of Eight Decades* is an anthology. Others working the vein are Cornelius Weygandt (*The Blue Hills, Philadelphia Folks,* etc.) and A. Edward Newton (*The Amenities of Book Collecting,* etc.), all very nice.

There are of course hundreds of other books on and about Philadelphia; I enjoyed some of these others too. But then I even enjoyed parts of the *Centennial History of the Pennsylvania Railroad.* I don't recommend it.

N.B.

Index

Index

Index

Family, in Philadelphia, 40-43, 67-70, 214-15, 264, 388. *See also "Old Philadelphia" and* Philadelphia Oligarchy
Family firms, in Philadelphia, 69, 169-75, 212
Fantasia (movie), 474
Far West. *See* West, the
Farmer, Major Robert, 184
Farmer's Club, 251-55, 260, 290, 409, 419, 488
Faust, opera by Gounod, 478
Faust, translation by Bayard Taylor, 379
Fawn Court, 8, 358
Federalist politics, 24, 121, 402
Fellowship, the (fire company), 142
Fetterman, Mrs. Gordon, 65
Fidelity Trust Building, 246
Field hockey, 313
Fields, W. C., 448
Fifth Street, 243, 244, 245
Filbert Street, 194, 197
Fire companies, in Philadelphia, 142-43
First Bank of the United States, 154, 158, 160
First Troop, Philadelphia City Cavalry. *See* Philadelphia City Troop
Fish House. *See* State in Schuylkill
Fish House Punch, 261, 524
Fisher family, 176, 186, 211, 264, 297, 378, 481
Fisher, Eddie, 483
Fisher, Henry, 29
Fisher, Joshua, 360
Fisher, Lindley, 304
Fisher, Sidney, 23, 29, 35, 110, 174, 186, 211, 252, 304, 323, 360, 370, 378, 395, 423, 443, 462, 474, 527, 595; diary and observations, 23-32, 49-51, 60-61, 75, 99, 132, 179, 283, 301, 321, 441-42, 517, 532, 536, 543
Fisher, Sydney, 301
Fiske, Minnie Maddern, 433
Fitzgerald, F. Scott, 89, 367
Fitzgerald, Michael, 133
Fitzsimmons, Thomas, 574-75
Fleisher family, 570
Fleming, John, 569
Flight of Time (pageant), 499
Flippen, Mrs. Harrison, 313
Florence, Italy, 333
Florida, 184
Foch, Marshal Ferdinand, 221, 489
Fonthill, home of Edwin Forrest, 438
Food Distribution Center, 560
Football, 316-17
Ford, Henry, 407, 590
Ford, Henry, II, 175
Forest Hill, Ingersoll house, 127, 255
Forrest, Catherine Sinclair (Mrs. Edwin Forrest), 436-38
Forrest, Edwin, 372, 434-39, 444, 446-47
Forrest Home for Actors, 438
Forrestal Research Center, 510
Forster, John, 436, 437
Fort Wilson, home of James Wilson, 130

Fourth Street, 134, 145, 148, 531
Fox family, 44, 162, 443
Fox, Joseph, 144
Fox, William Logan, 144
Fox, William Logan (twentieth century), 242
Fox hunting, 10, 63, 187, 214, 285-96, 316, 378-79, 597
Foxhunting Formalities, by J. Stanley Reeve, 291
Fraley, Frederick, 255
Francesca da Rimini, play by George Henry Boker, 374, 431, 439
Francis family, 117, 129, 153
Francis, Tench, 116-17, 129, 211, 250
Frankenstein, by Mary Godwin Shelley, 369
Franklin, Benjamin, 13, 44, 47, 60, 70, 104, 106, 135, 147, 148, 228, 229, 245, 247, 286, 321-22, 327, 400, 406-8 *passim,* 456, 501, 509, 596, 598; and University of Pa., 81-84 *passim,* 398; founds insurance and fire companies, 142-44, 146; and Pennsylvania Hospital, 220, 222-23, 226, 234; Fund, 233; and Philosophical Society, 234-37, 239; library, 240-42; family, 271, 400-3, 432; as writer, 368-69, 410; as printer and publisher, 397-99, 404, 413, 424, 562; and Old Philadelphia, 397-99; character, 398; musical activities, 458-59; scientific activities, 502-3, 506
Franklin, Sarah, 400
Franklin, Walter, 197
Franklin, William, 401
Franklin Inn, 269, 381, 408
Franklin Institute, 13, 247-48, 344, 359
Franklin Park, 556
Franklin Square, 71, 132
Frankford, 530
Franks family, 565
Franks, Abigail, 565
Franks, Becky, 565
Franks, David, 284, 565
Frederiksted, St. Croix, Virgin Islands, 65
Free Library, 13, 191, 246-47, 344, 570
Freed, Isaac, 576
French, Mrs., 461
French, in Philadelphia, 64, 167, 272-73
French West Indian names, 64
Freneau, Philip, 367, 369
Frick, Henry, 547
Friday Evenings, the, 93
Friendly Society for Mutual Insurance, Charleston, 143
Friends and Fiddlers, by Catherine Drinker Bowen, 395, 492
Friends Central School, 79
Friends Hospital, 266
Friendship, the (fire company), 142
Frill, Benjamin, 283
Froggy Fairy Stories, by A. D. Biddle, 54
Frost, Arthur, 335, 336
Fry, Joseph, 465

Fry, William Henry, 465, 477-78, 493, 494
Furness family, 238, 382-83
Furness, Frank, 194, 246, 260-61, 383
Furness, Horace Howard, 260, 380-82
Furness, Horace Howard, Jr., 383
Furness, the Rev. William H., 382
Furness, William M., Jr., 383
Furness, William H., III, 383

GAFFNEY FAMILY, 577
Gaffney, Joseph, 128
Gallatin, Albert, 236
Galsworthy, John, 22
Garber, Daniel, 342
Garbo, Greta, 474
Garden Club of America, 524
Garden Club of Philadelphia, 524
Gardeners (club), 524
Garfield, James A., 131
Garret, Robert, 253
Garrick Club, London, 436
Gas lamps, 35-36
Gas Ring, 549
Gates family, 215
Gates, Thomas, 138, 237, 275
Gautier, Théophile, 497
Genealogical Society, 247-49 *passim*
General Electric Company, 212; cricket club, 307
"General Idea for a College of Mirania," by William Smith, 83
General Magazine and Historical Chronicle for All the British Plantations in America, 413
Geographical Society, 247
George II, of England, 226
George III, of England, 326
Georgian Court, Gould palace, 312
German Jewish names, 65
Germania Orchestra, 466-67
Germans, in Philadelphia, 64, 72, 104, 115, 322, 542, 567-68, 571, 577; musical influence, 331-32, 454, 455, 466-67, 562-63
Germantown, 30, 32, 105, 117, 304, 311, 454, 532, 557, 564, 575; battle of, 117
Germantown Academy, 79, 304
Germantown Cricket Club, 303, 305, 307, 308, 310-11, 313
Germantown Friends School, 79
Gerstley family, 570
Gertrude J. Mieterer Fund for Charity, 233
Gettysburg, battle of, 541, 575
Geyelin family, 64
Giannini, Vittorio, 494
Gilbert and Sullivan, 21, 136, 489
Gilchrist, William, 469, 493
Gilkyson, Walter, 393
Gilpin, Mrs., 408
Gimbel family, 570
Girard, Stephen, 152-53 *passim,* 158-59, 160-63 *passim,* 165, 167, 201, 228-30, 243, 245, 273, 404, 555; will of, 131, 158, 228-32, 236, 579
Girard Avenue, 228
Girard Bank, 373
Girard Beneficial Association. *See* Girard Trust Corn Exchange Bank

Index

Philadelphia Lyric Opera Company, 480, 599-600
Philadelphia Museum of Art, 8, 122, 131, 200, 237, 262, 341, 343, 350, 352, 354, 355-56, 359, 596; architecture, 344-45; art collection, 346-48, 349-50
Philadelphia National Bank, 152
"Philadelphia novel," 388-89, 390, 393
Philadelphia Oligarchy, 12, 28-29, 40-43, 114, 211, 214, 257, 321-22, 361, 388, 410, 453, 596-97. See also "Old Philadelphia" and Philadelphia: gentry
Philadelphia Orchestra, 197, 214, 321, 346, 453, 464-65, 467, 469-76, 494, 498, 500, 597
Philadelphia Record, 3, 390, 426
Philadelphia Renaissance. See Politics, in Philadelphia and Redevelopment project
Philadelphia Saving Fund Society (PSFS), 165, 167-69, 190, 202, 219, 364, 460, 596
Philadelphia Scrapple, by Harold Eberlein, 520
Philadelphia Skating Club and Humane Society, 314
Philadelphia Society for the Promotion of Agriculture, 157, 250-52
Philadelphia Story, by Philip Barry, 3, 433, 434, 449-50
Philadelphia Symphony Society, 469, 485
Philadelphia Zoological Garden, 61, 100
Philadelphian, The, by Richard Powell, 4, 42, 91, 279, 394, 451
Philco Radio, 484
Philharmonic Society, 485, 486
Phillips, Walter, 550, 553, 600
Philmont Country Club, 258, 572
Philosophical Hall, 238-39, 241
Philosophical Society. See American Philosophical Society
Philosophy Four, by Owen Wister, 383
Phipps, Ogden, 312
Physick, Dr. Philip S., 36, 104; house, 36-37
Pickering Hunt, 172, 288
Pickwick Club, 298
Pindar, 321
Pine Forge, 180, 183
Pine Street, 8, 13, 220, 483, 529, 531, 534
Pittsburgh, Pennsylvania, 20, 179, 188, 189, 191, 212
Platt family, 297
Platt, Charles, 151
Plays and Players, 452, 499
Pocono Mountains, 535-36, 538
Poe, Edgar Allan, 367, 370, 416, 500
Poems and Plays, by George Henry Boker, 373
Pohlig, Carl, 471, 472
Point Breeze, Joseph Bonaparte estate, 272-73
Politics, in Philadelphia, 69, 90, 125-26 passim, 137-38, 159, 540-55, 600
Polk, James, 70, 128

Polo, 295
Polock family, 568
Polock, Moses, 569
Polyceen, James, 283
Pont Reading (house), 519
Pool Forge, 180, 183
Poor Richard's Almanac, by Benjamin Franklin, 368, 398
Port Folio, 370, 371, 386 414-15
Portland, Maine, 420
Portuguese Jewish names, 65
Potter family, New York, 69
Potts family, 182-85 passim
Potts, Horace C., 183
Potts, Thomas, 183
Pottsgrove, home of Thomas Potts, 183
Pottstown, Pennsylvania, 183
Pottsville, Pennsylvania, 183, 205
Poulsen, Zachariah, 245, 330
Powel family, 153, 155
Powel, Ida (Mrs. John G. Johnson), 349
Powel, John Hare, 156-57, 251, 276, 323, 387, 440, 516, 524
Powel, Samuel, 156-57, 250, 349, 531
Powell, Richard, 42, 91, 279, 394, 451
Powelton, home of John Hare Powel, 157, 518
Presbyterianism, 74, 80, 88, 107, 173
Price family, 59
Price, Eli Kirk, II, 344, 348
Price, John Sergeant, 314
Pride and Prejudice, by Jane Austen, 582
Primrose, Violet, 277
Prince of Parthia, by Thomas Godfrey, Jr., 431
Princeton, New Jersey, 509-10; battle of, 274
Princeton University, 58n., 67, 80-82 passim, 84-86 passim, 101, 105, 172, 177, 193, 274, 317, 412; history, 88-89; ties with Philadelphia, 88-92; reputation, 89; Nassau Hall, 90, 360; architecture, 90; Board of Trustees, 91; Museum, 331, president's house, 360; literary magazine, 373; Triangle Club, 490, science department, 509
Principato, Dr. Luigi D., 223
Printing. See Publishing, in Philadelphia
Printz, Johan, 301
Prix de Rome, 493
Providence, Rhode Island, 71
Provident Tradesmen's Bank and Trust Company, 152, 165, 596
Public Ledger, 161, 252, 307, 418, 419, 425, 428, 465
Publishing, in Philadelphia, 397-428
Puccini, Giacomo, 433
Pugh family, 44, 59, 209
Pugh, Gainor (Mrs. John Roberts), 191
Pugh, Robert, 191
Pulitzer Prize, 433, 493
Punch magazine, 21, 136
Push-ma-ta-ha (Choctaw chief), 435
Pyle, Howard, 335-37
Pyramid Club, 258, 343, 563

QUAKERISM AND QUAKERS, 45, 70, 92, 135, 136, 172-73, 412; influence, 9, 21, 32, 41, 64, 70-76, 99, 102-3, 114, 140, 157, 186, 191, 201, 220, 234, 284, 324, 410, 431, 453-54, 513, 515, 573-74, 594; Welsh settlement, 59, 62; schools, 77-80; and insurance, 144, Keithian schism, 183, 399; addresses, 529, 530-31
Quay, Matthew, 173, 542-43, 546

RABBIT, THE (club), 261-62, 265, 276, 524, 566
Racquet Club, 207, 268, 312, 363, 566
R.C.A. Victor Corporation, 484
Radnor, Pennsylvania, 59, 196, 288
Radnor Hunt, 286-90 passim, 293
Radnor Hunt Races, 294
Radnor Reminiscences, by J. Stanley Reeve, 291-92
Raguet, Condy, 167, 201, 273
Railroad industry, 69, 178, 182, 187-209, 532
Rambo's Rock, 260
Ramsey, Mr., 24-25
Randolph family, Virginia, 204
Randolph (Nicholas Biddle's ship), 46
Rauch, Stewart, 168, 553
Rawle family, 117-20 passim, 129, 158, 215, 236, 297, 507
Rawle, Francis, 118, 211, 406, 542
Rawle, Mary Morris (Mrs. James Rawle), 78
Rawle, William, 118
Rawle, William (grandson of preceding), 118-19, 123, 124, 125, 141
Rawle, William Henry, 133
Rawle and Henderson (law firm), 119
Read family, 122, 129
Read, Deborah. See Rogers, Deborah Read
Read, George, 122
Read, Thomas Buchanan, 380, 500
Reading, Pennsylvania, 46, 130, 181, 185, 203, 207
Reading (forge), 180
Reading Railroad, 163, 198-99, 203-9, 211, 212, 307, 532, 533
Rebecca (forge), 180
Red City, The, by S. Weir Mitchell, 381
Red D Line, 176
Redevelopment project (Philadelphia Renaissance), 19, 70, 197, 213, 238, 357, 358, 365, 398, 464-65, 531, 538-40, 555-62, 571-72, 600
Redman family, 567
Redman, Dr. John, 104, 105, 108, 432
Reed family, 122
Reed, Joseph, 122, 130
Reeve, J. Stanley, 286, 290, 291
Reeves family, 182
Reinagle, Alexander, 460, 462, 463, 477
Religion, in Philadelphia. See under individual denominations
Remington, Frederic, 384

Index

Index

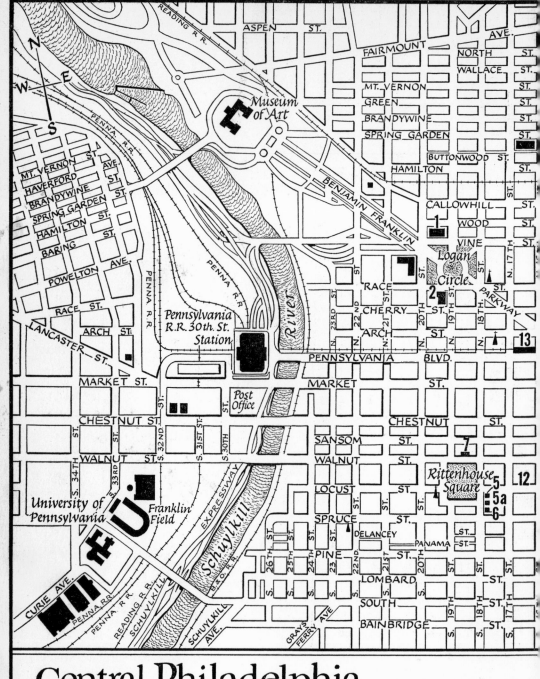

Central Philadelphia

1 *Free Library*
2 *Academy of Natural Sciences*
3 *Academy of Fine Arts*
4 *City Hall*
5 *Curtis Institute Free Library*
5a *Barclay Hotel*
6 *Art Alliance*
7 *Rittenhouse Club*
8 *Racquet Club*
9 *Bellevue Hotel*
10 *Union League*
11 *Philadelphia Club*
12 *St. Mark's*

0   1/4   1/2
One Half Mile